Essentials of Research Methods for Educators

Sara Miller McCune founded SAGE Publishing in 1965 to support the dissemination of usable knowledge and educate a global community. SAGE publishes more than 1,000 journals and over 600 new books each year, spanning a wide range of subject areas. Our growing selection of library products includes archives, data, case studies, and video. SAGE remains majority owned by our founder and after her lifetime will become owned by a charitable trust that secures the company's continued independence.

Los Angeles | London | New Delhi | Singapore | Washington DC | Melbourne

Essentials of Research Methods for Educators

Anastasia Kitsantas

George Mason University

Timothy J. Cleary

Rutgers, The State University of New Jersey

Maria K. DiBenedetto

University of North Carolina at Greensboro

Suzanne E. Hiller

Blue Swallow Farm Foundation

FOR INFORMATION:

2455 Teller Road
Thousand Oaks, California 91320
Email: order@sagepub.com

1 Oliver's Yard
55 City Road
London EC1Y 1SP
United Kingdom

Unit No 323-333, Third Floor, F-Block
International Trade Tower
Nehru Place, New Delhi – 110 019
India

18 Cross Street #10-10/11/12
China Square Central
Singapore 048423

Printed in the United States of America

Library of Congress Cataloging-in-Publication Data

Names: Kitsantas, Anastasia, author. | Cleary, Timothy J., author. | DiBenedetto, Maria K., author. | Hiller, Suzanne E., author.

Title: Essentials of research methods for educators / Anastasia Kitsantas, George Mason University, Timothy J. Cleary, Rutgers, The State University of New Jersey, Maria K. DiBenedetto, University of North Carolina at Greensboro, Suzanne E. Hiller, Blue Swallow Farm Foundation.

Description: First edition. | Thousand Oaks, California : SAGE, [2023] | Includes bibliographical references and index.

Identifiers: LCCN 2023041902 (print) | LCCN 2023041903 (ebook) | ISBN 9781071830697 (paperback : acid-free paper) | ISBN 9781071830703 (epub)

Subjects: LCSH: Education—Research—Methodology—Textbooks.

Classification: LCC LB1028 .K5167 2023 (print) | LCC LB1028 (ebook) | DDC 370.721—dc23/eng/20231012
LC record available at https://lccn.loc.gov/2023041902
LC ebook record available at https://lccn.loc.gov/2023041903

Acquisitions Editor: Leah Fargotstein

Content Development Editor: Darcy Scelsi

Production Editor: Veronica Stapleton Hooper

Copy Editor: Karin Rathert

Typesetter: diacriTech

Cover Designer: Gail Buschman

Marketing Manager: Victoria Velasquez

BRIEF CONTENTS

DETAILED CONTENTS

PREFACE

INSPIRATION AND PURPOSE

The inspiration for this textbook developed from our professional backgrounds and experiences and our shared goal of writing a research methods textbook that would motivate educators and students to conduct research. Each of us has a doctorate in educational psychology; expertise in student learning; and careers related to teaching, conducting research, and providing administrative and clinical services in school contexts. As experts in educational psychology, we are trained to develop ways to optimize learning, develop and sustain motivation, and help learners manage or regulate their cognition, affect, and behavior. From our training and professional experiences in working with novice researchers and educators, we recognized a need for a research methods book that was practitioner friendly. Students and educators often express concern about their ability to understand and learn content found in research methods books. This realization prompted us to describe research methods using a style of writing that is easy to comprehend. We did so by outlining research designs and related concepts using a conversational tone and approach and by focusing much attention on the application of research design and related concepts to real-world education-related situations.

In addition to the primary goal of providing information on research methods to practitioners, we framed the chapters and content using specific features that allow readers to interact with the content, thus giving educators opportunities to experience success in working through the mastery-oriented exercises. It is our hope and expectation that by reading and using this textbook, educators will gain a deeper understanding and a sense of competency about research methods and perhaps become motivated to conduct research in schools.

While the main purpose of this textbook is conveying important information about research methods, we intentionally use self-regulated learning as the guiding principle for helping educators think of themselves as potential researchers. Self-regulated learning refers to a process by which learners set goals and then proactively work toward reaching these goals. Self-regulated learning involves a three-phase cycle of planning (Phase 1), doing (Phase 2), and reflecting (Phase 3) and is often developed through engaging in a sequence of four levels characterized by observing and emulating models (Levels 1 and 2), engaging in self-control (Level 3), and practicing independently—the self-regulation level (Level 4). Research has shown self-regulated learning is a powerful mechanism to help individuals learn and achieve their goals. While self-regulated learning is explained in greater detail in Chapter 1, in the section that follows, we provide an overview of this book's key features and describe how they are connected to self-regulated learning to help readers learn about research methods.

KEY FEATURES OF THIS BOOK

An important underlying goal of this textbook is to embed self-regulated learning principles within the book features to support educators in becoming more research savvy in pursuing a critical issue through research. Due to the nature of the content within each chapter, readers will find that some chapters explicitly reference or discuss self-regulated learning while others do not. However, there are aspects of the three-phase cycle of self-regulated learning (planning, doing, and reflecting) or the four-level self-regulatory competency development model (observation, emulation, self-control, and self-regulation) present in every chapter in addition to the unique features used in this textbook. Table 1 lists the features we use to nudge readers toward a more self-regulated mindset and approach to learning. The features are presented in the first column, and the explanations of the features are found in the second column. The underlined words in Column 2 are aspects of self-regulated learning targeted by the features.

TABLE 1 ■ Key Features That Enhance the Chapter Content Connecting Them to Self-Regulated Learning	
Key Feature	**Purpose of the Key Feature**
Theoretical Foundation in Self-Regulated Learning	Three phases of self-regulated learning and developing self-regulatory competency in conducting research are embedded overtly or covertly, in every chapter.
Interactive	Research has shown that students learn best when they are actively learning, and that active learning can build self-efficacy (beliefs about one's capability to accomplish a task). This text provides several opportunities for active learning within the content through questioning, activities, and extension activities.
A Day at Work	Each chapter opens with an example (or a model) of a relatable real-world problem. This scenario is a situation used to demonstrate the content throughout the chapter to help make the information more relatable to educators.
Checklists	Checklists are present to help readers self-record their progress and understanding of the content.
Stop and Think prompts	Stop and Think prompts are present to help readers become more metacognitively aware of what they are reading.
Takeaway prompts	Takeaway prompts are present throughout each chapter linking the section to the chapter's learning goals to help readers monitor or keep track of the content.
Decision Trees	Decision Trees are present in several chapters to help readers plan and reflect on what factors to consider when making research methods decisions.
Data Sets	Several chapters include datasets for demonstration and practice purposes.
Let's See It!	*Let's See It!*—each chapter presents examples or models to demonstrate for readers ways to complete a similar activity.
Let's Do It!	*Let's Do It!*—each chapter presents opportunities for readers to practice what they just read, followed by answer keys to scaffold understanding of the content.

Key Feature	Purpose of the Key Feature

The following topics represent sections rather than features.

Ethics	Each chapter provides critical ethical information related to the chapter content that should be used in planning, conducting (doing), and reflecting on research.
Publication Manual of the American Psychological Association (APA)	Readers will find a section on the use of the *Publication Manual of the APA in each chapter beginning with Chapter 2*. Using this manual is relevant to each of the phases: planning, doing, and reflecting.
End of Chapter Content: End of Chapter Summary, Key Terms, Extension Activities (You Do It!), and References	Along with the Chapter Summary, Key Terms, and References is a *You Do It!* activity. These activities provide readers with a review and opportunities to self-reflect and demonstrate self-regulatory competency.

We believe the various features used in this textbook will not only help improve readers' understanding of research methods but also their strategic approach to conducting research. For example, each chapter is *interactive*. Readers will find that throughout the chapters, we pose questions, provide opportunities for practice, engage readers by using more of a conversational tone, colorful pictures, diagrams, and tables, and present relatable current topics in education. The interactive feature of this textbook exemplifies the three phases (planning, doing, and acting) and four levels (observation, emulation, guided practice, and independent practice) of self-regulated learning by strategically placing these elements within the chapter.

Each chapter begins with A Day at Work. This opening scenario presents a "hot topic" in education—one that is current and difficult to resolve and linked to the chapter content. We hope the scenarios engage readers by helping them see the relevance of research to common, real-world problems. As readers review the scenarios, it is expected that they will make their own observations and self-reflect as they relate their personal experiences or knowledge to the scenario.

The authors use Checklists to help readers engage in the planning and doing aspects of self-regulated learning on their own. Using checklists can be very helpful for enhancing people's self-awareness and overall organization and thoroughness. Checklists serve as reminders of important things to be considered or included for a given topic and can ultimately save time by improving efficiency. When conducting research, educators can use checklists to help delineate plans and then record (by a placing a checkmark) progress. Metacognitive prompts appear throughout each chapter as Stop and Think boxes. These prompts are strategically placed in chapters to help educators think about what they are reading and check for understanding. The Stop and Think prompts are associated with the doing phase of self-regulated learning because they typically occur in places where the authors want readers to stop and think and convey their understanding and knowledge about a particular issue.

Monitoring and reflecting prompts are represented as Takeaway boxes within chapters to help readers make connections with the chapter's learning goals. These boxes are also strategically placed in sections where readers should monitor their understanding of the content before proceeding to the next chapter section. Most of the chapters have Decision Trees diagrams that help educators in the planning and doing phases of self-regulated learning. Not only do they provide guidance, but they represent a type of exemplar or model of how to make appropriate decisions when conducting research. By observing and interacting (as readers think about the questions posed) with how these decision trees are used, educators could customize or create their own decision trees when conducting research.

The *Let's See It!*, *Let's Do It!*, and *You Do It!* activities are directly tied to the four levels of self-regulatory competency. In the *Let's See It!*, we present models or examples of how to complete a specific skill or activity. In the *Let's Do It!*, readers are prompted to try the activity on their own or with minimum support from their instructors, thus providing opportunities for emulation and guided practice. In the *You Do It!*, readers are asked to demonstrate their understanding of research concepts independent of the instructor. Thus, the *You Do It!* activities are aligned with the self-regulation level and inherently more challenging. *These You Do It!* activities are found at the end of the chapters as part of the extension activities.

Ethical considerations are critical when conducting research and thus are emphasized in every chapter. When educators embark on a research project, ethical issues should be considered in each of the three phases: planning—to ensure the plans for the research study will be ethical, doing—to make sure researchers are acting ethically while conducting the study, and reflecting—to safeguard that the data analyses, interpretation of findings, and communication of research are done in an ethical manner.

Each chapter beginning with Chapter 2 discusses pertinent issues reflected in the most recent publication of the *Publication Manual of the American Psychological Association*. The three phases as well as the four levels of competency of self-regulated learning are also relevant here as we provide information to consider that will help in the different steps of conducting a research study and in communicating the research to others.

Each chapter closes with a Chapter Summary, Key Words defined throughout the chapter, Extension Activities, and References. These items provide readers with opportunities to self-reflect as they review the content and demonstrate competency through the completion of the extension activities. These exercises are intended to help readers experience what it is like to be self-regulated.

Finally, we would like to emphasize to readers that we have a strong commitment to reflect diversity, equity, and inclusion (DEI) and have attempted to embed these values and related topics throughout the book. Chapter 1 further discusses DEI and its role in educational research.

ACKNOWLEDGMENTS

We would like to thank everyone who provided us with feedback, advice, and recommendations on this book. We have much gratitude for Jerry Higgins who helped launch this textbook; the staff at Sage who provided us with the opportunity to create this novel book; Darcy Scelsi and Leah Fargotstein who embraced the spirit of what we were trying to accomplish and guided us along the way; Karin Rathert and Veronica Stapleton Hooper who worked closely and patiently with us through the copyediting phase; the students, teachers, and colleagues who reviewed preliminary versions of the chapters; and our families for giving us the love, patience, time, and support we needed to complete our writing.

REVIEWERS

Gerald Ardito
Pace University

Noelle Banuelos
California State University Northridge

Amy Benton
SAMFORD University

Diane Bordenave
Southern University at New Orleans

Lois Cavucci
University of Dayton

Robert Ceglie
Queens University of Charlotte

Mary Chittooran
Saint Louis University

Libby Cohen
University of Southern Maine

Kenneth Elpus
University of Maryland

Brianna Grumstrup
University of Maine at Farmington

Joshua Guillemette
University of Central Florida

Jeff McLaughlan
West Chester University

Vanaja Nethi
Nova Southeastern University

Benjamin Ngwudike
Jackson State University

Victoria Sherif

ABOUT THE AUTHORS

Anastasia Kitsantas

Anastasia Kitsantas, PhD, is Professor of Educational Psychology and Director of the Office of Doctoral Studies in the College of Education and Human Development at George Mason University (GMU). She has also served as Director of the Educational Psychology, Research Methods, and Education Policy Division and as Academic Program Coordinator of the Educational Psychology Program. She received her PhD in Educational Psychology with a specialization in Development, Learning, and Instruction from the Graduate School and University Center of the City University of New York. She has previously served on the faculties at James Madison University in the School of Psychology and at Florida State University in the Department of Educational Research. Prior to working in higher education, she taught in K–12 settings.

Dr. Kitsantas' research interests focus on the development of self-regulated learning (SRL) and student motivation across diverse areas of functioning, including academic learning, athletics, and health. She has also studied the role of learning technologies in supporting student SRL. She finds joy in mentoring students to conduct research in these areas and has chaired more than 30 doctoral dissertations. She is the editor, coauthor, or author of three books and over 150 journal articles, book chapters, refereed proceedings, and reports, many of which are directed toward the training of self-regulation. Her publications have appeared in diverse outlets across many fields, such as educational psychology, teacher education, learning technologies, health psychology, and sport psychology. Her research output has been widely cited by others, with more than 19,000 Google Scholar citations. In fact, she has been recognized as ranking in the top 2% of scientists worldwide based on research conducted from Stanford University that covered ~7 million scientists in 22 major fields (Jeroen, Boyack, & Ioannidis, 2020). She has also presented over 200 papers or invited addresses at local, national, and international conferences. She has received funding support for her scholarship by various agencies. Currently, she is the Principal Investigator (PI) and a Co-PI on two projects funded by the Department of Education and the National Science Foundation, respectively. Both projects focus on the development of self-regulatory skills among school-aged students in literacy and STEM areas in preparation for postsecondary learning, the workplace, and lifelong learning.

Dr. Kitsantas was awarded the Outstanding Dissertation Award by Division 15 of the American Psychological Association (APA) in 1997 and had been honored to receive the 2019 Barry J. Zimmerman Award for Outstanding Contributions to the fields of studying and self-regulated learning research by the Studying and Self-Regulated Learning (SSRL) Special Interest Group (SIG) of the American Educational Research Association (AERA). She is a Fellow of the American Psychological Association's: Division 15, Educational Psychology. She has excelled at teaching in a variety of course modalities and was awarded a George Mason University Teaching Excellence Award, which is an institutional recognition for outstanding teaching and acknowledgment of the significant work that faculty members devote to teaching, advising, mentoring, and curriculum development. She is the former Editor-in-Chief of *The Journal of Experimental Education* and has served on the editorial boards of a number of professional journals, including *Contemporary Educational Psychology, Educational Technology, Research and Development, Metacognition and Learning, The Journal of Experimental Education,* and many others.

Dr. Kitsantas has been extensively involved in the profession and has held numerous leadership positions in professional organizations. She served as a Member at Large of the Executive Board of Division 15 of APA in 2011 and most recently served as the Chair of the Fellows Committee and the Webinar Committee. She has also been involved in the SSRLSIG of AERA as the SIG Chair, Program Chair, and Chair of the Barry J. Zimmerman Award Committee. She has been a panel reviewer for the Institute of Education Sciences, the National Science Foundation, and other funding agencies. She has developed partnerships with GMU and other universities abroad, taught abroad, and as an advocate for study abroad programs, continues to seed fruitful international collaborations.

Timothy J. Cleary

Timothy J. Cleary is Professor and Chair of the Department of School Psychology in the Graduate School of Applied and Professional Psychology (GSAPP) at Rutgers, The State University of New Jersey. He obtained his PhD in Educational Psychology with a specialization in School Psychology from the Graduate School and University Center of the City University of New York, CUNY Graduate School in 2001. Dr. Cleary began his professional career working as a licensed school psychologist in the public and private sector. He began his academic career as a Visiting Professor at CUNY before serving as Assistant and Associate Professor at the University of Wisconsin—Milwaukee prior to moving to Rutgers University in 2012.

Dr. Cleary's primary research interests include the development and application of self-regulated learning (SRL) and motivation assessment and intervention practices across academic, athletic, medical, and clinical contexts. Specifically, he has examined trends in school-based SRL assessment and intervention practices, developed and validated several types of SRL assessments (i.e., self-report, teacher rating scales, parent rating scales, microanalytic protocols), developed and tested academic intervention programs, and investigated links among SRL processes and performance indicators. He has published over 70 peer-review journal articles and book chapters specifically addressing SRL issues and applications, coedited a scholarly book on SRL, served as sole author on an edited volume targeting SRL intervention programs and a sole author for a research-to-practice book for K–12 teachers, *The Self-Regulated Learning Guide: Teaching Students to Think in the Language of Strategies* (2018). Most of his publications have appeared in top-tiered journals across multiple fields, including school psychology, educational psychology, medical education, teacher education, and sport psychology. His research productivity has been widely cited by others, with approximately 8,000 Google Scholar citations and 4,000 citations since 2018. He was the recipient of the 2021 Barry J. Zimmerman Award for Outstanding Contributions to the fields of studying and self-regulated learning research from the Studying and Self-Regulated Learning Special Interest Group of the American Educational Research Association (AERA).

Dr. Cleary's extramural grant funding is significant in both its quantity and quality, and most of his projects have been collaborative in nature. He is serving or has served as a Principal Investigator (PI) or Co-PI on grants from the National Science Foundation, the Department of Education's Fund for the Improvement of Postsecondary Education (FIPSE), Institute for Educational Sciences (IES), and the Spencer Foundation. Over the course of his career, Dr.

Cleary has served in a lead or collaborative scholarly role on grants totaling approximately $12 million.

Dr. Cleary has also taken on several leadership roles at the university and national levels. Across institutions, he has served as Program Director, Director of Clinical Training, and Department Chair. He also participated as a Fellow in the inaugural Rutgers Leadership Academy in 2015. At a national level, Dr. Cleary has served on the executive board for the Studying and Self-Regulated Learning Special Interest Group (SSRL SIG) of the American Educational Research Association (AERA), performing roles of Chair, Program Chair, and Secretary. He also served as Chair for the Graduate Student Mentoring Program of the SSRL SIG for four years and has participated in various mentoring programs sponsored by NASP and Division C of AERA. Dr. Cleary currently serves on prestigious editorial boards for school psychology journals (*Journal of School Psychology, School Psychology*) and educational psychology journals (*Journal of Experimental Education, Metacognition and Learning*) and served as a panel reviewer for IES grant for several years. Dr. Cleary is frequently asked to provide professional development workshops to school personnel, researchers, and psychologists across the country regarding the application and motivation and SRL principles.

Maria K. DiBenedetto

Dr. Maria K. DiBenedetto holds a doctorate in Educational Psychology with a specialization in Learning, Development, and Instruction from the Graduate School and University Center of the City University of New York. She has a rich history in working in various administrative positions in higher education, including admissions, recruitment, advisement, student services, assessment, and reaccreditation, as well as adjunct teaching of both undergraduate and graduate students (courses include research methods, educational psychology, counseling psychology, child and adolescent development, theories of learning in teaching, and management). She also has several years' experience teaching as a high school science teacher and Chair of the Science Department, as well as experience as a second- and fourth-grade elementary school teacher.

Dr. DiBenedetto's current position is at the University of North Carolina, Greensboro, in the Bryan School of Business and Economics where she is a member of the Dean's Leadership Team. In her position as Lecturer/Director of Assessment and Reporting, Dr. DiBenedetto oversees assurance of learning for the business school's reaccreditation by AACSB International (Association to Advance Collegiate Schools of Business), one of the most prestigious and internationally recognized organizations that reviews business schools throughout the globe. In addition, she ensures the business school is meeting the assurance of learning standards set by SACSCOC (Southern Association of Colleges and Schools Commission on Colleges) for all graduate programs, undergraduate majors, minors, and certificate programs. She also serves on various committees throughout the university and within the business school and is a senator on the university-wide staff senate.

Dr. DiBenedetto's research interests are focused on self-regulated learning, self-efficacy, and motivation. She has published numerous chapters and articles on these topics and has collaborated with world-renown scholars in the field of educational psychology. She is particularly interested in research on self-regulated learning for college-bound high school students as well as study strategies for undergraduate and graduate students and their impact on achievement. Her research has been widely cited; for example, in a recent article in *The Chronicle of Higher Education* on first-generation college students' study strategies, the authors cited one of her studies in their discussion of study strategies for success (https://www.chronicle.com/article/Kn owing-How-to-Study-Can-Mean/246644.).

Along with Dr. DiBenedetto's empirical research, she has written several theoretical/conceptual publications focused on assessment, standards-based instruction, self-efficacy within a sociocultural lens, the mentoring of doctoral students, and two books, one edited and one coauthored. In the edited book *Connecting Self-Regulated Learning and Performance With Instruction Across High School Content Areas* (2018), each chapter is cowritten by outstanding content area high school teachers throughout the United States and well-known educational psychologists on applying self-regulated learning to classroom instruction. *Self-Regulation and the Common Core: Applications to ELA Standards* (2015) was her earlier coauthored book that discusses how self-regulated and the common core can be used to teach ELA standards to students in grades K–12.

Dr. DiBenedetto has served on several prestigious editorial boards: *Journal of Experimental Education; The International Journal of Educational and Psychological Assessment;* and a special issue of *Theory Into Practice.* She has served as a guest reviewer for several premier journals including the *Journal of Educational Psychology; Journal of Advanced Academics; Learning and Individual Differences; and Assessment in Education: Principles, Policy, & Practice,* among others.

DiBenedetto is a member of the American Psychological Association (APA) and served as chair of Division 15's (Educational Psychology) Committee on the Development of Early Career Educational Psychologists. She served in several positions in the Studying and Self-Regulated Learning Special Interest Group (SIG) for the American Educational Research Association (AERA) including Chair, Program Chair, Secretary, and Editor of the SIG.

Dr. DiBenedetto has presented her research internationally and domestically and has conducted professional development workshops for teachers in middle schools and high schools in addition to guest lectures for doctoral students on student learning and assessment. In addition, Dr. DiBenedetto serves on doctoral dissertation committees and has served and serves as a consultant on many projects for organizations such as ACT (American College Testing), Pearson Education, Department of Education Institute of Education Sciences (IES), and the Portuguese Science Foundation.

Suzanne E. Hiller

Suzanne E. Hiller, PhD, has worked in the field of education as a practitioner, professor, researcher, and evaluator for over three decades. Notably, she was the Teacher Naturalist with the Smithsonian Institution's National Museum of Natural History. She has served as an assistant professor teaching educational psychology, program evaluation, research, and preservice teacher courses in curriculum and assessment. While affiliated with Wingate University, she was the Director of the Graduate Education Program and the Director of Multidisciplinary Studies in Education with Hood College.

Currently, she is the Executive Director of the *Blue Swallow Farm Foundation,* an organization dedicated to promoting inclusive, authentic experiences in outdoor education through research and training while motivating students in STEM careers. In light of this mission, Suzanne E. Hiller has been working with educators, administrators, researchers, and scientists on a variety of projects related to professional development, curriculum development, and research, with a particular emphasis on outdoor classrooms and citizen science. Most recently, she has conducted a series of research studies on the impact of water quality programs on student STEM achievement, career motivation, environmental attitudes, and social-emotional well-being. Through this type of research, professional development on designing and utilizing outdoor classrooms, curriculum resources for educators, and mentorship and support for doctoral students, she continues to encourage growing interest in providing students with exposure in STEM activities within natural settings.

In support of educational research at large, Suzanne E. Hiller has served on the editorial board for the *International Journal of Mathematical Education in Science and Technology* and the *Journal of Experimental Education.* She has also been a reviewer for a variety of journals, such as *Learning and Individual Differences; Learning, Culture, and Social Interaction; and Heliyon.* She has written one book on using metacognitive and self-regulatory strategies to promote student science achievement and coedited one book on fostering STEM career motivation through citizen science.

Her background in motivation and self-regulation was particularly relevant as a co-principal investigator on a grant from the Maryland Governor's Emergency Relief Fund to provide assistance for teachers during the recent health crisis. Using an online format, the program serviced teachers across the state of Maryland with presentations, mentorship, and projects related to social-emotional learning, trauma-informed practices, mind-brain education, and self-regulation, all topics that were critical for student success during the pandemic. The experience of working on this grant serves as a model for several upcoming programs to train educators and administrators in outdoor instruction through the *Blue Swallow Farm Foundation* as well as to develop curricular materials for outdoor learning, Grades K–12.

1 INTRODUCTION TO RESEARCH

LEARNING OBJECTIVES

Upon completion of this chapter, students should be able to

1.1   Explain the benefits and characteristics of educational research

1.2   Construct the steps of the scientific method in conducting research

1.3   Differentiate between the approaches of basic research and applied research

1.4   Elaborate on how self-regulated learning can help educators become educator—researchers

1.5   Consider key logistical constraints and diversity, equity, and inclusion considerations in conducting research

1.6   Demonstrate knowledge of ethical issues when conducting research on human subjects

1.7   Identify the various content features in the individual chapters of this book

A DAY AT WORK

Helping Struggling Students Succeed!

Educational research can help educators use effective approaches to instruction.
©iStockphoto.com/SDI Productions

Mr. Hibachi and Ms. Pérez were just hired as fifth-grade teachers in an urban elementary school for students who consistently struggle and achieve poor performance scores on their report cards and on the state's standardized tests. Both teachers previously taught for several years, and each of them is confident their approach to teaching works well—although they differ widely from one another. Mr. Hibachi prefers a more student-centered approach called *constructivism*, whereby students work together in groups to problem-solve and construct their own knowledge with minimal talking or interfering from the teacher. Ms. Pérez prefers a more traditional approach called *direct instruction*, whereby she lectures or disseminates knowledge to students. They then work on small group activities or on worksheets on their own at their desks. However, after speaking with Mr. Hibachi, Ms. Pérez is beginning to have second thoughts about which instructional approach to take—although Ms. Pérez is confident that she can help her students learn and succeed if she identifies the best approach for them! How does one know whether the instructional approach one is using is most effective? Reading and/or conducting educational research can help provide Ms. Pérez with the answers to these and other questions.

INTRODUCTION

Educators often do not visualize themselves as researchers. Research is frequently viewed as the work of university faculty or scientists trying to solve a broad array of problems. But what educators may not realize is that it is possible to conduct research, and doing so can be extremely rewarding and beneficial to one's work as an educator!

In this chapter, we provide an overview of the benefits and characteristics of educational research and the common approaches to conducting educational research. We explain the steps of the scientific method using examples of critical issues of practice and discuss the role of self-regulated learning in helping educators learn how to conduct research. Following our discussion of self-regulated learning, we discuss key logistical constraints and diversity, equity, and inclusion considerations in conducting research. We then discuss ethical considerations in conducting research followed by a brief description of each chapter in the textbook. As you read this chapter and subsequent chapters, try to envision yourself as an educator who is not only capable of conducting research, but one who can use research to make school contexts a more productive, positive, and effective place to learn and work.

THE IMPORTANCE OF EDUCATIONAL RESEARCH

LEARNING OBJECTIVE
1.1   Explain the benefits and characteristics of educational research.

Educational research is a process that involves the organized or systematic collection of information to examine teaching and student learning. Educational research may include simple and straightforward activities, such as reviewing the literature on a specific topic, or more complex activities, such as conducting a true experiment on the use of a new instructional approach. While some educators may be excited about taking a research methods class, many are apprehensive about taking courses titled Research Methods. Educators often associate research methods courses with statistics or mathematics and worry the content will be difficult to understand. In our direct interactions with pre-service teachers or administrators, we have even heard them talk about how they did not see the importance of educational research, stating that their goals are to teach or work in schools not conduct research! But educational research has taken on increased importance in recent years due to the many complex and challenging situations educators encounter, as well as the need for data-driven decision making in schools. It is imperative for practitioners to understand educational research to make informed decisions about problems they are facing in the classroom, school, and beyond.

Educational research can help educators solve critical problems, such as alleviating test anxiety among students, narrowing the achievement gap, and improving student retention.

©iStockphoto.com/GoodLifeStudio

Benefits of Conducting Educational Research

Before we describe the benefits of conducting research, we would like to emphasize that we use the term *educator* throughout this book in a broad sense to include teachers, school counselors, special education educators, psychologists, and administrators. There are several direct benefits to educators at all expertise levels to conducting research, such as providing solutions to problems directly related to practice, solving more broadly defined critical problems, and informing policy decisions and procedures.

Educational research can assist educators in addressing critical issues of practice by helping them learn about new ways to problem-solve and novel approaches that can enrich their experiences and performance as educators. By learning about educational research or even conducting their own research, educators can also gain an understanding about the causes of various problems and reflect upon best practices. For example, if Ms. Pérez conducted research to identify an instructional approach that best supports students who are struggling to perform well on biweekly exams to, she may be able to refine her teaching so that it ultimately has a positive and significant impact on students' achievement outcomes. A larger scale research-to-practice application could involve a national study on middle-school students' science achievement and using that data to change curriculum and instructional practices across the country.

An additional reason that educational research is beneficial is that it can be used to solve more broad critical problems. Critical problems usually extend beyond the scope of a classroom and include situations that have not been studied before. For example, Dr. Corvino is headmaster of a high school that consists of students who have been diagnosed with neurodiverse conditions. She has become increasingly concerned about student morale and its potential effects on attendance, learning, and participation in extracurricular activities. After searching through the literature, Dr. Corvino realized that minimal research has been conducted on student morale in schools similar to her own, and she decided to conduct a research study with her former university professor from her education program. This type of research can provide educators with strategies and solutions to problems that otherwise might not seem solvable.

The third benefit of educational research is that it can be used to inform policy decisions and procedures. Educational research can provide information to government and local officials, school boards, administrators, and other relevant stakeholders to help make evidence-based decisions about education. By relying on findings from educational research, policy decisions can be made that are grounded in empirical evidence and data rather than merely opinions, stories, or subjective experiences. For example, superintendents may conduct research on whether providing students with annual programs on substance abuse can help reduce drug and alcohol use among teenagers within the schools in their districts. Administrators or school board members may have suggestions or ideas on how to reduce substance abuse, but unless these suggestions are backed by scientific evidence, it is unlikely they will be implemented, financially supported, or enforced as part of a new policy. In sum, educational research can help educators become more effective practitioners by providing them with useful insights and information that may be incorporated into their work. But what exactly is meant by research methods and what are some of the characteristics of educational research?

Characteristics of Educational Research

A big part of being an educator involves reflecting on issues related to one's profession. Throughout this book, we will describe scenarios where the educators reflect about different problematic topics and think through and identify potential solutions. Educational research typically begins with first identifying a problem or a critical issue and then conducting a literature review to develop research questions and/or hypotheses. Researchers would then collect, analyze, and interpret the data, and then finally provide written or verbal communication of the results. Research methods refers to specific procedures for collecting and analyzing data to provide information or uncover a new finding. We describe four characteristics of educational research that help explain this definition in greater detail (Figure 1.1).

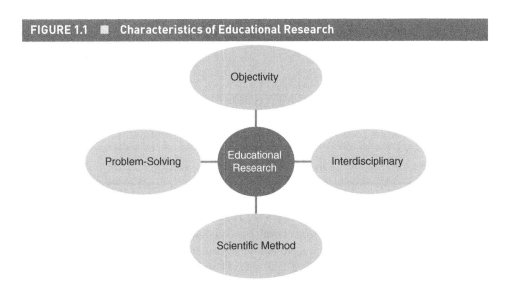

FIGURE 1.1 ■ Characteristics of Educational Research

The first characteristic of educational research is that it usually sets out to solve a specific problem. For example, in our opening scenario, Ms. Pérez wanted to provide her students with the opportunity to achieve the best possible outcomes. In addition to Ms. Pérez figuring out which teaching approach to use, there are a multitude of concerns that educators may encounter—such as school safety, faculty motivation, cyberbullying, standardizing curriculum, high-stakes testing, student diversity, and student connectedness and resilience. Conducting research can help guide decision-making and the use of problem-solving strategies that would not have been available otherwise.

A second characteristic of educational research is objectivity, or an unbiased view of things. In subsequent chapters, we delve into the different research methodologies and designs for conducting research; however, regardless of which methodology or design one chooses, it is critical for researchers to be objective in every aspect of the research process. Maintaining objectivity can be challenging when researchers have implicit biases that naturally and unintentionally skew the collection, analyses, and interpretation of data. It is necessary for educators who are conducting research to reflect on their biases and to remain objective or impartial and to focus on the facts in conducting research.

A third characteristic of educational research is that it tends to be interdisciplinary. While conducting educational research on a specific educational problem can appear straightforward, addressing that problem can also draw from multiple perspectives and disciplines. For example, if Ms. Pérez were to conduct some preliminary research on effective instructional strategies for fifth-grade students who struggle academically, she would likely find journal articles that are discipline specific—such as teaching mathematics, English, or history. However, in doing so, she would also likely come across research on instructional approaches that are specific to special education or neurodiverse students.

The fourth characteristic of educational research is that it is grounded in the scientific method. The scientific method is essential for conducting research and thus is used by scientists and educators alike. We detail the scientific method in the following section given its central role in most educational research.

THE TAKEAWAY

Educational research and its characteristics are essential to educators to help them with problem-solving and difficult issues of practice.

RESEARCH AS A SCIENTIFIC METHOD

LEARNING OBJECTIVE

1.2   Construct the steps of the scientific method in conducting research.

Many of us learned about the scientific method in high school or earlier grades. The scientific method is a dynamic process that helps researchers conduct research by following six distinct steps. One may think the scientific method only applies to scientists or students conducting experiments in science classes; however, the scientific method is naturally intertwined with educational research in that it provides an objective systematic framework that can be followed and replicated. Most educators, which include teachers, school psychologists, school social workers, school therapists (i.e., speech and physical therapists), and administrators, can act and think like scientists as they problem-solve and make decisions about their work or address concerns in the school community. Even when not fully aware of it, educators are constantly reflecting, questioning, assessing, and evaluating in ways that mirror the research activities of scientists.

The use of the scientific method provides a systematic approach for scientific inquiry. Many education programs require a course in research methods because it is important for students to learn about the power and value of conducting research and using the research literature to enhance their work as educators.

Learning how to conduct research and understanding how to critically evaluate published research are professional responsibilities of all educators. In conducting research, educators may decide to collaborate with colleagues, administrators, university faculty, or stakeholders. When conducting research, educators take on two distinct roles: scientist and educator. These two roles provide educators with the power to improve problems of practice and create transformative changes in themselves and others. The six steps to the scientific method as outlined in Figure 1.2 consist of identifying a research problem, reviewing the literature, developing hypotheses, collecting data, analyzing and interpreting the data, and drawing conclusions and communicating the research. This framework provides educators with a systematic approach to conducting research.

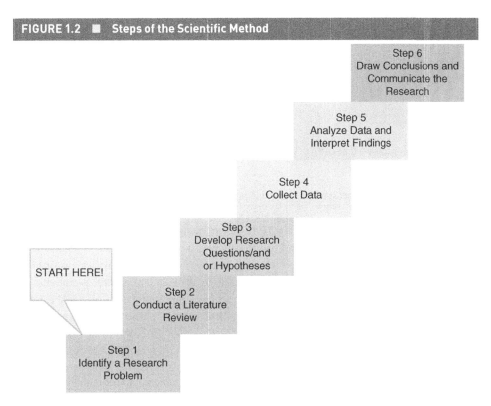

FIGURE 1.2 ■ Steps of the Scientific Method

START HERE!

Step 1
Identify a Research Problem

Step 2
Conduct a Literature Review

Step 3
Develop Research Questions/and or Hypotheses

Step 4
Collect Data

Step 5
Analyze Data and Interpret Findings

Step 6
Draw Conclusions and Communicate the Research

Identifying a Research Problem

The scientific method begins with the identification of a critical issue or problem in education that needs to be resolved. The research problem provides direction, purpose, and structure for the remaining steps of the scientific method. Research problems may be identified by focusing on aspects of a particular theory (for example, testing a statement of a theory), the desire to replicate previous studies, or by one's personal experiences. The research problem should be a critical issue that can be investigated via research; realistic in terms of available time, resources, and skills; and it must be ethical. For example, in terms of a realistic research problem it would be much more manageable and doable for Ms. Pérez to study two types of instructional approaches (constructivist instruction versus direct instruction) across all fifth graders in her school district rather than many different instructional approaches one could use to teach K–6 students nationally.

Once educators have identified a problem, they need to articulate a statement of the problem that includes a description of the key constructs and characteristics of the participants. A statement of the problem refers to an explanation of the problem that one would like to investigate and is written as a declarative statement or as a question. These statements can range from a few sentences to several paragraphs and should include an explanation of the research problem, your claim or position on the issue, and a rationale for the significance of the study.

The statement of the problem helps to guide the development of research questions. A research question is a question about some aspect of your problem that you want to explore or understand. Research questions are explained in further detail in Chapter 2, where we discuss the key components to writing a research question. In our opening scenario, Ms. Pérez knows the students in her school struggle academically, and she has questions about which teaching approach is most effective given the characteristics of these students. In the *Let's See It!* activity, we provide examples of a statement of the problem and research questions using Ms. Pérez's interest in instructional approaches. Following the *Let's See It!* is a practice opportunity for you in the *Let's Do It!*. Keep in mind that the intention of this activity is to help you to begin thinking like a researcher, and we do not expect you to write perfect research questions since we have not yet described the important elements of a writing a good research question. That will come in Chapter 2!

Let's See It! 1.1

Goal: Understand How to Write a Statement of the Problem and Research Questions

Directions: Review the statement of the problem and the sample examples of research questions.

Statement of the problem: Many fifth graders perform poorly in school and on standardized tests. Fifth grade is a critical year for students, as it is the last grade one takes before entering middle school. Research on which instructional approach (constructivist or direct instruction) to use for students who struggle academically is important because the findings can help educators best support their students' achievement. Success in fifth grade can lead to access to high-performing middle school placement that can ultimately lead to entrance to competitive high schools, thus providing the foundation for admission to more competitive colleges. Therefore, fifth-grade performance can possibly impact the future of these learners.

Examples of Research Questions

- Which instructional approach (i.e., constructivist versus direct instruction) will result in higher achievement on standardized test scores for fifth-grade students who are struggling academically?
- Will there be a difference in student achievement on standardized tests' scores depending on which instructional approach they receive (i.e., constructivist versus direct instruction)?

Let's Do It! 1.1

Guided Practice: To Practice Writing a Statement of the Problem and Research Questions

Directions: Imagine you are a principal of a rural elementary school and have been asked by the superintendent to separate all boys from girls for instructional purposes because the superintendent believes students will be less distracted from one another, which will ultimately lead to greater student achievement. Imagine that you do not agree with this approach and, along with several of your colleagues, believe it can be detrimental to students' achievement and socioemotional development to separate boys and girls throughout the day.

Write a statement of the problem as you see it and then describe a couple of research questions you might ask if you were going to conduct a study on this.

Statement of the Problem

_____

_____

_____

Examples of Research Questions

_____

_____

_____

Now that you have completed the *Let's See It!* and the *Let's Do It!* activities, you can independently practice these skills further by completing the *You Do It!* exercise included at the end of the chapter. In that exercise, we ask you to identify a critical problem in education that is of concern to you and then to write the statement of the problem and potential research questions you would seek to have answered.

Reviewing the Literature

Conducting a literature review is the second step in the scientific method, and involves searching databases to identify, review, and synthesize findings from published journal articles, books, and other relevant publications. When conducting a literature review, researchers may discover that research has already been done on this topic, or they may uncover variables not previously considered. The process of conducting a literature review is also discussed in greater detail in Chapter 2, as a critical step in the scientific method that can help researchers fine-tune their research questions and/or formulate hypotheses. It can also provide researchers with information about relevant theories on the topic, which helps to make a stronger rationale and explanation for conducting a particular research study.

STOP AND THINK 1.1

Describe an example of a critical issue related to education that you could search for on Google? Conducting a literature review is a more scientific approach to searching for answers!

Formulating Research Questions and/or Hypotheses

Educators conducting research will often reflect and think about the concerns they have about critical issues they experience or have observed in schools. These reflections often help to formulate research questions that depending on the methodological approach might lead to hypotheses for their study. A hypothesis is a stated belief about the relationship between two or more variables or a proposed explanation stemming from observations and a literature review. It is an essential component of the scientific method because it provides the standards against which researchers evaluate and interpret their results. To formulate a hypothesis, the researcher specifies the relevant variables and the potential relationships among them.

Hypotheses can make predictions about expected outcomes. In many cases, researchers seek to draw a conclusion about the presence of a real effect or relationship among variables. Researchers may also formulate a hypothesis based upon what they think is true. For example, Ms. Pérez may write a hypothesis such as the following: "District-wide fifth-grade students who struggle academically and receive direct instruction perform better on school achievement and on standardized tests than those who receive constructivist instruction." After making this hypothesis, she would then conduct a study to determine if her hypothesis is correct or not.

One common strategy is to write a hypothesis as an "if . . . then . . ." statement. This guideline can be a helpful strategy because it requires the researcher to specify exactly what it is they are interested in studying. Mrs. Pérez may write her hypotheses as follows: (1) If district-wide fifth-grade students who struggle academically receive direct instruction, then their achievement in school and their scores on standardized tests will improve. (2) If district-wide fifth-grade students who struggle academically receive constructivist instruction, then their achievement in school and their scores on standardized tests will improve. Hypotheses derive from the statement of the problem and provide information on what researchers are investigating when they conduct their studies. They are typically the result from fine-tuned research questions that differ from questions posed in the first step of the scientific method because now they will likely be more specific and incorporate variables and relationships uncovered in the literature review that remain unanswered.

Collecting Data

The next step in the scientific method is to collect data. Data collection methods and the type of data collected depend on the type of research being conducted. For example, data may be generated from data collection instruments or tools that may include artifacts, observations, test scores, self-report scales, interviews, surveys, or a combination of different assessment instruments. Regardless of the type of research study one is conducting, it is necessary that data are collected objectively without any preconceived ideas or biases. The data must also be collected in a systematic way such that if another researcher wanted to replicate the research study, they would be able to follow the same procedures using the same instruments.

Analyzing and Interpreting Data

Data analysis is an essential aspect in all research designs. Statistical techniques are often used to analyze data that are numerical or easily quantifiable, such as if Ms. Pérez were to analyze teachers' responses on surveys to predict end-of-the-year student performance. The choice of data analysis should be directly tied to the research hypothesis and/or answer the research questions.

In some research designs, data analysis involves using language-based or non-numeric data to uncover themes and trends to understand or explain a phenomenon. If Ms. Pérez conducted interviews of the teachers in her school district, she might look for themes or patterns in their responses that provide insight into her research questions about which instructional approach seems most effective. Analyzing data usually involves the use of one or more techniques, depending on the type of design implemented and the types of data collected.

Interpreting the results from data analysis is the second part of this step in the scientific method. Here researchers will study the analyzed data or trends to understand its meaning. When examining the results from the data analysis, researchers will interpret the data in the context of the hypotheses and/or research questions or in terms of patterns or new insights. Regardless of the research design, the interpretation must also be honest and free from bias. Data alone are meaningless. It is how one interprets and presents the data that brings the data to life, and these interpretations provide the foundation for drawing conclusions and communicating about the research.

STOP AND THINK 1.2

As educators, what are some of the ways in which you would encounter data outside of the research context? What information might you observe from the data?

Drawing Conclusions and Communicating the Research

The final step in the scientific method is to draw conclusions from the findings and to communicate the research to others. After analyzing and interpreting the data, the researcher will reflect on the findings and draw conclusions that must be supported by the evidence (the data), and these conclusions may or may not support the researcher's hypotheses, answer the research questions, or explain a phenomenon. Conclusions from research should contribute to our knowledge and understanding about a problem or critical issue and can help educators find solutions to localized problems in their classrooms, school, or community, or more broadly—such as finding solutions to statewide or national problems. If Ms. Pérez found at the end of her study that there was no evidence that one instructional approach was more effective than the other, she may conclude that the type of instruction she uses will have less effect on student achievement than other variables. An example of how research can have an impact beyond a classroom or school would be if a group of educators and policymakers conducted a research study that involved second language vocabulary instruction in high schools across the United States and found one instructional method helped students more easily learn and remember new language vocabulary than all other methods. This finding could ultimately influence the recommended approaches for teaching a foreign language across the country.

Communication of the research study is an important part of this last step. Research may be communicated through presentations at conferences or professional workshops, in scientific journals, journals of practice, in blogs, and on websites related to the topic. There are several benefits related to communicating about your research. One in particular is the possibility of influencing your work as well as the work of others. Research findings often are used to help educators make informed decisions along with suggesting problem-solving strategies that may help issues of practice. An additional benefit is that when research is communicated to others, the authors typically conclude with recommendations for further research. These recommendations can provide others interested in conducting research with some topics for future studies.

THE TAKEAWAY

Using the scientific method provides the necessary structure for objectively and rigorously conducting research!

BASIC RESEARCH VERSUS APPLIED RESEARCH

LEARNING OBJECTIVE
1.3   Differentiate between basic and applied approaches to conducting research.

There are many different types of research methods that educators can use to find solutions to their work-related problems or educational topics of concern; however, research methods tend to be categorized as either basic research or applied research. These two categories can be differentiated based on the purpose of a given study and its applicability to one's professional work or practice. Understanding the differences between basic research and applied research can help educators make decisions about which research methods to use before embarking on a research investigation.

Basic research is a type of research that is focused on the understanding of observable events or developing or expanding a theory. In trying to understand the causes of an observable event, basic research is focused on conceptual ideas and processes and will attempt to explain how or why things happen. Broadly speaking, basic research can also be very useful in theory development. Theories, which involve a set of integrated ideas to explain something, often take years to form. Conducting basic research can help develop and demonstrate key components of the theory. Another important aspect of basic research is that it is frequently employed in laboratories or artificial settings. For example, the psychologist B. F. Skinner developed his theory of operant conditioning using animals he placed in his "Skinner box." By providing animals with positive reinforcements (food) in the Skinner box, he was able to shape, control, predict, and record the animals' behaviors.

Applied research focuses on solving a specific problem or testing a theory to determine its usefulness to problems of practice. Unlike basic research, applied research studies typically do not typically contribute to a knowledge base about a phenomenon or theory; rather they contribute to a knowledge base regarding solutions to a particular problem. In other words, applied research is usually not generalizable or universally applicable because it is focused on addressing critical issues that educators grapple with in their schools. For instance, if teachers in a middle school decide to conduct an experiment using a new intervention program to help promote resilience among students who have lost family members, they would be conducting applied research.

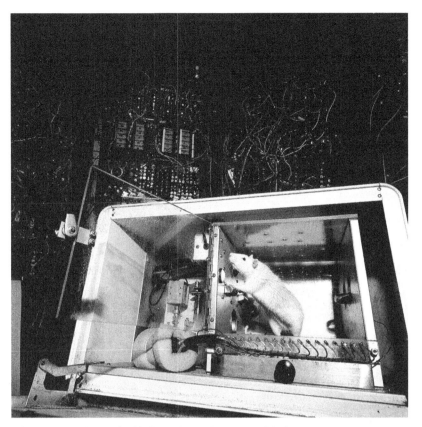

Skinner trained animals using his Skinner box and operant conditioning.

Walter Dawn / Science Source

Basic research and applied research are conducted with different purposes in mind. As indicated, the purpose of basic research is for the advancement or contribution of knowledge. This differs from applied research where the nature of the investigation is a problem or solution focused with participants, instruments, and data collected. In basic research, studies are often aimed at providing information that is generalizable and universally applicable. Thus, basic research studies can often lay the foundation for applied research. Due to the purpose of contributing knowledge, basic research studies tend to be exploratory, descriptive, or explanatory in nature. Table 1.1 presents some of the main differences between basic research and applied research.

In sum, the differences between basic research and applied research involve the purpose and practical focus of a given study. Perhaps an easy way to understand the difference is to think of basic research as research designed to help clarify concepts, make predictions, expand theories, or supply general information needed to solve problems, whereas applied research provides data that can help solve specific problems. While these two approaches seem very different from one another, they are not mutually exclusive, and some studies integrate both purposes.

In the *Let's See It!* we provide some examples of basic research and applied research questions, followed by an opportunity for you to practice in the *Let's Do It!* activity. At the end of the chapter, readers are provided with a self-directed exercise in the *You Do It!* activity.

TABLE 1.1 ■ Differences Between Basic Research and Applied Research	
Basic Research	**Applied Research**
Purpose is to acquire new knowledge or expand on existing knowledge	Purpose is to find solutions to practical or specific work-related problems
Motivated by interest to better understand a phenomenon or advance theory development, thus the research tends to be more conceptual	Motivated by educators' concerns about issues of practice, thus the research tends to involve students, parents, colleagues, and confidential information
Pertains to expanding the understanding of concepts or events to explain a phenomenon or advance theory development	Pertains to examining the relationships among variables and generating data for the purpose of problem solving
Usually occurs in an artificial setting such as a laboratory that is highly controlled	Usually occurs within an authentic setting, such as a classroom or school
Findings or research outcomes are more generalizable and universal	Findings or research outcomes are most relevant to the sample studied
Often exploratory, descriptive, or explanatory—primary goal is to understand or explain things	Often includes action research, research and development, and program evaluation studies—primary goal is to generate data to solve problems

Let's See It! 1.2

Goal: Understand the Differences Between Basic Research and Applied Research Studies

Directions: Read the following different types of research questions to gain an understanding of the different purposes of the studies.

Examples of Basic Research Questions

1. How does alcohol consumption affect the adolescent brain?
2. What are the causes of forgetting for children?
3. Are there cultural differences in participation in after-school extracurricular activities?
4. Do pop quizzes increase the time spent studying after school?

Examples of Applied Research Questions

1. Will eliminating homework increase participation in extracurricular activities for high school freshmen across the school district?
2. What are the ways that school administrators can help improve student attrition for students in marginalized communities?
3. Will offering students laptops improve science retention for African American girls in our state?
4. What is the impact of a meditation intervention program on student achievement scores for middle school students in California?

Let's Do It! 1.2

Guided Practice: To Gain Better Insight Into the Differences Between Basic Research and Applied Research by Practicing Writing Questions Related to Each Approach.

Directions: Using the examples in the *Let's See It!* as models, practice writing two basic research questions and two applied research study questions.

Examples of Basic Research Questions

1. _____

2. _____

Examples of Applied Research Questions

1. _____

2. _____

Hopefully, these examples and practice opportunities have helped you understand the differences between basic research and applied research. Because applied research tends to be focused on specific practical problems, it includes action research, research and development, and program evaluation research studies. It is important to note that applied research can be beneficial because it provides educators with opportunities to conduct research and make a positive difference on students and school communities.

THE TAKEAWAY

Research methods tend to be categorized as either basic research or applied research, depending on the goals and objectives of the research.

WAYS IN WHICH EDUCATORS CAN BECOME REFLECTIVE EDUCATOR-RESEARCHERS

LEARNING OBJECTIVE

1.4   Elaborate on how self-regulated learning can help educators become educator-researchers.

Self-regulated learning, which refers to setting personal goals and utilizing one's motivational and strategic skills for reaching these goals, is a useful framework for educators to envision themselves as educator-researchers. In all chapters of this textbook, we use self-regulated learning principles as features, such as the *Let's See It!, Let's Do It!* and the *You Do It!* activities, to help you learn about research methods. We believe that becoming more strategic, self-aware, and reflective as you learn from this textbook will help you to independently think about and conduct your own research study. We now provide a brief overview of what we mean by self-regulated learning and how it can be a tool for reading and learning about research methods and eventually, conducting your own research study.

Self-regulated learning consists of a cycle of three phases: planning, doing, and reflecting (see Figure 1.3; Zimmerman, 2002). Planning (in self-regulated learning) includes setting goals, deciding what strategies you need to implement to reach these goals, and how motivated you are to work on these plans and goals. Doing refers to actively implementing or acting on the plans you made and monitoring these actions, while self-reflecting refers to thinking about the outcomes and making judgments on what worked well and what needs improvement. The nature and quality of one's self-reflection impacts how one plans before a new attempt at learning. This cyclical model of self-regulated learning is not only embedded in several key features used throughout this book, it can also serve as a "thinking guide" for educators when conducting research or as part of their professional activities.

FIGURE 1.3 ■ Self-Regulated Learning Cycle

Planning can help all of us be more effective in learning new things because it involves setting goals, developing strategies to reach our goals, and feeling a sense of self-efficacy—beliefs in our capability to reach our goals. Self-efficacy beliefs, which one can also think of as self-confidence, can help motivate us as we learn or engage in behaviors.

STOP AND THINK 1.3

Using the phase of planning, think about your goals and plans for how to read and learn the material presented in this book. Do you have a clear plan? How confident (self-efficacious) do you feel about being able to understand the content of this book now that you know it is presented in an easy-to-understand way?

Doing involves carrying out the plans that were made during the planning phase. During the doing phase of the cycle, we keep track of our progress and use metacognitive monitoring Keeping track of our progress can be done in a number of ways such as using a checklist or daily planner—it provides us with overt information about our progress. Metacognitive monitoring is more covert, by thinking about what is working well or not, it allows us to make on-the-spot adjustments to help us reach our goals. Metacognitive monitoring involves being aware of our thoughts as we carry out our plans. These subprocesses can be used by educators to help them sustain their motivation to learn about research or to conduct research. As you begin to read this textbook, it is important to think about the different ways in which you can monitor or keep track of your understanding and progress. We developed several features in this book to help you do this very thing!

STOP AND THINK 1.4

Give some examples of how you monitored your progress on an important task? Did you find it a helpful strategy for reaching your goals?

Self-reflection is a process that most educators engage in on a regular basis that involves evaluating and reacting to outcomes. Self-reflecting is an important professional skill in that it can help educators identify strengths and weaknesses in their performance at work and in their research and can highlight new possibilities on how to improve. For example, if Ms. Pérez from our opening scenario uses direct instruction to carry out her lesson plan, she may observe that while teaching, many students appeared bored and disengaged. Using this self-monitored information, Ms. Pérez may decide to add some group activities to her new lesson plan. In this simple example, she began with a specific lesson plan (planning), followed by implementing a direct instructional approach. Based on the information she gathered about the effects of her teaching (doing), she reflected on whether her instructional approach needed to be modified (reflecting)—thus she incorporated all three phases of the cycle.

In reading the chapters in this textbook, you will find each chapter provides readers with many practice opportunities to self-regulate their learning. As you complete these activities, you will gain a sense of your own understanding. We encourage you to openly reflect on whether you need to go back to the text and review the material or whether you can move forward with the next section or chapter. In addition to using the three phases of self-regulated learning as you read this book, you can also consider using them in each of the steps of the scientific method as one embarks on conducting research.

Now that we have discussed the three phases of self-regulated learning and how they can be tools to help you learn and conduct research, we would like educators to understand the ways in which they can become self-regulated or develop competency to learn research methods and successfully conduct research.

STOP AND THINK 1.5

Have you been in situations where you stopped to reflect on your behavior and the outcomes? Has that helped you perform better next time?

Developing self-regulated learning competency in conducting research is a gradual process that consists of four developmental levels (Schunk & Zimmerman, 1997; see Table 1.2). The first level is observation level: watching a model demonstrate an activity or reading or seeing examples in written form. This is followed by the emulation level: practicing what was observed under the watchful eye of someone with more expertise who will scaffold as needed. Next is the self-control level: performing what was previously practiced but with greater autonomy and minimal supervision or help. Lastly is the self-regulation level: independently engaging in the original activity or a similar activity to what was observed and making adaptations as needed.

It is important for readers to understand that becoming a competent researcher is more of a journey than sprint. You first need to see or hear what good research looks like (e.g., *Let's See It!*) and then get the necessary practice and feedback (e.g., *Let's Do It!*) to apply what was learned. A primary goal of this textbook is to model key research concepts, provide guided practice opportunities for readers, and then offer more independent practice activities. In Table 1.2, we provide a scenario demonstrating the development of self-regulatory competency in conducting research where Dr. Rebecca Schwartz, a faculty member, is mentoring Bradly, a master's student in the higher education leadership program at her college. Bradly expressed an interest in assisting Dr. Schwartz in her research study that involved conducting focus groups on principals' thoughts about standardized curriculums. While the study protocol requires asking the focus group participants specific questions, the follow-up questions are made "on-the-spot" because they are based on the participants' responses to the standardized questions. It is these on-the-spot questions that seem to generate interesting information for Dr. Schwartz's study. Dr. Schwartz assists Bradly in becoming self-regulated enough to run his own focus group for her research study. Each level is presented in the left column, followed by a brief description of the level in the middle column, and an example in the third column.

TABLE 1.2 ■ The Four Levels of the Development of Self-Regulated Learning Competence		
Level	**Explanation of the Level**	**Example of the Level**
Observation	Learn by watching a model demonstrate an activity or learn by reading or seeing examples in written form	Bradly sits quietly during a focus group meeting and observes how Dr. Schwartz asks questions and encourages discussion among the participants with follow-up questions.
Emulation	Emulate what demonstrated under the close supervision of someone more experienced who may scaffold as needed	Dr. Schwartz gives Bradly the list of questions she created and encourages him to ask the questions as she did with the other participants. Bradly models asking the questions in the same way that Dr. Schwartz asked them. Dr. Schwartz jumps in with follow-up questions at times to get the participants to further elaborate or expand on the discussion.
Self-Control	Engage in tasks with limited direct supervision of the model or someone more experienced	Dr. Schwartz asks Bradly to create his own follow-up questions after the initial questions are asked. Dr. Schwartz remains available but is not part of the focus group.
Self-regulation	Engage in tasks independent of others	Bradley is able to now run an entire focus group meeting independently. He begins using the standardized questions and is comfortable asking his own follow-up questions to increase discussion on the topic.

We have highlighted these levels and their importance because this model is foundational for educators developing into researchers. In the next section, we discuss several logistical issues relevant to education-researchers and the importance of diversity, equity, and inclusion in conducting research.

THE TAKEAWAY

Self-regulated learning can help educators develop into educator-researchers.

KEY LOGISTICAL FACTORS AND DIVERSITY, EQUITY, AND INCLUSION CONSIDERATIONS IN CONDUCTING RESEARCH

LEARNING OBJECTIVE
1.5 Consider key logistical constraints and diversity, equity, and inclusion considerations in conducting research.

As you read the chapters in this book and the many examples and scenarios that we provide, you will hopefully see that conducting research can be exciting, enjoyable, rewarding, although somewhat challenging at times. In this section, we describe some of those challenges to help educators anticipate obstacles that may arise so that they are better equipped to deal with them. The three challenges we believe are most common that must be confronted before conducting a research study are knowledge or expertise in research design and methodology (which you will learn from this textbook), the time and resource demands to conduct school-based research, and the constraints that naturally exist within and across many schools. Finally, diversity, equity, and inclusion considerations are discussed as they relate to research in educational contexts.

Expertise in Research Design

Many educators or other school personnel either do not feel self-efficacious about their capability to conduct research or do not believe they have sufficient expertise in research design and methodology without coursework or training. We believe, however, that educators who carefully read and study this textbook will become more knowledgeable and competent in conducting research or will develop the background knowledge needed to seek additional resources to help them in conducting their own research study. By studying and practicing the many activities within the chapters, in particular the *Let's See It!*, *Let's Do It!*, and *You Do It!* sequence of exercises, you will enhance your knowledge, skills, and confidence in conducting research.

Managing Time Limitations

Educators are often inundated with teaching and other professional responsibilities and may feel as if they have little to no time for new activities, let alone the time to conduct a research study! However, what may seem like additional work may actually save time for educators, improve the quality of their work, and perhaps most importantly, enhance the quality of education for students. While conducting research *is* time-consuming, it provides educators with the opportunity to solve a problem related directly to student learning or one that may already be taking time away from other academic-related activities.

Consider a district with historically low school attendance rates. As a result of low attendance, teachers and administrators rotate daily to call students and their families to check on why they are absent. In addition, teachers need to continually set aside time for students to make up missing coursework. The attendance office staff must also devote substantial time to monitoring student attendance and sending emails and written notices to the homes of students who are absent. The various deans or administrators are required to spend time reviewing students' records to determine whether they have been absent too many class days to be promoted to the subsequent grades. These activities reflect hours of time not dedicated to other important education-related activities. While conducting a research study may take time to develop, implement, and analyze, the results from a study may lead to preventative remedies to help these schools and benefit all the educators and students who are missing out on learning. Conducting a research study can also reflect a proactive approach to making innovative improvements or substantial changes. Either way, the time spent conducting research can be offset by the benefits from the findings.

STOP AND THINK 1.6

Are there other constraints that might make conducting research difficult in your school?

School Characteristics as Constraints

Schools vary in terms of financial stability and availability of educational resources. In urban contexts or marginalized communities, schools may lack adequate funds for purchasing books, enrichment programs, computers, and other academic support programs. To further complicate matters, these types of schools and communities may, at times, need to reallocate and use funds earmarked for educational initiatives to address more emergent concerns, such as school safety and school building repairs and updates. Collectively, these issues underscore the need for researchers and educators to collaborate and pool resources for developing a stronger research infrastructure. Educators who are interested in conducting research may seek to collaborate with faculty members from universities who may have access to funding. Many university faculty would welcome the opportunity to collaborate with educators and gain access to schools and students. In addition, there is always the possibility of applying for financial support through grants. Grant money can be used for a variety of research-related activities, such as professional development workshops, classroom supplies, school equipment, and instructional intervention programs for students.

Diversity, Equity, and Inclusion in Conducting Research

Diversity, equity, and inclusion (DEI) considerations in conducting research should be in the forefront and addressed in each aspect of the research process beginning with the research topic. Research topics, for example, could include racial inequalities in grading, the tendency to over-diagnose boys and children of color with attention deficit hyperactivity disorder, the over-disciplining of children of color, the digital divide—a phrase used to describe the critical issue of

Conducting research can ultimately save educators time and improve student learning.

©iStockphoto.com/gradyreese

not all students having equal access to technology—and the achievement gap between groups of students based on race and ethnicity.

Educators should critically examine their theoretical framework, hypotheses, and/or research questions to ensure they are relevant to the populations they are targeting. . It is also important for educators to make decisions about their sample selection to ensure the participants reflect the school, community, and nation, depending on the intent to use the findings. Samples should be selected based on the research design and researchers ought to include a diverse sample based on race, sexual orientation, gender identification, ethnicity, socioeconomic status, giftedness, disabilities, and underrepresented and marginalized groups when appropriate. Researchers have a responsibility to use measurement instruments that are gender neutral, free from bias, and designed to be culturally appropriate for diverse populations.

The protocol for conducting research studies must also be sensitive to DEI and be administered by researchers who are objective and free from bias. Analyzing findings, drawing conclusions, and communicating results should take diversity, equity, and inclusion into account and again be gender neutral and free from racism and bias.

As you can see, there are many logistical challenges to consider when deciding to conduct research in schools, and the importance of DEI should be considered in all aspects of conducting research.

THE TAKEAWAY

Expertise in research; time and logistical issues; school characteristics; and diversity, equity, and inclusion are important considerations when embarking on a research study.

ETHICAL CONSIDERATIONS

Ethical considerations are critical when conducting research and emphasized throughout this book. We begin by introducing this topic with a focus on the importance of using ethics in working with human subjects. Research studies that involve humans must be submitted to the institutional review board (IRB) for review and approval and must meet a number of standards for research in public school systems and universities. While in Chapter 3 we discuss the IRB and the need to obtain permission from students and parents to conduct research in greater detail, we want to emphasize the importance of ensuring that all research presents no risks of harm to human subjects.

Several decades ago, there was little-to-no regulatory oversight on what researchers could do with participants. Institutional review boards, which are designed to protect human subjects from harm, were nonexistent. For example, the infamous study by Milgram (1963) on obedience to authority violated many codes of ethics, particularly deception. In this research (see Milgram, 1963), Milgram obtained participants from newspaper ads advertising for males to participate in a study on learning at Yale University. The procedure involved pairing the participant with another person. Milgram had the two people draw lots to find out who would be the "teacher" and who would be the "learner." The drawing was fixed so that the participant was always the *teacher* and the *learner* was always someone who was pretending to be a participant but was actually working with Milgram on the study. The learner was taken to a room where electrodes were attached to his arms, and the teacher and researcher went into another room that had a fake electric shock generator and a row of switches with voltages ranging from 15 volts (Slight Shock) to 450 volts (Danger: Severe Shock).

Milgram was interested in seeing how far someone (the teacher) would go in administering the shocks to the learner when told to do so by the researcher who represented an authoritative figure. The learner was given a list of words to recall, and he intentionally made mistakes when the teacher tested him, thus prompting the researcher to tell the teacher to punish the learner by shocking him. Every time a (fake) shock was administered, the learner screamed out in pain (although he was not really in pain), and the screams intensified as the voltages increased. Even with the screams, 26 of the 40 participants administered the highest voltage shock on the generator. According to Milgram, "The procedure created extreme levels of nervous tension in some Ss (participants). Profuse sweating, trembling, and stuttering were typical expressions of this emotional disturbance. One unexpected sign of tension—yet to be explained—was the regular occurrence of nervous laughter, which in some Ss (participants) developed into uncontrollable seizures" (p.1, 1961). Milgram's study showed that people will obey an authority figure, even if it involved inflicting pain on others. Clearly, there are several breaches of ethics in this study—such as deception, failure to protect participants, and the right to withdraw at any time during the experiment. Many of the participants suffered long-term emotional and psychological disturbances from participating.

A second research study that breached ethical issues was conducted in the medical field. In 1932, the United States Public Health Service conducted research with the Tuskegee Institute in Alabama to study the course of syphilis in men. Six-hundred African American males, 399 of whom had syphilis and 201 of whom did not have the disease, participated in the study. Syphilis is a sexually transmitted disease that can cause serious health problems if left untreated—such as nerve and brain damage, paralysis, tumors, blindness, and death. Researchers targeted mainly poor rural men who had never been treated by a doctor, and when visiting them, told the men they were being studied for "bad blood"—a local term used to describe several conditions, such as fatigue, anemia, rashes, and flu-like symptoms, among others. The men who agreed to participate in the study received free medical exams, free meals, and free burials. Without knowing they had a contagious disease, many of the men passed the disease on to their partners. Pregnant women who had syphilis passed the disease to their children. In the mid-1940s, penicillin became the nationwide treatment for people who have syphilis, but this was not made available to the men in this study who were viewed as participants in this research and not considered patients. Forty years later, in 1972, an investigation took place. The investigation was prompted when the information about the study was leaked to the media: newspapers, television, and radio. Many of the participants had died of syphilis or related symptoms, infected their wives, and had children born with congenital syphilis. This study remains one of the most unethical research studies conducted on human subjects and the impetus for the *Belmont Report*.

The *Belmont Report* created from the National Research Act of 1974 developed guidelines for conducting ethical research due to a series of harmful and unethical studies, such as the Tuskegee Syphilis Study and Stanley Milgram's Obedience to Authority Study. The *Belmont Report* outlines three areas of focus in protecting participants: respect for persons, beneficence, and justice (U.S. Department of Health and Human Services, 2022).

When conducting research, respect for persons entails that participants in the study must be treated as autonomous human beings. Lack of respect is shown when a researcher rejects a participant's ability to act on their judgment or information. However, not all participants are capable of acting autonomously. For example, children need guidance developing autonomy, individuals who struggle with mental illness, and those who are imprisoned may lose the capacity to act autonomously. Respect for these vulnerable individuals requires that protections are offered because they cannot act autonomously.

Beneficence centers on maintaining the well-being of all participants by conducting research that does not cause harm and that maximizes the possible benefits for the participants. For example, deceiving a participant about the purpose of a study could potentially cause harm if what the participants are engaging in goes against their own beliefs and restrictions (e.g., providing sensitive information that could be used in a manner that is not clearly stated to the participant can result in discrimination and harassment). A critical issue related to beneficence is that participants cannot be coerced to participate. All participants need to be informed that they can withdraw from the study at any time without penalty. If a teacher asked a trained colleague to interview eighth-grade students about anti-bullying campaigns in the school, they would need to obtain informed parental consent forms and minor assent forms from the students. If a participant who was in the middle of an interview wanted to stop, the interviewer would have to honor the request without coercion. This would ensure that the well-being of the student is taken into account and that they are not put in jeopardy for the sake of the study.

The third section of the *Belmont Report* is known as justice. To have a framework of justice within a research study, the educator/researcher should ensure that all potential participants have an equal opportunity to be selected to participate in a study. Thus, the principle of justice requires vulnerable individuals to receive special protections regarding the benefits of the study. The vulnerable should be assured of receiving their fair share of the benefits and also be protected from having more than their fair share of the burdens of research imposed on them. If a researcher chooses to study an after-school STEM program, all eligible students in the school need to have an equal chance of being selected for the research study, according to justice. This action ensures that no one is denied access to a beneficial program without a fair system of selection in place. If the researcher wants to select one of six fourth-grade classrooms to participate in a research study on STEM education during the school day, the classroom could be randomly selected, and then students in the selected classroom could be invited to participate in the study.

As you can see from the two studies described previously, it is critical that researchers read and adhere to the guidelines provided in the *Belmont Report*.

THE TAKEAWAY

Research that involves human subjects must maintain ethical standards, and researchers should review the Belmont Report to understand the ethical principles prior to beginning a study.

A LOOK AHEAD: ORGANIZATION OF THIS BOOK

LEARNING OBJECTIVE
1.7   Identify the various content features in the individual chapters of this book.

In this section, we describe the organization and overall content of the book. Across the various chapters of this book, we describe multiple effective approaches for conducting research. Each chapter begins with learning objectives that correspond to the various sections of the chapter and then discusses ethical considerations in conducting research. Beginning with Chapter 2, the last learning objective in each chapter discusses guidelines from the latest edition of the *Publication Manuel of the American Psychological Association*.

We have organized and sequenced the chapters into what we believe is a natural flow to learning about research methods. Beginning with Chapter 2, "Reviewing the Literature," we provide readers with information about how to explore, review, and analyze challenges in the workplace to identify critical issues in education. Most importantly, this chapter provides an overview of the purposes and steps to conducting, reviewing, and synthesizing a literature review and how to articulate a research problem or question using the planning, doing, and self-reflecting phases of self-regulated learning. In our opening scenario, given that Ms. Pérez had already identified a critical issue (i.e., direct versus constructivist instruction) of interest to her, she is ready to complete Step 2 of the scientific method, conducting the literature review. Her plan is to conduct a literature review on different instructional approaches and their effectiveness before developing her research questions and hypotheses.

Chapter 3, "Research Design: The What, When, and How of Research," helps readers understand the broad distinctions between research methodology and designs. This chapter provides information on the differences and similarities between qualitative and quantitative methodologies as well as some of the key designs subsumed within each methodology. This chapter introduces readers to various research designs and provides decision-making guidelines to help readers determine the most effective designs for addressing a particular research question. Given her interests, Ms. Pérez may ultimately decide to survey teachers in her district (quantitative methodology) or conduct personal interviews of teachers in her district (qualitative methodology), or she may choose to do a combination of both (mixed methods). This chapter presents foundational concepts and principles linked to subsequent design chapters.

In Chapter 4, "Non-experimental Research Designs," we discuss the key features of non-experimental designs and provide insight into the types of research questions that can be best addressed with such designs. Specifically, we compare and contrast descriptive, correlational, and comparative non-experimental designs in terms of the nature of relevant research questions, measurement-related issues, and sample-related issues. In our opening scenario, Ms. Pérez was concerned about which teaching approach is most effective for students who struggle academically. She decided to develop and administer a survey to teachers in her school district to uncover non-teaching variables that could contribute to students' academic success. The survey targeted multiple variables, such as years of teaching experience, instructional approaches, attitudes toward marginalized populations, beliefs about student motivation, and teacher self-efficacy. This chapter could be useful to Ms. Pérez and others who are interested in using research to describe the nature or relationships among different variables.

In Chapter 5, "Experimental Research Designs," we begin with a discussion of the common threats to internal validity and the link between experimental design features and internal validity. This is followed by descriptions of true experimental, quasi-experimental, and single-participant experimental designs. In addition to administering her survey, Ms. Pérez also collected end-of-year student grades and found that instructional approaches were, in fact, highly correlated with students' end-of-year grades. While this information was useful, Ms. Pérez wanted to examine the effects of different instructional approaches on student learning. Given that she recognized the limitations of correlational studies for drawing conclusions about cause and effect, she decides to conduct an experiment to determine if the two instructional approaches differentially impact end-of-year grades. Chapter 5 is the go-to chapter for educators who want to examine issues pertaining to the causal effects of intervention or instructional activities within the classroom.

Chapter 6, "Qualitative Research Designs," is dedicated to helping educators understand the characteristics of qualitative research. Qualitative research is dynamic and adaptable by nature, and this chapter identifies the types, purposes, and process of conducting qualitative research as well as the breadth of designs (i.e., case studies, phenomenology, grounded theory). If Ms. Pérez decided she wanted to gain insights about the perspective, attitudes, or lived experiences of teachers and administrators when working with students who struggle academically, she could read Chapter 6 for guidance about the characteristics of conducting a good qualitative research design as well as the roles of the researcher when using such designs.

Chapter 7, "Mixed Methods Research Designs," describes the nature of a mixed methods research design and when it is most appropriate to use. We identify the types of commonly used mixed methods research designs and the steps involved in planning, conducting, analyzing, and interpreting the findings from mixed methods research. If Ms. Pérez decides to conduct a mixed methods research design, she will combine information from surveys, focus groups, and individual interviews with teachers. She believes this approach will provide her with a more comprehensive picture of what teachers' beliefs and experiences are before moving forward with an experimental design. This chapter would help guide her in using this methodology.

In Chapter 8, "Action Research for Educators," we define action research and its origin, distinguish it from other research designs, and underscore the benefits of conducting action research within school contexts. In addition, we provide an overview of the differences between practical and participatory action research and describe how the cycle of self-regulated learning overlaps with the action research cycle. Ms. Pérez read about action research in her research methods class and has decided that rather than conduct a larger study involving other teachers, administrators, and students, she will conduct an action research study in her classroom. For the first half of the school year, she will use direct instruction, and for the second half of the school year, she will use a constructivist approach to determine which approach results in higher grades. Action research can help educators conduct research within their own classrooms or school settings and create transformative changes in themselves and others.

In Chapter 9, "Program Evaluation," we describe the characteristics of program evaluation. We identify the purposes, types, characteristics, and typical logic model of program evaluation initiatives. In addition, we identify how to create, conduct, analyze and report findings of a program evaluation. At Ms. Pérez's school, the principal wants to assess the benefits of developing professional development workshops on constructivist practices. This chapter can help Ms. Pérez's principal make decisions on the evaluation of using a constructivist approach before requiring it in her school.

In Chapter 10, "Sampling and Measurement Learning Objectives," we present information about how to select a sample for a research study. In addition to discussing sampling-related terminology, probability and non-probability sampling techniques, and sampling error, we compare sampling across quantitative, qualitative, mixed methods, and action research designs. We clarify the differences between measurement and measurement error, differentiate levels of measurement, and discuss the different types of validity and reliability in measurement. If the superintendent in Ms. Pérez's school district decided to conduct a statewide research study on instructional strategies, they would gain some insights into the best approaches to use in obtaining a sample of participants rather than attempting to use participants from all schools within the state.

In Chapter 11, "Data Collection," we discuss tools and methods for gathering and organizing data within educational settings and the advantages and disadvantages of quantitative and qualitative data. Central to this chapter is the critical role of data collection instruments (e.g., surveys, interviews, observations) in the research process and how data collection sets the stage for data analysis. Before Ms. Pérez conducts a study on instructional approaches, she needs to make decisions about the specific data collection instruments or approaches to use in her study. Chapter 11 can help provide guidelines that can assist her in making these decisions.

Chapter 12, "Descriptive Statistics," focuses primarily on descriptive statistics, an aspect of statistics that focuses on numerically and visually summarizing the data included in a dataset. In addition to presenting an overview of the key characteristics of datasets and the purpose of descriptive statistics, we describe the most effective ways of visually depicting a distribution of scores, discuss measures of central tendency, and identify and explain different metrics of variability of scores in a distribution. We also discuss procedures for determining where an individual's scores rank in relation to others and highlight the use of correlational analysis as a descriptive statistic. When Ms. Pérez was in her teacher education program, she read through several articles that presented different types of data, including measures of central tendency and variability. By reading this chapter, she will understand what these concepts mean in the context of research and how this information is essential when analyzing and interpreting results from her research study.

In Chapter 13, "Inferential Statistics," we define and describe inferential statistics and provide information on probability and what it means to indicate research results are statistically significant. We also provide information on conducting hypothesis testing, interpreting statistical significance, and comparing and contrasting commonly used inferential tests, including the distinction between parametric and nonparametric statistics. Ms. Pérez knows it is not realistic to conduct her study on every teacher in her school district. Thus, she selects a sample to collect data from and then hopes to determine whether the results with the sample is what one would expect to see in the broader population. This chapter will help her understand when to make inferences about whether the research results represent real and meaningful effects.

In Chapter 14, "Qualitative Analysis," we discuss foundational principles of qualitative analysis and detail coding techniques. We provide readers with methods for analyzing qualitative data across different qualitative designs and various ways to organize and present data. If Ms. Pérez used teacher focus groups and interviews as her primary data collection instruments, she will need to use an analysis approach for identifying codes and themes or broad ideas in the qualitative data. For example, she may notice that several teachers express lacking self-efficacy and feelings of frustration in obtaining adequate funding to help their students. This chapter will help Ms. Pérez understand the various ways to create meaning about the lived experiences and perspectives of the sample.

Chapter 15, "Communicating Research," shifts the focus from conducting to communicating research. We identify best practice approaches to written and oral communication, discuss key considerations when communicating research, and underscore how self-regulated learning principles apply equally well to helping educators not only become successful researchers but also effective communicators. Ms. Pérez plans to publish her research in an academic journal upon completion. This chapter will help Ms. Pérez understand the components of a journal article and how to engage in self-regulated learning to accomplish her goal.

Chapter 16, "Using Research to Guide Practice," describes the ways in which research can be directly linked with practice. We provide insights into how to evaluate the quality of research and discuss the specific ways in which research can be used to support practice for teachers, administrators, and the community. We describe the impact of research on higher education programs and professional and personal growth and discuss the use of self-regulated learning to implement research-based change. Ms. Pérez was initially motivated to conduct research on teaching strategies because she was concerned about ensuring her students were provided with the best instructional approach. However, after speaking with professors from her teacher education program, she realized that student achievement was an issue with which many schools were struggling. Ms. Pérez is hoping that with her research, she will learn ways to improve student learning and importantly, have an impact on the current literature on teaching students who struggle academically.

CHAPTER SUMMARY

This chapter provides an overview of the benefits and characteristics of educational research and describes research methods in the context of educational settings. The chapter presents six steps of the scientific method for conducting educational research and differentiates between basic and applied approaches to conducting research. This chapter also describes how educators can become better learners and users of research methods and prepare themselves for conducting research using self-regulated learning followed by a discussion of logistical issues to consider and the importance of taking into account diversity, equity, and inclusion when conducting research in schools. The chapter closes with a discussion of the ethical considerations in conducting research on human subjects and a brief summary of the subsequent chapters.

EXTENSION ACTIVITIES

You Do It! 1.1

Self-Directed Practice: Writing the Statement of the Problem and Research Questions on a Critical Issue in Education

Directions: Describe a critical issue in education, then write a statement of the problem and potential research questions you would seek to have answered.

Description of the Critical Issue

_____

_____

_____

Statement of the Problem

_____

_____

_____

Research Questions

_____

_____

_____

You Do It! 1.2

Self-Directed Practice: Practice Distinguishing Basic From Applied Research

Directions: Using Table 1.1, list four differences between the basic research and applied research from the abstracts that follow

Basic Research Example

Schunk, D. H., & DiBenedetto, M. K. (2020). Motivation and social cognitive theory. *Contemporary Educational Psychology*, *60*, 1–10. https://doi.org/10.1016/j.cedpsych.2019.101832

This article discusses motivation from the perspective of Bandura's social cognitive theory. Motivation refers to processes that instigate and sustain goal-directed activities. Motivational processes are personal/internal influences that lead to outcomes—such as choice, effort, persistence, achievement, and environmental regulation. Motivation has been a prominent feature of social cognitive theory from the early modeling research to the current conception involving agency. The conceptual framework of reciprocal interactions is discussed, after which research is summarized on behavioral, environmental, and personal influences on motivation. Key internal motivational processes are goals and self-evaluations of progress, self-efficacy, social comparisons, values, outcome expectations, attributions, and self-regulated learning. Critical issues confronting the theory include diversity and culture, methodology, and long-term effects of interventions. The article concludes with additional recommendations for future research on contexts, conceptual clarity, and technology.

Applied Research Example

Pickering, J. D., Bickerdike, S. R. (2017). Medical student use of Facebook to support preparation for anatomy assessments. *Anatomical Science Education*, *10*(3), 205–214. https://doi.org/10.1002/ase.1663.

The use of Facebook to support students is an emerging area of educational research. This study explored how a Facebook page could support Year 2 medical (MBChB) students in preparation for summative anatomy assessments and alleviate test anxiety. Overall, Facebook analytics revealed that in total, 49 (19.8% of entire cohort) students posted a comment in preparation for either the first (33 students) or second (34) summative anatomy assessments. Eighteen students commented in preparation for both. In total, 155 comments were posted, with 83 for the first and 72 for the second. Of the 83 comments, 45 related to checking anatomical information, 30 were requiring assessment information, and 8 wanted general course information. For the second assessment, this was 52, 14, and 6, respectively. Student perceptions on usage and impact on learning and assessment preparation were obtained via a 5-point Likert-style questionnaire, with 119 students confirming they accessed the page. Generally, students believed the page was an effective way to support their learning and provided information that supported their preparation with increases in perceived confidence and reductions in anxiety. There was no difference between gender, except for males who appeared to be significantly less likely to ask a question as they may be perceived to lack knowledge ($P < 0.05$). This study suggests that Facebook can play an important role in supporting students in preparation for anatomy assessments.

Basic Research	Applied Research

KEY TERMS

Applied research
Basic research
Beneficence
Doing
Educational research
Emulation level
Hypothesis
Justice
Observation level
Planning (in self-regulated learning)
Research methods

Research questions
Respect for persons
Scientific method
Self-control level
Self-efficacy
Self-reflecting
Self-regulated learning
Self-regulation level

ANSWER KEY

Stop and Think Activities

STOP AND THINK 1.1

Most students will have used Google to search for information. Unlike much of the information on Google, the literature review typically provides information that is credible and has been reviewed by peers in the field.

STOP AND THINK 1.2

Answers may vary, but for teachers, the data may include assignments and test grades, students' responses to questions, conversations with students, meeting with parents, and classroom observations. Administrators may look at admissions and enrollment data, attrition data, diversity data, cost of attendance data, graduation rates, percentages of students attending colleges, and students' performances in competitive athletic or cultural events, to name a few. All of these data provide educators with information that can be very useful in understanding their current situations, making decisions, and in developing problem-solving strategies.

STOP AND THINK 1.3

Answers will vary. Some plans may be the following: to skim the chapters before reading them, to take notes on the chapters, to complete all activities, to work with a study partner, and so forth. We are hoping that readers will indicate they feel self-efficacious about learning the material in this textbook.

STOP AND THINK 1.4

While answers will vary, there is considerable research to support that self-monitoring can help us keep track of progress to reach our goals.

STOP AND THINK 1.5

Responses will vary, but like Stop and Think 1.4 research supports the idea that self-reflection can help us perform better in subsequent tasks. When we self-reflect, we are able to review what we have done and think about whether we can make improvements in our behavior in the future to lead to more positive outcomes.

STOP AND THINK 1.6

Responses will vary depending on the school setting, but an example of a constraint not already discussed includes accessibility to students—some schools may not be receptive to having research conducted among their students, and parental consent may be difficult to obtain. Parents may not approve of their children participating in a research study.

Let's Do It! Activities

LET'S DO IT! 1.1
Guided Practice: To Practice Writing a Statement of the Problem and Research Questions

Directions: Imagine you are a principal of a rural elementary school and have been asked by the superintendent to separate all boys from girls for instructional purposes because the superintendent believes students will be less distracted from one another, which will ultimately lead to greater student achievement. Imagine that you do not agree with this approach and believe it can be detrimental to students' achievement and socioemotional development to separate them throughout the day. Write a statement of the problem as you see it, then describe a couple of research questions you might ask if you were going to conduct a study on this.

Statement of the problem: Segregating students based on birth gender can have detrimental effects on students' achievement and socioemotional development. Single sex education can promote harmful gender role stereotypes among students and faculty. In addition, it can promote discrimination among students who identify as the opposite sex or who are nonbinary.

Examples of Research Questions

1. Will there be a difference in student achievement among students who are separated by gender for instruction?

2. Will students who are separated by gender feel as if they are being discriminated against as they are forced to conform to gender-role stereotypes?

Let's Do It! 1.2

Guided Practice: To Gain Better Insight into the Differences Between Basic Research and Applied Research by Practicing Writing Questions Related to Each Approach

Directions: Using the examples in the *Let's See It!* as models, practice writing two basic and two applied research study questions.

Examples of Basic Research Questions

Examples can vary greatly, however here are two additional examples:

1. Do courses in teacher education programs that focus on cultural diversity impact curriculum choices in schools?

2. What are the ways that parental involvement in homework promotes accountability among students?

Examples of Applied Research Questions

Examples can vary greatly, however here are two additional examples:

1. What are the perceptions of teachers regarding a professional development program on mathematical instructional effectiveness across high schools in the district?

2. Do 12th-grade students feel more self-efficacious about learning science than ninth-grade students in our school?

2 REVIEWING THE LITERATURE

A DAY AT WORK

When Learning Doesn't Stick!

©iStockphoto.com/skynesher

Mrs. Burnett is an experienced fourth-grade teacher in a diverse, suburban elementary school who specializes in math and science. As with all educators, she and her colleagues grapple with a range of dilemmas in helping students learn. The fourth-grade teachers on her team all agree that one of the most frustrating challenges is when students say, *"We never learned this!"* or *"I don't really remember."* These are phrases teachers hear regularly; however, forgotten information seems especially problematic in math instruction where each skill builds upon the next. Even when third- and fourth-grade teachers work together to ensure a smooth transition for learners between grade levels, students seem surprised to hear some math topics in fourth grade were previously learned.

For the teachers on Mrs. Burnett's team, students forgetting math concepts and processes seems to occur on a regular basis; from month to month, week to week, or even day to day. Because this is an ongoing concern, Mrs. Burnett and her colleagues often brainstorm ways they can improve this situation. Together, they are constantly trying new strategies, searching for ideas, and discussing possibilities. What can they do to *make learning stick?* Perhaps, there is another way to solve this problem.

INTRODUCTION

Mrs. Burnett has many questions about why students do not retain information from class. She wonders if these questions have been previously examined by researchers. Mrs. Burnett decides to read some journal articles in order to determine if there is research on this topic that can help her identify an effective solution. As educators review the research literature, they will often be able to more clearly define the critical issue. Literature reviews provide the opportunity for educators like Mrs. Burnett to dive deeply into their critical issue and read about what other scholars in the field have explored. By conducting a literature review, Mrs. Burnett and her team can see what has been done, where the gaps in the literature are, and either articulate research questions or identify solutions based on a synthesis of the existing literature. The literature review functions much like a funnel (see Figure 2.1). The educator will first identify a critical issue and how

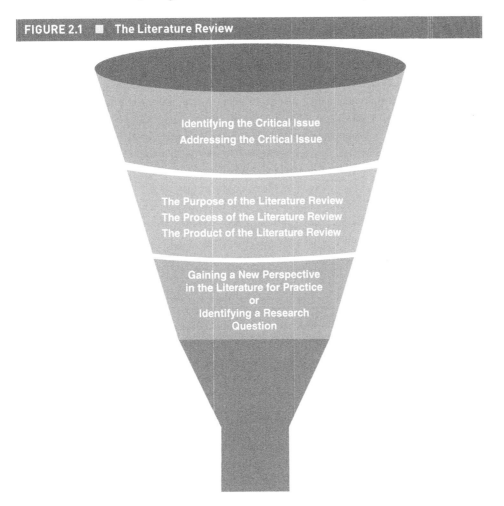

FIGURE 2.1 ■ The Literature Review

Identifying the Critical Issue
Addressing the Critical Issue

The Purpose of the Literature Review
The Process of the Literature Review
The Product of the Literature Review

Gaining a New Perspective
in the Literature for Practice
or
Identifying a Research
Question

it may be addressed. The educator will then work through the purpose, process, and product of the literature review and, hopefully, will gain a new perspective about the critical issue or relevant research questions.

CRITICAL ISSUES IN THE WORKPLACE

LEARNING OBJECTIVE
2.1   Investigate a critical issue in the workplace.

There are many professionals working in school settings, such as administrators, teachers, school psychologists, school counselors, special education assistants, and social workers. While learning and performance in the classroom often take center stage, these professionals have different roles and areas of focus. Teachers, who tend to have the most contact with students, spend a lot of their time thinking about how best to get students to learn and perform well on class assignments, tests, or projects. Administrators, who are also interested in student learning, would likely focus on "broader" issues, such as overall student performance on standardized state tests or final year-end tests. Other support staff, like school counselors or school psychologists, tend to work individually with students, oftentimes to address personal or social-emotional difficulties.

Regardless of the type of school-based professional, these individuals will all encounter obstacles and challenges in their work. Administrators may struggle with the number of teacher observations they need to conduct, while teachers may get frustrated because their students come to class unprepared or fail to perform well on exams. Now, the purpose of this section is not to speculate about whether educators encounter challenges in their roles but rather to figure out whether such challenges are simply "a normal part of the job" or whether they represent a critical issue—that is, an issue that needs to be systematically explored, reviewed, and analyzed in greater depth.

Schools have many mechanisms (e.g., how to support student needs) to deal with noninstructional and instructional problems or situations. When a problem (e.g., student discipline issues) persists after several attempts to solve a problem, educators may think, "Now what? What do we do about it?" These types of issues can be addressed at a departmental level or through collaborations between administrators and faculty. As a first step in generating solutions to important issues, problem-solving teams rely on existing support structures and services within their schools. Beyond such practice, it is again relevant for us to ask, *Is this a daily problem or a critical issue?*

STOP AND THINK 2.1

Principal Jiménez consistently hears concerns from teachers that students are not prepared for class. Is this a "daily problem" or a "critical issue?" Why?

Although a critical issue is difficult to define, in general, it can often be thought of as a type of problem that has strong implications for student learning or teaching, persistently occurs over time despite attempts to correct the problem, or adversely impacts a certain group of individuals. These issues are distinct from daily problems, which tend to be relatively more localized, minor in intensity, and resolvable using our existing knowledge or available information. A few guiding questions to help distinguish between a critical issue and a daily problem are listed in Table 2.1.

TABLE 2.1 ■ Guiding Questions to Distinguish Between Critical Issues and Daily Problems	
Critical Issue?	**Daily Problem?**
Does the issue seem unresolvable with the information you have available?	Is the problem something that can be resolved in straightforward way?
Does the issue seem to be on a larger scale—for example, include multiple classes, groups of students, across the school or district?	Is the problem more localized and not consistent among similar students, teachers, or situations?
Does the issue have a significant impact on teaching and learning?	Is the problem troublesome (and perhaps annoying or bothersome) but does not significantly interfere with teaching and learning?

Importantly, a broader and problematic critical issue in school-based settings can often emerge from common day-to-day experiences. For example, when a teacher has a nagging feeling that students seem confused about their lesson or they notice many students seem bored by the content, they may be prompted to reflect on the pedagogical changes that can be made to improve understanding and interest. Unfortunately, modifications that educators may make do not always work. It is in these instances when more extensive or intensive changes are needed that one notices the emergence of a critical issue. Other examples of critical issues involve students who have difficulty with reading fluency even after multiple interventions have been put in place, the availability of unbiased procedures for honors-based placement, or the achievement gap for under-represented students. To grapple with these critical issues, educators may need to systematically explore the research literature that addresses these issues.

THE TAKEAWAY

A critical issue is a topic of significance that occurs frequently or with regularity and may warrant further research and exploration.

THE PURPOSE OF A LITERATURE REVIEW

LEARNING OBJECTIVE
2.2 Describe the purpose of a literature review by reading through research articles..

Finding solutions to critical issues in education often requires extending beyond one's personal experiences, discussions with colleagues or other professionals, or utilizing existing school resources. In situations where solutions cannot be readily found, educators may turn to a more systematic, investigative approach to examining a critical issue. From a research perspective, this process is called a literature review.

In a sense, the educator who is conducting a literature review is like a detective who is searching for clues, answers, or ideas for cracking the case when there is no obvious solution. The literature review provides the backdrop or explanation to frame the search and ultimately can lead to providing the answer to the critical issue. Figure 2.2 illustrates a general process of using a literature review to address a critical issue and to identify ways to hopefully resolve the critical issue.

FIGURE 2.2 ■ Purposes of Conducting a Literature Review

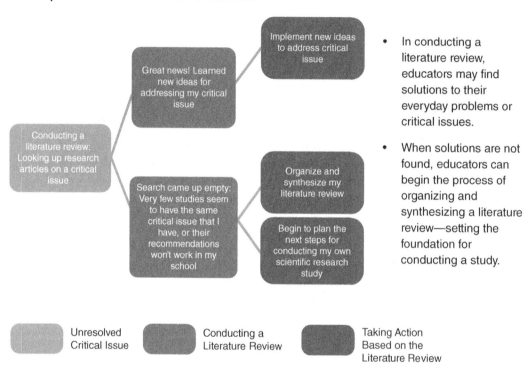

The research literature is important for several reasons. Educators can review selected aspects of the literature to learn about theories or models that underlie student learning and functioning, instructional approaches, and teacher motivation. With this new information, educators can potentially make more effective decisions about promoting positive changes in schools, and identifying new areas for conducting research. In short, conducting a literature review can enable educators and others to (a) become familiar with the theories, findings, methods, and data collection instruments of other researchers; (b) refine and clarify the critical issue or research problem; (c) provide support for current practices; and d) identify new research to address the critical issues of interest.

THE TAKEAWAY

Conducting a literature review is an important first step to tackling a critical issue or solving a research problem. A literature review provides important information on what is already known about a specific area of interest and what future research may need to address.

CONDUCT A LITERATURE REVIEW

2.3   Conduct a literature review from start to finish.

We discuss the literature review as a process that leads to a product (Figure 2.3). It is common for educators and researchers to use the term literature review to refer to the steps, procedures, and tactics for identifying relevant and important research about a given topic. However, in this chapter, we distinguish the "how" of conducting a literature review from the "what" that the literature review produces. It is common to hear people talk about a literature review simply in terms of a written summary and formal critique of research-related information about a particular subject area. While this product or written summary is important, it is equally relevant to clarify the many steps or processes needed to produce this final product.

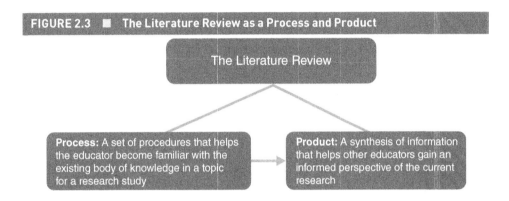

FIGURE 2.3 ■ The Literature Review as a Process and Product

In this regard, literature reviews can vary across two broad dimensions: (a) scope (i.e., selective or comprehensive) and (b) structure of the search (i.e., informal or systematic).

In terms of scope, an educator/researcher interested in studying academic performance may choose to focus specifically on group differences (e.g., special education students versus general education students) or on a selective issue, such as paired reading strategies. However, if educators wanted to take a more comprehensive approach, they could search for and evaluate articles on a range of topics, such as socioeconomic status, parental education levels, and reading materials in the home.

The intensity and urgency of the critical issue will often dictate whether the literature review is informal or systematic. Perhaps a school-based professional wants to present information about paired reading strategies to a collaborative team. In this case, a less structured review may be most appropriate. However, if students' reading scores across several grade levels in a school district have been declining for the past couple of years, with subsets of students not meeting proficient levels of understanding, a more systematic and targeted review of the literature could be helpful. In short, when the stakes or standards are higher, one will likely commit to conducting the more systematic review.

Figure 2.4 shows the literature review process as a five-step process that results in a final product or synthesis of information. Regardless of the scope or structure of the literature review, the process to product pathway includes several overlapping and reciprocal procedures: (1) searching, (2) identifying, (3) evaluating, (4) organizing, and (5) synthesizing information. In the following section, we review each of these five steps.

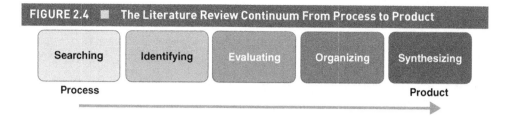

FIGURE 2.4 ■ The Literature Review Continuum From Process to Product

Searching   Identifying   Evaluating   Organizing   Synthesizing

Process   Product

Searching for Sources of Research

University libraries, public school libraries, and community libraries offer a range of databases for educators to locate empirical research. This is research centered on observations and measurements of a particular event based on the experiences of a researcher. Prior to conducting the search, the interested party should identify key concepts associated with the research problem. This step is necessary because databases operate through keyword searches and often contain a thesaurus to identify the general keywords. Here are a series of steps to follow in conducting a search using keywords:

1. Select and narrow a topic.

2. Identify the key concepts in the research problem. Write a list of key terms.

3. Develop a list of synonyms for key terms. Check the thesaurus to find synonyms.

4. Conduct a database search by starting with the most important key term and sequentially adding additional terms.

5. Narrow or broaden the search as needed. The command "and" between two key terms during a database search narrows the search results; the command "or" broadens the search by telling the search engine that these two key terms are synonyms.

6. Repeat the process as needed.

7. Check the references cited by the articles located to identify other related studies.

8. Create a reference list using the American Psychological Association's (APA) style.

9. Consider if other information would be helpful.

When most people talk about the research literature what likely comes to mind are peer-reviewed journal articles produced by researchers whose conclusions and interpretations are reviewed by their peers or colleagues; however, the literature is broader than that. For example, the education literature includes a vast number of publications including books, journal articles, technical reports, papers presented at professional conferences, and curriculum guides, among others based on primary and secondary sources. Given that this broad set of resources can be overwhelming for educators, a key first step is to figure out how to distinguish between primary and secondary sources.

Primary Versus Secondary Sources

Generally speaking, primary sources reflect first-hand accounts of a situation or phenomenon, while secondary sources analyze and review information provided by the primary sources. While our perspective is that understanding the difference between primary and secondary sources is valuable, . . . you may be asking yourself, "Does the difference even matter? I am just really looking for a solution to my problem!" We believe the answer is yes! Although both types of sources are important, they do different things.

Primary sources are documents, research studies, images, and artifacts reflecting firsthand information. These sources represent new knowledge, discoveries, personal accounts, or original thinking about a topic. Often times, these sources are typically the first formal appearance of original research. For example, Cleary and Kitsantas (2017) published a study on middle school students' motivation and performance in mathematics. The authors collected data from a large sample of middle school students, analyzed and interpreted the data, and then reported the findings in a published manuscript. The information provided in that article *added* to the current knowledge base about how contextual factors, student motivation, and self-regulated learning relate to mathematics achievement.

In contrast, secondary sources involve analyses, syntheses, and interpretations of primary sources. They are often persuasive as they attempt to describe or explain primary sources in the form of conceptual articles, book chapters, and nonacademic work, such as blogs, newspaper articles, and website information. For example, Schunk and DiBenedetto (2020) wrote an article about motivation in an education journal. Unlike Cleary and Kitsantas (2017), however, Schunk and DiBenedetto did not conduct the studies discussed in the article but rather they provided an overview of the literature that addressed motivational factors in education. Secondary sources can be helpful in integrating data findings from different primary sources. They can also help build a framework of understanding by forming a general picture of research conducted about a particular topic. However, it is also important to be wary of and vet your sources for credibility and accuracy.

Some things to consider as you evaluate research sources include the age of the source (i.e., relevant and current, the author and their background or experiences, the domain extension of the site, which will help you determine who is funding the source (e.g., .org, .com, .gov, etc.); consistent citation of sources; publication sources (e.g., *New York Times, National Geographic,* etc.); and the credibility of the source. Determining whether a publication is a primary or secondary source can sometimes be tricky. While the distinction may be clear in some situations, at other times, it is not so obvious. Thus, educators will often need to dig deeper to figure this out. Table 2.2 presents a few guiding questions and examples to help educators differentiate between primary and secondary sources.

TABLE 2.2 ■ Guiding Questions for Primary and Secondary Sources Related to Education Research		
Ask the Question . . .	Primary	Secondary
Does the publication describe a current and new study, and were the findings (data and results) collected by the authors?	✓	
Does the publication ONLY present a review of research conducted by other scholars or educators?		✓
Does the publication present a review of research conducted by other scholars or educators but also offer new and novel information based on the review?	✓	
Is an educator presenting a paper at a conference considered a primary or secondary source?	It depends! If the paper is describing research conducted by the educator, it is primary. If the paper synthesizes research conducted by someone else, it would likely be a secondary source.	

An essential goal when searching for research articles is not only ensuring that they are relevant and current but also peer-reviewed. Thus, some common guidelines for accessing articles are to search for peer-reviewed works published within the last 10 years, but seminal work or articles published by prominent researchers in the field are often widely used regardless of the timelapse. *Peer-reviewed* journal articles that are published in a refereed journal are high quality manuscripts determined suitable for publication by experts in the field. When researchers submit an article for publication, they remove their names and identifying information. The article is then distributed to people who are considered experts on the particular topic. These experts are blinded (i.e., unaware) to the author who wrote the article or conducted the study. Typically, two or three experts are asked to review and to convey their recommendations for each article submitted for publication in a journal. This peer-reviewed process is important because it helps to ensure that the only articles that are published have been vetted and reviewed by scholars in the field.

Use of the Planning, Doing, and Reflecting Cycle to Conduct Searches

Now that we know how to effectively search for literature and to discern between primary and secondary sources, and peer-reviewed articles it is time to practice! Following is the *Let's See It!* activity, which is an example of the process involved in locating research for learning strategies used by elementary students to retain knowledge in math.

Let's See It! 2.1

Goal: Connect the Planning, Doing, and Reflecting Cycle of Self-Regulated Learning to Conducting a Literature Search

Mrs. Burnett's observations are leading her to think that working memory issues are affecting students' knowledge retention. Using the backdrop of working memory in mathematics classrooms, Table 2.3 illustrates how the procedures for conducting a literature search correspond with the planning, doing, and reflecting cycle of self-regulated learning. The planning, doing, and reflecting cycle represents the processes of self-regulated learning that you, the learner, can use to plan how to complete a literature review assignment, make an attempt to do the assignment with guidance and feedback, and then reflect upon the final product to figure out what worked or what needs to be improved regarding your literature search skills.

TABLE 2.3 ■ Mrs. Burnett Illustrates How She Searches for Sources of Research in Math Knowledge Retention		
Searching for Sources of Research	**Guiding Procedures**	**Mrs. Burnett**
Planning	1. Select and narrow a topic. 2. Identify the key concepts in the research question. Write a list of key terms. 3. Develop a list of synonyms for key terms. Check the thesaurus to find synonyms.	Mrs. Burnett and her team decide to conduct research on working memory and mathematics retention. Keywords/phrases: "mathematics," "learning strategies," "elementary students," "working memory," "knowledge retention."

Searching for Sources of Research	Guiding Procedures	Mrs. Burnett
Doing	1. Conduct a database search by starting with the most important key term and sequentially adding additional terms. 2. Narrow or broaden the search as needed. The command "and" between two search key terms narrows the search, and the command "or" broadens the search by allowing synonyms. 3. Repeat the process as needed.	Mrs. Burnett, using the preceding key terms, adds one key term at a time to the options in the search bar. She uses other options, including the use of "math" instead of "mathematics" and adds the word "and" to further refine her search: "elementary education" and "mathematics."
Reflecting	1. Check the references cited by the articles located to identify other related studies. 2. Create a reference list using APA format. 3. Consider if other information would be helpful.	Mrs. Burnett reviews the reference list in the articles located on mathematics and memory retention. She decides that comparing articles for regular education and special education students would be helpful. Perhaps the term "differentiation" would assist with the search.

Using our example with Mrs. Burnett and the various guidelines presented in this section, take a moment to practice conducting a literature search using the planning, doing, and reflecting cycle using the following *Let's Do It!* activity.

Let's Do It! 2.1

Guided Practice: Connect the Planning, Doing, and Reflecting Cycle of Self-Regulated Learning to Conducting a Literature Search

You have been teaching seventh-grade math for two consecutive years. Your observations are leading you to think that your students' lack of self-efficacy in themselves considerably undermines their capability to succeed in mathematics. You are looking for instructional strategies to increase seventh-grade student self-efficacy beliefs in mathematics. Use key words related to the critical issue (planning) and conduct a quick search using those key words (doing). What did you find? Did you discover additional search terms you originally did not think of (reflecting)? Fill out the Table that follows to help you organize your thoughts, following the example in the *Let's See It!* 2.1.

Searching for Sources of Research	Guiding Procedures	Your Responses
Planning	1. Select and narrow a topic. 2. Identify the key concepts in the research problem. Write a list of key terms. 3. Develop a list of synonyms for key terms. Check the thesaurus to find synonyms.	

Searching for Sources of Research	Guiding Procedures	Your Responses
Doing	1. Conduct a database search by starting with the most important key term and sequentially adding additional terms. 2. Narrow or broaden the search as needed. The command "and" between two search key terms narrows the search, and the command "or" broadens the search by allowing synonyms. 3. Repeat the process as needed.	
Reflecting	1. Check the references cited by the articles located to identify other related studies. 2. Create a reference list using APA format. 3. Consider if other information would be helpful.	

Identifying Sources of Research

After conducting an initial literature search, one would likely have a list of several studies to potentially include in the research synthesis. Oftentimes, there are more articles than necessary to include in a synthesis, but once the articles are reviewed, it is determined that many of them do not actually fit with what the educator/researcher needs. When screening all the articles from the search, there are several things to keep in mind (see Figure 2.5). Each article selected should correspond with the overall problem (i.e., critical issue) emphasized in the literature review. More importantly, articles should reflect the key headings within the literature review. For example, if a research team wants to learn about issues with absenteeism and history achievement, it is

When identifying relevant sources of research for the literature review, researchers should keep in mind the specific context of their critical issue, such as grade level or subject of interest.
©iStockphoto.com/Halfpoint

important to include research and then under subheadings, use key terms, such as *absenteeism and history achievement*. Further, if the research team also wanted to consider general education versus special education as part of the review, then they should include some studies related to these topics. As a general benchmark or guidepost as you navigate this process, seek to identify at least two to three key articles per subheading.

Moreover, it is key to not only align the sources with the overall purpose of the literature review, but to also target contemporary and seminal studies that are considered scientifically valid; that is, they are empirically-based and peer reviewed as part of a reputable journal. In addition, as previously indicated, another guidepost is to select articles published within the last 10 years, unless the writing is from a seminal author. A useful tactic in conducting a literature review is to look up the references in a recently published article that addresses the same critical issue you wish to target. By simply reading the titles of the articles in the reference section, educators may find some additional and helpful articles to consider and locate. Finally, the research questions, methods, and findings should all correspond to the educator's critical issue.

Checklist for Searching for and Identifying Research Articles

1. Does the research study address the critical issue?

2. Is the research study empirically based on information presented?

3. Is the research study peer reviewed?

4. Was the research study conducted within the past 10 years?

5. Did I check the references of the articles for other potentially relevant studies?

Evaluating Sources of Research

Once the search and screening of the initial set of studies is completed, educators need to do a more thorough, nuanced analysis of these targeted studies. Before getting into specifics about the evaluation process, let's discuss the standard format or structure of a primary source or peer-reviewed article.

Research articles tend to follow a similar sequence of heading and section in a research paper (e.g., abstract, introduction and literature review, method, results, discussion, references). Identifying and understanding this standard format will help educators in their search for articles as well as in the writing of one's own research study. We will delve deeper into each component of a research article next.

Abstract

The abstract is a comprehensive summary of the key sections of the study. It typically includes a brief statement of the topic, a summary of the method used, and the findings. All in all, an abstract includes approximately one or two sentences for each major section of the paper. Abstracts are important because they can help educators get an immediate sense regarding the potential relevance or importance of a study to the target critical issue. It is quite common that after reading the abstract, the educator may realize the study is not addressing the topic of interest and will decide to exclude it from the literature review.

Take a look at the following abstract from a study conducted by Bell and Pape (2012). What information can you gather about the study from reading this portion of the article only?

In this study, we take a sociocultural perspective on teaching and learning to examine how teachers in an urban Algebra 1 classroom constructed opportunities to learn. Drawing on analyses of discourse practices, including videotaped classroom lessons as well as other classroom artifacts and telephone interviews, we describe ways that two teachers and their students interacted to develop mathematical understanding. Through descriptive narrative, we highlight practices that positioned students as competent mathematical thinkers and provided evidence of students' mathematical agency. This study suggests that critical awareness of discourse practices in conjunction with teacher mediation of other affordances for learning within the classroom environment might engage students in mathematical practices such as problem solving, explaining mathematical ideas, arguing for or against specific solutions to problems, and justifying mathematical thinking.

Introduction

The introduction sets the stage for the research study by identifying the problem or critical issue and providing a rationale regarding its overall importance and significance. The authors will often review the theory and background of the key topics and strive to weave together related topics to produce a compelling rationale and a set of research questions. Ideally, the main body of the literature review situates the study within a theoretical framework and presents a logical presentation of information and gaps in the literature that lead to the purpose statement and the research questions of the study.

Method

A method section identifies the participants (sample), research design, procedures used to carry out the study, data sources (dependent variables), instrumentation (where relevant), and a process for analyzing the data. The description of the methods and procedures is the heart of any research study; thus, this section needs to be very clear and explicit, so other educators or researchers can easily replicate the study. Educators will be introduced to the key elements of a methods section in the subsequent chapters.

Results

The results section helps a reader understand the nature of the data that were collected as well as the answers to the research questions listed in the introduction. It typically includes several tables and figures to illustrate the important findings.

Discussion

The discussion provides a thoughtful and analytical discussion of findings of the study and its link to the established literature on the topic. In this section, the authors will address both expected and unexpected findings. Thus, the discussion section is not based solely on the authors' perspectives and opinions. It also references implications for practice, when appropriate, and will discuss the various limitations of the study and future directions of research.

References

In this section, the authors provide a list of primary and secondary sources that were included across all sections of a research article. The majority of citations (i.e., when an author references or cites a source) will appear in the introduction and discussion sections, although some may also be included in the methods. This list in most educational outlets should be presented in APA style.

Now that you have a sense about the key components of research articles, how do you evaluate them to determine their relevance and importance? As mentioned previously, when you are searching and reading through articles, you may decide to eliminate some that are not closely linked to the critical issue. Further, conducting research is analogous to being a detective; you need to pay attention to certain clues or details that convey information about the quality and relevance of the articles to your critical issue or student population. For example, in searching for articles on working memory and mathematics, you may find an article that initially seems relevant. However, when reading the article, you discover that it actually focuses on helping engineers resolve spatial memory problems that arise in building construction.

Hopefully, for any literature review that is conducted, educators will find plenty of articles that are closely tied to the critical issue. These articles should be put aside and used as part of the formal literature review (to be discussed in a subsequent section). But please keep the following point in mind as you embark on this journey: Conducting a thorough literature review is a necessary but time-consuming process. As educators, we strive to make a positive impact on those we teach and work with. Conducting an effective literature review is critical for helping us improve teaching and learning and or for stimulating ideas about needed educational research.

STOP AND THINK 2.2

If you were to conduct a literature review on a critical issue, what sort of articles would you search for?

Organizing Sources of Research

The next key step in the literature review process is to organize the details and key features of the targeted studies. This step in the process is akin to teachers encouraging their students to keep binders with separation tabs to categorize different aspects of their coursework—homework, classwork, quizzes, projects, and so forth. Similarly, teachers often turn to *Google Drive* or other similar platforms to create folders for a similar purpose. These organizational strategies are useful to students because it is easy for students to get overwhelmed with information or mixed up. The same logic applies to educators sifting through the literature on a given topic—they can also become overwhelmed.

In organizing research studies and information prior to synthesizing and writing the literature review, we encourage educators to use a table or annotated bibliography (see Table 2.4). This type of visual display is often helpful for examining each individual study and for identifying trends or themes across them. Grouping your studies according to themes or main ideas will help you see how your sources relate to each other. Table 2.4 incorporates the key aspects of research articles previously displayed according to related themes.

TABLE 2.4 ■ Example Matrix of How to Organize Your Articles							
	Full Citation	Purpose/ Research Questions	Definition of Terms	Research Method	Sample	Data Collection Instruments	Analysis	Key Findings
Theme A								
Theme B								

The last step in conducting a literature review is to synthesize what you have discovered; thus the next section will tackle the synthesis step in more detail.

SYNTHESIZE RESEARCH

2.4   Synthesize research when writing a literature review.

Much like a detective who has completed their investigation, we are now ready to analyze and synthesize the targeted studies into a meaningful narrative—that is, to report an accurate and compelling story about what was found in our review. However, this story is not one that can be formed in one sitting. As shown in Figure 2.5 and as we have frequently mentioned, the literature review is both a process and a product. To make this easier to follow, we conceptually break down this journey into two phases: the pre-synthesis phase and the synthesis phase.

The pre-synthesis phase steps entail the following:

1. Communicating the problem clearly

2. Summarizing key research studies (one or two short paragraphs) and emphasizing how each article relates to the critical issue

The synthesis phase elaborates on the following:

3. Comparing and contrasting studies that address the critical issue

4. Developing a rationale, if appropriate, when interested in conducting a new study

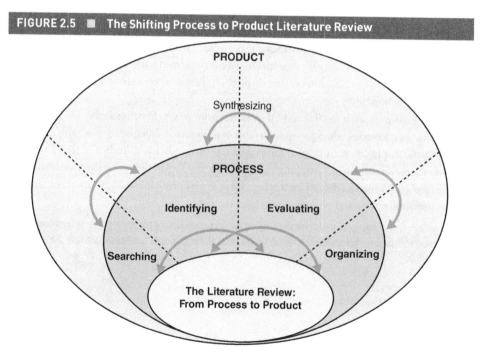

FIGURE 2.5 ■ The Shifting Process to Product Literature Review

By analyzing the literature review journey in two phases (i.e., pre-synthesis and synthesis) encompassing the four steps, you have all of the information to lay out the blueprints for the story you want to tell. Now, this story crafted by a researcher will not only summarize findings from the research articles, but will also integrate and weave the articles together to relate them back to the original critical issue or problem identified at the beginning of the journey. Later in this chapter we will walk you through the journey of crafting your own story.

The Pre-synthesis Phase: Communicating the Critical Issue and Summarizing Key Studies

In the first four steps of the literature review process, you have already done the research and prepared summaries (your annotated bibliographies). Now, you need to take this information and craft the story you want to tell. The pre-synthesis phase represents the activities authors use to organize their thinking about how to write their summary most effectively—making sure they communicate and summarize the key studies that relate to their critical issue. An important feature to include early in the outline involves the conceptual definitions of key terms. A conceptual definition is a dictionary-like definition that helps one clearly communicate the essence or nuances of the key terms or variables in a study. These definitions help the educator to state more clearly what is meant and can be taken from all reference works, including journals, books, and other sources. Table 2.5 lays out the steps for the planning involved in the pre-synthesis phase.

TABLE 2.5 ■ The Planning of the Pre-synthesis Phase—Summary of Steps

Step 1.	**Review and Select**
	Review the summaries you prepared on the articles you thought were directly relevant to your critical issue and select the ones that seem the *most* relevant; be sure to include seminal articles.
Step 2.	**Organize and Order**
	Think about the flow of your story and organize your articles in the order you want to "tell" or write about using that order. Articles are typically described in a story in chronological order, but you must also keep in mind other information such as sample characteristics, themes, and methodologies that are related to your critical issue.
Step 3.	**Outline Your Story**
	Statement of the problem: Add a few bullets highlighting the significance of the critical issue and why it is an issue that needs further research.
	Key terms: Use your key terms to identify and prepare an outline of subtopics based on the articles you have selected—these will be your *headings or subheadings* (themes you want to emphasize).
	Gaps in the literature: Add a few bullets on where research is needed.
	Rationale: Write a few sentences or bullets about why your proposed research study is important in light of the critical issue.
	Research questions/hypotheses: Draft two to three research questions or hypotheses. While we provide guidance on how to write a research question in the following section, during this phase, you can begin to generate questions that remain after your research on the critical issue.

Overall, as you outline the story it is important to read other literature reviews to get a sense of the types of themes you might want to cover or ways to organize this section of the paper. Take advantage of your reference list if you find a well-conducted literature review. The reference section of similar sources might help to identify studies to emulate. The following checklist provides a review of elements to consider when conducting a pre-synthesis of the literature.

Checklist for Literature Review Pre-Synthesis

Checklist for Literature Review Pre-Synthesis

1. Review and select

2. Organize and order

3. Outline your story
   a. Statement of the problem
   b. Key terms subheadings
   c. Gaps in the research
   d. Rationale
   e. Research question/hypothesis

The Synthesis Phase: Analysis and Developing a Rationale

The synthesis phase involves compiling all components from the pre-synthesis phase into a narrative story. The researcher will begin by comparing and contrasting all the studies that were gathered, followed by an analysis of how exactly empirical research studies fit together to develop a rationale related to the critical issue. Using the outline of your topic, pull together all the research you have gathered as part of your "investigation" and then start thinking about how you can weave these research sources all together to create a narrative. Look for patterns, similarities, and differences between studies and between groups of studies that will help you identify gaps or areas for further research.

In Table 2.6 we provide an overview of the key steps in this synthesis process.

TABLE 2.6 ■ The Doing of the Synthesis Phase—Summary of Steps

Step 1. **Stay Focused, Read, and Emulate**

Use the outline to begin writing but stay focused on your critical issue. The key is to weave the critical issue into each of the sections you are writing. In your introduction, describe and emphasize the importance of the critical issue and the need for research in this area. By now you should be familiar with reading the introductions to research studies. Use one that you particularly like as a "model" of how you would like to write.

Step 2. **Compare and Contrast**

As you describe the studies using your annotated bibliographies, compare and contrast the strengths and weaknesses of these studies. Be sure to keep your subheading themes in mind and always stay focused on your critical issue.

Step 3. **Emphasize Gaps**

Do not hesitate to indicate gaps in the research. Think of yourself as the detective who discovered some clues but not everything to solve the case—this means further research is needed. Weave these weaknesses in as you write about the research findings. This helps with the development of your research questions and strengthens your rationale for conducting research.

Step 4. **Writing Tips**

Use the reference list summaries to integrate in the writing. Whether the writing is a summary or quotes, be sure to include a citation. Excessive use of quotes should be minimized in the synthesis. Use primary sources to synthesize information and secondary sources to further support ideas and as transitions.

Report the findings of authors in past tense as concisely as possible.

Double check that the articles you cite are documented and formatted appropriately in APA.

The doing of the synthesis phase is in essence the integration of existing knowledge. The next phase, the reflecting of the synthesis phase will help you reflect on the synthesis product and make revisions as needed. Write, revise, and rewrite to ensure accuracy of content and formatting. It might be also beneficial to have another pair of eyes to read and critique your synthesis. In Table 2.7 we provide a list of the "should" and "should nots" of the literature synthesis product.

TABLE 2.7 ■ The Reflecting of the Synthesis Phase: The "Should" and "Should Nots" of the Literature Synthesis Product		
	"Should"	**"Should Not"**
Step 1	● Adequately cover previous research on the topic ● Cite findings directly from original studies (primary) ● Cover seminal (classic or often-cited) research ● Be organized hierarchically and logically by topic ● Discuss "major" studies in detail and "minor" studies more broadly ● Establish a theoretical framework for the research problem ● Make an argument or compelling rationale for the significance of the research	● Only reflect an educator's own research ● Reflect others' "opinions" about previous research ● Focus primarily on outdated materials of research ● Be organized by author-related studies ● Reflect studies that are unrelated to the research problem or methods of the study ● Be a simple summary or list of studies ● Use anecdotal evidence as the primary part of the rationale
Step 2	● Go slowly; write, revise, rewrite, revise . . . ● Keep your eyes on the goal and continuously monitor your progress ● Ask another colleague to provide feedback	● Rush or be sloppy and leave important information out ● Underestimate a writing assignment as it typically takes more time than expected ● Avoid seeking help

We now provide a checklist on some key questions to consider when developing a literature review synthesis. Using this checklist, take a look critically at your synthesis product and reflect on the steps you took to complete this task, focusing on adjustments and revisions needed to improve the final product.

Checklist for Literature Review Synthesis

1. Did I identify and adequately review the two or three essential ideas or areas related to my overall critical issue?

2. Are my headings appropriate and logically sequenced and presented?

3. Did I include a relevant theory or model that links the various studies?

(Continued)

4. Did I present and discuss the key or seminal studies that support my overall rationale?

5. Did I present a compelling, logical case or "story" regarding why my research questions and proposed study are important?

At first glance, it could seem as if you are writing a report or summary of the articles, but a literature review is much more than that. While a report may be written to provide an overview of a topic or persuade readers to understand an argument, the overall goal of the literature review extends further. In this sense, the literature review frames current understandings of a topic to inform research questions, synthesize information across studies, and highlight gaps in the literature. It is helpful to remember that the literature review is an iterative process, and it takes much time to finalize a fully developed product. The purpose is to determine what has been done and what still needs to be done.

The story generated from the literature review will either help educators

- resolve the critical issue of interest, or

- identify questions that need to be answered—that is, to conduct a research study!

STOP AND THINK 2.3

Over the course of his academic career, Martin has written many book reports. Is a literature review synonymous with a "book report"? Why or why not?

FORMULATE RESEARCH PROBLEMS OR QUESTIONS

LEARNING OBJECTIVE

2.5   Articulate a research problem or question.

At this point in the chapter, you have learned about the steps educators can take to better understand, refine, and synthesize the literature around critical issues. You also learned how school-based problems can often serve as stimulating factors for conducting a comprehensive and systematic literature review. A literature review represents both a process of uncovering what research has to say about the critical issue as well as how one might best analyze and synthesize that research. Ideally, doing the investigative work of a literature review will help educators or other professionals do one of two things:

- Find solutions or deeper understanding of the critical issue—this is akin to the "Aha!" moment educators arrive at when realizing how to help their students or improve instruction.

- Develop questions that need to be examined in a research study—think of this process as a jigsaw puzzle where all the pieces fit nicely but there are a few pieces missing. What does one need to make the puzzle more complete?

Research questions are directly linked to the target critical issue but typically go beyond this issue or capture it in investigative or measurable terms. Research questions developed for new research studies shine the light on unresolved problems or questions that have not been previously studied in the literature. In the next section, we describe in more detail how to develop effective and clear research questions

Parts of the Research Question

Well-stated research questions can do one or more of the following: (1) describe characteristics, trends, or processes in a specific context, (2) identify and compare groups based on specific characteristics, and/or (3) relate variables or factors under investigation. For example, a research question may specifically examine how frequently middle school students use self-regulatory strategies while solving math problems in class. An educator interested in a comparison research question might also want to examine whether males and females differ in their use of self-regulatory strategies. Or one might want to examine relationships between use of self-regulatory strategies and mathematics achievement. Regardless, combinations of these factors, while aligning with the critical issue and purpose of the study, can open up the opportunity for quality research questions that can be addressed by researchers in the field, respectively.

Strategies for Writing Good Research Questions

Writing a good research question is not easy. It is a revision-oriented process that takes time, reflection, and refinement. Albert Einstein emphasized strong questioning techniques and curiosity as the impetus for discovery. In fact, Einstein's theory of relativity developed from his initial question, *"What if I rode a beam of light across the universe?" So how does an educator know when and how to write a research question?* Some questions or critical issues that might arise in school are not necessarily questions that can be answered even after completing a thorough literature review.

Developing effective research questions includes whether or not the critical issue is measurable and whether it will contribute to our understanding and educational practice. Specifically, five general factors should be considered when thinking about research questions: (a) feasibility, (b) measurability, (c) clarity, (d) significance, and (e) ethicality.

Feasibility

For *feasibility*, an educator may have a topic of interest; however, collecting data may not be possible because of resources like time, money, personnel, and equipment. For example, districts may limit when research takes place because of testing windows, so it might not be possible to answer a question for an issue that only occurs in the spring.

Measurability

Measurability reflects the extent to which the key variables or construct can be clearly and effectively assigned values or meaning. An example of a research question not able to be answered or measured is one based on subjective value judgements lacking concrete measurable variables—such as "Is Mr. Jones or Mrs. Smith a better math teacher?" This research question is vague and subjective and does not offer a construct that can be measured. A better research question in this situation might be "Does Mr. Jones exhibit more effective forms of student questions and feedback than Mrs. Smith?" You may hypothesize that the time of day the classes are taught or the level of enjoyment students feel while in the class—two measurable constructs—might have something to do with the answer to this research question.

A research question formulated to assess teacher mathematical knowledge should be readily measurable.

©iStockphoto.com/PeopleImages

Clarity

Clarity relates to whether the research question accounts for conceptual and operational definitions of key terms. As mentioned previously, a conceptual definition provides the meaning of a construct and often relates to a theoretical basis, whereas the operational definition delineates how a variable will be identified, measured, or assessed by providing a clear, concise, detailed definition of a measure. Vague conceptual and operational definitions create poorly defined research questions.

Another aspect of clarity that is really important is making sure that your research question aligns with your critical issue and your purpose for the study. For example, it would not make sense to have a research question on family dynamics if your critical issue is students having trouble retaining what was learned during lessons, with the purpose for your study being to explore different pedagogical approaches to presenting the curricula. Although family dynamics and how the students' caregivers view learning could impact student retention, a research question of this nature would not align well given differing characteristics (e.g., key words used during literature search, different set of participants, different context/setting for the study).

Significance

As a researcher, a key question to ask is whether the research question is worth exploring. That is, does the answer to a research question provide an additional contribution to address the given critical issue? When addressing the issue of *significance*, keep in mind two reflective notions:

- Why would it be important to answer this question practically or theoretically?

- How might answers to this question contribute to the field?

Designing questions that are not significant and will not improve practice or conditions for students may not be useful.

Ethicality

One of the most important things to consider when writing a research question is *ethics*. In other words, the intent of the study should not cause or should seek to minimize physical or psychological harm to the participants. For instance, asking some students about their educational experiences during a major climate event, such as a hurricane, might stir up traumatic memories. Research conducted through universities and public school systems are reviewed by an institutional review board (IRB) to ensure the study is ethical.

THE TAKEAWAY

A good research question is well defined, feasible, measurable, significant in terms of its contribution to existing literature, and ethical to answer.

Reflecting the Methodology Within the Question

There are many different types and formats of research questions. In quantitative research designs, research questions will often emphasize the nature of relationships or effects among variables, whereas qualitative research designs utilize questions that focus more on the nature, aspects, or characteristics of processes, issues, and events. Table 2.8 shows examples of quantitative and qualitative research questions.

TABLE 2.8 ■ Examples of Quantitative and Qualitative Research Questions

Example

Describe characteristics, trends, or processes in a specific context.

What are elementary teachers' perceptions of their experiences in using manipulatives in the math classroom?

Compare groups based on specific characteristics.

What is the impact of math manipulative instruction on English language learners (ELL) as compared to their typical peers?

Relate variables.

What is the relationship between math achievement and student math self-efficacy in a math manipulatives intervention?

After a research question has been formulated, the educator will need to decide what research design will be used to test the research question. Thus, the first consideration is whether the question relates to the methodology or broad approach of the study (e.g., quantitative or qualitative). For instance, in a quantitative study, the emphasis will be on examining trends or relationships among variables (e.g., achievement, interest, socioeconomic status). On the other hand, qualitative studies aim to capture the meaning of processes and events, focusing on the "why and how," often from the perspectives or lived experiences of participants. Qualitative questions are framed very differently from quantitative questions because questions relate closely to the research goals and methods as part of the research framework. Consider the following scenario to frame quantitative and qualitative questions: An elementary school has a growing population of gifted and talented children. Presently, these students are immersed in classrooms with little or no individual support except for a 1-hr-a-day class of advanced instruction. To supplement enrichment programs, these students were invited to an after-school STEM camp. A team of elementary school educators were interested in understanding the day-to-day school experiences of these students as well as the impact of the after-school STEM camp based on student STEM interest and problem-solving skills. Like many issues or situations that educators face, this scenario can be investigated from a quantitative or qualitative research perspective.

Quantitative and qualitative research questions may be used separately or in tandem to gain a more in-depth understanding of a critical issue, such as evaluating the impact of an after-school STEM camp on student learning.

©iStockphoto.com/kate_sept2004

An example of a quantitative question related to this scenario could be "Does participation in the after-school STEM camp impact gifted and talented elementary students' STEM interest and problem-solving skills?" This question is more quantitative in nature because it is examining effects on specific variables, interest in STEM, and problem-solving skills. On the other hand, to gauge the perspective of student experiences in their daily activities in comparison to the STEM camp, an appropriate qualitative question might be "What are the perspectives and attitudes of gifted and talented elementary students on the experiences of a STEM camp?" While both questions require data collection, the quantitative question underscores the use of measures (i.e., STEM interest scale) to determine changes for the students receiving the program. On the other hand, the qualitative research question reflects the need to do a deeper analysis or investigation of students' thoughts and feelings (i.e., perspectives) about the after-school program. The quantitative question relies on numbers and statistical analyses, whereas the qualitative question will likely be answered through analyses of interview transcripts or other forms of qualitative data. The quantitative–qualitative distinction is addressed thoroughly in Chapter 3. Table 2.9 provides some guidance to question starters for both styles of questions.

TABLE 2.9 ■ Quick Sentence Starters for Quantitative and Qualitative Research Questions	
Quantitative	**Qualitative**
"Is there a relationship . . ."	"What is the perspective . . ."
"Are there differences . . ."	"What are . . ."

In this section, we use the *Let's See It!* and *Let's Do It!* activities to help you learn how to write qualitative and quantitative research questions. For further practice, please complete the "*You Do It!*" activity.

Let's See It! 2.2

Goal: Identify Research Questions That Meet the Conditions of Feasibility, Measurability, Clarity, Significance, and Ethicality

Having reviewed the literature and refined her research study, Mrs. Burnett is interested in finding out if the use of math manipulatives improves working memory and math achievement for elementary students. She has decided to look at both quantitative and qualitative data and will write questions for each. Following are the questions she writes, which also meet the conditions of feasibility, measurability, clarity, significance, and ethicality. What do you think?

Quantitative Question

Are there differences in fourth-grade students working memory and math achievement following use of manipulatives in a math classroom?

Qualitative Question

What are the experiences of fourth-grade students regarding use of math manipulatives in the recall of math concepts?

Using our scenario as an example, when looking at Mrs. Burnett's quantitative research question, we see they are based in the measure of achievement, which will require an analysis of numbers and statistics that can be answered with a yes or a no. Mrs. Burnett's qualitative question on the other hand requires a deeper understanding of the students' perspectives (i.e., thoughts and feelings) and will most likely consist of data in the form of words from interviews or observations. Now, based on the preceding example, try writing your own research questions using the "*Let's do it!*" activity.

Let's Do It! 2.2

Guided Practice: Learn How to Write Quality Research Questions

Recall that quantitative questions focus on relationships among variables or trends and differences between groups, whereas qualitative questions describe perceptions, processes, and meanings. Use the following purpose statements to write one quantitative and one qualitative research question for each scenario. Then check the answer key at the end of the chapter for possible options.

Practice 1: The purpose of this study is to examine the impact of an anti-bullying program on tenth-grade student achievement.

Research Question

Practice 2: The purpose of this study is to examine the effect of a reading intervention on student reading performance.

Research Question

Articulating Research Questions With Data

Educators can attempt to address critical issues by first engaging in a literature review and then by generating specific research questions. For example, teachers in the classroom collect data on their students throughout the year like unit test scores. These data can raise a red flag about a problem in the school or classroom and can be used to assist teachers in defining a critical issue that involves investigating as shown in Figure 2.6. This process might involve generating research questions related to these initial data.

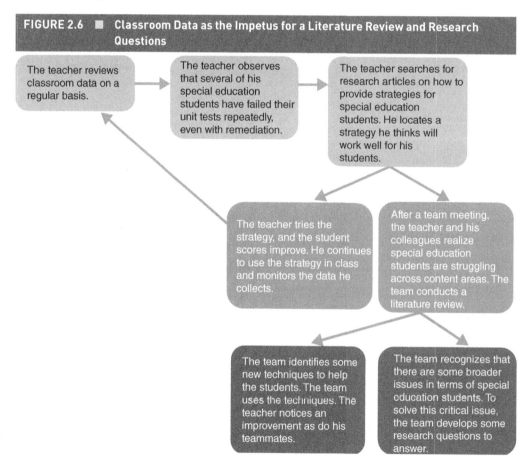

FIGURE 2.6 ■ Classroom Data as the Impetus for a Literature Review and Research Questions

Most classroom teachers naturally become concerned or anxious when they review their gradebook and realize some students are struggling. But this type of classroom data are important because they can spur the teacher to take action on a critical issue and ultimately frame research questions to find a solution based on what they find after conducting a literature review.

Within the daily school responsibilities of educators, administrators often request that data are collected for students so teams within the school can meet, assess student progress, and make plans to shift instruction. Examples of possible data sources would be unit tests and benchmarks. In addition, administrators often request that teachers collect other information, such as attendance, intervention strategies (e.g., one-on-one instruction, paired reading, preferential seating), and socioeconomic status (SES), as some examples. Table 2.10 is a sample classroom dataset with two variables (SES, memory retention) and four-unit tests.

Student ID Number	SES	Memory Retention Issue	Test 1	Test 2	Test 3	Test 4
01543	1	1	75	70	76	80
23678	1	0	88	90	83	100
14222	2	1	58	60	55	70
12874	2	0	47	50	45	56
23691	1	1	60	57	49	62
82905	2	0	90	94	94	98
10032	1	0	87	88	95	96
17431	1	1	35	39	37	50
58237	2	0	95	93	90	95
37920	2	1	55	49	60	48
61888	1	0	86	93	94	92
43267	2	0	77	83	71	74
82913	2	0	93	90	91	94
44357	2	0	88	85	90	94
76548	1	1	10	35	40	30

TABLE 2.10 ■ Mrs. Burnett's Mathematics Gradebook

Note. SES (1 = Low; 2 = High); memory retention (0 = no; 1 = yes)

The dataset in Table 2.10 could be used in multiple ways. Data analysis of such a secondary dataset can identify a potential critical issue, can serve as the impetus to begin conducting a literature review, and can also help educators to think about important questions to ask if one were to conduct a research study.

STOP AND THINK 2.4

What trends do you notice?
What questions might you ask Mrs. Burnett about the test scores?
What more do you want to know about these students?

Now, here is an opportunity to use the *Let's See It!* and the *Let's Do It!* activities to help you further learn how to write research questions with data.

Let's See It! 2.3

Goal: Understand How to Write Research Questions With Data and Situations in Which More Data May Need to Be Collected to Answer the Research Questions

Even before conducting a formal literature review, Mrs. Burnett can use the dataset presented in Table 2.10 to articulate tentative research questions, such as the following:

Research Question 1: Are there differences in test performance based on memory retention issues?

Research Question 2: To what extent do test scores differ based on SES?

However, classroom datasets are not always useful to answer all potentially relevant questions. For example, Mrs. Burnett could not answer the question, "Are there differences in test performance for at-risk students as compared to their peers?" because she does not have an at-risk variable in her dataset. She also could not address, "What are student perceptions of math manipulatives in the classroom?" because this is a qualitative research question, and the data would come from methods such as interviews. These unanswered questions, which are related to Mrs. Burnett's original critical issue, can be addressed in one of two ways that were emphasized in this chapter:

1. Conduct a systematic literature review to identify a solution.
2. Propose and conduct a new research study.

Let's Do It! 2.3

Guided Practice: Practice Writing Research Questions With Data

Now, let's practice writing research questions using a sample set of data included in Table 2.11. This dataset includes data from a research study designed to assess whether a "learning how to learn" intervention implemented in a rural and an urban school improved students' standardized scores in mathematics before and after the intervention. Review the data and write two research questions that could be answered with this dataset. Then write two questions that could not be answered with the dataset. Check your answers in the answer key at the end of the chapter.

Two Research Questions That Could Be Answered

Research Question 1

Research Question 2

Two Research Questions That Cannot Be Answered

Research Question 1

Research Question 2

TABLE 2.11 ■ Example Dataset			
Student ID Number	Location of School	Math Standardized Score Before the Intervention	Math Standardized Score After the Intervention
12345	Urban	390	400
24567	Rural	330	350
34578	Urban	464	358
43456	Rural	436	451
57894	Rural	476	416
64567	Urban	425	432
74567	Rural	492	479
84564	Urban	421	380
95673	Urban	353	401
10345	Rural	464	396
11345	Urban	307	474
12444	Rural	491	439
23345	Urban	503	421
94678	Urban	436	435
23549	Rural	337	416
16234	Urban	449	493
57567	Rural	404	430
18456	Urban	400	420
19456	Rural	480	496
20456	Urban	418	450

ETHICAL CONSIDERATIONS

LEARNING OBJECTIVE
2.6   Demonstrate knowledge of ethical issues when engaging with literature.

Ethics should always be at the forefront of all decision making when engaging in research. You might think that research ethics should be considered when you are carrying out a study while engaging in collecting or analyzing data for your study. However, there are many ethical dilemmas specific to the literature review process that a researcher should consider before they even begin working on the study, including (a) maintaining an unbiased approach, (b) avoiding plagiarism, and (c) proposing ethical research questions.

Maintaining an Unbiased Approach

Educators and researchers should recognize their own values and biases in relation to the issues in the topic being identified. It is important to maintain objectivity as much as possible when evaluating research and to be aware of personal needs, interests, and belief systems in relation to your study and topic of interest. For example, a researcher studying high school dropout rates assumes the rates are higher in urban areas as opposed to rural areas. This bias could steer article selection and summaries. The research may focus only on factors that attribute to dropout rates in urban areas, disregard factors that impact students in other areas, and inaccurately make claims that extend to students in suburban and rural areas. It is the responsibility of the researcher to determine whether a topic can be ethically studied and ensure objectivity while planning and designing a study. In summary, as you gather published research, you will need to remain objective and examine all sources with a critical eye.

Avoiding Plagiarism

Having an understanding of intellectual property or the ownership of knowledge matters in the literature review process. Plagiarism is considered a type of copyright infringement that protects an author's work from being used without their permission. Thus, when you use someone else's ideas or material, you will need to acknowledge it. Some strategies in avoiding plagiarism are to (a) use quotation marks when copying something verbatim from an article; (b) learn how to paraphrase; and (c) correctly cite and reference sources. It is also possible to plagiarize yourself; thus, you should always paraphrase rather than directly copy your text from a previously published work.

Proposing Ethical Research Questions

As we discussed earlier, one of the most quintessential aspects of ethics to remember is to carefully reflect as you are making evaluations and judgments about research findings and consider research questions that are ethical. Scholars of peer-reviewed articles selected for the literature review have followed IRB requirements prior to conducting research. Some key questions to consider when writing ethical research questions include the following: (a) How will I recruit my participants? (b) How will I ensure the safety of my participants? (c) How will I ensure confidentiality and anonymity of my participants? These questions might help you determine if you are asking an ethical research question. It is the responsibility of the researcher to ensure that all participants have equal opportunities to be selected to participate in a study and have access to and can benefit from programs, procedures, or other services. If a researcher choses to study an after-school math program, all eligible students in the school would need to have an equal chance of being selected for the research study. This action ensures that no one is denied access to a beneficial program without a fair system of selection in place. It is also the responsibility of the researcher to ensure the well-being of all participants by conducting research that does not cause harm and maximizes the possible benefits for the participants. Finally, as drafting a research question, it is important to consider the ethical issue of maintaining anonymity for participants. Participants are willing to share sensitive aspects of their lives, and so in return, they should be guaranteed privacy to their identities in order to potentially avoid discrimination or harassment. This concern applies to school-based professionals as well as researchers.

THE TAKEAWAY

Educators should be aware of all potential sources of personal biases to ensure that their review of the literature is conducted in a professional and competent manner.

AMERICAN PSYCHOLOGICAL ASSOCIATION STYLE

LEARNING OBJECTIVE

2.7 Utilize the *Publication Manual of the American Psychological Association* when synthesizing literature for research.

Have you ever had to complete an assignment but felt that your professor was not providing you with adequate guidelines? This can be a very frustrating experience, especially if your professor grades for style, formatting, citations, and references. One of the benefits of writing scientific research is that there is a manual that provides detailed information and examples on how to write an effective literature review. The American Psychological Association (APA) provides a manual for publications and is the standard guide used in the scientific community.

Since 1929, the *Publication Manual of the American Psychological Association* has sought to set standards for the communication of scientific information. These standards, commonly known as "APA style," are the most frequently used manuscript standards in the social sciences. What is APA style? APA style is a format for academic documents such as scholarly journal articles and books. APA style mostly deals with in-text citations, references, headings, and tables and figures.

However, APA is more than a format; it is a system for synthesizing research—and covers everything you need to prepare and write your literature review. Whether you are writing a synthesis paper for a class or you are working on an empirical study for publication, you will need to use APA style to organize your manuscript and list the references you used. If you have never used this format before, you may find it is quite a bit different from some of the other writing styles, which may be somewhat challenging. However, learning how to write an APA manuscript is a useful skill that will serve you well.

Each chapter of this book will highlight a different component of a publication using APA style. You can also refer to the *APA Publication Manual* (7th ed.) for help. For this chapter, we will focus on APA citations in-text, references, headings, and tables and figures.

In-Text Citations

From what we have discussed so far, the literature review is based on research and scholarly work rather than personal opinion. For this reason, educators will use the scholarly publications identified from the literature review process to write the literature review product. When using these publications, researchers must cite them in the body of the text (e.g., within a paragraph). Here are a few guidelines for citing sources in-text:

1. When writing in-text citations, include the author(s) last name and publication year (e.g., Hiller & Kitsantas, 2016).

2. For three or more authors, write only the first author's last name followed by "et al." (e.g., Kitsantas et al., 2011).

3. If an author was mentioned in a paragraph, followed by a date in parentheses, the date does not need to be repeated in parentheses within the same paragraph unless the author and date are both in parentheses (e.g., Hiller and Kitsantas [2016]) versus (Hiller & Kitsantas, 2016)].

4. For government documents without an author, list the name of the government agency.

5. For website articles, list the name of the website if there is no author.

These are just a few guidelines. For the exhaustive list of guidelines, check out the seventh edition of the APA manual.

References

We mentioned earlier that educators can look at references at the end of articles to find additional sources of information on the critical issue. You must also provide this information to readers of your literature review; therefore, anyone you cite must have an accompanying reference at the end of a document. Referencing differs depending on whether the source is a journal article, book, chapter in a book, and so forth. This is the part that most educators find challenging because there are several subtle requirements on alphabetizing, capitalization, punctuation, and listing how to find the article on the internet. When creating your reference section, follow these guidelines:

1. Alphabetize references.

2. Review the APA manual to cite publications based on the type (e.g., journal articles, books, chapters in edited books, reports, etc.).

3. Include URL addresses for websites.

4. Include digital object identifiers (DOIs) for journal articles when possible. DOI numbers can be located on the front of publications or at crossref.org.

5. Some websites (like https://www.easybib.com/) will create reference lists; however, it is a good idea to check the references in comparison to the APA manual.

Headings

Headings are very helpful in cueing readers as to the organization of the literature review. APA format uses a specific *level of headings* depending on the placement in text. See Table 2.12 as an example of the different level headings based on an outline of working memory and math retention.

TABLE 2.12 ■ Model of APA (7th ed.) Heading Levels

Heading Levels	APA Format	Example
Level 1	Centered, Bold, Title Case Heading	Student Working Memory and Math Retention in Elementary School
Level 2	Flush Left, Bold, Title Case Heading	Difficulties with Working Memory
Level 3	*Flush Left, Bold, Italic, Title Case Heading*	*Compounding Difficulties with Working Memory*
Level 4	Indented, Bold, Title Case Heading, Ending with a Period.	Special Education Students.
Level 5	Indented, Bold, Italic, Title Case Heading, Ending with a Period.	*Special Education Students Who Are English Language Learners.*

Tables and Figures

Throughout writing, authors often include tables and figures, and so it is highly recommended to follow APA style in terms of formatting these graphics. For both tables and figures, list **Table X** and **Figure X** in bold above the image. Then list the title in italics with the first letter of each word capitalized. For tables, include a total of three solid, horizontal lines, and include an appropriate table note (if needed) underneath the third horizontal line. Please see the examples of an APA table and figure in Figures 2.7 and 2.8, respectively.

FIGURE 2.7 ■ Model of APA (7th ed.) Table

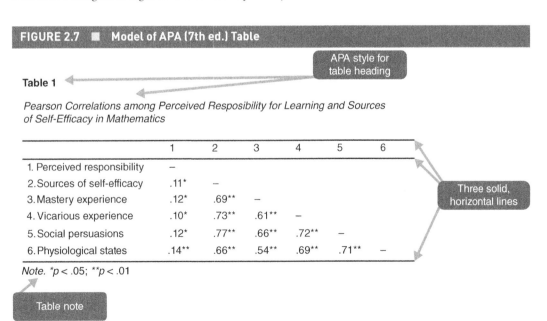

Table 1

Pearson Correlations among Perceived Resposibility for Learning and Sources of Self-Efficacy in Mathematics

	1	2	3	4	5	6
1. Perceived responsibility	—					
2. Sources of self-efficacy	.11*	—				
3. Mastery experience	.12*	.69**	—			
4. Vicarious experience	.10*	.73**	.61**	—		
5. Social persuasions	.12*	.77**	.66**	.72**	—	
6. Physiological states	.14**	.66**	.54**	.69**	.71**	—

Note. $*p < .05$; $**p < .01$

FIGURE 2.8   ■   Model of APA (7th ed.) Figure

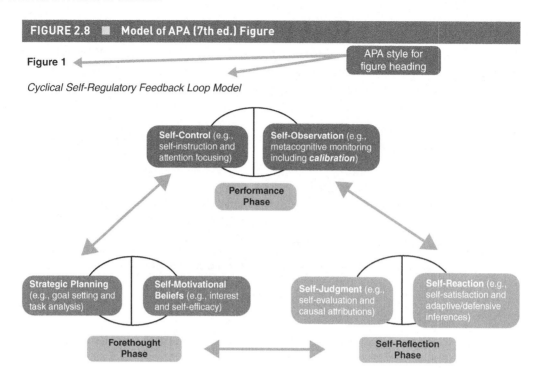

In closing, whether you are writing a synthesis paper for a class or you are working on an empirical study for publication, you will need to use APA format to organize your manuscripts and list the references you used. Learning how to write a manuscript in APA is a useful skill that will serve you well in the future. Please complete the *You Do It!* exercise in the extension activities as you review a paper that you are working on and pay particular attention to the headings, in-text citations, tables, figures, and references.

CHAPTER SUMMARY

Chapter 2 provided an overview of how an educator can investigate a critical issue by conducting a review of the literature, transition through the process of a literature review, synthesize information to create a literature review product, and determine whether or not further research is required to answer a critical issue. Assuming that a literature review does not yield an answer or solution to the problem then, an educator can articulate their own research questions and conduct a study. As an inherent part of the research process, we also provided guidance on ethical considerations and APA style. The following sections provide supplemental activities for enrichment and guidance.

EXTENSION ACTIVITIES

YOU DO IT! 2.1

Practice Writing Research Questions With Data

Self-Directed Practice: Practice Writing Research Questions

Please use the attached dataset to develop two to three research questions. In addition, identify two to three questions that cannot be answered with the dataset.

You Do It! 2.2
Practice Using APA Style

Self-Directed Practice: Practice Checking for Errors in APA Style

Use a paper that you are working on and check for APA errors.

KEY TERMS

Publication Manual of the American
    Psychological Association
Conceptual definition
Critical issue
Empirical research
Literature reviews
Operational definition

Peer-reviewed
Pre-synthesis phase
Primary sources
Secondary sources
Seminal work or author
Synthesis phase

ANSWER KEY

Stop and Think Activities

Stop and Think 2.1

It depends on the nature and extent of the problem. Not having a pencil each day may not be a critical issue. Educators are likely not going to want to do a full-fledged investigation into the causes of why students do not have pencils. However, if certain groups of students do not have internet access at home to complete work or if something more pervasive appears to be influencing the problem, this could point to a critical issue and be a sign that a more systematic investigative approach is necessary to remedy the problem.

Stop and Think 2.2

After identifying a critical issue of interest, the researcher should search for articles that are closely related to the critical issue and that are peer reviewed and/or empirical in nature. As a general guideline, researchers should look for research that is current and published in the last approximately 10 years. However, it may also be important to include seminal works or authors depending on the nature of the critical issue.

Stop and Think 2.3

A literature review and a book report are not the same thing. A literature review is more than a report or summary of the articles. The goal of a literature review is to frame current understandings of a critical issue to inform research questions, synthesize information from various studies, and identify gaps in the current literature, while a book report primarily seeks to provide an overview of a topic. The literature review is an iterative process.

Stop and Think 2.4

In general, Test 1 scores were the lowest, with most students improving their performance by Test 4. Students who have a memory retention issue appear to score significantly lower across all four tests than students who do not. One might ask Mrs. Burnett to explain more about this memory retention issue and how that might influence performance on math tests given that math is largely an applied subject. One may also want to know if any of these students are exceptional learners and how that may impact their academic performance and/or predisposition to memory retention issues.

Let's Do It! Activities

LET'S DO IT! 2.1

Guided Practice: Connect the Planning, Doing, and Reflecting Cycle of Self-Regulated Learning to Conducting a Literature Search

Searching for Sources of Research	Guiding Procedures	Your Responses
Planning	1. Select and narrow a topic. 2. Identify the key concepts in the research problem. Write a list of key terms. 3. Develop a list of synonyms for key terms. Check the thesaurus to find synonyms.	**Key Concepts/Terms** • Mathematics • Academic achievement • Mathematics self-efficacy • Self-efficacy interventions • Middle school **Potential Synonyms** • Mathematics education • School learning • Academic self-esteem • School-based intervention • Secondary school
Doing	4. Conduct a database search by starting with the most important key term and sequentially adding additional terms. 5. Narrow or broaden the search as needed. The command "and" between two search key terms narrows the search, and the command "or" broadens the search by allowing synonyms. 6. Repeat the process as needed.	**Potential Articles** Chen, P. P. (2003). Exploring the accuracy and predictability of the self-efficacy beliefs of seventh-grade mathematics students. *Learning and Individual Differences, 14*(1), 77–90. https://doi.org/10.1016/j.lindif.2003.08.003 Kitsantas, A., Cheema, J., & Ware, H. W. (2011). Mathematics achievement: The role of homework and self-efficacy beliefs. *Journal of Advanced Academics, 22*(2), 310–339. https://doi.org/10.1177/1932202X1102200206 Pajares, F., & Graham, L. (1999). Self-efficacy, motivation constructs, and mathematics performance of entering middle school students. *Contemporary Educational Psychology, 24*(2), 124–139. https://doi.org/10.1006/ceps.1998.0991
Reflecting	7. Check the references cited by the articles located to identify other related studies. 8. Create a reference list using APA format. 9. Consider if other information would be helpful.	Usher, E. L. (2009). Sources of middle school students' self-efficacy in mathematics: A qualitative investigation of student, teacher, and parent perspectives. *American Educational Research Journal, 46*(1), 275–314. https://doi.org/10.3102/0002831208324517 There are numerous potential answers to this question. An example could be looking at socioeconomic status.

LET'S DO IT! 2.2

Learn How to Write Quality Research Questions

Practice 1: The purpose of this study is to examine the impact of an anti-bullying program on tenth-grade student achievement as well as differences between males and females.

Quantitative: To what extent does the anti-bullying program decrease reported bullying behaviors and increase tenth-grade student achievement? Does this effect differ based on location of school?

Qualitative: What are the perspectives of tenth-grade students on the anti-bullying program?

Practice 2: The purpose of this study is to examine the effect of a reading intervention on student reading performance.

Quantitative: Does participation in the reading intervention have an impact on fourth-grade students' reading comprehension?

Qualitative: What are fourth-grade students' perceptions about the reading intervention?

LET'S DO IT! 2.3

Practice Writing Research Questions With Data

Two Research Questions That Could Be Answered

1. Are there any differences in students' math standardized scores before and following the intervention?

2. Do students' math scores vary based on location of the school?

Two Research Questions That Cannot Be Answered

1. In what ways did students in the intervention group find the "learn how to learn" intervention to be helpful in supporting their overall academic achievement?

2. Is there a relationship between math standardized scores and math course grades for these students?

©iStockphoto.com/Chainarong Prasertthai

3 RESEARCH DESIGN

The What, When, and How of Research

LEARNING OBJECTIVES

Upon completion of this chapter, the reader should be able to

3.1   Discuss the key features and philosophical distinctions between research methodology and research design

3.2   Describe areas of similarity and distinction between quantitative and qualitative research methodology

3.3   Explain specific research designs used within quantitative and qualitative methodologies

3.4   Explain a general decision-making approach for selecting quantitative and qualitative research designs

3.5   Describe several research principles that cut across research methodology and design

3.6   Demonstrate knowledge of the governing structure and oversight of ethical practices when conducting research

3.7   Utilize the *Publication Manual of the American Psychological Association* (APA) for different research methodologies and designs

A DAY AT WORK

Implementing Research Design in The Workplace

©iStockphoto.com/SDI Productions

Dr. Darrelle Jones is a superintendent of an urban school district with eight elementary schools, two middle schools, and one high school. Given the recent COVID pandemic and the need to bolster the district's technological infrastructure and support system for staff, he applied for a grant and received the funding. He would like to initiate a 3-year plan for effectively infusing technology in the classroom and for creating effective pathways for home-school communication and collaboration.

Dr. Maria Rodriguez, a principal in one of his schools, has a strong background in research design and evaluating school reform initiatives. Dr. Rodriguez has agreed to lead the efforts to implement and evaluate the effects of the technological and curricular innovations. She will rely heavily on Ms. Joanna Nichols, a science and mathematics teacher in her school who is widely recognized for her instructional innovations and overall teaching quality, to support and lead some of these initiatives. Knowing that Dr. Rodriquez has a strong background in research design, Dr. Jones and Ms. Nichols realize they need to do some review of basic concepts and approaches to conducting research if they are going to work successfully together, but what exactly do they need to know to get started?

INTRODUCTION

As emphasized in Chapter 2, researchers typically begin the research process by conducting a literature review on a particular topic and then developing specific research questions to address critical issues observed in the real-world situations or gaps in the literature. Developing research questions early in the research process is essential because they help researchers identify the most appropriate methods and procedures for selecting and interacting with a sample and for gathering and analyzing data. More simply, the questions that researchers wish to examine naturally point them in a particular direction regarding the most appropriate research methodology and design to select. In this chapter, we provide a conceptual overview of research methodology and design and highlight the key characteristics and distinctions among quantitative, qualitative, and mixed research methodologies. We also present an overview of various quantitative and qualitative research designs, a general process for guiding design selection, and several cross-cutting research principles linked to all research approaches. We end the chapter by reviewing important ethical considerations when structuring a research study and underscoring a few key APA principles when communicating results from different research methodologies or designs.

INTRODUCTION TO RESEARCH METHODOLOGY AND DESIGN

LEARNING OBJECTIVE

3.1   Discuss the key features and philosophical distinctions between research methodology and research design.

Drs. Jones and Rodriguez are interested in evaluating the implementation and effectiveness of computer adaptive technology for supporting instruction and enhancing students' academic success. To explore these issues, they need to identify an appropriate research methodology and one or more specific research designs that address their primary questions. Broadly speaking, research methodology reflects the philosophical and theoretical perspective about research that is linked by its shared assumptions, practices, and concepts. In contrast, a research design represents the specific plan for executing a study; that is, its specific procedures or methods for selecting and interacting with research participants, and for collecting and analyzing data.

Three types of research methodologies are frequently discussed in educational and applied contexts: quantitative, qualitative, and mixed method. Quantitative methodology emphasizes the importance of gathering numerical data and information about variables and then describing how certain variables (e.g., quality of instruction, phonemic awareness, vocabulary) relate to, predict, or cause other variables (e.g., reading comprehension). A key objective of quantitative research is to gather numerical information about a sample (i.e., the specific group who participates in a study) and then use statistical approaches to draw conclusions about how likely the results would appear in broader population (i.e., larger group of individuals from whom a sample is selected). In contrast, qualitative methodology is more concerned with gathering language-based information about the perspectives, attitudes, and lived experiences of an individual or group of individuals. This type of research focuses on the richness and meaningfulness of responses from one or more individuals and applies qualitative analyses approaches (e.g., thematic analysis, coding) to discover or identify important patterns or themes. Finally, mixed methodology involves the integration of quantitative and qualitative methodologies (a more detailed discussion of the comparison of quantitative and qualitative approaches will come later in the chapter).

Research Philosophies Linked to Research Methodology

It is difficult to discuss research methodology without considering the philosophies that underlie them. Research philosophies reflect broad perspectives and assumptions about how people learn and generate knowledge. These philosophies, which include interpretive/constructive, positivistic, realistic, and pragmatic perspectives, extend beyond the meaning of any one research methodology. However, some philosophies are more aligned with a particular methodology than others. In this section, we focus on two philosophical perspectives, positivist and interpretivist, and their overlap with quantitative or qualitative methodologies.

Contrasting Research Philosophies in Educational Research
©iStockphoto.com/DrAfter123

Positivism originated from the field of physical science in the 19th century and has typically been linked with quantitative research methodology. A positivist philosophy espouses the viewpoint that objective, systematic, and numerical-based methods represent the best approaches for understanding the world in which we live. It focuses on objective reality (i.e., without subjective viewpoints and opinions) and absolute truths in the world. To examine this type of reality, positivism embraces the scientific method. Thus, it focuses on objectively collecting data (i.e., without using subjective opinions) and then using statistical analyses to describe well-defined variables or the relationships among them. For example, suppose Dr. Jones wanted to examine the influence of computer adaptive assessments and technology on student confidence, interest in school, and overall achievement. Based on prior research, he hypothesizes that the intervention would have a positive effect on those variables. His objective aligns with a positivist philosophical stance given that he will use objective measures (e.g., tests, questionnaire, rating scales) to gather data about specific variables (i.e., confidence, interest, achievement), and then descriptive statistics (e.g., means, correlations; Chapter 12) and inferential statistics (e.g., pairwise *t*-tests and ANOVAs; Chapter 13) to examine these effects.

In contrast, an interpretivist perspective closely aligns with qualitative research methodology. Interpretivism emerged from sociology and anthropology and in response to a focus on objective, numerical focus of the 1800s (i.e., positivist). It places primary emphasis on the lived experiences of individuals. This philosophical perspective assumes that individual experiences and the social world in which they operate shape reality (i.e., not one objective or absolute truth). Interpretivists emphasize that researchers construct an understanding of the experiences of participants by gathering data about their perspectives and behaviors. If Dr. Jones adopted an interpretivist perspective regarding the implementation of computer adaptive assessments, his research questions would shift towards a focus on the lived experiences of students and or teachers (e.g., their thoughts about the utility and value of computer-based approaches). He would rely on naturalistic types of data derived from assessment tools, such as interviews, observations, or reflection journals. The data and corresponding analyses (e.g., coding, analysis, and interpretation) would lead to a rich set of language-based or qualitative information about individuals' perspectives, experiences, and beliefs.

STOP AND THINK 3.1

This section outlined the philosophical traditions behind quantitative and qualitative methodologies. From your perspective, is there one philosophy or approach that resonates with you? Why?

Research Designs Linked to Each Research Methodology

Research methodology is the umbrella term that includes various research designs (see Figure 3.1). In a general sense, a research design represents the basic structure of a study. It reflects the specific action plan or *blueprint* regarding the "what" and "how" of a research study, such as methods for recruiting the sample, interacting with the sample, collecting data, and analyzing data (see Chapters 10 through 14 about specific methods and procedures). Thus, within each of the two broad methodologies (i.e., quantitative, qualitative) are different types of research designs. Whereas quantitative research includes non-experimental designs (e.g., descriptive, correlational, comparative; see Chapter 4) and experimental designs (e.g., true experiments, quasi-experiments, single participant research designs; see Chapter 5), qualitative research includes case study, narrative inquiry, phenomenological, grounded theory, and ethnographic approaches (see Chapter 6). The selection of a research design is one of the most important decisions researchers can make as it specifies how the study should be conducted.

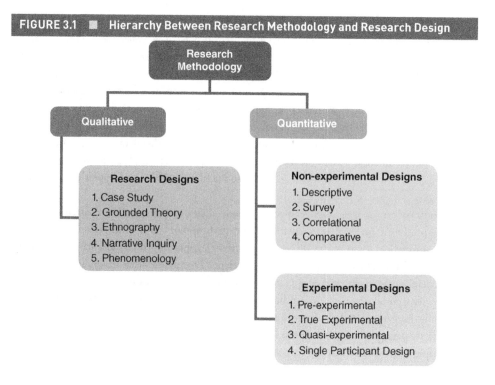

FIGURE 3.1 ■ Hierarchy Between Research Methodology and Research Design

THE TAKEAWAY

When conducting a research study, consider two steps: (1) Identify the research methodology that best aligns with your research objectives or questions, qualitative, quantitative, or mixed; (2) select a specific design within that methodology to address your research questions.

COMPARISON OF QUANTITATIVE AND QUALITATIVE METHODOLOGIES

LEARNING OBJECTIVE

3.2   Describe areas of similarity and distinction between quantitative and qualitative research methodology.

Quantitative and qualitative methodologies are both useful perspectives for generating knowledge about people and the world in which we live. However, these two research worldviews can be differentiated in terms of their overall purpose, logic or reasoning, and approaches to recruiting a sample, collecting data, and analyzing data (see Table 3.1). In general, quantitative research focuses on gathering numerical information about well-defined variables and directly testing a priori hypotheses (i.e., predictions about what the results may show). Quantitative methodology emphasizes a high level of control over the procedures used in a study and relies on objective forms of measurement to gather data. This methodological framework strives to minimize subjective interpretation and thus utilizes formal statistical procedures to understand how different variables (e.g., anxiety, self-efficacy, writing skill) relate to each other. The central goals of quantitative research are to use collected data to confirm hypotheses or predictions (i.e., deductive reasoning) and to generalize data from the participating sample to a broader population. As mentioned previously, Dr. Jones' investigation of the effects of computer adaptive assessments and technology on student confidence, interest, and achievement in school represents a quantitative methodological perspective.

TABLE 3.1 ■ Primary Differences Between Quantitative and Qualitative Methodologies		
Qualitative Research	**Point of Comparison**	**Quantitative Research**
Examines a particular context, phenomenon, or group of people through deep exploration and analysis. Uses observations to develop hypotheses and theories, but does not develop a priori hypotheses. Also, they focus on constructs but not variables.	*Overall Goals*	Examines the variables and or nature of the relationship among variables. Measures variables to make inferences about underlying constructs. Uses statistical procedures to confirm accuracy of a priori hypotheses or theory.
Emphasizes the use of subjective measures to understand the perspectives, beliefs, or attitudes of individuals (e.g., in-depth interviews, narrative observations, field notes). Perspectives of the researchers are recognized to influence the nature and interpretation of data.	*Measurement Focus*	Emphasizes the use of objective measures and a consistent, structured way to interpret data, regardless of other factors or personal perspectives of the researcher or participant (e.g., rating scales, tests, frequency count observations).
Relies on an inductive approach; methods that identify broad themes, hypotheses, or theory from specific observations of the participants.	*Reasoning Strategy*	Relies on a deductive approach; methods that involve starting with a theory and a priori hypotheses and then collecting and interpreting data to test and confirm hypotheses.
Emphasizes non-random sampling determined with preset criteria (e.g., purposeful).	*Sampling Methods*	Emphasizes random sampling to identify a representative sample from a larger population.
Asks participants to be integrally involved in the data generation process to express individual viewpoints.	*Role of Participants*	Asks participants to complete a specific set of measures and or to participate in experimental or non-experimental procedures.

On the other hand, qualitative methodologies are more dynamic and fluid in nature. They encourage the use of in-depth, exploratory assessment approaches to understand the attitudes, experiences, and/or perspectives of individuals, context, or phenomenon. Given that qualitative methodology is more exploratory and seeks to discover themes and truths as expressed by participants, they do not focus on testing hypotheses about relations between variables. Qualitative methodology emphasizes the importance of gathering large quantities of information about individuals and devoting considerable efforts to discovering important themes that underlie specific participant responses (i.e., inductive reasoning). Dr. Jones would likely use a qualitative methodology lens if he wanted to understand teachers' perceptions and attitudes about the feasibility and acceptability of using computer-based approaches in school contexts. Importantly, while the data generated in a qualitative study is typically language-based or verbal in nature, some numerical information can be used in certain circumstances (e.g., number of participants who endorsed a particular theme). The results from qualitative research designs also tend to be generative in nature; that is, the results can lead to hypotheses that can be tested with quantitative research designs.

Although Table 3.1 provides a summary of the key topics for which quantitative and qualitative methodologies can be distinguished, a few of these ideas warrant elaboration and further discussion.

Constructs and Variables

Qualitative and quantitative studies vary in their focus on constructs and or variables. Quantitative research focuses on both, while qualitative research only addresses constructs. A construct can be defined as an abstraction or concept that is not directly observed. Common constructs include intelligence, executive functions, motivation, attitudes about a bullying intervention program, or teacher satisfaction. We do not directly measure constructs per se; rather, we speak about them through analysis of observed data. Constructs are important because they represent important ideas or concepts that we use to understand and/or label behaviors or observations in the world. Qualitative researchers discuss constructs in terms of the themes that are discovered or generated during the qualitative analysis or coding process, while quantitative researchers make inferences about constructs based on scores generated from specific assessment tools (e.g., tests, questionnaires).

A variable represents a numerical indicator of a construct that can take on a range of potential values (i.e., it is quantified in some way). Variables are important in quantitative methodologies because they help to define or "provide evidence" about the degree to which individuals possess or reflect the construct of interest. Qualitative methodology does not typically focus on numerical variables because of its emphasis on language-based or verbal information. Generally speaking, two types of variables are emphasized in quantitative research: independent and dependent. Independent variables are those that are manipulated, changed, or directly influenced by a researcher. The most common example of an independent variable is the type of treatment or intervention used in an experiment. For example, if Dr. Jones wanted to examine the effects of a technology-enhanced mathematics curriculum relative to a standard instructional approach, he would randomly assign one group of students to the technology-enhanced instruction and a different group to the standard curricular approach. In this sense, he is actively directing or manipulating type of instruction (i.e., the independent variable). In this textbook, we use the term independent variable specifically in relation to experimental designs. However, we reference two other terms, predictor and grouping variables, that overlap to some degree with independent variables. Predictor variables are used in the context of correlational designs and represent variables that predict or explain certain outcomes, while grouping variables represent naturally occurring groups that may be similar in some ways yet differ in others (e.g., gender, grade level). Predictor, grouping, and independent variables are similar in that they all are used to explain scores on dependent variables:

- Independent variables *cause* or have an influence on a dependent variable.

- Predictor variables *predict or relate to* a dependent variable.

- Grouping variables are *differentiated* in terms of a dependent variable.

Dependent variables (also known as criterion variables) tend to represent what is being explained in a study. Oftentimes the variable reflects important outcomes or performance, such as test grades, academic skills, homework completion, academic productivity, mental health (e.g., anxiety), or other indicators of academic, behavioral, or mental health functioning.

THE TAKEAWAY

Constructs are key concepts emphasized in both quantitative and qualitative research designs. However, because variables reflect the quantification of a construct (i.e., use of numbers), they are more strongly emphasized in quantitative designs.

Hypothesis Testing

Another way in which quantitative and qualitative methodologies differ involves how researchers think about hypotheses (i.e., proposed explanations about some phenomenon). Quantitative research places a high value on developing a priori hypotheses (i.e., predictions about what one expects to observe in the results) while qualitative research does not. From a quantitative lens, researchers develop specific hypotheses about potential truths that exist in the world and then collect data and use formal statistical procedures to evaluate the viability or accuracy of these hypotheses. Thus, quantitative research is conducted to evaluate hypotheses that are generated before a study begins and are based on theory or prior research. Qualitative researchers have a different goal in mind. Rather than stating hypotheses at the outset, they gather rich amounts of data and engage in exploratory analyses to discover themes within the data and potentially new hypotheses about a phenomenon. Thus, qualitative research is much more focused on *using data to generate new ideas and potential hypotheses* than the quantitative perspective of *using data to confirm hypotheses*. In a sense, one can say that quantitative research espouses a "confirmation" mindset while qualitative research espouses more of a "discovery" mindset.

To illustrate this distinction in the use of hypotheses, consider an example with Dr. Rodriguez and her focus on implementing computer-adaptive assessment instruments in the school district. It is common for public schools to work with commercial vendors in providing teachers access to a bank of test items for their use as formative and/or summative assessment tools. A question on Dr. Rodriguez's mind was qualitative in nature: "How does a computer-adaptive assessment platform support reading achievement from the perspective of middle schoolers?" Consistent with this methodology, she used interviews and open-ended questions on a survey (as opposed to Likert-type scales) to gather rich data about student attitudes and perspectives. She also felt the need to adapt the data collection process based on emerging insights from initial information gathered during the process. Because Dr. Rodriguez was more interested in discovering or learning about participant perspectives and feelings, it did not make sense for her to make any a priori predictions or hypotheses about the results. However, she was interested in identifying themes in the data to draw conclusions about student perspectives about computer-adaptive assessments.

On the other hand, Dr. Jones was interested in a more quantitative-oriented question: "To what extent does a computer-adaptive assessment platform impact reading achievement, and do any observed differences vary based on biological sex?" This question is much more empirical in nature in that he hoped to quantify whether the computer-adaptive platform improved student reading. After reading about this type of technology, he believed the system should lead to improved reading performance. Thus, he stated an a priori hypothesis that the computer-adaptive system would be effective. By starting out with this prediction, he needed to then collect data and use deductive reasoning (i.e., starting with a theory or broader concept and testing and understanding its parts) to "confirm" that his initial predication or hypothesis was correct. This was in direct contrast to her initial question, which required him to use inductive reasoning (i.e., identifying how the patterns among specific observations can be used to develop a hypothesis or broader idea or principle).

Qualitative and Quantitative Research Can Address Common Educational Issues

©iStockphoto.com/monkeybusinessimages

Choosing Between Qualitative and Quantitative Methodologies

At this point in the chapter, you may be wondering whether researchers interested in the same general topic must choose between using either a quantitative or qualitative approach. The simple answer to this question is no, they do not have to choose one over the other. Researchers can and often use features from both qualitative and quantitative methodologies within a single study; a type of methodology called a mixed methods approach. However, you should keep in mind that the primary reason for choosing one methodology or design over another involves the nature of the research questions that one chooses to ask. Consider a scenario whereby Ms. Nichols and Dr. Rodriguez were both interested in studying a professional development program about emergent classroom technologies and their potential link to teachers' interest in technology, self-efficacy in using technology, and quality of lesson plans. On the one hand, Dr. Rodriguez was interested in addressing, "To what extent does access to professional learning experiences in technology predict teacher self-efficacy and interest in using technology in the classroom?" Dr. Rodriguez systematically reviewed the literature on this topic and conjectured (i.e., developed a hypothesis) that there should be a positive relationship between having a professional development experience (i.e., some received the professional development while others did not) and interest, enjoyment, and efficacy for using learning technology. Given that Dr. Rodriguez wanted to examine the relationship among variables and developed a priori predictions about these relationships, a quantitative methodology would be most appropriate for her to follow.

On the other hand, Ms. Nichols was more interested in focusing on the processes involved in the professional development program as well as teacher perspectives about program implementation. She had two questions in mind: (a) "In what ways does a technology integration professional learning program influence how teachers think about teacher lesson design?" and (b) "What are teachers' experiences and attitudes about developing technology-embedded lesson plans following a professional learning program?" Ms. Nichols did not have any preconceived ideas about teacher perceptions or experiences and thus she made no a priori predictions. In addition, her questions appeared to be more concerned with identifying underlying patterns in teacher thinking and attitudes than assessing and evaluating relationships among variables. Thus, while Dr. Rodriguez and Ms. Nichols were both interested in the same topic of teacher professional development training for technology, the nature of their research questions directly informed the research methodology that best suited their interests.

Thus, a key first step that researchers need to take as they design their research is to answer the broad question, "Should I use a quantitative, qualitative, or mixed method design?" In Figure 3.2, we provide a guide to help you address this question. To begin, look at the questions listed on the left-hand side of the figure under quantitative designs. After reading through these questions, if your general response is yes, then you likely want to adopt a quantitative perspective and chose a relevant quantitative design (e.g., experimental, descriptive, or correlational). If you answer no to these questions, then shift your focus to the right-hand side of the figure. It is likely that you would answer yes to most of the questions linked to a qualitative methodology. As noted previously, however, it is possible for you to answer yes to questions under both types of methodologies. In this instance, you would utilize a mixed methods approach.

FIGURE 3.2 ■ Decision-Making Guide for Qualitative, Quantitative, and Mixed Methodologies

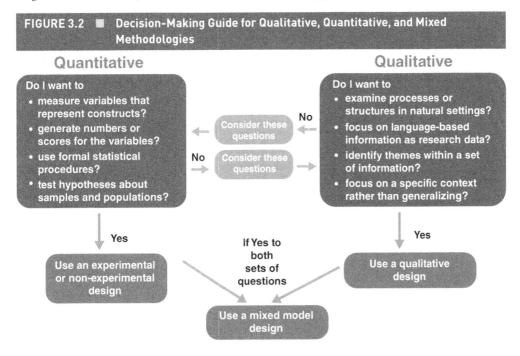

Assessing Critical Issues From a Qualitative or Quantitative Perspective

To deepen your understanding of the quantitative–qualitative methodological distinction, we have structured *Let's See It! Let's Do It! You Do It!* activities that focus on the types of research questions and approaches to collecting data to address those questions. We encourage you to complete the full sequence of activities to bolster your understanding of how research questions are linked to a given methodology.

Throughout this textbook, you will be exposed to several types of research questions linked to different research methodologies and research designs. In this set of *Let's See It!* and *Let's Do It!* activities, we provide you with illustrations and practice opportunities for distinguishing quantitative and qualitative designs for common situations in school contexts. For the *Let's See It!* activity, we provide examples of research questions linked to each methodology but that address the same critical issue (i.e., social media use). In the *Let's Do It!* activity, we provide you with a scenario but then ask you to develop example quantitative and qualitative research questions. Finally, we provide a *You Do It!* exercise as an Extension Activity at the end of the chapter. In this activity, you will be asked to create a qualitative and quantitative study based on a topic of interest to you.

Let's See It! 3.1

Goal: Identify Distinctions in Scope and Purpose of Qualitative and Quantitative Research Questions.

The primary objective of this activity is to illustrate differences in quantitative and qualitative research questions that address the same general topic. We provide a summary of the scenario background, the critical issues linked with that scenario, and example research questions. We also provide a summary of key methodological features (see Table 3.2 as a reference).

Scenario background: Mrs. Johnson and several of her fellow teachers at the same high school are concerned about the rising use of social media and its impact on student experiences in school and their learning. They suspect that students do not fully understand or appreciate the negative impact that social media can have on their studies and ability to focus on school. On one hand, they want to explore student experiences and perceptions about media use. However, they also think it's valuable to get a more objective sense about the potential influence of social media on student performance.

TABLE 3.2 ■ Critical Issue: Use of Social Media Among High School Students		
	Qualitative Methodology	**Quantitative Methodology**
Research question	What are high school students' experiences with social media? What are their attitudes and perceptions about its impact on their learning and performance.	Does the extent to which social media use predicts high school students' achievement vary based on student grade?
Hypothesis	None.	The relationship between social media use and achievement would be strongest for freshman students.
Likely measures	Interview; focus groups.	Questionnaires (use of rating scale 1 (low) through 5 (high)) to assess frequency of students' social media use. Review records of students' GPA.
Analysis approach	Interested in identifying themes across interviews to develop ideas or hypotheses about student reactions and attitudes.	Use of statistical techniques (e.g., correlations) to examine the relationship between social media and achievement.

Let's Do It! 3.1

Guided Practice: To Practice Distinguishing Quantitative and Qualitative Methodology

The primary objective of this activity is to practice generating your own research questions, using both a quantitative and qualitative lens. Please read the scenario about westward expansion and write a critical issue that seems relevant. With that critical issue in mind, develop an appropriate qualitative and quantitative research question in Table 3.3 and fill in the relevant information for hypothesis, likely measures, and analysis approach. You can check your work by reviewing the answer key provided in the appendix at the end of the chapter. Although the responses provided in the answer key may not directly relate to your responses, it will provide guidance about appropriate questions and features for each methodology.

Scenario background: Mrs. Marshall is curious about her middle school students' use of different types of learning strategies (e.g., graphic organizers, concepts maps) and their potential impact on student learning. Over the course of a month, she models and provides guided practice for students to use visualizations, graphs, or concept maps to organize information during learning. She then wanted to examine their use of these strategies for a specific lesson on westward expansion within the United States during the 1800s.

TABLE 3.3 ■ Critical Issue		
	Qualitative Methodology	Quantitative Methodology
Research question		
Hypothesis		
Likely measures		
Analysis approach		

THE TAKEAWAY

Although qualitative and quantitative research designs are both important, they are distinct in many ways. These differences can be captured by remembering a few key terms or phrases:

Quantitative: numerical information, deductive thinking, statistical tests, and hypothesis testing

Qualitative: language-based information, inductive thinking, thematic, or qualitative analysis

DIVERSITY OF RESEARCH DESIGNS ACROSS METHODOLOGIES

LEARNING OBJECTIVE
3.3   Explain specific research designs within quantitative and qualitative methodologies.

Although distinguishing quantitative and qualitative research methodologies is important on a conceptual level, a more practical or pragmatic concern involves identifying the most appropriate research design to use for a particular study. After all, research designs encapsulate the key components and blueprint for conducting the study—the recruitment of the sample, the process for interacting with research participants, and the procedures for collecting and analyzing data. Although we discuss specific research designs in several other chapters within this textbook, in this section, we provide a brief introduction and overview of the most popular and common designs linked with quantitative or qualitative methodology. We hope this overview further clarifies the qualitative–quantitative methodological distinction emphasized in this chapter while also addressing other important research principles linked to each methodology.

Quantitative Designs: Examining Distinctions Between Experimental and Non-experimental Designs

Quantitative designs can be classified into two broad categories, experimental and non-experimental designs.

Experimental Designs

Experimental designs, which include true experiments, quasi-experiments, or single participants research designs (see Figure 3.3), are designed to help researchers draw conclusions about cause and effect between variables. In educational contexts, experiments can be used to address questions such as, "Does direct teaching (the cause) lead *to* higher reader scores (the effect) then reciprocal teaching?" "Does the Good Behavior Game lead to decreases in disruptive behavior in middle school students with ADHD?" or "Does the use of a mental number line (the cause) enhance student mathematics skills (the effect)?" Thus, experiments are used to help researchers draw cause-and-effect conclusions and will often include phrases such as "effects of," "influence of," "leads to," or "impact on."

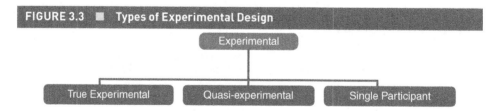

FIGURE 3.3 ■   Types of Experimental Design

Experimental

True Experimental   Quasi-experimental   Single Participant

Many scholars assert that true experimental designs represent the gold standard of experimental research because they provide a highly rigorous approach for testing the causal effects of an intervention. Using methodological features, such as random assignment (i.e., students are placed in experimental conditions using a random process) and control or comparison groups (i.e., the groups that do not receive the target intervention), true experiments enable researchers to more confidently make claims that a particular intervention or instructional program was the primary cause of an observed change in outcomes.

Quasi-experimental designs represent an effective alternative to true experiments but are less rigorous due to the absence of random assignment, which is a process whereby students have an equal chance of being in any of the intervention conditions. However, quasi-experiments are particularly important in educational settings given that they are more flexible and less constraining than true experiments.

Single participant research designs are a special class of experiments that focuses on one or a few students rather than large groups (i.e., as is the case with true and quasi-experiments). Despite the relatively limited number of individuals included in a single participant design, these designs can be used to examine the effects of interventions or instructional programs in schools.

Non-experimental Designs

Non-experimental designs represent a second category within the quantitative methodological framework. With non-experimental designs, researchers do not manipulate variables (e.g., creating different types of groups in an experiment), nor do they instill the level of control and rigor as with experimental designs (see Table 3.4). Thus, non-experimental research designs are not typically used to address questions about cause-and-effect. However, these types of designs are excellent choices when interested in describing people or situations (i.e., descriptive or survey design), examining the statistical relationship between different variables (i.e., interest in mathematics, confidence in mathematics, and mathematics achievement; correlational design), or comparing naturally existing groups (e.g., gifted versus non-gifted students; comparative design; see Figure. 3.4). Thus, non-experimental designs can address a broad range of research questions, including "How frequently do middle school students use time management strategies?" (descriptive design), "To what extent does student engagement relate to end of year report card grades?" (correlational design), and "Do gifted students differ from non-gifted students in their motivation and strategic skills? (correlational design)."

TABLE 3.4 ■ Comparison of Experimental and Non-experimental Designs		
	Experimental Designs	**Non-experimental Designs**
Key features	Actively and intentionally manipulate variables and seek to control all other factors or conditions of the study	Examine variables or naturally occurring groups not involving the manipulation of variables
	Primarily concerned with cause and effect	Primarily concerned with describing things as they are or how variables relate to one another
Design types	1. True experiments 2. Quasi-experiments 3. Single participant	1. Descriptive 2. Surveys 3. Correlational 4. Comparative studies
Study example	Ms. Thompson randomly assigns her four science classes into two groups: (a) technology informed inquiry-based learning, (b) traditional inquiry-based learning format. Her goal is to determine whether inquiry-based learning with technological supports leads to (or causes) higher student achievement than the traditional instructional format	Mr. Eberling administers a questionnaire to all eleventh-grade students in his school to examine whether student attitudes about math and their self-efficacy in math predict or explain student performance on statewide mathematic exams (correlational study)

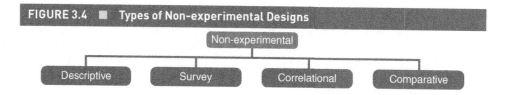

FIGURE 3.4 ■ Types of Non-experimental Designs

Thus, descriptive designs are those in which researchers seek to describe the characteristics of a sample, setting, measurement tool, or some other phenomenon. In these designs, researchers emphasize the use of descriptive statistics, such as frequency counts, percentages, means, and standard deviations.

Survey designs are like descriptive approaches in that they also describe phenomena. However, survey designs typically focus on the perceptions, beliefs, and attitudes of a group of people about a specific topic or situation, such as teachers' perspectives and knowledge about bullying prevention initiatives, and often go beyond mere description.

The final two non-experimental designs, correlational design and comparative design, are distinct from descriptive research because they focus on statistical relationships among variables (i.e., examines the pattern of whether changes in one variable is consistent with changes in another variable). Although similar to some degree, correlational and comparative designs can be most easily distinguished by the name of the explanatory variable. In comparative designs, researchers attempt to explain differences among well-defined groups (e.g., giftedness, biological sex, disabled), whereas correlational research often seeks to explain how one or more variables (e.g., anxiety, confidence, reading skills) predict or explain other variables (e.g., GPA).

Qualitative Designs: Key Distinguishing Concepts and Principles

Qualitative methodology entails a creative and dynamic process with the aim of providing rich, contextualized information about people or phenomenon. As noted previously, qualitative methodology emphasizes an inductive reasoning approach (i.e., determining how specific details converge to form a theme), which requires flexibility and introspection on the part of the researcher. At times, a qualitative researcher may engage with the community and participants as a privileged observer (i.e., someone who makes observations of a group but does not actively engage) while other designs cast the researcher as a participant observer (i.e., someone who functions as part of the group or community under study). Regardless of this researcher role, qualitative methodology requires researchers to be transparent about all aspects of the research process, including their preconceived notions about the topic as well as the specific research design, analysis, and interpretation techniques that are used. This level of transparency is needed given that qualitative research often focuses on subjective forms of assessment and because it will enhance the rigor and trustworthiness of the data—a key component of strong qualitative research.

We briefly introduce five of the most common qualitative research designs: (a) grounded theory, (b) narrative inquiry, (c) ethnography, (d) case study, and (e) phenomenology (see Figures 3.5). We use the general scenario of a school district implementing computer assessment technology as the context and backdrop for briefly reviewing these designs.

FIGURE 3.5 ■ Types of Qualitative Research Designs

A grounded theory design deploys a highly systematic process for developing a theory (i.e., a clear explanation of some phenomenon) based on data that are collected in a study. Interviews are a common assessment approach used in grounded theory. Researchers use a sequence of interviews, analyses, and interpretations as part of an iterative cycle; that is, they keep conducting interviews until no new information or insights are reached—a process called saturation). A research question such as, "What are the experiences of teachers in terms of the effectiveness of computer adaptive technology?" can easily be addressed using a grounded theory approach. Several people convey their experiences, and the researcher seeks to develop a model or theory using the data collected about these experiences.

A narrative inquiry design focuses on exploring the life of an individual or group of individuals (e.g., experiences of adolescent males who are incarcerated; experiences of teachers implementing computer adaptive technology in schools). A researcher records the personal stories and experiences of participants and then retells the story of their experiences (i.e., re-storying). While the narratives can derive from one or several individuals, the focus is on recounting the narratives using the participant's perspective rather than the researcher's perspective. In an educational context, a research question that can be addressed by re-storying individual experiences is, "What has been the experience of veteran and novice special education teachers as they shift to computer adaptive technology within their classrooms?"

The ethnographic design reflects a third type of qualitative research design that can be used in educational research. Ethnographers seek to analyze and highlight the norms and behaviors of a specific cultural group. This design is unique in its long-term study and analysis of cultural groups or community. Ethnographers typically recognize the challenges of capturing all nuances of interactions and dynamics in a given context and thus strive to describe these contexts based on the lived experiences of individuals and the ethnographer's approach to research. In an educational setting, a representative research question targeted by an ethnographer could be, "How do middle school and high school teachers from a rural community collaborate over time to meet the challenges of shifting away from unreliable internet to fiber optic services and in using computer adaptive assessment tools?" The ethnographer could also study how changes in technology services, collaborative efforts among teachers, and real-time assessment tools impact the educational experiences of students from the perspective of faculty members.

Researchers use a case study design when interested in conducting an in-depth description and analysis of the lived experiences of an individual, small group of individuals, organization, or other entity. While there are several types of case studies (see Chapter 6 for more detail), the key objective is to thoroughly explore the meaning and processes experienced by specific individuals and/or members of an organization. Central to this design is using a multi-method assessment approach (e.g., observations, interviews, work products, etc.) to generate a comprehensive and in-depth account of the individuals' experiences. The researcher is then charged with examining the extent to which the data from the multiple sources or assessment tools converge or diverge. Relative to the scenario about computer adaptive technology, an educator may wish to conduct a case study with a small group of early career teachers and their experiences using this type or other forms of technology. A research question that can be aptly addressed with a case study design is, "How do early career teachers navigate the challenges and potential pitfalls of using unfamiliar technology?"

A phenomenology design is an especially unique qualitative research approach due to its focus on the shared experiences of members within a group or community about the same phenomenon. In other words, phenomenology focuses on understanding the essence of participants' experience regarding some situation, event, or phenomenon. Phenomenologists tend to rely on interviews or observations and focus on the interpretations and overall consciousness of the participants. In phenomenology, there is no singular reality given that reality is subjectively determined by each individual's interpretations of the situation. Typically, the phenomenon under investigation is life-altering or intensive in some other way (e.g., school shooting, natural disaster). Thus, with this design, a researcher could examine the ways in which teachers within a school district instruct and leverage technological forms of assessment during an emergency. For example, suppose a high school in a particular school district was shut down due to an emergency; toxic industrial chemicals were found in the school and surrounding campus. School administrators relocated students to a Macy's store in an abandoned mall to sustain instruction and ongoing assessments of students. A relevant research question that may be relevant to this situation and design is, "What is the nature of the instructional and assessment experiences of teachers during emergency or crisis situations?"

Qualitative Methodology in Addressing the Lived Experiences of Others
©iStockphoto.com/SolStock

Identifying Key Methodological and Design Features

In this next series of *Let's See It!, Let's Do It!, You Do It!* activities, we ask you to review published studies that address issues pertaining to computer adaptive testing. Through these activities, you can hone your understanding and skills in applying methodological concepts to specific studies.

For the *Let's See It!* activity, we provide a summary of a study conducted by Martin and Lazendic (2018). In this example, we identify its overall purpose, the methodology and design, and specific components of the design, such as sample, measures, analyses. After reviewing this study, turn to the *Let's Do It!* activity to get some practice in identifying these concepts for a different study (Hrastinski & Wilbur, 2016). We provide responses to the *Let's Do It!* activity as part of an answer key in the appendix.

Let's See It! 3.2

Goals: To Demonstrate How to Identify the Research Design, Methodological, and Methods Choices of a Research Study.

The primary objective of this activity is to illustrate some of the key concepts and ideas that should be considered when reading a research article. Pay particular attention to the overall methodology and design used and the extent to which the various design features (i.e., sample, measures, analyses) are consistent with that methodology and design.

Study: Martin, A. J., & Lazendic, G. (2018). Computer-adaptive testing: Implications for students' achievement, motivation, engagement, and subjective test experience. *Journal of Educational Psychology, 110*(1), 27–45. http://dx.doi.org/10.1037/edu0000205

Purpose/Results

The purpose of this study was to examine the impact of computer adaptive testing (both fixed test and adaptive test) on student achievement, motivation, engagement, and subjective experience as well as differences based on gender and age.

Design Components

> **Methodology:** Quantitative
> **Research Design:** Experimental
> **Method**
> **Sample:** 12,736 elementary (years 3 and 5) and secondary (years 7 and 9) in Australia.
> **Data Sources:** Demographic information—grade level, gender, socioeducational advantage NAPLAN—National Assessment Program-Literacy and Numeracy
> **Data Analysis:** Multi-level modeling (regression)

Let's Do It! 3.2

Guided Practice: Identifying Research Methodology and Design Features

Using the *Let's See it!* activity and other tables and figures within this chapter, review the Hrastinski and Wilbur (2016) article and complete all the sections that follow. You can check your work by looking up the answer key in the appendix.

> **Study:** Hrastinski, I., & Wilbur, R. B., (2016). Academic achievement of deaf and hard-of-hearing students in an ASL/English bilingual program. *Journal of Deaf Studies and Deaf Education, 21*(2), 156–170. https://doi.org/10.1093/deafed/env072
>
> **Purpose/Results**

_____

_____

_____

Design Components
Methodology: _____
Research Design: _____
Method
Sample: _____
Data Sources: _____
Data Analysis: _____

THE TAKEAWAY

Qualitative and quantitative methodologies each include an array of unique research designs used to address different research questions.

MAKING DECISIONS ABOUT RESEARCH METHODOLOGY AND DESIGN

LEARNING OBJECTIVE
3.4   Explain a general decision-making approach for selecting quantitative and qualitative research designs.

Now that you understand the distinction between quantitative and qualitative methodologies and have some basic working knowledge of common designs within each framework, the next logical question to consider is, "How do I select the most appropriate design within a given methodology to address my specific research questions?" Although it is well beyond the scope of this chapter to consider the broad range of factors influencing this decision-making process, we present a couple of general decision-making guides to help classify studies as quantitative (see Figure 3.6) or qualitative (see Figure 3.7). Please note, these guides are not exhaustive of all potential designs that may exist within a given methodology. Further, there may be reasons other than those included in Figures 3.6 and 3.7 for selecting a particular design (e.g., practical or logistical considerations). For example, even though Mrs. Prentice may believe a true experimental design is ideal for answering a question about the causal effects of computer adaptive technology on her students' learning, she may not be able to use an experimental approach if she is unable to randomly assign students to each condition. Nonetheless, these figures can be of great assistance to novice or beginning researchers in understanding some of the fundamental distinctions among different designs.

Quantitative Methodologies

Figure 3.6 reflects the general decision-making process for selecting an experimental or non-experimental quantitative design. To use this guide, researchers first need to address a broad yet foundational question, "Am I going to manipulate (i.e., modify, alter, change) any variables?" If you answered yes to this question, you most likely are interested in using an experimental design, such as a true experimental, quasi-experimental, or single participant design. These design options are presented on the left-hand side of the decision-making guide. You would then proceed through

FIGURE 3.6 ■ Decision-Making Guide for Quantitative Designs

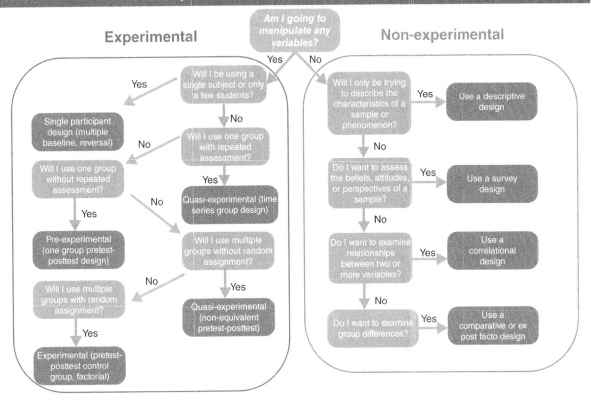

FIGURE 3.7 ■ Decision-Making Guide for Qualitative Research

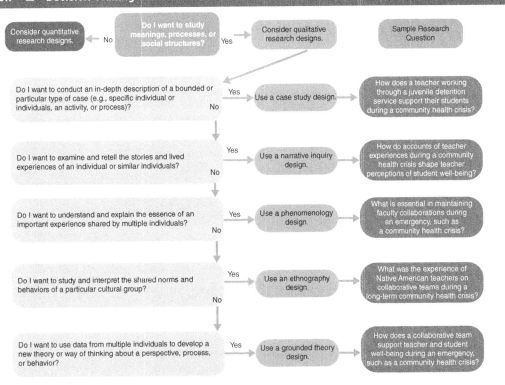

each question in sequence to identify the most suitable design. When you answer yes to a question, you have likely identified the design that is most suitable to addressing your research questions.

If you answered no to the general question at the top of Figure 3.6 about manipulating variables (i.e., a researcher creates different groups), you would shift your focus to the non-experimental approaches listed on the right-hand side of the figure. The potential non-experimental design options include descriptive, survey, correlational, and comparative. It is important to recognize that while Figure 3.6 can assist you in identifying key differences across experimental and non-experimental designs, all the designs listed in this figure are similar in that they focus on variables and numerical information and rely on formal statistical procedures to analyze the data.

Qualitative Methodologies

A general decision-making process can also be used to identify the most appropriate qualitative research design for a given study. Unlike quantitative designs, which were divided into two general categories (i.e., experimental, non-experimental), we present a decision-making guide for distinguishing five qualitative designs (see Figure 3.7).

All five qualitative designs presented in Figure 3.7 share several important features. They all seek to gather language-based information from respondents, use some type of coding or analysis process to create meaning within the data, and focus primarily on the subjective experiences and perceptions of individuals. However, these qualitative designs differ in several ways, including the number of individuals selected for a study. For example, case studies can be effective for examining only one individual, but grounded theory and ethnographic designs typically involve the use of a larger group. Another key difference among qualitative designs involves the particular experience being targeted. As an example, narrative inquiry designs target the personal stories of experience expressed by participants, while phenomenology approaches examine the experiences of participants for a shared and unusual or intense experience.

THE TAKEAWAY

Selecting an effective research design involves addressing two key questions:

1. Which research methodology is most appropriate to use (qualitative, quantitative, mixed)?
2. Which design within a particular methodological structure most closely aligns with my research question?

CROSS-CUTTING THEMES FOR RESEARCH METHODOLOGY AND DESIGN

LEARNING OBJECTIVE
3.5   Describe several research principles that cut across research methodology and design.

A common theme in this book is that research designs serve as a bridge between the questions posed by a researcher and the interpretations or conclusions they wish to make (see Figure 3.8).

Each research design discussed in this textbook has a specific purpose and function and thus can be used to address unique aspects of topics or critical issues. However, there are many research principles that hold true or cut across research methodology (i.e., qualitative, quantitative) and design (e.g., experiment, comparative, case study, ethnographic).

FIGURE 3.8 ■ The Central Role of Research Designs in the Research Process

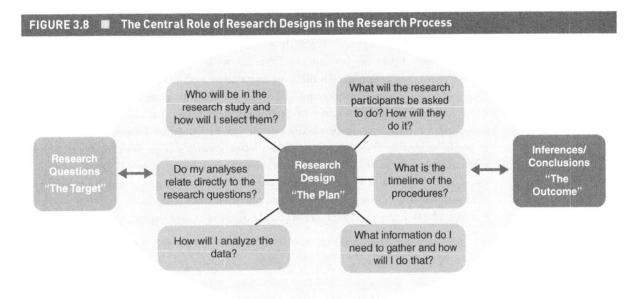

Cross-Cutting Theme 1: Building Knowledge of Research Design

Foundational knowledge in measurement, sampling procedures, and data analysis is required to successfully execute or implement any research design.

Research is a complex, multi-phased process. To execute a research plan or course of action, researchers need to possess foundational knowledge of research concepts and principles. Thus, regardless of whether Dr. Rodriguez wanted to conduct an experiment to examine the effects of an innovative online tutoring support program (i.e., quantitative methodology—experimental design) or to conduct an in-depth case study regarding the experiences of students with learning disabilities participating in the tutoring program, (i.e., qualitative methodology—case study design), she needs to possess adequate knowledge and skills for the following:

- Obtaining an appropriate sample
- Collecting data from the sample
- Analyzing the data
- Identifying the most effect ways to communicate and disseminate the results

Developing this broad knowledge base and skillset is not something that occurs easily or quickly; it takes time, practice, and feedback from others. Thus, becoming a skilled researcher is a marathon, not a sprint. Reading this textbook and taking a course in research methods represents your first steps in becoming a more knowledgeable consumer and or producer of research.

Cross-Cutting Theme 2: Making Valid Statements in Research

Research designs have a direct influence on the nature and type of conclusions and inferences that can be made from data and research results.

Research designs represent the central mechanism for conducting a research study. As mentioned previously, a research design consists of the plans and methods a researcher uses to address their research questions; it also sets the stage for how to interpret or make meaning about the results of the study. In a sense, research designs create the rules or parameters from which valid interpretations of data can be made. In Table 3.5, we provide examples of different types of conclusions that are aligned with different quantitative and qualitative designs. Suppose Dr. Rodriguez wanted to examine the causal effects of a new web-based reading intervention targeting decoding, fluency, and reading comprehension skills. Given that making statements about cause and effect are typically best accomplished with experimental designs, she elected to use a specific experimental design (e.g., pretest–posttest control group). What makes this design effective in drawing causal conclusions from the data is its reliance on control group and random assignment—essential features for isolating the effects of his reading program). If Dr. Rodriguez used a different quantitative design (e.g., comparative study, correlational) for his study, she would not be able to make these types of causal inferences or conclusions.

TABLE 3.5 ■ Linking Research Questions to Specific Research Methodologies, Designs, and Types of Conclusions

Example Research Questions	Type of Research Methodology	Type of Research Design	Example Valid Inferences or Conclusions
Do gifted students exhibit similar types of goals and self-reflection skills when using a web-based reading program as their non-gifted peers?	**Quantitative**	**Comparative** "differences between naturally occurring groups"	On average, gifted students and non-gifted students do not show *significant differences* in their goals or in their self-reflection skills about performance.
Do fifth-grade students receiving a web-based reading program intervention exhibit superior decoding and reading comprehension skills than a comparison condition (i.e., students who did not receive the intervention)?	**Quantitative**	**Experimental** "effects of a variable on one or more outcomes"	The reading intervention had a *causal effect* on fifth-grade students' decoding and use of reading comprehension strategies.
What are the experiences and attitudes of a middle school student with ADHD when learning in an online learning environment?	**Qualitative**	**Case study** "deep exploration into some phenomenon or individual"	A student with ADHD enjoys the autonomy and novelty of online learning but often struggles with self-directing and managing their attention and behaviors in these environments.
What are the experiences of veteran teachers enrolled in a technology-based Professional development workshop?	**Qualitative**	**Grounded theory** "A systematic method for creating theories about a topic of study, often based on themes"	Veteran teachers involved in technology-based professional development Workshops benefitted generally from the experience. Themes which emerged related to greater self-efficacy for technology usage, engagement with technology, and technology-based lesson integration.

Being able to make accurate, appropriate, and meaningful conclusions about the results in a study is of concern within both quantitative and qualitative researchers, although different terminology is emphasized. Quantitative researchers refer to this concept as validity whereas qualitative researchers typically reference trustworthiness. Validity (in quantitative research) represents a multi-dimensional construct involving the meaningfulness of conclusions about variables or statistical results. Four types of validity evidence are typically considered: internal validity, external validity, statistical conclusion validity, and construct validity. We provide a brief definition of these terms here but expand on them in greater detail throughout the book:

- Internal validity refers to the extent to which conclusions can be made that one variable (e.g., reading intervention) causes another variable (i.e., growth in fluency).

- External validity refers to the extent to which results of a study can generalize across settings, people, or situations outside the parameters of a study.

- Statistical conclusion validity reflects the extent to which the conclusions derived from statistical analyses are appropriate.

- Construct validity reflects the extent to which scores from a measure or research study accurately reflect a clearly defined construct.

In short, validity is a concept linked to the conclusions or inferences that are made from the results in a study. It does not reflect the characteristics of an assessment tool or research design. Thus, quantitative researchers should not seek to draw conclusions about the validity of a standardized reading test or intelligence test, nor should they attempt to make claims that experimental designs are a more valid design than a correlational or case study design.

In qualitative research, trustworthiness is the term most often used to describe the credibility and overall transparency with which the data are collected and interpreted. Given subjectivity is inherent to many qualitative research designs (i.e., in terms of assessment tools and the interpretation process), it is critical for researchers to be explicit and fully transparent in how all aspects of the study were conducted. Four domains of trustworthiness are frequently referenced: credibility, transferability, dependability, and confirmability. Credibility centers on steps researchers take to develop accurate interpretations. For example, when preparing a method section, the researcher will describe the data analysis procedures in detail, while in the results section, they will provide explicit details about the analysis and interpretation processes. Transferability describes how findings are relevant to other educational contexts, whereas dependability relates to the ability of other researchers to replicate a given study. The fourth component includes confirmability, which reflects the degree to which the conclusions can be corroborated by other people. In short, both quantitative and qualitative methodologies and research designs are both concerned with ensuring that researchers communicate the results and conclusions in an accurate, appropriate, and meaningful way.

Cross-Cutting Theme 3: Ruling Out Alternative Explanations

Ruling out alternative explanations or the influence of extraneous variables is an important aspect of quantitative and qualitative methodologies and designs.

A critical component of making accurate and valid interpretations is the need to rule out alternative explanations. In short, an alternative explanation is a description about the relationship or connection among variables or the nature of some experience that is different from a researcher's interpretations. Ruling out alternative explanations is important for both quantitative and qualitative methodologies. Let's revisit the issue of causation to illustrate what is meant by alternative explanations. In the quantitative literature, an important distinction is made between correlation and causation. Most quantitative researchers will, at the very least, strive to examine whether one variable (e.g., academic skills, emotions, type of academic support or instruction) *correlates* or *covaries* with one or more other variables (e.g., course grades, anxiety). The concept of correlation or covariation simply means that the pattern of scores for one variable "fit" or go together in some way with the pattern of scores for different variable. Thus, if Dr. Jones wanted to examine the relationship between laptop use (measured in minutes) and student learning, he would need to measure or gather information (i.e., scores or other numerical information) for each of these variables. If Dr. Jones observed that students who spend more time using their laptops in the classroom also exhibit higher report card grades, then he can conclude that as the amount of laptop use increases there is a tendency for students to achieve at a higher level. Making this latter statement is not the same as claiming that spending more time on your laptop will cause one to get better grades.

STOP AND THINK 3.2

Based on the scenario with Dr. Jones and his findings of a significant correlation between laptop use and grade, is the following statement valid? Why or why not?
   "Laptop use directly influences report card grades."

Although researchers have begun to argue that qualitative designs may be able to address issues of causality (see Maxwell, 2012, for an extended discussion of this issue), quantitative designs have historically been the recommended choice to drawing causal inferences. Regardless of the design, however, the most important research principle to recognize is that cause-and-effect claims can *only be made when alternative explanations of some phenomenon or results are ruled out*. Quantitative approaches attempt to rule out alternative explanations by attempting to control all or almost all aspects of the procedures and methods of a study and include features such as random assignment and the use of comparison or control conditions.

In contrast, qualitative researchers do not seek to constrain or control many aspects of a study. To rule out alternative explanations, they rely on specific techniques, such as searching for data or cases that contradict the preferred explanation, using triangulation of data (i.e., assessing convergence of data), and asking research participants to convey whether they agree with the conclusions that were drawn (i.e., member checks). Suppose Dr. Rodriguez used a case study design to examine the processes that early career teachers with a learning disability use to implement a new type of educational technology for enhancing students' data practice skills in science (i.e., data collection, data analysis, etc.). A key theme emanating from this study was that the teachers who had doubted themselves and their ability to work with technology (i.e., teachers with low self-efficacy) tended to avoid practicing the technology and often opted to use technology that was most familiar to them. To help bolster the case that self-efficacy and not other factors lead to or cause disengagement and avoidance, Dr. Rodriguez can take one of several actions. She could review the qualitative dataset to identify information or situations that contradict his conclusion. Perhaps there are teachers with higher self-efficacy who also avoided using the new technology, or conversely, there was a teacher with low self-efficacy who fully engaged with the technology. This information would contradict the conclusion that self-efficacy was the cause of disengagement. She could also meet with the teachers who participated in the study to share the key findings and to explore whether other factors may have been at play or caused their avoidance of the new technology.

Cross-Cutting Theme 4: Time Perspective in Research Designs

Some research designs collect data at one time point whereas others engage in data collection at multiple points.

Another important research concept that is relevant to both quantitative and qualitative designs involve the time dimension of a study (i.e., how often and when data are collected). Cross-sectional designs provide a one-time assessment or "snapshot" of a sample or some other phenomenon. Cross-sectional research offers several benefits to researchers, most notably the efficiency with which data can be collected. As an educator, although Dr. Rodriguez is quite busy with her administrative responsibilities, she is interested in examining changes in student attitudes and confidence when using different learning technologies during the middle school years. To gather this information, Dr. Rodriguez decided to administer a couple of student questionnaires and gather learning analytic data about students' real-time use of school-based technologies. He gathered this information from students in all three grade levels (i.e., sixth, seventh, and eighth grade) at the conclusion of the second marking period (i.e., single point in time).

Although this cross-sectional design can help Dr. Rodriguez and his colleagues better understand technology use in middle school, this one-time assessment approach limits the conclusions she may wish to make, such as drawing conclusions about developmental trends across the grade levels. For example, suppose eighth-grade students showed more frequent use of certain technologies than sixth and seventh graders. It might be tempting to conclude that middle school students show an increasing trend in technology use over time. However, it is also plausible that the observed grade level differences reflect idiosyncratic characteristics of the eighth-grade cohort (e.g., they were exposed to a technology initiative in sixth grade that the current sixth and seventh graders were not).

To assess developmental changes or actual shifts in individuals' thinking, attitudes, or behaviors over time, researchers often rely on longitudinal designs. With a longitudinal design, researchers administer the same measures or assessment approaches at multiple time points. In the case of quantitative designs, researchers will administer questionnaires, tests, or other types of objective measures, whereas for qualitative designs they will repeatedly administer interviews, focus groups, or other approaches that yield language-based data.

THE TAKEAWAY

Despite the clear distinctions between quantitative and qualitative methodologies and designs, they often address overlapping and parallel issues.

ETHICAL CONSIDERATIONS

LEARNING OBJECTIVE

3.6 Demonstrate general knowledge of the governing structure and oversight of ethical practices when conducting research.

In each chapter of the textbook, we discuss various ethical issues and concepts related to the specific chapter content and topics. At a broad level, the chapters will reference one or more aspirational ethical principles contained within the American Psychological Association's *Ethical*

Principles of Psychologists and Code of Conduct, such as beneficence (i.e., strive to benefit others and do no harm), fidelity and responsibility (i.e., build trust with others and be accountable for actions), integrity (i.e., promote accuracy, honest, and truthfulness), justice (i.e., promote fairness and strive to avoid injustice to others), and respect for peoples' rights and dignity (i.e., ensure privacy, self-determination, and welfare of others). In addition to recognizing these five general principles and other specific ethical standards, one of the most important initial steps in conducting ethical research is to seek out permission or approval from relevant stakeholders to conduct research in school settings.

In 1974, the U.S. Congress passed the National Research Act to provide funding, support, and guidance for developing and monitoring the use of agreed-upon ethical standards and procedures when conducting research (National Research Act, 1974). Over the past few decades, most colleges, universities, hospitals, and school districts employ an internal review group to monitor and ensure compliance with ethical research practices. In many contexts, these review groups are called an institutional review board (IRB), but they can also be labeled independent ethics committees (IEC), research ethics board (REB), ethical review board (ERB), or human subject review committee (HSRC). For simplicity, we use the term IRB throughout this chapter to denote an ethics review group.

To get approval for a research study, researchers must submit a proposal or summary of the study to the IRB for review. Within this proposal, the researcher provides information about the purposes and significance of the study, its core design, methods, and procedures, and the mechanisms and processes for collecting, managing, and storing research data. Of particular interest to an IRB is the nature of the target sample (e.g., children, adults, prisoners, pregnant women, etc.) and the process through which the sample is recruited and involved in the study. In most circumstances, researchers will need to get informed consent from the research participants or from parents or guardians of participants who are either below 18 years old or are not able to legally provide their own consent (e.g., individuals with the cognitive disability). The IRB helps to ensure that the informed consent documents appropriately inform the participants about a range of topics, including the duration of the study and participation, risks and benefits to participants, steps or safeguards taken to minimize any negative effects of participation, anticipated uses of the research data, and the process through which the participants identifiable personal information is protected. When school-aged children are involved (i.e., those under 18 years of age), parents or legal guardians are required to provide consent, but the participating children or adolescents are also provided the opportunity to provide assent; a process very similar to the consent procedures except that the person providing consent is under the age of 18 years. Thus, when conducting research in schools, it is very common for researchers to first get parental consent and then obtain student assent.

In most institutions, researchers are also required to engage in ongoing professional development and evaluation of their ethical knowledge and application skills through the Collaborative Institutional Training Initiative (CITI Program) or other similar programming. These types of programs provide a range of ethics-based courses regarding legal and ethical training for researchers. The courses are developed by panels of experts to ensure the quality and representativeness of the information to different populations. These ethics training courses tend to be self-directed and self-paced but also include checks for understanding and a final quiz. In short, being a researcher in the 21st century requires individuals to not only possess adequate knowledge of research design and methodology and the emerging critical issues in their respective fields but also ethical principles and practices for minimizing harm to participants as part of a research study.

THE TAKEAWAY

Before conducting research in schools, researchers need to take ethics-based training and coursework and receive permission from an IRB.

AMERICAN PSYCHOLOGICAL ASSOCIATION STYLE

LEARNING OBJECTIVE

3.7 Utilize the *Publication Manual of the American Psychological Association* for different research methodologies and designs.

When writing an article for publication, researchers typically report information in different sections or parts, including an *abstract* (i.e., a concise summary of the entire study), *introduction* (i.e., summary of related research, rational for study, research questions), *methods* (i.e., sample, measures, procedures, and overall design), *results* (i.e., nature of the statistical or analytical procedures and the corresponding numerical or thematic/qualitative findings), and *discussion* (i.e., summary of key findings, connection with the prior literature, implications, future research directions; see Chapter 16 for a more detailed analysis). The following sections are typically included when writing a research report using APA style:

APA Style Writing: Steps to Writing a Report
Follow the linear roadmap:

1. Title
2. Abstract
3. Introduction
4. Methods
5. Results
6. Discussion
7. References

And remember to BE ACCURATE and DETAILED but STAY CONCISE!

The guidelines for communicating information are similar across all research methodologies for certain sections of an article, such as the abstract and introduction. However, when considering the methods, results, and discussion sections, the reporting guidelines can vary across quantitative and qualitative research. To illustrate this point, we focus specifically on the similarities and differences for the methods or research design sections in quantitative and qualitative articles (see Table 3.6).

A fundamental distinction between a qualitative and quantitative research article is the structure, flow of information, and length of a research design section. Because qualitative research tends to be more dynamic and fluid in nature, such as an on-going iterative data

TABLE 3.6 ■ Reporting Standards for Methods Section of Qualitative and Quantitative Studies

Aspects of the Design Section	Quantitative	Qualitative
Sequence of design description	A description of the design often follows information about the sample and measures or data collection	A description of the design often occurs at the outset of the methods section
Key sections of a method section	• Characteristics of participants, recruitment and selection, sample size, and power analysis • Data collection (i.e., definition of measure and description of psychometric rigor) • Research design (i.e., type of design, conditions or subgroups, procedures to be followed for each condition/subgroup) • Data analysis strategies to address hypotheses (e.g., descriptive and inferential statistics)	• Research design overview (i.e., type of design and rationale) • Researcher description • Characteristic of study participants, recruitment, and selection • Data collection and coding • Data analysis strategies (e.g., coding, thematic analyses) • Methodological integrity (e.g., triangulation, checks on interview quality, how research perspectives were managed)
Format of design section	Format tends to be highly structured, adhering to a sequence of sample, measures, design and procedures, and data analysis	Format can vary from paper to paper based on specific aspects of the inquiry process. For example: • Data analysis and data collection may be placed in combined or separated sections • Can be written in narrative or chronological order
Key principles in description of research design	• High level of detail and specificity regarding the sample characteristics, psychometric rigor of measures • Clarity regarding whether conditions were manipulated or naturally occurring (i.e., experiment versus non-experiment) and the corresponding name of design	High level of clarity and an appropriate rationale regarding how the chosen design best captures the lived experiences of research participants Inclusion of a lengthier design description than for a quantitative study given the fluid, nuanced nature of the qualitative data collection and analyses

collection process, researchers often need to devote much attention in a research article to address these details. The research design section in a qualitative research article will often be addressed in the initial part of a methods section and will explicitly detail the background and perspectives of the researcher. Because some qualitative research involves researchers frequently interacting with the research participants and being directly immersed in the data collection and subjective interpretive process, they need to take great care in explaining how their personal perspectives and biases were considered and did not adversely affect data interpretation. Such a focus helps to enhance the trustworthiness and credibility of the interpretations that are communicated in a qualitative research article. Finally, because the data collection process and level of interaction with research participants is highly variable across qualitative studies, the basic structure and flow of information in a methods section will often vary significantly from study to study.

In contrast, the methods section in quantitative research articles tend to be more structured and pre-determined, although some variability in format is permitted. The typical sequence of a methods section includes the sample (i.e., characteristics, size, recruitment process), measures (i.e., description of measures and their psychometric quality), research design and procedures, and a data analysis plan. Further, because quantitative studies are often concerned with hypothesis testing and generalizing results to a broader population and context, researchers will also provide an explicit and detailed description of sample characteristics (age, gender, educational history, socioeconomic status, etc.) and the contexts in which the participants operate. The methods section of a quantitative article is also contrasted with qualitative research articles in that the former provides extensive information about the measures used to collect data, including their purpose, administration and scoring procedures, and psychometric rigor. Because quantitative studies rely on numerical information, they typically do not need to focus on coding or transcription procedures that are so prevalent with qualitative studies.

THE TAKEAWAY

The nature of the format and structure of the methods section of a research article will vary depending on the specific methodology one uses (i.e., quantitative, and qualitative).

CHAPTER SUMMARY

In this chapter, we compared and contrasted quantitative and qualitative methodology and discussed the corresponding research designs linked to those methodologies. Researchers can elect to use qualitative and quantitative methodology or some combination of both (i.e., mixed method). They can seek to examine differences among groups or explore the statistical relations between different variables (i.e., quantitative), or they can strive to understand the perspectives and experiences of individuals or groups of individuals, such as the perspective of teachers when implementing a new curriculum or the lived experiences of individuals experiencing suicidal thoughts and behaviors (i.e., qualitative). One research methodology is not inherently superior to the other. Each methodology is used for specific objectives and purposes. Further, as researchers increasingly recognize the unique value and contribution of each approach and acknowledge that neither methodology can fully encapsulate or examine a situation, phenomenon, or group of people, there has been an increased focus on using mixed methods approaches.

Further, there are several research principles that cut across research methodology. On some level, research across both methodologies is concerned with recruiting and selecting a sample, identifying key constructs to interpret, deciding how frequently to collect data over time during the study (i.e., cross-sectional, longitudinal), and making appropriate, accurate, and meaningful inferences about the collected data (i.e., validity or trustworthiness).

EXTENSION ACTIVITIES

You Do It! 3.1

Using Quantitative and Qualitative Methodology

Self-Directed Practice: To Practice Distinguishing Quantitative and Qualitative Methodology

The primary objective of this activity is to give you an opportunity to think about a topic that is of personal interest to you (e.g., cyberbullying, effectiveness of reading programs, understanding the experiences of incarcerated youth). Using the basic framework and structure for the *Let's See It!* (Mrs. Johnson scenario) and *Let's Do It!* (Mrs. Marshall scenario), identify a topic or scenario of interest to you. After thinking through the details and critical issues of a topic you wish to explore, identify the methodology that makes the most sense for your investigation and how selecting that methodology influences the nature of your research questions, use of hypotheses, type of measures to use, and analysis approach. Try creating a study from both a qualitative and quantitative perspective.

Area of Personal Interest

Critical Issue

Qualitative Methodology	Quantitative Methodology
Research Question:	Research Question:
Hypothesis:	Hypothesis:
Likely measures:	Likely measures:
Analysis approach:	Analysis approach:

KEY TERMS

A priori hypothesis

Alternative explanation

Case study design

Comparative design

Construct

Correlational design

Cross-Sectional design

Deductive reasoning

Dependent variable

Descriptive design

Experimental design

Ethnographic design

Grounded theory design

Grouping variable

Independent variable

Inductive reasoning

Informed consent

Institutional review board

Interpretivist

Longitudinal design

Mixed methodology

Non-experimental design

Narrative inquiry design

Phenomenology

Positivism

Predictor variable

Qualitative methodology

Quantitative methodology

Quasi-experimental design

Research design

Research methodology

Single participant research design

Survey design

True experimental design

Trustworthiness

Validity (in quantitative research)

Variable

ANSWER KEY

Stop and Think Activitities

STOP AND THINK 3.1

There is no correct answer for this Stop and Think. The intent was to get you to reflect on whether you have a natural tendency to think about research in a certain way or whether a particular methodology speaks to how you think about the world in which you operate. Quantitative research is incredibly valuable as it can uncover how variables occurring in school contexts (e.g., reading skills, test grades, problem-solving skills) relate to each other or can be influenced or enhanced by school-based interventions. On the other hand, qualitative research can provide an authentic and deep understanding of the lived experiences of important stakeholders within a school context (e.g., students, teachers, principals) and how their perceptions and attitudes play a role in their professional activities.

STOP AND THINK 3.2

"Laptop use *directly influences* report card grades."

Just because two variables are related to each other does not mean that one variable caused the other. To make claims of causality (i.e., one variable causing another), researchers need to consider whether three basic conditions are met:

- The target variables are *correlated* to some degree.

- The presumed cause *occurs prior* to the outcome (temporal sequence).

- *Alternative explanations* regarding the cause-outcome link have been ruled out.

In the example with Dr. Jones, a statistical relationship between laptop use and achievement was clearly established, thereby satisfying condition #1. The temporal sequence condition (i.e., cause must precede effect) was also met given that he assessed students' laptop use during the second semester of the school year but collected data achievement using end-of-year grades; thus, the presumed cause (laptop use) occurred prior to the outcome. In addressing the first two conditions, Dr. Jones has some credible foundation for potentially drawing a causal link between laptop use and achievement. However, he still needs to think about and consider whether other factors or alternative explanations exist regarding the determinants of student achievement.

Let's Do It! Activities

Let's Do It! 3.1

Guided Practice: To Practice Distinguishing Quantitative and Qualitative Methodology

The primary objective of this activity is for you to practice generating your own research questions, using both a quantitative and qualitative lens. Please read the scenario about westward expansion and write a critical issue that seems relevant. With that critical issue in mind, develop an appropriate qualitative and quantitative research question and fill in the relevant information for hypothesis, likely measures, and analysis approach. You can check your work by reviewing the answer key provided in the appendix at the end of the chapter. Although the answer key may not directly relate to your responses, it will provide guidance about appropriate questions and features for each methodology.

Scenario background: Mrs. Marshall is curious about her middle school students' use of different types of learning strategies (e.g., graphic organizers, concepts maps) and their potential impact on student learning. Over the course of a month, she provided modeling and guidance to half of her social studies classes in how to use visualizations, graphs, or concept maps to organize information that they were learning. She then wanted to examine their use of these strategies for a specific lesson on westward expansion within the United States during the 1800s.

Critical Issue: Utility of graphic organizers to improve learning

Qualitative Methodology	Quantitative Methodology
Research question: What are student attitudes and perceptions about graphic organizers? What are the key challenges and benefits of these strategies from the perspective of students?	**Research question:** Do students who received the graphic organizer instruction show improved learning relative to the group who did not use the graphic organizer?
Hypothesis: None.	*Hypothesis:* Students who received the strategy instruction would exhibit higher unit exam grades than those who did not receive the instruction.
Likely measures: Interviews with a small number of students who received the graphic organizer instruction; work products when using graphic organizers.	*Likely measures:* Classroom-based multiple-choice exams.
Analysis approach: Identify the most common themes related to the perception and use of graphic organizers.	*Analysis approach:* Use of statistical techniques (e.g., t-tests) to examine group differences in achievement.

LET'S DO IT! 3.2

Identifying Research Methodology and Design Features

Study: Hrastinski, I., & Wilbur, R. B., (2016). Academic achievement of deaf and hard-of-hearing students in an ASL/English bilingual program. *Journal of Deaf Studies and Deaf Education, 21*(2), 156–170. https://doi.org/10.1093/deafed/env072

Purpose/Results

To examine differences between highly proficient and low proficient groups in American Sign Language (ASL) in terms of reading comprehension, language skills, and mathematics.

Design Components

Methodology: Quantitative

Research Design: Comparative

Method

Sample: Eighty-five deaf and hard of hearing students from sixth to eleventh grade who attended a deaf school. Forty-seven were highly proficient in ASL while 38 were not proficient.

Data Sources: Northwest Evaluation Association (NWEA) Measures of Academic Progress; Stanford Achievement Test, 10th edition)

Data Analysis: Descriptive statistics and ANOVA procedures were used to assess group differences.

 NON-EXPERIMENTAL RESEARCH DESIGNS

LEARNING OBJECTIVES

Upon completion of this chapter, the reader should be able to

4.1   Recognize when the use of non-experimental designs is most relevant

4.2   Apply the core features of descriptive designs

4.3   Apply the core features of correlational designs

4.4   Apply the core features of comparative designs

4.5   Demonstrate knowledge of ethical issues when conducting, analyzing, and communicating non-experimental research

4.6   Utilize the *Publication Manual of the American Psychological Association* in reporting and presenting findings in non-experimental designs

A DAY AT WORK

My Students Struggle to Manage Things!!

©iStockphoto.com/monkeybusinessimages

Ms. Judy Berry and Mr. Sungwoo Kim are members of a tenth-grade instructional team at a local high school. Like many of their colleagues, they are concerned with the large number of students who struggle with the demands and expectations of high school. From their perspective, many students simply go through the motions when completing schoolwork and are not fully invested or engaged in their learning.

In subsequent months, Ms. Berry, Mr. Kim, and a few of their colleagues decided to review the research literature about student motivation and self-regulated learning.

Specifically, they wanted to learn about the reasons why some students try harder and are more successful in managing their learning than others. They also attended a few professional development workshops to learn about effective regulatory strategies that help students succeed, such as time management, help seeking, and self-quizzing. Although the teachers were excited to learn about these strategies, they still had some nagging questions about the sources of student motivation and regulation. When someone suggested they conduct their own research to examine these issues, the teachers seemed interested but were at a loss because they did not know what needed to be done and how to do it.

INTRODUCTION

The "what needs to be done" and "how to do it" pertains to the research design of a study. In this chapter, we introduce readers to the basic features and characteristics of three non-experimental designs: descriptive, correlational, and comparative designs. As noted in Chapter 3, non-experimental and experimental designs are distinguished by whether researchers manipulate variables (i.e., intentionally alter or create conditions for different groups). Researchers *do not* manipulate variables in non-experimental designs but do so with experimental approaches. Non-experimental designs are versatile in that they can be used to describe the characteristics of people or situations as they naturally occur (i.e., descriptive design), explore the statistical relationships between variables (i.e., correlational design), or examine differences among naturally occurring groups (gifted versus non-gifted; comparative design). For each of these non-experimental designs, we address the same core topics: research questions, measurement-related issues, sampling, and data analysis approaches. While we do not delve deeply into all the nuances for these core topics across the non-experimental designs, we address some of the most pertinent details for each respective design. We also use the Mr. Kim and Ms. Berry scenario throughout the chapter to illustrate how the different designs can be applied and used in school contexts. The chapter ends with a discussion of ethical issues and the key recommendations from the American Psychological Association regarding the dissemination and communication of results from non-experimental studies.

USING NON-EXPERIMENTAL DESIGNS

LEARNING OBJECTIVE
4.1   Recognize when the use of non-experimental designs is most appropriate.

When researchers design a quantitative study, the initial question they must consider is, "Will I seek to manipulate any variables (e.g., type of reading program, nature of feedback), or will I simply observe and examine variables that naturally exist?" As reflected in Figure 4.1, the answer to this question plays a key role in selecting a research design. If researchers wish to manipulate variables, they will use an experimental design (e.g., true experiment, quasi-experiment, single-participant design). Manipulation of variables in an experiment simply means that the researcher exposes different groups of individuals to varying levels of an intervention, instructional approach, or some other experience. When no manipulation occurs, a non-experimental design becomes the focal point. Although some may consider experimental designs to be superior to non-experimental approaches, we do not adopt the position; rather, we assert that every design is useful and appropriate for addressing particular questions and issues. Because experimental designs help to illustrate cause and effect relations, they are ideally suited to examine the effectiveness of interventions. In contrast, non-experimental designs are most often used when researchers wish to examine variables as they naturally exist (e.g., teacher satisfaction, reading comprehension skill) or in situations when variables cannot be manipulated and changed by an experimenter (e.g., biological sex).

FIGURE 4.1 ■ Comparison of Experimental and Non-experimental Designs

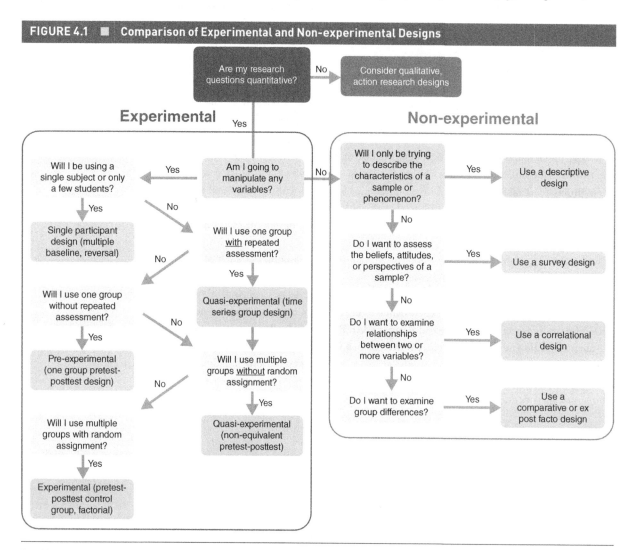

Consider the dialogue between Ms. Berry, Mr. Kim, and one of their colleagues, Ms. Melinda Johnson, to illustrate the applicability and use of non-experimental designs in schools.

Ms. Berry: *"I often wonder about how frequently students use strategies when they complete their homework or study. Like how well do they manage their time, plan out how best to study, or quiz themselves before tests? I don't need to do any fancy or complex research, but I just want to learn more about the types of strategies that middle school students use and maybe how well they use them."*

Mr. Kim: *"That's a great idea. So how would you do that?"*

Ms. Berry: *"Well, I'm thinking the best thing to do is to administer a questionnaire that asks students to rate how often they use these strategies. There are many questionnaires that assess these things. I think it makes sense to also observe students in different classrooms so I can directly see how often they do things like ask for help, stay on task, and come prepared to class."*

Mr. Kim: *"Nice. I often wondered about the ways in which gifted and non-gifted students differ. Not every student who is intelligent will perform well in school. I think other things lead to student success, regardless of their intelligence. That is something I always wondered about."*

Ms. Johnson: *"I think about similar things. It often seems there are many differences between boys and girls, such as their attitudes and interests in math or science."*

Mr. Kim: *"Yes . . . biological sex is an important variable to think about."*

Ms. Johnson: *"But I also have wondered about other types of demographic variables, like the financial situation of their family or the quality of their education prior to high school. I think these types of variables may be even more important for explaining student performance in school. I also think about how much student motivation or their ability to cope and manage with the demands of high school impact their grades. I guess what I am saying is that I am curious about whether some variables are more important than others in explaining why some students do well in school and others do not."*

Ms. Berry: *"I think on some level, we are all interested in doing the same thing. We just want to understand and explain what our students do and how they think and feel and whether these things can explain their performance in school."*

Non-experimental designs are typically used when researchers wish to

- Describe how people think or what they do or the characteristics of a learning program or curriculum **(Ms. Berry)**

- Compare groups of similar students who differ in terms of some characteristics or ability **(Mr. Kim)**

- Examine to what extent different variables relate to or predict student outcomes **(Ms. Johnson)**

The key non-experimental designs discussed in this chapter include descriptive (which often includes survey designs), correlational, and comparative designs. Descriptive designs are those in which researchers seek to describe the characteristics of a sample, setting, measurement tool, or some other phenomenon. They tend to rely on descriptive statistics, such as frequency counts, percentages, means and standard deviations (see Ms. Berry). Survey research designs, which are often considered a type of descriptive design (although they can also consider relationships among variables), typically focus on the perceptions, beliefs, and attitudes of a group of people about a specific topic or situation. Examples of topics addressed by survey research designs may include teacher perspectives and knowledge about bullying prevention initiatives in their school, parental perceptions regarding the quality of home school collaboration, or the beliefs and attitudes of school psychologists about their professional roles in working with students who return to school following concussion (i.e., return-to-learn initiative).

The final two non-experimental designs, correlational and comparative, are considered more "advanced" non-experimental approaches because they attempt to explain how multiple variables predict or explain each other. Since Mr. Kim was interested in comparing gifted versus non-gifted students, he would use a comparative design. Melinda's ideas about examining relationships among multiple variables (e.g., family financial background, biological sex, prior school experience, motivation, and school success) can be addressed with a correlational design. While she cannot claim that one variable causes another variable she can draw conclusions about which variables are most important in explaining school success.

THE TAKEAWAY

Non-experimental designs are just as important as experimental designs. They just have a different objective; to describe, explain, or examine different variables as they naturally exist.

DESCRIPTIVE DESIGNS

LEARNING OBJECTIVE

4.2   Apply the core features of descriptive designs.

For each of the non-experimental designs addressed in this chapter (i.e., descriptive/survey, correlational, comparative), we focus on four essential features and characteristics: (1) nature of research questions, (2) sampling, (3) measurement, and (4) statistics. We first turn to descriptive designs (see Figure 4.2).

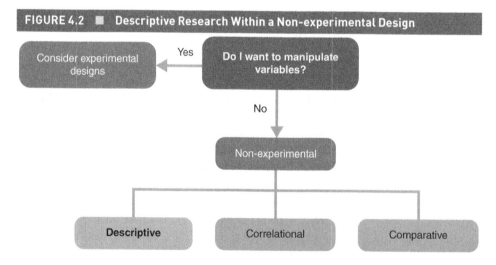

FIGURE 4.2 ■ Descriptive Research Within a Non-experimental Design

Nature of Research Questions

As emphasized in several chapters of this textbook, the questions a researcher elects to investigate in a study have a direct influence on the selection of a research design. In Figure 4.3, we present several research questions that are aligned with a descriptive design. As you review these questions, pay particular attention to the following points: First, descriptive designs can be used to address a variety of topics with different types of research participants, or samples. They can help researchers better understand the skills, abilities, and behaviors of individuals or their perceptions, beliefs, and feelings about specific issues or situations. For example, descriptive studies can be used to understand teacher perceptions of a cyberbullying intervention in schools, the number of out-of-seat and inattentive behaviors exhibited by middle school students with learning disabilities, or the key characteristics of Head Start programs implemented in urban communities.

FIGURE 4.3 ■ Example of Descriptive Design Research Questions

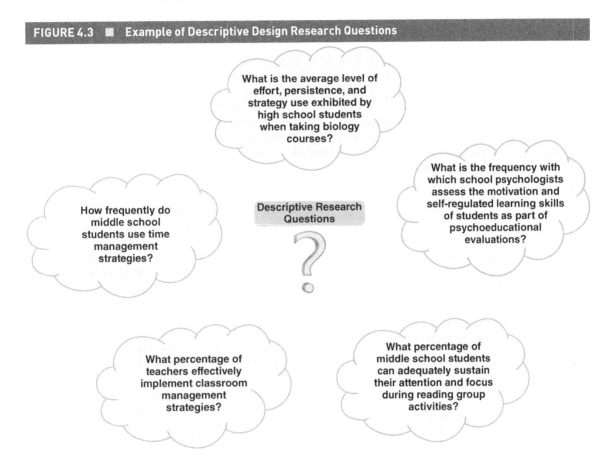

A second point to note involves the specific wording of the five questions. None of these questions mention anything about *relationship* between variables or the *effect* of one variable on another one. Descriptive designs focus primarily on gathering information that describes the characteristics, beliefs, perceptions, or attitudes of people. In other words, they focus on sample or contextual characteristics that naturally exist. Further, all five example research questions either directly use quantitative or numerical language or imply that some type of quantification of information is needed. Examples of numerical language used in descriptive research include the following:

- Number of times students get out of their seats (frequency)

- Average scores on a measure of student self-efficacy for learning (mean or average)

- Percentage of students enrolled in an after-school reading program (percentage)

Finally, although descriptive studies can be viewed as being more simplistic than other designs, particularly in terms of the statistical analyses, they are quite nimble and useful for addressing a wide range of critical issues in today's schools, such as teachers' instructional practices, the feasibility of implementing a new intervention (i.e., how easily the intervention can be implemented in schools), or student attitudes and perspectives about suicide prevention programming. When researchers elect to use descriptive designs, they often attempt to shine a light on an important topic and issue that has not yet been studied at great length. Addressing research questions with a descriptive design can provide a foundation for addressing more complex questions with correlational and experimental approaches.

Sampling

In looking back at the research questions in Figure 4.2, it should be apparent that descriptive studies intentionally target a particular group of people, such as teachers, middle school students, or school psychologists. Thus, when researchers are thinking about using a descriptive design, a critical initial question to consider is, "*To whom do I wish to generalize the results of my study?*" Ms. Berry wanted to understand the strategic behaviors of middle school students in mathematics contexts. Given her role as a seventh-grade teacher, Ms. Berry could simply examine the SRL and motivational characteristics of all students at her middle school. This type of study may yield compelling information that is directly relevant to her role as a teacher, but the key issue is whether she wants to produce results that generalize to middle school students more broadly.

This latter issue of external validity or generalizability is an important consideration for quantitative researchers. Ultimately, researchers try to select a sample that is representative of a particular population. For example, if Ms. Berry works at a predominately upper middle-class school with over 85% White students and elects to conduct a descriptive survey with students only at that school, her ability to draw conclusions about middle school students throughout the state would be greatly restricted. Thus, two key sampling-related principles to consider when using descriptive research designs is to (1) first determine the population to whom one wishes to make interpretive statements and conclusions and (2) then take the necessary steps to appropriately sample from that population.

Measurement

In any quantitative research study, researchers assess or measure things about people, situations, or contexts. For a descriptive study, researchers can use assessment tools (i.e., the method for gathering quantitative information or scores) that require direct involvement of the sample (e.g., using a survey, questionnaire, or interview) or that are less obtrusive in nature (e.g., direct observations, video or audio recordings). The choice of assessment tool depends on the nature of the situation and the overall objectives of the study. As an example, Ms. Berry wanted to examine student engagement and help-seeking behaviors during classroom instruction, so she decided to conduct a series of direct observations in several classrooms over the course of a few weeks. She recorded the number of students who actively participated in class discussions as well as those who asked for help during unstructured academic activities. Ms. Berry's assessment approach consisted of using direct observation techniques to gather numerical data about the strategic behaviors of middle school students (e.g., number of times students participate per minute). In contrast. if Ms. Berry was more interested in describing the attitudes of students about their sense of belongingness or their confidence for earning an A in the course, she would likely use a survey or questionnaire (i.e., measures that includes several statements to which respondents are asked to rate themselves). In the remainder of this section, we focus primarily on a specific type of descriptive research that uses questionnaires to assess the attitudes, opinions, and beliefs of individuals (i.e., descriptive survey design).

Multiple Purposes of Descriptive Survey Designs

The term *survey* can have different meanings depending on its use in research. Survey assessment tools typically involve questionnaires or interviews that are used to get participants to convey their beliefs or perceptions about a particular topic. Survey assessments can be used in any quantitative research design (i.e., experimental, correlational, comparative, descriptive). In some situations, the surveys are used to assess variables representing well-defined, theoretical constructs (e.g., self-efficacy, use of learning strategies, anxiety, school connectedness). However, surveys can also be used more generally to assess the perceptions, beliefs, opinions, abilities, or behaviors of a sample of individuals about an emerging or critical issue, such as teacher and student perceptions about race relations in their school. Using this type of design in school contexts can be quite enlightening for educators and administrators because it can reveal critical gaps or unmet needs of educational professionals or students. In this chapter, we emphasize the use the term *survey* to reflect a specific type of descriptive design, a *descriptive survey design*.

To illustrate this approach, let's revisit one of the research questions presented in Figure 4.3 ("What is the frequency with which school psychologists assess the motivation and self-regulated learning (SRL) skills of students as part of psychoeducational evaluations?"). In recent years, Mr. Kim and several of his colleagues have encountered a fairly large number of students who give minimal effort when completing their schoolwork and who get overwhelmed with school demands. Given that many students referred for a psychoeducational evaluation due to academic concerns also tend to exhibit motivational difficulties, Mr. Kim often wonders why information about students' motivation beliefs (e.g., self-efficacy, interest in school, sense of belonging) or their strategic or self-regulated learning behaviors (e.g., time management, help seeking) is not typically discussed during Child Study Team meetings involving teachers, school counselors, administrators, and parents. After speaking with colleagues in other school districts about this topic, Mr. Kim increasingly began to speculate that school personnel (e.g., school psychologists, counselors) do not typically assess these variables as part of a student evaluation. However, this was his hypothesis that needed to be tested by conducting a study. Thus, he conducted a descriptive survey study with school psychologists to formally assess their perceptions, knowledge, and actual use of motivation and strategies assessments. The underlying driving force behind this study was Mr. Kim's interest in addressing a critical practice issue; that is, whether school psychologists neglect motivation and self-regulated learning assessments even though these constructs appear to be quite important to student school success.

When using surveys for descriptive purposes, researchers need to have a clear understanding of the *critical issue* as well as the relevant *target sample*. A few guiding questions can be used to identify a critical issue relevant with this design:

- Is there a gap or disconnect between what teachers or other school professionals want or need to perform their job versus what they actually do in practice?

- Is there some ongoing problem or issue that adversely affects teachers,' other school professionals,' or parents' ability to successfully help children learn and to have positive mental health or well-being?

- In what ways will gathering information about the perspectives of teachers, other school professionals, or parents lead to a better understanding of the critical issue or to potential solutions?

> ## STOP AND THINK 4.1
>
> Consider the three guiding questions for identifying critical issues in a survey design. Do you see how these questions would help Mr. Kim sharpen his focus for the study? Explain.

Survey Development and Dissemination

When attempting to examine the perceptions, opinions, and attitudes of a particular group of people rather than well-defined constructs (e.g., the situation with Mr. Kim), researchers often need to develop their survey. These surveys typically consist of a questionnaire or interview format. Interviews are conducted using telephone, videoconferencing, or in-person formats. Regardless of the format, interviews offer the opportunity to generate in-depth and nuanced information that may not be possible with a paper and pencil (or electronic-based) questionnaire. They also provide opportunities for a researcher to ask follow-up questions when respondents provide ambiguous or vague answers. Unfortunately, interviews can be time intensive for both the researcher and research participant. On the other hand, questionnaires, which involve a series of statements to which individuals respond via a rating, are easier to administer and can generate an extensive amount of information in an efficient way. For this reason, questionnaires tend to be the most frequently used approach in descriptive survey designs. However, a challenge for researchers using this type of design is to either create an original survey or to customize an existing survey measure to meet the specific needs of the study.

We developed a checklist of key question prompts researchers can ask themselves when developing a new survey tool (see Table 4.1). When reviewing the questions in this checklist, three key themes and principles emerge: (1) survey items should directly pertain to the overall purposes, research questions, and prospective analyses to be used, (2) survey items should be clear, easy to understand, and sensitive to specific needs of the sample, and (3) an iterative process of survey development should be emphasized.

Regarding the link between survey items and planned analyses, it is important for researchers to have a specific plan in mind for how they want to analyze the survey data. For example, if they decided to use a free-response question format (i.e., participants write in narrative answers to questions) but are specifically interested in calculating frequency counts or percentages of participants who display a certain behavior, then there is a misalignment between their assessment approach and the planned analyses. In Mr. Kim's situation, because he wanted to assess the frequency or percentage with which school psychologists performed certain types of assessments, he reasoned that it would be more effective to use questionnaires rather than open-ended or free response formats. In short, when developing a new survey, researchers should think about the content of the items or questions as well as the format (e.g., Yes/No, Likert scale) that best aligns with the target research questions and their desired data analyses.

In terms of the clarity of survey items or questions, researchers should use simple language and ensure that the items are brief and direct. Thus, we caution against including superficial or unnecessary information or technical jargon that increases the complexity or length of a survey. We also encourage researchers to be cognizant of the reading level and native language of prospective participants. If you believe some or all your participants will include English language learners, for example, you need to take appropriate steps to either translate the survey into the appropriate language or to adapt the reading level of items. Along a similar vein, researchers need to be mindful of the overall attractiveness or appeal of the survey. Creating a survey that lacks

TABLE 4.1 ■ Checklist for Developing Items for Questionnaires in Survey Design Research			
Did I write the directions in a simple and clear manner?	☐ Yes ☐ No	Did I clearly define all key terms for the reader?	☐ Yes ☐ No
Do the items on the questionnaire adequately address target problem and research questions?	☐ Yes ☐ No	Do I know specifically how I want to use the results generated from the questionnaire?	☐ Yes ☐ No
Did I only include items that are relevant to the study (reduce length whenever possible)?	☐ Yes ☐ No	Did I create different sections to help with flow and clarity of transitions?	☐ Yes ☐ No
Did I think about the potential of using open-ended question formats only when it was completely necessary?	☐ Yes ☐ No	Do I have a plan for how to analyze data gathered using different types of questions?	☐ Yes ☐ No
Would it be helpful to use different item formats (Likert scale, ranked items, checklists, free response)?	☐ Yes ☐ No	Did I proofread the questionnaire?	☐ Yes ☐ No
Are the items simple, clear, and focused on only one issue (i.e., not double-barreled)?	☐ Yes ☐ No	Did I have other people proofread the questionnaire?	☐ Yes ☐ No
Did I organize the items so that the more sensitive or potentially personally invasive questions are asked at the end?	☐ Yes ☐ No	Did I pilot the questionnaire with the target population?	☐ Yes ☐ No
Did I organize the items from more general to more specific?	☐ Yes ☐ No	Is the survey format and structure appealing and easy to navigate?	☐ Yes ☐ No
Did I include all relevant demographic characteristics that would be important to data analysis (i.e., comparing groups)?	☐ Yes ☐ No	Did I create a cover letter that is clear and appealing to potential respondents?	☐ Yes ☐ No
Did I consider the reading level of the respondents?	☐ Yes ☐ No		

appeal, is excessively long, does not flow naturally from section to section, or does not provide a friendly, thought-provoking cover letter, may lead to poor response or completion rates.

Finally, researchers should adhere to an iterative process of survey development. A critical component of this iterative process is the use of pilot testing. Pilot testing involves administering the survey to a small group of individuals who represent the target sample. Pilot testing is useful for generating feedback regarding the clarity of directions, items, and item format, while also providing initial evidence for reliability and validity. Typically, researchers ask a pilot test group to complete the survey and to also provide comments or suggestions. Time permitting, researchers can also debrief the pilot test group respondents via telephone or in person to gain a deeper understanding of questionnaire weaknesses and the most effective ways to optimize the clarity and or formatting of the items. Researchers may also ask collaborators and other professionals to proofread the survey to further ensure clarity and accuracy.

After the survey is developed and refined, researchers need to develop a plan for distributing it to the target sample. Historically, researchers have used postage mailing as the primary mechanism for survey dissemination and sample recruitment. In this approach, the researcher identifies the mailing addresses of prospective respondents, mails the questionnaire, and then asks them to complete and return the survey in a stamped return-addressed envelope. When educators conduct research in schools, they also may give envelopes with a description of the study and parental consent forms and ask students to share it with their parents. Although these types of approaches are still utilized in certain situations (e.g., when the target sample does not have access to computers and other forms of technology), they are expensive and can increase the workload for both the researcher and survey participant. It is for this reason why most survey studies rely on software technologies or website applications to disseminate surveys.

When using technological tools, it is customary for researchers to send an email to prospective respondents that includes the survey (i.e., either as pdf attachment or via a website link). Both approaches can be effective, but having an email attachment does add to the burden on the respondents; they need to open the attachment, complete the survey, and then email the survey back as an attachment. Increasingly, researchers utilize web-based surveys within specific platforms, such as Survey Monkey, Qualtrics, SoGoSurvey, or Zoho Survey. These platforms vary in price, format, and features, but collectively, they represent an important advance in conducting descriptive survey research. Across these platforms, researchers gain access to survey templates and have extensive options for customizing survey questions and disseminating the survey. These platforms also enable researchers to directly download data from the website to facilitate database management and data analyses.

THE TAKEAWAY

Developing a survey that targets the perceptions, beliefs, and attitudes of research participants is one of the most critical aspects of successfully implementing a descriptive survey design.

Statistics

In a descriptive study, researchers will use many types of assessments, such as record reviews, interviews, questionnaires, or direct observations. In most instances, researchers rely on descriptive statistics (e.g., means, standard deviations, percentages, frequency counts; see Chapter 12) to summarize and interpret the data. In the scenario with Ms. Berry, suppose she used self-report questionnaires and direct observations to collect data about student motivation and SRL skills across sixth-, seventh-, and eighth-grade students in her middle school. Her overall design is cross-sectional in nature because the survey was administered at a single point in time across different grade levels of the target sample. To analyze the data, Ms. Berry calculated the mean (average) scores for all survey measures across grade level. She also calculated the frequency and percentage of students who attended extra help sessions and those who were able to complete at least 90% of the homework per week (see Table 4.2). Consistent with a descriptive design, these results simply describe the sample in terms of their behaviors and perceptions using numerical language (e.g., percentage, average score, etc.).

TABLE 4.2 ■ Descriptive Statistics of Student Motivation and SRL Strategies for Ms. Berry Scenario			
	Sixth grade (n = 175)	Seventh grade (n = 193)	Eighth grade (n = 162)
Self-report measures	*M (SD)*	*M (SD)*	*M (SD)*
Effort	3.78 (.65)	3.22 (.56)	2.82 (.91)
Persistence	3.01 (.66)	3.21 (.66)	2.02 (.73)
Time management	3.01 (.76)	2.90 (.81)	3.99 (.67)
Organization	2.67 (.87)	3.67 (.71)	3.76 (.58)
Behavioral indicators	*n (%)*	*n (%)*	*n (%)*
Students attending extra help sessions	7 (4.0%)	40 (20.7%)	45 (27.8%)
Students completing at least 90% homework	145 (82.8%)	139 (72.0%)	112 (69.1%)

Note. All self-report measures were based on a five-point Likert with high scores reflecting more adaptive skills. *M* = mean (average score). *SD* = standard deviation (average variation of score about the mean). *n* = sample size. The behavioral indicators are reported in terms of frequency counts and percentages.

STOP AND THINK 4.2

In looking at the data in Table 4.2, does anything jump out to you or do you see any patterns? Do you see how this table reflects a descriptive design?

Examining Descriptive Survey Research in the Empirical Literature

In this section, we present two research studies using descriptive research designs. After reading and reviewing the summaries of these studies (*Let's See It!*), you will be asked to independently summarize a different descriptive study (*Let's Do It!*). To further cultivate your understanding and use of descriptive design principles, please complete the *You Do It!* activity.

Let's See It! 4.1

Goal: To Understand the Key Features of Descriptive Survey Designs

The primary objective of this activity is to help you identify the key features of two published articles using a descriptive survey design. Copur-Gencturk and Rodriguez (2021) descriptively examined the noticing skills of a national sample of elementary school teachers when watching multiple video clips of classroom situations (Table 4.3). The authors coded teacher responses to create the numerical information necessary for conducting descriptive analyses. Hendricks (2011) used a survey design to explore the knowledge and practices of special education teachers in their work with students with autism (Table 4.4). Please read the two study summaries to learn about the information linked to the different design features. It may also be helpful to access and read the entire methods section of the two articles to obtain a more detailed overview of the methodological procedures and approaches used for each study.

TABLE 4.3 ■ Descriptive Survey Design	
Study	Copur-Gencturk, Y., & Rodrigues, J. (2021). Content-specific noticing: A large-scale survey of mathematics teachers' noticing. *Teaching and Teacher Education, 101.* https://doi.org/10.1016/j.tate.2021.103320
Purpose	To examine the types of issues that elementary school teachers (i.e., target sample) notice when watching real video clips of teacher-student interactions during mathematics problem-solving and instruction.
Critical Issues	To determine the specific types of content-noticing (mathematics related) while watching video clips of unknown teachers. Few studies have examined teaching noticing capacity on their own; that is, outside of a professional development or other structured learning experience. Teacher noticing is important as it relates to instructional adaptability.
Sampling	496 fourth- and fifth-grade teachers across 48 states. Sample was primarily White (81.1%) and female (86.5%). There was a 21% response rate.
Measurement	Teachers were asked to list the three most significant things they noticed after watching four video clips. A 4-point rubric was used to code teacher response (i.e., create numerical values) for depth and content-specific topics.
Statistics	Descriptive statistics (frequency, percentage).
Results	More than two thirds of the teachers noticed pedagogical topics (e.g., teaching modeling or questioning) for all four videos, but less than one third of teachers noticed issues with student mathematical thinking in any of the videos. A broad conclusion was that many teachers do not attend to important issues in mathematical practices or student thinking.

TABLE 4.4 ■ Descriptive Survey Design	
Study	Hendricks, D. (2011). Special education teachers serving students with autism: A descriptive study of the characteristics and self-reported knowledge and practices employed. *Journal of Vocational Rehabilitation, 35*(1), 37–50. https://doi.org/ 10.3233/JVR-2011-0552
Purpose	To examine various characteristics of special educators serving students with autism (i.e., target sample) and to identify teacher knowledge and practices regarding their work with students with autism (i.e., dependent variables).
Critical Issues	To determine whether teachers who work with students with autism possess sufficient knowledge about autism and effective instructional practices to adequately serve this population.
Sampling	498 special education teachers from Virginia with experience teaching students with autism (21% response rate). To be eligible, teachers needed to deliver instruction to students with autism for a minimum of 25% of the school day. The sample was primarily from suburban schools (60.2%), followed by rural (32.5%) and urban districts (7.2%). The teachers were evenly distributed in terms of years of teaching experience, with almost all participants having their full teaching license (87.3%).

Measurement	The survey was based on Virginia Skill Competencies and was developed in three phases: (1) generation of items using a 5-point Likert scale targeting knowledge and implementation, (2) expert review of items to ensure appropriateness, and (3) pilot study with former special education teachers and private school teachers of students with autism. Cover letters and links to the web-based surveys were distributed to all teachers through school email. Teachers were given three weeks to complete the questionnaire.
Statistics	Descriptive statistics (i.e., mean, standard deviation, frequencies, percentages).
Results	Teachers from different specialties and grade levels teach students with autism. More than half of teachers served students with autism in self-contained classrooms. Overall, teacher knowledge of autism and instructional practices and implementation of practices is low to intermediate.

Let's Do It! 4.1

Guided Practice: Practice Summarizing the Key Features of Descriptive Survey Designs

The primary objective of this activity is for you to independently review and identify the key features of a descriptive research article. To guide your thinking, we encourage you to use the *Let's See It!* exemplars as well as the guiding questions in Table 4.5. We also provide an answer key at the end of the chapter for you to check your work.

TABLE 4.5 ■ Descriptive Survey Design	
Study	Cleary, T. J., Gubi, A., & Prescott, M. V. (2010). Motivation and self-regulation assessments: Professional practices and needs of school psychologists. *Psychology in the Schools, 47*(10), 985–1002. https://doi.org/10.1002/pits.20519
Purpose	Is the overall purpose clear?
Critical Issues	Does the issue appear to be a critical educational issue?
	Is a strong rationale provided for the critical issue? (may need to read the introduction to the article)
Sampling	Is the target group appropriate given the research purposes?
	Do the authors target one sample as a whole or was there interest in subgroups?
	Does this seem appropriate?
Measurement	To what extent were the following issues addressed:
	• Self-generated or existing survey
	• Well-defined, theoretical constructs or opinion, attitude, perspectives
	Process of dissemination (in person, email, etc.)
Statistics	What are the different types of descriptive statistics that were used?
	Were inferential statistics used (i.e., *t*-tests, chi-square tests, etc.)?
	If yes, why were they used? Does this mean the study is no longer descriptive?
Results	What are the key findings that relate to the research questions?

THE TAKEAWAY

Descriptive research designs represent an effective approach for identifying the characteristics, beliefs, behaviors, or attitudes of a group of people. They focus on describing rather than explaining relationships among variables.

CORRELATIONAL DESIGNS

LEARNING OBJECTIVE

4.3   Apply the core features of correlational research designs.

Describing the characteristics of people or other phenomena can be quite informative, but most researchers and educators are interested in more complex issues, such as the relationship between two or more variables (i.e., correlational designs) or differences that exist among naturally occurring groups like ethnic groups or gifted versus non-gifted students (i.e., comparative designs). We focus on the characteristics and features of correlational designs in this section and address comparative designs in the subsequent one (Figure 4.4).

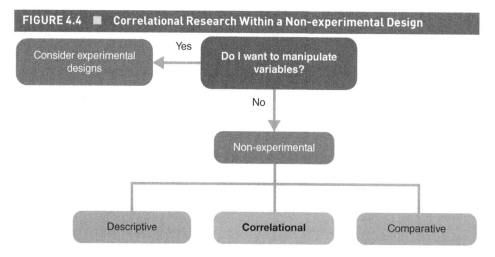

FIGURE 4.4 ■ Correlational Research Within a Non-experimental Design

Correlational designs examine the nature of the numerical or statistical relationship between two or more variables. Although we describe the meaning of a correlation more fully in Chapter 12, we briefly introduce it here for illustration purposes. A correlation involves the extent to which scores from a particular group on one variable shows a discernable pattern with the scores from the same group for a second variable. This bivariate correlation (i.e., relationship between two variables) is the simplest and most common type of correlation used in research studies. To illustrate, suppose Ms. Berry wanted to examine the correlation between student self-efficacy for solving math problems (i.e., one type of variable) and scores on a midterm mathematics exam (i.e., another variable). In order to dertermine if these two variables are related, Ms. Berry would first need to give students a questionnaire assessing their self-efficacy or confidence for learning in math. Getting access to the exam grades is fairly straightforward given that she is the one administering the exam. For each variable, there will be a range of scores (e.g., total self-efficacy score ranged from 10 to 40 while the test scores ranged from 35 to 90). To assess the correlation between self-efficacy and mathematics grade, Ms. Berry is essentially trying to figure out whether the pattern in the scores across these two variables is clear and predictable. To understand the phrase "clear and predictable," consider the three most common patterns described following. When student's self-efficacy scores increase . . .

- their test performance also increases (*positive relationship*)

- their test performance decreases (*negative relationship*)

- no clear pattern in test performance can be detected (i.e., *no relationship*)

Thus, the most basic question researchers address when using a correlation design is, "How much would one expect the scores on one variable to change as the scores on a different variable change?" The more predictable the pattern of scores between variables, the higher the correlation. Although all correlational designs address this question to some degree, there is variability in the complexity and scope of these designs. We address such complexities across the following four design features: (1) nature of research questions, (2) sampling, (3) measurement, and (4) statistics.

STOP AND THINK 4.3

Can you identify a few bivariate correlations (i.e., relationship between two variables) that are of interest to you as an educator?

Nature of Research Questions

In Figure 4.5, we present five research questions that can be addressed with a correlational design. In reading these questions, you may notice areas of convergence and divergence. For example, all questions are similar in that they include at least two variables—the minimum number needed to calculate a correlation value. However, the number of variables that were included in each question varied quite a bit; some questions included only two variables whereas other questions included four or five. Due to the inherent complexity of human functioning, most correlational research includes four, five, six, or more variables in a single study.

You may have also noticed that most questions were phrased to reflect how scores for certain variables (i.e., predictor variables) explain or predict scores for other variables (i.e., dependent variables). In most situations, predictor variables are those that researchers believe can explain certain outcomes. For example, student engagement scores (i.e., predictor variable) were conceptualized as a predictor of report card grades (i.e., dependent variable) in one question, while teacher self-efficacy, biological sex, and teaching experience (i.e., three predictor variables) were identified as predictors of teacher satisfaction (i.e., dependent variable). We discuss the distinction between predictor and dependent variables in greater depth in the measurement section.

Finally, you may have also noticed the underlined words in all questions. We intentionally underlined these words to highlight the distinctions in purposes and complexity of correlation designs. The simplest research question presented in Figure 4.5 ("To what extent does student engagement <u>relate to</u> end-of-year report card grades?") involves a simple bivariate correlation (i.e.,

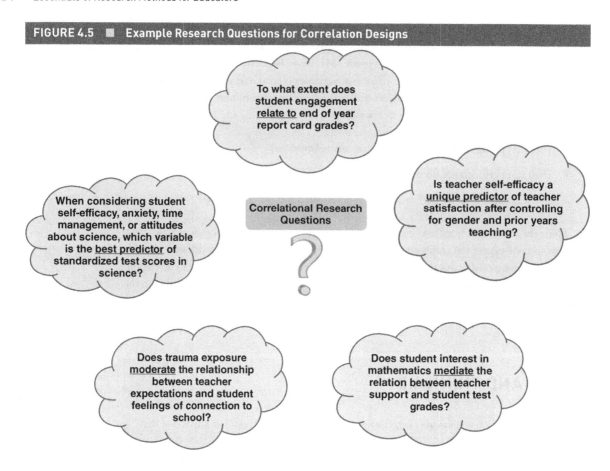

FIGURE 4.5   ■   Example Research Questions for Correlation Designs

relationship between two variables). While informative, this bivariate correlation does not adequately represent real-life complexities. For example, is it reasonable to think that student engagement is the *only* useful variable in predicting achievement? Of course not. Achievement can be influenced by myriad factors, including student confidence, their interest in school, prior academic skills (i.e., reading, math, writing), emotional functioning (anxiety, depression), quality of instruction, and level of academic support they receive at home. Thus, most correlational studies will often include many variables. When using these more complex designs, researchers can focus on how well *all the variables* predict the key outcome and/or how well one, two, or some other combination of variables predict. For example, consider the question, "Is teacher self-efficacy a <u>unique predictor</u> of teacher satisfaction after controlling for gender and prior years teaching?" This question may seem complex at first glance, but the phrase "unique predictor" is communicating something important about the goal of the study; that is, to examine pattern of scores between teacher self-efficacy and satisfaction after controlling for the effects of all other predictor variables (i.e., biological sex, prior years teaching).

Two other underlined words, mediate and moderate, are also often used in complex correlational designs. Simply put, these terms are used when researchers want to examine whether the relationship between two variables is best understood by a third variable (i.e., a mediator or moderator). As an example, consider the mediation question in Figure 4.5. With this question, the researcher is asking whether teacher support has a direct effect on student grades (i.e., it predicts grades regardless of student interest) or whether student interest mediates this relationship (i.e., the effects of teacher support on grades operates through student interest). If you turn to the moderation question, the focus of the question shifts. In moderation, a researcher examines the extent to which the relationship between two variables (e.g., relationship between teacher expectations and students' perceptions of connection to school) depends or varies based on the moderator variable (i.e., trauma exposure). In this case, it is possible that the link between teacher expectation and student connection is stronger for those who have not experienced trauma relative to those who have. Although mediation and moderation concepts extend beyond the scope of this chapter and textbook, they are useful to keep in mind because they are often necessary for capturing the complexities of human functioning.

Sampling

In quantitative research, sample selection is especially important. Ideally, researchers select samples that are representative of the target population. Although we delve into sampling-related issues and procedures later in this book, a particularly important issue when using correlational designs involves the sample size (i.e., the number of research participants included in a study). Some scholars have recommended a minimum of 30 participants for a correlational design, but this general guideline will vary based on several factors:

- Reliability and validity of the measures (i.e., larger samples are needed when measures have lower reliability)

- The effect size that one expects to observe (i.e., larger samples are needed when trying to detect very small effects)

- The complexity of the statistical procedures (i.e., larger samples are typically needed when more complex inferential statistics are used)

Measurement

When planning a correlational study, researchers need to consider the *number and breadth* of variables to include as well as the approaches for measuring these variables. The most fundamental step in virtually all correlation research is to decide which variables *do* the prediction or explanation (i.e., predictor variables) versus those *being* predicted or explained (i.e., dependent variable). To select the most appropriate variables, researchers need to have knowledge of the existing empirical literature and relevant theory that explains how the variables should fit together. For example, suppose Ms. Johnson wanted to evaluate variables that best explain middle students' mathematics achievement. In reviewing the mathematics literature, Ms. Johnson learned that several motivational belief variables (e.g., student's self-efficacy in math, interest in math, growth mindset) relate to achievement. She was particularly interested in examining the role of student self-efficacy (i.e., student confidence in their abilities) and growth mindset (i.e., believing that ability or intelligence can be improved or changed) in predicting their grades. In reviewing the literature, Ms. Johnson also discovered that different mathematical concepts, such as number sense and computational skills, and "thinking" skills, like metacognition (i.e., how students think about their own thinking) were also related to math success. When taking all this information into account, Ms. Berry decided to include a broad set of predictor variables, such as self-efficacy, number sense, computational skills, metacognition, and prior achievement, in her design so she could identify which predictors were most helpful in explaining the mathematics test scores.

STOP AND THINK 4.4

In looking at each research question in Figure 4.5, can you identify the predictor and dependent variables?

While selecting the most relevant predictor variables is a key step, researchers must also decide the best ways to measure the variables. To select appropriate measures, researchers will often focus on the reliability of scores and the validity of conclusions that one makes about the scores. As discussed in greater detail in Chapter 10, reliability pertains to the stability or consistency of scores generated by a measure, while validity reflects the accuracy and meaningfulness of the conclusions one makes from those scores. When planning a correlational study, researchers should engage in the following basic steps to ensure the adequacy of their measures:

- Review the research literature to identify the most relevant variables in explaining or predicting target dependent variables

- Select measures that have evidence to support the consistency of scores (reliability) and that assess the target constructs of interest (validity)

- Determine whether the measures have been used with students who are similar to those included in your study

Statistics

When specifically addressing data analysis with correlation designs, a few key principles should be addressed. At minimum, researchers should include a correlation matrix that includes all variables addressed in the study. A correlation matrix refers to a tabular representation of the numerical relationships between each pair of variables included in a study (see Table 4.6).

TABLE 4.6 ■ Example of a Correlation Matrix						
	1	2	3	4	5	6
1. Effort	–					
2. Persistence	.65	–				
3. Time management	.49	.32	–			
4. Organization	.18	.12	.40	–		
5. Extra help	.23	.45	-.23	-.13	–	
6. Homework completion %	.56	.54	.38	.44	-.23	–

Note. The numbers included in the table reflect correlation coefficients that range in value from –1 to 1.

Correlation coefficients (often conveyed with the letter *r*) range in size from –1 to 1. Numbers that approach the extreme points (1 or –1) reflect strong relationships, while scores close to 0 reflect weak or no relationship. Thus, as observed in Table 4.6, the relationship between effort and persistence ($r = .65$) is stronger than the relationship between persistence and organizational skills ($r = .12$). The use of correlation matrices is emphasized in quantitative research because they can help readers quickly and efficiently identify how each pair of variables included in a study are related. As emphasized repeatedly throughout this section, however, correlational designs do not simply focus on how two variables relate to each other. In fact, many researchers utilize advanced statistical analyses (e.g., multiple regression, mediation analyses, structural equation modeling) to answer more complex and nuanced research questions involving a large number of variables. Although a focus on these more complex statistical approaches is well beyond the scope of this textbook, in Table 4.7 we summarize the purposes and features of different statistical procedures that are frequently used in correlational research.

TABLE 4.7 ■ Common Statistical Approaches Used in Correlational Designs		
Type of Analysis	**Purpose**	**Number of Variables**
Bivariate correlations (correlation matrix presents a series of bivariate relations)	To examine whether the pattern of scores for one variable covary with the scores on a different variable.	Two variables (e.g., anxiety and school achievement).
Multiple regression	To examine the collective and/or unique effect of multiple predictor variables on a dependent variable.	Three or more variables. Two or more predictor variables (e.g., anxiety, self-efficacy) and one dependent variables (school achievement) are specified.
Mediation	To examine whether the relationship between two variables operates through or is mediated by a third variable (i.e., mediator).	At least three variables, with the mediator (e.g., self-efficacy) helping to explain the relationship between a predictor (e.g., anxiety) and dependent variable (e.g., school achievement).
Moderation	To examine whether the relationship between two variables *depends on* or *varies* across levels of a third variable (i.e., moderator).	At least three variables, showing that the relationship between two variables (e.g., anxiety and school achievement) depends on the levels of a moderating variable (e.g., biological sex). That is, the relationship between anxiety and achievement is not the same for men and women.
Structural equation modeling	A complex extension of multiple regression that seeks to simultaneously explore relations among a large number of variables, often including mediation and moderation effects.	Typically, the number of variables ranges from four to eight variables. Complex models will often include several mediating or moderating variables.

Examining Correlational Research in the Empirical Literature

In this section, we use the *Let's See It!* and *Let's Do It!* activities to help you learn and refine your understanding of the essential principles of correlational designs. The *Let's See It!* activity will help you become more familiar with the key information to think about when reviewing correlational research, while the *Let's Do It!* activity provides practice opportunities to apply your understanding and knowledge.

Let's See It! 4.2

Goal: To Understand the Key Features of Correlational Designs

In this activity, we ask that you read the summaries of the two correlational studies. Kremer and Kremer (2019) examined the predictive influences of bullying victimization on students' television watching (Table 4.8), while Cleary and Zimmerman (2017) examined the relations among motivation, self-regulated learning behaviors, and mathematics performance of middle school students (Table 4.9). Each of these studies investigated complex relationships (e.g., moderation, mediation) but as you proceed through the *Let's See it!* and *Let's Do It!* activities, do not get hung up on these terms. For now, just focus on the general features of the correlational designs. As you complete the *Let's See It!* activity, it would be helpful to think about the ways in which the studies overlap or exhibit similar features. It may also be helpful to access and read the entire methods section of the two articles to obtain a more detailed overview of the methodological procedures and approaches used in each study.

TABLE 4.8 ■ Correlational Designs	
Study	Kremer, K. P., & Kremer, T. R. (2019). Bullying victimization and disability status are associated with television watching in adolescence. *Journal of Child and Family Studies, 28*(12), 3479–3486. https://doi.org/10.1007/s10826-019-01530-5
Purpose	To examine the predictive influences of bullying victimization on students' television watching and the moderating role of disability status on that relationship.
Sampling	6,529 eighth-grade students from the Early Childhood Study-Kindergarten Cohort were used. The sample was primarily White (60%), with Black (16%) and Hispanic (17%) the next largest groups. The sample consisted of 51% female, with 13% eligible for free or reduced lunch. Further, over 60% of the sample came from homes making less than $75K, and approximately 63% of parents did not have a formal college degree.
Measurement Predictor variables	(a) Bullying victimization, (b) disability status, (c) demographics (e.g., race, gender, family income, parent education, reading test scores)
Dependent variable	Daily television watching
Statistics	Descriptive statistics (e.g., means, standard deviations) and multiple linear regression
Results	While bullying victimization was a significant predictor of daily television time, disability status moderated this relationship. Students who were bullied at school demonstrated the highest level of television watching. Demographic variables that were unique predictors of television watching included race, gender, reading scores, and parent education.

TABLE 4.9 ■ Correlational Designs	
Study	Cleary, T. J., & Kitsantas, A. (2017). Motivation and self-regulated learning influences on middle school mathematics achievement. *School Psychology Review*, *46*(1), 88–107. https://doi.org/10.1080/02796015.2017.12087607
Purpose	To use advanced statistical procedures (structural equation modeling) to examine the relations among a large set of variables. This study considered the relations among background variables, motivation, self-regulated learning behaviors, and math performance of middle school students. The authors also were interested in examining the role of self-efficacy and self-regulation as mediators in the model.
Sampling	331 middle school students. The sample was ethnically and racial diverse (e.g., White [49%], Hispanic [25%], Asian [21%], Black [5%]). Approximately 59% of the sample was female, and 25% were eligible for free or reduced lunch.
Measurement Predictor variables	Developed a hypothetical model based on (a) background (SES, prior achievement), (b) motivational variables (self-efficacy, task interest, school connectedness), (c) self-regulated learning strategies. Reliability and validity information for all formal measures were included.
Dependent variable	Mathematics achievement
Statistics	Descriptive statistics (e.g., means, standard deviations), correlational analysis, and structural equational modeling (SEM).
Results	Student self-efficacy, SRL behaviors, socioeconomic status (SES), and prior achievement were unique predictors of mathematics achievement. The effects motivation variables (i.e., interest, connectedness) on student SRL and achievement were mediated by students' self-efficacy.

Let's Do It! 4.2

Guided Practice: Practice Summarizing the Key Features of Correlational Designs

In this *Let's Do It!* activity, you will have the opportunity to review and identify the key features of a study using a correlational research design. To assist you in this process, we encourage you to refer to the articles included in the *Let's See It!* activity and to use the guiding questions in Table 4.10. We also provide an answer key in the appendix at the end of the chapter for you to check your work.

TABLE 4.10 ■ Correlational Designs	
Study	Huk, O., Terjesen, M. D., & Cherkasova, L. (2019). Predicting teacher burnout as a function of school characteristics and irrational beliefs. *Psychology in the Schools*, *56*(5), 792–808. https://doi.org/10.1002/pits.22233
Purpose	Does the study address an important and meaningful area of research?
	Is a strong rationale provided for targeting the specific variables of interest?
	Do some variables seem more important than others?

(Continued)

TABLE 4.10 ■ Correlational Designs (*Continued*)	
Sampling	Is the target group appropriate given the research purposes?
	What was the sample size?
	What were the key characteristics of the sample?
Measurement	Did the authors clearly identify the predictor and dependent variables?
	Did the authors select appropriate measures (evidence for reliability and validity; used with similar students in prior research)?
Statistics	Was a descriptive summary table or a correlation matrix provided in the results section?
	Were inferential statistics used? Which ones (e.g., multiple regression, moderation, structural equation modeling)?
Results	What are the key findings that relate to the research questions?

COMPARATIVE DESIGNS

LEARNING OBJECTIVE

4.4   Apply the core features of comparative designs.

As an educator, you may have wondered whether certain groups of students differ from other groups. For example:

- "Do gifted students differ from non-gifted peers in their level of motivation?"

- "Do students taking honors or other types of advanced courses show higher levels of anxiety and depression than students in regular education classes?"

- "Do students who experience bullying display lower levels of achievement than those who are not bullied?"

To examine group differences, researchers can use either a *comparative* (i.e., a non-experimental design) (Figure 4.6) or *experimental design.* However, these two designs can be distinguished across several key features:

- The formation of the target groups (comparative designs target naturally occurring groups while experiments create groups or conditions through manipulation by the researcher)

- The level of control over the research procedures (comparative designs typically exert less control over extraneous variables)

- Their capacity to draw conclusions that one variable *caused* the other (comparative designs do not permit casual and effect conclusions while experimental designs do)

When discussing comparative designs, we consider the same four features addressed for descriptive and correlational designs (i.e., nature of research questions, sampling, measurement,

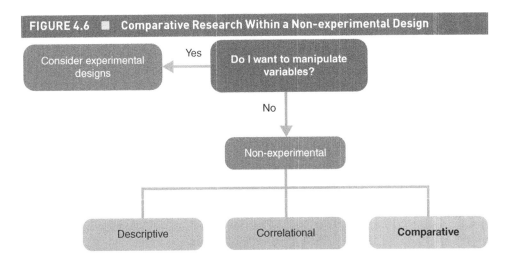

FIGURE 4.6 ■ Comparative Research Within a Non-experimental Design

and statistics) but add one new feature: *exploring causality and ruling out alternative explanations.* Adding this section for the comparative designs is important given that researchers occasionally attempt to use this design to tentatively talk about cause and effect relationships among variables.

Nature of Research Questions

As you have been learning throughout this chapter, one of the reasons why research questions are important is because they guide the selection of a research design for the study. When reviewing the five research questions in Figure 4.7, one of the first things that should jump out to you is the link between a grouping variable and one or more dependent variables. For example, when considering the question, "Do gifted students differ from non-gifted students in their motivation and strategic skills?" the grouping variable pertains to student giftedness while the two dependent variables include strategic skill and motivation. It is also important to note the similarity but subtle distinction in terminology of the variables for comparative and correlational designs. Whereas correlational designs focus primarily on the link between *predictor variables* and dependent variables, comparative studies examine the link between *grouping variables* (e.g., teacher experience, biological sex, giftedness) and the dependent variable. In some sense, examining differences between gifted and non-gifted students (i.e., grouping variable) across some dependent variable (e.g., motivation) is akin to examining the relationship or correlation between the grouping variable and dependent variables. If significant groups differences are observed between the gifted groups, then one can conclude that giftedness is related to motivation and strategic skills. We elaborate on this overlap or intersection between comparative and correlational designs in the statistics part of this section.

STOP AND THINK 4.5

In looking at each research question in Figure 4.7, can you identify all of the grouping variables and the levels (i.e., subgroups of those variables)?

FIGURE 4.7 ■ Typical Research Questions for Comparative Designs

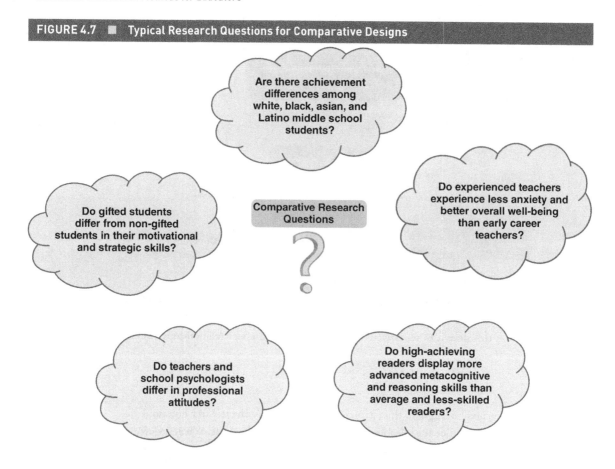

In also reviewing the example research question, please note the broad range of populations and issues that can be addressed using a comparative approach. That is, comparative designs can examine differences among subgroups of teachers (e.g., experienced vs early career) or other school-based professionals (e.g., teachers vs school psychologists), as well as for different types of students (e.g., gifted vs non-gifted). Given the wide variety of naturally occurring groups within school contexts, comparative research designs represent a viable option to address many questions relevant to administrators, educators, and other school personnel.

Sampling

As emphasized in the prior section, the nature of the grouping variable is one of the most critical components of a comparative design. Grouping variables tend to be categorical in nature; that is, the subgroups will vary across some feature, characteristic, or dimension, such as grade level or family status. Mills and Gay (2019) provided a useful categorization scheme for grouping variables that involves five broad categories: (a) *organismic* (e.g., biological sex, age); (b) *ability* (e.g., intelligence, perceptual ability); (c) *personality/attribute* (e.g., anxiety, self-esteem); (d) *family-related* (e.g., parental marital status, socioeconomic status); and *school-related* (e.g., size of school, type of instruction). In some sense, each of these grouping variables reflects an abstract idea or construct that varies across levels or dimensions. For example, when reviewing the research questions in Figure 4.7, *teacher experience* is a construct represented by two subgroups or levels (i.e., experienced, inexperienced), while *reading level* is a construct represented by three subgroups (i.e., high, average, and low). When thinking about a grouping variable for a comparative study, make sure you clearly define the variable and then specify the criteria needed to create the different subgroups. Grouping variables are typically created in one of two ways:

- *Present or absent designation:* Identify a group that possesses the defining characteristic while other groups do not (i.e., gifted students possess superior intelligence while non-gifted students do not).

- *Different levels or degree:* All groups possess the defining characteristic to some extent but vary in degree or level (i.e., all students display some level of achievement but vary across high, medium, and low levels).

Regardless of how the grouping variable is created, researchers should clearly define the different subgroups and then recruit participants for each subgroup. Consider Mr. Kim and his interest in examining student giftedness. Mr. Kim was primarily interested in exploring whether giftedness (i.e., the grouping variable) related to student self-efficacy and interest in school (i.e., two dependent variables). He defined giftedness as students who displayed an IQ of 130 or higher. Using this cutoff, Mr. Kim was able to identify two populations that varied in giftedness status (i.e., gifted versus non-gifted). These subgroups are *naturally occurring* in the sense that Mr. Kim did not create or assign the students to the different groups (i.e., as would be the case with experimental designs addressed in Chapter 5)—these groups can be identified based on specific definitions and criteria. After establishing the two subgroups, Mr. Kim randomly selected students from each subpopulation and then administered the self-efficacy and interest measures. He then used a test of statistical inference called *independent* t-*test* to formally examine group differences.

THE TAKEAWAY

The key issue in creating a grouping variable is establishing a clear definition and inclusion criteria for that variable.

Measurement

The measurement issues considered in comparative studies closely parallel those addressed in correlational studies. That is, researchers strive to use reliable and valid measures given the specific purposes of the study and the target sample. As underscored in the prior section, however, a unique aspect of comparative studies is the use of measures and or criteria to conceptualize the grouping variable. For example, suppose Ms. Berry was interested in examining differences in anxiety and well-being between teachers with varying levels of experience (i.e., early career versus veteran teachers; see Figure 4.7). Ms. Berry would first need to operationally define teaching experience (e.g., number of years teaching full time in a K–12 context) and then specify the criteria to establish different subgroups. In this situation, she was mostly interested in comparing early career teachers (i.e., defined as less than 2 years of full-time teaching) to veteran teachers (i.e., defined as more than 10 years of full-time teaching). Thus, in terms of measurement, Ms. Berry would simply perform a record review to obtain the necessary information about teacher experience. In other situations, however, researchers may need to administer formal assessments to obtain the necessary information to form the subgroups (see Mr. Kim scenario in the Sampling section).

Exploring Causality and Alternative Explanations

Another critical issue when using comparative designs (and correlational designs to some degree) involves the issue of *causality* or *causal influence*. That is, can researchers ever make the claim that the grouping (or predictor) variable has a causal influence or effect on the dependent variable (i.e., the outcome or what is predicted both other variables)? Before addressing this issue, we need to qualify a key point at the outset:

> *Researchers should never make definitive claims that one variable causes another variable when using a non-experimental design.*

The use of cause-and-effect language (e.g., effects of, influences, impacts etc.) is typically reserved for experimental designs. However, there are times and instances when researchers may wish to make a case that a causal connection could possibly exist between a grouping variable and one or more dependent variables. Suppose Mr. Kim wanted to consider the possibility that student giftedness is a direct cause of student motivation. He identified a group of 30 gifted middle school students in two local school districts and then randomly selected a group of 30 non-gifted middle school students from the same schools. Mr. Kim administered a few measures of motivation (e.g., effort, persistence, growth mindset) after the second quarter of the school year. He conducted statistical analyses (e.g., *independent t*-test) to assess group differences and found that gifted students were in fact more motivated than non-gifted youth. When speaking to Ms. Berry about these results, Mr. Kim concluded, "Wow. Giftedness really does influence student motivation!" Is Mr. Kim's statement a valid conclusion? What do you think?

From our perspective, his statement is not appropriate or valid! Technically speaking, Mr. Kim's use of a comparative research design is acceptable and appropriate given the situation. However, his use of the word *influence* suggests that he believes giftedness caused higher motivation. As a general rule of thumb, one should never use causal language unless they are able to rule out most or all alternative explanations about an observed effect. In a simple sense, an alternative explanation refers to a statement about the cause of an observed effect that differs from what one presumes, hypothesizes, or desires to be the causal explanation. As you may recall from Chapter 3, there are three conditions for establishing cause and effect relations. In the scenario with Mr. Kim, two conditions were satisfied (i.e., giftedness and achievement are related; giftedness occurred prior to the achievement scores); however, the third condition (i.e., controlling or ruling out alternative explanation) was not addressed.

STOP AND THINK 4.6

Using the Mr. Kim scenario, can you identify alternative explanations about why gifted and non-gifted students may have differed in motivation besides giftedness (use the following as a guide)? Another reason why gifted and non-gifted students differed could have been because _____.

To build an argument for a possible causal link between giftedness and motivation, Mr. Kim should have utilized a more rigorous comparative design called a causal comparative or ex post facto approach. With this type of design, a researcher strategically and explicitly attempts to rule out alternative explanations. Thus, the basic logic underlying causal comparative designs is that by controlling for or ruling out one or more potential alternative explanations, researchers can strengthen the argument that a grouping variable *could be* the cause of the dependent variable (please note that we again caution readers that establishing a clear or definitive causal connection is not possible with a causal comparative design).

To achieve a higher level of control when using a comparative design, researchers can use a variety of different tactics:

1. Establish homogeneous comparison groups (i.e., create groups that are highly similar in most ways)

2. Use matching procedures (i.e., select students based on certain variables that are equivalent to other students)

3. Use statistical procedures to control for other variables that could explain the effects.

Establishing homogeneous subgroups is an effective approach for controlling initial differences among the subgroups. Creating homogeneous subgroups essentially involves identifying individuals who are similar across many variables yet differ with respect to the grouping variable. For example, if Mr. Kim believed that school connectedness was a strong predictor of student motivation, he may opt to control for this variable by only selecting participants from the gifted and non-gifted populations who exhibited similar levels of perceived connectedness. By following this procedure, Mr. Kim is, in a sense, "equating" the groups on the perceived connectedness variable. If two groups are virtually identical on perceived connectedness, it would not be possible for this variable to be a plausible alternative explanation of the observed group difference in motivation.

Researchers could also use a matching procedure to increase the chances that the subgroups are highly similar. When using matching, Mr. Kim would first need to identify one or more variables that relate to motivation (e.g., school connectedness). Then, during the sampling selection process, Mr. Kim would match a gifted student with a specific level of school connectedness to a non-gifted student with the same or highly similar connectedness scores. Finally, Mr. Kim could use certain statistical procedures to control these extraneous variables in a statistical sense (e.g., analysis of covariance, factorial analysis of variance). In sum, although comparative designs never permit researchers to make strong claims about cause and effect, researchers can strengthen these types of claims by using procedures that can rule out one or more alternative explanations.

Statistics

In comparative designs, the primary objective is to examine group differences across one or more dependent variables. If there are two groups (e.g., a class of gifted students versus a class of typical students), then a *t*-test for independent means can be used. If there are more than two groups (e.g., Class A, Class B, and Class C), then an analysis of variance should be utilized. We mention a few of the most common inferential statistical approaches here, but these approaches are addressed in greater depth in Chapter 13.

Let's circle back to an idea that was discussed when we first introduced comparative designs. We noted that an observed group difference (e.g., gifted verses non-gifted) on a dependent variable is synonymous with saying there is a *relationship* between giftedness and the dependent variable. Let's explain why this is the case. Using statistical language, grouping variables are categorical (i.e., variables consisting of distinct labels or categories) rather than quantitative in nature (i.e., numbers vary along a continuum such as 10 to 90). When using categorical or grouping variables in statistical analyses, researchers ordinarily assign arbitrary numerical values to represent each of the groups. In the situation with Mr. Kim, he followed the standard procedure of assigning a 0 to represent one group (e.g., non-gifted students) and a 1 to represent the other group (i.e., gifted students). Thus, the giftedness variable had two possible values (i.e., 0 and 1). If Mr. Kim found that gifted students were more motivated than non-gifted students, it would be entirely accurate for him to conclude that motivation and giftedness are positively correlated. That is, as the scores for giftedness get larger (i.e., going from a 0 [non-gifted] to 1 [gifted]), so do the scores on motivation. Thus, comparative designs should be considered as a special type of correlational design, one in which the predictor variable is categorical in nature.

THE TAKEAWAY

Comparative designs are most useful when interested in examining group differences and, in certain situations, for making tentative speculations about cause-and-effect claims among variables.

Examining Comparative Research in the Empirical Literature

The last set of *Let's See It!* and *Let's Do It!* activities in this chapter parallel the format and structure of previous activities. By first reading example summaries of two comparative studies and then independently reviewing and analyzing a different comparative study, you will gain important knowledge and skills for interpreting and using comparative designs.

Let's See It! 4.3

Goal: To Understand the Key Features of Comparative Designs

To begin this practice activity, please review summaries of the two studies presented in the following section. Cleary and Zimmerman (2001) examined self-regulatory and motivational differences among three groups varying in their level of expertise in shooting basketball free-throws (i.e., expert, non-expert, and novice) (Table 4.11). Hoogeveen et al. (2012) examined social-emotional differences across two groups of gifted students who varied in terms of their achievement or levels of acceleration (i.e., accelerated gifted versus non-accelerated gifted) (Table 4.12).

TABLE 4.11 ■ Comparative Designs	
Study	Cleary, T. J., & Zimmerman, B. J. (2001). Self-regulation differences during athletic practice by experts, non-experts, and novices. *Journal of Applied Sport Psychology, 13*(2), 185–206. https://doi.org/10.1080/104132001753149883
Purpose	To examine differences in self-regulatory and motivational differences (i.e., dependent variables) among expert, non-expert, and novice basketball players (i.e., grouping variable with three levels) during a free-throw practice session.

Sampling	Three groups of high school students (*n* = 43) were recruited: expert, non-expert, and novice basketball players. All participants were male and primarily White (60%) and African American (33%).
Measurement Grouping variable	Three categories of expertise were noted based on two key criteria (i.e., free-throw shooting percentage and playing experience): (a) experts played high school varsity and shot 70% or higher, (b) non-experts played high school varsity and shot below 55%, (c) novices did not play organized team basketball beyond the seventh grade.
Dependent variables	Student self-efficacy, satisfaction, and several measures of self-regulation.
Attempts to Rule Out Explanations	All three groups were shown to possess similar knowledge of shooting technique; the expert and non-experts were equivalent in terms of their shooting knowledge, playing experience, and status as a varsity high school basketball player. Thus, differences in knowledge, experience, or membership on the varsity team could not explain any of the observed group differences between experts and non-experts.
Statistics	Descriptive (e.g., means, standard deviation), correlation analyses, and inferential statistics (e.g., MANOVA; chi-square).
Results	The expert free-throw group exhibited higher levels of self-efficacy and more adaptive goals, strategic plans, and reflective thinking than both other groups. Significant relationships were observed between students' goals, strategic plans, attributions, and adaptive inferences.

TABLE 4.12 ■ Comparative Designs

Study	Hoogeveen, L., van Hell, J. G., & Verhoeven, L. (2012). Social-emotional characteristics of gifted accelerated and non-accelerated students in the Netherlands. *British Journal of Educational Psychology, 82*(4), 585–605. https://doi.org/10.1111/j.2044–8279.2011.02047.x
Purpose	To examine differences in self-concept, behavioral characteristics, and social contacts (i.e., dependent variables) between accelerated gifted students (skipped grades) and non-accelerated gifted students (i.e., grouping variable is type of gifted student).
Sampling	Data were collected from 203 children, adolescents, and young adults in the Netherlands who had previously been diagnosed as gifted; 148 of the participants were identified as accelerated. The sample was 67% male. Gender breakdown was provided across each of the three developmental levels.
Measurement Grouping variable	Two levels of giftedness were identified based on status as an accelerated student: (a) accelerated gifted students (i.e., those who were placed in grades higher than their development status), (b) non-accelerated gifted students. All participants were formally identified as gifted by psychologists.
Dependent variables	Student self-concept, behavioral characteristics, and social contacts.
Attempts to Rule Out Explanations	Both groups were identified as gifted by psychologists working at a giftedness center at a university; moderator variables (e.g., gender, birth order, grade level, classroom size) were included to examine whether group differences in the dependent variables varied by these moderators.

(Continued)

TABLE 4.12 ■ Comparative Designs History (*Continued*)	
Statistics	Descriptive statistics (e.g., means) with primary focus on inferential statistics (e.g., MANOVAs, *t*-tests).
Results	The key results were that the two groups did not differ across most measures of social-emotional functioning (e.g., self-concept) and social contacts, but differences did emerge in terms of underground (e.g., refusal to join social programs, resists challenges) and risk-avoidance behaviors (e.g., takes no risks). Accelerated gifted students were reported by parents to engage in *less* underground and risk avoidance behaviors. A few moderation effects were observed across self-concept, social contacts, and behavioral characteristics.

Let's Do It! 4.3

Guided Practice: Practice Summarizing the Key Features of Comparative Designs

Now it's your turn to review and summarize a comparative research article. Like the other *Let's Do It!* Activities in this chapter, you will need to read the assigned article: Hartley et al. (2015). Using the guiding questions in Table 4.13 and what you have learned in this chapter, please summarize the key features of the study. Feel free to look back to the *Let's See It!* activities for assistance if you need it. You can also check your work by reviewing the answer key provided in the appendix at the end of the chapter.

TABLE 4.13 ■ Comparative Designs	
Study	Hartley, M. T., Bauman, S., Nixon, C. L., & Davis, S. (2015). Comparative study of bullying victimization among students in general and special education. *Exceptional Children, 81*(2), 176–193. https://doi.org/ 10.1177/0014402914551741
Purpose	Is the overall purpose clear?
	Is a rationale for the study provided?
	Does it make sense that the authors are interested in comparing naturally occurring groups?
Sampling	Is the description of the target sample clear?
	What was the sample size?
	What were the key characteristics of the sample?
Measurement Grouping variable	How did the authors define and identify the different groups?
	Did they need to use specific inclusion criteria to define the grouping variable? Explain.
Dependent variables	Across which variables did the authors compare the different groups?
	Did the dependent measures appear appropriate given the purposes of the study?
Attempts to Rule Out Explanations	To what extent did the authors try to ensure that the groups were similar aside from the grouping variable?
	Did the author consider or attempt to control for any other variables?

Statistics	Did the authors use any descriptive statistics to summarize the results?
	What type of inferential statistics were used (i.e., *t*-tests, ANOVA, chi-square tests etc.)?
Results	What are the key findings that relate to the research questions?

ETHICAL CONSIDERATIONS

<table>
<tr><td colspan="2" align="center">LEARNING OBJECTIVE</td></tr>
<tr><td>4.5</td><td>Demonstrate knowledge of ethical issues when conducting, analyzing, and communicating non-experimental research.</td></tr>
</table>

Research designs represent a type of detailed action plan that facilitates the execution of a given research study. In a simplistic sense, research designs reflect what needs to be done, how it should be done, and with whom it is done. Ideally, researchers *intentionally* choose a research design that addresses a critical issue and/or set of research questions. In many educational contexts and situations, however, the selection of a research design is constrained by logistical challenges and barriers as well as ethical considerations. Our goal in this section is to briefly identify key ethical issues when conducting research in schools, with specific attention to non-experimental designs.

During all aspects of the research process (identifying research questions, selecting a research design, sampling research participants etc.), educators need to be cognizant of ethical issues and their responsibility to act in ethical ways during research endeavors. An aspirational ethical principle emphasized in this chapter is *integrity*, which reflects the extent to which researchers advocate for honesty, accuracy, and truthfulness in data collection, interpretation, and dissemination. For school-based researchers, it is essential to *never* go beyond the data when making interpretations (i.e., talk about the results in a way that is misleading or overstating). For example, researchers should never make cause-and-effect claims when using non-experimental designs. Although some non-experimental approaches, such as causal comparative studies, can help strengthen the case about potential cause-and-effect, they are not structured to make these claims. When educators or researchers make misleading or inaccurate conclusions from research data, negative consequences can occur.

In revisiting the scenario with Mr. Kim, he made a comment that was misleading ("Wow. Giftedness really does have some *effect on* student motivation?"). While Mr. Kim was obviously excited about his research findings, his comment suggested that giftedness may cause (i.e., "effect on") student motivation. Because giftedness is typically defined in terms of innate cognitive abilities and competencies, one may erroneously infer from Mr. Kim's comments that student motivation is the result of intellectual capacity and/or other inborn characteristics of individuals (which we know is not really the case). Thus, one aspect of having integrity as a researcher is to never draw conclusions or inferences about data that are not supported by a particular research design. Non-experimental designs are fabulous for describing people or the relationships among variables, but they should never be used to evaluate the effects of an intervention program or make claims that a certain variable causes another variable.

THE TAKEAWAY

Given that non-experimental designs are highly relevant and practical for use in school contexts, it is important for educators and researchers to be mindful of the circumstances and the ways in which these designs should be used.

AMERICAN PSYCHOLOGICAL ASSOCIATION STYLE

LEARNING OBJECTIVE
4.6 Utilize the *Publication Manual of the American Psychological Association* in reporting and presenting findings in non-experimental designs.

One of the most important issues addressed by the APA Publication Manual involves bias-free language. That is, to write and communicate information that does not offend, demean, or perpetuate negative assumptions about groups of people based on biological sex, sexual orientation, disability status, and/or myriad other factors (e.g., socioeconomic status, religion, etc.). Although we specifically address the use of bias-free language in this chapter (in part because sample description is especially important when using non-experimental designs), the use of bias-free language is relevant for all research designs (e.g., experimental, non-experimental, qualitative).

In this section, we underscore two key principles that underly bias-free communication about research participants: (a) be specific and clear when describing the sample, (b) use the most appropriate phrases or terms to describe the sample. Being specific, precise, and accurate in communication is a key characteristic of professional writing. As an example, suppose Ms. Berry included seventh-grade students in her sample. However, when communicating her results to others, she described them as middle school students. At first glance, the term middle school appears appropriate and may even be technically accurate (i.e., seventh-grade students are typically in middle school). However, given that seventh-grade students are not representative of all grade levels within middle school, it would have been more appropriate for her to communicate the participants' grade level. Further, consider Mr. Kim and his use of a comparative design to examine differences between gifted and non-gifted students. Given that definitions of giftedness often vary in the research literature, he should provide a clear operational definition and/or the specific criteria used to identify those groups (e.g., IQ and/or achievement score). Providing this level of specificity and detail fosters a clear and precise foundation from which readers can understand the results and implications from a study.

A second key issue involves the use of appropriate terms and language when describing a sample. In Table 4.14, we summarize suggestions made by APA about appropriate and inappropriate phrases when describing people. This table is not exhaustive of all demographic characteristics and thus is primarily illustrative in nature. As you review the table, you likely will come across terms and phrases that are frequently used in casual conversation or in writing. An important aspect of professional growth is to become self-aware of the language you use in communication and to recognize that certain words or phrases can have an offensive, demeaning, or otherwise negative influence on others.

TABLE 4.14 ■ Suggestions for Avoiding Biased Language When Describing a Sample in School Contexts			
Characteristic	Consider Using . . .	Avoid Using . . .	Overarching Principle
Age	• The specific age range of individuals • Children • Adolescents • Adults	• Under or over a specific age (under 21) • Seniors or elderly	Preference is to use labels that are free from potential bias or stereotype and that promote clarity.
Gender	• Men or women • Gender • Terms that reflect gender identity	• Males or females • Sex (unless referring to sex assignment) • Binary only gender assumptions	Preference is to use a broader concept of gender and emphasize how people self-describe.
Disability	• Person-first language (youth with ADHD)	• Condition-first language (hyperactive youth) • Disability language when not needed • Terms that are negative or construed as slurs	Preference is to use terms that are consistent with how groups of disabled individuals describe themselves.
Research participants	• Respondents • Specific descriptors (middle school students, children) • Participants • Subjects	• Patients (in non-medical contexts) • At-risk (unless clear descriptions of at-risk are provided)	Preference is to use terms that are clear, specific, and representative of the context in which the participants operate.

THE TAKEAWAY

Clear descriptions of a sample is vital for all research designs but is especially relevant to non-experimental approaches. Thus, when using these designs, be clear, precise, and sensitive in the language used to describe people.

CHAPTER SUMMARY

The non-experimental designs presented in this chapter are highly applicable in school settings. Collectively, they help researchers describe people's perceptions, attitudes, skills, or behaviors and can address questions related to the relationship between two or more variables. Correlational designs are highly flexible in that they can examine simple correlations between two variables or more complex approaches to exploring how seven or eight variables relate to each other. Comparative designs are quite useful in examining differences among naturally occurring groups, such as grade level, giftedness, or type of courses in high school (e.g., honors, advanced placement, standard). Regardless of the specific differences among descriptive, correlational, and comparative non-experimental designs, they all seek to describe situations, events, or people in some way. They also do not manipulate variables. When researchers wish to manipulate variables (e.g., creating three different reading group conditions), they will likely turn their attention to using experimental designs.

EXTENSION ACTIVITIES

You Do It! 4.1

Self-Directed Practice: Thinking Through Important Issues When Developing a Descriptive Survey Design

Descriptive survey research designs generate important information about the attitudes and beliefs of teachers, parents, and other important stakeholders in education. In this *You Do It!* exercise, you will be asked to create a plan and outline for a survey research study addressing a topic of interest to you. We encourage you to use Figure 4.8 and Table 4.15 to assist in developing ideas for your study. Figure 4.8 (i.e., Descriptive Survey Design Decision-Making Guide) represents a type of troubleshooting scaffold to help you think through key issues as you attempt to apply this design to your research questions of interest.

FIGURE 4.8 ■ Descriptive Survey Design Decision-Making Guide

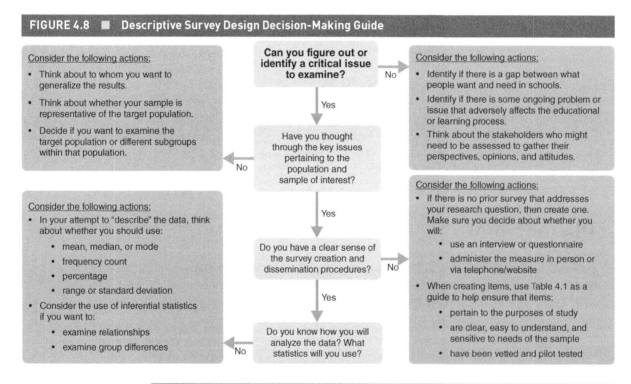

TABLE 4.15 ■ Descriptive Survey Designs Guiding Questions

Purpose	Is there an important gap or problem in teaching practices or student functioning that you want to better understand?
	Are you trying to understand a problem that you experience in practice?
Critical Issues	What is the nature of the critical issue you want to examine?
	How does this critical issue relate to a potential practice gap?

Sampling	Which group or groups of stakeholders are most important to assess for your idea?
	Are there important subgroups within this general population that you want to examine? Why?
Measurement	Are there any existing surveys related to your topic that you can review? Will you need to generate a new survey?
	Are you clear about the item format and content to include in the survey? What is your plan for disseminating the survey?
Statistics	What are the different types of descriptive statistics you want to use (i.e., means, standard deviations, frequencies, percentages)?
	Will you use inferential statistics (i.e., t-tests, chi-square tests, etc.)? Why?

You Do It! 4.2

Correlational Designs

Self-Directed Practice: Thinking Through Important Issues When Developing a Correlational Study

In this *You Do It!* exercise, you will have the opportunity to generate the basic framework for a correlational study that addresses a topic of interest to you. The overall purpose of your study does not need to be complex, but it is important to reflect on the key issues and topics that are most relevant. To assist this type of independent practice, please refer to the Correlation Design Decision-Making Guide (Figure 4.9) and the guiding questions in Table 4.16.

FIGURE 4.9 ■ Correlational Design Decision-Making Guide

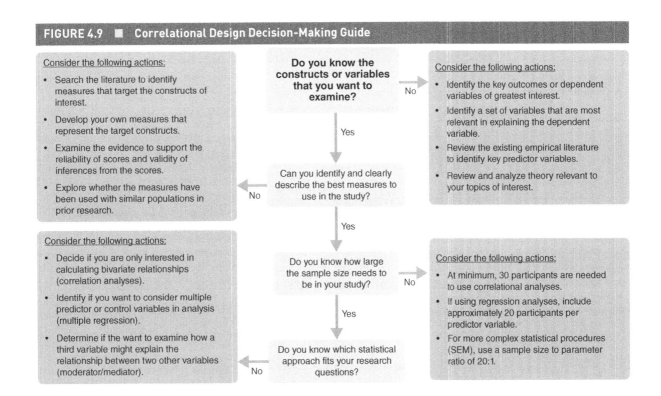

TABLE 4.16 ■ Correlational Designs Guiding Questions	
Purpose	What is the nature of the critical issue you want to examine?
	Is there an emergent or important gap in practice that you have noticed?
	Can you create any specific research questions that relate to the critical issue?
Sampling	What is the nature of the sample of students you want to target?
	To whom do you want the results to generalize?
	About what size of the sample should you select?
Measurement Predictor variables	What are the key variables that you believe can explain the dependent variable?

Is there one or two variables that are of primary interest to you?

Should you include some variables that prior research has shown to predict the dependent variable?

Dependent variable	What is your primary outcome that you want to explain with the predictor variables?

Do you want to include more than one dependent variable? Which ones?

Statistics	Which of the following statistical approaches is most relevant to addressing your research questions:

- Bivariate correlations?
- Multiple regression?
- More complex approaches? Moderation/mediation/structural equation modeling?

You Do It! 4.3

Comparative Designs

Self-Directed Practice: Thinking Through Important Issues When Developing a Comparative Study

Now is your chance to put on your creative hat and develop your own comparative study. Like all other *You Do It!* exercises, you are not expected to fully describe or articulate how you would conduct an actual study. Your goal is to think through the issues linked with this design and to develop an initial plan for conducting a comparative study. To assist you in this type of independent practice, please refer to the Comparative Design Decision-Making Guide figure 4.10 and the Table 4.17 to troubleshoot or problem-solve as you work through this design.

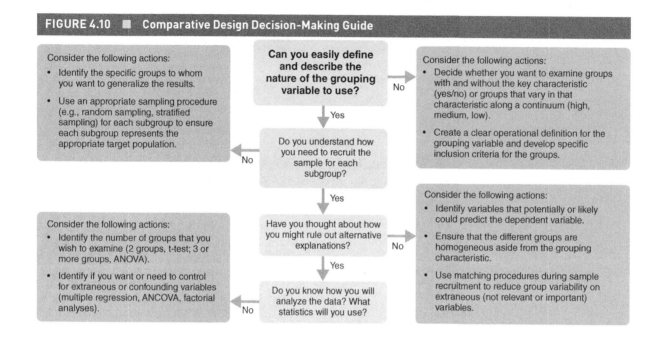

FIGURE 4.10 ■ Comparative Design Decision-Making Guide

Can you easily define and describe the nature of the grouping variable to use? — No →

Consider the following actions:
- Decide whether you want to examine groups with and without the key characteristic (yes/no) or groups that vary in that characteristic along a continuum (high, medium, low).
- Create a clear operational definition for the grouping variable and develop specific inclusion criteria for the groups.

↓ Yes

Do you understand how you need to recruit the sample for each subgroup? — No →

Consider the following actions:
- Identify the specific groups to whom you want to generalize the results.
- Use an appropriate sampling procedure (e.g., random sampling, stratified sampling) for each subgroup to ensure each subgroup represents the appropriate target population.

↓ Yes

Have you thought about how you might rule out alternative explanations? — No →

Consider the following actions:
- Identify variables that potentially or likely could predict the dependent variable.
- Ensure that the different groups are homogeneous aside from the grouping characteristic.
- Use matching procedures during sample recruitment to reduce group variability on extraneous (not relevant or important) variables.

↓ Yes

Do you know how you will analyze the data? What statistics will you use? — No →

Consider the following actions:
- Identify the number of groups that you wish to examine (2 groups, t-test; 3 or more groups, ANOVA).
- Identify if you want or need to control for extraneous or confounding variables (multiple regression, ANCOVA, factorial analyses).

TABLE 4.17 ■ Comparative Designs Guiding Questions

Purpose	What is the nature of the critical issue you want to examine?
	How would your idea contribute to the literature or improve knowledge?
	Can you create any specific research questions that relate to the critical issue?

Sampling	What is the nature of the sample of students you want to target?
	To whom do you want the results to generalize?
	About what size of the sample should you select?
Measurement Grouping variable	What is the nature of the grouping variable?
	Are these groups defined by specific criteria? Explain.
Dependent variables	What is your primary outcome on which to differentiate the subgroups?
	Do you want to include more than one dependent variable? Which ones?

(Continued)

TABLE 4.17 ■ Comparative Designs Guiding Questions (*Continued*)

Attempts to Rule Out Explanations	Are there any ways to ensure that the levels of the grouping variable are as similar as possible (i.e., aside from the grouping characteristic)?
	Could matching be used to create more homogeneous subgroups?
	Are there other important variables that you would want to "control" that could potentially explain any observed group difference?
Statistics	Would there be any descriptive statistics you want to use (e.g., means, standard deviations, frequencies, percentages)?
	Are inferential statistics relevant to your research questions? What types of inferential statistics might you use to examine group differences (i.e., *t*-tests, chi-square tests, etc.)?

KEY TERMS

Bias-free language

Bivariate correlation

Causal comparative design (ex post facto)

Correlation matrix

Matching

Mediation

Moderation

Pilot testing

ANSWER KEY

Stop and Think Activities

STOP AND THINK 4.1

Guiding Questions to Identify Critical Issues	Purpose of the Guiding Question
Is there a gap or disconnect between what teachers or other school professionals want or need to perform their job versus what they actually do in practice?	This question should stimulate thinking about critical issues, emergent concerns, problems in professional practice, and so forth, that educators may encounter. A critical issue often arises when there is a gap or mismatch between the needs of educators, parents, or school and the services or program that should address those needs. David identified a gap between the perceived importance of student motivation and strategic behaviors and the extent to which school psychologists assess these processes as part of school-based evaluations.
Is there some ongoing problem or issue that adversely affects teachers,' other school professionals,' or parents' ability to successfully help children learn and to have positive mental health or well-being?	This question focuses on a problem or issue that creates negative consequences for others. Because David and his colleagues do not routinely receive this type of information about students, they often are confused about how best to improve student motivation and functioning in school.
In what ways will gathering information about the perspectives of teachers, other school professionals, or parents lead to a better understanding of the critical issue or to potential solutions to the issue?	This question addresses the importance, value, or contribution that a survey study might have on both the research literature and practice. David believed that addressing the target practice gap may stimulate thinking and research about new and effective ways for evaluating student motivation and strategic behaviors.

STOP AND THINK 4.2

Table 4.2 represents a common descriptive summary table reported in most quantitative studies but is particularly relevant in descriptive studies. A couple of key things to note include the following:

- The use of different types of descriptive statistics (i.e., mean, standard deviation, frequency count, and percentages; see Chapter 12 for a more detailed overview)

- Clarity with which one can observe numerical distinctions in some variables across grade levels. For example:
  - Very few sixth-grade students attend extra help sessions, but most seem to complete their homework with 90% accuracy
  - Eighth-grade students display numerically lower effort and persistence but better time management skills than the other two grades

Please note our use of the word numerical in the preceding description was intentional. Clearly there are differences in the values of the numbers across the grade levels. Although one can say there is a numerical difference in some variables, you will learn in Chapter 13 that numerical difference is not the same thing as a *statistically significant difference.*

STOP AND THINK 4.3

There are no correct or incorrect correlations that you could have identified. The purpose of this Stop and Think activity was simply to get you thinking about whether you have any curiosity about how certain variables fit together or explain each other. Some potential correlations may include the relationship between the following:

- Quality of instruction and report card grades

- Student social-emotional skills and behavioral difficulties exhibited in class

- Homework completion and test performance

- Student bullying victimization experiences and student depression

STOP AND THINK 4.4

Research Question	Predictor Variable(s)	Dependent Variable
To what extent does student engagement relate to end-of-year report card grades?	Student engagement	Report card grades
Is teacher self-efficacy a unique predictor of teacher satisfaction after controlling for gender and prior years teaching?	Self-efficacy Gender Prior years teaching	Teacher satisfaction
Does student interest in mathematics mediate the relation between teacher support and student test grades?	Teacher support Student interest (mediator)	Test grades
Does trauma exposure moderate the relationship between teacher expectations and student feelings of connection to school?	Teacher expectations Trauma (moderator)	School connectedness
When considering student self-efficacy, anxiety, time management, and attitudes about science, which is the best predictor of student performance?	Self-efficacy Anxiety Time management Science attitudes	Student performance

STOP AND THINK 4.5

Research Question	Grouping Variable	Subgroups/Levels
Do gifted students differ from non-gifted students in their motivation and strategic skills?	Giftedness	Gifted Non-gifted
Are there achievement differences among ethnicity groups?	Ethnic/Racial groups	White Black Latino Asian

Research Question	Grouping Variable	Subgroups/Levels
Do high-achieving readers display more advanced metacognitive and reasoning skills than average- or less-skilled readers?	Reading level	High Average Low
Do teachers and school psychologists differ in personality traits?	Professional type	School psychologist Teacher
Do experienced teachers have less anxiety and better overall well-being than early career teachers?	Teacher experience	Experienced Inexperienced

STOP AND THINK 4.6

Presumed Cause of Motivational Group Differences	Potential Alternative Explanations of the Observed Motivational Group Differences
Being gifted leads students to exhibit higher level of motivation	Gifted students were exposed to several enrichment classes over the past several years. These enrichment opportunities, *rather than being identified as gifted,* were the primary cause of their higher motivation.
	Gifted students differed from the non-gifted students across many other variables, such as demographics (i.e., SES, parent education), prior achievement, anxiety levels, and so forth. Those demographic variables represented the primary causes of the observed motivational differences *rather than being identified as gifted.*
	Gifted students may be treated differently by teachers in school. Thus, gifted students may be more motivated than their non-gifted peers because of the more positive support they receive from teachers *rather than because they are identified as gifted.*

Let's Do It! Activities
Let's Do It! 4.1

Descriptive Survey Design

Study

Cleary, T. J., Gubi, A., & Prescott, M. V. (2010). Motivation and self-regulation assessments: Professional practices and needs of school psychologists. *Psychology in the Schools, 47*(10), 985–1002. https://doi.org/10.1002/pits.20519

Purpose — To examine the professional practices, knowledge, and needs of school psychologists regarding motivational and self-regulated learning assessment and intervention practices. Researchers also examined differences in these variables across school psychologists working in urban and suburban schools.

Critical Issues — The rationale for studying this issue was strong due to a perceived gap between school psychologist perceptions of the value and importance of assessing student motivation and self-regulation (very high) versus the frequency with which they assess these processes (very low).

(Continued)

Sampling	143 school psychologists from a mid-western state were sampled. They were shown to be representative of school psychologists across the country in terms of gender, ethnicity, and years of experience. The sample was primarily female (72%) and White (87%), with most having an EdS degree (93%). The authors elected to focus on differences between school psychologist working in urban and suburban schools, given the lack of attention devoted to these subgroups.
Measurement	The authors created a questionnaire (Likert scale) to address the perceptions, beliefs, and practices of school psychologists regarding their motivation and self-regulation assessment and intervention practices with children. The paper and pencil survey was administered in person to school psychologists during a school-based meeting.
Statistics	Descriptive statistics (e.g., mean, frequency, percentages) were emphasized, but inferential statistics (e.g., t-test, chi-square) were used. The descriptive statistics addressed the importance versus actual practice of using motivation and self-regulation assessments. Inferential statistics were used to examine differences in assessment practices among school psychologists across suburban/urban contexts.
Results	Regardless of school context (urban and suburban), school psychologists frequently encountered students with motivational and regulatory difficulties and perceive those processes to be important (motivation and self-regulation ranked in top 3). However, they do not routinely evaluate or target these processes during assessments or interventions.

Let's Do It! 4.2

Correlational Designs

Study

Huk, O., Terjesen, M. D., & Cherkasova, L. (2019). Predicting teacher burnout as a function of school characteristics and irrational beliefs. *Psychology in the Schools, 56*(5), 792–808. https://doi.org/10.1002/pits.22233

Purpose	The study examined the relationship between irrational teacher beliefs (i.e., predictor variable) and teacher burnout (i.e., dependent variable) after controlling for several other variables (e.g., student behavior, teacher support). The authors provided a rationale for the importance of addressing teacher burnout as a dependent variable and for examining other personal and contextual factors as predictors. The authors referenced a few theories to support their inclusion of several variables in their study (transactional model of stress and coping).
Sampling	The authors sampled teachers from 10 high schools from multiple states. They selected high school teachers due to higher levels of stress in those grade levels. Of the total 77 teachers, the majority worked as a regular education teacher (83.1%), with a little more than half teaching core curriculum classes (53.2%).
Measurement	The authors focused on teacher burnout as the primary dependent variable (3 subscales included for this measure). There was an extensive number of predictor variables, including teacher perceptions of student behavior, teacher perceptions of support from others, teacher satisfaction, teacher self-efficacy, and teacher irrational thinking. The irrational thinking variable appeared to represent the primary predictor variable in their model (four subscales). The authors provided evidence to support the psychometric properties of the measures.

Statistics   The authors included a descriptive statistics table (means, standard deviation, etc.) for all measures. A paired sample *t*-test was used to examine differences relative to a normative sample. A correlation matrix was provided to illustrate pairwise correlations between predictor variables and the dependent variable (total score and 3 subscales). Multiple regression was used to examine the collective effects of all predictors on teacher burnout and to examine the separate effects of school characteristics (e.g., support, student behavior) and irrational beliefs on teacher burnout.

Results   The regression model with all predictor variables accounted for approximately 46% of the variance in teacher burnout. When considered separately, school characteristics accounted for 25% of teacher burnout variance, while irrational beliefs accounted for an additional 18% of the variance in burnout. Thus, irrational beliefs represented a unique and important variable in understanding teacher burnout.

LET'S DO IT! 4.3

Comparative Designs

Study

Hartley, M. T., Bauman, S., Nixon, C. L., & Davis, S. (2015). Comparative study of bullying victimization among students in general and special education. *Exceptional Children, 81*(2), 176–193. https://doi.org/10.1177/0014402914551741

Purpose   The authors sought to examine differences in bullying victimization experiences and corresponding psychological distress (i.e., dependent variables) across general and special education students (i.e., grouping variable). The authors discussed the negative consequences of bullying and noted the lack of research that examines bullying experiences across students in different educational contexts. They also noted that students who received special education services are particularly vulnerable to experience bullying.

Sampling   A national sample of students in Grades 5 to 12 were selected from 31 states in the U.S. Students were eligible if they had reported experiencing bullying at least two times per month. There were 2,874 general education students and 361 students receiving special education services.

Measurement
Grouping variable   Two levels of students (i.e., special education, general education) were identified based on the status as a general education or special education student. All students in both groups reported frequent bullying experiences.

Dependent variables   The authors examined group differences across several variables, including frequency of physical and emotional harm, specific bullying events, and psychological distress. The two groups were also compared across several demographic variables (age, grade level, free or reduced lunch, ethnicity, etc.).

Attempts to Rule Out Explanations   The authors identified students in both groups who had experienced bullying victimization at least two time per month (this helped to roughly match groups in terms of exposure to bullying).

The authors compared the two groups after the data were collected across age, grade level, gender, race, SES, and immigrant status. There were differences across most variables; a larger percentage of special education students were recent immigrants, had lower SES, were of minority status, and were male. Thus, there were many alternative explanations to the premise that special education alone predicts bullying experiences.

(Continued)

Statistics   The authors reported a descriptive summary table and conducted ANOVAs or chi-square analyses to examine group differences across demographic variables. The authors used complex statistical procedures (e.g., MANOVA, logit modeling analysis) to examine group differences across frequency of physical and emotional harm and psychological distress and to examine patterns of verbal, physical, and relational bullying.

Results   The results converged with prior evidence that students with disabilities are more likely to be bullied and to report greater physical and emotional harm and psychological distress than their non-disabled peers. Patterns of bullying are similar across the two groups, although students in special education were more likely to report greater levels of physical bullying. Male peers were more likely to bully students in special education than female peers.

5 EXPERIMENTAL RESEARCH DESIGNS

LEARNING OBJECTIVES

Upon completion of this chapter, the reader should be able to

5.1   Explain the most common threats to internal validity

5.2   Explain the link between experimental design features and internal validity

5.3   Identify the core characteristics and limitations of pre-experimental designs

5.4   Apply the core features of true experimental designs

5.5   Apply the core features of quasi-experimental designs

5.6   Apply the core features of single participant experimental designs

5.7   Demonstrate knowledge of ethical issues when conducting, analyzing, and communicating experimental research

5.8   Utilize the *Publication Manual of the American Psychological Association* in reporting and presenting findings from experimental studies

A DAY AT WORK

Does What I do Actually Improve Student Learning?

©iStockphoto.com/monkeybusinessimages

Jennifer is a student teacher at Lee Avenue Elementary School, a K–5 school located in an urban community. Jennifer has enjoyed a very successful year thus far and often receives positive feedback regarding the quality of her teaching. Jennifer appreciates the support provided by her supervisor, Ms. Douglas, and is grateful to have been placed in a district that emphasizes innovative and evidence-based instructional practices. In fact, Jennifer participated in a district-wide initiative to enhance the quality of reading comprehension instruction for elementary and middle school students. This broad reading initiative included many components, such as implementation of a classroom-wide reading program, development of a school-wide reading support center, and at-home reading collaborations.

Jennifer and Ms. Douglas were particularly excited about the potential of the classroom-based reading program for improving students' reading comprehension skills. They began implementation of the program in March and continued it for approximately eight weeks. They also administered a reading test to students a few weeks before (i.e., pretest) and after (i.e., posttest) the reading program was implemented. Large gains in students' reading skills were observed. Ms. Douglas and Jennifer were excited because it looked like the new reading program had a direct impact on students' reading . . . or did it?

INTRODUCTION

In this chapter, we consider several variations of an experimental design: pre-experiment, true experiment, quasi-experiment, and single participant experiment. Many of the basic characteristics of experiments parallel those of non-experimental designs, such as developing research questions, recruiting, and selecting a sample, collecting data about important variables, and conducting statistical analyses. However, experimental approaches are used for a unique purpose; they enable one to make these types of cause-and-effect claims.

In this chapter, we devote a lot of attention to the concept of internal validity. As you may recall, in Chapter 3 we defined internal validity as the extent to which researchers can confidently claim that an experimental manipulation (e.g., administering an intervention or instructional program) resulted in or caused some effect (e.g., improved reading scores). After presenting a detailed discussion about the various threats to internal validity, we focus on the different types of experimental designs (i.e., pre-experiments, true experiments, quasi-experiments, and single participant experiments). In addition to discussing the specific features of each design, we analyze why certain experimental approaches are more effective than others in strengthening the internal validity of a study. We reference the Jennifer and Ms. Douglas scenario and other real-life examples to illustrate key experimental design concepts and provide several *Let's See It!*, *Let's Do It!*, and *You Do It!* activities to further strengthen and apply your knowledge about these designs. We end by discussing ethical considerations when conducting experiments and best-practice approaches for disseminating and sharing experimental data with the scholarly and broader community.

DEEPENING KNOWLEDGE ABOUT THREATS TO INTERNAL VALIDITY

LEARNING OBJECTIVE
5.1   Explain the most common threats to internal validity.

When researchers conduct experiments, they typically make predictions or hypotheses about what they expect or hope to observe in the results. For example, Ms. Douglas and Jennifer believed the new class-wide reading program they implemented had a significant influence on students' reading comprehension skills. To be able to make this type of claim, however, they need to think carefully about the validity (i.e., accuracy or meaningfulness) of this statement. That is, was the intervention the primary cause of the improved comprehension skills or could the observed changes in reading skill have been the result of other factors, such as student intelligence or motivation, access to other reading resources, or the level of reading support from parents at home? Ruling out or controlling these other variables or alternative explanations is at the very heart of the internal validity concept. When researchers are able to show that other variables or explanations could not possibly be a cause of the observed change, the internal validity of a study is strengthened. But when these alternative explanations are possible, internal validity is undermined. Researchers typically call these alternative explanations threats to internal validity.

The most common internal validity threats include history, maturation, testing, instrumentation, and selection. Ruling out these and other threats requires researchers to adopt a detective-like mindset and frequent use of the question, *"IS IT POSSIBLE."* Although simplistic, this question is one of the most important questions researchers can ask themselves when interpreting data from most research designs. This guiding question helps researchers maintain a healthy level of skepticism about whether the target intervention caused any changes observed in the sample. Following, we provide definitions and a brief example for the five threats to internal validity. We use the *IS IT POSSIBLE* prompt to stimulate the appropriate skeptical mindset.

History

History as a threat to internal validity involves events, experiences, or situations that occurred during the same approximate time as the intervention. For example, suppose researchers administered a 10-week social skills intervention to a group of fifth-grade students who also participated in several after-school activities, the latter of which were highly social in nature. The researchers observed significant changes in students' social skills following the 10-week intervention. Of interest to the researchers was whether the social skills intervention caused this observed change in students' social skills or *IS IT POSSIBLE* that students participating in the after-school activities impacted the change?

Maturation

Maturation as a threat to internal validity reflects developmental or maturational changes that naturally occur within research participants. As an example, consider a group of participants who received a writing intervention over the course of six months. The researcher assessed students' writing skills before the intervention began and following the 6-month program and observed large gains in their writing skills. Did the target writing intervention cause the observed change in writing skill or *IS IT POSSIBLE* that natural changes in student's abilities and skills over the course of the school year was the primary cause?

Testing

Testing as a threat to internal validity occurs when the experience of taking an assessment at one point in time influences participant responses or performance when the assessment is re-administered. For example, students across several seventh-grade classrooms received a bullying intervention program at the beginning of the school year. Students were asked to complete a survey about bullying before and after the program. Based on the collected data, students showed more positive and adaptive behaviors and beliefs about bullying after the program. However, because many of the questions included in the pretest measure (i.e., before the program began) may have prompted students to begin thinking more deeply about their own bullying behaviors and experiences, *IS IT POSSIBLE* that the act of completing the survey inadvertently led to changes in students' behaviors and reactions? In other words, was it the effects of the pretest that caused the change rather than the bullying intervention?

Instrumentation

Instrumentation as a threat to internal validity involves changes in the nature or accuracy of an assessment tool over time. An instrumentation effect can occur if there is a change in the assessment tool or the quality and consistency with which it is used. For example, consider a teacher who applied a more stringent criteria in grading essays at pretest than for the posttest. Thus, the observed change could have been the result in the quality of the grading procedure rather than intervention. An instrumentation effect can also occur when different assessment tools are used. For instance, as part of a 3-month reading intervention study, researchers used a *multiple-choice format* for assessing reading at pretest (i.e., before the program began) but a *short-answer format* at posttest (i.e., after the program was completed). The researchers observed significantly higher scores at posttest. Did the reading intervention cause the observed change, or *IS IT POSSIBLE* the difference in the difficulty of the two reading measures (i.e., multiple choice at pretest versus short answer at posttest) was the cause of the observed group difference?

Selection

Selection factors as a threat to internal validity reflect differences in the characteristics, attitudes, and beliefs of participants prior to receiving an intervention. For example, suppose researchers placed students from *Ms. Johnson's class* in a math intervention group and students from *Mr. Jackson's class* into a group that did not receive the intervention (i.e., control group). Thus, students were assigned to the intervention condition based solely on their membership in a certain math class. Students from Ms. Johnson's class demonstrated significantly higher test scores than students from Mr. Jackson's class at posttest. Is there enough information to claim that the math intervention caused the observed change, or *IS IT POSSIBLE* that *initial* student differences across the groups (e.g., math ability, prior achievement, motivation) was the source of the observed posttest differences?

When considering the scenarios for each of the five threats to internal validity, the answer to IS IT POSSIBLE prompt in each instance was the same: "Yes, it is possible!" When researchers encounter situations when different factors could explain a particular effect, the strength of the internal validity of the study is weakened. Without strong internal validity, researchers can never confidently claim that a target intervention was the cause of the effect.

Examining Threats to Internal Validity

It is now your chance to deepen your knowledge and understanding of internal validity threats. In the *Let's See It!* activity, you will read a brief scenario about Ms. Douglas and her colleague, Ms. Mustapha, and their implementation of a reading program. You will learn how the *IS IT POSSIBLE* prompt can be used to identify history, maturation, testing, instrumentation, and selection as potential threats to internal validity. For the *Let's Do It!* activity, you will be asked to read a dialogue between Jennifer and her college professor, Dr. Floyd, and then use the *IS IT POSSIBLE* prompt to identify the threats to internal validity addressed in their conversation.

Let's See It! 5.1

Goal: To Understand how Specific Threats to Internal Validity Are Linked to Specific Research Situations

Ms. Douglas administered a classroom-based reading intervention to all students in her fifth-grade class. The reading intervention lasted approximately eight weeks. She then administered a reading comprehension posttest to her students following the intervention. Students from the other fifth-grade classroom in the school (i.e., Ms. Mustapha) did not receive the reading program but were posttested on reading comprehension. The posttest scores for the two classes were examined. The results showed that the students in Ms. Douglas' class exhibited superior reading comprehension skills than students from Ms. Mustapha's class. Is it valid to conclude that the reading intervention program used by Ms. Douglas caused the observed group difference in reading comprehension? Look at Table 5.1 to determine the plausibility of each potential threat in this study.

TABLE 5.1 ■ Threats to Validity		
Threat to Internal Validity	IS IT POSSIBLE?	Explanation of Threat
History	Yes	Based on the information presented in the scenario, it is not clear whether external factors (e.g., extra help, frequent parental involvement) were more prevalent in one classroom than the other. Thus, was it the reading program that caused the observed differences or other potential factors unique to Ms. Douglas' classroom?
Maturation	Not likely	Because there was a comparison group composed of students of similar age, grade level, and so forth, it is not likely that maturational or developmental factors only occurred with students in Ms. Douglas' class. If a maturation effect was present and the cause of the outcomes, one would observe that change in both classes.
Testing	No	Because a pretest was not administered, it is not possible to have a testing effect.
Instrumentation	No	Because a pretest was not administered, the issues about changes in the assessment tools over time are not relevant.
Selection	Yes	Based on the details of the scenario, it is possible that students from the two classes exhibited differences in reading ability, motivation, or other relevant variables *before* the reading intervention was even implemented. Thus, initial group differences could be a causal factor of the observed change rather than the reading program.

Let's Do It! 5.1

Guided Practice: To Practice Applying Threats to Internal Validity

Goal: To Identify Key Threats to Internal Validity in the Study

Please read the following dialogue between Jennifer and Dr. Floyd. Jennifer is enrolled in a research methods course as part of her pre-service teaching degree requirements. As a capstone requirement for this course, Dr. Floyd asks students to conduct a project that utilizes some type of research design to evaluate an aspect of their work as a teacher. Jennifer wanted to use her experience with implementing the 8-week reading program to fulfill the requirements of the project. She was excited given her very positive experiences with the program and the strong improvement displayed by her students. The research design used by Jennifer and Ms. Douglas entailed administering a pretest reading comprehension measure to all students in their class (i.e., before the reading program began), providing the reading intervention program for eight weeks, and then administering a different type of reading comprehension measure at posttest (i.e., after the intervention was completed) to the same students. She scheduled a meeting with Dr. Floyd to discuss this assignment and her experiences with the reading program.

After reading the dialogue, please use Table 5.2 to identify threats to internal validity that Dr. Floyd referenced in his conversation with Jennifer. Please explain your answers. An answer key is provided at the end of the chapter so you can self-check your work.

TABLE 5.2 ■ Threats to Validity		
Threat to Internal Validity	**IS IT POSSIBLE?**	**Explanation of Threat**
History		
Maturation		
Testing		
Instrumentation		
Selection		

Jennifer: "*I can't believe it. Do you remember the reading comprehension program that I have been using with my fifth graders as part of my student teaching?*"

Dr. Floyd: "*Of course, yes. How is it going?*"

Jennifer: "*Well, I just completed the 8-week program, and it really helped them. I will be using this experience for our capstone assignment. I would like to describe how the reading program improved their reading comprehension skills.*"

Dr. Floyd: "*That is great. Sounds like you really made a difference with the kids. What made you think your intervention worked?*"

Jennifer: "*The students just read so much better in class. We also tested their reading comprehension skills in May to see if their scores were higher than when we tested them in February. I used SPSS to run a paired sample t-test with the 25 students. The results showed a statistically significant improvement from pretest to posttest. It feels so good to not only have learned about the reading comprehension program but to also understand how to evaluate whether it actually worked.*"

Dr. Floyd: "*That certainly sounds promising. It is great that the students performed better at the end of the school year. But, let me ask you a question. How do you know that it was the classroom reading program that you implemented that made the difference?*"

Jennifer: Jennifer was a bit surprised by the question, but responded, "*Because I could see it in their behavior and how they were reacting during the intervention. The data do not lie. The students clearly showed better reading comprehension skills in May.*"

Dr. Floyd: *"No doubt, the students showed better comprehension skills in May relative to February. But let me clarify my question. How can you be so sure that it was the classroom reading program and not something else that caused the change?"*

Jennifer: Jennifer, who now appeared puzzled and somewhat surprised that Dr. Floyd did not share in her enthusiasm, stated, *"I am not sure what you mean."*

Dr. Floyd: *"Well, let me play devil's advocate. I remember you telling me that many of the students in your class also began to attend the reading support center in November. Is it possible that the improvement you observed was due to the support students received from the reading specialist and not the program you provided in the classroom? Also, didn't several parents provide additional reading supports to their children at home during this same year?"*

Jennifer: *"I guess this is true . . . but come on. I really saw improvement in their skills over time. I know that they improved from what we did in the classroom. It was a great program."*

Dr. Floyd: *"Don't misunderstand . . . you may be right. But I am simply trying to get you to question how confident you can be in making a claim that it was the reading program you provided over the 8 weeks that truly made the difference. Let me ask you another question. Isn't it possible that the reading gains showed by the students were simply due to natural improvement in reading that they would have shown over the course of the school year? Perhaps the key factor impacting the change in their reading skills was natural growth in their cognitive or reading abilities that one would expect from receiving regular classroom instruction in fifth grade."*

Jennifer: *"I guess that is possible. But let me ask you this . . . how do you know for sure that the change was due to natural growth in the students rather than the reading program?"*

Dr. Floyd: *"Ahhhh . . . that's a very good question and actually part of my point. The reality is that I don't know. When thinking about whether a reading program or some other intervention caused or directly influenced an outcome, it is essential that you think about other possibilities besides the program that you are focused on."*

Jennifer: *"I think I am getting a little confused."*

Dr. Floyd: *"Ok, let me give you another example. I recall you saying that you used two different reading comprehension tests. If I am correct, I believe the test you used in February utilized fill-in-the-blank questions while the posttest in May was multiple choice."*

Jennifer: *"Yes, that is true."*

Dr. Floyd: *"I understand why you used the two different tests, but isn't it possible that the changes in reading comprehension scores were simply due to differences in the reading tests that you used? Couldn't some kids have found the fill-in-the-blank format much more difficult than the multiple choice? Thus, the observed growth could have been due to the test in May being easier for the students?"*

Jennifer: *"Whoa. I think I see your point. I guess what is confusing me is how one can ever know for sure about these other possible causes. How can I know whether what I do in the classroom makes a difference? It is almost as if you need to be like a detective."*

Dr. Floyd: *"For sure . . . that is something we will be talking about as a class this week. To be able to say one thing causes another, you do need to think analytically, like a detective, to rule out other explanations. While detectives may ask the question "who done it?" researchers ask "what caused it?" The experimental designs we will talk about in class should help to answer this question.*

THE TAKEAWAY

If you ever want to make claims that a school-based intervention or instructional approach caused a change in some outcome, you must think about all potential threats or alternative explanations about why those changes occurred.

INTERNAL VALIDITY WITHIN EXPERIMENTAL DESIGNS

LEARNING OBJECTIVE
5.2   Explain the link between experimental design features and internal validity.

To understand how experimental designs control threats to internal validity, it is essential to first learn about the key features of these designs. In Table 5.3, we list several experimental design features and explain how each relates to two questions underlying the concept of internal validity:

- Was there an observed effect?

- What are the most likely causes of that effect?

To make claims that an intervention caused some outcome, researchers must first establish that an effect occurred. Researchers determine an effect by collecting data from the research participants at different points in a study. For example, most experimental designs involve administering a pretest (i.e., assessment before an intervention) and/or a posttest (i.e., assessment after an intervention) and then examine differences across those two time points. For example, if Ms. Douglas used a pretest–posttest approach to identify the effects of a reading fluency intervention, she could administer a measure of reading fluency before the students received the intervention and then again after the intervention was completed. She would then use a test of statistical inference (e.g., paired *t*-test; see Chapter 13) to determine whether the pretest–posttest difference is statistically significant (i.e., a real effect not due to chance).

Another common approach for identifying an effect is to compare the posttest scores for different groups. This method is only possible when researchers include two or more groups within the design. Thus, if Ms. Douglas administered the reading fluency posttest to her class and another fifth-grade class that did not receive the intervention (i.e., control group), the intervention effect could be determined by comparing the posttest scores of the two groups.

Finally, some experimental designs incorporate a time series component to measure change—that is, collecting multiple data points over time. You can think of a time series

TABLE 5.3 ■ Design Features for Identifying Effects or Enhancing Internal Validity		
Internal Validity Features	**Definition**	**Connection With Intervention Effects or Internal Validity**
Pretest (O_{pre})	An observation or measure of individuals' attributes, skills, or characteristics prior to receiving an intervention	• When compared to posttest scores, can be used to determine the presence of an effect • Can play a role in establishing initial group equivalence
Posttest (O_{post})	An observation or measure of individuals' attributes, skills, or characteristics after they receive an intervention	• Key metric used to determine the presence of an intervention effect
Intervention group (I)	One or more groups in an experiment that receive an intervention or program as stipulated by the researchers	• Performance by this group is the basis for making claims that an effect has occurred
Control group	One or more groups in an experiment that do not receive any intervention or program	• Serves as a reference against which to evaluate changes in the intervention group • Helps to rule out threats to internal validity, such as history, maturation, testing, and so forth
Comparison group	One or more groups in an experiment that receives an alternative intervention or program relative to the intervention condition	• Serves as a reference point against which to evaluate changes in the intervention group • Helps to rule out threats to internal validity, such as history, maturation, testing, and instrumentation
Time series component	Continuous or repeated administration of an assessment before (i.e., pretest) and after (i.e., posttest) an intervention begins	• Helps to illustrate whether patterns of scores at baseline differ from patterns of scores during the intervention phase • Helps to rule out threats to internal validity, such as maturation, testing, and instrumentation
Random assignment (R)	A procedure whereby each participant in a sample has an equal chance of being placed in any of the conditions or groups	• Helps to ensure that all groups in a study are equivalent across extraneous variables (i.e., variables not controlled for by the researcher) • Helps to rule out selection threats to internal validity

component as having *multiple* pretests and *multiple* posttest data points. The basic logic for identifying an effect with a time series design parallels the reasoning for using a pretest–posttest approach. That is, all data points collected prior to the intervention (i.e., multiple pretest scores) are compared to the data following the intervention (i.e., multiple posttest scores). With the time series approach, an effect is observed if, collectively, the pre-intervention scores differ from the post-intervention scores.

When no intervention effect is observed in a study, researchers do not need to be concerned with threats to internal validity. In other words, identifying the causes of an effect does not make sense when there is no effect in the first place. When an effect is observed, however, the concept of threats to internal validity takes center stage. For example, if Ms. Douglas observed a significant change in students' reading comprehension scores from pretest to posttest, her primary thought should be to determine whether the comprehension intervention was the most viable explanation of the observed change or whether it was due to an alternative explanation (i.e., threats to internal validity).

All the design features listed in Table 5.3 play a role in helping researchers identify an intervention effect and or to control potential threats to internal validity. Designs that use most of these features tend to have stronger internal validity than those without these features. Before reading on with the chapter, we encourage you to complete the brief Stop and Think exercise to reflect more deeply on the different experimental design features and their link to the internal validity of a study.

STOP AND THINK 5.1

In reviewing the information presented in Table 5.3, can you identify which features address the issue of an effect and which ones address the causes of that effect?

THE TAKEAWAY

When thinking about internal validity, you need to first consider how you will measure an effect (e.g., pretest/posttest). Then, ask whether the features of a design are sufficient for concluding that the intervention (or some other factor) was the likely cause.

PRE-EXPERIMENTAL DESIGNS

LEARNING OBJECTIVE
5.3 Identify the core characteristics and limitations of pre-experimental designs.

To get you thinking more deeply about experimental design features and the various threats to internal validity, we introduce the highly simplistic pre-experimental design. As the prefix "pre" suggests, these types of designs are not truly experimental in nature because they *do not* include most of the design features listed in Table 5.3. To be frank, pre-experimental designs are largely ineffective in ruling out most or all threats to internal validity. Thus, we encourage researchers not to use these approaches when the interest is showing that an intervention caused a particular outcome. However, we do spend some time discussing these designs given the ease with which they can be administered in school contexts, and they can often serve as a useful pilot study about an intervention.

A common pre-experimental design is the single group pretest–posttest design. This design includes three key features; administering a pretest (i.e., assessment before the intervention) to a single group, providing an intervention to that group, and administering a posttest after the intervention is completed; see highlighted in second column of Figure 5.1. In the first column of

FIGURE 5.1 ■ Checklist of Experimental Features of Single Group Pretest–Posttest Design (pre-experimental)			
Sequence of Assessment and Intervention	**Design Features**	**Determination of Effect**	**Internal Validity**
O_{pre} I O_{post}	Pretest (O_{pre})	An effect is determined by examining the difference between the pretest score and posttest score for the group. This type of effect is known as a gain score.	Without a control or comparison group, no threats to internal validity can be ruled out. Random assignment is not relevant in this type of design given that only one group is typically used.
	Posttest (O_{post})		
	Intervention group (I)		
	Control group (C)		
	Time series component		
	Random assignment of participants (R)		

Note: The highlighted areas reflect features that are included as part of the design, whereas gray highlights denote features that are not present. O_{pre} = pretest observation; O_{post} = posttest observation; X = intervention; I = intervention group; C = control or comparison group; R = random assignment.

Figure 5.1, we use specific notation to represent the key design features. The O_{pre} and O_{post} reflect the use of assessment measures. The O_{pre} reflects the pretest (i.e., assessment before intervention is delivered) while the O_{post} reflects the posttest (i.e., assessment after the intervention is completed). The use of a single (I) in the diagram indicates that one group was used in the study and received the target intervention.

The single group pretest–posttest design should be somewhat familiar to you as it was the approach used by Ms. Douglas and Jennifer in the opening scenario. By administering the reading program to students from her class and gathering pretest and posttest data about their reading comprehension scores, Ms. Douglas and Jennifer were able to determine that the students improved their reading skills. Thus, they were able to make definitive claims about the *presence of an effect*—the first key issue in establishing the internal validity of their study. However, as we have emphasized in previous sections, demonstrating the presence of an effect is a necessary but *not sufficient* condition for concluding that the intervention was the cause of that effect. Because this design did not include a control group, a time series component, or random assignment, there is no way to rule out any threats to internal validity (e.g., history, maturation, testing). Please see the Stop and Think activity to explore why the absence of these three design features prevented Ms. Douglas and Jennifer from ruling out these threats. Completing this activity will help set the stage for learning about more effective and rigorous experimental designs.

STOP AND THINK 5.2

In examining Table 5.3, can you explain why the one group pretest–posttest design cannot rule out any threats to internal validity (note: we will provide a detailed explanation of this "ruling out" process as we discuss the experimental designs)?

THE TAKEAWAY

Although pre-experimental designs are easy to implement, they lack the essential features and overall scientific rigor needed to rule out threats to internal validity.

TRUE EXPERIMENTAL DESIGNS

LEARNING OBJECTIVE
5.4   Apply the core features of true experimental designs.

When researchers want to show that an intervention or instructional program directly causes some outcome, they will use a *true experimental design*—the gold standard of experimental designs (Figure 5.2). At the most basic level, a true experiment involves randomly assigning participants to different treatment or control conditions. Although there are several variations of a true experiment, we focus on two designs: (1) pretest–posttest control group design and (2) factorial experimental design. For each design, we address the following three topics: (a) nature of research questions, (b) design features linked to internal validity, and (c) statistics.

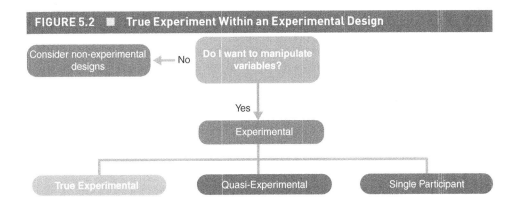

FIGURE 5.2 ■ True Experiment Within an Experimental Design

Pretest–Posttest Control Group Design

The pretest–posttest control group design is widely recognized as a strong experimental design because it incorporates several features that greatly enhance internal validity. When researchers administer assessments before and after an intervention (i.e., pretest, posttest), create different conditions or groups (e.g., one group receives an intervention while the other(s) does not), and decide how to best allocate research participants to the treatment and control groups (i.e., random assignment), they have created the necessary conditions for ruling out all or most alternative explanations or threats to internal validity.

In the simplest version of the pretest–posttest control group design, there are two groups: an intervention group and a control group. While the intervention group (i.e., the group that receives the intervention) is of primary interest, the control or comparison group (i.e., the group that does not receive the target intervention) is equally important, albeit for a different reason. In an experimental design, a control group and a comparison group serve the same basic function; that is, a benchmark against which to evaluate the results of the intervention group. However, control and comparison groups are slightly different. A control group refers to individuals in an experimental study who do not receive any intervention or program as part of their participation in the study. In contrast, a comparison group receives some type of program or initiative but not the target intervention given to the intervention group.

Nature of Research Questions

In Figure 5.3, we present four research questions that can be investigated using an experimental design. As you review these questions, we encourage you to take note of the following points. First, all questions reflect the desire of the researcher to examine the effect or influence of some program, intervention, or other experience on one or more dependent variables. The different interventions represent independent variables—that is, variables the researcher manipulates to create different conditions. Using the example research questions, the independent variables included (1) type of reading program, (2) type of therapeutic modality, (3) presence or absence of a professional development workshop, and (4) presence or absence of the Good Behavior Game.

From a practical point of view, the research questions also collectively show that experimental designs can be used to examine the effects of a wide range of instructional or intervention programs implemented in school contexts and across myriad outcomes and people. In short, experiments allow researchers to draw conclusions about whether some intervention, program, or other activity worked in improving the functioning of students, teachers, paraprofessionals, and so forth.

As reflected with these research questions, there will always be at least two groups in true experimental designs. Thus, research questions will often be worded to reflect comparisons among different groups or conditions (e.g., intervention group versus a control or comparison group). In fact, two of the example questions referenced a comparison group (e.g., type of reading

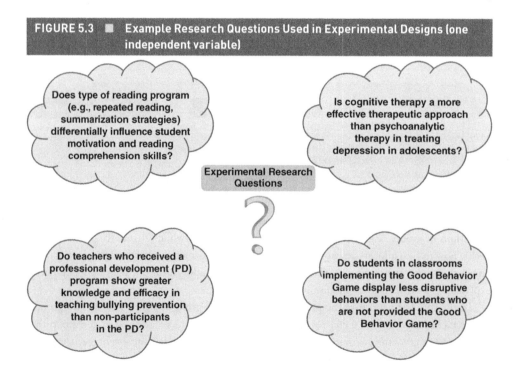

FIGURE 5.3 ■ Example Research Questions Used in Experimental Designs (one independent variable)

Does type of reading program (e.g., repeated reading, summarization strategies) differentially influence student motivation and reading comprehension skills?

Is cognitive therapy a more effective therapeutic approach than psychoanalytic therapy in treating depression in adolescents?

Experimental Research Questions

Do teachers who received a professional development (PD) program show greater knowledge and efficacy in teaching bullying prevention than non-participants in the PD?

Do students in classrooms implementing the Good Behavior Game display less disruptive behaviors than students who are not provided the Good Behavior Game?

program, type of therapeutic intervention) whereas the other two questions reflected control groups (i.e., presence or absence of professional development or the Good Behavior Game). Please note that comparison groups are often preferred over control groups when research is conducted within schools. Creating conditions when students do not receive any type of support service, like a control group, is typically viewed in a negative fashion by parents and/or administrators. For this reason and for the sake of clarity, we emphasize the use of comparison groups throughout the remainder of the chapter.

Design Features Linked to Internal Validity

Pretest–posttest control group designs include all the design features listed in Figure 5.4 except for the time series component (see highlighted areas). The pretest and posttest features are used to detect the presence or absence of an effect, while random assignment and the use of a comparison group are the primary ways in which researchers control for threats to internal validity. Let's explore how these design features foster the internal validity of a study.

When reading through this section, please remember that experimental researchers are always interested in addressing two key questions related to internal validity: (1) Was there an effect? and (2) What was the cause of the effect? Let's consider these two questions in relation to Mr. Fredericks and his desire to evaluate the effects of an upward extension of the reading comprehension program used by Ms. Douglas and Jennifer in their fifth-grade classroom. Mr. Fredericks is a seventh-grade language arts teacher in the same school district as Ms. Douglas. Prior to the school year, Mr. Fredericks approached the principal, Dr. Adams, about possibly randomly assigning students to the four sections of his English class. Random assignment simply means that every student who is eligible to participate in the study has an equal chance of being placed in the intervention or comparison condition. Although randomly assigning students can be difficult in school contexts, Dr. Adams was supportive of this effort because he understood its value in ruling out threats to internal validity. Upon hearing that random assignment would be used, Mr. Fredericks became excited because he knew that this design feature would help to ensure that the different groups in the study were as similar as possible (i.e., minimizes selection threat to internal validity).

FIGURE 5.4 ■ Components and Features of Pretest–Posttest Control Group Design

Sequence of Assessment and Intervention	Design Features	Determination of Effect	Internal Validity
(I) R O_{pre} X O_{post} (C) R O_{pre} O_{post}	Pretest (O_{pre})	There are two options: (1) compare change in scores from pretest to posttest for each group (2) directly compare posttest scores of the groups.	Very strong; high potential for controlling all or most threats to internal validity
	Posttest (O_{post})		
	Intervention group (I)		
	Control group (C)		
	Time series component		
	Random assignment of participants (R)		

Note: The highlights reflect features that are included as part of the design, whereas gray highlights denote features that are not present. O_{pre} = pretest observation; O_{post} = posttest observation; X = intervention; I = intervention group; C = control or comparison group; R = random assignment.

In October of the school year, Mr. Fredericks administered a pretest measure of reading comprehension to all students across the four sections. He decided that his first and second sections of the day (i.e., both in the morning) would receive the new reading program (i.e., intervention group) while the third and fourth sections (i.e., both in the afternoon) would receive the standard reading program (i.e., comparison group). Mr. Fredericks made this decision given that it was more practical and easier from an instructional and preparation point of view to administer the intervention in back-to-back classes in the morning.

After delivering the 6-week reading program, Mr. Fredericks re-administered the same reading comprehension measure to all students. Thus, Mr. Fredericks obtained two sets of scores for each of the two conditions: a pretest and posttest for reading comprehension. Mr. Fredericks first examined the pretest scores for the intervention and comparison groups to confirm that their reading skills were similar prior to beginning the intervention. He was thrilled that these groups did not differ on the pretest. Establishing the equivalency between intervention and comparison conditions at pretest helped to remove a major threat to internal validity (i.e., initial group differences or selection). Please consider completing the Stop and Think activity to further explore the relevance and importance of using both pretests and random assignment in a study.

STOP AND THINK 5.3

In the situation with Mr. Fredericks, why would a pretest be needed when random assignment was used? Isn't random assignment supposed to guarantee that groups are equivalent?

Now that the study was completed, Mr. Fredericks wanted to identify if the reading skills of the intervention group improved and whether he could conclude that the reading program was the cause of that effect. To identify the effect, Mr. Fredericks used a *t*-test for independent samples to compare the posttest reading scores of the intervention group (i.e., first- and second-class sections) and the comparison group (i.e., third- and fourth-class sections). As you will learn in Chapter 13, a *t*-test or an analysis of variance procedure (ANOVA) are the most common approaches to examine group differences. To his excitement, Mr. Fredericks found that the intervention group displayed significantly higher reading comprehension scores than the comparison. With demonstrating this observed effect, Mr. Fredericks now turned his attention to figuring out whether the reading program was the likely cause of the effect.

In Figure 5.5, we summarize the common threats to internal validity and how well the pretest–posttest control group design ruled out these threats as potential causes of the reading gains. When reviewing this table (and other similar tables in different sections of this chapter), please keep a couple of points in mind. First, the table does not include all potential threats to internal validity. We focus on the most common threats or alternative explanations emphasized by researchers. Second, we use the IS IT POSSIBLE prompt to remind you about the need to be skeptical and cautious before concluding that any intervention or instructional program played a causal role in in the observed change. We use the following nomenclature to reflect the extent to which the threat to internal validity was a possible explanation of the observed effect:

FIGURE 5.5 ■ Threats to Internal Validity in the Mr. Frederick's Experiment

Threat to Internal Validity	Explanation of Potential Threat	Controlling for Threats to Internal Validity
History	IS IT POSSIBLE that some external factor operating in the school or for the seventh-grade students caused the observed reading group differences? **Highly unlikely**	If there was some external causal factor influencing reading skills, then Mr. Fredericks would have likely observed the effect in both the intervention and comparison conditions.
Maturation	IS IT POSSIBLE that some natural developmental change led to the observed reading group differences? **Highly unlikely**	If there was an internal or developmental change happening among the 7th grade students, then Mr. Fredericks would have likely observed that effect across both conditions (i.e., maturation would occur similarly in both groups).
Testing	IS IT POSSIBLE that taking the pretest reading comprehension test naturally led students to perform better on the posttest? **Highly unlikely**	If administering the pretest influenced the posttest scores, this effect would have been observed across both conditions (i.e., because both groups took the pretest).
Instrumentation	IS IT POSSIBLE that changes in the nature or accuracy of a measurement occurred across different time points? **Highly unlikely**	In this specific scenario, the threat of instrumentation is not possible because of the nature of the reading test. The same test was administered at pretest and posttest and the scoring was objective and standardized, so it does not seem possible that instrumentation played a role in the observed group reading differences.
Selection	IS IT POSSIBLE that the two conditions (which consisted of two seventh-grade classes each) had initial differences before the intervention began? **Highly unlikely**	The use of random assignment and testing for initial group with pretest data helps to control for the potential threat of selection.

Note: Blue shading reflects threats that are likely controlled. No shading reflects threats that are not controlled.

- *Yes:* the threat is real; thus, the internal validity is undermined
- *Highly unlikely:* the threat is not plausible; internal validity is enhanced
- *Not applicable/possible:* the threat is not a consideration given the nature of the specific study or design feature

It is important to note that we use the phrase "highly unlikely" rather than "no" in most situations to underscore that even in tightly controlled experimental designs (like the pretest–posttest control group design), it is possible that some unknown variable influences the dependent variable. The use of a strong experimental design mimimizes the likelihood that the threats influenced the results, but no research design can ever guarantee that all threats, both common and unforeseen, will be controlled. The only time we use "no" is when a threat is not possible in any circumstance.

These qualifications aside, the pretest–posttest control group design is a highly robust and effective approach for eliminating most threats to internal validity. In fact, in the scenario with

Mr. Fredericks, the first four threats to internal validity (i.e., history, maturation, testing, and instrumentation) appear to be adequately controlled because a comparison group was used. The basic logic of using a comparison group is that if threats to internal validity were truly occurring and had a causal impact on students, these effects would be observable to researchers across *both* the intervention and comparison groups. As an example, suppose administrators at Mr. Fredericks' middle school invested in computer software technology designed to enhance the quality of reading instruction for the entire school. If all students had access to this computer software and it turns out that this software did indeed influence students' reading performance (i.e., and not the target reading intervention), then both the intervention and comparison groups should exhibit improved and comparable reading skills. However, because the intervention group outperformed the comparison group, there was something unique in the experience of the intervention group that made a difference; that is, having access to the target reading intervention.

Despite the value of using comparison groups, they cannot fully control all threats to internal validity. Another important threat involves the equivalency of the groups before the intervention is implemented. When researchers recruit a sample to participate in a study, it is generally expected that the participants naturally show differences in personal attributes, abilities, or attitudes, such as ethnicity, self-efficacy, prior achievement, feelings of connectedness, or anxiety. The presence of differences at an *individual level* within a group is expected, and this is not typically a problem in experimental designs. It is when these differences occur at the *group level* that problems with internal validity may arise. For example, if the reading intervention group with Mr. Fredericks showed higher levels of cognitive ability and motivation at pretest than the comparison group, he will likely have lingering doubts regarding whether these factors or the intervention caused the observed effects. Students who are more motivated will work hard and display high levels of effort and persistence in the face of a challenge. Similarly, students with strong cognitive abilities will naturally be able to engage in high levels of inductive or deductive reasoning; factors that can clearly influence reading comprehension. In this situation, how can Mr. Fredericks ever know with a reasonable degree of certainty that the reading program was the cause of improved reading comprehension scores and not students' cognitive abilities or level of motivation?

To rule initial group differences (i.e., selection) as an alternative explanation, experimental researchers strive to randomly assign students to condition. The "magic" of random assignment is that it helps to ensure (although does not guarantee) that the differences in characteristic, abilities, or skills that naturally exists among research participants are equally distributed across the groups *before* an intervention is provided. As you may recall, Mr. Fredericks worked with his principal to help ensure that randomization occurred at the student level before the school year began. Thus, each student had an equal chance of being placed in the reading intervention group (first and second sections) or the comparison group (third and fourth sections). Although the use of random assignment in schools can be challenging, it was well worth the effort for Mr. Fredericks because it greatly increased the odds that the intervention and comparison groups were the same before the reading intervention was administered.

Random assignment is one of the most important features of an experimental design, but it still does not guarantee initial group equivalence. When sample sizes are small or when researchers do not truly use a randomization process, it is possible that groups can differ. For these reasons, we strongly recommend that researchers, whenever possible, gather relevant demographic information about the sample (i.e., race, SES, etc.) and administer pretests for variables that may relate to the dependent variable. Gathering this additional information can be used to check or verify that the random assignment procedures worked. Because Mr. Fredericks used the pretest–posttest control group design (i.e., which includes both random assignment and pretests), he had a very high level of confidence that initial group differences were not a threat to internal validity in his study.

There are situations, pariticularly in school settings, when the use of pretests may not be advisable (see Stop and Think 5.4 activity to explore these situations). If Mr. Fredericks did not include a pretest in his study, the new design would simply be referred to as a posttest-only control group design. As long as the intervention or control groups are equivalent at pretest (which is highly likely due to the use of random assignment), the logic and rigor of the posttest-only control group design is equivalent and may even be stronger than the pretest–posttest control group design (see Table 5.4). While both of these experimental designs rule out the same threats to internal validity, the posttest-only control group design can be viewed as superior because threats to testing or instrumention are not possible. In other words, these two threats cannot exist when a pretest is not administered. Thus, with the posttest-only design, the testing and instrmentation threats shift from being labeled as "highly unlikely" to "no" or "not applicable."

STOP AND THINK 5.4

Including a pretest in an experimental design is a positive and effective thing to do. However, can you identify situations when including a pretest may be inappropriate or problematic?

Statistics

In journal articles using experimental designs, researchers report descriptive statistics (e.g., means, standard deviations) for all dependent variables and often include a correlation matrix to illustrate the relations among these variables (see Chapter 12). When specifically addressing the observed effects of an intervention, researchers will use inferential statistics (see Chapter 13). Regardless of the experimental design, researchers use inferential statistics to draw conclusions about whether an observed difference is large enough to be considered "real" or whether it occurred by chance. For studies with only two groups, independent t-tests are often utilized. When three or more groups are included, researchers will use some variation of an analysis of variance procedure (one-way ANOVA or ANCOVA).

Factorial Designs

Factorial designs represent an expansion and more complex variation of the basic pretest–posttest control group design. Central to factorial designs is that they include more than one independent variable As we will highlight in subsequent sections, the use of multiple independent variables changes the nature of the questions that researchers address.

Nature of Research Questions

The four research questions presented in Figure 5.6 can be addressed with a factorial design. A couple of major themes can be identified when reviewing these questions. First, each of the research questions references two independent variables. When researchers use a factorial design, they are no longer only interested in examining the main effect of one variable; rather, they want to explain outcomes by considering the individual or main effects for all independent variables.

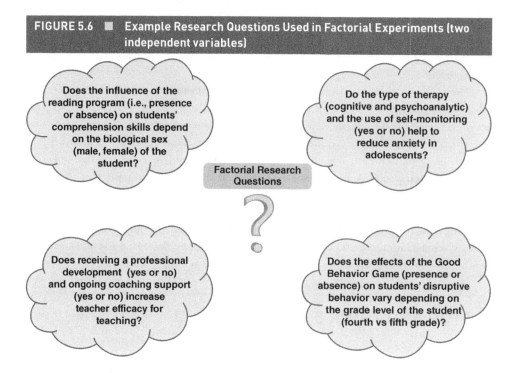

FIGURE 5.6 ■ Example Research Questions Used in Factorial Experiments (two independent variables)

Does the influence of the reading program (i.e., presence or absence) on students' comprehension skills depend on the biological sex (male, female) of the student?

Do the type of therapy (cognitive and psychoanalytic) and the use of self-monitoring (yes or no) help to reduce anxiety in adolescents?

Factorial Research Questions

Does receiving a professional development (yes or no) and ongoing coaching support (yes or no) increase teacher efficacy for teaching?

Does the effects of the Good Behavior Game (presence or absence) on students' disruptive behavior vary depending on the grade level of the student (fourth vs fifth grade)?

Second, in factorial designs, researchers must pay attention to another potential explanation of observed effects, an interaction effect; that is, the extent to which the effect of one independent variable on the outcome varies or differs across the levels of a second independent variable. To consider the issue of main and interaction effects in a more detailed way, we recommend that you complete the Stop and Think 5.5.

STOP AND THINK 5.5

Please answer the following two questions:

1. Can you identify the independent and dependent variables for the four research questions in Figure 5.3?
2. Which of the questions deal with an interaction effect? How do you know?

Design Features Linked to Internal Validity

As you may recall, Mr. Fredericks administered the new reading program to his four sections of English language arts; the two intervention classes were in the morning, while the comparison classes occurred in the afternoon. After thinking through the potential use of a pretest–posttest control group design (a design which included only one independent variable), he began to wonder whether *time-of-day* (i.e., morning versus afternoon sections) was a potential threat to internal validity. From his experience, students in his afternoon sections tend to have more difficulty staying focused and on-task than students in the morning sections. Thus, he began to worry that by only implementing the intervention in the morning he was inadvertently "stacking the deck" in favor of the reading intervention group.

If the intervention was only implemented in the morning time slots, he would never be certain whether it was the reading program that produced the change in reading scores or if it was due to higher levels of attention and focus that he believed students exhibited in the morning sessions. Thus, in designing his study, he inadvertently introduced time-of-day as a potential threat to internal validity. The use of a factorial design can help remediate this problem.

Mr. Fredericks decided to include the time-of-day variable as a second independent variable to create a factorial design. Thus, he provided the reading program to one morning and afternoon class, and the traditional reading curriculum (i.e., comparison condition) to the other morning and afternoon sections. By directly manipulating time-of-day (i.e., he decided when the intervention was implemented throughout the day), Mr. Fredericks was now able to examine the main effects of each of the two independent variables: (1) *intervention condition* (i.e., reading program versus traditional reading program) and (2) *time-of-day* (i.e., morning or afternoon; see Figure 5.7).

FIGURE 5.7 ■ Experimental Design With Two Independent Variables (factorial design)

		Time of day	
		Morning Classes	Afternoon Classes
Type of reading instruction	Intervention group (new reading program)		
	Comparison group (traditional reading curriculum)		

Although the inclusion of a second independent variable naturally creates a more complex design, the core features of this design mirror those of the pretest–posttest control group design (i.e., one independent variable; see Figure 5.8). For example, in the factorial design with Mr. Fredericks, students were randomly assigned to one of the four classroom periods and were pretested on reading comprehension skills before the intervention was introduced. Mr. Fredericks delivered the 6-week reading comprehension program to only students in the intervention condition and then re-administered the reading comprehension measure to all students at posttest. By including random assignment, a comparison condition, and pretest–posttest measures, the internal validity of this factorial study is quite strong (i.e., for the same reasons as with the pretest–posttest control group design).

The unique characteristic of Mr. Frederick's factorial design (i.e., when compared to the pretest–posttest control group design) was the inclusion of a second independent variable (i.e., varying the reading intervention across morning and afternoon sections). In using a factorial design, Mr. Fredericks created an opportunity to examine two distinct main effects: intervention (i.e., presence or absence) and for time-of-day (i.e., morning or afternoon). In other words, he could now address the following questions: (1) "Did the intervention group show higher reading scores than the comparison group (i.e., effect of intervention)?" and (2) "Did the students receiving morning reading instruction display better reading than those in afternoon sections (i.e., effects of time-of-day)?"

FIGURE 5.8 ■ Components and Features of Factorial Group Design

Sequence of Assessment and Intervention	Design Features	Determination of Effect	Internal Validity
(I) R O_{pre} X1X2 O_{post} (C) R O_{pre} O_{post}	Pretest (O_{pre}) Posttest (O_{post}) Intervention group (I) Control group (C) Time series component Random assignment of participants (R)	When a research design includes two independent variables, researchers can address: (1) two main effects (i.e., one for each independent variable) (2) an interaction effect (i.e., different combinations of the two independent variables)	Very strong; high potential for controlling all or most threats to internal validity

Note: The highlights reflect features that are included as part of the design, whereas gray highlights denote features that are not present. O_{pre} = pretest observation; O_{post} = posttest observation; X1X2 = reflects different levels that exist across the two independent variables; I = intervention group; C = control or comparison group; R = random assignment.

In addition to the separate effects of each independent variable, Mr. Fredericks also needs to be mindful about a potential interaction effect. An interaction effect can be phrased as a question: "Does the effect of the reading intervention (i.e., one of the independent variables) on student reading comprehension scores (i.e., dependent variable) vary or depend on the time-of-day (i.e., the second independent variable) the intervention was administered?" If Mr. Fredericks observed a statistically significant interaction, this communicates to him that while the positive effect of the reading intervention was possible, it likely had different effects depending on whether it was administered in the morning or afternoon. In other words, the difference in reading scores between the intervention and comparison group for the morning session might be much larger than the differences between groups in the afternoon.

THE TAKEAWAY

Regardless of the complexity of a true experimental design, random assignment and the use of multiple groups are key factors in controlling most threats to internal validity.

Statistics

All experimental designs, regardless of whether researchers use a pretest–posttest control group design, posttest-only control group design, or a factorial design, rely on inferential statistics to draw conclusions about group differences and whether those difference are large enough to be considered real. Because factorial designs include multiple independent variables, there is a need for more complex statistical approaches, such as two-way or three-way ANOVAS or ANCOVAS. Although we do not delve into much detail regarding the statistical nuances and complexities that exist with factorial design, we underscore the general premise that as the complexity of research designs increase (i.e., number of independent variables), the complexity of the corresponding statistical approaches will also likely increase.

Examining Experimental Research in the Literature

In this section, we present two peer-reviewed articles in the literature that used an experimental design to examine the effects of an intervention. We encourage you to complete the sequence of *Let's See It!*, *Let's Do It!*, and *You Do It!* activities to refine your understanding of experimental design principles and to begin developing your skills in applying them to your own research ideas.

Let's See It! 5.2

Goal: To Understand the Key Features of True Experimental Designs

The primary objective of this activity is to identify the key design features of two studies using an experimental design. Please review the summaries of Ansely et al. (2021) (Table 5.4) and Zimmerman and Kitsantas (1999) (Table 5.5). In addition to overall purpose and results, we identified issues pertaining to sample characteristics, nature of the intervention, design features that control for threats to internal validity, and statistical approaches. Pay particular attention to the description of the independent variable manipulation (i.e., describe the intervention) and the features used to control threats to internal validity. If you are interested in reading more specific or nuanced aspects about the design, please review the full article.

TABLE 5.4 ◼ True Experimental Designs	
Study	Ansley, B. M., Houchins, D. E., Varjas, K., Roach, A., Patterson, D., & Hendrick, R. (2021). The impact of an online stress intervention on burnout and teacher efficacy. *Teaching and Teacher Education, 98.* https://doi.org/10.1016/j.tate.2020.103251
Purpose	To examine the *causal effects* of an online stress intervention (i.e., independent variable) on teacher burnout, use of coping strategies and teacher self-efficacy for teaching (i.e., three dependent variables).
Sample	Fifty-nine participants volunteered for the study; however, 26 participants completed the entire intervention, while 25 participated in the control group. Majority of participants were active teachers with 0–5 years of experience (69%), female (80%), and working in traditional public schools (77%).
Nature of Intervention	Included eight, 30-minute asynchronous modules focused on strategies for coping with stress and developing social-emotional competencies that nurture positive learning experiences. Participants also developed goals and plans for independent practice of coping strategies. Five weeks were allotted to complete the program.
Design Features and Internal Validity	Pretest–posttest control group design was used. Use of a *control group* (controls for history, maturation, testing, and instrumentation). Participants were *randomly assigned* to an intervention group (*n* = 29) and a control group (*n* = 30) (controls for selection threat).
Statistics	Descriptive statistics (i.e., means, standard deviation); MANCOVA used to assess group differences on multiple variables and to control for background variables.
Results	In terms of the one *main effect*, the intervention group reported significantly greater reductions in stress, greater amount of time using coping strategies, and more positive perceptions of teaching self-efficacy than the control group teachers.

TABLE 5.5 ■ True Experimental Designs	
Study	Zimmerman, B. J., & Kitsantas, A. (1999). Acquiring writing revision skill: Shifting from process outcome goals self-regulatory goals. *Journal of Educational Psychology, 91*(2), 241–250. https://doi.org/10.1037/0022–0663.91.2.241
Purpose	To examine the *causal effects* of goal-setting and self-recording (i.e., two independent variables) on the writing skill, self-efficacy, self-reactions, interest, and attributions (i.e., five dependent variables) of high school students.
Sample	A total of 84 high school girls from a single high school were selected. The sample was ethnically diverse (Caucasian, 18%; African American, 15%; Hispanic, 45%; Asian, 14%), collectively exhibited above average writing skills (average score at 75th percentile).
Nature of Intervention	The intervention involved self-regulation features in a writing context. *Goal setting* had three levels (outcome, process, shifting goals). Students in the outcome goal focused on rewriting sentences with a minimum number of words; the process goal condition was prompted to focus on using the correct writing strategy; the shifting goal condition was prompted to start with an outcome goal but would shift to process goals. The *self-recording* condition had two levels (present or absent). Those who were asked to *self-record* either wrote down the number of words used in the writing revision or the number of steps of the writing strategy on which they focused.
Design Features and Internal Validity	Factorial design with two independent variables (i.e., goal setting, self-recording).
	Use of a *control group* (controls for history, maturation, testing, and instrumentation).
	Participants were *randomly assigned* to a control group or one of six intervention groups that varied across goal setting and self-recording: (1) outcome-recording, (2) outcome-no recording, (3) process-recording, (4) process-no recording, (5) shifting-recording, (6) shifting-no recording (controls for selection).
Statistics	Descriptive statistics (means, standard deviations, correlations among dependent variables) and inferential statistics (3 x 2 factorial ANOVA and *t*-tests).
Results	In terms of *main effects:* (1) The shifting goal group exhibited superior writing skills and psychological processes across all dependent variables than the other two groups (2) the recording condition resulted in more positive writing skills, self-efficacy, and self-reactions. Virtually all *interaction effects* were not statistically significant.

Let's Do It! 5.2

Guided Practice: To Practice Summarizing True Experimental Design Research

Goal: To Apply Knowledge of Experimental Design Features

The primary objective of this activity is for you to read an experimental study and practice identifying the essential features of the design. Cleary et al. (2017) examined the effects of a self-regulation intervention program across achievement and other important academic outcomes. As you read the article, we encourage you to use the materials addressed in the Let's See It! activity and the worksheet (Table 5.6). We also provide an answer key at the end of the chapter for you to self-check your work.

TABLE 5.6 ■ True Experimental Designs	
Study	Cleary, T. J., Velardi, B., & Schnaidman, B. (2017). Effects of the Self-Regulation Empowerment Program (SREP) on middle school students' strategic skills, self-efficacy, and mathematics achievement. *Journal of School Psychology, 64*, 28–42. http://dx.doi.org/10.1016/j.jsp.2017.04.004
Purpose	Is the overall purpose clear?
	Is a rationale for the study provided?
	Does it seem appropriate to examine the effectiveness of the intervention?
Sample	Is the description of the target sample clear?
	What are the key characteristics of the sample?
	How many participants were included?
Nature of Intervention	How did the authors define the independent variables? How many levels to the independent variable are there? What are the key components of the intervention?
Design Features and Internal Validity	To what extent did the authors try to ensure that the groups were similar aside from the grouping variable?
	Did the author consider or attempt to control for any other variables?
Statistics	Did the authors use any descriptive statistics to summarize the results?
	What type of inferential statistics were used (i.e., *t*-tests, ANOVA, chi-square tests etc.)?
Results	What are the key findings that relate to the research questions?
	Could conclusions be drawn about the causal effects of the intervention?

QUASI-EXPERIMENTAL DESIGNS

LEARNING OBJECTIVE	
5.5	Apply the core features of quasi-experimental designs.

Quasi-experimental designs approximate or come close to an experimental design but fall short in terms of controlling threats to internal validity. In a quasi-experiment, researchers will use *comparison groups* and/or a *time series feature* to minimize threats to internal validity but do not utilize *random assignment* (Figure 5.9). In most school settings, the use of random assignment procedures is not possible. Students are typically enrolled or placed into groups (e.g., sections of a class, type of reading) based on their individual academic needs or due to logistical or administrative constraints. When one also considers that most educational supports or interventions are administered during school hours and within a classroom setting, the prospect of a researcher randomly assigning students to an intervention or comparison condition is a daunting challenge. Thus, quasi-experiments represent an important and viable research design in school settings.

Two quasi-experiments are addressed in this chapter: nonequivalent control-group design and the interrupted time series design. For both designs, we address the same topics addressed

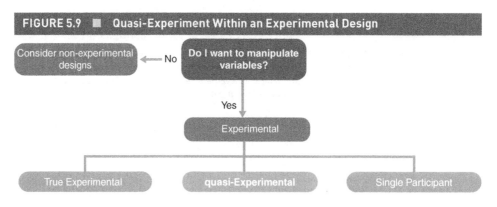

FIGURE 5.9 ■ Quasi-Experiment Within an Experimental Design

with true experiments: (a) nature of research questions, (b) design features linked to internal validity, and (c) statistics.

Nonequivalent Control Group Design

The nonequivalent control-group design is similar in structure and format to the highly regarded pretest–posttest control group design. In both designs, researchers use multiple groups, pretests, and posttests. The notable distinction is the absence of random assignment in the nonequivalent control group design.

Nature of Research Questions

In Figure 5.10, we present four research questions that can be addressed with quasi-experimental designs. As you review these questions, you likely will immediately notice that they are identical or very similar to the questions we included in the experimental design section (see Figure 5.3). In fact, the two questions highlighted in Figure 5.10 are identical to two questions in Figure 5.3.

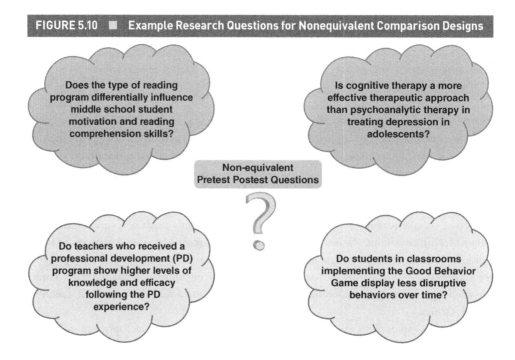

FIGURE 5.10 ■ Example Research Questions for Nonequivalent Comparison Designs

At first glance, this might strike you as odd; that is, how can different designs address the same question? The reality is that the difference between experimental and quasi-experimental designs has less to do with the target question being addressed (i.e., did the reading intervention cause improved reading scores) than it does in the level of confidence one can have in concluding the intervention was the cause of the effect. Our primary objective in this section is to help you understand how well quasi-experiments approximate or come close to the standards of a true experiment.

Design Features Linked to Internal Validity

In the simplest version of a nonequivalent control group design, researchers include two groups. One group receives the intervention or instructional program while the other group receives an alternative program (i.e., comparison group) or does not receive any type of program (i.e., a control group). The researcher would also administer measures before the intervention is implemented (i.e., pretest) and then again after it has been completed (i.e., posttest). Due to the presence of the comparison condition, the nonequivalent control-group design is a notable upgrade over the simplistic pre-experimental designs. As you may recall, the pre-experimental single group pretest–posttest design mentioned earlier in the chapter is identical to the nonequivalent control-group design *except* for comparison condition. The lack of a comparison condition is not a trivial matter, as it represents a key mechanism through which researchers can simultaneously rule out several threats to internal validity (e.g., history, maturation).

It is also important to note that the nonequivalent control-group design is very similar to the experimental designs mentioned in the prior section. However, this quasi-experimental is considered "less rigorous" because it does not utilize random assignment (see Figure 5.11). Let's consider a scenario with Mr. Fredericks to illustrate the strengths and limitations of the nonequivalent control group design. Unlike the prior example presented in the experimental design section, suppose Mr. Fredericks was not able to randomly assign participants to the different reading conditions. This constraint would prevent him from using a true experiment. Technically, he could use the pre-experimental single group pretest–posttest design, whereby he

---

FIGURE 5.11   ■   Components and Features of Nonequivalent Pretest–Posttest Design

Sequence of Assessment and Intervention	Design Features	Determination of Effect	Internal Validity
(I) O_{pre} X O_{post} (C) O_{pre} O_{post}	Pretest (O_{pre})	To determine the presence of an effect, one compares gain scores of the groups from pretest to posttest OR compares posttests for the groups. If groups show initial differences at pretest, researchers will statistically control for that variable	Moderately strong; does not take into account all potential group differences due to lack of random assignment
	Posttest (O_{post})		
	Intervention group (I)		
	Control group (C)		
	Comparison group (C_p)		
	Time series component		
	Random assignment of participants (R)		

Note: The highlights reflect features are included as part of the design, whereas gray highlights denote features that are not present. O_{pre} = pretest observation; O_{post} = posttest observation; X = intervention; I = intervention group; C = control or comparison group; R = random assignment.

gave the reading program to all students across his four sections. However, he is convinced that such a design is too weak to ever be considered.

After thinking through this issue, Mr. Fredericks had an idea. He decided to administer the reading program to the first and third sections (i.e., one morning and one afternoon) and then use his second and fourth sections (i.e., one morning and one afternoon) in the comparison condition. Thus, two of the classrooms received the new reading intervention while the other two classrooms received the standard reading curriculum. Mr. Fredericks also administered the same reading comprehension measure at pretest and posttest to students in all four classrooms. After collecting the posttest data, he compared the two conditions by using the independent *t*-test; a type of inferential statistic (see Chapter 13). The results revealed the students receiving the reading intervention displayed significantly higher levels of reading skill than the comparison classroom.

STOP AND THINK 5.6

In using a nonequivalent control group design, how confident can Mr. Fredericks be in concluding that the reading intervention was the primary cause of the observed effect? Explain.

In Figure 5.12, we provide an overview of the key strengths and weaknesses of the nonequivalent pretest posttest design with regards to internal validity. Using this table as well as your overall knowledge of internal validity, please complete the Stop and Think activity.

Statistics

The statistical approach used by researchers to examine group differences in quasi-experimental research parallels the approaches used in experimental designs; that is descriptive statistics (e.g., means, standard deviations) and some type of inferential statistic to assess group differences (e.g., *t*-tests or some variation of ANOVA)). However, because the nonequivalent control-group design does not control for selection (i.e., initial group equivalence), researchers will often gather background information about the sample (e.g., grade level, SES) as well as scores for other variables that may relate to the dependent variable. With this additional information, researchers can include these variables in statistical analyses to identify the presence of pretest-group differences on these variables prior to implementing the intervention. If no pretest-group differences are observed, the case for claiming that the reading intervention was the cause of the change is strengthened (although it will never reach the level of certainty as with experimental designs). On the other hand, if there are differences at pretest across these additional measures, researchers can use special procedures to "statistically control" for these variables (e.g., analysis of covariance [ANCOVA; see Chapter 13]). In practical terms, the phrase "statistically control" simply means that posttest scores for the groups are adjusted based on the pretest scores. Group differences are then evaluated using these adjusted scores.

Interrupted Time Series Design

Another common quasi-experimental approach is the interrupted time series design. Unlike the nonequivalent control-group design, which focuses on multi-group comparisons based on a single set of measurements at pretest and posttest, the interrupted time series design utilizes *repeated or continuous assessment* over time. This design is often used with a single group, although multiple groups can be used.

FIGURE 5.12 ■ Threats to Internal Validity in Mr. Frederick's Quasi-Experiment		
Threat to Internal Validity	Explanation of Potential Threat	Reason Why Threat to Internal Validity Is/is not Controlled or is not Applicable
History	IS IT POSSIBLE that some external factor operating in the middle school or for the seventh-grade students caused the observed reading group differences? **Highly unlikely**	If there was some external variable exerting an effect on reading in the seventh grade, Mr. Fredericks would have observed the effect across the intervention and comparison conditions.
Maturation	IS IT POSSIBLE that some natural developmental change led to the observed reading group differences? **Highly unlikely**	If there was an internal or developmental change happening among seventh-grade students, then that effect would have been observed across both conditions.
Testing	IS IT POSSIBLE that taking the pretest reading comprehension test naturally led students to perform better on the posttest? **Highly unlikely**	If there was a testing effect, then that effect would have been observed in the posttest across both conditions.
Instrumentation	IS IT POSSIBLE that the reading comprehension measure or the accuracy of this measure changed from pretest to posttest? **Highly unlikely**	In this specific scenario, the threat of instrumentation is not possible because of the nature of the reading test. The same test was administered at pretest and posttest. The scoring was also objective, so it is not realistic that any changes to measure occurred.
Selection	IS IT POSSIBLE that the different conditions demonstrated initial differences before the intervention began? **Yes, it is possible**	Given that there is no random assignment of students to groups, it is highly possible this design does not control initial group differences.

Note: Blue shading reflects threats that are likely controlled. Orange shading reflects threats that are not controlled.

Nature of Research Questions

In Figure 5.13, we present the same four research questions included in Figure 5.10. However, we now highlight two questions that are most logically addressed by the interrupted time series design. These two questions are distinct from the other questions because of their focus on a single group of individuals.

Design Features Linked to Internal Validity

The core distinguishing feature of a time series design is the repeated assessment of a specific behavior or skill across two distinct phases: baseline and intervention. A baseline phase is similar in concept to the pretest (i.e., data are collected before the intervention is introduced) but includes a minimum of three data points. The intervention phase also includes repeated assessments but reflects the period during which the intervention is implemented. In most situations for school-based research, a single group is utilized and assessed over time (see Figure 5.14 for essential features).

Multiple data points at baseline and intervention phases represent the central mechanism through which a time series design can rule out threats to internal validity. In all experimental designs discussed thus far in the chapter, researchers use a control or comparison group to rule

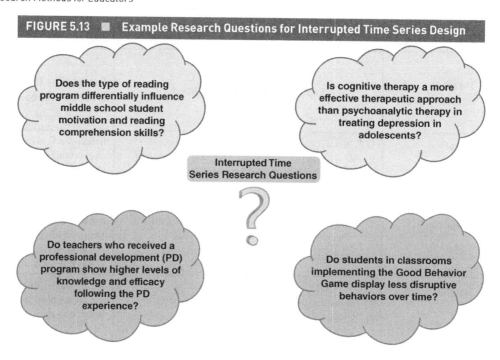

FIGURE 5.13 ■ Example Research Questions for Interrupted Time Series Design

FIGURE 5.14 ■ Components and Features of Interrupted Time Series Design

Sequence of Assessment and Intervention	Design Features	Determination of Effect	Internal Validity
(I) $O_{pre}O_{pre}O_{pre}$ X $O_{post}O_{post}O_{post}$	Pretest/Baseline phase (O_{pre})	Primary method is to compare changes in the level (i.e., average) and slope (i.e., trends or patterns) of data) from baseline to intervention phases	Moderately strong-does not control for historical factors or a potential interaction between pretest and the intervention
	Posttest/Intervention phase (O_{post})		
	Intervention group (I)		
	Control group (C)		
	Time series component		
	Random assignment of participants (R)		

Note: Green highlights reflect features that are included as part of the design, whereas blue highlights denote features that are not present. O_{pre} = pretest observation; O_{post} = posttest observation; X = intervention; I = intervention group; C = control or comparison; R = random assignment.

out most threats to internal validity. The comparison group serves as the benchmark against which to evaluate the effects on the intervention group. The basic logic is that if threats to internal validity are real (e.g., history, testing, etc.), researchers should observe these effects across both the intervention and comparison conditions. In the interrupted time series design, the repeated baseline assessments act as the essential comparison condition or point of reference needed to rule out threats to internal validity. Because the baseline is often extended over several weeks, a researcher could evaluate if changes in the dependent variable occurred before the intervention is implemented. If changes during baseline are observed, it is very likely that some external or internal factor is in effect. Thus, one of the key characteristics of a high-quality baseline is that the data collected during this phase is *stable.* Let's consider the time series design with Ms. Douglas and Jennifer and discuss how its features rule out threats to internal validity.

Suppose Ms. Douglas and Jennifer wanted to examine the effects of a supplemental reading program (i.e., pullout program) on the reading fluency of students scoring at the 25th percentile on a standardized measure of reading fluency. They did not have access to a comparison group given that most of the struggling readers wanted to participate in the supplemental program. Without a viable comparison group, Ms. Douglas and Jennifer could not use a true experimental or nonequivalent control group design. However, the interrupted time series design was a strong choice for evaluating intervention effects.

The supplemental reading program consisted of an additional 30-minute block of reading that emphasized the use of repeated readings and reciprocal peer tutoring. The program was administered three days per week over the course of 6 weeks (i.e., a total of 9 hours of additional instruction). Before administering this program, Ms. Douglas administered a one-minute reading fluency probe to all students two times per week over a span of three weeks. Thus, she gathered a total of six baseline data points. All students in her class then received the supplemental reading program for six weeks. During this six-week intervention phase, students were again administered the reading fluency probes two times per week, resulting in 12 intervention phase data points (see Figure 5.15).

To interpret the results, Ms. Douglas and Jennifer calculated the average reading score for the baseline data points and the average for intervention phase data. They then used a paired sample *t*-test and found that the group of at-risk readers demonstrated a significant level of growth in reading fluency scores from baseline to intervention. Because the time series design used by Ms. Douglas included only one group, you may be wondering whether this design is truly an improvement over the highly simplistic pre-experimental design discussed earlier in the chapter: the *one group pretest–posttest design.* Both designs use a single group and collect data prior to and after the intervention has been implemented. Thus, they both can clearly identify the presence or

FIGURE 5.15 ■ Interrupted Time Series Designs to Assess Effects of Supplemental Reading Program

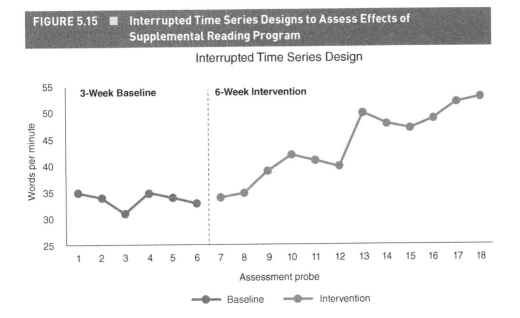

Interrupted Time Series Design

absence of an effect (i.e., change from pretest/baseline to posttest/intervention phase). The use of repeated or continuous assessment across the baseline and intervention phases, however, is what distinguishes the time series approach.

In Figure 5.16, we examine the various threats to internal validity and how the time series design handles these factors. As you can see, the time series design controls many threats but not all of them. As you review this table, please consider the following best practice guidelines for optimizing internal validity with a time series design:

- The pretest scores are stable (i.e., do not fluctuate) or exhibit a trend in the direction opposite of the intended intervention (i.e., students reading scores got worse during the baseline is the opposite effect of what one would expect of the reading intervention)

- The scores on the dependent variable change only after the intervention has been implemented

- The change in the data during the intervention phase occurs as quickly as possible after intervention implementation

To create the baseline, Ms. Douglas used brief reading comprehension probes twice a week over three weeks. As can be observed from Figure 5.15, the baseline data were stable (i.e., very

FIGURE 5.16 ■ Controlling Threats to Internal Validity in an Interrupted Time Series Design

Threat to Internal Validity	Explanation of Potential Threat	Reason Why Threat to Internal Validity Is/is not Controlled or is not Applicable
History	IS IT POSSIBLE that some external factor operating in the school or for the fifth-grade students caused the observed reading group differences? **Yes, it is possible**	Given the baseline and intervention phases occur at different points in time, it is possible that some external factor (i.e., besides the intervention) could have arisen or exerted its effects during the intervention phase only.
Maturation	IS IT POSSIBLE that some natural developmental change led to the observed reading group differences? **Highly unlikely**	If there was an internal or developmental change happening among fifth-grade students, then that effect would have likely been observed across both conditions.
Testing	IS IT POSSIBLE that taking the pretest reading comprehension test naturally led students to perform better on the posttest? **Highly unlikely**	If there was a testing effect, then that effect (change in scores) would have likely been observed during the baseline phase.
Instrumentation	IS IT POSSIBLE that changes in the nature or accuracy of a measurement occurred across different time points? **Highly unlikely**	If there was an effect based on the consistency or quality of the measurement tool, then one would likely have observed effects at some point during the baseline phase, rather than just when the intervention phase began.
Selection	IS IT POSSIBLE that the different conditions demonstrated initial differences before the intervention began? **Not applicable**	Given there is only one group in this design, the potential effect of selection is not applicable. Differential selection only can represent a problem when there are multiple groups being compared.

Note: Blue shading reflects threats that are likely controlled. Orange shading reflects threats that are not controlled. Red shading reflects that the threat is not applicable to this design and/or study.

little variation). With a stable baseline, it seems reasonable to conclude there was no external or internal threat to internal validity (i.e., if one of the threats was active, she would have observed changes in reading fluency during the baseline). Another important observation was that the reading fluency scores did not begin until the intervention was implemented. Thus, Ms. Douglas can feel confident about ruling out threats to maturation or testing.

However, this design does not rule out all threats to internal validity. In many cases, history threats are of primary concern (see Table 5.16). To rule out history, a design needs a comparison condition that occurs at the *same time* as the intervention condition. While the time series approach uses the baseline as the comparison, there is no distinct comparison condition that occurs during the intervention phase. The one situation in which history may not be a problem when using this time series design is in situations when the dependent variable changes immediately after the intervention is first introduced. If the effect is immediate and the baseline data are stable, it does not seem realistic that some external factor or event occurred at the precise moment when the intervention began. When the effect is delayed, however, things get murkier. As you can see in Figure 5.15, the observed effect occurred rapidly (i.e., began to emerge in Week 2 of the intervention). Thus, unless some external factor occurred during the first week of the reading fluency program, it does not seem likely that history was a key threat in this study (although a researcher cannot rule out this problem with full certainty).

To remedy the problem with a slow or delayed intervention effect, researchers can elect to incorporate a comparison group into a time series design. In this more complex design, two separate groups of individuals are repeatedly assessed at the baseline and intervention phases, but one group receives the intervention while the other does not. Although this design would effectively rule out all threats to internal validity, it is not a practical design in school settings because it requires repeated assessments across several classes and potentially grade levels (e.g., use of curriculum-based reading probes during the elementary school years). Most schools are not structured to accommodate this design, nor do they have the resources to routinely take on the level of testing and assessment that might be needed for the research study.

Statistics

To analyze time series data, researchers often use descriptive or visual analyses as well as inferential statistics. Visual inspection of data is typically performed in a descriptive sense; that is, researchers seek to identify trends and patterns in the data and look at changes in the data from baseline to intervention. Because visual inspection can only lead to speculations about an intervention effect, researchers strive to use formal statistical procedures to assess baseline to intervention phase changes within the single group. The most common analysis approaches include paired sample t-tests or repeated measures analysis of variance or even more complex approaches, such as latent growth modeling. Although there is variability in the complexity of these statistical methods, for the purposes of this textbook, just remember that the general objective in any time series design is to evaluate whether students' overall performance or trends in performance at intervention is better than what was observed at baseline.

THE TAKEAWAY

Although quasi-experimental designs do not control for all threats to internal validity, they represent a viable approach to examining intervention effects in school contexts.

Examining Quasi-Experimental Research From the Literature

In this section, we present two studies that utilized a quasi-experimental design. Consistent with the activities used for the experimental designs, we encourage you to complete all three: *Let's See It!*, *Let's Do It!*, and *You Do It!* activities. By going through each of these activities in sequence, you can further develop your basic knowledge of quasi-experimental designs and gain additional experience in applying your knowledge of this research design to your own unique research ideas.

Let's See It! 5.3

Goal: To identify and Explain the Key Features of a Quasi-Experimental Design

The primary objective of this activity is to help you identify the key features of a study using a quasi-experimental design. Please review the summaries of Bui and Fagan (2013) (Table 5.7) and McDaniels et al. (2016) (Table 5.8). In addition to overall purpose and results, we summarized sample characteristics, nature of intervention, design features to control for threats to internal validity, and statistics. Pay particular attention to the nature of the intervention and the mechanisms for controlling threats as they are central to understanding cause and effect. If you are interested in reading more specific or nuanced aspects of the design, please review the full article.

TABLE 5.7 ■ Quasi-Experimental Designs	
Study	Bui, Y. N., & Fagan, Y. M. (2013). The effects of an integrated reading comprehension strategy: A culturally responsive teaching approach for fifth-grade students' reading comprehension. *Preventing School Failure, 57*(2), 59–69. https://doi.org/10.1080/1045988X.2012.664581
Purpose	To examine the effects of two versions of the Integrated Reading Comprehension Strategy program (IRCS and IRCS Plus; 1 independent variable) on three reading skills in elementary school students: word recognition, reading comprehension, and story retell (i.e., 3 dependent variables)
Sample	Forty-nine 5th-grade students from two 5th-grade classrooms in an urban school district participated. Half of the students from each class received IRCS, while the remaining students received the IRCS plus a multicultural emphasis. The majority of the sample was Hispanic (84%), with all students receiving free or reduced lunch (100%).
Nature of Intervention	The two IRCS interventions were administered over five, 80-minute sessions. The sessions emphasized reading strategies, story grammar, and included modeling, guided practice, and independent practice. One version of IRCS utilized multicultural responsive teaching and cooperative learning while the other did not.
Design Features and Internal Validity	Nonequivalent pretest–posttest control group design.
	Use of pretest and posttest assisted with determining intervention effect.
	Use of a comparison group (IRCS vs. IRCS Plus; control for history, maturation, testing and instrumentation).
	Placing half of both classes in each condition ruled out threats to the teacher

Statistics	Descriptive statistics (mean, standard deviation) and inferential statistics (paired samples *t*-tests).
Results	The results showed that both IRCS groups displayed significant gains in word recognition, reading, comprehension and story retell, with no differences between the two groups at posttest.

TABLE 5.8 ■ Quasi-Experimental Designs

Study	McDaniels, S. C., Houchins, D. E., & Robinson, C. (2016). The effects of Check, Connect, and Expect on behavioral and academic growth. *Journal of Emotional and Behavioral Disorders, 24*(1), 42–53. https:doi.org/10.1177/1063426615573262
Purpose	To examine the effects of a behavioral intervention (i.e., 1 independent variable) on the daily progress reports, academic engagement, math skills, and reading skills (i.e., 4 dependent variables) of elementary school students
Sample	Twenty-two elementary school students with behavioral and or emotional disabilities from an alternative education school were recruited. Students ranged from Grades 2–4 but were primarily African American (64%) and male (86%).
Nature of Intervention	Check, Connect and Expect includes several components, including instruction in goal setting, progress monitoring, relationship building, and social skills and problem-solving. The program includes Basic Plus (faded monitoring plus home school collaboration), Basic (daily progress monitoring), and Self-Monitoring (i.e., student monitor own behavior).
Design Features and Internal Validity	Times series feature (controls for maturation, testing, maturation).
	Assessment at baseline and intervention phases.
	Single group interrupted time series design with baseline (4 weeks) and intervention phases (9 weeks).
Statistics	Descriptive statistics (mean, standard deviation) were used. Longitudinal growth models were used to examine differences in *level* (i.e., average, or mean value) and *slope* (i.e., pattern of data within a phase) of data across baseline and intervention phases.
Results	The single group showed a statistically significant improvement in the daily progress reports and their overall level of academic engagement, but no differences from baseline to intervention were noted for mathematics or reading skills.

Let's Do It! 5.3

Guided Practice: To Practice Summarizing the Quasi-Experimental Design

Goal: To Apply Knowledge of Quasi-Experimental Design Features

The primary objective of this activity is for you to get some practice in reading and reviewing a quasi-experimental study. To guide your thinking, we encourage you to use the information presented in the Let's See It! activities as well as the guiding questions in Table 5.9. We also provide an answer key at the end of the chapter for you to self-check your work.

TABLE 5.9 ■ Quasi-Experimental Designs	
Study	Fuchs et al. (2021). A quasi-experimental evaluation of two versions of first-grade PAKS: One with and one without repeated reading. *Exceptional Children, 87(2)*, 141–162. https://doi.org/10.1177/0014402920921828
Purpose	Is the overall purpose clear?
	Is a rationale for the study provided?
	Does it seem appropriate to examine the effectiveness of the intervention?
Sample	Is the description of the target sample clear?
	What are the key characteristics of the sample?
	How many participants were included?
Nature of Intervention	How did the authors define the independent variables?
	How many levels to the independent variable are there?
	What are the key components of the intervention?
Design Features and Internal Validity	To what extent did the authors try to ensure that the groups were similar aside from the grouping variable?
	Did the author consider or attempt to control for any other variables?
Statistics	Did the authors use any descriptive statistics to summarize the results?
	What type of inferential statistics were used (i.e., *t*-tests, ANOVA, chi-square tests, etc.)?
Results	What are the key findings that relate to the research questions?
	Could conclusions be drawn about the causal effects of the intervention?

SINGLE-PARTICIPANT DESIGNS

LEARNING OBJECTIVE

5.6   Apply the core features of single-participant experimental designs.

Most educators in K–12 contexts focus their instructional time and energy on large groups or entire classrooms of students. However, there are times when they work with specific individuals or perhaps a few students at a time. For example, students diagnosed with autism may require an intensive, individualized behavioral modification plan to enhance their functioning in the classroom, while students with a learning disability may need additional reading supports several times a week to improve their decoding, fluency, and/or comprehension skills. When the goal is to examine the effects of an intervention or remedial supports for a specific individual or very small group (e.g., 2–4 students), single-participant research designs (also called single-case or single-subject designs) represent a viable alternative to the more traditional group experimental design (Figure 5.17).

Single-participant research designs are similar in some respects to group experimental and quasi-experimental designs. At a general level, they all seek to examine whether intervention or

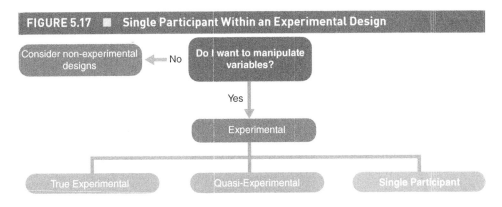

FIGURE 5.17 ■ Single Participant Within an Experimental Design

instructional programs are effective. Single-participant designs are very similar to the quasi-experimental interrupted time series design, given that they both rely on continuous or repeated assessment over time, collect multiple data points at baseline (labeled with A) and intervention phases (labeled with B), and use measures that are brief in nature and highly sensitive to change. All time series designs, regardless of whether they involve groups or individuals, establish a stable baseline of data points and then use that baseline as the benchmark against which to evaluate change or effects during the intervention phase. However, single participant and group time series approaches do differ in one critical way; the replication of the baseline-to-intervention phase sequence.

With single-participant designs, researchers replicate the baseline (A) to intervention (B) sequence in multiple ways to rule out threats to internal validity. The different ways in which the A-B sequence is repeated determines the specific nature of the single-participant design that is used: (1) withdrawal or reversal designs, (2) multiple baseline designs, and (3) changing criterion designs. In this chapter, we focus on the multiple baseline designs given its broad applicability and flexibility within most school contexts.

Multiple Baseline Designs

With a multiple baseline design, researchers replicate the A-B process across different *individuals, target behaviors*, or *settings*. This type of design is called "multiple baseline" because baseline data are gathered across multiple people (e.g., Michael, Gabrielle, and Walter), multiple behaviors of a single person (e.g., out-of-seat behavior, calling out, work completion), or multiple settings within which a single person functions (e.g., math class, science, class, art class). It is the use of these multiple baselines that enables researchers to rule out threats to internal validity.

Nature of Research Questions

In Figure 5.18, we present four research questions that can be addressed with a single-participant research design. As you review and reflect on these questions, consider the following observations: First, all the questions are geared around the issue of intervention efficacy. Thus, at a broad level, single-participant research designs, true experiments, and quasi-experiments all address the same core question, "Does the intervention work?" Second, if you identify the dependent variables for each question (e.g., out-of-seat behavior, reading fluency, self-efficacy beliefs, disruptive behaviors like calling out), you may notice that all of these behaviors can be assessed using time-limited, brief measures that can frequently and repeatedly be administered over the course of an intervention (e.g., 1-mintue reading fluence probe, single item self-efficacy

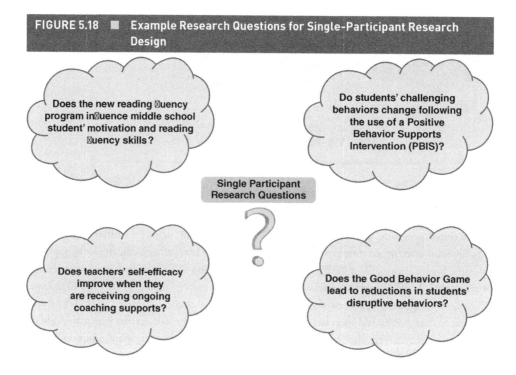

FIGURE 5.18 ■ Example Research Questions for Single-Participant Research Design

Does the new reading fluency program influence middle school student' motivation and reading fluency skills?

Do students' challenging behaviors change following the use of a Positive Behavior Supports Intervention (PBIS)?

Single Participant Research Questions

Does teachers' self-efficacy improve when they are receiving ongoing coaching supports?

Does the Good Behavior Game lead to reductions in students' disruptive behaviors?

questionnaire, direct observations of out-of-seat or disruptive behaviors). Due to the repeated assessment requirement of this design, it is not possible to administer lengthy or more comprehensive forms of assessment.

Design Features Linked to Internal Validity

The simplest version of a single-participant design is the basic A-B approach. With this design, multiple data points are gathered at baseline and intervention phases. To determine the presence of an effect, a researcher simply compares the average score or patterns of scores between these two phases (see Stop and Think activity). With a multiple baseline design, however, a researcher intentionally incorporates multiple A-B sequences. For multiple baseline designs across individuals, data within the A-B sequence is generated for each person in the design. If the multiple baselines reflect type of setting, then each A-B sequence reflects a different setting (e.g., science class, math class, social studies class).

STOP AND THINK 5.7

Which group designs discussed in this chapter does the simple A-B single-participant design appear to most closely resemble?

In Figure 5.19, we present the key features and components of the multiple baseline across individuals design. In looking at the first column of the table, you see two types of assessment: baseline (O_B) and intervention (O_I). Across all students (S1, S2, and S3), three data points are collected at baseline. Establishing the baseline across all individuals is always

FIGURE 5.19 ■ Components and Features of Multiple Baseline Designs

Sequence of Assessment and Intervention	Design Features	Determination of Effect	Internal Validity
(S1) $O_B O_B O_B$ $O_I O_I O_I$ $O_I O_I O_I$ (S2) $O_B O_B O_B$ $O_B O_B O_B$ $O_I O_I O_I$ (S3) $O_B O_B O_B$ $O_B O_B O_B$ $O_B O_B O_B$	Baseline phase (O_B) – similar to pretest Intervention phase (O_I) – similar to posttest Intervention at individual level – similar to intervention group Individuals as controls – similar to control group Time series component Random assignment of participants (R)	To determine the presence of an effect, one compares the change or discontinuity in data from baseline (pretest) to intervention phases (posttest).	Internal validity is established by comparing the intervention phases of one individual or condition relative to the baseline phase of the other individuals or conditions.

Note: Green highlights reflect features are included as part of the design; orange shading reflects features that could be applied but are often not applicable. O_B = baseline phase (pretest); O_I = intervention phase (posttest); S = student; R = random assignment.

the first step in this design. After a stable baseline is achieved for each person, S1 would be given the intervention *while the baseline assessment continues for S2 and S3.* Thus, the assessment of the dependent variable continues for all individuals regardless of whether they receive the intervention. After the first A-B sequence has been established (e.g., for S1), the researcher would then administer the intervention to S2. Again, the assessment continues for all students, but the data for S1 and S2 would be considered intervention phase data, while the data for S3 still reflect a baseline (i.e., they have not received the intervention yet). After the A-B sequence for S2 is established, S3 would then receive the intervention to establish the third A-B sequence. In short, when using a multiple baseline design across individuals, the number of A-B sequences should match the number of individuals included in the study.

Let's illustrate this design in the scenario with Ms. Douglas and Jennifer. Suppose there were a few students in their class (i.e., Michael, Gabrielle, and Walter) who, despite receiving the new classroom reading program, have not shown growth in their reading fluency skills. Ms. Douglas felt these students needed additional instruction and practice and thus wanted to provide them with a supplemental reading fluency program. Given the small number of students and their access to brief reading fluency probes, Ms. Douglas and Jennifer felt that a multiple baseline design across individuals was the best choice to evaluate the effects of the pullout program.

Before beginning the intervention, Ms. Douglas asked Jennifer to establish a reading fluency baseline for all three students. With the help of the reading specialist at the school, Jennifer administered 1-minute reading fluency probe to the students three times per week for two weeks (i.e., 6 total data points). These measures are easy to administer, brief in nature, and are sensitive to change. When establishing the baseline for each student, Ms. Douglas made sure the data were stable (i.e., the data points did not show a lot of variability; see Figure 5.15). As noted previously, a stable baseline is essential for any time series design because it rules out the presence of external or internal factors as causes of the target behavior.

After ensuring stability at baseline, Ms. Douglas then administered the intervention to Michael but *not* to Gabrielle or Walter. This "differential delay" (i.e., implementing the intervention with Michael but maintaining Gabrielle and Walter at baseline) is the most fundamental aspect of the multiple baseline design because it sets the stage or creates the opportunity for addressing the same two questions addressed by all experimental designs: (1) Was there an intervention effect? (2) What was the primary cause of that effect?

In the multiple baseline design, the first question is addressed by examining the pattern of *within-individual* A-B changes for each student. Because there were three students, three within-individual A-B changes are examined (see Figure 5.20). Given that Michael was the first individual to receive the intervention, Ms. Douglas is primarily interested in examining changes in his pattern of reading fluency scores across baseline and intervention. As you can see in Figure 5.20, the first six intervention data points for Michael represent a clear upward trend or improvement in his fluency skills. After this effect is established, Ms. Douglas continued providing the intervention to Michael but then also introduced it to Gabrielle. The reading fluency probes were continually administered to all three students. After the A-B effect for Gabrielle was identified, Walter began receiving the intervention. Again, because there were three students in this design, there are three opportunities to

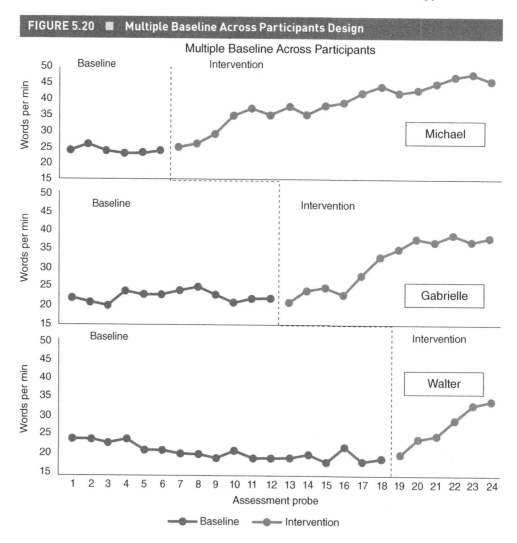

FIGURE 5.20 ■ Multiple Baseline Across Participants Design

observe or replicate the desired intervention effect (i.e., shift from A to B phases). Based on Figure 5.20, there is relatively strong evidence about the positive effects of the intervention because for all students

- The baseline fluency scores were stable and low prior to the intervention
- The fluency scores only began to change after the intervention was introduced
- A similar A-B effect was observed for all three students

Although Ms. Douglas was excited about these findings, she still needed to think about whether the fluency intervention was the actual cause of the A-B changes or if other factors could explain the changes. In other words, how strong was the internal validity of this study design? With a multiple baseline design, threats to internal validity are most effectively controlled by making *between-individual* A-B comparisons (see Figure 5.20). As you may recall, in group experimental designs researchers compare the average score of the intervention group to the average score of the control or comparison condition. The comparison condition is essential for ruling out threats to internal validity because it occurs during the same period as the intervention. This between-individual comparison enables researchers to assess changes in students who received and did not receive the intervention.

In single-participant designs, the multiple baselines serve as the comparison conditions. That is, the pattern of intervention phase scores for one individual is directly compared to the pattern of baseline scores of the individuals who have not yet received the intervention. In the scenario with Ms. Douglas, there were two possible between-individual comparisons to observe (see Figure 5.20):

- Michael's intervention scores compared to Gabrielle's and Walter's baseline scores
- Gabrielle's intervention scores compared to Walter's baseline scores

THE TAKEAWAY

It is through the replication of within-individual A-B changes that one determines the presence of an effect and the use of between-individual A-B comparison that one can rule out threats to internal validity.

In looking at Figure 5.20, Ms. Douglas would first look to determine whether the fluency scores for Michael changed only after the intervention is introduced (i.e., within individual A-B change). Once this effect is confirmed, she would then compare Michael's intervention phase data to the baseline fluency scores for Gabrielle and Walter. Because their fluency scores were maintained at the baseline level but Michael's fluency scores improved during this same period, it is not likely that a historical or any other factor produced the observed change. The next between-individual comparison would involve intervention phase data for Gabrielle and the baseline data for Walter. To deepen your understanding about these within-individual and between-individual A-B comparisons, please complete the *Let's See It!* and *Let's Do It!* activities at the end of this section.

Statistics

To analyze time series data, researchers often use descriptive or visual analyses as well as inferential statistics. Visual inspection of data is typically performed in a descriptive sense; that is, researchers seek to identify trends and patterns in the data and look at changes in the data from baseline to intervention. Because visual inspection can only lead to speculations about the presence of an observed effect, researchers tend to emphasize formal statistical procedures to assess baseline to intervention phase changes within the single group. Researchers can use simple inferential statistics, such as paired sample tests or repeated measures analysis of variance, or even more complex approaches, such as latent growth modeling. For our purposes in this textbook, just remember that with time series designs, researchers are most interested in understanding whether students' overall performance or trends in performance at intervention is better than what was observed at baseline.

Using Features of Single-Participant Designs to Rule Out Threats to Internal Validity

In this section, we present *Let's See It!* and *Let's Do It!* activities to enhance your skills in explaining how single-participant research designs can rule out threats to internal validity. The *Let's See It!* activity reflects the inherent limitations in using an A-B design, while the *Let's Do It!* activity reflects the more complex multiple baseline design.

Let's See It! 5.4

Goal: To Illustrate the Use of Within-Person and Between-Person A-B comparisons

The primary objective of this activity is to illustrate how a multiple baseline across individuals design can effectively rule out threats to internal validity. Please refer to Figure 5.20 as you review the summary Table 5.10. We also encourage you to use the IS IT POSSIBLE prompt to remind you take on a detective-like mindset to rule out threats to internal validity. The single-case research design scenario used in this activity is the same one discussed in the chapter with Michael, Gabrielle, and Walter.

TABLE 5.10 ■ Threats to Validity		
Threat to Internal Validity	Explanation of Potential Threat	Reason Why Threat to Internal Validity Is/Is Not Controlled or Not Applicable
History	*IS IT POSSIBLE that some external factor operating on the students caused the A-B changes in fluency scores rather than the fluency intervention?* **HIGHLY UNLIKELY**	In looking at Figure 5.11, please note two comparisons: (a) Michael's intervention data versus the baseline data for Gabrielle and Walter, (b) Gabrielle intervention data versus Walter's baseline. Because the baseline data for Gabrielle and Walter (when compared to Michael's intervention data) and for Walter (when compared to Gabrielle's intervention data) *did not change* until the intervention was introduced, it does not seem likely that external factors were at play.

Threat to Internal Validity	Explanation of Potential Threat	Reason Why Threat to Internal Validity Is/Is Not Controlled or Not Applicable
Maturation	*IS IT POSSIBLE that some natural developmental change led to the A-B changes in fluency scores rather than the fluency intervention?* **HIGHLY UNLIKELY**	Same rationale as preceding. If maturation effects were operational, then one would have likely observed this at some point for one of the cases.
Testing	*IS IT POSSIBLE that taking the pretest reading comprehension test naturally led to the A-B changes in fluency scores rather than the fluency intervention?* **HIGHLY UNLIKELY**	If the fluency assessment probe influenced performance on subsequent probes, one would likely have observed this effect as part of the lengthy baselines for Gabrielle and Walter.
Instrumentation	*IS IT POSSIBLE that changes in the nature or accuracy of a measurement led to the A-B changes in fluency scores rather than the fluency intervention?* **HIGHLY UNLIKELY**	The same measure was used throughout the entire data collection process. It does not make sense for the nature of the measurement tool to change only when the intervention was introduced for all three students.
Selection	*IS IT POSSIBLE that differences in the students selected for the study differed on some variables prior to receiving the fluency intervention and those differences led to changes in A-B scores rather than the intervention?* **HIGHLY UNLIKELY**	Although there could be pre-existing individual differences among the three students, this threat is not likely given that all three showed similar A-B changes and that their fluency skills did not change until they received the intervention.

Let's Do It! 5.4

Guided Practice: To Practice Summarizing the Single-Participant Designs

Goal: To Practice Examining Within-Individual and Between-Individual Comparisons

Tony, Robin, and Shalonda are third-grade students who struggle with mathematics computational skills. Ms. Thompson is a mathematics specialist in the school district and wants to provide an intervention program that research has shown to improve basic computational skills in elementary school children. However, she wants to examine its effectiveness with students within her district. Ms. Thompson used a multiple baseline across individual design to show these effects. She used a mathematic assessment probe shown to be effective for detecting intervention changes over time. Using the baseline and intervention data presented in Figure 5.21, please discuss using Table 5.11 and whether any factors undermine her ability to conclude that the math intervention improved math outcomes.

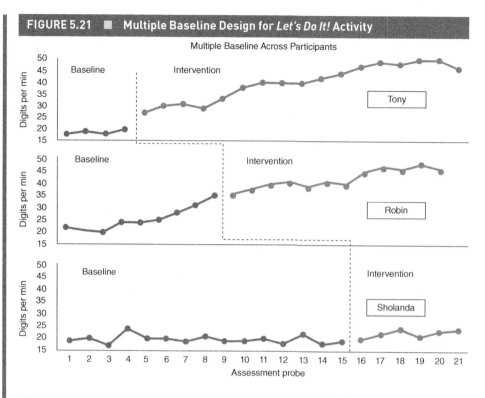

FIGURE 5.21 ■ Multiple Baseline Design for *Let's Do It!* Activity

Multiple Baseline Across Participants

TABLE 5.11 ■ Threats to Validity

Threat to Internal Validity	Explanation of Potential Threat	Reason Why Threat to Internal Validity Is/Is Not Controlled or Not Applicable
History	*IS IT POSSIBLE that some external factor operating on the students caused the A-B changes in computational scores rather than the mathematics intervention?* **Response:**	
Maturation	*IS IT POSSIBLE that some natural developmental change led to the A-B changes in computational scores rather than the mathematics intervention?* **Response:**	
Testing	*IS IT POSSIBLE that taking the pretest reading comprehension test naturally led to the A-B changes in computational scores rather than the mathematics intervention?* **Response:**	
Instrumentation	*IS IT POSSIBLE that changes in the nature or accuracy of a measurement led to the A-B changes in computational scores rather than the mathematics intervention??* **Response:**	
Selection	*IS IT POSSIBLE that differences in the students selected for the study differed on some variables prior to receiving the mathematics intervention and those differences led to A-B changes in computational scores rather than the intervention?* **Response:**	

ETHICAL CONSIDERATIONS

Given increased expectations among educators to make data-informed decisions about instructional and intervention initiatives, it is critical that they first learn the basics for evaluating effectiveness of these programs. In this chapter, we addressed how several concepts, such as comparison conditions and random assignment, enable educators to draw accurate and meaningful conclusions about the interventions or programs they implement. However, there are several ethical issues that may arise when using experimental designs in schools.

Access to Interventions and Programs

The general ethical principle of *justice* emphasizes the importance of ensuring that all individuals have equitable access to and can benefit from the programs, procedures, and services provided by professionals. As you might have already learned, the most rigorous experimental designs (i.e., true experimental and quasi-experimental designs) involve situations where some individuals receive an intervention or programs (i.e., intervention condition) while others do not (i.e., comparison or control groups). Although random assignment can be used to create a level of fairness in terms of who gets access to the intervention (i.e., all students have an equal chance and opportunity to receive the intervention), it does create the situation whereby some students receive a potentially effective intervention while others may not. With knowing that an interview is withheld from some students, what should a researcher do? Is the use of experimental methodology simply unethical in schools? The answer to this latter question is not a simple yes or no. On one hand, it is imperative to always place primary importance on the welfare of children and adolescents. However, it is also meaningful to use the most rigorous research designs possible so that educators have a clear sense of which instructional programs or initiatives make a difference. One reasonable solution to this dilemma is to ensure that all participants in a research study (i.e., regardless of intervention condition) receive the intervention, whether during the study or immediately thereafter. Thus, if a target intervention is shown to increase reading skills, then a control or comparison group should get access to that intervention after the study is completed. This methodological approach reflects the use of a waitlist control group feature as part of the design. That is, students who were initially in the control or comparison condition would receive the intervention following the initial intervention group receiving the intervention.

A similar ethical dilemma arises when using single-participant research designs. In reflecting back to the multiple baseline design scenario with Michael, Gabrielle, and Walter, you may recall that Walter did not receive the intervention until almost a month after Michael first received it. Is it ethical to delay the intervention for Walter for over a month even when Walter has been identified as academically at-risk? As educators, we all want to provide the most effective interventions to all students who may benefit from them. Thus, weighing the benefits and limitations of conducting experiments in schools must always be considered. A key benefit of using experimental designs is to identify whether an intervention program directly influences student outcomes. Implementing new instructional or intervention programs requires and allocation of time, personnel, and other resources. Thus, generating strong evidence about the casual impact of an intervention is essential within the data-based decision-making process in schools. As discussed, the key drawback of experimental designs is withholding the intervention from some students while others receive it. This latter issue can become a major problem when the students exhibit serious or highly disruptive behaviors, such as verbal or physical aggression or significant social difficulties. Thus, each situation needs to be closely examined to balance the need for scientific rigor in the work we do in schools versus the immediate needs of the students and teachers whom we serve.

THE TAKEAWAY

Researchers must always grapple with the tension between serving the needs of vulnerable students within schools and ensuring that high-quality research designs are used.

AMERICAN PSYCHOLOGICAL ASSOCIATION STYLE

LEARNING OBJECTIVE

5.8   Utilize the *Publication Manual of the American Psychological Association* in reporting and presenting findings from experimental studies.

As mentioned throughout this chapter, the main purpose of experimental designs is to establish a causal link among variables (see Table 5.12 for a summary of experimental designs discussed in this chapter). To identify this causal relationship, the researcher needs to manipulate one or more independent variables (i.e., creating different reading conditions) and then measure the impact of this manipulation on one or more dependent measures (e.g., reading comprehension skills). Because manipulating the independent variables is an intentional act of the researcher, they will normally have specific hypotheses in mind. For example, Ms. Douglas used the new class-wide reading program because she believed it would have a positive influence on students' reading skills. If she conducted her study and then wanted to write up her results for submission to a journal, she would need to clearly state her research questions and the corresponding hypotheses at the end of the introduction section. For example, she may state, "It is hypothesized that students receiving the reading comprehension program will exhibit higher levels of reading comprehension and fluency skills than students who did not receive the intervention."

Whenever communicating experimental hypotheses in a journal article, researchers also need to explicitly describe the rationale or justification for them. In most cases, hypothesis statements can be justified using theory or prior research. For example, if the new reading comprehension program emphasized social cognitive theory principles (e.g., modeling, guided practice) and had been shown in prior research to be effective with students different from the target sample, she can use this theoretical and empirical foundation to justify her hypothesis statement. Importantly, Ms. Douglas should revisit these hypotheses in the discussion section of the paper. Researchers are expected to not only state whether their original hypotheses were confirmed but to also provide an explanation if unexpected findings were observed. Thus, if Ms. Douglas observed that the reading comprehension program was effective, then she would make this statement while also providing evidence from the existing literature that aligns with her findings. Conversely, if the reading intervention was not effective, she needs to discuss these unexpected

Name of Design	Category of Design	Nature of Sample	Mechanisms to Enhance Claims of Effectiveness
TABLE 5.12 ■ Summary of Core Characteristics of Experimental Design Variations			
One group pretest–posttest design	Pre-experiment	One group	Pretest–posttest
Nonequivalent control group design	Quasi-experiment	Two or more groups	Pretest–posttest Control group
Interrupted time series design	Quasi-experiment	One group (could be expanded to multiple groups)	Baseline (stability) Comparing baseline and intervention phases
Pretest–posttest control group design (1 independent variable)	True experiment	Two or more groups	Pretest–posttest Comparison or control Random assignment
Factorial design (2 or more independent variables)	True experiment	Two or more group	Pretest–posttest Control group Random assignment
Single-participant research design	Single participant	One or several individuals	Baseline (stability) Comparing baseline and intervention phases

findings and offer potential explanations about why they might have occurred (see Chapter 15 for a more detailed discussion of communication of research).

Another critical aspect of communicating experimental research is to explicitly describe the experimental design procedures and the nature of the intervention. Regardless of whether one finds support for a given intervention, other researchers may want to replicate the study to confirm the findings. To do this, researchers need to describe the experimental design features clearly and explicitly (e.g., use of comparison condition, random assignment, nature of manipulation, etc.) as well as the nature of the intervention and how it was implemented. In the scenario with Ms. Douglas, she would need to describe the different modules of the intervention, the specific instructions that were provided to students, the individuals who administered the intervention, and information pertaining to the duration, length, and context of the sessions.

THE TAKEAWAY

Being explicit about the nature of the intervention and the overall procedure for implementation is a key ingredient for ensuring that research can be independently replicated by others.

CHAPTER SUMMARY

All experimental designs presented in this chapter address questions related to the causal effects of an intervention, instructional program, or other experience. The most essential quality of an experimental design involves its ability to rule out or control threats to internal validity. For group designs, researchers rely on comparison or control conditions, random assignment, pre-tests and posttest, or time series features. The use of comparison or control groups helps to rule out most threats to internal validity, while random assignment is essential for establishing initial group equivalence (i.e., controlling the threat of selection). When researchers are not able to randomly assign students to groups (i.e., quasi-experiments) and cannot form or use adequate comparison groups (i.e., pre-experimental designs), it is much more difficult to draw causal inferences regarding the link between an intervention and the target outcomes. With single-participant designs, researchers focus on replicating the basic A-B sequence across individuals, contexts, or behaviors to rule out threats to internal validity.

As we conclude this chapter, we hope you recognize the prior point made regarding the distinction between *scientific rigor* (i.e., how well a design enhances internal validity) and *practicality* and *feasibility* (i.e., the extent to which a design can realistically and practically be used in school settings) of research designs. As you likely will experience, there is often a tradeoff between high rigor (e.g., true experiments) and practicality (i.e., pre-experiments, quasi-experiments) when conducting experiments. When using a design with a high level of scientific rigor, one can more confidently claim that the target intervention was the cause of the desired outcomes. However, with increased rigor comes increased costs, time, and resource allocation. Thus, the most rigorous experimental designs are often difficult to implement in schools. On the flip side, with more simple experimental designs it is more practical and easier to implement them in schools, but the quality of the inferences or conclusions one can make about the effects of an intervention dramatically decrease.

EXTENSION ACTIVITIES

You Do It! 5.1

Devising an Experimental Design

Self-Directed Practice: Thinking Through Important Issues When Developing an Experimental Study

Experimental designs are a powerful but somewhat complex approach for determining the effects of an intervention on one or more outcomes. In this *You Do It!* extension activity, your task is to generate the basic ideas and framework for conducting an experimental study. We encourage you to think about a type of instruction, academic program, or intervention that is often used in school contexts. To help you create your study, use the *You Do it! Worksheet* (Table 5.13) and the *Experimental Design Decision Making Guide* (Figure 5.22) as a type of scaffold or guide to your thinking and generation of the study design.

You Do It! 5.2

Devising a Quasi-experimental Design

Self-Directed Practice: Thinking Through Important Issues When Developing a Quasi-experimental Design

Quasi-experimental designs can help you identify the effectiveness of school-based initiatives or even your own teaching on student learning. In this *You Do It!* extension activity, your task is to first identify a topic of interest to you that could be examined using either a nonequivalent pre-test–posttest design or an interrupted time series approach. We encourage you to use the *You Do it! Worksheet* (Table 5.14) and the *Quasi-Experimental Design Decision-Making Guide* (Figure 5.23) as

FIGURE 5.22 ■ True Experiment Design Decision-Making Guide

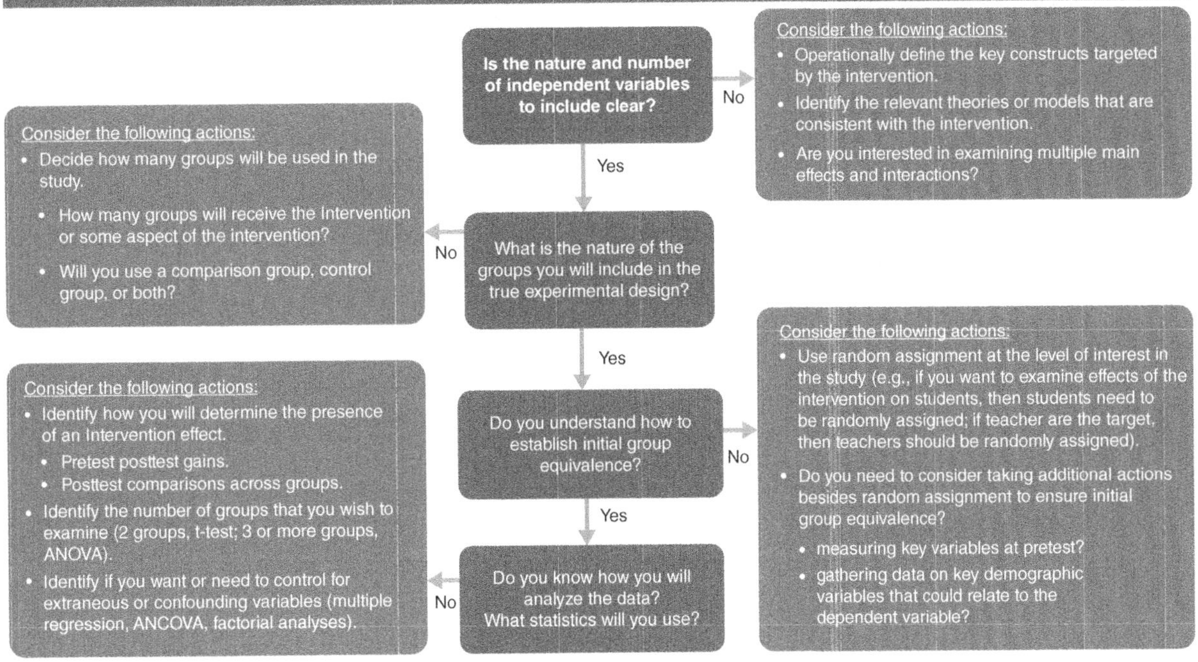

Is the nature and number of independent variables to include clear?

No → Consider the following actions:
- Operationally define the key constructs targeted by the intervention.
- Identify the relevant theories or models that are consistent with the intervention.
- Are you interested in examining multiple main effects and interactions?

Yes ↓

What is the nature of the groups you will include in the true experimental design?

No → Consider the following actions:
- Decide how many groups will be used in the study.
  - How many groups will receive the intervention or some aspect of the intervention?
  - Will you use a comparison group, control group, or both?

Yes ↓

Do you understand how to establish initial group equivalence?

No → Consider the following actions:
- Use random assignment at the level of interest in the study (e.g., if you want to examine effects of the intervention on students, then students need to be randomly assigned; if teacher are the target, then teachers should be randomly assigned).
- Do you need to consider taking additional actions besides random assignment to ensure initial group equivalence?
  - measuring key variables at pretest?
  - gathering data on key demographic variables that could relate to the dependent variable?

Yes ↓

Do you know how you will analyze the data? What statistics will you use?

No → Consider the following actions:
- Identify how you will determine the presence of an intervention effect.
  - Pretest posttest gains.
  - Posttest comparisons across groups.
- Identify the number of groups that you wish to examine (2 groups, t-test; 3 or more groups, ANOVA).
- Identify if you want or need to control for extraneous or confounding variables (multiple regression, ANCOVA, factorial analyses).

TABLE 5.13 ■ True Experimental Designs—*You Do It!* Worksheet

Purpose	What is the effect that you are trying to examine?
	Is the nature of the independent variable clear?
Sample	Who should be the sample used for this study.
	What are the key characteristics of this sample?
	Is the use of your specifically defined sample justified?
Nature of Intervention	What is the nature of your intervention?
	What specifically will be manipulated and what are the key defining features and procedures of the intervention?
	How many levels or subgroups will the intervention have?
Design Features and Internal Validity	What are the key design features that you will use to ensure that threats to internal validity are controlled?
	If your design cannot control all potential threats, are there any additional things you consider? (i.e., creative ways to control these threats).
Statistics	Which types of descriptive statistics are most relevant to present in your study?
	Which type of inferential statistics will be needed to examine group differences
	Did you consider the number of groups and the potential need to control certain variables when selecting the inferential test?

FIGURE 5.23 ■ Quasi-Experiment Design Decision-Making Guide

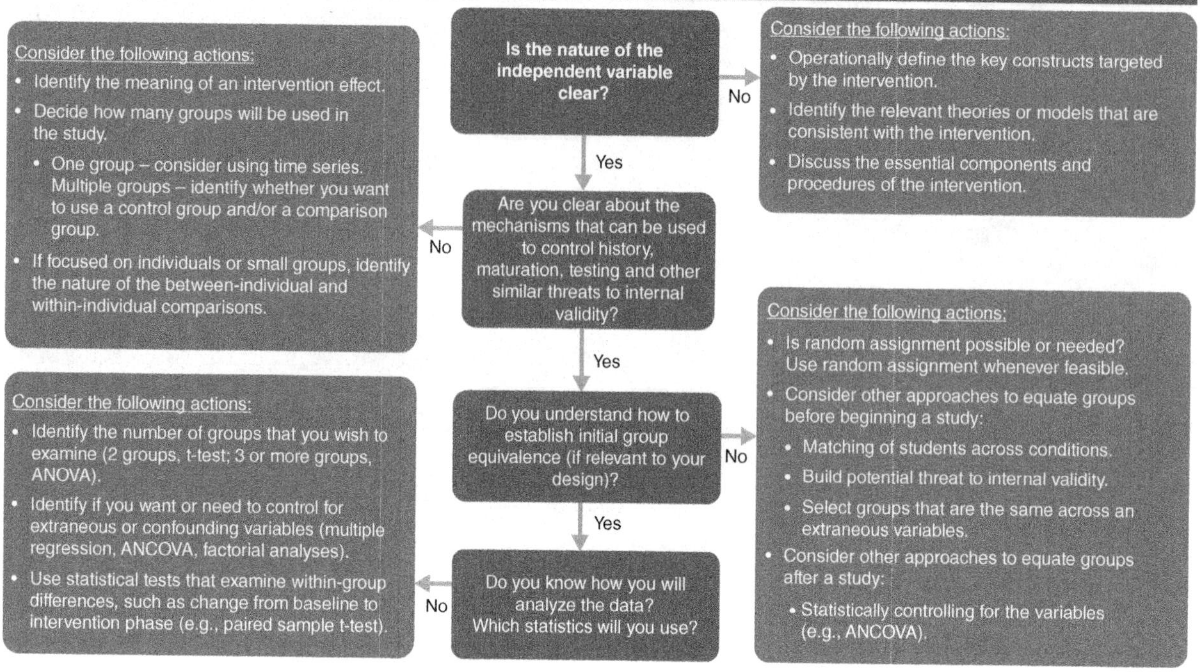

Consider the following actions:
- Identify the meaning of an intervention effect.
- Decide how many groups will be used in the study.
  - One group – consider using time series. Multiple groups – identify whether you want to use a control group and/or a comparison group.
- If focused on individuals or small groups, identify the nature of the between-individual and within-individual comparisons.

Is the nature of the independent variable clear?

Consider the following actions:
- Operationally define the key constructs targeted by the intervention.
- Identify the relevant theories or models that are consistent with the intervention.
- Discuss the essential components and procedures of the intervention.

Are you clear about the mechanisms that can be used to control history, maturation, testing and other similar threats to internal validity?

Consider the following actions:
- Identify the number of groups that you wish to examine (2 groups, t-test; 3 or more groups, ANOVA).
- Identify if you want or need to control for extraneous or confounding variables (multiple regression, ANCOVA, factorial analyses).
- Use statistical tests that examine within-group differences, such as change from baseline to intervention phase (e.g., paired sample t-test).

Do you understand how to establish initial group equivalence (if relevant to your design)?

Consider the following actions:
- Is random assignment possible or needed? Use random assignment whenever feasible.
- Consider other approaches to equate groups before beginning a study:
  - Matching of students across conditions.
  - Build potential threat to internal validity.
  - Select groups that are the same across an extraneous variables.
- Consider other approaches to equate groups after a study:
  - Statistically controlling for the variables (e.g., ANCOVA).

Do you know how you will analyze the data? Which statistics will you use?

TABLE 5.14 ■ Quasi-Experimental Designs

Purpose	What is the effect that you are trying to examine?
	Is the nature of the independent variable clear?
Sample	Who should be the sample used for this study?
	What are the key characteristics of this sample?
	Is the use of your specifically defined sample justified?
Nature of Intervention	What is the nature of your intervention?
	What specifically will be manipulated and what are the key defining features and procedures of the intervention?
	How many levels or subgroups will the intervention have?
Design Features and Internal Validity	What are the key design features that you will use to ensure that threats to internal validity are controlled?
	If your design cannot control all potential threats, are there any additional things you consider (i.e., creative ways to control these threats)?
Statistics	Which types of descriptive statistics are most relevant to present in your study?
	Which type of inferential statistics will be needed to examine group differences (i.e., t-tests, ANOVA, chi-square tests, etc.)?
	Did you consider the number of groups and the potential need to control certain variables when selecting the inferential test?

a type of scaffold or guide in your analysis of the design features. The troubleshooting guide is very similar to the ones used for the *You Do It!* extension activities for experimental designs.

KEY TERMS

Baseline phase	Nonequivalent control group design
Comparison group	Posttest
Control group	Posttest-only control group design
Factorial design	Pre-experimental design
History	Pretest
Instrumentation	Pretest–posttest control group design
Interaction effect	Random assignment
Interrupted time series design	Selection
Intervention group	Single group pretest–posttest design
Intervention phase	Testing
Main effect	Threats to internal validity
Maturation	Time series component
Multiple baseline design	Waitlist control group

ANSWER KEY

Stop and Think Activities

STOP AND THINK 5.1

To determine whether an effect has occurred for most of the group experimental or quasi-experimental designs, researchers rely on pretest and posttest scores for the groups. Researchers can compare the gain scores for each group (i.e., difference between pretest and posttest scores for each group) or simply compare the posttest scores for each group (i.e., assuming the pretest scores for the groups are equivalent). For time series designs, researchers identify an intervention effect by examining the patterns of scores at baseline to the score obtained during the intervention phase. They can use visual analysis of graphs to identify changes in trends in scores, or they can calculate the average baseline and intervention score and then compare those scores.

To address internal validity or the extent to which one can claim the intervention caused the observed effect, most group experimental designs rely on the use of comparison or control groups, random assignment (i.e., to equate the groups before the study begins), and or the use of pretest scores (i.e., to identify whether groups are equal on one or more specific variables before the study begins). The baseline to intervention phase comparisons of time series designs is the basis for ruling out threats to internal validity.

STOP AND THINK 5.2

One of the most effective ways to rule out threats to internal validity for any research design is to ensure that a benchmark or comparison condition exists. In most group designs, a comparison or control group serves this function. With the one-group pretest–posttest design, there is no comparison. Thus, there is no way to know whether a pretest to posttest change was the result of the intervention or other events or experiences occurring during the course of the intervention (i.e. . history), natural changes within the individuals (i.e., maturation), the effects of pretest assessment (i.e., testing), or changes to the assessment over time (i.e., instrumentation).

If any of these threats rather than the intervention had an effect on the posttest scores, researchers would be able to see these effects across both the intervention or comparison groups. Random assignment is another feature that rules out threats to internal validity but is not relevant in a one-group pretest–posttest design because there is only one group (i.e., all students get placed in the one intervention condition).

Stop and Think 5.3

Random assignment *helps to ensure* that multiple groups are equivalent at pretest, but it *does not guarantee* equivalency. Thus, the use of pretests and random assignments can help researchers confirm that the random assignment process worked as intended. Because pretests do not address every variable or factor, researchers will often use pretests to address the most important or relevant variables that may relate to the dependent variables of interest.

Stop and Think 5.4

Generally speaking, pretests represent an important aspect of an experimental design. They help to calculate gain scores and can be used to ensure initial group equivalence. However, they can create some problems in some situations. Because pretests are administered immediately prior to an intervention, there is potential for a testing-by-intervention interaction to emerge. That is, taking a pretest may influence how participants think or react to an intervention (e.g., taking a pretest may reveal the intent or purpose of the experiment, which causes a person to react differently). Thus, pretests can create a level of doubt about whether the intervention alone caused an observed change or if the change was due to the combined effects of the pretest and the intervention. From our perspective, pretests should be avoided when one suspects it can directly influence the posttest performance (i.e., a type of internal validity problem) or if it interacts with the intervention to produce the effect (i.e., an external validity problem).

Another problem with using pretests in school contexts involves issues of feasibility. Depending on the length of the pretest and the nature of the school or classroom in which it is administered, pretests can be costly in terms of time and resource allocation. Thus, school administrators who oversee the administration of school-based assessments to students may be sensitive or resistant to including both pretests and posttests as part of a research study.

Stop and Think 5.5

Research Question	Independent Variables	Dependent Variable	Addressed Interaction?
Does the influence of the reading program on students' reading comprehension skills depend on the gender of the student?	• reading program (i.e., present or absent) • gender (i.e., male, female)	Reading comprehension	Yes, interaction between reading group and gender Reading program **depends on** gender
Does type of therapy and the use of self-monitoring help to reduce anxiety in adolescents?	• type of therapy (i.e., cognitive vs psychoanalytic) • self-monitoring (i.e., yes or no)	Anxiety	No, the question references only the two main effects

Research Question	Independent Variables	Dependent Variable	Addressed Interaction?
Does receiving professional development and ongoing coaching support increase teacher efficacy for teaching?	• professional development (i.e., yes or no) • coaching support (i.e., yes or no)	Teacher self-efficacy	No, the question references only the two main effects
Does the effect of the Good Behavior Game (GBG) on students' disruptive behaviors vary depending on the grade level of student?	• Good Behavior Game (i.e., yes or no) • grade level (i.e., fourth or fifth)	Disruptive behaviors	Yes, interaction between GBG and grade level. Effects of GBG **varies across** grade level

STOP AND THINK 5.6

Mr. Fredericks can be reasonably confident given his use of the comparison condition. However, he would likely feel uneasy about the initial equivalency between the two groups. Without randomly assigning the students to the different conditions or using a variety of pretests or background variables, selection represents a major threat to internal validity.

STOP AND THINK 5.7

The basic A-B single-participant design resembles two types of designs discussed within this chapter. First, the A-B design is very similar to the pre-experimental, *one group pretest–posttest design* because they both assess variables before (i.e., baseline phase and pretest) and after the intervention (i.e., intervention phase, posttest). Further, there is no comparison condition used in either of the designs. Both designs examine pretest/baseline and posttest/intervention changes over time, but there is one targeted group (pre-experiment) or individual (A-B); thus, no comparisons are made across individuals.

The second design that mirrors the A-B design is likely more obvious. The quasi-experimental approach, *interrupted time series design*, is similar to the A-B design due to repeated assessment being conducted at both baseline and intervention phases. Again, both designs rely on the single group (or individual in the case of the A-B design).

Let's Do It! Activities

LET'S DO IT! 5.1

Dialogue With Jennifer and Dr. Floyd—Threats to Internal Validity

Threat to Internal Validity	IS IT POSSIBLE?	Explanation of Threat
History	Yes	Without a comparison group, it is impossible to determine if the observed gains in reading were due to the classroom intervention or the additional support from the reading specialist or from parental involvement.
Maturation	Yes	Because the pretest, intervention and posttest sequence took about two and a half months to complete, the lack of a comparison group prevents Jennifer from ruling out natural maturation or internal changes as the cause of the observed gain scores.

(Continued)

Threat to Internal Validity	IS IT POSSIBLE?	Explanation of Threat
Testing	Yes	This is a possible threat to internal validity, but it was not specifically addressed by Dr. Floyd in the conversation.
Instrumentation	Yes	Because different types of measures were used at pretest and posttest, there is no way to know whether the intervention was the cause of the reading gains or if the differences in assessment approaches was responsible.
Selection	Not applicable	Because there was only one group in this design, it is not relevant to think about initial group differences as the cause of the observed reading gains.

LET'S DO IT! 5.2

Summarizing Studies Using True Experimental Designs

True Experimental Designs	
Study	Cleary, T. J., Velardi, B., & Schnaidman, B. (2017). Effects of the Self-Regulation Empowerment Program (SREP) on middle school students' strategic skills, self-efficacy, and mathematics achievement. *Journal of School Psychology, 64*, 28–42. http://dx.doi.org/10.1016/j.jsp.2017.04.004
Purpose	To examine the causal effects of SREP (i.e., independent variable) on students' strategic behaviors (self-report questionnaire, scenario), attributions, adaptive inferences, self-efficacy, math achievement (i.e., six dependent variables)
Sample	Forty-two students were assigned to a SREP condition and a comparison condition. The majority of the sample was African American and Hispanic (77%), with 45% of the sample eligible for free and reduced lunch.
Nature of Intervention	There were two levels of the independent variable (i.e., SREP, comparison). Both groups received an identical number of training sessions and hours (i.e., 12 hours) over the course of three months. The intervention was provided to students in small groups (5–6 students). SREP focused on teaching students' various strategies and adaptive motivational processes while the comparison condition focused specifically on mathematics instruction.
Design Features and Internal Validity	A pretest–posttest control group design was used. Use of a comparison condition that received equivalent number of hours of an alternative program (controls for history, maturation, testing, instrumentation). Participants were randomly assigned (stratified random assignment) to condition (SREP, $n = 22$; comparison, $n = 20$; control for selection threats).
Statistics	Descriptive statistics (i.e., means, standard deviations, correlations) and several inferential statistics (i.e., independent t-tests, ANCOVA) were used to assess group differences. Two-way mixed model analyses were used to assess changes in math achievement over a two-year period.
Results	Students receiving SREP displayed more strategic and adaptive regulatory reactions and a statistically significant and more positive trend in mathematics achievement than the comparison condition. No differences emerged for any measure that used a self-report format.

Lᴇᴛ's Do Iᴛ! 5.3

Summarizing Studies Using Quasi-experimental Designs

Quasi-Experimental Designs	
Study	Fuchs et al. (2021). A quasi-experimental evaluation of two versions of first-grade PAKS: One with and one without repeated reading. *Exceptional Children, 87(2)*, 141–162. https://doi.org/10.1177/0014402920921828
Purpose	To examine the effects of different components of the Peer-Assisted Learning Strategies (PALS) (i.e., independent variable) on the phonological awareness, word meaning, reading, fluency, and reading comprehension skills of first-grade students (i.e., four dependent variables, although multiple measures were used to assess each of the four reading skills). The authors also examined whether initial phonological awareness skills moderated the effects of PALS.
Sample	Thirty-three teachers were assigned to one of three intervention conditions, while 491 first-grade students within those classes were examined. The sample was diverse (47% White, 32% Black, 21% other ethnicities/race). Forty-five percent qualified for reduced lunch while 12% were English language learners.
Nature of Intervention	There were three levels of the independent variable (i.e., PALS, PALS + repeated reading, and control).
Design Features and Internal Validity	A nonequivalent control-group design was used. Use of an expanded PALS comparison and a control allowed the authors to examine the advantages of adding repeated reading versus the original PALS program and a non-intervention condition (controls for history, maturation, testing, instrumentation). Teachers were randomly assigned to condition but not students. Thus, this does not control selection threats. The authors attempted to mitigate the selection threats by showing that the groups did not differ at pretest across demographic variables (sex, race, free or reduced lunch, etc.), teacher demographics, or pretest reading scores.
Statistics	Descriptive statistics (means, standard deviations, correlations) and several inferential statistics were used (i.e., regression or multi-level path models). Moderator analyses were conducted to examine whether PALS benefitted weaker students to a stronger degree than stronger readers.
Results	Both PALS conditions outperformed the control group.

Lᴇᴛ's Do Iᴛ! 5.4

Identifying Threats to Internal Validity in Single-Participant Designs

Please recall that internal validity is determined by (1) identifying the presence of an effect and (2) ruling out threats to internal validity. In looking at the graph for Tony, Robin, and Sholanda, the status of an intervention effect is not clear. Although both Tony and Robin showed an increase in math fluency over time, Robin's scores began to increase before she received the intervention while Sholanda's scores did not improve at all. Thus, it is difficult to make claims that the mathematics intervention worked. Review the information in the following table for answers to whether this design adequately controlled threats to internal validity.

Threat to Internal Validity	Explanation of Potential Threat	Reason Why Threat to Internal Validity Is/Is Not Controlled or Not Applicable
History	*IS IT POSSIBLE that some external factor operating on the students caused the A-B changes in fluency scores rather than the fluency intervention?* **Response: Yes, it is possible**	A major problem in the data is that Robin's fluency scores improved before she received the intervention. Further, because this improvement occurred at the same time as the improvement for Tony, it seems possible that some factor other than the intervention caused the change.
Maturation	*IS IT POSSIBLE that some natural developmental change led to the A-B changes in fluency scores rather than the fluency intervention?* **Response: Yes, it is possible**	Given that this design focuses on individual students and due to the unevenness in performance across the three students, it is possible that separate maturational factors facilitated Robin's performance but inhibited Sholanda's scores.
Testing	*IS IT POSSIBLE that taking the pretest mathematics fluency test naturally led to the A-B changes in fluency scores rather than the fluency intervention?* **Response: Highly unlikely**	Given that the baseline score for Tony and Sholanda were stable, it does not appear that administering the pretests on multiple occasions impacted the future performance.
Instrumentation	*IS IT POSSIBLE that changes in the nature or accuracy of a measurement led to the A-B changes in fluency scores rather than the fluency intervention??* **Response: Highly unlikely**	The same objective measure of mathematics fluency was used over time. Thus, a change in the measurement approach is not a viable explanation of the observed results.
Selection	*IS IT POSSIBLE that differences in the students selected for the study differed on some variables prior to receiving the fluency intervention and those differences led to changes in A-B scores rather than the intervention?* **Response: Yes, it is possible**	Given the uneven performance across students, it is difficult to determine whether external, maturational, or other individual differences (e.g., intelligence, motivation anxiety) were responsible for the results.

 **6** QUALITATIVE RESEARCH DESIGNS

LEARNING OBJECTIVES

Upon completion of this chapter, students should be able to

6.1   Describe characteristics of qualitative research

6.2   Outline the dynamic nature of qualitative research

6.3   Identify the types, purposes, and features of qualitative research

6.4   Detail the process of qualitative research

6.5   Demonstrate knowledge of ethical issues when engaging with qualitative research

6.6   Utilize the *Publication Manual of the American Psychological Association* in reporting findings in qualitative research

A DAY AT WORK

My Teacher Assistant Is a Lifesaver!

©iStockphoto.com/fizkes

I don't know what I would do without my assistant! She's a lifesaver! On any given day, you can hear Mrs. Marshall praise her teaching assistant, Louise, to students, parents, and other teachers. Louise, like any other teaching assistant in the classroom, is kind, patient, creative, organized, knowledgeable, and helpful. In fact, Louise is so skilled she often will interject in classroom activities because she has some information related to the topic or has an idea to help students remember information, such as mnemonic devices.

However, not all teachers are so adept as Mrs. Marshall at leveraging the skills of a teaching assistant, and not all teaching assistants are comfortable assuming teaching roles. Understanding the ways teaching assistants function can lead to improved practices, collaborations, and student achievement. Research can be an invaluable tool to understand the processes involved in co-teaching with teachers and teaching assistants, along with other critical issues that are common throughout the workaday experiences of teachers. Mrs. Marshall would like to conduct research on the advantages of co-teaching to help others understand the benefits, but what kind of research should she conduct?

INTRODUCTION

There are many topics in schools in which the research process could address critical issues. These concerns are common in the workplace of teachers, such as the impact of absenteeism, gaps in student performance, collaboration among school faculty, and the impact of educational strategies and professional development workshops, as some examples. In this chapter, we describe a methodological approach to researching critical issues known as qualitative research. This chapter begins with an overview of qualitative research. Next, we outline the dynamic nature of qualitative research and then provide a discussion of the types, purposes, and features of qualitative research. This section is followed by a description of the process involved in conducting qualitative research and concludes with issues related to ethics, APA style and reporting and communicating results.

WHAT IS QUALITATIVE RESEARCH?

LEARNING OBJECTIVE
6.1   Describe characteristics of qualitative research.

Throughout this book, we have discussed how critical issues can be addressed using a variety of research designs, depending on the setting, purpose of the study, and research questions. There are distinctions in research designs, driven by what the researcher aims to study; the specific research questions; the ways the study is implemented; and available participants, sites, and data sources. An analogy would be the many techniques used to prepare a tomato for cooking: dicing, slicing, cubing, mashing, baking, skinning, grilling, etc. In the same way a tomato can be prepared for the requirements of a meal, research designs vary to address the problem at hand with specific research questions.

©iStockphoto.com/sirichai_asawalapsakul

In the same way a tomato can be prepared for the requirements of a meal, research designs vary to address the problem at hand and specific research questions.

Qualitative research design focuses on examining phenomenon in natural settings based on the individuals involved in the situation and describing meanings, processes, and social/organizational structures, such as in a school setting. Qualitative research designs use inductive reasoning, where the researcher enters the study with broad questions to uncover the nature of a given context without any preconceived notions; the research questions help to narrow the field of study. There are no prescribed hypotheses to correspond with research questions as in the deductive approach. The aim is not to support or refute a research question or generalize to larger populations but rather to form a descriptive narrative of the web of systems and interactions within a given situation, often from the perspective of participants.

STOP AND THINK 6.1

Can you think of a critical issue in your school that could be studied in terms of processes, meanings, or social/organizational structures?

The experiences, beliefs, and values that participants and researchers bring to a study inherently shape the direction of the study and interpretation of findings. When considering the opening scenario and the potential role of teacher assistants, a qualitative researcher may use different lenses to examine the daily work experiences of these educators. Depending on the interest of the researcher, the topic of the role of teacher assistants lends itself well to many qualitative investigations: (a) diverse ways teacher assistants support classroom learning, (b) the teacher assistants' physical location in the classroom; (c) interactions between teacher assistants, students, and the classroom teacher; and (d) professional development opportunities. Faculty and staff in the school could provide valuable information on these issues through interviews, observational checklists, mapping, journal writing, and artifacts. These sources of evidence can illuminate the nature of interactions within the school that involve teacher assistants. An important element of qualitative research designs is the way the research question reflects the purpose of the study. For instance, "What were the initial training experiences of a teacher assistant working with special needs students?" is a question that could reflect a case study design focused on one person's perspective.

Qualitative research design is applicable to a vast array of topics in the education field. Notably, in this process, the researcher becomes immersed in the study of the operations, interconnections, and relationships within a social environment. Consider Principal Carter who, in collaboration with some university researchers, wants to study the impact of student to teacher ratios on reading achievement. From a qualitative lens, invested parties could focus on teacher perspectives of the processes in place to support students with multiple teachers and teacher assistants in the room. A research question might be "What are collaborative ways in which teachers and teacher assistants can support students in their reading development?"

STOP AND THINK 6.2

How would an examination of the interaction between teachers and teacher assistants be a topic that could be studied using qualitative research?

As qualitative research is a flexible, dynamic process, there is no formulaic way to construct a research question. The question stems from what the researcher is trying to learn and is the focal point from which the research design extends. One way to proceed in developing the research question is to start with a broad understanding of a topic, described through the literature review and gaps in existing research. This gap serves as the impetus for developing the research question. The question itself can be broad or narrow—descriptive or explanatory. For example, in the context of the way schools utilize teacher assistants to work with special education students, some research questions could be "How are decisions made as to where to assign special education teachers?" "How do the skill sets of teacher assistants align with the needs of students and the classroom?" and "What are some components of a special education program that effectively utilize teacher assistants to meet the needs of students?" All of the elements of the design (e.g., participants, data collection instruments, and analysis) form a nexus with the research question selected to address a critical issue. Each of these questions would generate specific methods to address the question.

The nature of a qualitative research question serves as the basis to describe social structures within school systems. Figure 6.1 depicts examples of research questions, which are indicative of qualitative studies in that the aim is to capture the meanings, processes, and social interactions within educational settings.

FIGURE 6.1 ■ Examples of Questions for Qualitative Research

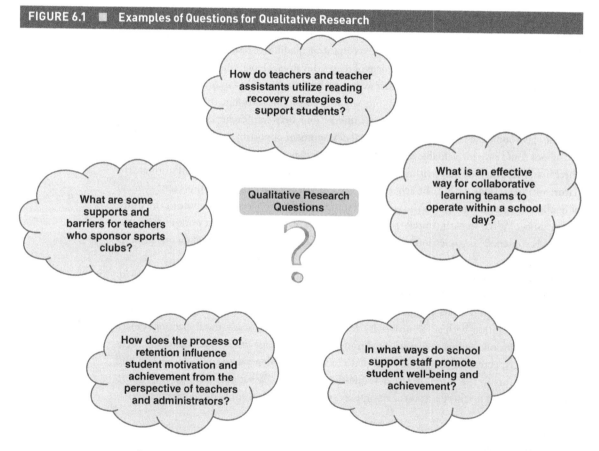

One way to write research questions is to use sentence starters. Some possible options include: "In what ways . . . ? " "What is the perspective . . . ?" "How do . . . ?" "What particular . . . ?" Starting research questions with words like what or how is useful in intimating that the framework of the study is from a broad and open stance. In this way, the researcher conveys that an inductive approach will be used to examine a critical issue.

Word choice is paramount when writing research questions. A useful suggestion is to avoid terms like "determine," "cause," "impact," "affect," or "influence," which are more commonly used in quantitative research. These types of terms suggest an investigation that includes quantitative measures testing relationships among variables.

A helpful guide for writing qualitative research questions is to consider (a) the context; (b) the topic of the critical issue; (c) ways the participants are involved in the process; and (d) a focus on the processes, meanings, and social interaction. In addition, the researcher should check the phrasing of the question to check for potential biases and/or assumptions.

Let's See It! 6.1

Goal: To Examine the Key Features of Qualitative Research Questions Using a Study by Scuichetti et al. (2018) as a Model

Background: Sciuchetti et al. (2018) examined special education teacher candidates' (TC) perceptions of the realities and demands of the teaching profession following a field placement.

Purpose Statement: The purpose of this study was to explore special education TCs' developing professional awareness in the context of strategically aligned coursework and early field experiences.

Qualitative Research Question

What insights regarding professional awareness, including professional roles and responsibilities, were evident in teacher candidates' (TCs') end-of-semester written reflections following a strategically aligned field experience?

No hypothesis.

Note: This question would be a viable research question because it frames the study to highlight the processes and elements of a qualitative study on teacher candidates' field experiences. In addition, the way the question is formulated, it is clear that data collection, analysis, and interpretations center on the experiences of individuals. The research question also provides some detail as to the context and participants.

Let's Do It! 6.1

Guided Practice: Creating Qualitative Research Questions

After reviewing *Let's See It!* 6.1, consider the following scenario and purpose statement. Create one to two qualitative research questions that align with the background information and purpose statement.

Background: Mr. Williams, the principal at a local elementary school, noticed that some teacher assistants seemed uncomfortable helping children with mathematics. He wondered if there were particular mathematics topics that teacher assistants needed training in and the best way to support his instructional staff.

Purpose Statement: The purpose of this study is to identify in what ways teacher assistants benefit from professional development in mathematics instruction.

Qualitative Research Questions

In this section, we described common features of qualitative research. Use the checklist in Table 6.1 to analyze a qualitative research study on instructional approaches for young children.

First review the sample model under *Let's See It!*, then, select a qualitative article to scan distinguishing features under *Let's Do It!*.

Let's See It! 6.2

Goal: To Analyze the Distinguishing Features Typical of Qualitative Studies

Table 6.1 incorporates both a checklist and reflection section as a model of how to analyse a qualitative research study in a broad approach using an early childhood study by MacDonald (2007). This type of activity can be useful in identifying if a research study is qualitative in nature.

Article Abstract

MacDonald, M. (2007). The use of pedagogical documentation in early elementary classrooms. *Early Childhood Quarterly, 22*, 232–242. https://doi.org/10.1016/j.ecresq.2006.12.001

In this study, a Reggio Emilia style of pedagogical documentation was introduced in five kindergarten classrooms in the New Westminster school district over a 6-month period from January to June 2005. The study investigated the potential of the Reggio Emilia style as a means of formative assessment in literacy instruction and to communicate learning to children and their families. Interviews with parents and classroom teachers followed; transcripts were analyzed using grounded theory methodology to determine common responses, and patterns in the perspectives articulated. A year later in June 2006, teachers were re-interviewed to determine if they had continued to use any of the techniques introduced and to ascertain barriers and challenges to its implementation. Based on these findings, two analytic stories were developed about the use of pedagogical documentation in traditional early elementary classrooms. The implications of these findings are then considered along with recommendations for further investigations.

TABLE 6.1 ■ Checklist for Qualitative Research Studies	
Checklist of Distinguishing Features	
Guiding Question	**Response**
_X_ Does the study start with a broad focus?	The writing starts with a broad overview of challenges for teachers and parents in identifying student progress in literacy growth during early childhood.
_____ Is the work free of a hypothesis?	The work includes a hypothesis, which is typically not used for qualitative research.
_X_ Does the work center on participant perspectives?	Teachers shared their perceptions of the effectiveness of the strategy of pedagogical documentation.
_X_ Does the work focus on interactions, meanings, and processes among participants within an organization or context.	The study is descriptive in nature and does not aim to suggest that the findings would be the same for larger populations.

Let's Do It! 6.2

Guided Practice: Analyze Basic Components of a Qualitative Research Study

After reviewing Let's See It! 6.1, review the qualitative article on recess time by Bauml et al. (2020) and complete the information below.

Checklist of Distinguishing Features		
Guiding Questions		Response
_____ Does the study start with a broad focus?		
_____ Is the work free of a hypothesis?		
_____ Does the work center on participant perspectives?		
_____ Does the work focus on interactions, meanings, and processes among participants within an organization or context?		

THE TAKEAWAY

Qualitative research designs are useful to study the meanings, processes, and social/organizational structures within an educational setting. These designs follow a dynamic, inductive approach, often reflecting the experiences and perspectives of participants.

THE DYNAMIC NATURE OF QUALITATIVE RESEARCH

Qualitative research designs, which aim to capture nuances within a study, tend to be intricate and flexible, which is a necessity in the process. There are many complexities within an educational setting, such as educational goals, interactions, strategies, and daily logistics. A researcher studying the interactions between teachers and teacher assistants during classroom instruction would likely want to consider many facets of the classroom environment and student needs. This example reflects the dynamic and multifaceted nature of qualitative studies. Since there are no predetermined outcomes, researchers will engage in an ongoing process of shaping the research design and methods (i.e., interviews, videos) as they uncover and analyze data.

Another distinguishing broad feature of qualitative research is the recognition that there are no absolute truths; analysis centers on the perspectives of the participants as well as the researcher. Later in this chapter, we outline several techniques a researcher can use to optimally report findings, such as being transparent about their data analysis and interpretation practices as well as their individual perspectives.

Qualitative research designs involve an adaptable process. From the broadest perspective, the nature of qualitative studies and role of the researcher are ever shifting to account for incoming data as the study unfolds. Figure 6.2 highlights two aspects distinctive to qualitative methodology: (a) the basic tenets of qualitative research design and (b) the role of the researcher during

FIGURE 6.2 ■ The Dynamic Qualitative Research Design and the Role of the Researcher

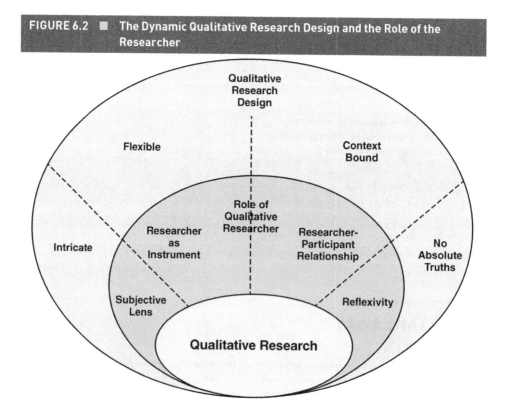

the process, both of which are consistently adapting throughout the course of a research study. The outer circle depicts the dynamic framework of qualitative research designs, which provide an outlet to make changes as needed throughout the research process. The inner circle depicts the role of the researcher in gaining information, shifting for the needs of the study, and reflecting on their role and potential biases. A description of each of the elements in these two layers is presented.

Qualitative Research Design

The process of qualitative research is inherently intricate, flexible, context bound, and framed with the supposition that there are no absolute truths. These features are necessary as qualitative studies start with broad general questions to uncover the essence of a contextual situation, a phenomenon, and/or the behaviors and insights of individuals. Just as a surfer shifts and adjusts their balance when barreling through a large wave, the foundational platform of a qualitative study is ever changing and requires modifications throughout the process.

Just as a surfer shifts and adjusts their balance when barreling through a large wave, the foundational platform of a qualitative study is ever changing and requires modifications throughout the process.

©iStockphoto.com/EpicStockMedia

Intricate

Regardless of the type of qualitative research design, as the researcher collects data and observational notes and then analyzes the data as they come in, the researcher will reflect on the information and make adjustments to data sources, such as semi-structured interview questions and additional sources/types of data, to continue the work. In this regard, the researcher uses both structured (e.g., interviews) and unstructured methods (e.g., naturalistic observations) as a blended approach to make sense of the topic of study. Since the nature of qualitative research is complex and multi-faceted, it is essential that the researcher take notes as analytic memos. Analytic memos are brief summaries in which the researcher assesses what they have learned over the course of the study. Analytic memos can be helpful throughout the research process to reflect on changes made, data analysis procedures and interpretations, as well as reflections of potential biases in the choices made.

Flexible

In the midst of a qualitative study, the researcher should be consistently reflective and flexible. Consider a qualitative researcher who is studying school staff member's' perceptions of homework and interviews several administrators, teachers, teacher assistants, and guidance counselors on the quantity and quality of homework assigned by teachers. As the interviews are transcribed, coded, and initially analyzed, the researcher may include some questions related to homework consistency and after-school activities in subsequent questions for future interviewees. In this case, some additional aspects have been revealed by the initial participants, which require further investigation. The qualitative researcher will need to be able to shift in terms of identifying new participants who can provide detailed explanations and consider potential alternative sources of data and/or data analysis techniques.

Content Bound

Given that each middle school in a district may have different homework policies, some schools may have consistent guidelines about quantity of homework; other schools may have inconsistent expectations across teachers; and for some sites, administrators may discourage homework altogether. On the topic of homework, educators can have strong opinions. A researcher studying faculty perceptions of homework will need to make shifts in the way they conduct research in each school to account for these homework policy differences and individuals' stances on homework requirements. For this reason, the nature of qualitative research tends to be highly malleable based on the study setting.

No Absolute Truths

Within the multi-dimensional realm of qualitative research, there is a recognition that there are no absolute truths but rather interpretations from varied perspectives. The viewpoints of the faculty on homework can be captured through a web of data sources; methods of analysis and interpretation; and the combined perspectives of administrators, teachers, teacher assistants, and the researcher. In this sense, there could be many ways to interpret findings based on the lens of the participants and researchers. For this reason, it is the responsibility of the qualitative researcher to be fully transparent about their role in the study and the methods and potential biases used to develop findings.

STOP AND THINK 6.3

Some individuals claim that qualitative research is more subjective than other types of research. Do you agree or disagree with this statement and why?

Role of the Qualitative Researcher

The role of the qualitative researcher is unique to the methodology. Since the researcher's perspective is central to the study, there are key elements related to the role of the researcher that are integral to the design process. Some of these features include the researcher as an instrument, the researcher–participant relationship, subjective lens, and reflexivity.

Researcher as Instrument

The qualitative researcher acknowledges that they play an essential part in the research study in all regards, which is shaped by personal experience, beliefs, attitudes, and values. In their role to collect, analyze, and interpret data, the researcher inherently serves as an instrument. A researcher observing an IB meeting will have specific past experiences, beliefs, values, and attitudes about professional development and IB programs, which inherently shape the research process. For this reason, it is essential that the researcher is transparent about their perspective on the subject matter, the methods used for analysis and interpretations, and consistent reflections on personal biases. High caliber qualitative studies are explicit in the way data are collected, analyzed, and interpreted to clearly illuminate the ways in which inductive reasoning occurred and actions taken to minimize potential biases.

Researcher–Participant Relationship

Depending on the nature of the study design, the researcher may have a relationship with the participants by engaging in activities as a participant observer or as a privileged observer. A participant observer has first-hand experiences in a community by participating in activities, whereas a privileged observer is permitted to analyze the interactions and behaviors but does not participate in day-to-day operations. A primary issue is how to curtail biases in all aspects of qualitative research design. Acknowledging the subjective lens and utilizing reflexivity are two ways a qualitative researcher can be transparent about their perspective on the topic of study. In addition, the term positionality describes an individual's worldview and the position they adopt about their research. This stance includes information about an individual's beliefs about the nature of knowledge and agency. The researcher strives to use their insights to highlight positionality of participants from their perspective. In essence, there is a balance between the role of the researcher and that of the participants.

Subjective Lens

Since personal factors can influence the overall course of the study and subsequent interpretations, a qualitative researcher should clearly describe their subjective lens. The subjective lens is the perspective of the qualitative researcher; identifying this viewpoint is critical in reflecting on personal bias throughout the study. The subjective lens entails a coordination between human experience and emotion based on background experiences. As a qualitative researcher enters a study, they monitor their subjective sensibilities to maintain rigor throughout the research process. That is to say, while it is not always possible to be completely objective, by reflecting on perspectives, the researcher aims to reduce partiality and reflect on how the subjective lens could influence analysis and interpretation of data.

For instance, a researcher interested in studying faculty perceptions of homework could state they enter the study with the supposition that "consistent homework is an effective way to promote student achievement." In this way, the researcher reveals they have a subjective lens that could influence findings of the qualitative study. This type of statement adds a layer of transparency to support the quality of work.

Reflexivity

To counter personal perspectives, qualitative researchers practice reflexivity wherein self-evaluation and reflection are essential to consider if findings have been influenced by the researcher's subjective lens. Reflexivity on the part of the researcher, demonstrated by noting and understanding how they perceive the world, is important in order for researchers to acknowledge and work with existing biases, as well as understand what they bring to the table during a research project. This process assists the researcher in making adjustments as the study unfolds and to check potential issues related to personal predispositions. It is a keystone step in the research process, regardless of design, to promote research practices with integrity.

Reflexivity is a fine-grained skill in which the researcher considers how their beliefs, values, and attitudes could be influencing the trajectory of the study and the way in which conclusions are drawn. Particular areas that are prone to possible biases are the methods used to collect data, analysis of data, and reporting of findings. Embedding reflexivity throughout the research process increases trustworthiness and rigor in conducting research and disclosing findings in an honest and credible manner.

THE TAKEAWAY

Qualitative research is a multi-faceted process wherein the researcher will use an iterative approach to adjust elements in the research process (e.g., participants, interview questions, coding techniques). In this way, the researcher continuously reflects on the choices made as well as their role in the study.

TYPES, PURPOSES, AND FEATURES OF QUALITATIVE RESEARCH DESIGNS

LEARNING OBJECTIVE

6.3   Identify the types, purposes, and features of qualitative research.

There are a range of qualitative research designs available depending on the needs of the study, the research questions, and available data sources. Figure 6.3 represents some common forms of qualitative research, and Figure 6.4 highlights the many ways the role of teacher assistants reflects different types of qualitative research designs. The overall purpose of the study is integral to the type of research design that will be selected. Consider how the type of research design shapes the focus and purpose of the study, all within the context of teacher assistants. As a preview to a more in-depth discussion, Figure 6.4 includes each type of design, a corresponding topic, and ways to design a study.

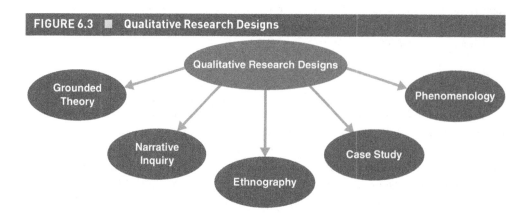

FIGURE 6.3   ■   Qualitative Research Designs

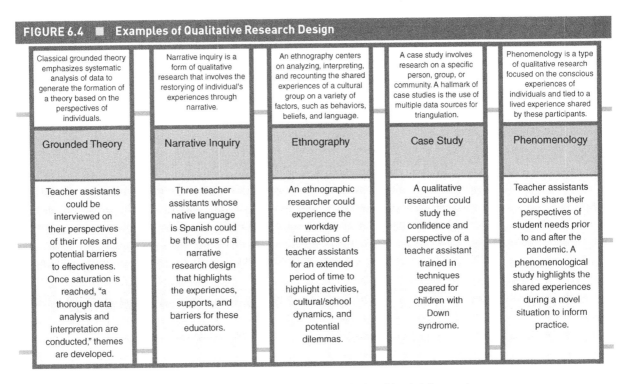

FIGURE 6.4 ■ Examples of Qualitative Research Design

While there are many types of qualitative research designs, including blended forms, these five types are often found in literature from various social science fields. Figure 6.5 provides a flow chart summary of the types of qualitative research designs, the purpose, and sample

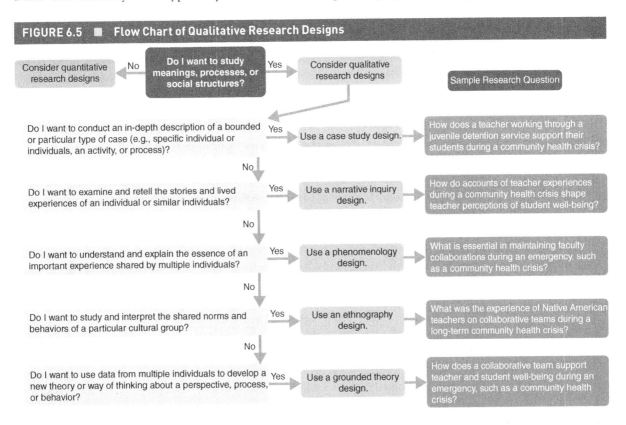

FIGURE 6.5 ■ Flow Chart of Qualitative Research Designs

research questions with the backdrop of teaching during a community health crisis, followed by a more in-depth discussion of each type of design. Utilizing the flow chart can be helpful in determining which type of research design is best suited for a specific critical issue.

The next section outlines the purpose and several essential features and characteristics for each of the five common qualitative research designs. The four features addressed in each section include: (1) nature of research questions, (2) sampling, (3) data collection, and (4) data analysis.

Grounded Theory

Grounded theory is an approach developed by Glaser and Strauss (1967) as a systematic method for creating theories about a topic of study (Figure 6.6). The researcher follows a system of data collection, analysis, and interpretation to build emergent themes that ultimately form an overarching theory to understand the intricacies of a study. The researcher continues to modify and refine the theory as an iterative process with the collection of data across time. For this reason, the type of data and participants identified throughout the study are critical to the overarching goals.

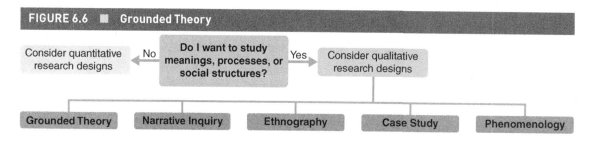

FIGURE 6.6 ■ Grounded Theory

Nature of Research Questions

A primary difference between grounded theory and other types of qualitative research design is the emphasis on developing theory, frequently rooted in the experiences of participants. For this reason, the research questions strive to mirror the practices of everyday events that are being studied through a context-specific theory rather than a general theory that is applicable to many situations. For example, constructivism is a broad theory that is applicable to many topics. When studying effective elements of an IB program, a researcher may focus on the theory of knowledge (focusing on the nature of knowledge), which is a foundational part of the IB curriculum.

The research question for grounded theory should be written in a way that is broad, open ended, and focused on practical ways to address a critical issue. The goal is to shape the study in a way that theories can emerge based on the participants' shared accounts rather than preset notions of the outcomes. In fact, grounded theorists often conduct the literature review after data analysis, so as to limit potential biases during analysis. Figure 6.7 shows sample research questions that meet these criteria with the context of teacher professional development workshops for each of the five highlighted research designs. The question in orange highlights a question applicable to grounded theory.

When writing research questions for a grounded theory approach, it is helpful to remember that a substantive theory will be developed and often described through a variety of themes interpreted from the data. The highlighted question in Figure 6.7 would be appropriate because it is broad enough to shape grounded theory with several iterations of interviewing, coding, and analyzing data. In addition, the backdrop of professional development workshops is a common event in the education field, so it would be possible to interview many cycles of teachers attending these types of events.

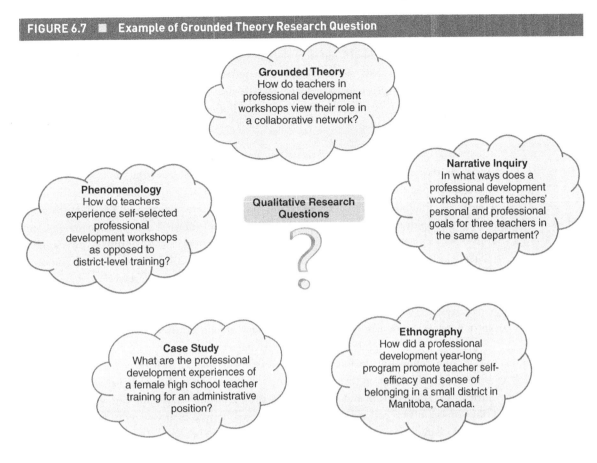

FIGURE 6.7 ■ Example of Grounded Theory Research Question

Sampling

In grounded theory, theoretical sampling is a method for selecting participants who can provide rich accounts to support theme development. In addition, this type of sampling method can occur in phases with several rounds of interviews, coding, and analysis. Theoretical sampling also differs from convenience sampling, another common approach to identifying participants; researchers invite participants who are readily available. If a researcher wanted to examine the role of teacher assistants during a remedial after-school program, there may be limits to finding available participants. Convenience sampling can shed light on how support staff can improve student reading progress; however, designing a study with specific criteria can address the questions more specifically (more information on the types of non-random sampling techniques is covered later in the chapter).

Data Collection

Interviews are often a primary way that researchers develop grounded theory; however, other options include observations, organizational documents, videos, field notes, and participant-created products (see Chapter 10 for a full discussion of types of data). A central issue when conducting interviews is to recognize that both the interviewees and interviewer have an equal role in the process. While predetermined interview questions form the basis of the interview, the participant shares their perspective and may sometimes veer away from the original question. At this point, the researcher adjusts subsequent questioning based on participant feedback. While the dialogue may have a positive tone where the interviewee feels comfortable sharing information, the researcher is listening attentively to steer the interview. Approaching the interview in this way empowers the participant and positions the interviewer as an active member of the discussion. In addition, the contributions of each participant aid in theoretical sampling. In other words, the researcher selects subsequent participants based on the analysis of transcripts from previous participants. While these guidelines are relevant for the use of interviews for any type of qualitative design, the findings can be particularly relevant in support of theory development.

Semi-Structured Interview Development and Implementation. Prior to interviewing participants, the researcher will generate a list of semi-structured interview questions, which typically receive approval from an institutional review board (IRB) prior to the start of the study. These questions form the backdrop of the interview and usually include five to ten questions that align with the purpose of the study and overarching research questions. A good initial question is one that sets the tone for the interview while relating to the critical issue. For instance, a researcher interviewing a teacher about their experiences with a professional development workshop could begin by asking, "How did you first become interested in attending the professional development workshop?" Subsequent questions could be "How did the professional development workshop meet your professional goals?" or "In what ways did the professional development workshop pertain to your work in the classroom?" These semi-structured interview questions align with the purpose of the study and the overarching research questions.

Prior to conducting the interview, the researcher may practice with a critical friend, a person who can give feedback on their interviewing techniques. Next, the researcher will contact participants to arrange a time and location. Typically, the participant will indicate where they would like to meet (office, park, library, etc.). One suggestion is to interview individuals in the same type of location and modality (e.g., online vs. in person) because differences in these formats may influence the outcome of the discussion.

The semi-structured interview questions will be the catalyst for the dialogue and transcriptions that will produce findings from the study. Once participants have been interviewed and transcripts have been coded and analyzed, some researchers will do a follow-up with the participants, particularly if any new questions emerge over the course of the study.

Data Analysis/Interpretation Techniques

With transcriptions, the researcher will begin to code data for further analysis and interpretation. One way to support theory development is with the constant comparative analysis approach (CCA); through this technique, data are coded in iterative phases of open coding (initial coding), axial coding (category formation), and selective coding to develop a theory. Enhanced information about the constant comparative approach appears in Chapter 14. *While this brief description falls under the section for grounded theory, this data analysis technique is applicable to many forms of qualitative research design.*

Open Coding. One way to approach the constant comparative analysis approach is for a researcher to (a) transcribe the interviews and code the transcripts with noun labels, (b) formulate categories, and then (c) analyze trends across categories to build emerging themes, resulting in theory formation. Through the coding system, the researcher highlights overarching themes to discuss in a narrative. For example, if a researcher was examining the role of teacher assistants in the classroom, a study could center on teacher assistants' perceptions of their responsibilities in the classroom. By interviewing participants on their perspectives, the research findings could reveal themes about teacher assistants' attitudes, beliefs, and values on their contributions to the work place. The overall process would entail interviewing teachers on the role of their assistants and then transcribing the dialogue.

Next, labels are applied in the open coding phase. An example, would be writing a "T" when "time management" was noted or "C" when "community" was mentioned. The individual coding the data would determine the label scheme from their perspective as shown in Figure 6.8. Creating codes in this way is an inductive method for coding. In contrast, some researchers may want to use a priori coding; this is a technique where codes are created prior to analysis and based on a theoretical framework.

Let's See It! 6.3

Goal: To Review an Example of the Initial Form of Coding of Qualitative Data Known as Open Coding

In Figure 6.8, a letter has been applied to each word in a transcript, often to represent a noun. This letter serves as a descriptive label. On the right is a key that shows the correspondence between the letters and noun labels.

FIGURE 6.8 ■ Open Coding With Descriptive Noun Labels

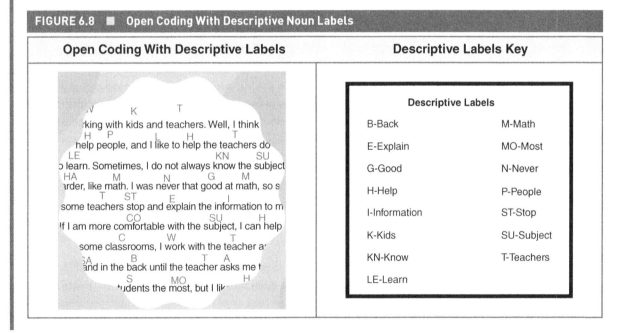

Let's Do It! 6.3

Guided Practice: Create an Open Coding Scheme With Noun Labels Using a Sample Transcript

After reviewing Figure 6.8, use the transcript data excerpt from a teacher on the curriculum. Practice your skills at open coding with some descriptive noun labels (Figure 6.9) and a corresponding key.

Excerpt of Qualitative Data From "Connor"

"You, know, there are a lot of great programs that could be taught in public education. But the day is only so long. It's like the old balloon theory. You squeeze one end; the other end is going to bulge out. So, you know, public school is trying to meet so many different demands that just time restraints keep some from being met. So those demands are not met. And for some reason, public school has been tapped on the shoulder as the institution that should impart all of the vast knowledge, and it just can't be done."

FIGURE 6.9 ■ Descriptive Noun Labels

Descriptive Labels

B-balloon	M-met
BU-bulge	P-program
D-demands	PE-public education
DA-day	PS-public school
DI-different	R-reason
DO-done	RE-restraints
E-end	S-shoulder
I-institution	T-time
K-knowledge	TH-theory

Axial Coding. While the focus of the open coding phase is to begin labeling data and grouping transcript sections based on these labels, the second phase, axial coding, is a process in which groups of descriptive labels are combined to form categories. From the initial coding phase (open coding), the descriptive groupings form categories (axial coding). Dialogue related to community, acceptance, and rules could be classified as cultural norms. Once these categories develop in the axial coding phase, then trends are described across categories during selective coding.

Selective Coding. Grounded theory studies employ an additional phase known as selective coding. During selective coding, iterative processes of interviews, data analysis, and interpretations create the basis for theory development. The process continues by interviewing additional teachers and integrating the data within existing information until grounded theory fully materializes through the use of saturation. *Saturation* refers to interviewing participants until no new information is revealed.

Saturation. An important note about grounded theory is that in order to use data to reveal thematic overtones, the researcher will continue to collect, analyze, and interpret data until saturation has been met. A qualitative researcher could study teacher assistants' perspectives of their role in the classroom and potential supports and barriers to their effectiveness by interviewing individuals. As interviews are transcribed, the researcher codes and analyzes data. Consider that a new wave of teacher assistants brings up the topic of training to meet the needs of special education students. The researcher would adjust interview questions with subsequent interviewees, and the process would continue until reaching the point of saturation. At this stage, the researcher would formulate theories based on the iterative process of coding, analysis, and interpretation.

Due to time constraints and limitation in access to participants, researchers are not always able to reach saturation to produce grounded theory. In this case, researchers can use constant comparative analysis to develop emergent themes rather than grounded theory; this is an approach that uses a tiered sequence of initial coding, formulating categories, and then describing emergent themes. If a researcher was conducting a study with a finite timeline and limited availability of participants with specific criteria, developing emergent themes would be more appropriate.

This CCA can be exemplified in the context of teacher assistants who work with children identified with dyscalculia, a learning disability in which individuals have difficulty understanding numbers and recalling mathematics-related information. There would not be the option of interviewing individuals to reach saturation if the researcher was running a one-time exploratory study as this is not a condition that is prevalent in all schools. Teacher assistants working with students who have needs related to this learning disability might not be available to reach saturation. In this case, analyzing staff perceptions would provide valuable insights but could not be extended to grounded theory, solely emergent themes.

Multiple Approaches to Grounded Theory

The overall process of grounded theory involves a dynamic web of observations, inferences, deductions, and the conceptualization of theories. Grounded theory is sometimes misunderstood as a vague and simplistic form of collecting data and writing narratives. The procedures actually require a great deal of reflexivity, transparency, and conceptual thought processes to develop an analytical framework. There are several approaches to conducting grounded theory, which include the classical grounded theory, interpretive grounded theory, and constructivist ground theory.

Classical grounded theory initially described by Glaser and Strauss (1967) and further detailed by Glaser (1992) describes a way to analyze and interpret qualitative data. Interviews from individuals are analyzed and interpreted to create thick descriptions that describe the intricacies of a social context. Originally coined by a social anthropologist (Geertz, 1973), a thick description moves beyond summaries to integrate both a description and the researchers' interpretations within an account.

Based on these individuals' perspectives, researchers involved in classical grounded theory aim to develop conceptual theories to explain processes and structures that influence these individuals. Classical grounded theory differs from other approaches in that the researcher has minimal knowledge of the topic of study prior to conducting research. While other forms of grounded theory accommodate some background knowledge to design the research study, classical grounded theory espouses that prior knowledge could inadvertently influence data analysis and interpretation.

The interpretive grounded theory approach, associated with Corbin and Strauss (1990), requires a complex and rigorous coding scheme as described earlier through open coding, axial coding, and selective coding. The key objective is often to develop themes or relationships across categories using the constant comparative analysis approach as the researcher actively engages with data throughout the coding process.

The third option is Charmaz's constructivist grounded theory approach (2006), which places emphasis on the joint efforts between the researcher and participant to discover the meanings and processes examined in the research study. In a constructivist approach, the researcher uncovers the findings through a flexible process that is not constrained to a set of methodological requirements. Theory emerges through the accounts of participants rather than a preexisting theory. The researcher determines the process for data analysis, interpretation, and dissemination of findings while adhering to principles of quality and transparency.

Each of these frameworks has commonalities in that the work is centered on understanding the essence of social structures with an inductive process. Regardless of the approach, there is a high level of accountability for the research to explicitly disclose how data were analyzed and interpreted in the development of themes/theories.

Examining Grounded Theory in the Empirical Literature

Grounded theory is a useful research design approach in educational literature, particularly in terms of theory development support. In the next section, we present a grounded theory research study (*Let's See It!*). Then you will be asked to summarize a grounded theory study with the first example as a model (*Let's Do It!*). To further cultivate your understanding and use of grounded theory principles, please complete the *You Do It!* activity.

Let's See It! 6.4

Goal: To Understand the Key Features of Grounded Theory Design

The primary objective of this activity is to help you identify the key features of a published article using grounded theory. Roybal-Lewis (2021) examined the experiences of early childhood teacher candidates in professional development schools. Roybal-Lewis utilized a constant comparative analysis approach to study participant experiences with a grounded theory lens. Read the summary in Table 6.2 to learn about the key information related to the grounded theory design. It may also be helpful to access and read the entire methods section of the article to obtain a more detailed overview of the methodological procedures and approaches used for each study.

TABLE 6.2 ■ Grounded Theory Design	
Study	Roybal-Lewis, A. (2021). Moving towards proficiency: A grounded theory study of early childhood teacher candidates and professional development schools. *Early Childhood Education Journal, 50*, 913–924. https://doi.org/10.1007/s10643-021-01229-7
Purpose	To examine the experiences of teacher candidates as they transition through professional development schools to make connections between effective pedagogical practices within the classroom and to create a framework known as the "Proficient Teacher Candidate."
Critical Issue	To highlight the processes of teacher candidates within an early childhood preservice teacher program that integrates learning within professional development schools.
Sample	The study utilized purposeful sampling and included (*n* = 50) early childhood teacher candidates in an education and licensure program in the Rocky Mountain region of the United States.
Data Collection	Data were collected through 43 semi-structured interviews. In addition, participants were asked to collect artifacts to help them make sense and meaning of their experiences (e.g., photographs, reflections, observation sheets, lesson plans).
Data Analysis	The researcher utilized the constant comparative analysis approach within a grounded theory design. NVivo 12.0 was a software program used to organize the data.
Results	The findings illuminated the elements that supported a "Proficient Teacher Candidate." These facets included teacher engagement (e.g., relationship with mentor teachers, applying course content), professional behavior and dispositions, and reflective practices. Candidates benefitted from applying course content, interacting with professional staff members, and reflecting and synthesizing their understandings and instructional effectiveness.

Let's Do It! 6.4

Guided Practice: Practice Summarizing the Key Features of Grounded Theory Design

The primary objective of this activity is for you to independently review and identify the key features of a grounded theory article. To guide your thinking, we encourage you to use the information from the *Let's See It!* (Table 6.2) as well as the guiding questions in the Table 6.3. We also provide an answer key in the appendix at the end of the chapter for you to check your work.

TABLE 6.3 ■ Grounded Theory Design	
Study	Benedict, A. E., Brownell, M., Bettini, E., & Sohn, H. (2021). Learning together: Teachers' evolving understanding of coordinated word study instruction within an RTI framework. *Teacher Education and Special Education*, 44(2), 134–159. https://doi-org.mutex.gmu.edu/10.1177/0888406420930686
Purpose	Is the overall purpose clear?
Critical Issue	Does the issue appear to be a critical educational issue?
	Is a strong rationale provided for the critical issue? (You may need to read the introduction to the article.)
Sample	Is the target group appropriate given the research purposes?
	What sampling technique was used to select participants?
	Were the techniques used to select participants clear and appropriate?
Data Collection	What types of data were used?
	How were the data collected?
Data Analysis	What approach was used to analyze data?
Results	What are the key findings that relate to the research questions?

Narrative Inquiry

Narrative inquiry research design describes the lives of individuals by gathering and restorying their experiences (Figure 6.10). Narrative analysis often develops from textual sources, such as accounts of individual experiences or historical information, while including the backdrop of personal accounts and storytelling in as much depth as the narrative itself. Moreover, narrative inquiry often focuses on how the participants make sense of the events in their lives. In a sense, this design has a biographical element as its basis.

FIGURE 6.10 ■ Narrative Inquiry

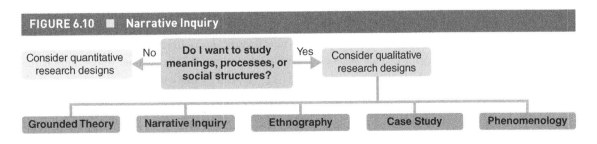

An example of narrative inquiry would be if a researcher interviewed English language learners who became classroom teacher assistants. The stories of these individuals, the transformative episodes during their career path, and the unfolding contextual factors are the framework for data analysis and interpretations. For these types of studies, the narratives could range in scope from one to several individuals, but the key objective is to center on the events in their lives.

Nature of Research Questions

The essence of research questions for narrative design is to frame the critical issue from the perspective of the participants. What will be essential in this type of study is the presentation of the experiences from the viewpoint of participant(s) rather than that of the researcher. The research questions set the tone for the study. As described earlier, integrating the topic and participants in the qualitative research question would be particularly useful since the study centers on the experiences of the participant(s). Figure 6.11 includes an example of a research question (highlighted in orange), which would be viable for narrative inquiry. In this case, the topic is the way in which a professional development workshop reflects the personal and professional goals of three teachers.

FIGURE 6.11 ■ Example of Narrative Inquiry Research Question

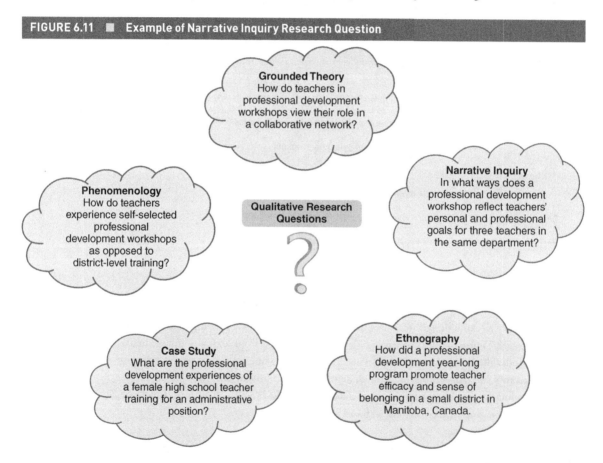

Narrative inquiry research questions move beyond describing a series of events to emphasize what can be gained in understanding the critical issue from the participants' voices. Some narrative inquiry research questions directly correspond with this notion. As a narrative inquiry study unfolds, one type of question to ask could be, "Why did teachers express their experience in the professional development workshop in this way?" or "How do the events expressed by teachers inform the way they perceive professional development workshops?" As the researcher develops narrative inquiry research questions, they will want to consider ways to capture how individuals interpret the events in their lives.

Sampling

This type of design does not require a large sample size given that the goal is to delve deeply into the stories of individual lives rather than generalizability. In fact, a large sample would not be effective in narrative inquiry as this is a systematic approach, often combining many types of data to highlight individual viewpoints. An open-ended survey with large numbers of responses would not lend itself well to this type of study. The most common form of sampling for narrative inquiry is purposeful sampling, in which criteria is specified prior to identifying participants.

Two possible complications with narrative design include exaggerations or inaccuracies recounted by participants. In this case, the data are not trustworthy. One way to counter this issue is to interview participants with similar backgrounds and experiences and then compare the data to shape the narrative. Researchers should practice reflexivity in their analysis, interpretations, and reporting to be sure the narrative does not deviate from the participants' accounts.

Data Collection

One prevalent form of data collection in narrative inquiries about an individual or groups of individuals' perspectives are field notes; the researcher takes observational records. In a sense, these notes become an experience shared by both researcher and participant. While field notes may be recorded by hand on site, it is helpful to transcribe these notes electronically for subsequent analysis. Tips include labeling the date, time, and location; integrating images with the text if available; and highlighting key terms within text.

Other possible sources of data include interviews, storytelling, letters, and biographies/autobiographies. Through each phase of the study and with each type of data source, the researcher should be systematic and transparent in their approach, always considering potential biases in recounting the experiences of the participants through reflexivity. While field notes are used in many forms of qualitative research design, the integration of this type of data lends itself well to recounting the perspective of participants.

One underlying assumption of narrative inquiry is the notion of temporality. In this case, temporality refers to people, events, and ideas as markers throughout time. This embedded concept highlights the continuum of events, not only what has happened in the past but how these aspects are relevant to the present and future. When collecting data, it is helpful to consider how to capture this continuum in the participants' lives. Two other elements in narrative inquiry include sociality (cultural and personal exchanges) and spatiality (environmental factors/place). In other words, the cultural, social, and environmental dynamics are integral to an individual's experiences.

Data Analysis

The way in which a researcher intends to present findings in narrative inquiry directly corresponds with data analysis. In the first instance, the researcher frames analysis around concepts developed from theory. Each narrative is then coded and categorized according to a pre-established theory. In a sense, this approach is akin to grounded theory, and in fact, the constant comparative analysis approach would be appropriate.

In the second case, the researcher collects stories of specific events, summarizes and synthesizes the information, and then creates a single narrative. The restorying of events follows a type of plot line. Various types of data including interviews, observations, and recordings are integral for either type of data analysis. Regardless of the data analysis approach, the researcher will want to be transparent and explicit in the description of how data were coded, analyzed, and interpreted. Creating figures to help with these corresponding accounts are particularly useful for the reader.

Examining Narrative Inquiry in the Empirical Literature

Narrative inquiry design is applicable to studying critical issues in educational settings, particularly from the perspective of individual accounts of events and perceptions. The following section highlights exemplars of narrative inquiry with the backdrop of professional development beginning with a *Let's See It!* activity. Then you will be asked to summarize a narrative inquiry study with the first example as a model (*Let's Do It!*). To further cultivate your understanding and use of grounded theory principles, please complete the *You Do It!* activity.

Let's See It! 6.5

Goal: To Understand the Key Features of Narrative Inquiry Design

The primary objective of this activity is to help you identify the key features of a published article using narrative inquiry. Brown (2022) focused on a professional development workshop targeting what early career secondary mathematics teachers notice using a Learning to Notice framework. Participants engaged in written replay to reflect on events within the mathematics classroom. Read the summary in Table 6.4 to learn about the key information related to the grounded theory design. It may also be helpful to access and read the entire methods section of the article to obtain a more detailed overview of the methodological procedures and approaches used for each study.

TABLE 6.4 ■ Narrative Inquiry Design	
Study	Brown, R. E. (2022). Using written teaching replays to learn what early career secondary mathematics teachers notice. *International Journal of Science and Mathematics Education 20*, 1635–1657. https://doi.org/10.1007/s10763-021-10220-y
Purpose	To highlight what induction level secondary mathematics teachers' focus on when writing narrative inquiries.
Critical Issues	The critical issue was training secondary teachers on how to use a Learning to Notice framework when reflecting on classroom instruction. The aim of the program was to train early career teachers in noticing.
Sample	The sample included 13 early career teachers who were in a cohort of an induction program, which included the Learning to Notice component.
Data Collection	The participants were asked to complete three teacher replay narratives about incidents within the classroom.
Data Analysis	Researchers coded 214 paragraphs in correspondence with three dimensions of the Learning to Notice framework (e.g., the role of the teacher, the topic, and the teacher perspective of lesson). Then coding schemes were analyzed for similarities and differences, including student solutions, task, or mathematical coding. Tiers of descriptive coding were used to develop emergent themes.
Results	Findings showed that teachers focused minimally on classroom management but emphasized an inquiry-based approach to instruction learned through professional development.

Let's Do It! 6.5

Guided Practice: Practice Summarizing the Key Features of Narrative Inquiry Design

The primary objective of this activity is for you to independently review and identify the key features of a narrative inquiry article. To guide your thinking, we encourage you to use the information from the *Let's See It!* (Table 6.4) as well as the guiding questions in Table 6.5. We also provide an answer key in the appendix at the end of the chapter for you to check your work.

TABLE 6.5 ■ Narrative Inquiry Design	
Study	Kuebel, C. R., Koops, L. H., & Bond, V. L. (2018). Cultivating teachers of general music methods: The graduate years. *Journal of Music Teacher Education, 28*(1), 10–23. https://doi-org.mutex.gmu.edu/10.1177/1057083718761812
Purpose	Is the overall purpose clear?
Critical Issue	Does the issue appear to be a critical educational issue?
	Is a strong rationale provided for the critical issue? (You may need to read the introduction to the article.)
Sample	Is the target group appropriate given the research purposes?
	What sampling technique was used to select participants?
	Were the techniques used to select participants clear and appropriate?
Data Collection	What types of data were used?
	How were the data collected?
Data Analysis	What approach was used to analyze data?
Results	What are the key findings that relate to the research questions?

Ethnography

The research design known as an ethnography, one of the earliest forms of qualitative research designs, centers on analyzing, interpreting, and recounting the shared experiences of a cultural group on a variety of factors (e.g., behaviors, beliefs, and language; Figure 6.12). Ethnographies derive from the tradition of cultural anthropology by assessing patterns in social interactions and human behavior. A discerning characteristic of this qualitative design is the focus on describing and interpreting cultural norms and behaviors. Ethnographers typically live within the culture they are studying for an extended period of time to develop a narrative of larger issues from day-to-day pictures.

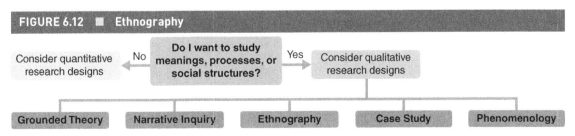

FIGURE 6.12 ■ Ethnography

This type of study requires prolonged experiences, so the researcher conducts participant-based observations to learn about the context first hand. Researcher observations, accounts of daily experiences, interactions, and behaviors in tandem reflect the variability of people, their perceptions, and the local site.

As an example, in some cultures in the world, English is the established language of instruction for mathematics, although it is not the native language of community members. This issue can pose some dilemmas for teachers who are not as fluent in English but teach mathematics. In an ethnographic study, a researcher could live in such a community. The researcher could study the English-based training program from the perspective of teachers, parents, administrators, school personnel, and students. The broad use of technology affords new opportunities for virtual ethnographies, so this type of study is less costly since it traditionally requires a lengthy time commitment in the past.

Ethnographers study the shared experiences of a cultural group on a variety of factors over a prolonged period of time.

©iStockphoto.com/ranplett

There are some underlying assumptions held by ethnographic researchers, one being that it is not possible to provide a complete description of any aspect of human nature and experiences. There is only an attempt to provide rich detail of a specific context at a snapshot of time. Another foundational assumption is that a researcher must experience the social norms and interactions through observation and participation, as well as gather data through a process of inquiry when questioning individuals about their thought processes, reactions, and behaviors. Since ethnographic studies take a long period of time, the quality and amount of participant engagement may vary over time. In order to obtain rich sources of information, the researcher will need to be persistent, methodical, and practice reflexivity throughout the process.

Nature of Research Questions

In an ethnographic study of teacher assistants, a researcher assimilates within a community for an extended period of time to follow the daily lived experiences of participants. Since the researcher's focus is typically based on behaviors and interactions, the research question will reflect this perspective. In addition, there are often inherent cultural/social influences and patterns within a community. These aspects shape the way a researcher will integrate questions that account for social structures. In an educational context, a researcher could describe the daily activities, school dynamics, and dilemmas faced by teacher assistants by asking the question, "What are the experiences of teacher assistants who work in Title I schools?" This type of question provides a framework to capture the nuances of social activities, beliefs, and attitudes central to ethnographic studies as shown in Figure 6.13 in orange.

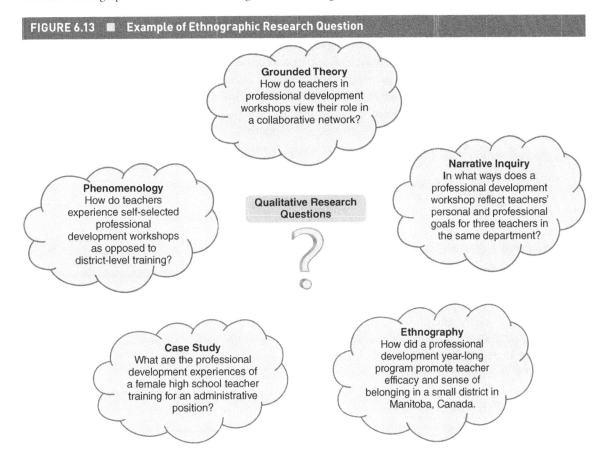

FIGURE 6.13   ■   Example of Ethnographic Research Question

Grounded Theory
How do teachers in professional development workshops view their role in a collaborative network?

Phenomenology
How do teachers experience self-selected professional development workshops as opposed to district-level training?

Qualitative Research Questions

Narrative Inquiry
In what ways does a professional development workshop reflect teachers' personal and professional goals for three teachers in the same department?

Case Study
What are the professional development experiences of a female high school teacher training for an administrative position?

Ethnography
How did a professional development year-long program promote teacher efficacy and sense of belonging in a small district in Manitoba, Canada.

Sampling

Ethnographers typically select a specific community to study over a long period of time. The non-random sampling method known as *purposeful sampling* (a.k.a. purposive sampling) is most applicable to ethnographies. There are several types of purposeful sampling (see Section 6.4); however, using a criterion approach would be suitable for an ethnography. In this regard, the researcher would specify a specific location of study and then detail the criteria used for selecting participants. A researcher conducting an ethnography could also use network/snowball sampling, although this technique may not garner participants who would provide the richest amount of detail.

Data Collection

Previously in this chapter, we discussed the use of interviews for qualitative research. While many of the guidelines for conducting interviews are appropriate across various types of researcher designs, ethnographic interviews focus heavily on cultural frameworks. For this reason, the researcher will want to create semi-structured interviews that target topics of culture, such as rituals, beliefs, ceremonies, oral history, myths, and folklore, as some examples.

There are several types of questions that would be helpful in collecting data from a cultural viewpoint. Research questions could center on the experiences and behaviors of individuals. For example, in a study of professional development workshops, a participant could be asked, "What was the first day of the professional development workshop like for you?" Not only should the questions ask participants to recall events, but individuals should be asked to explain what the event meant to them. In this way, participants can share their values, beliefs, and attitudes about specific situations. The researcher could state a question with a counter opinion: "Some teachers feel that it would be better to be in the classroom than to miss a day for professional development. What are your thoughts?" Participants could also recount how they felt when something happened to better understand the affective/emotional perspective.

Focus group interviews may be a useful tool in addition to individual sessions. This method enables the researcher to capture shared cultural norms as well as what the group emphasizes and chooses to ignore and where it diverges in opinions. As with other types of research designs, varied types of data include video recording, community artifacts, and documents, as some other examples. However, in ethnographic work, the dialogue during interviews and between individuals will be a prevalent type of data.

Data Analysis

Ethnographic research includes thick descriptions of the cultural and social exchanges within a community of individuals. Many types of qualitative research create a schematic system based on tiered coding of data (e.g., the constant comparative analysis approach) from the participant perspective. In an ethnographic approach, the researcher must also integrate their understandings of the processes, meanings, and exchanges within the description. Whatever coding and organizational system are put in place for this process, the researcher will want to be explicit about the coding and organization and the way inferences occurred. Keeping field notes and analytic memos of the thought process of the researcher is a helpful tool in remembering the sequence of events and rationale for decisions during data analysis.

A main goal in the dissemination of findings is for the researcher to give the reader the sense they are immersed in the setting. As such, ethnographers present the findings in a dynamic way rather than presenting findings in a dry manner. Collecting ample data to provide a rich narrative is paramount in ethnographic work.

Multiple Approaches of Ethnographies

Regardless of the type of ethnography, a commonality is that the nexus of each study centers on human culture, social structures, and interactions. More specifically, researchers study the day-to-day behaviors and experiences of individuals within a community as well as their beliefs, values, and attitudes. We have outlined a classical approach to ethnography; however, there is another approach known as a critical ethnography.

A critical ethnography is a specific type of research design in which the goal is to empower a marginalized group of individuals. The focus is on challenging the status quo to uncover disparities. Individuals involved in critical ethnographies engage in reflective practices prior to and during the process of research. Key issues for reflection are to examine the personal identity of the researcher, issues surrounding participant selection (inclusion and exclusion of individuals), and the targeted topic of study in the research design. In addition, the critical ethnographic researcher will extensively research the historical backdrop that frames current issues surrounding social injustices. If regional educational leaders and researchers noticed that there were disparities in the number of female superintendents in comparison to male counterparts, a critical ethnography could conduct a historical examination of educational leadership as well as potential supports and barriers to educational training, mentorship, and recruitment practices. Regardless of the type of ethnography, research questions often start with "what" to reveal patterns of social activity, such as the procedures of a school district in addressing the needs of talented students.

Examining Ethnographies in Empirical Literature

Ethnographies are a common form of qualitative research. This approach extends to many facets of education. The following example (*Let's See It!*) and activity (*Let's Do It!*) provide practice in analyzing published educational ethnographies.

Let's See It! 6.6

Goal: To Understand the Key Features of Ethnographic Design

The primary objective of this activity is to help you identify the key features of a published article using ethnographic design. Kaomea et al. (2019) conducted an ethnographic study of teachers and students in an elementary school with a focus on embedding Hawaiian indigenous cultural heritage within formal elementary classroom settings. Read the summary in Table 6.6 to learn about the key information related to narrative inquiry design. It may also be helpful to access and read the entire methods section of the article to obtain a more detailed overview of the methodological procedures and approaches used for each study.

TABLE 6.6 ■ Ethnographic Design	
Study	Kaomea, J., Alvaret, M. B., & Pittman, M. (2019). Reclaiming, sustaining and revitalizing Hawaiian education through video-cued makawalu ethnography. *Anthropology & Education Quarterly, 50*(3). 270–290. https://doi.org/10.1111/aeq.12301
Purpose	The purpose was to examine an initiative to integrate a culture-based curriculum aligned with indigenous Hawaiian communities.
Critical Issue	The critical issue was that Hawaiian teachers had been educated in mainstream schools with Western value. The current study focused on ways the school adopted a culturally responsive Hawaiian curriculum reflective of the 700 students of Hawaiian ancestry.
Sample	One Hawaiian classroom teacher, Mrs. Makao, teaching to her first-grade classroom.
Data Collection	The participant taught to her first-grade classroom. The video was condensed to a 20 min segment.
Data Analysis	The researchers utilized a Hawaiian methodology of *makawala*, which is a multi-linear, multi-dimensional way of utilizing data. The instructional video was viewed by the participant in terms of how the lesson reflected her values and that of Hawaiian culture. Next a focus group panel of experts in Hawaiian culture addressed similar questions after watching the clip. The researchers synthesized findings from the teacher's reflections, the focus group's reflections, and literature on Hawaiian culture.
Results	Findings from this ethnographic study centered on effective practices for homeschool connections, culturally responsive pedagogy, and teaching practices attuned to Hawaiian culture. Effective practices which were highlighted included Hawaiian fostering family-like atmospheres, building homeschool connections, and student collaborations.

Let's Do It! 6.6

Guided Practice: Practice Summarizing the Key Features of Ethnographic Design

The primary objective of this activity is for you to independently review and identify the key features of an ethnographic article. To guide your thinking, we encourage you to use the *Let's See It!* tables and information as well as the guiding questions in Table 6.7. We also provide an answer key in the appendix at the end of the chapter for you to check your work.

TABLE 6.7 ■ Ethnographic Design	
Study	Arrazola, B. V., & Bozalongo, J. S. (2014). Teaching practices and teachers' perceptions of group creative practices in inclusive rural schools. *Ethnography and Education, 9*(3), 253–269. http://dx.doi.org/10.1080/1745782 3.2014.881721
Purpose	Is the overall purpose clear?
Critical Issues	Does the issue appear to be a critical educational issue?
	Is a strong rationale provided for the critical issue? (You may need to read the introduction to the article.)
Sample	Is the target group appropriate given the research purposes?
	What sampling technique was used to select participants?
	Were the techniques used to select participants clear and appropriate?
Data Collection	What types of data were used?
	How were the data collected?
Analysis	What approach was used to analyze data?
Results	What are the key findings that relate to the research questions?

Case Studies

A case study is a research design of a specific person, group, or community (Figure 6.14). When creating case studies from a qualitative perspective (there are quantitative case studies), the goal is to investigate a single case as a way of learning about a particular topic. The study is sometimes thought of as a bounded system wherein the focus is specifically on a unit of analysis. The **unit of analysis** is an individual or group of individuals who are participants in the study. This bounded system encompasses the case, which can be an individual, a community of practice, an organization, or event. Identifying the unit of analysis from the onset is a defining feature of case studies, distinct from other designs.

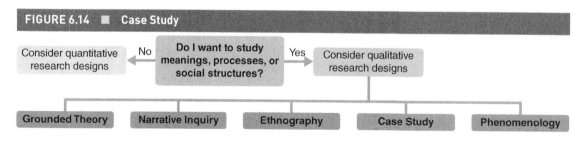

FIGURE 6.14 ■ Case Study

Since the primary focus of case studies is on the object of study, these designs apply to a wide range of contexts and disciplines. As the unit of analysis is inseparable to the context, the research itself should occur in a naturalistic setting to assess the lived experiences under specific parameters.

STOP AND THINK 6.4

How could the image that follows reflect a single case within a bounded system?

FIGURE 6.15 ■ Representation of a Single Case Within a Bounded System

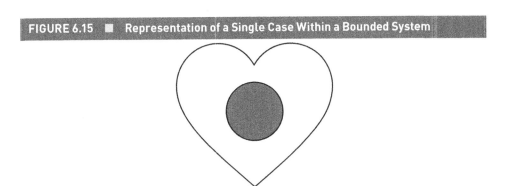

Nature of Research Questions

When working with case study design, the type of research design that is most helpful aims to answer the how, what, or why of a given situation. The research question highlighted in orange in Figure 6.15 reflects many of the tenets of case study research. For instance, asking "What are the professional development experiences of a female high school teacher training for an administrative position?" reflects a focus on one individual. In this case, the female high school teacher is the unit of analysis. The bounded system would be the instructional program and school context as she trains to be an administrator (see Figure 6.16). The case study itself would center on the lived experiences of this individual as she transitions from a teacher to a leadership role.

Sampling

A key issue in case studies include well-defined criteria for identifying a person or community to study. Equally necessary is to examine who or what is not included in the case study so as to fine-tune the criteria for purposeful sampling. In this type of design, the researcher should examine conditions in the most natural way possible to pinpoint the criteria. Well-defined parameters in case studies are known as "binding a case" and provide a buffer against an overly broad or narrow focus of study. Researchers can clarify the parameters of a study by time, setting, activities, and context.

As noted in the description of case studies, a defining aspect is the focus on the unit of analysis. Sampling procedures may differ based on the type of case study. For instance, a researcher may select an individual of interest. The researcher may want to learn more about a community or organization that they are unfamiliar with. In educational settings, a case study may be relevant to study needs within a particular school system. Regardless of the rationale for selecting the case, the researcher will want to clearly state the process used in the selection while addressing any potential biases.

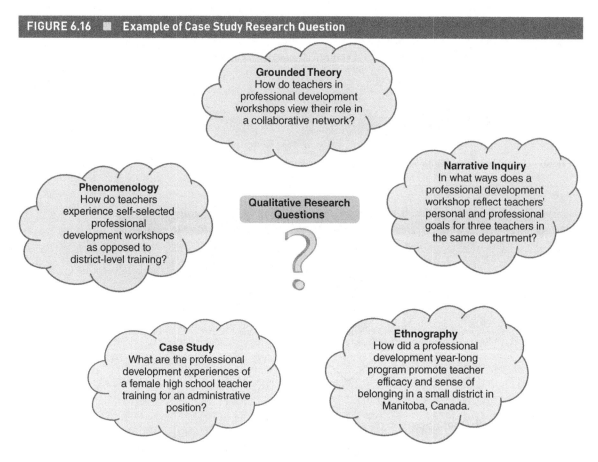

FIGURE 6.16 ■ Example of Case Study Research Question

When considering a teacher to study during the administrative training process, selecting any one individual training to be an administrator may be too broad of a case study. In contrast, a person with language processing difficulties, who has worked in five different schools, and who speaks French as a primary language, may be too narrow of a scope. Identifying the unit of analysis requires intentionality to study a person or setting for specific reasons. The researcher will need to clearly identify the characteristics of an individual or situation that are most suitable for the study to bind the case.

Data Collection

A hallmark of case studies is the use of multiple data sources to facilitate a clearer understanding through triangulation, a term that refers to reaching the same conclusion via multiple methods. There are many types of data that could be integrated as forms of triangulation (see Chapter 10 for more information). For example, a researcher studying the experiences of a female high school teacher transitioning to a leadership role through professional development workshops could collect many types of data, including interviews, the person's daily schedule, workshop agendas, school-based meetings, journal entries, and video recordings, as some examples. The overall aim would be to utilize a variety of sources that could provide a multi-faceted understanding of the unit of analysis as well as supporting methods for triangulation.

Data Analysis

A benefit of embedding a diverse range of data within case studies is to produce a highly descriptive and complex narrative of the case of study. If the unit of analysis is an organization, the researcher will want to approach the study with the notion that the individuals make up the whole case study collectively.

When analyzing data for a case study in which the unit of analysis is an organization, one approach is to analyze data from each individual and merge the findings to create a collective narrative. Collecting field notes and analytic memos during this process will enhance synthesis of subsequent information. These narratives will become a point of comparison when all information has been compiled. These narratives may be coded and categorized to check for patterns and inconsistencies across data.

Another useful suggestion is to create templates of each individual within an organization. These templates will assist in drawing accounts for individuals and the organization as a whole. Collecting information provides a way to form potential vignettes in the narrative. In addition, figures can be constructed to reflect findings across individuals within the organization.

Multiple Approaches to Case Studies

Another area to address is the type of case study that will best address the critical issue. There are many types of case studies, depending on the purpose of the study: intrinsic, instrumental, explanatory, exploratory, descriptive, and collective case studies.

The term intrinsic case study reflects the nature of this type of study where a particular individual, community, or event is selected based on a researcher's interest. While the unit of analysis may not seem to be unusual, a researcher makes the selection based on personal interest and to learn more about the person or context. An example would be the study of a teacher trained in naturalist studies who works with students in collecting stream turbidity samples in the outdoors. While there are many teacher naturalists who train children in this type of activity, the researcher has an interest for the specific techniques and viewpoints of this individual.

An exploratory case study is useful when the researcher has limited background information or experience with the unit of analysis. Studying how teachers involved in a local naturalist organization may warrant an exploratory approach. The researcher may have minimal knowledge on the training of these teacher naturalists, particular programs for the community, how the naturalists interact with the community, and variations based on school-aged students and adults.

In contrast, an explanatory case study has a specific question that considers the outcomes related to the implementation of an intervention. Stakeholders from a school district that implement a literacy-based program in outdoor contexts may want to determine the impact of training by naturalists on student reading achievement. A focus of the study would be to determine how teacher naturalists influence student reading achievement through an outdoor instructional medium.

In an instrumental case study, the goal is to use the case study to learn about a different topic outside of the parameters of the initial study. The case plays a subsidiary role in investigating another issue or supporting the development of a theory. For instance, investigating the perceptions of teacher naturalists in an organization about effective educational strategies in the outdoors may prompt further study into how to train teachers when forming collaborations with scientist and students. The researcher might enter the study with a broad question about how individuals in the organization perceive the best ways to train teachers working with children in the outdoors. Inadvertently, the information garnered could lead to studying specific outdoor programs and distinctive professional development opportunities.

A collective case study is when a researcher initially studies one case and then begins to study several cases on the same topic to make comparisons. These studies can occur simultaneously or sequentially. In this way, comparing several case studies provides added information on a topic of interest. A researcher might be interested to see how the perceptions of teachers affiliated with naturalist organizations in different regions vary based on the needs of the community and students.

Studying a teacher trained in naturalist studies who works with students in collecting stream turbidity samples in the outdoors could be an example of an intrinsic case study; in this instance, the researcher wants to learn more about the experiences of this individual.

©iStockphoto.com/John S Stewart

An example is the study of social supports and barriers in outdoor settings for a student with Down syndrome. A comparison of several students' experiences would be referred to as a collective case study. Or if a researcher studied the experiences of individuals with Down syndrome and compared analysis from participants in different geographic areas of the country, this technique would be considered a cross case comparison. During case studies, many different techniques can be used in analysis and interpretation. A typical approach would be to include observational notes of participants and in-depth interviews. If a teacher assistant was trained in a specialized program to assist children with Down syndrome, a case study research design could be used to examine the educator's perspective and confidence in using the strategies in the training program.

Examining Case Studies in the Empirical Literature

A case study is a useful research design approach in educational literature to learn about specific issues for an individual, organization, or community. In the next section, we present a series of published case studies. First, we will highlight elements of a case study in *Let's See It!* Then you

Studying social supports and barriers in outdoor settings for a student with Down syndrome would be a case study. A comparison of several students' experiences would be referred to as a collective case study.

©iStockphoto.com/DGLimages

will be asked to summarize a case study with the first example as a model in *Let's Do It!* To further enhance your understanding and use of case study principles, please complete the *You Do It!* activity.

Goal: To Understand the Key Features of Narrative Inquiry Design

The primary objective of this activity is to help you identify the key features of a published article using case study design. Kayi-Aydar (2019) conducted a narrative case study of the teacher agency and teacher identities of a Spanish language teacher through her daily work experiences. Read the summary in Table 6.8 to learn about the key information related to case study design. It may also be helpful to access and read the entire methods section of the article to obtain a more detailed overview of the methodological procedures and approaches used for each study.

TABLE 6.8 ■ Case Study Design	
Study	Kayi-Aydar, H. (2019). A language teacher's agency in the development of her professional identities: A narrative case study. *Journal of Latinos and Education, 18*(1), 4–18. https://doi.org/10.1080/15348431.2017.1406360
Purpose	The purpose of the case study was to describe the ways in which a Spanish language teacher utilized personal agency to form professional identities in the workplace.

Critical Issue	The critical issue was to examine how a teacher of Spanish language of Mexican descent navigated her workplace experiences, utilized personal agency, and formed her professional identities.
Sample	One teacher of Spanish language of Mexican descent.
Data Collection	Data collection encompassed transcripts from four semi-structured interviews focused on the participant's life history, particularly as a Spanish language teacher in various contexts in the United States.
Data Analysis	Analysis stemmed from discourse analysis. Transcripts were analyzed by identifying discourse markers for phrases starting with terms like "I mean . . ." "Oh well," and "You know" to identify areas where the participant was uncertain or had doubts and as a way to assess the participant's positionality within the context of school settings.
Results	Findings from the case study generated three themes centered on agency as a way to negotiate teacher identities for marginalized individuals, becoming "the teacher" role model for Latino students, and utilizing agency to reclaim a professional identity. Issues of race, ethnicity, language background, and power were elemental as part of these emergent themes.

Let's Do It! 6.7

Guided Practice: Practice Summarizing the Key Features of Case Study Design

The primary objective of this activity is for you to independently review and identify the key features of a case study design article. To guide your thinking, we encourage you to use the *Let's See It!* tables and information as well as the guiding questions in Table 6.9. We also provide an answer key in the appendix at the end of the chapter for you to check your work.

TABLE 6.9 ■ Case Study Design

Study	Bustamante, C. (2020). TPACK-based professional development on web 2.0 for Spanish teachers: A case study. *Computer Assisted Language Learning, 33*(4), 327–352. https://doi.org/10.1080/09588221.2018.1564333
Purpose	Is the overall purpose clear?
Critical Issue	Does the issue appear to be a critical educational issue?
	Is a strong rationale provided for the critical issue? (You may need to read the introduction to the article.)
Sample	Is the target group appropriate given the research purposes?
	What sampling technique was used to select participants?
	Were the techniques used to select participants clear and appropriate?
Data Collection	What types of data were used?
	How were the data collected?
Data Analysis	What approach was used to analyze data?
Results	What are the key findings that relate to the research questions?

Phenomenology

The form of qualitative research known as phenomenology derives from a philosophical tradition associated with Edmund Husserl (1859–1938), a German philosopher who was interested in the sentiments of groups of individuals who had experienced the same life event (Figure 6.17). Husserl (1913/2012) conjectured that information on material objects varied and was not based in reality. People's interpretations of these objects rooted in their consciousness was the only thing individuals could be certain of. In this way, Husserl espoused "bracketing" the external world from the nature of perceptions (Creely, 2018).

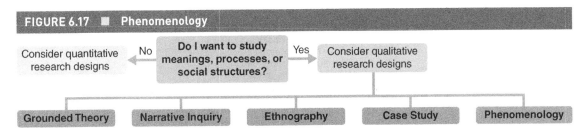

FIGURE 6.17 ■ Phenomenology

With a primary emphasis on those who have experienced a phenomenon in such a way that they can give detailed accounts, phenomenologists consider that individual's experiences and consciousness shape interpretations. In this type of design, the researcher aims to reveal the inner thoughts of the participants. This type of research has been applied to a variety of studies centered in sociology, nursing, health sciences, psychology, and education.

Nature of Research Questions

In order to develop research questions that are applicable to phenomenologies, it is helpful to understand some basic premises of this type of design. Phenomenologists adhere to the notion of Lifeworld; this term encompasses the way the human consciousness makes sense and meaning from everyday events. These influences are internal to the individual and guided by other people/relationships, animate and inanimate objects, technology, information taken in by the senses, and geographic location as many relatable factors. Another key term is the intentionality of consciousness, wherein the nature of a phenomenon cannot be separated from the perceptions of individuals.

Phenomenological studies inherently hold some underlying assumptions related to social interactions and behaviors. Therefore, researchers enter the field of study acknowledging that the vantage of individuals provides the backdrop for understanding lived experiences and those interactions shape all behavior, contextual factors, and viewpoints. Reality is part of individual's everyday encounters and linked to consciousness. Finally, phenomenologists are able to describe the essence of a phenomenon when participants with shared confrontations recount their Lifeworld, particularly when there is a revelation about the structure of the phenomenon.

Phenomenologists concern themselves with examining the structures and encounters that ultimately shape the individual's Lifeworld. This methodological focus is central to the design of research questions. In the case of a phenomenological study on collaborative teams, an applicable question could be, "Based on the perspective of core subject middle school teachers and teacher assistants, what is the essential structure of an effective collaborative team to meet the needs of students during a community health crisis?" The question draws attention to the collective experience of individuals who have experienced a distinct phenomenon.

Considering teacher professional workshops could be a backdrop for a phenomenological study. For instance, school districts often require professional workshops by grade level or subject area. As such, department members experience the training collectively. In contrast, teachers often select external workshops out of interest. Figure 6.18 shows another way to frame a question from the perspective of professional development workshop: "How do teachers experience self-selected professional develop workshops as opposed to district-level training?" The phenomenological design in this case could contrast collective experiences on professional development training.

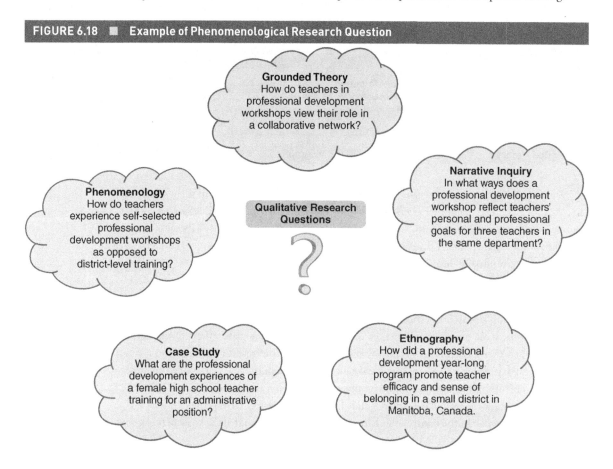

FIGURE 6.18 ■ Example of Phenomenological Research Question

What is notable about phenomenological designs is that the research questions not only focus on the perceptions of individuals from common experiences but also situate the researcher in the study. These questions provide a backdrop from which the researcher centers themselves among the views of the participants, examines the viewpoints of the participants engaged in the phenomenon, and draws meaning from data analysis and interpretation.

Sampling

During a phenomenology, a researcher would recruit participants who have first-hand, in-depth experiences of the phenomenon under study. For this reason, the purposeful sampling technique of criterion sampling is most appropriate. The first primary criterion would be that the participants have been involved in the phenomenon. Examples of these lived experiences from an educational lens could include individuals who started charter schools, teacher experiences opening a new school, homeschool enrichment mathematics programs, or the ways in which district programs support parents of children with autism. The ultimate aim of a phenomenological study is to ascribe basic meanings to an experience or phenomenon that straddles many individuals' accounts rather than repurposing an account based on one individual's impressions. This goal enables the researcher to attune to the context in greater detail.

Data Collection

As with many forms of qualitative research, interviews are a key type of data for phenomenological studies. The goal of analysis is to provide a unified understanding of the topic through multi-faceted lenses. Interview transcripts are particularly useful in this endeavor. In essence, the researcher is drawing inferences and meanings about the event based on the inferences and meanings drawn by the participants. The data collected should frame the ways in which the participants make meaning out of the event studied. A wide range of other types of data could be applicable, depending on the needs of the study (see Chapter 10 for more information on types of data).

Data Analysis

A term that is unique to phenomenology is epoché, which refers to refraining from drawing conclusions about the nature of reality of given circumstances or perceptions without further investigation; that is to say the researcher withholds drawing conclusions prior to amassing rich data from multiple sources. As noted earlier, phenomenologists adhere to the notion of Lifeworld; this term encompasses the way the human consciousness makes sense and meaning from everyday events. These influences are internal to the individual and guided by other people/relationships, animate and inanimate objects, technology, information taken in by the senses, and geographic location as many relatable factors.

STOP AND THINK 6.5

Mrs. Pauls, a counselor at the local middle school, wants to study student and teacher perceptions of an after-school homework club. Which types of qualitative research design would be appropriate and why?

A phenomenologist will begin by collecting data on the lived experiences of participants. After initial data collection, the researcher uses reflective analysis to interpret the shared stories. For example, if a researcher wanted to study the novel context of distance learning during a school closing, interviews from teachers who taught during this time period could be collected to reveal the nature of the phenomenon. Teacher assistants' perspectives of student needs prior to and after the community health crisis could be instrumental in shaping programs to meet individual learning needs. This scenario exemplifies how phenomenology differs from other forms of research; individuals who have experienced a specific event share their views so the researcher can fully understand the structure and shared experiences of the event. Other examples of phenomenological studies could be individuals who have experienced the loss of a loved one at an early age, a community that becomes central to a national news story, or parents challenging a specific school district policy that affects their children, families, and neighborhood.

Through analysis, the researcher aims to tease out individual perceptions to form a core understanding of the phenomenon. Utilizing a themed approach is one way to proceed with this type of investigation. To conduct this type of analysis, the researcher first codes phrases into units of meaning. Next, the researcher enters these units of meaning in a data table and then labels each unit by theme. When all units of meaning are labeled, themes are analyzed and combined into a cluster. In this sense, the themes become subthemes. Once subthemes are developed, the researcher creates one central theme that serves as the nexus for the narrative. It is especially helpful to draw insights from individual participants before drawing collective themes. As with all data analysis techniques, the researcher is explicit in the processes and rationale and checks for biases when describing data analysis procedures.

Multiple Approaches to Phenomenology

The discipline of phenomenology can be subdivided into two traditions: descriptive and interpretive phenomenologies. Both branches center on the shared experiences of individuals who have undergone a specific and often unique circumstance to share underlying meanings.

A descriptive phenomenology emphasizes the processes of exploring, analyzing, and describing shared and unique experiences. In this case, researchers utilize bracketing and frame the study in epoché, where there are no preconceived notions. Utilizing these processes allows the researcher to uncover hidden elements of the phenomenon. A distinct feature of this form of phenomenology is to make it clear to readers what the experience is like without any expectations prior to analysis.

The branch known as interpretivist phenomenology emphasizes gaining deeper understandings through interpretations, particularly when there are further implications for the topic of study. The view is that beyond recognition of the event, interpretivists aim to draw out rich extended meaning from the participants' expressions. Previous knowledge about the event, while bracketed in descriptive work, is embedded in the interpretations within the study. In this case, the participants' voices and the insights from the researcher are integral to the overall findings. An example of an educational context would be studying a school with flextime, in which there is a time in the school day where students can select their activity (e.g., working on assignments, help-seeking, off campus lunch, enrichment offerings). This would be a unique phenomenon as most secondary students are not given as much flexibility within the school day. A phenomenology could focus on teachers' perceptions of flextime based on workshop training and day-to-day experiences.

Examining Phenomenology in the Empirical Literature

Phenomenology is a useful research design approach in educational literature, particularly when analyzing unique contexts or events. In the next section, we present a phenomenology study (*Let's See It!*). Then you will be asked to summarize a phenomenology study with the first example as a model (*Let's Do It!*). To further cultivate your understanding and use of phenomenology principles, please complete the *You Do It!* activity.

Let's See It! 6.8

Goal: To Understand the Key Features of Phenomenological Design

The primary objective of this activity is to help you identify the key features of a published article using phenomenological design. Hite and Milbourne (2022) used a phenomenological approach to study the professional development and career paths of master K–12 STEM instructors. Read the summary in Table 6.10 to learn about the key information related to phenomenological design. It may also be helpful to access and read the entire methods section of the article to obtain a more detailed overview of the methodological procedures and approaches used for each study.

TABLE 6.10 ■ Phenomenological Design	
Study	Hite, R. L., & Milbourne, J. D. (2022). Divining the professional development experiences of K–12 STEM master teacher leaders in the United States. *Professional Development in Education, 48*(3), 476–492. https://doi.org/10.1080/19415257.2021.1955733
Purpose	The purpose of the interpretive phenomological case study was to examine the professional development opportunities of master K–12 STEM career teachers and leaders.
Critical Issue	The critical issue addressed in this study was ways to improve professional development opportunities to increase the quantity of STEM instructors and to improve STEM learning and instruction.
Sample	Ten teachers who had been nationally recognized for their mastery and leadership in STEM education with the Presidential Award for Excellence in Mathematics and Science Teaching or the Albert Einstein Distinguished Educator Fellowship.
Data Collection	Each participant completed a 60 min. online interview following an open-ended question format that encouraged think-aloud reflections of their past experiences in STEM and professional development.
Data Analysis	Thematic analysis occurred in a series of phases, with the first focused on individual interviews to develop emergent themes. The second phase was a formulation of themes across participant experiences, particularly in terms of similarities and differences.
Results	Findings revealed that participants emphasized the culture and community of a school, as well as outside individuals and organizations, which influenced their STEM career pathways as instructors. Participants also found that networks within professional learning communities led to new networks. Participants also highlighted service, altruism, and a commitment to the school community as a motivating factor in developing their mastery of STEM instruction.

Let's Do It! 6.8

Guided Practice: Practice Summarizing the Key Features of Phenomenological Design

The primary objective of this activity is for you to independently review and identify the key features of a phenomenological design article. To guide your thinking, we encourage you to use the *Let's See It!* tables and information as well as the guiding questions in Table 6.11. We also provide an answer key in the appendix at the end of the chapter for you to check your work.

TABLE 6.11 ■ Phenomenological Design	
Study	LeRoy, A. S., & Boomgaard, S. L. (2021). Empathy in isolation: Lived experiences of teachers of refugee children. *Integrative Psychological & Behavioral Science, 55*(2), 430–443. https://doi.org/10.1007/s12124-019-09508-0
Purpose	Is the overall purpose clear?
Critical Issue	Does the issue appear to be a critical educational issue?
	Is a strong rationale provided for the critical issue? (You may need to read the introduction to the article.)

Sample	Is the target group appropriate given the research purposes?
	What sampling technique was used to select participants?
	Were the techniques used to select participants clear and appropriate?
Data Collection	What types of data were used?
	How were the data collected?
Data Analysis	What approach was used to analyze data?
Results	What are the key findings that relate to the research questions?

While this section has surveyed major types of qualitative research design, we would like to note that these types of designs can be integral to mixed methods research, wherein both qualitative and quantitative methods address research questions (further described in Chapter 7). In addition, qualitative methods may be part of action research; these studies take place in educational settings to solve practical school-based problems as outlined in Chapter 8. Finally, this section provided a broad overview of qualitative research designs; many variations of these approaches are applicable to research studies depending on the context, research questions, and framework established by the researchers.

THE TAKEAWAY

There are a variety of qualitative research designs to address specific research questions. There is no one type of research design that is preferable over others. Researchers select the design that is most applicable to the purpose of the study, aligns with the research questions, and is feasible to conduct (e.g., availability of participants and data collection instruments).

THE QUALITATIVE RESEARCH PROCESS

LEARNING OBJECTIVE

6.4   Detail the process of qualitative research.

Preparing to conduct qualitative research involves a great deal of organization and planning in terms of research design, settings, participant selection, assessment tools, and logistical considerations, as some examples. The goals and requirements of a qualitative study will dictate the research process and frames the literature review, method, results, and discussion sections. In this section, we focus on some critical elements found in each section of the research process as well as issues that could arise in terms of the procedures of conducting qualitative research (see also Chapters 2 and 15).

The Qualitative Literature Review

The format of the literature review derives from the educational issue identified by the researcher(s). The literature review outlines aspects of the topic of study by summarizing and synthesizing literature based on previous research studies. Since qualitative research is inductive in nature, the literature review tends to be shorter than quantitative studies and does not end with a preset determination of an outcome in the form of a hypothesis. The research questions themselves focus on questions that would provide a rich, detailed account of the setting and/or unit of analysis and are the last element included in the literature review. Typically, the researcher has a minimal understanding of the intricacies of the problem, to limit the formation of predetermined understandings prior to data collection. In fact, some qualitative researchers refrain from writing the literature review until after data collection, analysis, and interpretation have occurred.

Sometimes a researcher will determine that a topic of interest has not been studied extensively in the literature. At this point, the researcher will draw on relatable topics, demonstrate gaps in the literature, and propose a new study. Regardless of the topic, the researcher should proceed with the literature review by emphasizing four essential elements: (a) writing article summaries concisely, (b) synthesizing articles across the literature review, (c) relating each article to the topic of study with a cohesive structure, and (d) integrating articles from other disciplines when necessary. Utilizing these principles will be instrumental in developing a well-constructed qualitative literature review.

The Method Section

For a qualitative study, the method section generally includes sections on the research design, setting, and participants; sampling; procedures; data collection; proposed data analysis; and quality and ethics.

Research Design, Setting, and Participants

An effective way to begin the method section is to begin by restating the purpose of the study as it relates to the overall research design. At this point, the researcher will indicate which type of qualitative research design will address the question.

When designing a qualitative study, a researcher may not always have access to individuals they would like to interview/study. An important part of the research design is identifying not only who will be studied but if there are any parameters that will create limitations in terms of resources, access to individuals, and limits on the time table.

Within this section, the researcher often provides demographic information about the participants (e.g., biological sex, racial/ethnic backgrounds, socioeconomic status, special education status, etc.). A critical element for qualitative research is to describe the identification of participants for the study. Following, is a basic overview of non-random sampling techniques that are applicable to qualitative research.

Sampling

Qualitative researchers customarily select participants through non-random sampling techniques as shown in Figure 6.21. Non-random sampling techniques are a way to select participants for a study, not by chance but rather through identified criteria and/or participant availability (for a detailed description of these sampling techniques, see Chapter 10). Figure 6.19 shows an initial classification of non-random sampling methods (convenience, purposeful, and quota). Next, purposeful sampling is further subdivided into five categories (criterion, maximum variation, snowball/network, by case, theoretical sampling).

FIGURE 6.19 ■ **Non-Random Sampling Methods**

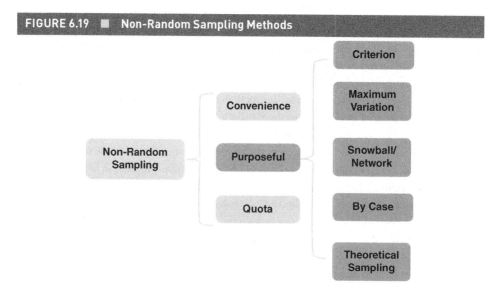

In convenience sampling, researchers invite participants who are readily available. This type of sampling can shed light on a context of interest; however, designing a study with specific criteria to identify participants can often address the questions more specifically. Quota sampling is a non-random technique used when researchers identify a set of characteristics for a population and survey/interview individuals who reflect these characteristics within a homogeneous group to capture a quick comparison. The third non-random sampling technique is purposeful sampling, which is most applicable to qualitative research. Since qualitative researchers often utilize the process of *restorying* (collecting, analyzing, and rewriting) the experiences of participants or describing phenomenon as they relate the nature of an educational setting, purposeful sampling (also known as purposive sampling) is a preferrable method for identifying participants. In this case, the researcher uses a set of pre-determined criteria to select the participants.

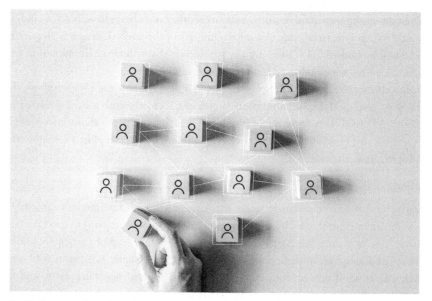

Qualitative researchers often utilize purposeful sampling (also known as purposive sampling) with a set of pre-determined criteria to select the participants.

©iStockphoto.com/oatawa

There are several ways the researcher can utilize purposeful sampling including (a) criterion, (b) maximum variation, (c) snowball/network, (d) by case, and (e) theoretical sampling. Each of these methods for selecting participants is steered by the study goals and the availability of participants.

Purposeful sampling through criterion sampling entails that a researcher identifies specific characteristics of individuals who would yield rich information as part of a study. For example, a researcher studying teacher assistants who are career switchers (individuals who had previous professions) could use the criteria of (a) career switchers, (b) less than 5 years' experience, and (c) elementary school.

A second framework for participant selection is maximum variation. This method is useful when the researcher wants to select individuals who represent high and low ends of a particular attribute, phenomenon, or situation. Researchers studying perceptions of teacher assistants' preference for training in mathematics instruction could identify individuals with high and low interest and then compare findings based on maximum variation.

Snowball or network sampling is a third option in selecting participants in qualitative research. In this case, the researcher interviews an individual and then asks for a referral. Perhaps a researcher studying teachers' perceptions of outdoor education is having difficulty locating individuals with diverse backgrounds to shed a multifaceted narrative of outdoor training. Participants make referrals of teachers with varying backgrounds to broaden the scope of the study following each interview. A drawback of this approach is that the initial person in the chain of referrals has great influence over the trajectory of the study. Figure 6.20 shows an intricate referral system across three geographical boundaries to illustrate the dynamics of snowball/network selection.

FIGURE 6.20 ■ An Example of Snowball/Network Participant Selection

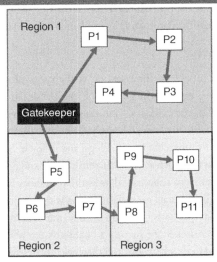

Note. P indicates a participant.

When using a snowball or network approach, a gatekeeper often helps to secure research participants. A gatekeeper is someone in an organization who assists the researcher in gaining access/permissions for individuals to participate in a study. The researcher should consider that the gatekeeper has influence over the direction of the study because of referrals to individuals who receive an invitation to participate in the study; the gatekeeper unknowingly steers the direction of the study. Figure 6.20 shows how the gatekeeper makes critical referrals to participants in two separate regions. From there, each participant makes additional referrals.

A fourth approach to participant selection is by case. In this instance, by case study refers to a situation in which an individual has specific characteristics, and a study would yield a rich discussion of an individual's daily interactions. Distinct from maximum variation, in which several individuals would be studied based on a range of characteristics, case studies focus on a smaller unit of study in more detail. An example would be a physical education teacher who teaches individuals with physical disabilities how to dance. A researcher may want to examine the lived experiences, training protocol, and challenges and highpoints of the individual.

Theoretical sampling is a type of purposeful sampling used in a specific type of qualitative research design discussed earlier in this chapter, known as grounded theory. Theoretical sampling as defined by Glaser and Strauss (1967) is a method of developing a theory by collecting, organizing, and categorizing data. In this process, once initial data have been collected, the researcher analyzes and interprets data, refines the inquiry, and collects additional data (e.g., interviews) as the basis for theory development.

Qualitative researchers strategically select the most appropriate participant sampling method based on the needs of the study. Outlining the choices for sampling informs subsequent procedures in the study.

Procedures

Another purpose of the method section is to describe the procedures involved in the research study, depending on the research design selected. When working in schools, a researcher will want to be mindful of the way they implement the research design so as not interfere with the school day and student learning. Coordinating invitations, permissions, and methods of study (e.g., interviews, observational notes) are all strategically planned with the on-site administrator, district research offices, university IRBs, and often with the assistance of a gatekeeper. One useful technique when presenting the procedures is to create a timeline of key aspects of the research study, such as starting and ending dates, and the implementation of collected qualitative data.

Data Collection

Another key element listed in the method section is the types of data included in the study. Qualitative data, designed to capture the essence of specific situations, range from interviews, observations, writing samples, and artifacts. Traditionally, interviews have been a bountiful way to gather information for a qualitative research study. Continual innovations in technology add to possibilities through online forums, chat rooms, blogs, and so forth. Moreover, other types of data can be in forms other than in text, such as artwork, music, film, and poetry, as some examples.

An important note in terms of collecting data is the misnomer that quantitative data always involves "numbers" and qualitative data excludes numbers with a focus on "quality." This explanation is an oversimplification as qualitative data can include numbers, although this is most often *not* the case. For instance, if a researcher conducting a qualitative study wanted to observe where the teacher assistant is positioned in the classroom and their role, the researcher may prepare a checklist in advance to note the number of times the teacher assistant is in the front of the room and what the assistant is doing to create a tally. This frequency describes the role and behavior of the teacher assistant. (For more information on qualitative frequency coding, see Saldaña, 2021.)

Under the data collection section, the researcher will provide an overview of each tool that is part of the research design. The writing will include the name of the tool, author, and a description of the purpose, and sample questions are common elements to include. Describing data collection tools is particularly important when considering alignment between the purpose of the study, research questions, and analysis. To address the critical issue, the data collection tools must be well-defined in order to gather applicable information.

Proposed Data Analysis

Within the proposed data analysis portion of the method section, the researcher will outline specifically how data analysis techniques correspond with each research question. Throughout this section, the researcher will provide detailed information about data analysis procedures, such as coding.

If tiers of coding are applicable to the data analysis approach, the researcher will describe the implementation of each phase of coding. At this point, it may be helpful to integrate figures to help the reader understand the process. The goal would be that other researchers could replicate the steps via a detailed explanation. In the results section, the researcher will continue the process by applying the system of analysis with the data unique to the selected researcher's study.

Quality and Ethics

The quality and ethics portion of the method section is where the researcher outlines the steps that have been taken to promote high levels of trustworthiness (see Section 6.5 for more information on trustworthiness). Further, it is helpful to refer to qualitative methodologists when addressing issues related to quality and ethics. Two broad ways to address trustworthiness are to describe the role of the researcher and steps taken to curtail potential biases.

When addressing the role of the researcher, a narrative on the subjective lens within the method section provides the reader with insights into the positionality of the researcher. In addition, the researcher will refer to the use of reflexivity and tools to support this process, such as field notes/analytic memos. These descriptions could include the way the principles of the Belmont Report were upheld, such as protecting participant identity throughout the research process.

Another important element is to describe specific steps taken to curtail researcher bias. In Chapter 14, we will provide detailed explanations of specific strategies including intercoder reliability, member checking, and triangulation.

During the qualitative research planning process, there are questions that can be used to steer the overall design. Figure 6.21 includes a flowchart with some critical decisions to

FIGURE 6.21 ■ Qualitative Research Method Section Decision Tree

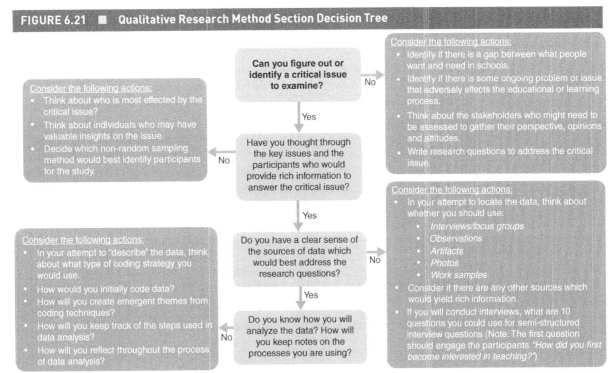

make, particularly for the method section. The middle boxes can be thought of as a form of troubleshooting—these questions can guide you in terms of issues you may not be sure how to address.

The Results Section

When developing the results section, the writing should include an explicit description of data coding, analysis, and interpretations. Once the procedure for data analysis have been described in detail, a narrative of the findings follows. One way to proceed is to arrange the section by themes. Each theme should be supported with participant quotes, which serve as data points to support overall theme development.

Notably, the researcher will want to reflect on the results from a multicultural perspective to frame the work from the perspective of participants. The research study conducted by Kaomea et al. (2019) on the integration of Hawaiian heritage within classroom instruction reflects the use of a multicultural lens throughout the study, including the results section. This multi-faceted lens framed the Hawaiian *makawulu* phenomenological design, the utilization of a focus group of Hawaiian cultural experts as part of the methods, and the integration of individual and group perceptions of Hawaiian cultural elements embedded within the curriculum as a form of culturally responsive practices. The nature of the study and social/cultural elements serve as the basis for the results section. A reflective researcher will be aware of how their cultural background and experiences can inadvertently steer the results. In this case, there is a balance between the role of the researcher and the participants' perceptions.

In the results section, the author should strive to maintain participant anonymity. The use of pseudonyms for participants is one way to protect individual identity. If there are very specific identifiers for participants, findings may be presented by changed descriptions of the participants.

The Discussion Section

Throughout the discussion, the researcher summarizes the findings without including numerical information or quotes at length. Importantly, the findings should be related to previous literature. The section concludes with limitations within the study, implications for educators and researchers, suggestions for future research, and educational implications.

A common weakness in the discussion section is to present minimal information that relates the findings of the proposed study to previous literature. In this situation, the researcher should include how the present work aligns with findings from past research and highlighting new discoveries if present. Another common deficiency in the discussion section is a misguided focus on limitations. In this section, the researcher only describes issues that would impact their ability to analyze data (e.g., difficulty accessing participants, restrictions in gathering data, etc.). Finally, the work should include implications as that is the overarching purpose of most research. The aim is to provide support or guidance for improved educational practices.

THE TAKEAWAY

The qualitative research process is ethically bound, interactive, and involves extensive planning, methodical analysis, and thoughtful interpretation.

ETHICAL CONSIDERATIONS

When developing and conducting qualitative studies, researchers aim to develop high quality studies. Central to this goal of designing, administering, and reporting findings is to relay information with integrity. In this way, the work reflects a high level of trustworthiness with a clear account of the topic of study, without being overly influenced by the researcher's perspective. Whereas reliability and validity are key factors in establishing accurate interpretations in quantitative research, qualitative researchers focus on issues related to *trustworthiness*. Elements of trustworthiness, which heighten the rigor of qualitative work, can be viewed as analogous to issues of validity and reliability often attended to and described in quantitative work as shown in Figure 6.22.

Establishing trustworthiness in qualitative research centers on credibility, transferability, confirmability, and dependability. Credibility describes how confident the researchers are that the findings are accurate and is comparable to internal validity assessed in quantitative studies. Transparency of data analysis procedures, the use of triangulation of data sources, and researcher consensus of findings are ways to bolster credibility.

Transferability details how key findings can relate to other situations and is analogous to external validity in quantitative work. Researchers who are mindful of transferability help readers make connections between the qualitative accounts and their own personal experiences. Attempts to neutralize findings to be free of researcher bias are known as confirmability, wherein objectivity is central to quantitative work. Lastly, dependability relates to the notion that other researchers could replicate the study with similar results and would be reflective of reliability in quantitative studies. Considering these elements within research design to establish trustworthiness elevates the quality of the research design.

FIGURE 6.22 ■ Analogous Elements of Trustworthiness, Validity, and Reliability

Qualitative Research	Quantitative Research
Confirmability	Objectivity
Credibility	Internal Validity
Dependability	Reliability
Transferability	External Validity

Qualitative researchers should always consider how writing results and disseminating findings could impact the participants by using pseudonyms and avoiding the use of clues in descriptions, which could connect the participant with other members in the study or readers. In presenting findings, the author should strive to maintain participant anonymity. These precautions reflect the principles of the *Belmont Report* (U.S. Department of Health and Human Services, 2022) related to beneficence in which the researcher takes steps to minimize harm to participants.

Once researchers obtain permission through IRB, interviewing individuals is a common way of gathering data to address research questions. Often, when researchers are conducting qualitative research, findings involve describing the life experiences of participants. In this case, the researcher needs to use reflexivity when developing the version presented and how personal biases may shape the presentation. As the researcher enters the study, the research design goal should be to take an *emic* approach or sometimes referred to as an "insider approach." The words, perceptions, and beliefs of the individuals are integral to understanding the context of study. This approach is in contrast to an *etic* approach or "outsider approach," which reflects the perceptions of the researcher. An etic approach can be problematic if the researcher imposes their own values, attitudes, and beliefs. In the past, historical ethnographies used *othering* to describe other people, which means a researcher presents a person or group of individuals as different or foreign to themselves, often with a negative connotation. For instance, some accounts may have referred to the practices of indigenous peoples as negative or unsophisticated, overlooking advanced technological contributions for the historical period of time.

As an example, an emic approach describes the experiences of teachers instructing in a gifted and talented school with shared voices of the faculty. In an etic approach, the researcher recounts their personal perceptions of the context at hand; an account which may be skewed based on personal beliefs, values, and attitudes. The researcher may recount the operations of the gifted and talented school in a way that is contrary to those faculty members who operate and work in the school structure. The difference in these two frameworks has been particularly integral to ethnographic studies centered on peoples from varying cultural backgrounds. A reflective researcher aims to account the lived experiences of individuals rather than researcher interpretations that may be steered by their own personal background. Sharing the subjective lens and strategies for reflexivity within the method section is one way to counter potential shifts from an etic approach.

THE TAKEAWAY

Maintaining quality and ethics is a keystone of qualitative research. Qualitative researchers aim to be transparent about the methods in place to adhere to rigorous standards.

AMERICAN PSYCHOLOGICAL ASSOCIATION STYLE

LEARNING OBJECTIVE
6.6   Utilize the *Publication Manual of the American Psychological Association* in reporting findings in qualitative research.

When presenting findings of a study, the American Psychological Association (APA) style is relevant to qualitative work. Many of the guidelines that apply to other forms of research are also used for qualitative research. Tables and figures follow the same format regardless of the type of writing or research. However, there are particular common errors in the presentation of findings related to quoting participants based on interviews.

Participant Quotes

Including quotes from participants in research manuscripts is a necessary element as these perspectives help to shape theme development and narrative support of findings. Qualitative work based on interviews and without these references to dialogue is a limitation. These quotes can be thought of as analogous to data points. To quote a participant within text, be sure to use the pseudonym of the person interviewed as in the following case of a teacher being interviewed about changes in mathematics education.

"I also see a decrease in mental math abilities and also just basic computational skills" (Maddie).

An important APA style guideline is that more than 40 words are listed as block quotes. In the example that follows, notice that there are no quotation marks. After the quote, the period follows the quote rather than the participant's pseudonym.

Well, this is a very large concern to me because you know we used to, for sixth graders, we had three options Math 6, Accelerated Math, and then Pre-Algebra. And basically, Accelerated Math was 1 year ahead and even at that level it was quite challenging because some of those skills I learned in high school, and we were asking 11- and 12-year-olds to absorb this information. (Maddie)

What is most important with using APA style is consistency in presentation. While quoting participants, be sure to use the same format in the use of quotes throughout the document.

THE TAKEAWAY

When quoting participants, be sure that you are not making it possible for others to pinpoint their identity. Researchers are ethically bound to protect participants' identities. Strategies that can be used are to use pseudonyms or change other key identifying features. If using a quote could potentially disclose the identity, consider omitting the quote in your report.

CHAPTER SUMMARY

Qualitative research designs have the potential to provide unique insights into a critical educational problem, which is often not perceptible through other types of research methods. This chapter provides a broad overview of the features, dynamic processes, and types and purposes of qualitative research design, as well as the process of conducting qualitative research. Variations of these designs are integral to addressing critical issues in educational settings. As with all forms of research, addressing ethical considerations and adhering to reporting findings in APA style are hallmarks of quality studies.

EXTENSION ACTIVITIES

You Do It! 6.1

Writing Qualitative Research Questions

Self-Directed Practice: Practice writing qualitative research questions.

Directions: Select a topic of interest and write two to three research questions that could be used in a qualitative study. Refer to Table 6.1 for assistance.

You Do It! 6.2

Analyzing Main Components of Qualitative Research

Self-Directed Practice: Analyze major design features of qualitative research.

Directions: Identify a qualitative research article and review the work for the following features: (a) a broad focus, (b) lack of hypothesis, (c) focus on interactions, meanings, and/or processes in a social setting. Refer to Table 6.2 for assistance.

You Do It! 6.3

Creating an Open Coding Scheme

Self-Directed Practice: Create an open coding scheme.

Directions: Create an open coding key with the provided transcript on a teacher's description of curriculum development. Share the key you created with a classmate and have them recode the work. Compare the coding schemes to see your level of agreement. Where there was no agreement on a coded word, discuss your interpretations to reach a consensus. See Figure 6.8 for assistance.

> As far as specific courses . . . there has to be a demand. I think that demand has created in most cases by a dynamic teacher who you know, has encouraged kids to become involved. That's what happened at [the local high school]. They actually wrote the curriculum . . . which has been offered in all 10 high schools. But I think it was due to primarily a couple of individual teachers who had a passion for environmental education, and they created that interest in kids. And so, someone took note and thought this is something we could beef up the curriculum . . . And I think it should be encouraged with time permitting.

You Do It! 6.4

Analyzing a Qualitative Research Study

Self-Directed Practice: Analyzing a qualitative research study.

Directions: Section 6.3 focused on identifying the types, purposes, and features of qualitative research. Using the *Let's See It! Let's Do It!* tables as models for each type of qualitative research design, locate a qualitative research article on a topic of interest. Analyze the major features per the models.

You Do It! 6.5

Utilizing a Qualitative Research Method Decision Tree

Self-Directed Practice: Reflect on important issues when developing a qualitative research design.

Designing a qualitative research study can pose many questions about how to proceed in the process. A decision tree can be helpful as a guiding tool. Using the Qualitative Research Method Section Decision Tree (Figure 6.21) and the accompanying Qualitative Research Design worksheet, create a qualitative research design on a topic of interest.

Section	Description	Alignment Comments (Does this section align with the original purpose and research questions?)
Research Design (What type of qualitative research design would you use?)		

Section	Description	Alignment Comments (Does this section align with the original purpose and research questions?)
Participants and Setting (Who will be the participants and how will they be selected?)		
Intervention (if applicable) (Is there a strategy or program being studied?)		
Data Collection Tools (What qualitative data will be collected to examine the topic?)		
Proposed Data Analyses (How will data be analyzed?)		
Quality and Ethics (What steps will be taken to curb potential biases and establish trustworthiness?)		

KEY TERMS

Analytic memo
Bounded system
Classical grounded theory
Confirmability
Collective case study
Constructivist grounded theory
Credibility
Critical ethnography
Critical friend
Cross case comparison
Dependability
Descriptive phenomenology
Emic
Epoché
Etic
Explanatory case study
Exploratory case study
Field notes
Gatekeeper
Inductive approach

Instrumental case study
Intentionality of consciousness
Interpretive grounded theory
Interpretivist phenomenology
Intrinsic case study
Lifeworld
Othering
Participant observer
Privileged observer
Positionality
Reflexivity
Restorying
Sociality
Spatiality
Subjective lens
Temporality
Thick description
Transferability
Unit of analysis

Stop and Think Activities

STOP AND THINK 6.1

There are many possible options to answer Stop and Think #1. A critical issue that describes individuals' perspectives, processes, or meaning of social structures within a school setting. Examples of critical issues, which could be addressed with a qualitative study, include (a) parents' perceptions of homeschool connections, (b) students' viewpoints on access to extracurricular activities, and (c) strategies to promote vertical alignment on topics across grade levels. Qualitative studies typically do not use selected response items but could include open response items on a survey, transcripts from interviews, and school artifacts as some examples.

STOP AND THINK 6.2

Studying interactions between teachers and teacher assistants would be a viable topic for a qualitative study. This context could be studied with data sources, such as individual interviews, focus group interviews, diagrams, observational checklists, meeting notes, and open-ended responses on surveys. Issues for consideration are how participants would be selected with corresponding criteria, methods for data collection, and explicit descriptions of data analysis and interpretations.

STOP AND THINK 6.3

Regardless of the type of methodology or research design, researchers strive to be as objective as possible and counter potential biases and/or validity threats. Because researchers select the topic of study, the participants, the methods, and the approach for data analysis and interpretations, there is an element of subjectivity in research. For this reason, reviewing elements of research designs for potential biases is a keystone of all research practices.

STOP AND THINK 6.4

A bounded case study can be thought of as circle encompassed by a heart shape. The circle represents the case or object of analysis and the heart frames the outer limits of the bounded case. For instance, if a researcher was studying a team of teachers who were developing a summer STEM curriculum following a professional development workshop, the case would be the experiences of the three teachers' collaboration. The limits of the bounded case could be the space and time of the workshops and collaborative meetings, the time and space of the summer camp, the needs of the students the camp would be serving, and the training and experiences of the teachers working together, as some examples.

STOP AND THINK 6.5

Two possible types of qualitative research that would work well in this scenario are narrative inquiry and case study. In a narrative inquiry, the researcher(s) could interview select teachers and students about the homework club experience. Using the individuals' accounts, the researcher could restory the experience both from the viewpoints of teachers and students.

Another option could be an intrinsic case study to study the inner workings of an after-school homework club. Multiple sources would serve well as a form of triangulation, a hallmark of case studies. Sources could include a comparison of adult and student perspectives, analysis of homework artifacts, classroom teachers' observations of student performance, and video analysis, as some examples.

Let's Do It! Activities

LET'S DO IT! 6.1

Guided Practice: Creating Qualitative Research Questions

Although answers will vary, here are two qualitative research questions that you could write based on the scenario.

1. In what ways do teacher assistants benefit from professional development in mathematics instruction?

2. What are the most effective aspects of professional development for teacher assistants working with students during mathematics instruction?

LET'S DO IT! 6.2

Guided Practice: Analyze Basic Components of a Qualitative Research Study

Regardless of the type of qualitative research study, answers for analyzing the basic components of a qualitative research study will center on (a) a broad focus, (b) the absence of a hypothesis, (c) a presentation of findings from the participants' perspectives, and (d) a focus on interactions, meanings, and processes for the specific context. Consumers of qualitative research should be aware to check for these components. The following answer key is based on the work of Bauml et al. (2020).

Guiding Question	Response
_____ Does the study start with a broad focus?	The article starts with a broad overview and benefits of unstructured play within the school day.
_____ Is the work free of a hypothesis?	The work is free of a hypothesis.
_____ Does the work center on participant perspectives?	The work centers on the experiences of 17 classroom teachers and one physical education teacher who participated in the LiiNK Project, an approach to integrating four 15-min breaks of unstructured play as part of the school day. Teachers participated in interviews. Findings were presented from their perspectives with integrated quotes within the descriptions.
_____ Does the work focus on interactions, meanings, and processes among participants within an organization or context.	The work focuses on interactions, meanings and processes for teachers working with the LiiNK projects. Thematic analysis centered on issues related to academics and cognitive development, social-emotional well-being, and instructional practices.

LET'S DO IT! 6.3

Guided Practice: Create an Open Coding Scheme With Noun Labels Using a Sample Transcript

There are many ways to conduct open coding. Once you have created a coding system (see Figure 6.8), check with a classmate and compare the coding systems. Below are some possible options for coding the excerpt based on using nouns as labels.

Descriptive Labels

B-balloon

BU-bulge

M-met

P-program

(Continued)

(*Continued*)

D-demands	PE-public education
DA-day	PS-public school
DI-different	R-reason
DO-done	RE-restraints
E-end	S-shoulder
I-institution	T-time
K-knowledge	TH-theory

LET'S DO IT! 6.4

Guided Practice: Practice Summarizing the Key Features of Grounded Theory Design

The primary objective of this activity is for you to independently review and identify the key features of a grounded theory article. To guide your thinking, we encourage you to use the *Let's See It!* tables and information as well as the guiding questions in the table that follows.

Grounded Theory Design	
Study	Benedict, A. E., Brownell, M., Bettini, E., & Sohn, H. (2021). Learning together: Teachers' evolving understanding of coordinated word study instruction within an RTI framework. *Teacher Education and Special Education, 44*(2), 134–159. https://doi-org.mutex.gmu.edu/10.1177/0888406420930686
Purpose	The purpose is to examine how a content/lesson study influences teacher understanding and application of phonological, orthographical, and morphological rules in word study to support students who are at risk for failing in reading.
Critical Issue	The issue is critical because teachers are implementing response to intervention initiatives to assist struggling readers. However, there is minimal evidence to relate workshop training to effective RTI implementations in the classroom. The rationale for this study is that a workshop program known as Project InSync assists teachers to learn about word study through an integrated content, curriculum, and lesson plan study.
Sample	The target group is (*n* = 7) regular education and special education teachers from one elementary school. The teachers work in collaborative teams and participated in a 1-year workshop series through Project InSync. In this case, purposive sampling was utilized and was appropriate to highlight how the processes of the workshop series informed instructional practices for low performing readers.
Data Collection	The data were collected through audio and video recordings of team discussions during specific phases of the five-phase cycle of workshops, particularly in lesson planning and debriefing.
Data Analysis	The data were analyzed in a tiered phase of coding, analysis, category formation, and theme development utilizing NVivo software.
Results	Findings showed that teachers were able to demonstrate an understanding of how to integrate content knowledge and instructional practices to meet the needs of struggling readers. In addition, over the course of 1 year, there was a shift in the areas that teachers focused on. Initially, teacher attention centered on understanding word study topics. Next, teachers began to draw connections between the content, pedagogical techniques, and student needs. In the third phase, teachers began considering interdisciplinary connections.

LET'S DO IT! 6.5

Guided Practice: Practice Summarizing the Key Features of Narrative Inquiry Design

The primary objective of this activity is for you to independently review and identify the key features of a narrative inquiry article. To guide your thinking, we encourage you to use the *Let's See It!* tables and information as well as the guiding questions in the table that follows.

Narrative Inquiry Design	
Study	Kuebel, C. R., Koops, L. H., & Bond, V. L. (2018). Cultivating teachers of general music methods: The graduate years. *Journal of Music Teacher Education, 28*(1), 10–23. https://doi-org.mutex.gmu.edu/10.1177/1057083718761812
Purpose	The overall purpose is to examine the experiences of three music educators in their career paths in developing professional identities over a period of time.
Critical Issue	The critical issue is exploring the experiences of three music educators, some of whom transitioned from being K–12 public school teachers, to navigating tenure track positions at universities. The focus in this article centers on the co-learner, collaborative, and mentorship roles of three individuals in this process.
Sample	The target group was three individuals who had "crossed paths" at one university over the course of 8 years. One completed a doctoral program, one was a student, and one was a faculty member who had served as a mentor. Participants had experience as public-school teachers prior to the university experiences.
Data Collection	Participants met once a month for a 9-month period online. Data were collected in the form of Google text chats and video conference calls. Data were collected for data analysis.
Data Analysis	Participants engaged in an auto-narrative inquiry design. Data were reread multiple times, while participants considered the meaning behind the story selections and the way they were told. Transcripts were reviewed for intersection and divergence by taking notes in margins. Recurrent ideas were also noted. Core ideas were organized around the themes of temporality, sociality, and place for restorying.
Results	Key findings from this study showed that the basis for the path of these music educators was a passion for music and teaching as a form of temporality. In terms of sociality, two themes that emerged were that of a sense of impostor syndrome when shifting from being a public-school music educator to working in higher education and balancing the mentorship role between providing support for a mentee while maintaining autonomy. In terms of place, the three participants viewed the university setting (although students were not always in the same place at the same time) and the online forum as a space for them to co-learn, collaborate, and mentor. The restorying of these three experiences show that the identity formation of a music educator changes over time and benefits from a mentorship process.

LET'S DO IT! 6.6

Guided Practice: Practice Summarizing the Key Features of Ethnographic Design

The primary objective of this activity is for you to independently review and identify the key features of an ethnographic article. To guide your thinking, we encourage you to use the *Let's See It!* tables and information as well as the guiding questions in the table that follows. We also provide an answer key in the appendix at the end of the chapter for you to check your work.

Narrative Inquiry Design	
Study	Arrazola, B. V., & Bozalongo, J. S. (2014). Teaching practices and teachers' perceptions of group creative practices in inclusive rural schools. *Ethnography and Education, 9*(3), 253–269. http://dx.doi.org/10.1080/17457823.2014.881721
Purpose	The focus of the study was to develop workshops and training for teachers working in rural areas of Spain to account for varying age levels, cultural backgrounds, ability levels, and disabilities.
Critical Issue	This issue was critical as teachers in rural areas of Spain work with very small class sizes where the groups of students are not homogenous based on age level, background, or capabilities. Researchers aimed to provide teachers with training to integrate innovative and creative approaches to working with students.
Sample	The participants included four teachers who taught in rural schools within the Autonomous Community of Aragon, in Northern Spain. Teachers had classrooms of 2, 4, 5, and 15 students. The researchers worked as participant observers over the course of the study.
Data Collection	Data included observations/field notes, informal conversations and video recordings. Data were collected over the course of 2008 through 2010.
Data Analysis	Data were analyzed according to teacher attention to meeting the needs of diverse learners, creative approaches, and relevance of instruction to student learning.
Results	The key findings following immersive training and workshops were that teachers were interested in developing creative assignments, encouraging student autonomy and student motivation, and meeting the needs of diverse students.

LET'S DO IT! 6.7

Guided Practice: Practice Summarizing the Key Features of Case Study Design

The primary objective of this activity is for you to independently review and identify the key features of a case study design article. To guide your thinking, we encourage you to use the *Let's See It!* tables and information as well as the guiding questions in the table that follows. We also provide an answer key in the appendix at the end of the chapter for you to check your work.

Case Study Design	
Study	Bustamante, C. (2020). TPACK-based professional development on web 2.0 for Spanish teachers: A case study. *Computer Assisted Language Learning, 33*(4), 327–352. https://doi.org/10.1080/09588221.2018.1564333
Purpose	The purpose of the study was to examine how teachers experienced a technology-based professional development program and its applications within the classroom.
Critical Issue	The critical issue is that technological advances have affected foreign language instruction. The focus of this research was to examine ways in which a professional development program known as TPACK altered teachers' pedagogical, content, and technology integration.
Sample	The sample included (n = 18) Spanish foreign language teachers on the secondary level. Criterion sampling was used with the condition that teachers taught Spanish at the middle or high school level.
Data Collection	Data collection included demographic information, journal reflections, interviews, focus groups, and lesson observations.

Case Study Design

Data Analysis	Data were analyzed through a software program known as MAXQDA. The program enabled researchers to create a coding system (invivo and descriptive coding) based on the categories of content, pedagogy, and technology. Through associated patterns, researchers were able to identify themes.
Results	Participants noted that utilizing the interconnected areas of technology, content, and pedagogy increased collaboration among students. In addition, teachers changed assessment practices by utilizing formative and summative assessments, including rubrics and peer-reviewed feedback. Teachers noted the strong connections between technology and pedagogy and valued technology based on professional development. Technology integration required more planning, and at times, access to technology was a barrier.

LET'S DO IT! 6.8

Guided Practice: Practice Summarizing the Key Features of Phenomenological Design

The primary objective of this activity is for you to independently review and identify the key features of a phenomenological design article. To guide your thinking, we encourage you to use the *Let's See It!* tables and information as well as the guiding questions in the table that follows. We also provide an answer key in the appendix at the end of the chapter for you to check your work.

Phenomenological Design

Study	LeRoy, A. S., & Boomgaard, S. L. (2021). Empathy in isolation: Lived experiences of teachers of refugee children. *Integrative Psychological & Behavioral Science, 55*(2), 430–443. https://doi.org/10.1007/s12124-019-09508-0
Purpose	The purpose of this study was to examine the perceptions of teachers working with refugee children, interactions between teachers and these children, resources, and professional development.
Critical Issue	This issue is critical in that the perceptions of teachers about refugee students can be an important factor in the quality of instruction and social interactions.
Sample	As part of the phenomenological design, participants served as co-researchers. Twelve individuals teaching refugee students.
Data Collection	Co-researchers completed eight open questions via a survey link.
Data Analysis	Based on responses, three collective themes emerged, including value in empathetic, reciprocal relationships; increased capacity through programming/resources; and meaningful impact from professional development. Responses from individuals were presented collectively via themes.
Results	Findings revealed that the traumatic experiences of refugee students were viewed with a great deal of empathy by teachers. In terms of programming and resources, co-researchers indicated that districts did not always have the human resources or programs needed for refugee students (e.g., access to counselors, communications training). In addition, co-researchers found that professional development could have positive (e.g., practical strategies for teachers) or negative consequences (inefficient meetings with case managers) on instruction. In general, teachers perceived that professional development for working with refugee students was scarce.

7 MIXED METHODS RESEARCH DESIGNS

A DAY AT WORK

Educating Students to Be Good Digital Citizens!

©iStockphoto.com/SolStock

Mr. Peter Millett is a biology teacher at a diverse suburban high school. Katie, one of his students, is a popular tenth grader involved in many clubs and sports with a seemingly well-rounded life and positive personality. However, recently Mr. Millett has noticed a change in Katie's sunny demeanor. Mr. Millett learned that Katie has fallen victim to cyberbullying after a group of girls posted unkind messages about her on social media. As Katie became moodier and more reclusive, Mr. Millett became concerned and turned to other teachers for advice. He determined that not only is this problem common but that many teachers are ill-equipped to address cyberbullying in K–12 settings.

Understanding the potentially detrimental effects cyberbullying can have on students, Mr. Millett and his colleagues agree to form a team to conduct a research study examining student, parent, and teacher perceptions and understandings of cyberbullying. The team of teachers decides they would like to incorporate both quantitative data collection methods, such as surveys using Likert-type scales, as well as qualitative data collection methods, including interviews and focus groups, to help them gain a more in-depth and complete understanding of the complex and multifaceted problem of cyberbullying in K–12 settings. However, is using assessment tools that gather both strands of data an acceptable way to conduct research?

INTRODUCTION

The combining of qualitative and quantitative strategies has been observed in various disciplines throughout history (i.e., the Greeks in their observations of astronomy; Galileo's use of the telescope; and astronomy, sociology, geology, medicine, and anthropology, to name a few) but were never labeled as mixed methods research. However, professionals in various disciplines have long recognized the benefit of approaching issues from a multitude of angles and perspectives and through gathering different types of data. Although mixed methods research was introduced in the late 1950s by Campbell and Fiske, researchers did not officially recognize and write about this new paradigm in methods until the 1990s. Today, researchers frequently use mixed methods designs while taking advantage of the individual strengths of both qualitative and quantitative methodologies (see Figure 7.1). In this chapter, we provide an overview of mixed methods research that can help educators gain a more complete picture of a critical issue being explored. We describe different types of mixed methods research designs as well as how to conduct a mixed methods design study. Finally, we discuss ethical issues to consider when engaging with mixed methods research and how to use the *Publication Manual of the American Psychological Association* when using mixed-methods approaches to research.

FIGURE 7.1 ■ Mixed methods research combines elements of quantitative (numbers) research and qualitative (experience) research to answer a set of research questions.

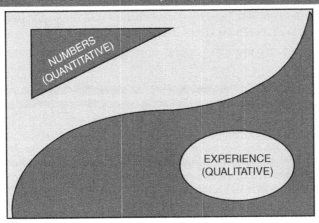

MIXED METHODS RESEARCH

Solving a critical and multifaceted issue such as cyberbullying often requires approaching a topic from different angles and perspectives. For these complex issues, using mixed methods methodology is helpful because this could entail mixing different research methodologies in order to strengthen findings and minimize the weaknesses of a single method. In general, mixed methods research is defined as one type of research method, typically involving a mix of qualitative and quantitative assessment approaches that integrates the results and draws inferences based on both strands of data.

Researchers apply different methods and approaches at the same time or one after the other to gain a more in-depth understanding of a critical, real-life, contextual issue such as cyberbullying in schools. The methodological approach is unique because it intentionally allows researchers to combine numerical or quantitative data (e.g., grades) with the richness of qualitative data (e.g., parental interviews). By intentionally combining quantitative and qualitative methods, researchers will have a greater opportunity to understand a critical issue or problem and can expand the scope of knowledge that is generated.

STOP AND THINK 7.1

What are some critical issues that an educator might want to examine using mixed methods research?

Most commonly, mixed methods research has been used in social, behavioral, and the health sciences to help integrate both qualitative and quantitative data. Integration of the qualitative and quantitative findings at some phase of the research process, such as during data collection, analysis of data, or at the interpretative stage of the research, is a key characteristic of mixed methods designs. Integrating data from qualitative and quantitative approaches requires an in-depth understanding of how each method can help educators answer their research questions. Depending on the purpose of the study and research questions, the level of integration of methodologies will vary. See Table 7.1 for a brief overview of the definitions and examples of quantitative and qualitative research methods.

TABLE 7.1 ■ Quantitative and Qualitative Research Methods		
Type	**Definition**	**Example**
Quantitative Research	Works with deductive inquiry; testing hypotheses, predicting and explaining phenomena, and standardizing data collection and analysis. Quantitative research is typically associated with numerical data.	Asking students to complete a survey on bullying or obtaining the grades of students who experienced bullying.

Type	Definition	Example
Qualitative Research	Works with inductive inquiry; the adaptation and evolution of methods as new data are collected. Provides more in-depth insights. Qualitative research is typically associated with rich, descriptive data.	Interviewing students who are experiencing bullying in a school or observing student interactions on the playground.

In the *Let's See It!* and *Let's Do It!* activities in this section, we illustrate and provide practice opportunities for you to explore how to use qualitative and quantitative data to explore critical issues in the workplace. We also provide a *You Do It! 7.1* activity at the end of the chapter for further practice.

Let's See It! 7.1

Goal: Identify Examples of Quantitative Data and Qualitative Data for the Cyberbullying Scenario

Going back to our opening scenario, Mr. Millett and his colleagues want to gain a better understanding of cyberbullying in K–12 settings and what can be done to address this complex issue. As part of their research question, Mr. Millett and his team of teachers want to determine "to what extent these types of cyberbullying behaviors are occurring within their school and how do some high school students describe the trauma associated with these experiences?" The team could employ quantitative methods, such as surveys administered to students, teachers, and parents using Likert-type scales. Quantitative data may give researchers a better sense of the magnitude of the problem (i.e., how many students like Katie are being affected by these behaviors). The team could also employ qualitative data, such as student focus groups, open-ended survey responses from affected students and their parents, interviews with administrators, and logs of discipline referrals related to cyberbullying at the school. Qualitative data may help researchers understand how these various groups feel about and are impacted by cyberbullying at school. Thus, these varied data sources provide many lenses and perspectives from which to examine the critical issue.

Table 7.2 provides examples of different types of data that fall under the quantitative and qualitative research paradigms. We also provide a brief statement that highlights the use of quantitative and qualitative data collection instruments to examine the critical issue of cyberbullying.

TABLE 7.2 ■ Quantitative Versus Qualitative Data Collection Instruments in Mixed Methods	
Quantitative Data	**Qualitative Data**
Surveys	Interviews
Preexisting Records (e.g., absenteeism)	Observations
Achievement tests	Documents (social media posts)

Example: Administering a survey to determine the prevalence of cyberbullying and following up with an interview of those who have been bullied about their experiences.

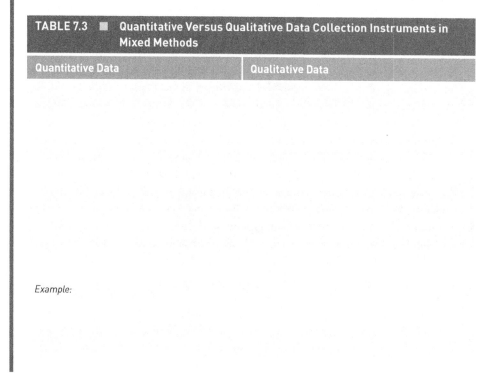

Let's Do It! 7.1

Guided Practice: Identify Additional Examples of Quantitative and Qualitative Data Instruments for a New Scenario

Suppose now that a team of researchers are interested in studying the impact of a new writing intervention on high school students' self-efficacy of writing and their experience with writing. They have formulated the following research questions: "Are there any differences in student self-efficacy for writing before and after the intervention?" that is accompanied by a secondary question: "How do students describe their experience with writing?" Think through these research questions and fill out Table 7.3 with potential quantitative and qualitative methods that the researchers might use to examine the effectiveness of the writing intervention.

TABLE 7.3 ■ Quantitative Versus Qualitative Data Collection Instruments in Mixed Methods	
Quantitative Data	**Qualitative Data**

Example:

When Is It Appropriate to Use Mixed Methods Research?

As was emphasized earlier in the chapter, mixed methods research uses both quantitative and qualitative methodological principles; it relies on both quantitative and qualitative data, combines deductive and inductive reasoning, and uses statistical and thematic or other forms of qualitative analysis to address a critical issue from multiple angles. These multiple angles provide a more comprehensive understanding of a broader question or multifaceted issue.

Problems most suitable for mixed methods research are those where quantitative or qualitative approaches alone are inadequate for answering the research questions. By including quantitative and qualitative research principles in a single study, researchers often obtain more rich types of data than if quantitative data alone were used. Figure 7.2 provides some examples of mixed methods research questions.

FIGURE 7.2 ■ Mixed Methods Research Questions

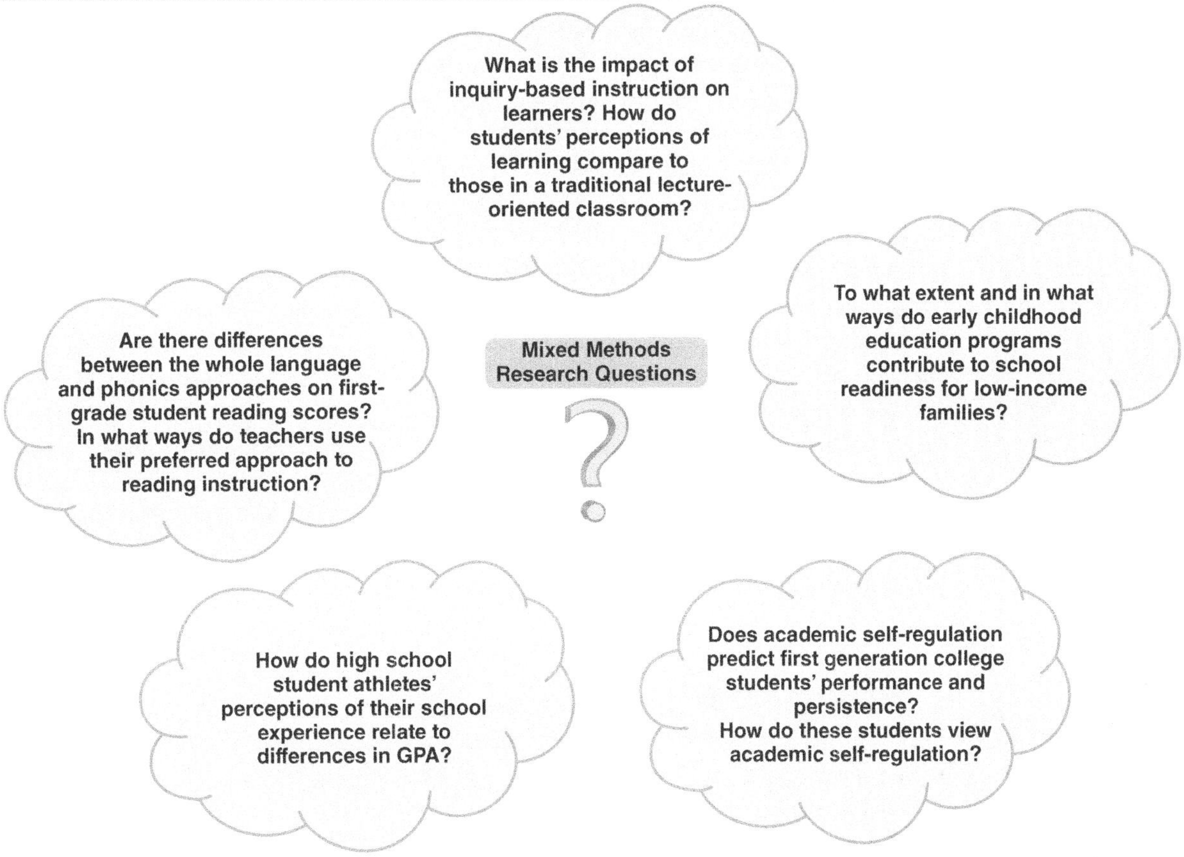

As you examine the research questions in Figure 7.2, you will notice that you can write separate quantitative questions and qualitative questions and you can also write a mixed question that clearly shows the intent for some integration between the quantitative and qualitative phases of the proposed study to understand a critical issue. Identifying multiple research questions and providing a strong rationale about how combining qualitative and quantitative methods will help you build on the strengths of both approaches is important to determine whether using mixed methods is an appropriate design to answer the research questions. To illustrate, imagine Mr. Millett and his colleagues wanted to study cyberbullying in the school district. They identify two research questions: "What are the prevalence and types of cyberbullying among high school students in their school district?" and "How do students describe their experiences with cyberbullying?" They believe that they can fully address the complexity and obtain a more comprehensive picture of this critical issue by collecting, analyzing, and integrating data from both methodological approaches. They first decide to invite students from all high schools in their district to respond to a survey regarding whether they had witnessed or experienced cyberbullying in the past year. After responses on this survey were collected, they select a purposive sample of students to participate in a focus group based on their experiences with cyberbullying reported on the survey. The teachers ask the students questions about their feelings about witnessing bullying, being bullied, or being the perpetrator of bullying. Interviewing students in this case may reveal new insights about cyberbullying that may not be possible through numeric survey responses. The two sets of data (quantitative and qualitative) can be used in tandem in the data analysis to provide a more complete picture of the experiences and emotional reactions students in the school have with cyberbullying. The findings could be tied into existing research on other students' experiences with cyberbullying (theoretical) and result in approaches to reduce it in Mr. Millett's school (practical). A mixed methods design approach in this case seems appropriate and useful for developing practical applications, such as interventions strategies as it provides a more comprehensive understanding of the critical issue.

There are several reasons for using mixed methods in educational research. Typically, researchers use mixed methods for complementarity, development of new research strategies and tools, triangulation, and expansion. First, the merging of quantitative and qualitative data might help the researcher develop a more complete understanding or a complementary picture of a problem like in the example study of cyberbullying described earlier. Researchers might also be interested in the development of research tools where qualitative data collection might inform the construction of questions for the proposed survey. Further, triangulation which describes the process of gathering data from a variety of different sources and perspectives to gain a more comprehensive understanding of the issue of interest can help the researchers obtain more rigorous conclusions by using these two methods. Finally, researchers might be interested in using mixed methods to extend and widen their inquiry with depth and breadth which might support better understanding a research problem.

STOP AND THINK 7.2

What are some reasons for conducting a mixed methods study? Use a practical example to help you think through your answer.

Overall, it is important for researchers to consider whether using a mixed methods approach is a feasible option and/or why mixed methods would be more beneficial than other approaches given the increased resources (i.e., more time and people) required to conduct a mixed methods study. If a researcher can fully evaluate a research question by using only surveys, then it is not necessary to include qualitative methods. Conversely, in situations where a research question cannot be answered using quantitative methods alone, adding qualitative data can help provide the missing information.

In summary, one way to think of a mixed methods approach is as a dialogue between the qualitative and quantitative methods. Throughout the course of the study, each technique informs the next to create a rigorous design. Once researchers understand the basics of mixed methods research and the advantages of using this approach, the next step is for them to learn how to conduct this type of research and when each of the two methodologies (i.e., quantitative and qualitative) should be incorporated. This question will be explored in the next section.

THE TAKEAWAY

Mixed methods research combines quantitative and qualitative methods to provide researchers with sufficient data and perspectives to gain a comprehensive understanding of a complex critical issue.

COMMONLY USED MIXED METHODS RESEARCH DESIGNS

LEARNING OBJECTIVE	
7.2	Identify types of commonly used mixed methods research designs.

Mixed methods research is typically conducted in phases that may take place at different points in the research process. When collecting data, a researcher—depending on the purpose of the study and the research questions—might place more weight or priority on qualitative or quantitative data. Possible reasons for giving priority to one data strand or the other may be based on previous research or personal experience. A researcher can also control the sequence of data collection. Data may be collected all at the same time, as in the case of concurrent designs, or data may be collected in separate phases, as with sequential designs. The three most common types of mixed methods research designs include concurrent triangulation, explanatory sequential, and exploratory sequential. As a researcher, it is important to keep in mind that regardless of the research design selected, the use of both qualitative and quantitative data collection methods in a single study is not sufficient to call it a mixed methods design. The heart of the mixed methods design is the integration or linking of the qualitative and quantitative phases of the study. Integration typically takes place at the design, methods, or interpretation levels where the results from the first phase of the research might be used to compare, explain, and build the second phase of the research design.

A concurrent triangulation (also known as convergent) design collects and analyzes both quantitative and qualitative data at the same time (concurrently) and gives similar or equal weight to the qualitative and quantitative types of data. The researcher hopes that the two data-sets lead to similar conclusions about a critical issue being examined. An explanatory sequential design incorporates quantitative data in Phase 1 of the study, followed by qualitative data in Phase 2. The qualitative data are used to *explain* the results of the quantitative data or to gain a more in-depth understanding of the critical issue. Finally, an exploratory sequential design incorporates qualitative data in Phase 1 of the study, followed by quantitative data in Phase 2. This type of design may be used when little is known about the critical issue. By collecting qualitative data first, researchers can *explore* the issue and potentially develop ideas about the necessary or important quantitative data to collect in Phase 2. We will explore these three designs in greater depth in the following sections. Table 7.4 summarizes key points of these three designs.

TABLE 7.4 ■ Types of Mixed Methods Designs		
Type	**Definition**	**Example**
Concurrent Triangulation	Quantitative and qualitative data are collected and analyzed at the same time. Data are merged (or triangulated) into a single dataset that links both types of data.	Mr. Millett conducts a study by administering surveys and conducting interviews at the same time and then combines the findings to create a more complete picture of cyberbullying in his school.
Explanatory Sequential	Quantitative data collection is conducted first followed by qualitative data collection in order to *explain* the results of the quantitative findings to learn more. The focus is on the quantitative data.	Mr. Millett begins by administering a survey to students about their experiences with cyberbullying followed by interviews with students who reported experiencing multiple instances of cyberbullying to assess the impact that cyberbullying has on students.

(Continued)

TABLE 7.4 ■ Types of Mixed Methods Designs (*Continued*)		
Type	**Definition**	**Example**
Exploratory Sequential	Qualitative data collection is conducted first followed by quantitative data collection in order to *explore* the critical issue to determine the necessary quantitative data to collect. The focus is on the qualitative data.	Mr. Millett begins by conducting interviews to learn more about the factors that play a role in cyberbullying. From the results of the interviews, he creates a survey to administer on a widespread scale to gather information on students' experiences and perceptions of cyberbullying.

STOP AND THINK 7.3

What might be some scenarios in your work where it would be beneficial to collect quantitative data before qualitative data, or vice versa?

Concurrent Triangulation Design

Triangulation involves the combining of two or more methods into one single approach to address a critical issue or phenomenon. Although there are many variants of triangulation designs, we are going to focus on just the concurrent triangulation (convergence) design. As part of a concurrent triangulation design, the researcher gathers quantitative and qualitative data simultaneously. The researcher's goal is to merge the two datasets, typically by bringing the separate results together with the expectation that the two strands of data will lead to similar conclusions about the critical issue being examined. For example, a researcher might want to examine whether middle school students' self-efficacy beliefs for self-regulated learning in mathematics overlap with themes identified in interviews about the use of various self-regulatory strategies. The researcher would collect and analyze quantitative and qualitative data and then merge the two datasets into one overall interpretation to assess the extent to which the findings converge or do not converge.

Nature of Research Questions

When considering research questions for concurrently triangulated mixed methods studies, a researcher can either write the question as one single question that can be addressed both from a quantitative and qualitative perspective, or to separate the question into two questions—one quantitative question and one qualitative. For example, looking at the research question "What are the perspectives of high school teachers who witness cyberbullying in their classrooms, and how do these perspectives predict classroom management?" there is both a quantitative aspect (How do these perspectives predict classroom management?) and a qualitative aspect (What are the perspectives of high school teachers who witness cyberbullying in their classrooms?). See Figure 7.3 for some further examples of research questions that can be answered with a concurrently triangulation mixed methods design.

FIGURE 7.3 ■ Concurrent Triangulation Research Questions

To what extent does a responsive classroom program influence classroom management, and how do classroom teachers and student teachers view their classroom interactions?

How do student teachers describe their classroom management, and to what extent does their self-efficacy for classroom management fluctuate during the course of their student teaching?

Concurrent Triangulation Research Questions

What is the relationship between classroom and student teachers' perceptions of classroom management and how they relate to teaching performance?

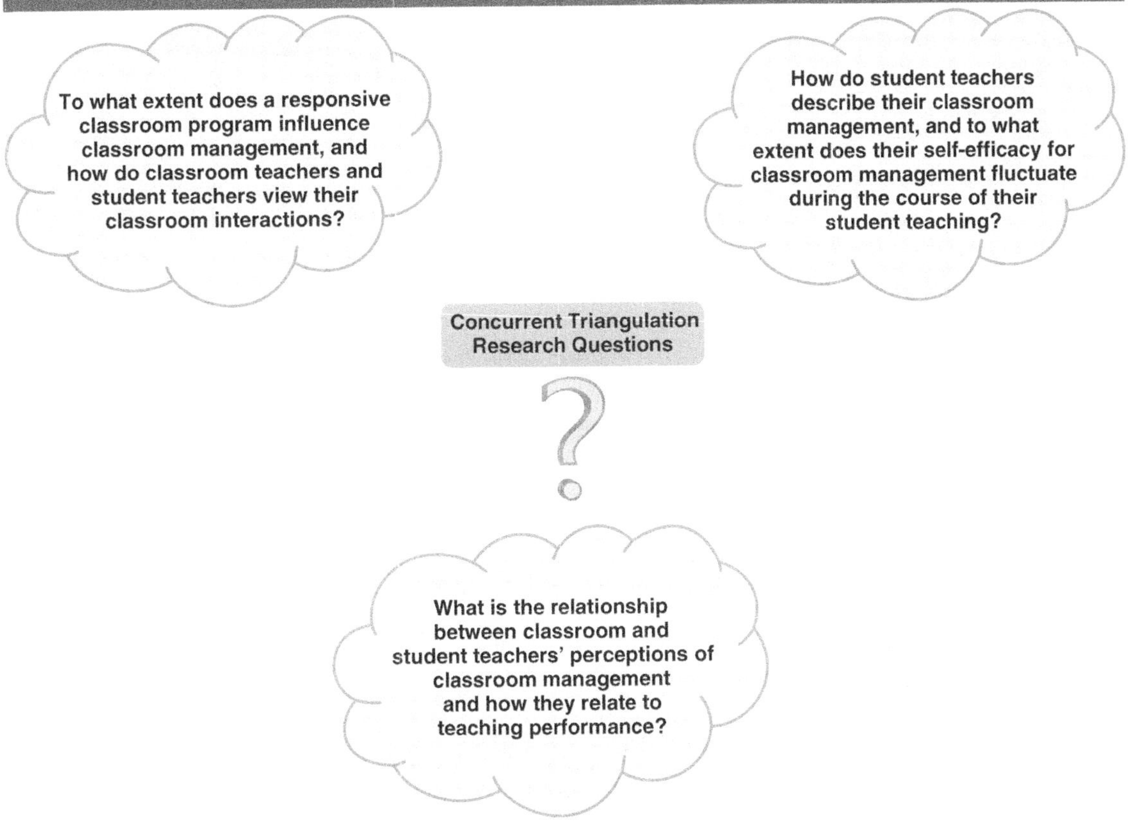

Sampling and Measurement

When sampling for a concurrent triangulation mixed methods study, the researchers will use a single sample throughout the study, meaning that the same participants will engage in both the quantitative and qualitative portions of the study. Although the two phases of the study are occurring concurrently, they may not be taking place at the exact same time. How the researchers obtain the participants (e.g., using purposive or probabilistic sampling; see Chapter 10 for more information on sampling) will set the stage for the remainder of the study. Regardless when engaging in a concurrent triangulation mixed methods design, the researcher should consider integrating multiple sampling methods for true triangulation.

Going back to Mr. Millett and his colleagues, if they wish to use a concurrent triangulation design, they could administer the survey mentioned previously to assess the frequency of students' experiences with cyberbullying in the past year. At the same time, they may seek out student and/or faculty volunteers to participate in focus groups on cyberbullying regardless of whether they have experienced cyberbullying in the past year. In this case, the survey focus group data would be collected simultaneously, and then combined and analyzed concurrently. In a concurrent design, it is possible that the results of one type of data may inform decision making regarding the analysis of the other type of data. For example, if Mr. Millett and his colleagues analyze the survey data and learn that students have distinct experiences with cyberbullying in the past year (i.e., some students report no bullying and others report significant amounts of bullying), they may choose to analyze the focus group data based on the frequency of cyberbullying experienced. The researcher, or educator needs to keep in mind that the two components are presented as one set of data, and there should be an emphasis on linking the data.

Data Analysis

One concept of concurrent triangulation is rooted in the idea that the results of the study should display both concurrent validity (constructs are related) and discriminant validity (constructs are different) at the same time. This design is helpful because the qualitative data can reinforce the findings from the quantitative data, and vice versa. This notion of convergence and divergence is at the heart of triangulation, where the intentional mixing and integration of quantitative and qualitative research occurs. Thus, the integration or linking of the two types of qualitative and quantitative data that defines mixed methods in concurrent triangulation designs happens typically at the interpretation level through comparing and connecting results from the two strands of data.

Explanatory Sequential Design

When the quantitative phase is followed by the qualitative phase, which constitutes an explanatory sequential design, the intent is typically to determine the best participants to follow up with or the processes or mechanisms underlying the quantitative results. A research team studying an integrative art program (a form of professional development for teachers) starts the study with a pre-assessment survey to assess the demographics of program attendees as well as their interest and attitudes about the art program. Based on the participants reported level of interest in the program (high and low interest), participants are selected for interviews following the intervention. In this case, the quantitative survey method is helpful because it informs the researchers about which participants to study in more detail through qualitative interviews. By collecting the quantitative and qualitative data in this particular sequence, the researchers have greater potential for creating a rich understanding of the context and for using qualitative data to enrich the meaningfulness and scope of the conclusions made from the quantitative data.

Nature of Research Questions

Research questions for explanatory sequential mixed methods designs will generally be presented as two separate research questions. The first question will always be quantitative in nature, followed by a qualitative question. The questions may either be two separate questions, where each describes the phenomenon from that perspective, or the second question (qualitative) will be built off of the first (quantitative). For example, "How frequently do middle school students experience cyberbullying? How do student experiences vary among sixth, seventh, and eighth graders?" is structured in a manner where the second question, which is qualitative in nature, is built from the first question. See Figure 7.4 for some additional examples of research questions that can be answered with an explanatory sequential mixed methods design.

Sampling and Measurement

In an explanatory sequential design, the quantitative data collection is performed first and may be used to identify participants who are good candidates for participation in the subsequent qualitative portion of the study. For example, returning to the opening scenario, if Mr. Millett

FIGURE 7.4   ■   Explanatory Sequential Design Research Questions

Are there relationships among responsive classroom practices, student behaviors and participation?
How do teachers account for these relationships?

To what extent do social-emotional strategies influence student sense of belonging and well being?
How do teachers conceptualize and discuss the importance of social-emotional learning in their classroom?

Explanatory Sequential Research Questions

To what extent does a student peer-mediation program influence behavior referrals?
How do peer mediators navigate student disputes?

decides to administer a questionnaire that captures student demographics and whether or not students have experienced cyberbullying, he may choose to select participants for the qualitative phase of the study from the pool of participants who took the questionnaire based on whether they have experienced cyberbullying. Those selected participants may then be asked to engage in either an interview or focus group to provide in-depth information that is critical for more fully understanding the critical issue or phenomenon. It is important to note that because the quantitative method occurs first in an explanatory study, the method of sampling must be probabilistic (e.g., simple random, systemic, stratified, or cluster sampling).

Data Analysis

During explanatory sequential designs, qualitative data are collected to *develop explanations* underlying the quantitative data. This analysis approach can provide researchers with a greater depth and understanding of the overall critical issue, problem, or phenomenon of interest. The qualitative portion of an explanatory mixed methods design will often be guided by the unresolved questions, limitations, or outliers uncovered in the quantitative portion of the study. This approach typically leads to a better understanding of the constructs being examined and will help provide a more nuanced understanding of the phenomenon. The integration or linking of the two types of quantitative and qualitative data that defines mixed methods in explanatory sequential designs takes place at the methods level. That is, the researcher selects the participants and develops qualitative data collection instruments for the qualitative follow-up analysis based on the quantitative results from the first phase to investigate those findings in more depth through analyzing the qualitative data in the second phase of the study.

Exploratory Sequential Designs

When a quantitative phase follows a qualitative phase, which occurs in an exploratory sequential design, the intent of the researcher is often to use quantitative assessments and analyses to examine a phenomenon or issue that was identified from qualitative data. More specifically, researchers may decide to develop a survey instrument, an intervention, or a program informed by qualitative findings. This approach is often used when researchers do not know much about a topic or issue. In a sense, researchers use the qualitative data to "discover" a new idea and then leverage quantitative data to examine this idea. For example, a school superintendent was interested in examining what kinds of classroom management issues teachers are facing in the classroom and what additional classroom supports teachers feel would be useful in helping to address these issues. He decided that observations and interviews with a small group of teachers might help him create a questionnaire to confirm that the majority of teachers in his school are facing similar issues in the classroom in order to ensure the most effective allocation of time and resources. The principal's most critical and meaningful data are collected in the Phase 1 qualitative interviews, and she uses quantitative data in Phase 2 to engage in hypothesis testing with a large sample of teachers.

Going back to the example from our opening scenario, suppose Mr. Millett and his colleagues wanted to examine the magnitude of cyberbullying offences in their school district among high school students. They would first conduct focus groups with a small group of students, teachers, and parents to determine the level and intensity of cyberbullying as a basis to conduct a systematic quantitative study. They then would use quantitative surveys as a follow-up in order to highlight the magnitude of these types of offenses both in terms of frequency and relationship to other variables, such as achievement and sense of belonging in the school community.

In closing, there are a few key points to remember when using exploratory mixed methods designs. Researchers emphasize the qualitative data by presenting an open-ended research question first followed by quantitative data. Qualitative data collection is followed by quantitative data collection. Finally, the goal of the initial exploration through qualitative data collection and analysis is to build a quantitative study that will yield generalizable findings.

Nature of Research Questions

Research questions for exploratory sequential mixed methods designs are similar to those of explanatory designs in that the research questions may be presented as two separate questions. However, for exploratory sequential designs, the first question will always be qualitative and the second a quantitative question. The questions may either be built off of each other starting with the qualitative question, or they may be two separate questions where each describes the phenomenon from that perspective. For example, "What are high school students' perceptions about cyberbullying? Does social persuasion moderate the impact of cyberbullying on well-being?" is structured in a manner where each question takes a different perspective in understanding the phenomenon. See Figure 7.5 for some additional examples of research questions that can be answered with an exploratory sequential mixed methods design.

FIGURE 7.5 ■ Exploratory Sequential Design Research Questions

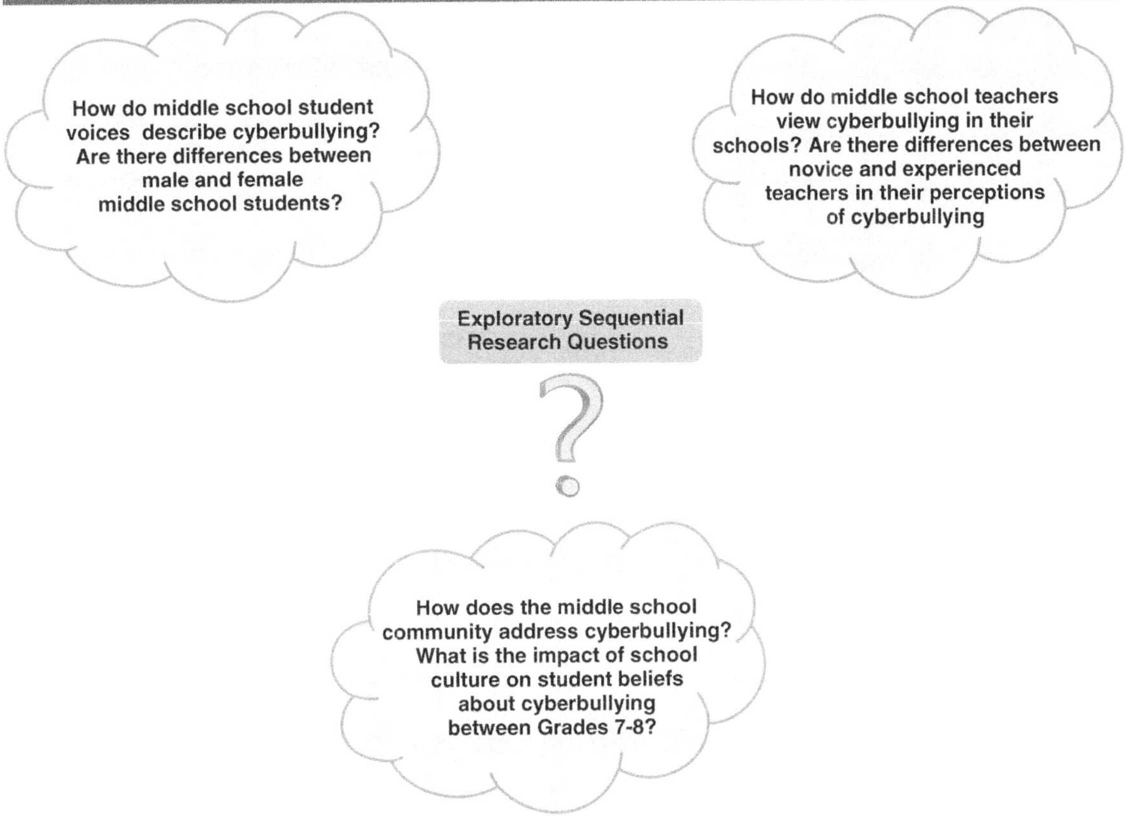

How do middle school student voices describe cyberbullying? Are there differences between male and female middle school students?

How do middle school teachers view cyberbullying in their schools? Are there differences between novice and experienced teachers in their perceptions of cyberbullying

Exploratory Sequential Research Questions

How does the middle school community address cyberbullying? What is the impact of school culture on student beliefs about cyberbullying between Grades 7-8?

Sampling and Measurement

In an exploratory sequential design, because the qualitative portion occurs first, the sampling method should begin with purposive sampling techniques (e.g., maximum variation, extreme case, or typical case sampling). Following sampling, researchers must determine their method of qualitative data collection. Once the qualitative phase is complete, researchers will sample for the quantitative phase through probabilistic sampling methods, followed by some method of quantitative data collection.

Data Analysis

During exploratory sequential designs, quantitative data are collected to formally test ideas or trends identified by the qualitative data. In the qualitative phase, researchers would conduct interviews with participants in order to gain a more complete understanding of the research topic of interest. In the quantitative phase, they may collect and analyze data on averages or trends related to the construct, and using that information modify or create an instrument or test newly developed hypotheses using inferential statistics. Thus, typically the integration or linking of the two types of qualitative and quantitative data that defines mixed methods in exploratory sequential designs takes place at design level where the results from the qualitative data are used to build the second quantitative phase of the research design.

Figure 7.6 summarizes where quantitative and qualitative methods fit in, in each of the three types of mixed methods research designs.

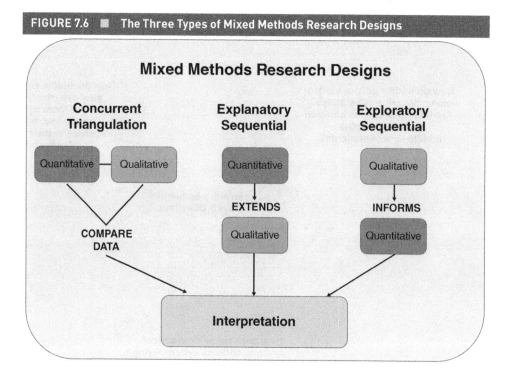

FIGURE 7.6 ■ The Three Types of Mixed Methods Research Designs

Now that we are familiar with the three main types of mixed methods designs we'll engage in a *Let's See It!* and *Let's Do It!* activity to practice identifying and justifying these types of designs using empirical research articles with a focus on critical issues within school contexts. Please also see the *You Do It!* 7.2 activity at the end of this chapter.

Let's See It! 7.2

Goal: Practice Identifying and Justifying Using Mixed Methods Research Designs

Using the Cleary et al. (2022) mixed methods study and the mixed methods decision tree in Figure 7.7 take a look at the answers to the questions in Table 7.5 regarding identifying and justifying the type of mixed methods design in this article.

Cleary, T. J., Kitsantas, A., Peters-Burton, E., Lui, A., McLeod, K., Slemp, J., & Zhang, X. (2022). Professional development in self-regulated learning: Shifts and variations in teacher outcomes and approaches to implementation. *Teaching and Teacher Education, 111.* https://doi.org/10.1016/j.tate.2021.103619

FIGURE 7.7 ■ Mixed Methods Decision Tree

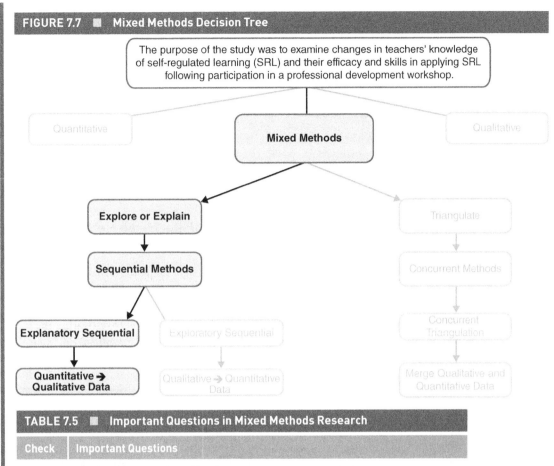

The purpose of the study was to examine changes in teachers' knowledge of self-regulated learning (SRL) and their efficacy and skills in applying SRL following participation in a professional development workshop.

Quantitative

Mixed Methods

Qualitative

Explore or Explain

Triangulate

Sequential Methods

Concurrent Methods

Explanatory Sequential

Exploratory Sequential

Concurrent Triangulation

Quantitative → Qualitative Data

Qualitative → Quantitative Data

Merge Qualitative and Quantitative Data

TABLE 7.5 ■ Important Questions in Mixed Methods Research

Check	Important Questions
✓	What are the research questions?
	1. Do high school science teachers show a statistically significant increase in their familiarity and knowledge with SRL, self-efficacy to apply SRL principles across students perceived as having different achievement levels, and their SRL conceptualization and application skills following an SRL PD workshop?
	2. What are the perceptions, attitudes, and experiences of science teachers regarding their attempts to infuse SRL principles in science lesson plans?
✓	How are the researchers collecting data? Researchers collected data in two phases. Phase 1 involved collecting quantitative data in the form of pretest and posttest teacher surveys. Phase 2 involved conducting individual interviews with a subset of teachers identified as advanced or emerging based on data collected in Phase 1.
✓	Are these methods more quantitative or qualitative in nature? Quantitative and qualitative methods are both equally represented in this study and make a significant contribution to the exploration of the research questions.
✓	Do they use qualitative or quantitative first, or are they being addressed at the same time? Researchers used quantitative methods first.
✓	Do the quantitative data influence the qualitative? Vice versa? The quantitative methods (collected first) influenced the collection of qualitative data. The quantitative data were used to identify two subgroups of teachers (advanced or emerging) in which to interview in the qualitative phase.

Check	Important Questions
✓	What type of design is used in this study? This study uses an explanatory sequential mixed methods design.
✓	Is the design appropriately identified? Why or why not? Yes. Researchers clearly state what design they used and the order in which quantitative and qualitative data were collected.

Let's Do It! 7.2

Guided Practice: Practice Distinguishing and Justifying Using Mixed Methods Research Designs

Hartwell and Kaplan (2018) represents another type of mixed methods design. Using the mixed methods decision tree in Figure 7.8, read this article and provide answers to questions in Table 7.6 using the Table 7.5 responses as a guide.

Hartwell, M., & Kaplan, A. (2018). Students' personal connection with science: Investigating the multidimensional phenomenological structure of self-relevance. *Journal of Experimental Education, 86*(1), 86–104. https://doi.org/10.1080/00220973.2017.1381581

FIGURE 7.8 ■ Mixed Methods Decision Tree

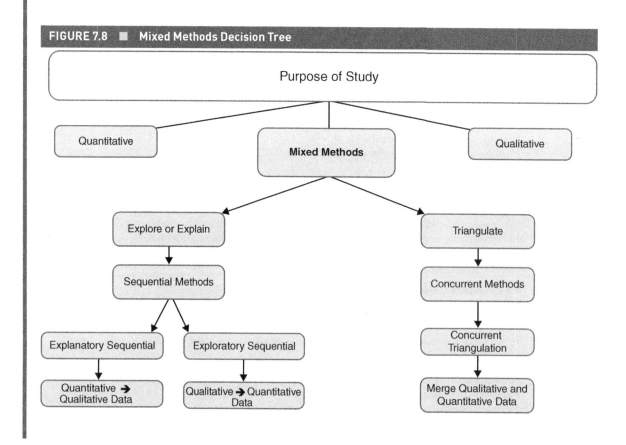

TABLE 7.6 ■ Important Questions in Mixed Methods Research	
Check	Important Questions
✓	What are the research questions?
✓	How are the researchers collecting data?
✓	Are these methods more quantitative or qualitative in nature?
✓	Do they use qualitative or quantitative first, or are they being addressed at the same time?
✓	Do the quantitative data influence the qualitative? Vice versa?
✓	What type of design is used in this study?
✓	Is the design appropriately identified? Why or why not?

THE TAKEAWAY

Selecting a proper mixed methods design for a particular research study can inform the data analysis and interpretation of results.

DEVELOPMENT OF A MIXED METHODS DESIGN STUDY

LEARNING OBJECTIVE	
7.3	Develop a mixed methods design study.

As discussed several times in this chapter, mixed methods research is unique and beneficial because it incorporates both quantitative and qualitative approaches to address a critical issue. When deciding to use this type of methodology, however, researchers typically need to plan and consider how all of the moving parts of the study should be put together. This might include deciding on which theories and designs to utilize in the study, providing a justification for the study, writing the purpose statement and research questions, determining the type of design, and finally outlining the methods section (sample, data collection instruments, etc.). All of these steps need to occur *before* beginning the actual study.

Table 7.7 provides a summary of key questions to be considered when planning a mixed methods study. Researchers can use this table to help them in the planning phase of conducting a research study. We will explore each question in further detail next.

Building a Theoretical Framework

Having a solidified theoretical framework will help to determine the direction of a study and whether or not it will be more explanatory (quantitative heavy) with deductive characteristics, or exploratory (qualitative heavy) with inductive qualities. Regardless of the initial approach, theoretical frameworks serve as the map and guide to integrating data collected from both methods into a single comprehensible set of data. For example, Bandura's (1986) social cognitive theory

TABLE 7.7 ■ Checklist for Planning a Mixed Methods Study
Planning a Mixed Methods Study: To Do List
1. Do I have a theoretical framework for my mixed methods study?
2. What is the rationale for examining this critical issue? How will this study expand upon the research that has already been conducted in this area?
3. What is the purpose of this study? What research questions do I seek to answer?
4. What mixed methods design is best for the purposes of my study? Why?
5. How will I select my sample? Does my chosen method of selection align with the purpose of the study and my research questions?
6. What instruments will I use to collect data? What have other researchers used?
7. What do I need to consider in order to seek approval from the institutional review board (IRB)? How will I collect and store data in an ethical manner?

emphasizes the importance of building students' self-efficacy beliefs. Self-efficacy beliefs refer to one's capability to accomplish a task. In a situation whereby students are preparing to take the annual state benchmark exams, a school principal might want to measure their self-efficacy for performing while looking into factors that influence student self-efficacy beliefs, including past performance, vicarious experiences (observing others perform), verbal persuasion, and physiological cues. Bandura's theory provides the theoretical framework, which might guide an educator's decision on how best to measure self-efficacy.

Developing a Rationale: The Gap in the Literature

After identifying the theoretical framework to guide the research study, the next step is to start sifting through the literature. Similar to all other research designs, reviewing the current literature regarding the critical issue of interest is essential for understanding what is known regarding an issue as well as the gaps that need to be addressed in a mixed methods study. By identifying an important gap in the literature, researchers can more easily develop the rationale (i.e., reasoning) for selecting the specific type of research methodology and design. Conducting a comprehensive literature review is also needed to determine appropriate research questions to be investigated (see Chapter 2), and to support the justification for employing a mixed methods design.

Articulating Aims and Research Questions

Like any study, the particular type of mixed methods approch should be based primarily on the nature of the research questions of interest and whether conducting a qualitative or quantitative study alone is not enough to assess the critical issue. For example, if Mr. Millett wanted to collect data on teacher and student beliefs, attitudes, and experiences about cyberbullying, he may become concerned that using only a survey will not capture the depth and level of nuance that he desires. Thus, using both a survey, interview, and/or other assessment tools would likely help Mr. Millet to develop a greater understanding of how different data sources inform each other.

The research questions should be connected and contain both qualitative and quantitative elements that focus to elaborate on findings identified in the literature review. Other components of a mixed methods research question to consider include the following: What is the goal(s) for conducting this research? Are the research questions targeting those goals? Does the research question imply a comparison between groups, a magnitude, description or contextualization from a unique perspective, or is it a combination of all of these components? It is important to note that the strategy for determining a research question will have an effect on other components in the research design (i.e., how data are collected, the particular design, sample, and even how the research question will be answered). Research questions can be constructed in a variety of ways. Some questions might be aligned with a qualitative foundation (broader and more focused on what something is or how something happens), and some may present quantitative style questions that include variables of interest and a specific hypothesis. Referring back to our example with Mr. Millett and his colleagues, Mr. Millett may conduct a study with an explanatory sequential design to answer the following research questions: "What is the prevalence of cyberbullying in this high school? How often does it occur? To what extent does cyberbullying impact victims socially, emotionally, and academically?" In mixed methods research, some overlap in the focus of the research questions will occur, and many times more questions will (and should) evolve out of the results, as is common in qualitative research. Most importantly, both the quantitative and qualitative data need to work to address the same critical issue and research questions.

Cyberbullying in high schools is one critical issue that may be a good fit for mixed methods research requiring multiple strategies to answer related research questions.

©iStockphoto.com/SolStock

Sampling and Data Collection Methods

Sampling is important in designing a mixed methods study and is largely determined based on whether the researcher focuses on the quantitative or qualitative data collection. When the data are collected concurrently, the researcher typically focuses on and collects data from the same participants. On the other hand, in sequential designs, a small or unequal qualitative sample is typically utilized. There are three main sampling methods for a mixed methods approach: probability sampling, purposive sampling, and convenience sampling. During probability sampling, the researchers take a sample of random individuals either from across a population or from designated subgroups of a population to get an accurate representation of the population of interest. Purposive sampling typically employed in qualitative research involves selecting specific members of a population based on specific characteristics these individuals have related to the problem at hand. Finally, convenience sampling employs volunteer participants that are easily accessible to the researcher. In general, mixed methods research will typically merge probabilistic and purposive methods. Table 7.8 summarizes the three primary sampling methods used in a mixed methods approach.

TABLE 7.8 ■ Sampling in Mixed Methods		
Type	Definition	Example
Probability Sampling	Random selection of participants from a population of interest.	In a study on sleep at a particular university, 100 students out of the 5,000 students enrolled at the university are randomly selected to report their average nightly hours of sleep.
Purposive Sampling	Non-random selection of participants based on certain characteristics.	A researcher is interested in high school students' motivations to attend college at a high school with historically low rates of college attendance. She asks all of the graduating seniors whether or not they plan to attend college. Those who do not plan to attend are excluded from the study.
Convenience Sampling	Non-random selection of participants that are easily accessible.	An educator interested in understanding how student self-efficacy beliefs in math fluctuate in cooperative versus direct-instruction learning environments recruits students from her school.

Once the sample has been selected, the next step is to determine the most useful data collection tools to address both the qualitative and the quantitative parts of the study. Researchers must carefully select instruments that are valid and reliable. The instrumentation used (i.e., surveys, focus groups, questionnaires, vignettes, etc.) will play a key role in the strategies used to analyze the data, such as coding of responses. In Table 7.9, we list some of the more commonly used tools for each type of methodology. It should be noted that there is some overlap in measures between methodologies, such as data obtained from observation instruments that can be in the form of more structured observations (i.e., numerical) as compared to naturalistic observations (i.e., text). Once the researcher has received permission to conduct the study from the institutional review board (IRB), they can begin the data collection process.

TABLE 7.9 ■ Instrumentation Tools	
Quantitative Tools	Qualitative Tools
Surveys	Interviews
Rating scales	Focus groups
Structured observations	Naturalistic observations
Preexisting data	Open-ended questionnaires

Sometimes planning a mixed methods study can be best approached by looking at the critical issue and reverse engineering it to help with understanding. This may entail examining the outcomes or end goal, and moving backward toward the research questions and hypotheses in order to understand what the design and intention of the study should be. For example, based on the cyberbullying scenario, if Mr. Millett were taking this approach, he would look at cyberbullying (the critical issue) and set a goal for what he would like to learn from this study. Let's say the outcome goal is to find strategies that are proactive in making a potential bully think twice before posting a comment that could bring harm to another person. Moving backward a researcher could then think of the different factors they want to focus on (i.e., school and home environment, attributions, self-efficacy, mental health, etc.), and from there formulate hypotheses and research questions. Ultimately the research designs a researcher implements will dictate the structure of the study. For example, if choosing a sequential approach, the results of the first part of the study assist in designing the second part of the study, whereas in concurrent triangulation both qualitative and quantitative methods will occur at the same time. Let's practice using *Let's See It!* and *Let's Do It!* activities that follow. There is also a *You Do It! 7.3* exercise as an extension activity at the end of the chapter.

Let's See It! 7.3

Goal: Mapping Out the Research Design of an Article

In this activity we ask that you read the summary about a study conducted by Schmidt, et al. (2018). Then, see if you can map out the purpose, research question(s), method, and findings of this article. It may also be helpful to access and read the entire methods section of this article to obtain a more detailed overview of the methodological approach used in this study.

Article Summary

Schmidt, J. A., Kafkas, S. S., Maier, K. S., Shumow, L., & Kackar-Cam, H. Z. (2018). Why are we learning this? Using mixed methods to understand teachers' relevance statements and how they shape middle school students' perceptions of science utility. *Contemporary Educational Psychology, 57*, 9–31. https://doi.org/10.1016/j.cedpsych.2018.08.005

In this article, the researchers used a mixed methods design to investigate how middle school science teachers perceived and communicated the relevance of science content to their students along with their student's perception of utility of the science content. The authors explored three research questions: "How do the science teachers in the study describe the relevance of their course content and communicate these views in their daily interactions with students?" "To what degree do the students in the study perceive their daily course content and the domain of science as useful?" and "To what extent is the way that teachers describe and communicate relevance related to students' beliefs about the utility of daily course content and the domain of science more generally?" Four middle school science teachers participated in interviews and repeated observations along with their seventh-grade students (N = 306 from 14 seventh-grade classrooms) who responded to self-reported measures on the usefulness and utility of the science content. Quantitative data were collected from students during the same period when their classrooms were being observed. Following separate analyses of the quantitative and qualitative data, the data sources were merged to examine how teachers' relevance statements related to their own beliefs and to students' perceptions of science utility. The results of the study showed that teacher's beliefs were strongly mirrored by their perceptions of science relevancy, which influenced how they discussed science relevance in their instructional practices. Findings also showed that students only found the science content to be moderately relevant unless the utility of the content was explicitly discussed by the teacher.

Now follow the decision tree to determine how we concluded what is the type of study.

Let's Do It! 7.3

Guided Practice: Practice Mapping Out the Research Design for an Article

Using Table 7.10 showing the example article by Schmidt et al. (2018) for the *Let's See It!* activity, read through the Mishna et al. (2020) article and see if you can map out the purpose, research question(s), method, and findings for this mixed methods research study in Table 7.11.

TABLE 7.10 ■ Mixed Methods Article Example	
Study	Schmidt, J. A., Kafkas, S. S., Maier, K. S., Shumow, L., & Kackar-Cam, H. Z. (2018). Why are we learning this? Using mixed methods to understand teachers' relevance statements and how they shape middle school students' perceptions of science utility. *Contemporary Educational Psychology, 57*, 9–31. https://doi.org/10.1016/j.cedpsych.2018.08.005
Purpose	To investigate middle school science teachers' beliefs and perceptions on the utility of the science content they are teaching as well as their student's perception of science content utility.
Research Questions	1. How do the science teachers in the study describe the relevance of their course content and communicate these views in their daily interactions with students? 2. To what degree do the students in the study perceive their daily course content and the domain of science as useful? 3. To what extent is the way that teachers describe and communicate relevance related to students' beliefs about the utility of daily course content and the domain of science more generally?
Method	Four middle school science teachers and their seventh-grade students (*N* = 306 from 14 seventh-grade classrooms). Convergent mixed methods design was employed. Data were collected using • Quantitative data included daily end-of-class self-reported data from students • Qualitative data included teacher interviews and classroom observations After all data were collected were collected concurrently. Data were then triangulated and interpreted.
Findings	Findings showed that teacher beliefs of the relevance of the science content had an influence on how they were teaching the content, including how often they explicitly addressed the utility and relevance of the content, which in turn impacted how students perceived the utility of science content being taught.

TABLE 7.11 ■ Mixed Methods Article Example	
Study	Mishna, F., Birze, A., & Greenblatt, A. (2022). Understanding bullying and cyberbullying through an ecological systems framework: The value of qualitative interviewing in a mixed methods approach. *International Journal of Bullying Prevention, 4*, 220–229. https://doi.org/10.1007/s42380-022-00126-w
Purpose	
Research Questions	
Method	
Findings	

THE TAKEAWAY

Using a mixed methods design requires advanced planning and a solid understanding of both quantitative and qualitative methods.

MAKING SENSE OF THE FINDINGS FROM MIXED METHODS RESEARCH

LEARNING OBJECTIVE

7.4　Demonstrate understanding of how to describe findings from mixed methods research.

After the study is planned, the sample is identified, and the data are collected, the researcher is ready to begin what many consider the most exciting part of doing research, which is analyzing and interpreting the study findings. When analyzing data in mixed methods designs, there are three general steps to follow: (1) prepare data, (2) describe, analyze, and interpret data, and (3) present the findings (Step 3 will be covered in the next section). Generally, there are many ways to analyze the data depending on the mixed methods design used in the study. For example, the researcher in the concurrent triangulation design typically compares results from the analyses of qualitative and quantitative data and makes an interpretation regarding the extent to which the findings converge or do not converge. Refer to Table 7.12 for a helpful guide to think through how a researcher might prepare, analyze, and interpret the study findings when conducting a mixed methods study.

TABLE 7.12 ■ Checklist for Quick Steps to Analyzing Mixed Methods	
Step 1: Prepare data	Preparing data for analysis (i.e., clean, explore, reduce, sort, code, transform the data)
Step 2: Describe analyze, and integrate data	Describe what is revealed by the data Use comparative analyses to examine differences and deeper meanings: • Sequentially, where one starts with one method then the other (i.e., exploratory or explanatory) • Concurrently, where one links the data as one dataset and analyzes at the same time (i.e., triangulation)
Step 3: Present findings	Engage in the most effective way to depict findings: Graphics Quotes Joint visual displays (i.e., models, matrices, tables)

Preparing Data for Analysis

Once data are collected preparatory work is needed to clean, explore, organize, and transform the data for analyses. In the case of qualitative data, the first step is to discern meaning from all data sources, such as interviews, focus groups, field notes, documents, and journals. This process entails converting the data into textual form which may include transcribing word for word data from focus groups and interviews. Transcribing involves converting spoken data (i.e., an audio recorded interview) into written text, usually word for word. Transcription allows interview answers, for example, to be examined for patterns. The review of textual data for patterns helps researchers determine appropriate ways to code the data. Coding the data involves reading through the transcriptions and looking for words or phrases that occur most frequently and creating codes for those words and phrases. For example, if we interviewed five students on their thoughts and feelings about cyberbullying and their responses included words such as angry, frustrated, unhappy, mad, and uncomfortable, we might choose to categorize all of these responses as "negative reactions." Finally, researchers would develop a codebook when all textual data have been analyzed along with an explanation for each code and quotes that illustrate the code. Once codes are constructed, patterns are observed and themes are developed from the codes.

In case of quantitative data, the first step is to develop a codebook in order to create records for each data source. A computer spreadsheet is used to clean the data of any outliers. Descriptive statistics might generate additional input on ensuring accuracy of the dataset, such as outliers or errors in the data. Data transformation might also be necessary for some mixed methods designs (i.e., concurrent triangulation designs). This might entail transformation of one data type into the other so that both can be analyzed together. In this case qualitative data are coded, codes are assigned numerical values and included with quantitative data in statistical analyses. On the other hand, qualifying quantitative data might involve using factor analysis (i.e. data reduction) to develop factors that become themes to be compared to themes generated from the qualitative data. Additional information on how to describe, analyze, and integrate both quantitative and qualitative data is provided in the following sections.

Describing and Analyzing Quantitative Data

When analyzing quantitative data independently researchers can use one of several statistical approaches, although the best approach depends on the design of the study. Descriptive statistics should always be run regardless of the methodological approach. Descriptive statistics allow researchers to better understand the nature of the sample as well as summaries of the variables of interest. If the researcher is interested in hypothesis testing, then the researcher can use various approaches, such as a *t*-test or an ANOVA, depending on the nature of the data and the research questions of interest. If determining the relationship between two variables, a correlation or regression analysis will be appropriate. When looking at inferential statistics (refer to Chapter 13).

Describing and Analyzing Qualitative Data

When describing qualitative data separately, there are various techniques researchers might use (see Chapter 14). Researchers may choose to describe qualitative data in a variety of different ways depending on the data collected. One of the more common analysis methods is thematic analysis, which helps identify patterns in qualitative data though transcription and then coding of the data, such as when using an interview transcript, and then engage in coding of responses or other text by similarity. Other types of qualitative data analysis include narrative inquiry, which focuses on an individual's story or experience, and grounded theory, where a theory can be developed through analysis.

Integrating Data

Integrating data in mixed methods research requires a thorough understanding of both the quantitative and qualitative components of a study in order to effectively address the overall goal of the study. Strategies to integrate qualitative and quantitative data can be implemented at the design, methods, and interpretation levels of research. Depending on the conceptualization of the design the options for integration are many and rather complex. Simply put, integration at the design level depends on the design selected. In sequential designs, the goal is to have one phase of the mixed methods study build on the other, whereas in the concurrent triangulation designs the goal is to merge the data in order to compare and contrast the findings. At the methods level, integration can happen via linking sampling, data collection, and analysis. For example, in an explanatory sequential design, data from surveys informs how participants are sampled for phase 2 of the data collection, whereas data collection instruments might also be revised based on the subsample of the participants. Finally, integration of qualitative and quantitative data at the interpretation level happens via integrating through narrative, data transformation (e.g., involving concurrent triangulation designs), and joint displays. Generally, researchers describe the qualitative and quantitative findings in a single report using two separate sections for the quantitative and qualitative data, or they weave the findings together within one section. Use of joint visuals such as tables and matrices can provide additional information gained from the separate quantitative and qualitative data.

Integrating multiple types of data is one of the biggest issues regarding validity in mixed methods research, especially since the various kinds of data can be collected and combined in so many different ways. It can be challenging to determine how much emphasis to place on each type of data, the level of importance of different findings, and how to handle findings that are contradictory. Thus, is it important that experienced researchers and/or experts for both methodologies be included as part of an analysis. Technological tools and programs designed to integrate both quantitative and qualitative data can also be invaluable to the research process. In these programs, qualitative data can be transformed into quantitative data, and vice versa to facilitate the integration, analysis, and interpretation of findings. In summary, being able to successfully analyze both sets of data and integrate is heavily dependent on complementary and related research questions that require mixed methodologies to answer. The trustworthiness of mixed methods studies can be enhanced using many strategies, such as obtaining a representative sample of participants and ensuring that the instruments used are psychometrically sound and appropriate for the research questions of interest. Additionally, any treatment or interventions that are delivered must have applicability and fidelity. Finally, data obtained must be thorough, copious, and useful for analysis and interpretation. These steps ensure that findings are sound and appropriately generalizable to the population of interest.

THE TAKEAWAY

Approaches to integrate qualitative and quantitative data can be implemented at the design, methods, and interpretation levels of research.

ETHICAL CONSIDERATIONS

LEARNING OBJECTIVE
7.5   Demonstrate knowledge of ethical issues when engaging with mixed methods research.

Now that you have learned some information about how to properly conduct a mixed methods study, describe, analyze, and integrate the results, it is important to consider ethical considerations in the context of mixed methods research. As with any research study, when conducting mixed methods research, the same ethical considerations that pertain to the quantitative and qualitative methods designs also apply in terms of protecting research participants from harm; ensuring voluntary participation, privacy and confidentially; and obtaining informed consent/assent. With regards to mixed methods research designs, we focus on two areas that researchers should take extra steps to ensure ethical conduct: design, sampling, data collection; and the researcher's role in quality and ethics.

Design, Sampling, and Data Collection

Regardless of the methodology used in research, it is imperative that a researcher adheres to the rules and guidelines of conducting research. In terms of using mixed methods, the researcher should provide a strong justification for selecting a design in a way that elaborates on why that specific design was chosen and how it adds value for a particular study. Thus, in regards to our opening scenario, Mr. Millett may be interested in assessing the impact of the number of likes a social media post gets that has been deemed harmful by the victim and bully perceptions of cyberbullying. It would make sense for Mr. Millett to identify harmful social media posts and the frequency of likes as a first step in the study and then follow up with a survey (quantitative) to the participants on how these posts made them feel. He would need to provide a rationale for conducting subsequent interviews (qualitative) to add to a deeper understanding of the phenomenon and examine certain themes (i.e., explanatory sequential design).

The researcher should also be aware of sampling and data collection issues that might arise during mixed methods research in each methodological paradigm. Typically, participants in mixed methods research are asked to participate more than once, such as responding to a survey as well as participating in a focus interview. This additional demand might result in an increased burden placed on the participants. Thus, researchers should make intentional study design modifications to reduce burden on the participants. Time commitments for both strands of data collection must be clearly described on the informed consent form.

Furthermore, speaking of the informed consent form, it is also critical for researchers to outline and fully understand ethical standards and principles before using mixed methods research. It is particularly important to examine how participant consent translates between the qualitative and quantitative phases of research. Explicit consent must be obtained to access data from a participant in one phase of a study and again in the second phase. Researchers must ensure that participant consent covers all phases of the study. Additionally, researchers must consider the de-identification of data and other similar privacy concerns. Finally, when the researcher is linking data (especially data obtained through a public domain) to participants across study phases, the researcher must ensure the consent of participants has been received and that privacy, especially through the internet and social media has been appropriately addressed). With mixed methods designs continuing to evolve in the field, researchers will likely encounter new ethical issues while conducting research. Researchers should share any ethical issues that may arise during the research process with the research community.

STOP AND THINK 7.4

How does ethical research improve the trustworthiness of the findings of a mixed-methods study?

Quality and Ethics

The ethical considerations pertaining to the important role that the researcher plays in conducting mixed methods research can not be underestimated. The researcher in mixed methods research can be seen as an instrument in the research process, including design, data collection, and data analysis. They must reflect on how their particular goals might cross ethical boundaries in mixed methods studies. In fact, reflexivity (i.e., judgments, practices, and belief systems) is necessary because the researcher interacts closely with the research design, method, and interpretation. Providing reflexivity of a study allows the researcher to open the reader to a greater level of analysis and interpretation of the study's results, adding a level of credibility, trustworthiness, and transparency. In summary, when communicating and conducting research, the researcher should be aware of the role they play in the research and be able to reflect on preexisting mindsets and biases so they have a greater awareness of their own biases and can be mindful of them in conducting research.

THE TAKEAWAY

It is important for researchers to recognize their own biases and worldviews when conducting a study in order to enhance the study's credibility and trustworthiness.

AMERICAN PSYCHOLOGICAL ASSOCIATION STYLE

Currently, there is no standard method of writing a mixed methods report. Researchers have autonomy in how to communicate or convey the results (i.e., APA style, narratives, story form, etc.). Researchers can be creative in presentation of the material as long as it increases the reader's understanding and conceptualization of the critical issues and overall results.

In general, the type of the mixed methods design used has some impact on how the study is organized in a journal article. For example, in a concurrent triangulation study where the researcher focuses heavily on both quantitative and qualitative components, the report should give equal attention to the quantitative and qualitative results. In a sequential design approach, the paradigm that was administered first should be presented first. It is important to include a paragraph that introduces the design when writing about a study in the methods section of the manuscript, identifying the type of mixed methods design, and describing the level of timing, weight and priority, and analyses decisions. Most importantly though, a researcher needs to state the rationale for selecting this design for the study.

All material should be written in a scholarly fashion with relevant information. Standard APA format in mixed methods writing is linear in that there is a clear chronological order beginning with an introduction, literature review, methods, results, and ending with a discussion. Benefits of following standard APA format include the fact that the sections are clearly delineated, which allows the reader to anticipate the information included in each section. Further, concise writing in mixed methods research is especially important because most mixed methods reports will be longer in comparison to reports of other studies that used either a qualitative or quantitative methodology alone.

Ways of Presenting Quantitative and Qualitative Data in an Integrated Manner

Regardless of the type of mixed methods used, studies should incorporate a section on the integration of the two methods. A well-rounded and balanced inclusion of both numerical data and qualitative quotes in a journal article is important. Overall, determining how the predetermined, objective, third-person quantitative style of reporting and the more fluid, reflexive, and oftentimes first-person qualitative style of reporting are integrated is largely determined by researchers. In many studies, the quantitative findings and qualitative findings are reported in separate sections. A contrasting approach would be to present both quantitative and qualitative findings together. This technique can be challenging and should be avoided due to the intricate nature of each methodology. In summary, the goal is to address each research question by integrating quantitative and qualitative findings. In this way, the methodologies function as a dialogue or conversation in relationship to each research question. Perhaps the most important information about presenting results of a mixed methods design is identifying ways to connect the qualitative data from Phase 1 of the study with the quantitative data from Phase 2 of the study using a joint display. A joint display allows the researcher to depict the data visually together where exemplary quotes from the qualitative interviews can be compared and contrasted to results from the statistical analyses of another source of data.

THE TAKEAWAY

The focus that is given to the quantitative and qualitative portions of the study in the report should correspond to the design of the mixed methods study.

CHAPTER SUMMARY

Mixed methods research involves integrating qualitative and quantitative methods in such a way that it allows researchers to develop a deeper understanding of critical issues, people, or other phenomena of interest. When mixed methods research is effectively used, researchers emphasize the strengths of each method while minimizing their inherent weaknesses. There are many variations of mixed methods designs depending on the research questions, and the resources available. In this chapter we covered three types including the concurrent (convergent) triangulation, the explanatory sequential, and the exploratory sequential designs and provided some general steps for conducting mixed methods research. We also discussed challenges associated with conducting mixed methods research, such as additional resources, sampling, ethics and using multiple analyses and interpreting approaches to deal with the varied forms of data. To overcome these challenges, it is recommended that mixed methods research teams include experienced researchers or experts from each of the two methodologies. This range of methodological expertise and the development of a multidisciplinary team can be time consuming, but is necessary for executing a thorough and well-developed mixed methods study.

EXTENSION ACTIVITIES

You Do It! 7.1
Self-Directed Practice: Identify Examples of Quantitative and Qualitative Data Instruments for a Critical Issue of Your Choice

After reviewing Table 7.2, which focuses on cyberbullying, think about your own mixed methods study that you would like to conduct in order to address a critical issue of interest to you. What types of quantitative and/or qualitative data might you collect to answer your research question(s)? Would some combination of these two types of data in a mixed methods study offer more than either type of data could offer alone? Complete Table 7.13 to help you think through your research questions and study.

You Do It! 7.2
Self-Directed Practice: Practice Distinguishing Using Mixed Methods Research Designs

Identify a mixed methods study of your choice, review it and provide answers to questions in Table 7.14 Use the mixed methods decision tree (Figure 7.8) to help you determine what type of study this is.

TABLE 7.13 ■ Quantitative Versus Qualitative Data Collection Instruments in Mixed Method	
Quantitative Data	**Qualitative Data**

Example:

TABLE 7.14 ■ Important Questions for Your Own Mixed Methods Research	
Check	**Important Questions**
✓	What are the research questions?
✓	How are the researchers collecting data?
✓	Are these methods more quantitative or qualitative in nature?
✓	Do they use qualitative or quantitative first, or are they being addressed at the same time?
✓	Do the quantitative data influence the qualitative? Vice versa?
✓	What type of design is used in this study?
✓	Is the design appropriately identified? Why or why not?

You Do It! 7.3

Self-Directed Practice: Mapping Out the Research Design of an Article of Your Choice

Think about a critical issue that you would like to examine. Using Table 7.15 identify a mixed methods article related to this critical issue and then map out the purpose, research question(s), method, and findings.

TABLE 7.15 ■ Mixed Methods Article Example
Study

Purpose

**Research
Questions**

Method

Findings

KEY TERMS

Concurrent designs

Concurrent triangulation

Explanatory sequential design

Exploratory sequential design

Mixed methods research

Sequential designs

Theoretical framework

Triangulation

ANSWER KEY

Stop and Think Activities

STOP AND THINK 7.1

There are a wide range of answers to this Stop and Think. Some examples of critical issues might be student struggles with academic self-regulation, parental absence in early childhood, and lack of student interest or motivation in the classroom. Regardless of the critical issue at hand, using mixed methods research can help to holistically investigate an issue using both qualitative and quantitative strands of data to bring in multiple perspectives.

STOP AND THINK 7.2

To tackle this Stop and Think the first step is to think about your critical issue as it relates to the purpose and research questions. Let's say you are interested in developing an instrument to measure student self-efficacy for self-regulating learning in mathematics. Both types of data are important in this case as qualitative interviews will help you write appropriate questions informing the development and further testing of a quantitative scale.

STOP AND THINK 7.3

As a teacher you are expected to try different methods in supporting your students' achievement. For example, if your students are having challenges in reading comprehension, you may consider implementing a reading comprehension intervention. Using an exploratory mixed methods design could help you gain a better understanding about the benefits of the intervention by conducting interviews with students to learn more about their experience and then follow up with a reading assessment. Alternately, you could administer a reading assessment first and then identify students that did not benefit from the intervention to gain further insights on how to improve the intervention for these students.

STOP AND THINK 7.4

Researchers should engage in reflexivity as they interpret the data. Specifically, they should reflect on their assumptions and biases as they conduct their research which leads to overall better analyses and interpretation, and help build trustworthiness in the findings of an individual study as well as in the field as a whole.

Let's Do It! Activities

LET'S DO IT! 7.1

Quantitative Versus Qualitative Data Collection Instruments in Mixed Methods	
Quantitative Data	Qualitative Data
Writing self-efficacy scale	Interviews
Writing scores	Focus groups

Example: The researcher might want to administer a self-efficacy of writing scale to students in order to gain more information about their perceived beliefs of their writing capabilities. She could follow up with interviews or focus groups to give students an opportunity to talk more about how they go about responding to a writing prompt and their experience with the intervention. Writing test scores over the course of the year would provide the researcher with a way to measure their progress as she implements changes.

LET'S DO IT! 7.2

Important Questions in Mixed Methods Research	
Check	Important Questions
✓	*What are the research questions?*
	1. How does the identity-based model of relevance capture the content of students' relevance constructions?
	2. What structural dimensionality manifests in the conceptual space of students' self-relevance constructions?
✓	*How are the researchers collecting data?* Researchers collected data using open-ended writing assignments and surveys with high school students.
✓	*Are these methods more quantitative or qualitative in nature?* Both quantitative and qualitative methods were used in a meaningful way to answer the research questions.
✓	*Do they use qualitative or quantitative first, or are they being addressed at the same time?* Researchers used qualitative methods first.
✓	*Does the quantitative data influence the qualitative? Vice versa?* The qualitative data (collected first) were used to collect information on relevant constructs (i.e., identified dimensions underlying students' perceived self-relevance of biology content), and it influenced the instrument design of the second phase of the study.

Check	Important Questions

✓ *What type of design is used in this study?*
This study uses an exploratory sequential mixed methods design.

✓ *Is the design appropriately identified? Why or why not?*
Yes. In this study, the type of mixed methods design is stated less outright than in the study included in the previous *Let's See It!* activity; however, design information is still easily identifiable and well explained.

Let's Do It! 7.3

Mixed Methods Article Example

Study	Mishna, F., Birze, A. & Greenblatt, A. (2022). Understanding bullying and cyberbullying through an ecological systems framework: The value of qualitative interviewing in a mixed methods approach. *International Journal of Bullying Prevention*, 4, 220–229. https://doi.org/10.1007/s42380–022–00126–w
Purpose	To examine bullying and cyberbullying through an ecological systems lens using a mixed methods approach.
Research Questions	Although no research questions were mentioned, the authors listed five objectives of the study with a focus on uncovering prevalence rates, risk and protective factors, consequences of cyberbullying, and exploring youth experiences and perspectives along with their parents' and teachers' perceptions of cyberbullying.
Methods	The sample included students in fourth ($n=160$), seventh ($n=243$), and 10th ($n=267$) grades and their teachers ($n=103$); and (3) their parents ($n=246$). Qualitative interviews followed with a subset of the sample including students, teachers, and parents. Survey data were collected first to gain information on the constructs of interest followed by interviews with middle school students and their parents.
Findings	The authors discussed the findings of study with an emphasis on how qualitive interviews helped them gain a better understanding of the complexity of bullying and cyberbullying among school-aged students.

 8   ACTION RESEARCH FOR EDUCATORS

LEARNING OBJECTIVES

Upon completion of this chapter, the reader should be able to

8.1   Describe action research and its origins

8.2   Distinguish between action research and other research methods

8.3   Provide a rationale for conducting action research for work-related problems

8.4   Differentiate between practical and participatory action research

8.5   Use the cycle of action research to conduct a study on a work-related problem as a self-regulated educator

8.6   Demonstrate knowledge of ethical issues when engaging with action research

8.7   Utilize the *Publication Manual of the American Psychological Association* in reporting and presenting action research designs

A DAY AT WORK

This Bullying Has to Stop!

©iStockphoto.com/Highwaystarz-Photography

Mrs. Ortez is an eighth-grade teacher in a small private middle school who is troubled about bullying toward students with disabilities. She noticed that some students will snicker and roll their eyes at each other when Sabrina, a student who is in special education, enters the room. She worries Sabrina feels isolated from her classmates because she does not seem to have any friends and is often not selected as a class partner. Mrs. Ortez also noticed that Sabrina eats alone in the cafeteria and is also concerned that bullying is not only prevalent among students but among faculty. For example, on a professional development outing, Mrs. Ortez overheard two teachers discussing how "hopeless" it was to teach a particular student who has a writing and math disability.

Mrs. Ortez, feeling frustrated and concerned, approached the principal about conducting a research study to explore bullying. The principal liked this idea and suggested Mrs. Ortez invite the school counselor, other teachers, and students with and without diagnosed disabilities to participate. Unsure of exactly how to go about conducting research, Mrs. Ortez remembers reading about action research when she was in her teacher education program and is wondering if that is the appropriate method to use.

INTRODUCTION

Throughout this book, we make the link between educators daily work and conducting research. In each chapter, we provide *A Day at Work* scenarios—real-life situations that educators struggle with; content information on different research methodologies; and the tools for planning, doing, and reflecting for conducting research. In this chapter, we describe a method of conducting research called action research. This chapter will begin with an overview of action research followed by descriptions of the two most common types of action research. We then provide a rationale for conducting an action research study, followed by information on the cycle of action research and how it overlaps with self-regulated learning. The last two sections are focused on ethical issues when engaging in action research and recommendations on how to communicate about action research using guidelines from the American Psychological Association (APA). Believe it or not, it is likely you have already engaged in some of the activities related to action research. It is also possible you have been a subject of action research when you were a student. Let's begin by defining action research.

WHAT IS ACTION RESEARCH?

LEARNING OBJECTIVE	
8.1	Describe action research and its origins.

Action research is defined as a research method in which the practitioner has a real-life problem or issue in their school that needs to be resolved. They may want to improve, change, correct, fix, or even eliminate the problem. The research is conducted by the educator and helps them figure out what is the best action to take.

For example, Mr. Karam, who is a first-grade teacher in a public housing community, is frustrated by the frequent absenteeism of students. When he called the parents of the students with high absenteeism rates, the parents gave a variety of explanations, such as the child is needed for babysitting a younger sibling, or they overslept and were too tired to bring their child to school. From these conversations, Mr. Karam suspects the students' parents do not fully grasp how important education is for their child. Hence, he decides to develop a program that would increase parental involvement as well as educate the parents on the benefits of regular attendance. The plan would be to conduct a literature review to see if he can come across programs that may have been successfully used in the past. Mr. Karam believes that if he finds a program that was used with students similar to his own, he could implement it in class to see if attendance improves. In addition, the Mr. Karam is hoping for something even greater than improving attendance: that the implementation of parental involvement may lead to a change in parental understanding of the importance of education for their children. Mr. Karam also knows it may be challenging to get parents involved in an intervention program and that the experiment must be done in a systematic way to ensure the validity of the results. As these thoughts run through his head, the Mr. Karam begins the literature review and takes notes as outlined in Chapter 2 of this book.

The preceding scenario is much like the example at the start of the chapter in that it reflects an opportunity to conduct research on an existing issue of practice. In both scenarios, the teachers feel frustrated. Conducting action research empowers educators to find potential solutions to these puzzles. Mrs. Ortez wants to explore students' understanding of bullying and develop an intervention program to address it. The problem as Mrs. Ortez sees it is that the bullying is targeted toward students with disabilities, and she is concerned about these students' socioemotional well-being. From this scenario, we know that she suspects students may not understand the experiences, feelings, and challenges that students with disabilities encounter, and she thinks an intervention might help.

Implied in these examples is that the intervention will cause a transformative educational experience in students and parents—one that will create a powerful change in them. Action research not only transforms learners but can empower educators by giving them a sense of control over student outcomes and a remedy for existing issues of practice.

Origins of Action Research

Kurt Lewin (1890–1947) was a social psychologist who is credited with coming up with the term action research in the 1940s. He believed the best way to obtain the solution to problems was to study them in the context within which they were occurring. Lewin's action research design overlaps with self-regulated maps closely against the processes of self-regulated learning described in Chapter 1 and used throughout this book because it involves four components: reflecting, planning, acting, and observing on a current situation. This includes examining potential changes or improvements that will ultimately lead to better practice and reflecting upon the outcomes.

Lewin developed his idea of action research by examining two concerns that many educators experience: motivation and performance, particularly among underrepresented students. Only Lewin's research initially consisted of examining motivation and performance among workers who were underrepresented in a factory in the 1930s. After dividing factory workers who were experiencing low levels of work morale and self-esteem into two groups, he provided two types of instruction. Group 1 received what educators might call direct instruction—an instructor taught a group of learners and provided little opportunity for interaction or discussion. Group 2 learners received what educators might call whole-class instruction, where the instructor taught the learners by encouraging questions, discussions, and interactions by allowing factory workers to provide feedback on the type of training they received. Motivation and workplace performance increased in the group of workers who were encouraged to be actively engaged in their learning.

While Lewin initially found that action research was an effective method of conducting research in work settings, it was quickly identified as an appropriate design for educators to use within school-based contexts. Because schools are dynamic institutions with a diversity of personalities, programs, and goals, these early studies on employees laid the foundation for conducting research in authentic settings (such as classrooms) where the participants (such as the educators and students) were directly involved in the research.

THE TAKEAWAY

Action research refers to a research method in which the practitioner has a real-life problem or issue in their schools that needs to be resolved.

ACTION RESEARCH AND OTHER RESEARCH METHODS

LEARNING OBJECTIVE
8.2   Distinguish between action research and other research methods.

Participant involvement is one of the core components of action research. Participants can include a teacher and their students, a team of teachers, administrators, school counselors and psychologists, as well as principals in a school district. It may also include families or communities. While action research is systematic in that it follows specific steps, it is different from research conducted by scientists who are outside of the authentic setting or using participants who are not directly a part of the educator's practice or community. A faculty member at a local university interested in conducting research on the attendance rates of students in neighboring schools is not an example of an action research study, while a principal concerned about the attendance rates in their own school *is* potentially an example of a potential action research study. This is because the issue under examination involves the students in the principal's school where the principal has a vested interest in their overall success.

Action research provides educators with the power and control to regulate instruction and learning and to improve professional practice. It focuses on specific situations and differs from other research in that its primary goal is to resolve or improve a situation in the context of where the educator is working. Action research also differs from other research methodologies because the latter approaches seek to create knowledge that is generalizable to other contexts and settings. For example, a group of scientists examining an outdoor classroom program for kindergartners may develop a program and test it on students in a school district. Upon examining the results, the scientists write a manuscript describing the study for publication in a peer-reviewed journal. The scientists, while participating in the study, are not directly affected by the results of the study whereas a teacher wanting to improve motivation among her students or a principal concerned about the high rate of violence in her school are directly affected by the outcomes of an action research investigation.

The following presents a few additional situations when action research may be an ideal approach to investigate an issue or problem in schools:

- English teacher Mrs. Walker is troubled about the reading comprehension skills in her classroom and performance on statewide examinations.

- The science department faculty suspect that students' lack of fundamental mathematical skills is interfering with science understanding.

- A school principal is trying to decide on whether to purchase Chromebooks to increase overall attendance and achievement for the students in their economically disadvantaged school.

- A guidance counselor has an idea for a program involving group activities that could help students who have lost a parent.

- Dr. Wolinski, the school superintendent, wants to increase enrollment and achievement in STEM courses among the underrepresented girls in their district.

STOP AND THINK 8.1

What are some issues you might want to investigate to make improvements in your work?

In the *Let's See It!* activity that follows we provide examples of the differences between conducting action research and other research methods followed by the *Let's Do It!* activity asking readers to provide their own examples of when one might conduct an action research study or a research study using a different design. At the end of this chapter, you have an opportunity to practice what you have learned using the *You Do It!* activity.

Let's See It! 8.1

Goal: Learn to Differentiate Action Research From Other Types of Research

Directions: Table 8.1 provides examples or models of differences between conducting action research and other types of research; notice how each approach has a different focus.

TABLE 8.1 ■ Action Research Compared to Other Research Methods	
Action Research	**Other Research Methods**
Educator is the scientist conducting the research. Mr. White is frustrated with his students' lack of motivation to complete their homework.	Research is conducted by scientists often disconnected from the classroom or school. Two professors from local universities contact the school district about conducting an intervention study on vaping among middle and high school students.
Participants are students directly connected with the educator. A teacher's classroom, a counselor's clientele, a principal's school are examples of this.	Participants are recruited. A research scientist may contact the school principal and ask if the students in the principal's school can be used for a research study.
Research topic has a direct impact on the educator and participants. Mrs. Ortez wants to stop the bullying by providing an instructional program to help students understand what it is like to have a disability.	Research topic contributes to a larger body of knowledge that may or may not impact a specific classroom or school. Dr. Brookman investigated the impact of afterschool activities on students' homework completion using a group of students in a gifted school and published the findings in a peer-reviewed journal on gifted students.

Action Research	Other Research Methods
Action research can have a transformative effect on the educator and participants. Providing students with opportunities to work and play with students with disabilities may result in changed feelings and behaviors toward others who are different.	Research scientists may conduct research with the intention of creating transformative experiences that are generalizable to others beyond the scope of the study. Afterschool programs that have been found to reduce truancy in low-income communities are recommended for students attending schools in similar settings.
There may be minimal to no generalizability of the results because educators are trying to better understand practices, students, or the school community of immediate concern. A guidance counselor is frustrated with students' tardiness in submitting college applications, therefore the counselor's research is focused only on the students in their school and those students' tardiness.	One of the goals of scientific experiments is generalizability. Researcher scientists are studying problems to contribute to the existing base of knowledge and hope that their findings could be generalized to similar participants and schools. Scientists attempt to find a sample of participants that are representative of a larger group—this helps in ensuring generalizability of their findings!

Let's Do It! 8.1

Guided Practice: Generate Examples of When to Use Action Research

Directions: Using the examples from the *Let's See It!* as models, write two examples of when educators would use action research and two examples of when research scientists would conduct research.

Write Two Examples of When Educators Would Use Action Research

_____

_____

_____

Write Two Examples of When Research Scientists Would Conduct Research

_____

_____

_____

THE TAKEAWAY

Action research differs from other research methods in that the educators and participants are personally vested and involved in the research and outcomes.

RATIONALE FOR CONDUCTING ACTION RESEARCH FOR WORK-RELATED PROBLEMS

LEARNING OBJECTIVE
8.3   Provide a rationale for conducting action research for work-related problems.

Teachers may wonder, why conduct action research when I am already so busy with lesson planning, grading, and after-school activities? Can I really make an impact on my students, teachers, and administrators through action research?

Benefits to Conducting Action Research

Questions such as these provide the catalyst to conducting research in authentic settings such as a classroom, school, or a community and can provide several benefits. Action research, when conducted in a systematic and rigorous way, can benefit all involved by enhancing opportunities for self-reflection, improving instructional practice and curriculum, assisting in making decisions that will impact and transform students, classrooms, and school communities, and by promoting professional development. Action research must be an organized process that can also be conducted within educators' day-to-day routines. The process of conducting action research can provide educators with many benefits, including answers to the questions they encounter in problem-solving an issue at hand. In Table 8.2 we outline several benefits to conducting action research.

TABLE 8.2 ■ Benefits to Conducting Action Research	
Reflective practice	Action research provides the means to make changes and improvements as educators typically know when something is working well and when it is not.
Professionalism	Action research empowers educators to make an impact and contribution to their field and provides opportunities for collaboration with others.
Problem solving	Action research can provide evidence for implementing problem-solving strategies. Educators know where there is a problem and how serious it is because they are directly involved with the students, colleagues, and school.
Educator efficacy	Action research builds educators' self-efficacy and motivation—believing you can have a positive impact on practice is empowering.
Participant participation	Action research engages participants in the research process. Research is conducted *with* learners, not on learners.
Personal growth	Action research provides opportunities for personal growth—you will gain new understandings about the problem, students, and yourself!

The Purposes of Conducting Action Research Align With Educators' Goals

The purpose and process of action research align well with the overall goals of teachers and administrators interested in improving student learning and motivation, school efficiency, and the allocation of resources. A critical decision point in determining whether to conduct an action research study is whether the problem you are trying to solve is one which is found only within your classroom, school, district, and community. In other words, is it a localized concern that may or may not be prevalent in other schools or among other students? In addition, the problem involves transforming one's understanding and learning experiences; therefore, the research is directed toward improvements in practice stemming from self-reflection and a desire for things to get better.

Action research is also iterative and dynamic, meaning educators are continually reflecting, planning, acting, observing, and re-planning as they monitor improvements that have been made and noting where additional or different plans need to be implemented. As educators, we are constantly bombarded with problems that seem to have no solution. We may feel challenged and concerned about a situation and have questions that need to be asked and answered. Decisions may need to be made about a student or curriculum or how to get colleagues and students to collaborate on finding solutions to long-standing dilemmas, such as racial discrimination and social justice. This ability to have an impact on the decisions made that affect others can be empowering to educators as they gain a sense of control over their work environment. This sense of control is also boosted as educators learn and engage in research. In Table 8.3, we provide an overview of the purposes to conducting action research highlighted by examples within authentic academic contexts.

TABLE 8.3 ■ Summary of Purposes for Conducting Action Research With Examples	
Purposes	**Examples**
Provides opportunities to self-reflect	Frankie continues to frustrate his fourth-grade history teacher, Mr. Richardson. During history class, Frankie walks across the room while the teacher is speaking, laughs in an inappropriately loud manner at students' jokes, and rarely completes the classwork. Mr. Richardson reflects on what might be triggering Frankie's behavior and keeps track of Frankie's disruptions. He decides to interview Frankie and his parents to learn more about Frankie's interests. Mr. Richardson then modifies the topics used to teach history, connecting them to topics Frankie seems to enjoy; Mr. Richardson also continues to record Frankie's behavior during class. After a month, Mr. Richardson follows up with a second set of interviews of Frankie and his parents.
Improves instructional practice	Mrs. Viscovich is a special education teacher who wants to develop a new strategy for building students' self-efficacy for completing writing assignments. Mrs. Viscovich conducts a pretest, provides an intervention that includes writing scaffolds and organizes the students' writing samples into individual portfolios, then conducts a posttest. This is repeated for several weeks with each week's writing assignment increasing in rigor.
Helps guide decision-making process	Principal Marlene Richter is undecided about whether teachers in her school should adopt a new approach to teaching mathematics. She plans to have two teachers pilot the new approach, conduct interviews of the students and teachers who participated, and look at pre- and post-intervention mathematics grades.
Promotes professional development	Being a researcher is not something Mr. Iurillo would identify with until deciding to conduct an action research study with a team of other administrators in his school. From the experience, Mr. Iurillo learned how to conduct focus groups with parents and students, to be more objective in evaluating data, and to establish a sense of credibility among his peers.

THE TAKEAWAY

The rationale for conducting action research is that it can help educators grow professionally while finding solutions to difficult issues that arise at work.

PRACTICAL AND PARTICIPATORY ACTION RESEARCH

LEARNING OBJECTIVE
8.4   Differentiate between practical and participatory action research.

While there are several different approaches to conducting action research, we describe two designs we are think are often effective within educational contexts: *practical* and *participatory action research.*

Practical Action Research

I have this nagging feeling that students are just not getting it, no matter how many different ways I present the material! Practical action research is a widely used approach in schools and class-rooms that involves an educator or team of educators working together to solve a pressing issue of practice of their choice. Through self-reflection and "insider" knowledge, the educator decides what problem needs to be examined, determines what sources of data to obtain, how data will be analyzed, and what action plans are to be implemented upon data analysis. Typically, the focus of practical action research rests on this insider knowledge. That is, through reflecting about one's own personal strategies for teaching and learning along with the students' personalities, needs, demeanors, abilities, and personal circumstances, the teacher will often come to realize there is a problem that needs to be addressed.

In our opening scenario, Mrs. Ortez is concerned about bullying in the classroom and school. Mrs. Ortez also wonders if bullying negatively affects student motivation and learning as well as students' tolerance and acceptance of diversity. Mrs. Ortez realizes there are several options available. One approach would be to involve other teachers, counselors, administrators, and par-ents. In fact, many individuals in the school might have an interest in this issue. Individuals such as nurses, custodians, and cafeteria workers may have raised concerns about bullying based on observations. Another idea is to conduct action research exclusively with the students in her classes. Either approach involves action research, so regardless of which one she chooses, Mrs. Ortez needs a method that is thoughtful, methodological, valid, and is focused on the "*how to . . .*" solve this bullying dilemma!

STOP AND THINK 8.2

What purposes would an action research study have for Mrs. Ortez and her school? What kind of changes would she hope to instil in the students?

Participatory Action Research

Sometimes concerns arise that are larger in scope and can include larger communities. Participatory action research refers to research on social issues that aim to improve the quality of schools, districts, families, and communities through the development and implementation of some action plan. Participatory action research emphasizes equal collaboration in the process of research and targets societal issues. Most importantly, the main goal of this type of research is to improve the lives of people affected, and it is typically focused on explicating unfair practices that can result in the marginalization of groups or individuals. One of the key differences between practical and participatory action research is that in participatory action research, all members are considered co-researchers, including those most affected by the actions that will result from the research.

Participatory research in action.

©iStockphoto.com/kali9

For example, teachers in a low-income district may feel stress and frustration at the lack of motivation among their students and at a loss for ways to motivate them without the resources and financial backing of the state. Together, the participants decide on the nature of the study to be undertaken, plans, actions, and the intended outcomes of the study that can include sources of inexpensive professional development opportunities and ways to generate funding for field trips and technology or academic-based festivals that involve students and families.

The topic of anti-bullying could also be at the forefront of a participatory action research study as well as practical action research. Suppose that in a particular district, reports of bullying are on the rise for special education students, who are often perceived by other students and educators as "different." This perception may have been due to an ineffective structure and policies within the schools. In the schools where bullying was prevalent, it was noted that special education students were not included in school activities in an equitable fashion—such as school plays, sports, or extracurricular activities. Without inclusive practices, these students may be more vulnerable to bullying attacks due to a lack of opportunities to interact with students who do not have a disability outside of the classroom. Educators within the district and the students (with and without disabilities) would work collaboratively to conduct a participatory action research study to improve conditions for special education students.

STOP AND THINK 8.3

How is participatory action research different from practical action research?

As with practical action research, it is important for the research study to be conducted following a process. Practical and participatory action research are each conceptualized as cyclical in nature, meaning emphasis is placed on the iterative and reflective nature of conducting action research. In the following section, we describe this cycle of conducting action research.

THE TAKEAWAY

Practical action research refers to research that involves an educator or team of educators working together to solve a pressing issue of practice of their choice, whereas participatory action research refers to research that is focused on social issues that aim to improve the quality of schools, districts, families, and communities

---

THE CYCLE OF ACTION RESEARCH

LEARNING OBJECTIVE
8.5   Use the cycle of action research to conduct a study on a work-related problem as a self-regulated educator.

Action research can be exciting and rewarding because it gives educators the opportunity to create transformative changes in themselves and students while helping "solve" issues that are concerning and warrant action.

The Four Components to the Action Research Cycle

Lewin's action research model involves four basic components: reflecting, planning, acting, and observing, which are described in detail in the following section. Collectively, these components form a cyclical process. This cycle is relevant to educators because we are constantly thinking about our work and about how to make improvements. Figure 8.1 displays the cycle of action research; notice how the components of action research embody the self-regulated processes of planning, doing, and reflecting phases of self-regulated learning discussed earlier in this book.

FIGURE 8.1   ■   Action Research Within a Self-Regulated Learning Framework

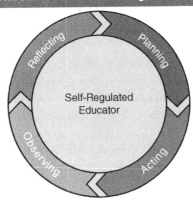

Reflecting Is Critical

Reflecting (in action research) is a process in which we not only make observations about ourselves and others but also about what we think about these observations and what they might mean. While we discuss reflecting as the first component of action research, self-reflection is actually prevalent throughout the cycle. Although reflection is often thought of as what we see when we look in a mirror, it involves much more than that. As educators, we strive for many things and care about our students and their emotional, psychological, and social well-being. Educators are concerned with topics such as student achievement, classroom and school environment, diversity and inclusion, and stakeholders' perceptions of the school. Emphasized throughout this chapter is that action research provides educators and administrators with an opportunity to self-reflect on practice and to explore potential solutions in systematic ways.

Educators constantly ask themselves questions to try to understand a phenomenon and find a remedy. In the scenario that follows notice on how Mrs. Ortez reflects on bullying in her school. In the *Let's Do It!* activity, we provide another scenario and ask you to identify how a principal makes observations and my reflect on these observations. Finally, at the end of this chapter, we invite you to describe your own observations and reflections on critical issues in education in the *You Do It!* activity.

Let's See It! 8.2

Goal: Reflect on Issues of Practice

Directions: As you read through the scenario, notice how Mrs. Ortez reflects on bullying from her daily experiences and how these reflections are inspiring her to take action.

Mrs. Ortez has made several observations with which she was uncomfortable. As she thinks more about it, she begins to realize there are many times over the past two years when she has witnessed discrimination or meanness toward students with disabilities in her school. She recalls that several months ago, on the way to a professional development workshop, she overheard two teachers complaining about a student who has a reading and writing disability and appears to be very unmotivated. Not to mention, at last year's field day, several teachers gave the students with disabilities non-meaningful tasks to do (such as distributing score cards) rather than having them participate in the competitive events.

This fall, students in her class seem particularly mean. They make faces and whisper about the students who have disabilities in her class. Last year, she heard that a group of popular boys put leaves and soil in the locker of a boy who has been diagnosed with attention deficit hyperactivity disorder (ADHD). The dirt and leaves came tumbling out and all over him when he opened the locker door. As Mrs. Ortez reflected on these situations, she realized they are not isolated events and that something must be done immediately. Her reflections are meaningful and critical for developing a plan of action to address the bullying.

Let's Do It! 8.2

Guided Practice: Reflect on Issues of Practice

Directions: As you read through the scenario, identify the reflections Principal Joseph Henritkson is making based on his observations and how these observations may direct him to take action.

Principal Joseph Henritkson is newly in charge of a large public high school with a large diverse student body. He has noticed that many of the students who are frequently given detention are non-White male students. He also observed a trend in which non-White students' end-of-year grades were significantly lower than White students' grades and that there were proportionately fewer minority students on the sports teams and in theatre club. Principal Henritkson is aware that the majority of teachers and coaches in the school are White and have been working in the school for many years. As he reflects on these observations, he becomes concerned that these educators may be biased and have differential expectations for students. What plan of action might the principal take to research this further?

Planning Is Proactive

As a natural result of reflecting, educators can make decisions on the specific topic they want to address. This lays the groundwork for the subsequent component of the cycle: planning. Planning (in action research) involves delineating the steps needed to take action and to reach one's goals. It is a forward-thinking activity because you are making plans in anticipation of doing something. In action research, educators make plans based on their observations and reflections before carrying out the research.

Most educators make daily adjustments in response to students, teachers, parents, and colleagues while "in the moment." Action research differs from these regular activities in that the refinements are thought-out, well-planned, and involve the future. The planning component of the cycle involves making important decisions about how you will conduct your study and with whom. To make these important decisions, there are few steps to the planning component.

Step 1 of Planning: Writing Research Questions

The first step in planning is to articulate a research question for your action research. In Chapter 2, we discussed the importance and skill needed to write a good research question. Research questions differ from the day-to-day informal questions educators have related to work in that they are specific and target unanswered questions. In addition, in action research, the nature of the questions will be different from those asked when conducting other types of research in that they are practice based. There are several characteristics to consider, such as whether the questions are open-ended, are clearly worded, are specific enough to address the issue at hand, and are meaningful. Effective action research questions should also address critical or emergent themes or issues; in other words, the questions should not be ones that you could easily address by making a slight modification in practice or infer from common sense.

In the *Let's See It!* activity, we provide examples of effective and ineffective research questions, with explanations of what makes the question good or poor (see Table 8.4). This is followed by a "quiz" in the *Let's Do It!* where you can test yourself.

Let's See It! 8.3

Goal: Distinguish Effective From Ineffective Research Questions

Directions: Review the questions in Table 8.4 and ask yourself about the characteristics of the question and whether the question is something easily answerable or if it represents a problem that is not easily solvable.

TABLE 8.4 ■ Comparison of Effective and Ineffective Action Research Questions	
Examples of Ineffective Action Research Questions	**Explanation**
Will playing music while third graders are doing seatwork keep them more on task?	This is a very simple thing to test and does not require a literature review or research study.
Are boys innately more gifted than girls in science?	This question taps on gender bias. There are many factors that go into school performance.
Examples of Effective Action Research Questions	**Explanation**
Will changing the current class schedule from a rotation schedule to a standard schedule result in less student tardiness and absenteeism?	This is a good action research question because it is not something that can be resolved without conducting research, and it is an issue related to this particular school.

Let's Do It! 8.3

Guided Practice: Practice Distinguishing Good From Poor Research Questions

Directions: In Table 8.5, the left side of the column are questions addressing problems of practice. Read the questions and think about whether they represent a good action research question or a poor one and why. Once you are done, check your responses at the end of this chapter.

TABLE 8.5 ■ Analyzing Research Questions	
Action Research Question	**Good or Poor Action Research Question and Why?**
Are my third graders struggling with spelling because the vocabulary words I use are too challenging?	
What are the ways in which cellphones are interfering with my middle school students' ability to concentrate on their classwork?	
Will more teachers attend a professional development opportunity if they are paid an additional stipend?	
To what extent is it a good idea for counselors in a school district to get together and share best practices?	
What are some approaches I can use as the principal to help my teachers feel valued?	

Step 2 of Planning: Conducting a Literature Review

Once educators have articulated a few good action research questions, a plan for conducting the literature review becomes more focused and directed. As the second step in planning, literature reviews help educators narrow down goals, inform current practice, and suggest possible solutions to existing concerns without necessitating the need for a study. Suppose a teacher is interested in using a new strategy to improve reading comprehension among their first graders. After conducting a literature review, the teacher may learn about programs that are not only easy to implement but have shown to be very effective among a wide variety of young students; thus, they are developmentally appropriate. The teacher can then decide to learn more about this program and implement it in class without having to conduct an action research study!

In addition to these benefits, literature reviews are an important activity for professional development. Reading articles in our field of practice can provide insight into new trends, teach us about new instructional methods and theoretical discoveries, expose us to topics we are unfamiliar with, and sharpen our skills as action researchers.

When conducting a literature review for action research, it is recommended that you search through a variety of sources—such as books and primary sources published in a variety of journals in your field. These primary sources should include other action research studies to help guide you as you prepare to conduct your own action research study.

Step 3 of Planning: Making Decisions

After research questions are articulated and the literature review is completed, educators should be ready for the third step; making plans on the intervention they would like to use or the types of information they would like to collect. Selection of programs should be based on best practices found in the literature and should include the following:

- Consideration of the participants (Who will they be and is parental consent needed?)

- School policies (Will you need the approval of school administrators?)

- Collaboration opportunities (Is this a study you would like to conduct with colleagues in your department, school, or community?)

- Timeline (What are the dates and length of time for the study implementation?)

- Cost (Are there additional costs, such as hiring a mathematics specialist to help improve mathematics performance or an educational psychologist to conduct professional development workshops with teachers and administrators?)

- Additional equipment purchases (Do you need technology resources, new books, videos, or to purchase laboratory materials?)

- Evaluation (What data will you collect from your action research and how will they be analyzed?)

Unlike the experimental research designs described earlier in this text, you will likely not have randomization or a control group because you are working with *your kids, your teachers, your staff, your community.* This highlights one of the most important characteristics of action research that we have been emphasizing—that it is practice based—giving educators the power to make a direct impact. This is because teachers usually know their students better than anyone in their school, and principals know their staff better than those in other schools, just as superintendents know their schools and the communities they serve.

Other sources of measurements that can be used in lieu of an intervention or to supplement an intervention include interviews, journal writing, focus groups, observations, surveys, questionnaires, samples of students' work, photos, field notes, running records, portfolios of students' performance, checklists, lesson plans, and school records. These sources may be generated by students, teachers, parents, the administration (including professional and nonprofessional staff), and externally generated (such as information obtained by outside consultants or community residents).

Step 4 of Planning: Engaging in Ethical Behavior

Lastly, yet most importantly, ethics must be considered. While we discuss ethics in more detail later in this chapter, there are several basic ethical considerations that must be considered when planning your action research, such as ensuring there is no coercion, that confidentiality and anonymity are adhered to, and that there is no chance any physical, emotional, or intellectual harm can come to the participants. As action research educators, you have several important things to consider during the planning component of the cycle. Once these have been decided, the "acting" begins!

Acting and Observing Are Repetitive and Ongoing

During the acting component of action research, the self-regulated educator implements the plans to address the school issue while making observations along the way. Most action researchers in education want to apply an intervention to create a transformative change. Therefore, the educators should begin by first collecting information on the participants before the intervention to determine a baseline. A baseline is typically followed by implementation of an intervention and then a post-test. As indicated in the planning component, the data collected could vary depending on the participants and the nature of the intervention. The observation component, not unlike the reflecting component, is a constant throughout the action research cycle. Observing in action research involves making a concerted effort to pay careful attention, to be watchful, and to gather information by taking note of the observations in all aspects of the cycle.

Acting provides educators with the opportunity to implement activities that may help improve practice. Through observations, educators can evaluate and make adjustments as needed. Following, are a couple of scenarios in the *Let's See It!* of how acting and observing can play out. Notice how each scenario uses different sources of data to make the observations and involves collecting a baseline, an intervention, and a follow-up post-test. Following is an opportunity for you to practice in the *Let's Do It!* activity. At the end of the chapter, we provide a *You Do It!* activity where you can demonstrate your understanding of the processes in the action research cycle.

Let's See It! 8.4

Goal: Examples of How Educators Can Use Different Data Sources to Make Observations That Lead to Action Research

Directions: In the two scenarios provided, notice how the educators use their classroom observations to pursue conducting action research.

Example Scenario 1. Data Sources: Observations and Student Reports

Every year, some of Mrs. Sanchez's students make comments that they feel inferior to their peers in the honors- and advanced-level foreign language classes. Given that Mrs. Sanchez repeatedly hears these comments, she reflects on how to help improve the motivation and self-efficacy of these struggling students. She decides to conduct a literature review and comes up with the idea of a student-lead festival. With the principal's permission to conduct the festival, she begins the following action research study.

Students dress up in preparation for the cultural festival.
©iStockphoto.com/Gerry Justice

Baseline

Mrs. Sanchez begins by assigning her students an essay to write on their thoughts and feelings about learning a foreign language. Mrs. Sanchez is not surprised to read that her students report low efficacy for learning a foreign language and perceive themselves as "dumb" and weak in the eyes of others in the school.

Acting

Since action research involves the participants working together on a study, Mrs. Sanchez asked the students if they would like to put on a school-wide festival where all the activities would be focused on the language they are learning in class. The students unanimously agreed that it would be fun.

Students dressed up, cooked food that was an important part of the culture they were studying, and played music in the language they were learning during the event. The festival was widely attended and created a buzz of excitement in the school. Throughout the entire process of preparing and conducting the festival, Mrs. Sanchez observed the students and noticed some exciting changes taking place.

Observing

Following the festival, Mrs. Sanchez asked the students to write another essay reflecting on the festival and whether their thoughts and feelings about learning foreign language have changed. Students reported feeling proud and more confident in themselves after all the work they did in preparation for the festival. Mrs. Sachez also noticed that students seem much happier, more excited and motivated in class, and that their grades have improved!

Mrs. Sanchez's reflections lead her to ask her students if they want to do a quarterly "cultural festival day" on different aspects of a culture. After doing this for a year, Mrs. Sanchez's plan is to reflect on her observations and decide whether this will remain part of her curriculum. Thus, the cycle continues!

Example Scenario 2. Data Sources: Observations and Artwork

In this simulated scenario, Jackie, a first grader in Mr. Lee's class, seems troubled. She is always wearing the same clothes, and her hair seems messy and uncombed. Mr. Lee, an experienced teacher, notices that she is a "loner" and does not mingle with her classmates during recess. Mr. Lee read articles that discussed how artwork can help younger children explain how they are feeling and instructs the students to complete daily drawings of their feelings, families, school, homes, and their friends.

After one week, he notices a pattern among Jackie's drawings (Figure 8.2):

Acting

Upon looking at the drawings, Mr. Lee meets with the school counselor (Mrs. Tamarallo) and together, they conclude that Jackie is experiencing homelessness. The counselor decides to hold a meeting with the assistant principal, Jackie's teachers, and the school's homeless liaison (a social worker available to all schools with expertise in students who are experiencing homelessness). The team decides to split up the task of conducting a literature review to learn about programs for young children who are in similar situations as Jackie and to

FIGURE 8.2 ■ Baseline Drawings

reconvene in a week. From the literature review, they agree to implement an intense intervention that will last three months. The intervention includes providing Jackie with breakfast and lunch along with snacks to take home, clothes donated from teachers in the school who have children Jackie's age, enhancing opportunities for play and developing friendships, counseling once a week, and one-on-one tutoring after school. Mr. Lee and the school counselor also visit Jackie's mother once a month at the shelter to help form a "connection" between them, the school, and Jackie.

Observing

It was also agreed that Mr. Lee would take notes as he observes Jackie's behavior in the classroom. He notices that Jackie's behavior seems to gradually change; she seems happier and more comfortable in school, and several teachers notice her playing with her classmates for the first-time during recess. He reflects and thinks the program is having a positive effect on Jackie. Upon completion of the intervention, he asks his students to draw the same themed pictures. Following are Jackie's (Figure 8.3):

FIGURE 8.3 ■ Post-Intervention Drawings

Mr. Lee meets with the team again and shares Jackie's drawings and his observations. The team discusses their observations and the second set of drawings. They conclude the intervention program is working and decide to continue with the program throughout the rest of the academic year. The team agrees to meet after each 3-month period and discuss making modifications as needed.

Guided Practice: Practice Using Different Data Sources to Make Observations That Lead to Action Research

Directions: As you read through the scenario, imagine yourself as the principal and identify the data sources, baseline observations, and the actions you might take.

Dr. Sheila McDonald is the principal in a public middle school that consists of Grades 6 through 8. While most of her students speak English as a second language, many of their parents do not speak any English. As a result, very few parents attend the fall and spring teacher–parent conferences. Several teachers have expressed concern at not being able to effectively communicate with parents about their children, who are excelling or struggling academically. In addition, the annual school play that finishes off the academic year is rarely attended by parents. Principal McDonald is disturbed by this situation and believes parental involvement is important for student success. She speaks with the superintendent and receives permission to conduct an action research study.

Principal McDonald begins by hiring a translator and by asking parents to complete a survey in Spanish asking them for feedback and ideas on how to increase parental involvement. She is not surprised to learn that parents want to be more involved but feel uncomfortable or unable to do so because they do not speak or understand English.

Identify the Data Sources

Identify the sources that Principal McDonald used to make her baseline observations.

Identify the Observations Dr. McDonald Has Made. What Would You Deem to Be the Baseline?

What has Dr. McDonald observed about parental involvement and what are parents indicating on the surveys?

Actions

What actions would you suggest the principal take? Who should be included in this study?

As witnessed from each of these scenarios, this cycle of reflecting, planning, acting, and observing can have a powerful transformative effect on participants and educators. At the end of this chapter, we provide a *You Do It!* extension activity on using the four components of action research.

ETHICAL CONSIDERATIONS

8.6   Demonstrate knowledge of ethical issues when engaging with action research.

As educators, you are in a position of power and authority. Classroom teachers have influence over students' grades, course placement, the classroom culture and safety, and whether students who choose not to participate will be treated equally to those who opt to be part of the study.

Principals and other administrators are also in positions of power and control. Principals make decisions on teacher placements, curriculum, promotions, suspensions and expulsions, and dress codes, among many other things. School administrators have influence over a variety of academic and nonacademic aspects, such as college admission applications, counseling and support services decisions, detention policies, athletics, and extracurricular activities.

Ethics in Conducting Action Research

These positions of power may influence whether a student decides to participate in an action research study and therefore highlights the importance of checking if you are required to apply for approval to conduct your study by the institutional review board (IRB). Whether that is a requirement or not, we strongly recommend educators provide students with written informed consent and/or assent letters. Chapter 3 discusses the importance of applying for approval with the IRB and explains the different letters one must obtain prior to conducting research. Receiving permission from the principal and school district are also critical for action research studies that involve collecting data to be shared with others or to be written up and published, and many school districts are requiring these written permissions, even if the intention is not to publish the research

These few steps can protect educators from being accused of being unethical, breaking any confidentiality laws, or being unprofessional in their research. Regardless of what level of an educator you are, it is important for all individuals to feel safe in their decisions of whether to participate and to know that they can withdraw from the study at any time. In sum, very often educators conducting action research studies will need to obtain approval from the IRB and their district to conduct an action research study.

Ethics in Analyzing Action Research

As emphasized throughout this chapter, action researchers rely heavily on self-reflections. Reflecting as part of the process of conducting research provides practitioners with opportunities to not only think about the action research study as it is occurring but to reflect on one's personal lens that may include biases, assumptions, and outcome expectations that can shape our observations. In other words, educators have a challenge over outside researchers in that they need to maintain a level of objectivity that can be difficult because they are working with their students or staff to find solutions of practice. Recommendations for reducing bias and subjectivity include discussing one's reflections with other teachers, colleagues, and administrators who can provide you with feedback and clarity and using pseudonyms, numbers, or other nonidentifiable characteristics to maintain confidentiality.

STOP AND THINK 8.4

If you were a high school counselor interested in conducting an action research study in your school on students vaping on campus, what are ethical issues that you might consider?

Ethical Issues in Communicating Action Research Findings

As indicated throughout this text, it is critical to protect the participants in your study. It is particularly important when you are working in a school where others teach, counsel, know, or are familiar with the participants to maintain confidentiality. Another important consideration is that when communicating findings to others, educators should be careful not to make sweeping statements regarding one's findings or to make statements that involve generalizing findings to other groups, as this is not the focus of an action research methodology. Further, it can be tempting to share findings about students in your class, for example, to the principal or to colleagues, but it in doing so, as a practitioner researcher you must ensure confidentiality and anonymity and take caution in discussing the study and its findings. One must also carefully consider possible alternative interpretations and explanations for the findings.

An additional and more subtle ethical consideration is that educators who conduct action research may be presumed to be in a position of authority by others (such as teachers, students, peers), just by the sheer fact they are conducting the research. This could influence the way participants and colleagues respond or influence the outcomes of the study. For example, a department colleague may encourage their homeroom students to participate in Mr. Arnaud's study because now that he is conducting research, they have begun to think of him as very intelligent and potentially making an important contribution. While this consideration does not involve the communication of the results via a publication, the way in which we, as educators communicate with colleagues and others about our action research study needs to be carefully thought out prior to commencing the study.

THE TAKEAWAY

Ethical considerations are extremely important in all types of research, but particularly so when the participants are part of your daily practice as educators!

AMERICAN PSYCHOLOGICAL ASSOCIATION STYLE

LEARNING OBJECTIVE

8.7 Utilize the *Publication Manual of the American Association* in reporting and presenting action research designs.

Educators who conduct action research may not realize their research presents an opportunity to share their work with others in and outside of the school community. Many educators belong to professional organizations that hold annual conferences or meetings where teachers and administrators can present their research. In addition, many of these organizations have publications in which educators can contribute. Sharing one's research can potentially influence the practice of others and motivate colleagues to pursue conducting their own action research studies. In addition, the process of sharing one's work requires the researcher to be able to think clearly in order to articulate information about the participants, research design, and findings without jeopardizing the participants' (who are usually students) confidentiality and anonymity.

Unlike other chapters in this book, it is not expected that the tone of a practitioner will be the same as that of a researcher or university professor. The language style is likely to be more personal in that it can reflect the tone and vocabulary of one familiar with the issue at-hand, such as teachers, administrators, students, or community leaders.

While action researchers should continue to follow the recommended APA formatting in describing their study, listing citations and references and including figures and tables, many action research studies are written up as reports and shared among colleagues, with others at industry or professional development conferences, and online on websites, blogs, and other internet-related platforms. More formal reports that include the problem, literature review, methodology, data analyses, discussion of findings, and implications for educators may be written-up and submitted to pedagogical journals and journals that specifically publish action research studies in addition to organizations that supply grants or external funding. Although the *Publication Manual of the American Psychological Association* stipulates that texts, figures, and tables be in black and white, for action research reports that are to be used internally, using colors in tables and figures can help convey meaning and grab viewers' attention.

Regardless of the format and audience, we recommend sharing your action research among the participants and your colleagues. Doing so gives others the opportunity to learn from your findings and replicate your study while providing you with a justification for implementation of changes to improve practice. As you probably can tell from reading this chapter, we see action research as an opportunity for practitioners to create transformative changes in themselves and others and to have a vital impact on their work and those they serve.

THE TAKEAWAY

Action research can not only benefit those directly involved but should be shared with others to provide them with the opportunity to learn from the findings.

CHAPTER SUMMARY

Action research exemplifies self-regulation in that it is a continuous cycle of four basic components: reflecting, planning, acting, and observing. By engaging in action research, practitioners can create transformative changes in themselves and others, impact practice, and find solutions or remedies to problems they encounter in their day-to-day work. It can also provide educators with a rationale for implementing changes in practice. The two types of action research discussed in this chapter are practical and participatory. Ethics must be considered when conducting action research and communicating the results. The communication of an action research study can be done formally, using APA guidelines, or informally if being used to communicate directly to colleagues and other nonpeer-reviewed formats.

You Do It! 8.1

Self-Directed Practice: Practice Understanding When Action Research Is More Appropriate than Other Research Methods

Directions: Read the action research study conducted by teachers Haines and Westmeyer (2023). Explain why they conducted an action research study versus another type of study. Do you think they made the right decision to use an action research design instead of another research design, and if so, why?

Haines, J., & Westmeyer, R. (2023). Show what you know: How girls' academic confidence increases with multiple and differentiated ways of sharing what the learned, *Journal of Teacher Action Research, 10*(1), https://www.teacheractionresearch.com/index.php/JTAR/article/view/67

You Do It! 8.2

Self-Directed Practice: Reflect on Issues of Practice

Directions: Think about problems you have observed as a preservice educator or practicing professional with no obvious remedies in sight. Make a list of those pressing concerns and rank them in order of importance, with Number 1 being of utmost importance. As you reflect on these observations, describe why some are more critical than others.

You Do It! 8.3

Self-Directed Practice: Practice Writing Good Action Research Questions

Directions: Using the problems of practice you identified earlier in the You Do It! 8.2, write action research questions for at least four of them.

You Do It! 8.4

Self-Directed Practice: Practice Using the Four Components of Action Research

Directions: Mrs. Ortez in our opening scenario has decided to conduct a practical action research study to help promote empathy, understanding, and inclusion of students with disabilities. Following is an excerpt from an actual dialogue between an educator and a middle school student who has a history of experiencing bullying. The student in this scenario is an exceptional learner and yet the situation is not that different from the one described by Mrs. Ortez. If you were the educator in this situation, would you do a practical or a participatory action research study? Using the four components of action research, how might you carry out an action research study?

> **Educator:** "What type of bullying are they doing to you?"
> **Student:** "Well, it started off as name calling and it escalated into the stabbing with pencils, then shoving into walls, and then it kind of died down. Then it went back up. And . . . now it's really only in P.E. . . . it's . . . they yell at me and sometimes when we're doing big group activities and like especially if I'm doing something that everybody else is doing . . . they will yell at me and call me out on it. They will come up to me . . . they've sworn at me before. There hasn't been really a lot of physical contact. There was one time that

a girl did kind of like put her hand on me and shoved me out of the way and then turned around and yelled at me and swore at me . . ."

Educator: "Why do you think they target you?"

Student: "Cause I realized with bullies, they tend to go after the ones that look weaker. Like the ones that won't stand up or the ones that are a little bit different from everyone else cause you can easily pick them out. And . . . I . . . tend to be different from everyone else . . .

"It takes me a little to get adjusted so if I'm going into a new grade level or if I am with a new teacher it takes me a little while to actually trust and to actually like talk out. Cause especially like in middle school I was very nervous, and I was like quiet the first week. And then I started speaking out more like giving answers and . . . And they saw that as me being the nerdy type and the smart one. And I would get bullied for being the smart one. But here's one thing that I never understood. If I got a question right and came off as being the smart one. I would get bullied. If I got a question wrong or was not doing too well in class. I would get bullied because I'm supposed to be the smart one . . .

"I do want to answer more cause I'm sitting there, and I know the answer, and nobody else is really giving the answer. And I'm just sitting there, and I know the answer, I know the answer. I know the answer, I know the answer. But I'm too afraid to answer because I know . . . even if I'm not going to get bullied it's still there. The fear that I'm going to get bullied, and it just will start like the beginning and then it's just going to escalate."

Educator: "And how does that make you feel?"

Student: "It's very frustrating because it's amazing how just one little comment can stay with you forever. And me having a pretty low confidence and low self-esteem to start with. I've tried building up confidence . . . like since third grade I have been building up my confidence cause I had very low confidence. I've tried so hard to build it up, but that one comment or that one case of bullying completely brings it back . . . all back."

KEY TERMS

Action research	Reflecting (in action research)
Transformative education	Planning (in action research)
Practical action research	Acting
Participatory action research	Observing

ANSWER KEY

Stop and Think Activities

STOP AND THINK 8.1

Answers will vary for this stop and think depending on the educators and the issues they are confronted with.

STOP AND THINK 8.2

Mrs. Ortez is hoping to find a way to increase students' self-efficacy and motivation for learning a foreign language. She thinks that having students create and prepare for a schoolwide cultural festival will help build their self-efficacy and motivation as they experience and witness enjoyment and support from others in the school and as they engage in active foreign language learning activities for the festival.

Stop and Think 8.3

Participatory research consists of research on social issues that aim to improve the quality of schools, districts, families, and communities, whereas practical research consists of research that involves an educator or team of educators working together to solve a pressing issue of practice *of their choice* that is more localized (for example, one's classroom or school).

Stop and Think 8.4

There are many ethical considerations that counselors would need to face in this action research study. For example, counselors may be concerned about confidentiality and the health of students who admit to vaping or whether parents are aware that their children may be vaping. Examples of some questions that counselors should consider include the following: Must counselors alert parents and administrators of students who admit to vaping? Will students respond honestly if they know their parents will find out they are vaping? If students agree to participate in the study, are there any academic, social, and personal consequences to admitting they are vaping? Will other students who do not participate in the study automatically assume the participants vape? How will counselors use the information they obtain from their research? How will they protect participants' anonymity?

Let's Do It! Activities

Let's Do It! 8.1

Answers will vary, however educators conducting action research would be focusing their studies on critical issues of practice, whereas scientists are typically more focused on broader issues and generalizability of their research findings.

Let's Do It! 8.2

Principal Joseph Henritkson has made several observations:

- Non-White male students tend to serve detention more often than White males

- Non-White students' grades are significantly lower than the grades of White students

- There are fewer non-White students on teams and in the theater club than White students

- The majority of educators in the school are White and have been working in the school for many years

Principal Henritkson's reflections include concern over individual biases against non-White students and a concern that non-White students are being held to different standards than White students.

While answers may vary on the actions that Principal Henritkson could take, one approach would be to conduct an action research study in his school to identify biases among faculty and staff. This could be done by collecting both quantitative (e.g. surveys) and qualitative data (e.g. focus groups or interviews) with faculty, staff, and students in the school. Assuming he finds that biases exist, he could provide professional development and educational workshops to faculty, staff, and students as part of the action research study.

Question	Good or Poor Action Research Question and Why?
Are my third graders struggling with spelling because the vocabulary words I use are too challenging?	Poor; teachers can easily test this in their classroom by varying the level of vocabulary words.
What are the ways in which cellphones are interfering with my middle school students' ability to concentrate on their classwork?	Good; the teachers would have to pursue this through a literature review and possibly an action research study.
Will more teachers attend a professional development opportunity if they are paid an additional stipend?	Poor; the principal can easily test this with the teachers to determine if attendance improves with financial incentives.
Counselors in a school district get together and share best practices. Is this a good idea?	Poor; common sense suggests that sharing of best practices can be beneficial to counselors and their students.
What are some approaches I can use as the principal to help my teachers feel valued?	Good; the principal would have to pursue this through a literature review and possibly an action research study testing different approaches to help her staff feel more valued.

Guided Practice: Identify Acting and Observing in the Following Scenario

Identify the Data Sources
What sources would Principal McDonald use for her observations?

- Personal observations
- Teachers
- Survey results

What Would You Deem to Be the Baseline?
What has Dr. McDonald observed about parental involvement, and what are parents indicating on the surveys?

- Parents are not participating in school events.
- Teachers are expressing concerns about lack of attendance at parent–teacher conferences.
- Parents would like to be involved but do not attend school meetings and events because they do not speak or understand English.

Actions
What actions would you suggest the principal take? Who should be included in this study?

Possible Actions

Responses may vary; following are a few possibilities:

- Focus groups to ascertain more from parents and students about the level of involvement they would like and what would be most helpful to their students

- Hire additional translators for school events and for communications to and from the school to parents

- Offer professional development workshops for educators to learn Spanish

- Offer workshops for parents to learn English

- Have cultural and Spanish-speaking events at the school

The study should include parents, students, teachers, and administrative staff (and translators!).

9 PROGRAM EVALUATION

LEARNING OBJECTIVES

Upon completion of this chapter, the reader should be able to

9.1   Describe characteristics of program evaluation

9.2   Distinguish between research studies and program evaluations

9.3   Identify elements of program theory and logic models

9.4   Distinguish between the types and purposes of program evaluations

9.5   Identify how to engage in a program evaluation

9.6   Demonstrate knowledge of ethical issues when engaging in program evaluations

9.7   Utilize the *Publication Manual of the American Psychological Association* in reporting and presenting findings in program evaluation

A DAY AT WORK

I Never Know What to Do Out There

©iStockphoto.com/stevecoleimages

Mr. Jameson, the principal at the local middle school, was very proud of the school's outdoor classroom. He viewed the setting as an important part of the school structure, where teachers could take children out to learn as an authentic way to teach the curriculum and as a positive resource to build home–school connections. He thought the outdoor classroom was heavily used by teachers and students, until he overheard a conversation:

Mr. Rork:	*I was really happy with my students today. They did a great job on their math quiz, so I took them to the outdoor classroom.*
Ms. Silva:	*That's nice. I really like it outside, but I never know what to do out there besides having the kids play and socialize.*
Mr. Rork:	*I know what you mean. I don't have any idea how to use the outdoor classroom to teach math.*

Overhearing this conversation made Mr. Jameson wonder if there was an underutilization of the space and if staff, students, parents, and community members had different perspectives on the topic. He questioned whether the effort, time, and funds utilized to create the outdoor classroom was an effective and meaningful approach for teaching students?

INTRODUCTION

The opening scenario reflects an issue that commonly occurs in schools and districts—it is not always evident whether the outcomes of a program truly reflect the initial goals and requirements of educational stakeholders. It was not clear in this scenario if teachers knew how to use the resources constructively and if the outdoor space truly advanced student skills and knowledge. Conducting a program evaluation yields information about whether there is a misalignment between interested parties' goals and actual outcomes (see Figure 9.1). A streamlined connection between instruction and assessment often leads to effective practices (e.g., adopted reading programs) and/or smoother operations (e.g., transportation services) within a school environment. This chapter provides a broad overview of the program evaluation in terms of characteristics and how this approach differs from research. Next, we outline the elements of program theory and logic models in developing program evaluations. We distinguish between the types of program evaluations and their purposes. The final portion of this chapter centers on how to conduct program evaluations, ethical issues in program evaluations, and presenting findings in APA style.

FIGURE 9.1 ■ Program Evaluation

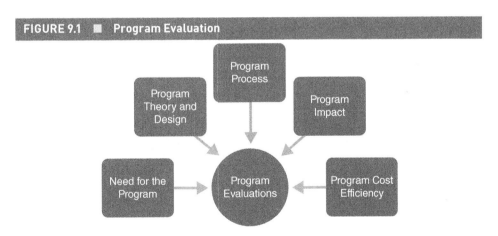

CHARACTERISTICS OF PROGRAM EVALUATION

LEARNING OBJECTIVE

9.1   Describe characteristics of program evaluation.

There are many ways that conducting program evaluations can support educators. Areas of attention include making program improvements, assessing the impact of a strategy/initiative, improving societal structures, sharing information and clarifying expectations, and informing instructional and policy decisions. Throughout this text, we have focused on three broad research methodologies (quantitative, qualitative, and mixed methods) and corresponding techniques used to address critical issues and research questions. Although these research methods may be applicable when conducting program evaluations, the purposes and processes utilized within program evaluation approaches differ substantially.

The Purpose of a Program Evaluation

Program evaluation refers to the systematic process of collecting, analyzing, and interpreting data to determine whether educational initiatives are meeting the needs and requirements of schools and school districts. This process is in accordance with preset objectives that were established by district stakeholders (e.g., superintendent, curriculum supervisors) when implementing a new program. The goal of program evaluations is to assess the effectiveness of a program, to further program development, and to make improvements. In contrast, researchers aim to generalize findings to the population or expand on a theory. There are many initiatives that are relevant to program evaluations, including school-based initiatives, logistical processes, and/or informal natural learning settings, such as museums and science learning settings. In addition, the target of the evaluations can be in the form of programs, curriculum design, procedures/processes, and instructional practices, to name a few examples.

The topic of the evaluation is known as an object or evaluand, which can take many forms. For example, an appropriate topic for a program evaluation would be to evaluate whether unencumbered teacher planning time improves teacher self-efficacy for instruction using the outdoor classroom. A curriculum, such as International Baccalaureate, a reading curriculum, or restorative practices for classroom management would be examples of a suitable topic. School personnel may want to investigate the way procedures and processes impact the overall efficiency of their schools. Examples of this type of evaluand would be studying the clarity and efficiency of online course registration, the impact of lunch schedules on academic planning, and the processes underlying transportation needs within a school district. As a case in point, a school district concerned about absenteeism may want to study whether changes in the morning breakfast routine increases student attendance. The focus of evaluands range from incorporating new instructional techniques, collaborative planning, changes in the school schedule, or transportation needs, like attracting and retaining bus drivers.

There are several reasons why stakeholders seek a program evaluation. For instance, a preexisting program may need improvement. Educators may want to analyze program outcomes and use these data to make better decisions about ways to optimize student learning or some other important aspect of school operations. Program evaluators provide a report to educational stakeholders about effective/ineffective elements of a program as well as clarify the expectations of interested parties at the outset of a program or after an evaluation. The findings of an evaluation can advance politically based initiatives or inform district policy (e.g., personnel in a school district considering the adoption of an outdoor classroom for every middle school). In this process, an evaluator will rely on several types of individuals to develop a program evaluation design, as shown in Figure 9.2. Input from the program evaluator, stakeholders (e.g., members of the Parent Teacher Association [PTA]), and clients/evaluation sponsors (e.g., district leaders) is central to the design of the evaluation. The audience generally learns of the findings through a written and/or oral presentation.

The focus of evaluands range from assessing the impact of instructional strategies (e.g., health and nutrition curriculum); logistical operations (e.g., cafeteria operations); or home–school programs (community/school gardening programs).

©iStockphoto.com/fstop123

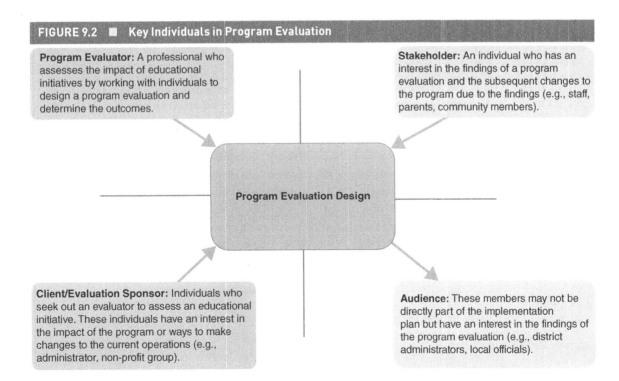

FIGURE 9.2 ■ Key Individuals in Program Evaluation

Program Evaluator: A professional who assesses the impact of educational initiatives by working with individuals to design a program evaluation and determine the outcomes.

Stakeholder: An individual who has an interest in the findings of a program evaluation and the subsequent changes to the program due to the findings (e.g., staff, parents, community members).

Program Evaluation Design

Client/Evaluation Sponsor: Individuals who seek out an evaluator to assess an educational initiative. These individuals have an interest in the impact of the program or ways to make changes to the current operations (e.g., administrator, non-profit group).

Audience: These members may not be directly part of the implementation plan but have an interest in the findings of the program evaluation (e.g., district administrators, local officials).

Key Individuals in Program Evaluations

When researchers conduct an evaluation, generally the participants or other stakeholders do not design the research study. In contrast, program evaluations are dependent on the individuals involved in the initiatives. Intrinsic to many types of projects, program evaluators require feedback from those impacted by an evaluand. For this reason, individuals other than the evaluators play critical roles in the shaping of the program evaluation. These people include clients/evaluation sponsors, stakeholders, and the audience.

Commonly, evaluations require contract services in which a client or evaluation sponsor (e.g., a local government agency, politician, school board members, or nonprofit organization) requests an external program evaluator for a specific purpose (e.g., person not directly involved in the evaluand). These clients/evaluation sponsors are instrumental in outlining the goals of the program evaluation; their input drives the overall plan as the evaluator checks the original intentions with processes and outcomes.

Client/Evaluation Sponsor

While school officials and teachers are able to analyze program processes and impacts, at times, a professional evaluator receives a contract to conduct a program evaluation. School organizations may seek the help of an outside evaluator to gain an external perspective. In this case, they are working for a client or evaluation sponsor who is responsible for coordinating an outside evaluation. The sponsor could be an individual, such as a school district administrator, a nonprofit/for profit organization, or a business. The client or evaluation sponsor will be instrumental in clarifying the origin of the program, the issue under investigation, and ultimate oversight for change based on program evaluation findings. Other program evaluations can be run by stakeholders, school administrators, and school personnel without hiring a professional evaluator.

Stakeholders

Stakeholders are individuals who have an interest in the findings of the program evaluation and the implementation of a program; these individuals have varied backgrounds. In a school setting, potential stakeholders range from teachers, administrators, students, parent volunteers, community members, custodians, nurses, and so forth. Stakeholders serve an important function in evaluation design as they have an interest in the outcomes, and evaluators should carefully identify who they include as potential stakeholders to gain insights from everyone involved. In the program evaluation of the outdoor classroom, it may seem obvious to identify the administrator, teachers, parents, and students as potential stakeholders. However, there are other individuals who may have an understanding of the framework from a different lens: custodian workers who maintain the grounds, nurses who deal with allergic reactions to bee stings, special education assistants working with students in wheelchairs, and neighbors affected by noise levels. All of these individuals have unique perspectives on the integration of the outdoor classroom within the school day. Program evaluators should carefully consider whether they have identified all stakeholders to account for varying perspectives on an issue.

STOP AND THINK 9.1

Have you ever been asked to provide information for a program evaluation or attended a presentation on the findings of an evaluation? What was the purpose of the program evaluation? Were you a/an client/evaluation sponsor, stakeholder, or audience member?

Audience

Another important consideration for the program evaluator is who the audience will be for the evaluation findings. Audience members have a stake in the outcomes; however, they may not directly implement aspects of the program. If a district initiates the building of outdoor classrooms for every middle school based on the program evaluation of one site, the audience members for the report could extend beyond school officials and personnel to neighbors and/or taxpayers in the community. Regardless of an individual's level of participation in program outcomes, the ultimate goal is to address the needs of each person affected by the structure of an organization.

Program Evaluators and Types of Programs

The role of the evaluator ties into the nature of the evaluation and the interactions with individuals on site. The classification of program evaluations center on the role of the evaluator: (a) independent evaluations occur when evaluators create the design of the program with input from stakeholders on a commissioned basis, independent of the organization; (b) collaborative evaluations (also known as participatory) reflect the dual roles of evaluators and stakeholders in shaping all aspects of the program evaluation process; and (c) empowerment evaluations involve transferring the knowledge from evaluator to stakeholders so they can take ownership of the evaluation process. Studying the impact of an outdoor classroom, for example, is plausible with all three approaches. For an independent evaluation, a local PTA hires a consultant to evaluate the needs of teachers to improve the use of the outdoor classroom. For a participatory evaluation, a team of stakeholders from the school and evaluators work together to design an evaluation to assess the utility of the outdoor space. In the third category (empowerment), an evaluator trains stakeholders, teachers, and administrators on how to evaluate the outdoor classroom program over time. Regardless of the type of collaboration between evaluator and interested parties, the overarching goals of a program evaluation are distinguishable from research. We will discuss these differences in greater detail in Section 9.2.

The role of the evaluator ties into the nature of the evaluation and the interactions with individuals on site. For example, it would be appropriate to use one of three types of evaluations to study an outdoor classroom (independent, collaborative, or empowerment), depending on the needs of the program evaluation.

©iStockphoto.com/FatCamera

Issues in Program Evaluation

When conducting program evaluations, the setting and underlying social dynamics at play are critical in assessing outcomes; educational evaluations intrinsically connect to the social structures within a school. A social structure refers to the patterned infrastructure in an organization and the way that individuals function in this arrangement (e.g., the way students and teachers teach, learn, and interact in an outdoor classroom). Figure 9.3 shows different issues that are integral to conducting a program evaluation.

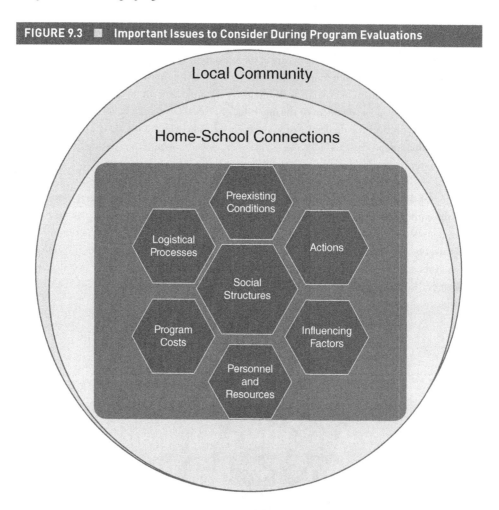

FIGURE 9.3 ■ Important Issues to Consider During Program Evaluations

A program evaluation design would account for an array of factors in order to analyze the desired program outcomes in contrast to the actual outcomes. Areas that would impact the design include preexisting conditions, actions and activities, other influencing factors (e.g., low parental attendance due to work conflicts and language barriers), personnel and resources, the cost to run the program, and the logistical processes involved in the workings of the initiative.

Preexisting Conditions

Consider an elementary school in which the teachers and administrators create a home–school connection program every Saturday morning where parents and children learn about activities that reinforce skills taught at school in reading and mathematics. When reflecting on preexisting conditions (e.g., school personnel, characteristics of students, educational needs), the evaluators might ask: "What was the impetus for developing this program?" Perhaps there was an influx of English language learners in the community and language barriers prevented parents from interacting and communicating with the school effectively. In addition, the children come from a variety of educational settings, creating some lags in their mathematical understandings. These preexisting conditions created a need to develop a program that fosters home–school connections. In a novel and motivating approach, the educators and stakeholders select the outdoor classroom as an engaging way to reinforce skills and build rapport with community members.

Personnel and Resources

Personnel and resources are principal factors to consider when planning a program evaluation. In the outdoor home–school connection program, stakeholders decide to include a stipend to support school personnel and parents to offset the need for part-time weekend jobs so that individuals may conduct/attend the workshops. Teachers, administrators, and assistants run the Saturday program as well as purchase materials and resources. Other individuals who may be critical for this workshop include custodians, administrative assistants, librarians and librarian assistants, and technology resource teachers.

Actions

The actions required to develop the program would center on the planning and coordination of school staff, and the activities during the Saturday workshops would relate to the interaction between educators, administrators, parents, and students. Actions could reflect the steps teachers and administrators take prior to the actual workshop, such as designing lesson plans, obtaining workshop materials, identifying workshop sponsors in the community, inviting attendees, marketing the workshop, communicating with parents, and arranging the physical environment. These types of steps are integral to the processes of the workshop, the dynamics of individuals involved, and the overall effectiveness of the program.

Influencing Factors

When analyzing the home–school connection program, the evaluator considers possible influencing factors that could limit the impact of the program. For example, many of the parents contacted work an overnight shift at a local factory and would be unable to attend a morning workshop. In another example, if flyers sent from the school to parents are not in the native language of the parents, communication gaps are a barrier to attendance. Sometimes parents who have newly immigrated to the United States are unfamiliar with the structure of local schools and may be hesitant to come to the schools, or parents may not have weekend transportation to get to the building. Many factors can limit participation, and these issues are not always immediately apparent to parties who create and implement workshops. The evaluator needs to use a multi-faceted lens to account for these additional factors.

Program Costs

As expenditures are integral to understanding the value of an evaluand, the evaluator will want to assess the program costs (both direct and monetized) to make a determination about the overall program. In this case, direct valuation would include the purchasing of materials and stipends for the workshop facilitators and parents. Other considerations would be the impact on weekend custodians, electricity and water usage, transportation allocations to transport parents, and administrators' workloads. Later in this chapter, there is an expanded discussion on assessing program cost efficiency.

Logistical Processes

Conducting workshops, such as a home–school connection program, has specific logistical requirements that center on the availability and use of space, technological equipment, food preparation, material preparation, and transportation needs. The evaluator will want to examine these processes and the impact on the target population. For instance, if parents do not have transportation to come to the workshop, the program developers have options to support the families, which include scheduling school buses, arranging for carpools, dispersing Uber cards, or making individual arrangements. The ways in which the program developers deal with logistical processes greatly influences the social interactions, the tone between facilitators and participants, and the overall program impacts.

STOP AND THINK 9.2

Reflect on a program or initiative in a school setting that you are familiar with. What conditions and processes would be important to consider when evaluating the program (e.g., remedial mathematics instruction, bell schedule)?

Formative and Summative Evaluations

This section outlines important issues for conducting program evaluations. The evaluators will want to take into account how to collect data when examining the underlying processes of an evaluand. Most educators are familiar with the term formative and summative assessments as a way to determine student misconceptions during the process of learning and to gauge student mastery of content. Similarly, program evaluators need to consider what types of evaluations would yield the most relevant information and when, how, and to whom to administer the evaluations.

Formative evaluations target the continuous improvements of a program in increments throughout the duration of an initiative. For an outdoor classroom program, relevant questions are "To what extent is the classroom being used for its original intent?" "What resources/professional development are needed to improve the program?" or "Are classroom teachers using the outdoor space with fidelity across grade levels?" Formative evaluations are critical in determining the consistency of an evaluand, the processes that support the program, and the performance of students across time on the same measure. Tracking progress over time assists in making improvements and modifications to evaluands.

In contrast, summative evaluations would occur at the end of the program to determine how well the outcomes reflect the original objectives, whether the program should continue as is, the need for systematic modifications and refinements, or if it is advisable to discontinue the program. In the context of a partnership between a local school district and local naturalists to train teachers on the use of outdoor classrooms, a summative evaluation would target the implications of this type of training. A viable set of summative evaluation questions include: "Were the outcomes consistent across grade levels?" "Under what conditions was the program most effective?" and "Are teachers able to utilize the outdoor space effectively to instruct students?"

Figure 9.4 reflects how formative and summative evaluations would span across the timeline of a professional development program for teachers on using the outdoor classroom for instructional purposes. In this example, the figure shows the calendar year with three professional development workshops planned. Formative evaluations would occur three times between August and March to determine if the workshop planners need to make adjustments to improve the quality of the program and support teachers in their work. At each checkpoint, quantitative and qualitative methods range from (a) surveys for quantitative data and (b) focus groups and lesson plans for qualitative data. Prior to the initial workshop, teachers would complete initial surveys and participate in focus groups about the role of the outdoor classroom in the school. Following the professional development workshops, evaluators would collect lesson plans and follow-up surveys to assess the needs of the group for upcoming training. In April in the figure below, a summative evaluation would be conducted with surveys, lesson plans, and focus group interviews to determine if there were gaps in the objectives of the program and the final outcomes.

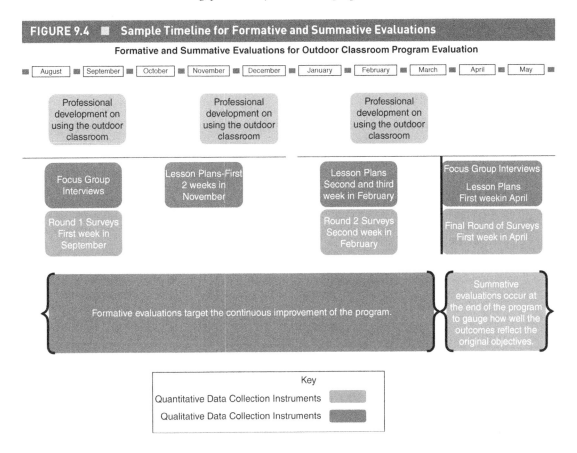

FIGURE 9.4 ■ Sample Timeline for Formative and Summative Evaluations

Formative and Summative Evaluations for Outdoor Classroom Program Evaluation

When detailing the intricacies of a specific program evaluation, it is helpful to remember that the main goal is to address a dilemma that has arisen in an organization. Evaluations provide support and inform the direction needed for change within the social environment of the evaluand.

THE TAKEAWAY

Societal needs and social conditions serve as a basis for program evaluations, which aim to make judgments about the outcomes of programs, initiatives, and processes.

RESEARCH STUDIES AND PROGRAM EVALUATIONS

LEARNING OBJECTIVE	
9.2	Distinguish between research studies and program evaluations.

While many of the research techniques described in previous chapters are applicable to program evaluations, the two approaches often differ in terms of overarching purpose, formation of research/evaluation questions, use or lack thereof of generalizations to broader populations, and standards used for analyzing and interpreting data. Evaluators will use tools/procedures necessary for research, such as reliability checks, and internal and external validity threats; however, the primary goals in a program evaluation are bound to a specific societal organization with an emphasis on the utility of the evaluation findings rather than being able to make generalizations about other similar programs. Table 9.1 shows some broad differences between program evaluations and research based on goals, overall focus, roles of individuals, and evaluation questions as described in the following section.

TABLE 9.1 ■ Major Differences Between Program Evaluation and Research		
Program Evaluation	**Point of Comparison**	**Research**
The goal is to make judgements about programs, strategies, or processes to improve program effectiveness and/or efficiency.	*Overall goals*	Research extends theories or tests hypotheses to contribute to new knowledge to broader literature.
Program evaluations inform decision-making strategies for creating change within a social structure.	*Overall focus*	Research draws conclusions that correspond with theories and previous literature and may generalize to broader populations.
The program evaluator integrates the perspective of individuals, such as clients and evaluation sponsors, into the research design.	*Individual roles*	The researcher typically designs elements of the research design and then collects data from participants and data sources.
Evaluation questions determine the merit and worth of a program by centering on the utility of a program.	*Questions*	Research questions align with theory and support hypothesis testing (quantitative) and/or questions about processes, dynamics, and meanings (qualitative).

Program Evaluation Goals

A pivotal feature that distinguishes program evaluation from research is the overall goals. Whereas research often extends theories or tests hypotheses to contribute new knowledge to the broader literature on educational topics, program evaluations deal with analyzing outcomes, conditions and/or processes at a particular site. The goal of evaluations is to make judgements about programs, strategies, or processes as a way to improve program effectiveness and/or efficiency. The goals could include assessing student mastery of learning, changes in affective states, or improvements in terms of how the school functions, as some examples. Ultimately, the goal of the program evaluation is to help clients, sponsors, and stakeholders accept, modify, or reject the evaluand based on findings. These decisions provide practical implications rather than enhancing intellectual pursuits.

Focus of Program Evaluations

The focus of program evaluations typically centers on a specific organization. The school setting is thought of as a socially constructed environment. The target of a program evaluation is to study the specific environment to solve a societal problem. This focal point is quite different from research studies, which often aim to establish/support a theory, extend findings to inform the comprehensive body of literature on a topic, and sometimes generalize to a broader population. With program evaluations, the focus is typically on a localized problem. Methods of data collection and analysis center on addressing a specific issue and offering tangible solutions.

Roles of Individuals in Program Evaluations

At the center of program evaluation is the notion that the goal is to improve the experiences of those individuals most affected by the evaluand. For this reason, program evaluators collect information from interested parties to first inform the program goals and focus. To correspond with the goals, the program evaluator will create evaluation questions. The individuals who work in the environment and who benefit from the program are critical in the refinement of these questions. This approach differs from research studies in which the researcher typically designs the study and creates research questions. In program evaluations, stakeholders can take on pivotal roles in the formation of a program evaluation design.

Unlike research studies, many types of individuals can be involved in the design of a program evaluation (e.g., teachers, support staff, administrators, parents, students).

©iStockphoto.com/SDI Productions

Evaluation Questions Based on Merit and Worth

As noted earlier, a way to distinguish between traditional research and program evaluation is that research studies aim to draw conclusions that correspond with theories and previous literature, while program evaluations inform decision-making strategies for creating a change within a social structure. In other words, an emphasis on the interaction in a specific situation is essential as evaluations center on a societal need that will bring about program adjustments. The criteria for evaluating objects center on judging the worth and merit of the program. With input from evaluation sponsors/clients/stakeholders, the evaluation questions directly align with the goals of the evaluation and reflect merit and worth.

Merit is a term that refers to the value a program adds to an organization. In contrast, worth centers on the utility of the program to the community at large. The question, "Is a career development program good at providing STEM career information?" reflects intrinsic merit to a school district. The district would want to know if the career development program had value to students and parents interested in STEM careers. Asking "Do students in the career development program enter STEM majors in universities?" would be reflective of extrinsic worth in adding value to the community at large. Researchers strive to relate findings to previous literature and theory, whereas evaluators target relevant factors to address practical questions, notably related to merit and worth. Figure 9.5 provides some examples of program evaluation questions.

FIGURE 9.5 ■ Sample Program Evaluation Questions Based on Merit and Worth

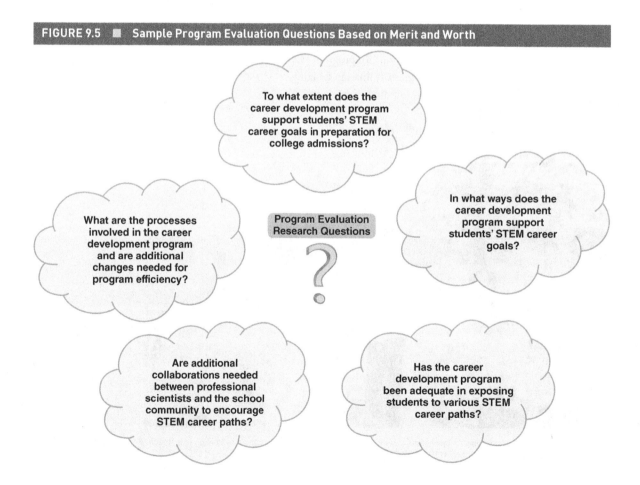

These types of questions differ from research questions. A research question on a career development program might be framed to check relationships among variables in support of a hypothesis or preexisting theory. A researcher might ask, "What is the relationship between student achievement and STEM interest based on a career development program?" In contrast, program evaluation questions focus on merit and worth with the end goal being to provide practical solutions to specific problems.

Many school-based initiatives would benefit from program evaluations that center on the worth and merit of a program. Innovations in instruction are continuously implemented within school districts, sometimes without discernment about ways to best meet the needs of student populations. For instance, an administrator may choose to shorten academic sessions once a week to allot for school clubs in order to build a sense of community and to help students identify new interests. However, there may be influencing factors that undermine the effectiveness of this type of program. Students may prefer to have longer academic sessions, the need to prepare for clubs detracts from teachers' planning time, and student academic performance may decline due to less time in class. Utilizing a program evaluation to assess the worth and merit of these programs is instrumental in making determinations about which tools and resources best meet student needs.

For example, Mr. Wilson, the superintendent of a local school district, has targeted a STEM career development program as an evaluand. He wants to know if the program is good (has merit) and if the funds allocated were worth the investment in terms of raising student achievement in science and mathematics. In this case, Mr. Wilson wants to make a judgment related to the resources. The questions he seeks to answer are reflective of merit and worth. When Mr. Wilson and the district stakeholders consider whether the STEM career development program is a good resource, they are considering the merit of the tool, or the intrinsic value to the local school district. On the other hand, wanting to know if the funds were well spent is a question of worth; this focus is reflective of extrinsic value to the school district. Table 9.2 presents examples of questions based on merit and worth for specific program evaluations.

Writing evaluation questions that reflect merit and worth are very essential in framing the design of a program evaluation. Consider the context of a STEM career development program to encourage students to enter STEM related fields. The following *Let's See It!* provides an example of how to write evaluation questions based on merit and worth with STEM for this topic. The *Let's Do It!* is a guided follow-up activity on writing evaluation questions based on merit and worth.

Let's See It! 9.1

Goal: Identifying Evaluation Questions Based on Merit and Worth

The primary objective of this activity is to identify merit and worth evaluation questions. Table 9.2 shows examples of merit and worth questions followed by a Let's Do It! activity. Remember, merit refers to programs that add value to an organization (intrinsic value), whereas worth describes the utility of a program and its impact on a larger community (extrinsic value). For this table, review the following questions based on merit and worth for a STEM career development program.

TABLE 9.2 ■ Identifying Merit and Worth Evaluation Questions	
Merit (intrinsic value)	**Worth (extrinsic value)**
How well does the STEM career development program align with the science curriculum?	Is it worth the initial cost and the cost of upkeep for a district to run a STEM career development program?
Is project-based learning a good STEM teaching strategy?	Is project-based learning improving student college admissions rates in STEM majors?
Is the STEM career development program a worthwhile initiative?	Are students in the STEM career development program entering 4-year colleges?
Is a science probe a good tool for instruction?	How well are students able to collaborate with local professional scientists with science probes?

Let's Do It! 9.1

Guided Practice: Merit and Worth in Evaluations

Goal: Identifying Evaluation Questions Based on Merit and Worth

The purpose of this exercise it to identify evaluation questions based on merit and worth. Remember, merit refers to programs that add value to an organization (intrinsic value), whereas worth describes the utility of a program and its impact on a larger community (extrinsic value). After reviewing Table 9.2, consider a school district that wants to implement workshops on improving instruction in the outdoor classroom. Table 9.3 provides a series of evaluation questions. Identify whether the questions are examples of merit or worth and provide the rationale. To guide your thinking, we encourage you to use the Let's See It! Table 9.2. We also provide an answer key in the appendix at the end of the chapter for you to check your work.

TABLE 9.3 ■ Analyze Merit or Worth		
Evaluation Question	**Merit (intrinsic value)**	**Worth (extrinsic value)**
How effectively are teachers able to utilize the strategies from the outdoor classroom workshops?		
Will the benefits of the outdoor classroom workshops outweigh the financial costs associated with program implementation?		
Are the outdoor classroom workshops leading to increased student achievement?		
Has there been increased enrollment in environmental science courses with the implementation of outdoor classroom workshops?		

In this section, we described the difference between program evaluation and research. Specifically, the section distinguished between the two broad approaches in terms of overall goals, focus, role of individuals, and evaluation versus research questions. We concluded by differentiating between evaluation questions based on merit and worth. In the next section, we discuss the elements of program theory and logic models to construct program evaluations.

THE TAKEAWAY

Program evaluation questions center on merit and worth, typically for a specified educational setting. In short, the evaluators consider whether an object/evaluand is good and if allocated funds are well spent. This focus differs from research questions, which often aim to test theories, generalize to a broader population, or inform the general body of literature on a specific topic.

ELEMENTS OF PROGRAM THEORY AND LOGIC MODELS

LEARNING OBJECTIVE
9.3   Identify elements of program theory and logic models.

The purpose of program evaluations is integral to the implementation and/or clarification of an evaluand. While the full process of program evaluation is beyond the scope of this chapter, there are three integral facets: (a) needs assessment, (b) program theory, and (c) program cost efficiency. Once these elements have been clearly addressed, the evaluator(s) will create a logic model. The following section describes each of these elements in detail.

Needs Assessment

School districts adopt a variety of programs to raise student achievement and increase overall well-being. Say for example that a local school district has noticed a drop in attendance and test scores across grade levels for the last 5 years, and district leaders and teachers are not sure what factors are responsible for this change in student performance.

Stakeholders decided to adopt an integrative art program to encourage attendance and increase student performance. However, they did not conduct a needs assessment prior to implementing the change. In this case, the lack of a needs assessment may hamper the effectiveness of instructional programs, misallocate funds, or create a lack of alignment between the needs and resources of school communities. The stakeholders have no way of knowing whether other programs would be more advantageous, such as adopting an art and technology-based reading program, increased professional development for teachers, or hiring additional reading and art specialists. The program developers may be overlooking other influential factors negatively impacting student achievement, including long commutes after school, lack of nutritious breakfasts prior to school, or after-school activities/jobs affecting study habits. In the case of this school district, a needs assessment would be an essential aspect of program evaluation to help interested parties make effective decisions to assist students. To conduct a needs assessment, the evaluator focuses on identifying gaps between how well the students are performing based on the implementation of instructional strategies as compared to the desired outcomes. These gaps could be particularly crucial when considering performance differences between groups of students (e.g., gifted/special education, and general education).

STOP AND THINK 9.3

Is there an issue in your workplace that would benefit from a needs assessment? What are some possible factors impacting this issue? Who are potential stakeholders?

Typically, needs assessments include three phases: pre-assessment, assessment, and post-assessment. During the pre-assessment, evaluators make initial inquiries about a problem from both an educational and social perspective. The assessment (in program theory) informs the evaluators and stakeholders about the program at hand in more detail, and the post-assessment proposes a solution to mitigate the problem under study. As with various forms of program evaluations, the clients and stakeholders are influential in steering the needs assessment. Once the evaluator collects initial information, a needs assessment provides details about the issue and associated factors. Based on the findings gathered from the needs assessment, the post-assessment delivers a plan of action.

Program Theory

The term program theory describes a proposed framework to tackle a specific problem in an educational setting. Figure 9.6 and the discussion that follows highlight some general considerations for program theory.

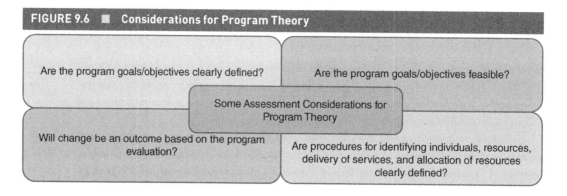

FIGURE 9.6 ■ Considerations for Program Theory

Are the program goals/objectives clearly defined?

Are the program goals/objectives feasible?

Some Assessment Considerations for Program Theory

Will change be an outcome based on the program evaluation?

Are procedures for identifying individuals, resources, delivery of services, and allocation of resources clearly defined?

In the example of the school district evaluating an integrative art program to improve student attendance and achievement, an evaluator developing the program theory would want to start with some initial steps. First, an evaluator would analyze the original design of the integrative art program in terms of logistics and processes.

While collecting this information from stakeholders, the evaluator considers the original design, the underlying assumptions, and the stakeholders' expectations for the program. Before advancing further in the process, the evaluator assesses the feasibility of the evaluation. For instance, a clear delineation of the program goals and objectives are necessary in order to create a program theory and evaluation design. Most importantly, the evaluator will want to take into account whether the stakeholders have a willingness to make changes based on the evaluation outcomes. For instance, the team of curriculum developers and stakeholders may have such a strong investment in the original creation of the integrative art program that they are not willing to make adjustments regardless of the program evaluation findings. In this case, proceeding with the program theory and evaluation design would not be advisable as adoption of any recommendations would be unlikely.

School initiatives like art integration programs are appropriate evaluands for a program evaluation. Gathering information on the origins of the program, the stakeholders' assumptions and expectations, the program goals and objectives, and stakeholders' willingness to make changes are essential considerations prior to conducting a program evaluation.

©iStockphoto.com/shironosov

If stakeholders are open to make changes, the evaluator will draw conclusions about the underlying assumptions interested parties have about the evaluand, logistical processes, personnel interactions, and resources entailed in the integrative art program. Examples would be determining assumptions related to the effectiveness of the program and potential barriers. The evaluator could analyze how the school's personnel obtain and allocate resources; the interaction between teachers, specialists, and teachers' assistants during the program; and areas for improvement within the program.

Finally, the evaluator assesses how well the program theory reflects the program goals and objectives. One of the key features would be for the evaluator to determine if there are some hurdles for the target population of students to receive resources and instruction. While the stakeholders and school staff may feel that the integrative art program is valuable in promoting attendance and achievement, evaluators determine the program is having more of a positive impact for students in the lower elementary grades than for upper elementary grades, primarily because teachers (Grades 3–5) need more professional development on how to integrate art within instruction while accounting for curriculum demands, for example.

Two components comprise the program theory: program impact theory and program process theory. The program impact theory addresses which factors need attention to bring about change. The program process theory focuses on the processes that will bring about the desired change. Both the program impact theory and program process theory are critical elements in program evaluation. Figure 9.7 summarizes these two components of program theory.

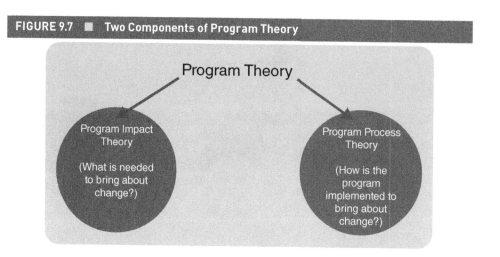

FIGURE 9.7 ■ Two Components of Program Theory

Program theories incorporate aspects of the program that need adjustments (program impact theory) and the implementation of changes (program process theory). Often evaluators develop the program theory from stakeholder feedback. If stakeholders wanted to create an outdoor classroom, they may seek feedback from many individuals, such as the custodian. This individual could provide valuable information in terms of lawn maintenance, issues related to adding a gravel path, and potential issues of vandalism. Understanding what would need to be done to make the outdoor classroom feasible would reflect the program impact theory. Next, stakeholders explore the steps needed to create an outdoor classroom program as a reflection of the program process theory. Both the program impact theory and the program process theory fall under the umbrella term of *program theory.*

Program Cost Efficiency

In addition to creating a program theory, a central task of schools and school districts is to select resources and allocate funds for programs that are most likely to generate optimal learning outcomes. One of the primary responsibilities of school officials and stakeholders is to identify resources and programs that produce the greatest impact with the least cost. Cost effectiveness analysis is integral to helping school administrators make decisions about how to allocate resources. In this endeavor, school officials will make the most precise estimates possible to determine how to maximize returns on investments. Preferably, adopted programs will garner the greatest impact with the lowest costs. Stakeholders and administrators aim to avoid a situation in which costs are high and there are minimal benefits. For example, a reading initiative adopted by the state of North Carolina reflected the low cost-to-benefit ratio as noted by Bell (2019): "Reading scores have not improved in years despite the state's multi-million-dollar efforts to increase third-grade proficiency—a benchmark that research says is closely tied to high school graduation." This quote reflects why studying program cost efficiency is such a necessary enterprise.

Beyond the cost of purchasing reading resources, there are additional costs for adopting this type of plan, which could extend to teacher training, the cost of technology hardware and software, and required adaptations within the school day to accommodate the reading program, including the time frame for training implementation. Stakeholders want to maximize the benefits of these types of program costs, allocating time and resources to evaluate the program cost efficiency. Ultimately, evaluations that incorporate program cost efficiency, both in terms of monetary and monetized benefits, aim to appraise whether the benefits of the evaluand exceed the costs.

When considering program cost efficiency, two areas of focus include cost-benefit analysis and cost-effectiveness analysis. A cost-effectiveness analysis would analyze costs of a program in comparison to the final outcomes. The goal is to identify the least costly program with the most benefits, keeping in mind that the most impactful practices are typically not low in cost.

Suppose a school district in a rural area has had difficulty hiring and retaining high quality teachers. To attract a strong pool of applicants, the district implements several strategies, including competitive health care and retirement packages and advanced degree reimbursement plans. Added incentives include ongoing professional development in effective teaching practices and volunteer mentorship programs. Ultimately through a cost-effectiveness analysis, stakeholders in the district would want to determine if the benefits of these strategies (e.g., the retention of high-quality teachers) as an outcome would outweigh the overall costs. Well-designed, cost-effectiveness analysis accounts for as many variables as possible, for unanticipated costs can skew the cost-to-benefit ratio.

From another perspective, the district pursues establishing an apartment complex with a shared workspace, so teachers may easily collaborate and have an affordable living space. For other services, such as a volunteer mentorship program, it is advisable to monetize resources to evaluate the cost-to-benefit ratio. Other cost-related factors include time saved by the district's human resources in the searching and hiring processes and time and resources allocated for initial teacher training for new hires. A cost-benefit analysis uses a fine-grained approach to further evaluate the costs and benefits by comparing these types of program components in the same monetary unit as the costs.

While the intricate processes involved in evaluating program cost efficiency are beyond the scope of this text, for evaluators and stakeholders interested in this aspect of program evaluation, some key steps would include how to (a) measure the costs and benefits, (b) monetize benefits, (c) estimate the overall costs of the program, and (d) compare the costs and benefits.

To implement an outdoor classroom program, there may be obvious costs. School staff requests to purchase materials, like soil sampling tubes and magnifying glasses. Additional costs relate to hiring a naturalist to run professional development on the use of an outdoor classroom. An evaluator would need to determine a way to measure the costs as well as the benefits (e.g., improved social emotional well-being of staff and students, less absenteeism of staff and students, etc.). It would be relatively straightforward to determine the cost of substitutes based on a decrease in teacher absences; however, estimating resources for maintaining the outdoor space would be calculated differently. Unexpected costs are a consideration, such as maintenance due to community vandalism. Ultimately, the program sponsors would want to assess the balance between overall costs and benefits for running the program as accurately as possible.

Program evaluations often integrate cost-effectiveness analysis and cost-benefit analysis. The many activities, training, and roles of school personnel as well as their salaries and benefits are factored into these two components of program evaluations.

©iStockphoto.com/monkeybusinessimages

Logic Models

Once the program theory has been clarified, the evaluator will design a logic model, a visual representation of the intended relationship between the objectives and outcomes. Typically, logic models follow a flowchart format and lend themselves well to prioritizing program needs, strategic planning, and outcome evaluations.

Four elements commonly found in a logic model are the inputs, activities, outputs, and outcomes. The inputs are the resources that provide a structure to the program. For an outdoor classroom initiative, examples are trained school staff, enhancements to space (pond, picnic tables), materials (stop watches, magnifying glasses, thermometers, soil sampling tubes), personnel to maintain the outdoor space, and funding for advanced professional development with naturalists. Maintenance of the grounds, outdoor structures, and materials would be reflective of maintenance concerns.

The activities in the logic model relate to actions or resources used to reach the needs of the target audience (e.g., students at the school). For an outdoor classroom, evaluators would meet with stakeholders; collect data on the uses, needs, supports, and barriers in using the outdoor space; and identify potential collaborations, such as with local naturalists, soil and water conservation groups, or naturalists who can train teachers.

The outputs are the types of activities and participants involved in a program. In the case of an outdoor classroom, the outputs could be the school staff attending professional development with naturalists; the number of and quality of lessons conducted outside; the utilization of materials for student learning; the purchase of additional materials (e.g., probes, plastic beakers and graduated cylinders); and collaborations to maintain, enhance, and extend the space (native plant species, wooden log benches, signage).

The outcomes include indicators of effective changes to the program; these outcomes are a way to assess the merit and worth of an evaluand. There are several ways to evaluate the outcomes: tiered outcome levels (e.g., short term, medium term, long term) or by intermediate and final outcomes. In the outdoor classroom scenario, short-term outcomes would be an increase of teacher use in the classroom, medium-term outcomes would be changes in teacher self-efficacy for instruction in the outdoors and improved lesson-planning skills. Long-term outcomes would be increases in student achievement and advanced lesson-planning skills in the outdoors. Figure 9.8 represents a logic model for the outdoor classroom scenario.

FIGURE 9.8 ■ Logic Model for Outdoor Classroom Program Evaluation

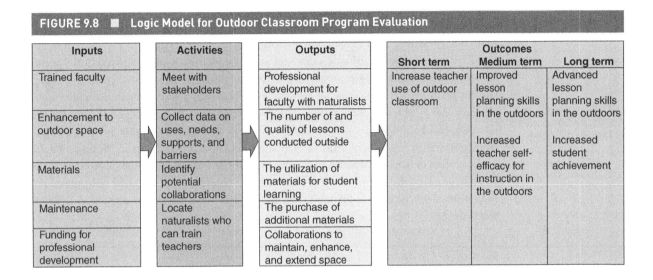

Inputs	Activities	Outputs	Outcomes		
			Short term	Medium term	Long term
Trained faculty	Meet with stakeholders	Professional development for faculty with naturalists	Increase teacher use of outdoor classroom	Improved lesson planning skills in the outdoors	Advanced lesson planning skills in the outdoors
Enhancement to outdoor space	Collect data on uses, needs, supports, and barriers	The number of and quality of lessons conducted outside		Increased teacher self-efficacy for instruction in the outdoors	Increased student achievement
Materials	Identify potential collaborations	The utilization of materials for student learning			
Maintenance	Locate naturalists who can train teachers	The purchase of additional materials			
Funding for professional development		Collaborations to maintain, enhance, and extend space			

Logic models provide a helpful visual to show the relationship between the program objectives and outcomes. This visual assists in the processes of assessing alignment between program goals and subsequent impacts. Notably, there are many types of logic models, the details of which are beyond the scope of this text. Once the program theory and logic model have been solidified, the evaluators can identify the specific type of program evaluation best suited for the object of study.

THE TAKEAWAY

The program theory and the corresponding logic model frame the program evaluation. If the stakeholders are not willing to make a change, it may be best not to proceed with the program evaluation.

TYPES AND PURPOSES OF PROGRAM EVALUATIONS

LEARNING OBJECTIVE

9.4 Distinguish between the types and purposes of program evaluations.

Continuous societal changes spur the need for program evaluations that are tailor-made to evaluate program outcomes. While many models of program evaluations have evolved since the 1800s, we outline five major approaches (objectives-oriented, management-oriented, consumer-oriented, expertise-oriented, participant-oriented), which are applicable to educational settings.

Objectives-Oriented Evaluation

The objectives-oriented evaluation approach, first described by Ralph W. Tyler in the 1930s, centers on alignment between program objectives and outcomes. The seminal work of Tyler emphasized the inherent connection between clearly defined learning objectives, instructional curriculum and design, and evaluation procedures. The Tylerian approach was the first structured system of program evaluation that accounted for the relationship between initial objectives and final outcomes. Tyler broadened the focus of program evaluations beyond individual student performance to account for varied educational objectives that included curriculum elements and logistical processes within school systems. For Tyler, the way to determine the effectiveness of a program was to consider embedded elements, such as the purposes, objectives, and student experiences within a curriculum, as a total process. Further, he proposed the incorporation of behavioral learning objectives prior to conducting evaluations so that it was possible to gauge the alignment between the stated objectives and program outcomes. One limitation of this type of evaluation is that there is less emphasis on processes of instruction and learning.

Management-Oriented Evaluation

Management-oriented evaluation highlights the use of information (e.g., needs of clients, input from stakeholders, budgetary constraints) to assist individuals in the decision-making process. This approach distinguishes between decisions and a hierarchy level of decision makers wherein administrators have a pivotal role in determining and utilizing the findings for effective decision making. The CIPP (context, input, process, and product), a widely used model developed by Daniel Stufflebeam (1971), is an example of a management-oriented evaluation, which outlines a process of informed decision-making with systematic evaluations. All four phases are essential in the CIPP model to help determine how an organization can best meet the needs of a target population by providing services that revolve around the program's ultimate core values.

The context evaluation (sometimes referred to as a needs assessment) considers how an organization can address gaps in a current societal structure. In this phase, the evaluators identify the target population, assess the needs of these individuals, determine problems and impacting factors, and examine whether the project goals correspond with the needs of the service group. For the Saturday home–school connection workshop, evaluators examine the goals of the program (e.g., build better home–school connections through the use of the outdoor classroom and improve student performance) and whether this approach can meet the needs of the community (e.g., parents, teachers, and students can work together to improve student performance with instructional training). The evaluators will work with clients, evaluation sponsors, and stakeholders to determine if there are other factors that are limiting student performance and if the proposed project truly meets the program goals and objectives.

Determining how the project should be run through the perspective of these individuals is reflective of the second phase, input evaluation. Individuals involved in the Saturday workshop, such as administrators, teachers, custodians, librarians, and parents, will have valuable insights into the best ways to administer the program. Formative assessments are useful for both the context evaluation and input evaluation, particularly if the program has been conducted previously.

The process evaluation describes the implementation of a program to see if the initiative runs as planned logistically to meet the objectives. Maintaining fidelity in terms of instruction would be one way the process could be undermined. For instance, if parent–student groups were given instruction in different rooms by several school staff members, the evaluators would want to examine if the experiences were similar in terms of instructional delivery, materials, and quality and if parents and students engaged in the activities to the same extent. Lastly, the product evaluation uses summative tools to determine how well the program met the needs of the target population via the objectives. Table 9.4 shows the description of the CIPP approach with considerations and examples based on a home–school connection program.

TABLE 9.4 ■ CIPP Model Description Based on a Home–school Connection Program

CIPP component	Description	Considerations	Example
Context evaluation—goals ● Target population ● Needs ● Resources ● Problem ● Underlying factors Environment	The context evaluation examines how an organization can address gaps in a current societal structure by determining the needs of a target population and assessing if program goals align with these needs.	Appropriateness of objectives; alignment of objectives with the needs of target population	Program developers identify parent–student teams based on students performing in the lowest quartile in reading and mathematics. The objective is for students to increase reading and mathematics performance with strategies taught at a home–school connection workshop.
Input evaluation—plans ● Clients Evaluation sponsors ● Stakeholders ● Objectives ● Curriculum ● Budget ● Personnel Theory and research	The input evaluation focuses on how a project should be run through the perspective of clients, evaluation sponsors, and stakeholders.	Theoretical literature on home–school connections; empirical research on home–school connections; appropriateness and acceptability of home–school connection training methods	Students form stronger beliefs about their capabilities (self-efficacy) when they are supported by family members and teachers (Bandura, 1997). Jeynes (2005) analyzed 41 home–school connection studies through a meta-analysis and found that strong parental involvement had a positive influence on elementary students. The workshop includes authentic problem-solving activities, which encourage critical thinking (McTighe & Silver, 2020).

(Continued)

TABLE 9.4 ■ CIPP Model Description Based on a Home–school Connection Program (*Continued*)

CIPP component	Description	Considerations	Example
Process evaluation—actions • Program development • Program implementation • Program monitoring Feedback	The process evaluation centers on the implementation of a program to see if the program is run as planned logistically to meet the objectives.	Extent to which the program was implemented with fidelity; participation of parent–student teams and task completion; attendance of parent–student teams; parent–student satisfaction with framing	Checklists and observations capture the processes involved in the implementation of the program. School personnel are interviewed about the program and processes utilized.
Product evaluation—outcomes • Impact • Effectiveness • Transportability • Sustainability • Application	The product evaluation determines how well the program met the needs of the target population via the objectives.	Parents' knowledge of content information on nutrition; parents' ability to apply skills; student engagement and performance behavior	Parent–student tasks are analyzed with a rubric. Parent–student attendance is noted with frequency distributions. Parents and students complete satisfaction surveys. Parents are interviewed on the experiences of the program.

In this model, adjustments can be made whenever there are gaps or inefficiencies within the system founded on improving a program rather than establishing a program's legitimacy. For this reason, the CIPP model is suitable in educational settings as a cyclical model to continuously improve the evaluand, although this type of evaluation is complex and difficult to implement.

Consumer-Oriented Evaluation

A common need within school districts and schools is to determine the need and impact of resources and materials. The consumer-oriented evaluation focuses on assessing the effectiveness and worth of resources available for purchase. This form of program evaluation stems from the work of Michael Scriven (1967). A consumer-oriented evaluator considers ways to conduct a systematic evaluation of intricate factors related to school operations, strategies, or resources. In this regard, educational resources are seen as a product, while educational institutions fulfill a service. The focal point is on the needs of the target population as consumers. A setback in this type of approach is that it does not take into consideration the motivational needs of curriculum experts and teachers within organizations.

Expertise-Oriented Evaluation

The inception of expertise-oriented evaluation with the implementation of standardized tests as collegiate entrance exams. Widely used in education since that time, subject matter experts conduct expertise-oriented evaluations to make judgments about the merit and worth of programs. Individuals with content expertise assess evaluands based on preset standards.

Evaluations managed by accreditation bodies would be an example of expertise-oriented evaluations. These evaluations include subject matter experts to make judgments about the merit and worth of programs. For instance, educational psychologists with expertise in career motivation could be part of an evaluation team to evaluate the worth and merit of a district's career development program.

STOP AND THINK 9.4

Consider an issue in your workplace/school setting which could be an evaluand for a program evaluation. Which type of program evaluation would be most appropriate and why?

Participant-Oriented Evaluation

Unlike the other four approaches, participant-oriented evaluations spotlight the opinions of participants impacted by the evaluand. This form of program evaluation emerged in the 1980s in tandem with action research based on the work of Robert Stake. Participant-oriented evaluations differ from the other forms in that the individuals most affected by the evaluand are part of the evaluation process. The evaluator's role is to engage directly with stakeholders and the target audience in a continual cycle to assess the impact of the evaluand.

When preparing a program evaluation, identifying the type of design needed can be instrumental in conjunction with the program theory. Figure 9.9 provides a flow chart with examples of each type of program evaluation design. Understanding the types and purposes of program evaluations will support the overarching goals in assessing the impact of an evaluation.

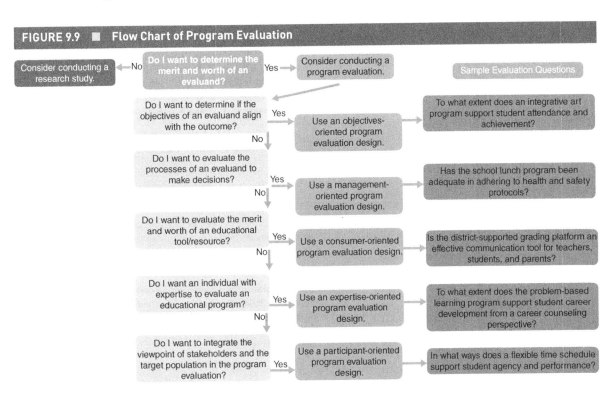

FIGURE 9.9 ■ Flow Chart of Program Evaluation

In this section, we have provided an overview of five common approaches to program evaluation. Regardless of the design, there are some consistent components of program evaluation, such as the description of the evaluand and purpose of the program evaluation. *Let's See It!* 9.2 highlights the components of program evaluations with a model by Roberts et al. (2014) on school food safety programs. *Let's Do It!* and *Let's See It!* 9.2 provides further practice in identifying program evaluation components.

Let's See It! 9.2

Goal: Identifying the Components of a Program Evaluation

The objective of this activity is to identify the components of a program evaluation. Review the program evaluation conducted by Roberts et al. (2014) on school nutrition. Then, look at Table 9.5 to see how we identified the type and purpose of the program evaluation, as well as design components of the evaluation.

TABLE 9.5 ■ Identifying the Components of a Program Evaluation	
Study	Roberts, K. R., Sauer, K. L., Sneed, J., Kwon, J., Olds, D., Cole, K., & Shanklin, C. W. (2014). Analysis of school food safety programs based on HACCP principles. *The Journal of Child Nutrition & Management, 38*(1). https://schoolnutrition.org/5—News-and-Publications/4—The-Journal-of-Child-Nutrition-and-Management/Spring-2014/Volume-38,-Issue-1,-Spring-2014—Roberts,-Sauer,-Sneed,-Kwon,-Olds,-Cole,-Shanklin/
Type of Program Evaluation	Objectives-oriented program evaluation
Evaluand	The evaluand was the food safety procedures implemented in school district cafeterias.
Purpose	The purpose of the program evaluation was to examine how school districts have implemented food safety programs based on Hazard Analysis Critical Control Points (HACCP) guidelines set forth by the Child Nutrition and WIC Reauthorization Act of 2004.
Data Collection Tools	Food Safety Observation form, Facility Observation form, Food Safety Observation and Facility Observations forms
Data Analysis	Data were analyzed using descriptive statistics (e.g., means and percentages) as well as qualitative analysis based on researcher observations.
Findings	HACCP guidelines were adhered across 34 schools analyzed. Particular issues related to covering and labeling food before storage, adequate temperatures for food storage, and the use of proper handwashing techniques prior to handling food.
Recommendations	Safety program operations should be customized to the needs of the school. Online documents to track these processes should be integrated in food safety programs. Continued improvements should focus on employee behaviors related to food production and contamination.

Let's Do It! 9.2

Guided Practice: Identifying the Components of a Program Evaluation

Goal

The objective of this activity is to identify the types and purposes of program evaluation designs. Identify the components of the program evaluation using the guide sheet as a Let's Do It! activity. To guide your thinking, we encourage you to use the Let's See It! Table 9.6 and the program evaluation article by Berk (2018) on out-of-school academic support. We also provide an answer key in the appendix at the end of the chapter for you to check your work.

TABLE 9.6 ■ Program Evaluation Designs	
Study	Berk, S. (2018). Assessment of public schools' out-of-school time academic support programs with participant-oriented evaluation. *Journal of Education and Learning*, 7(3), 159–175. https://doi.org/10.5 539/jel.v7n3p159
Type of Program Evaluation	
Evaluand	
Purpose	
Data Collection Tools	
Data Analysis	
Findings	
Recommendations	

Herein, we outlined the major types of program evaluations and the purposes of each. When analyzing an evaluand, the goals of the evaluation will be instrumental in determining the type of approach required. In the following section, we provide an overview of creating, conducting, analyzing, and presenting findings of a program evaluation.

THE TAKEAWAY

There are many types of program evaluations. Program evaluators utilize the approach that is most applicable to examining an evaluand and may also use a blended approach of multiple evaluation models.

ENGAGING IN A PROGRAM EVALUATION

LEARNING OBJECTIVE
9.5 Identify how to engage in a program evaluation.

The program evaluation process entails a great deal of preparation, planning, and organization. Interviewing stakeholders to develop elements of the evaluation, including the program theory, are essential. The goals and requirements of the program evaluation as well as the audience will steer the formation of evaluation questions, program theory, logic models, data collection, and the sharing of information. This section provides a broad overview of these elements with some specific suggestions in creating, conducting, analyzing, interpreting, and presenting findings of a program evaluation.

Program Evaluation Reports

Program evaluation reports include specific sections to inform the stakeholders, clients, and sponsors about the findings. Reports generally begin with the background of the problem; the program theory and logic models; a method description of the target population, timelines, procedures, and data collection tools; and a description of analyses and interpretations. The following section provides a description of each of these aspects of the program evaluation plan and concludes with a discussion of how to present findings.

Background of the Problem

Both the program evaluation plan and final report begins with background information. In this section, the evaluators include information on the context and the initiative or dilemma that serves as the evaluand. A general description of the organization, organizational model, and target population for the program would fall under this section. At this point, the evaluator cites the type of program evaluation design (e.g., expertise-oriented, objective-oriented, etc.).

Following this writing, the evaluator(s) should state the purpose of the evaluation and potential challenges. At this point, the work may reference other sources (e.g., other program evaluations, government reports) to further illuminate the issue. Since the evaluation sponsors are central to defining the program evaluation goals, these individuals and their positions are part of the description followed by the overarching goals of the evaluation and proposed evaluation questions. Examples of evaluation goals for a school district interested in improving the science curriculum map and resources to encourage student STEM career paths would be as follows: (1) identify the strengths and weaknesses of the current science curriculum, (2) outline specific curricular changes and timelines, (3) identify the best ways to form collaborations with professional scientists in the community, and (4) make recommendations for needed resources.

Program evaluations include a description of the background of the problem and the program goals. Stakeholders are key players in defining the program goals. For a STEM initiative, an example could be identifying the strengths and weaknesses of the program.

©iStockphoto.com/SolStock

Once the broad goals for the evaluation have been described based on feedback from evaluation sponsors/clients, the evaluator forms questions reflective of these goals. Sample evaluation questions that align with the goals of a district science curriculum overhaul include the following: "In what ways does the science curriculum support student achievement?" "Are the core lab experiences adequate in advancing student performance?" or "Is the current scope and sequence an effective means for supporting student performance?" The stakeholders' perspectives will be useful in developing surveys as part of the method section.

Program Theory

Earlier in this chapter, we described program theory as an essential element in the overall evaluation plan. For this portion of the design, the evaluator will want to clarify both the impact theory and process theory, particularly if a needs assessment of the initiative has been conducted previously. The overview of the program theory centers on both the program impact theory (What is needed to bring about change?) and the program process theory (How does the way the program is implemented impact the ability to create change)? Considerations for this section include a description of the feasibility of the program, the changes as an outcome of the evaluation, procedures for individuals who are part of the program, and the dissemination of resources. Finally, the description includes a discussion of the delivery and allocation of resources, such as materials. Considering program cost efficiency may be a component of this description depending on the needs of the program evaluation.

Logic Model

A logic model reflects all of the elements in an evaluand that contribute to the issues of study and ways to bring about change. One way to create a logic model is to consider the inputs in the situation to run a program, the activities of individuals and the target population within the program, and the outputs of these activities. For a career development program, examples of outcomes include (a) improved student work habits and (b) increased interest in science and STEM-related courses. Next, the model can include short-, medium-, and long-term outcomes as described earlier in this chapter. Other types of models may use similar features. For instance, the sample model in Figure 9.10 specifies the type of outcomes based on knowledge, actions, and conditions, while integrating assumptions and external factors. Table 9.7 provides guiding questions and sample responses to analyze the model.

Creating logic models is a common tool for program evaluators. The following *Let's See It!* 9.3 introduces the features of logic models with the backdrop of an outdoor classroom. The *Let's Do It!* 9.3 is a guided follow-up activity with the WonderBox logic model (Sharp & Mason, 2021) from the Mississippi Children's Museum based on makerspaces.

Let's See It! 9.3

Goal: Creating a Logic Model

Logic models serve as a visual representation of how program objectives correspond with outcomes. The objective of this activity is to demonstrate how to analyze and create a logic model. In this example, the outcomes are listed based on knowledge, actions, and conditions for the participant. In addition, assumptions of the program and external factors are part of the logic model. Review the logic model for the outdoor classroom program evaluation in Figure 9.10 and look at Table 9.7 for helpful questions to consider when analyzing this logic model.

FIGURE 9.10 ■ Logic Model for Outdoor Classroom Program Evaluation

Situation	Inputs	Activities	Outputs	Outcomes		
				Knowledge	**Action**	**Conditions**
The middle school has an outdoor classroom that parents, teachers, and administrators had built several decades earlier.	A local government agency has worked with administrators to expand the pond, renovate the boardwalk, create paths, and put in picnic tables.	Integrate a series of professional development workshops for staff to learn about using the outdoor classroom.	There is a school-wide curriculum that integrates natural sciences in instruction.	Participants increase knowledge of the ways to utilize the outdoor classroom.	Participants integrate the outdoor classroom within lesson plans several times a year.	Participants have greater self-efficacy for utilizing the outdoor classroom.
While the outdoor classroom was falling in disrepair, an administrator worked with local government officials to make improvements.	Funds for materials to be ordered for outdoor classroom use.	Integrate the use of the natural world within the curriculum.	At least 40 teachers are involved in implementing instruction in the outdoor classroom and representing all subject areas.	Participants increase knowledge of tools and resources that can be used in the outdoor classroom.	Participants order and utilize tools and resources in the outdoor classroom.	There is an increase in the number and quality of lesson plans developed for outdoor classroom use.
Some teachers have privately attended workshops on using the outdoor classroom.	Collaborations with naturalists for expertise.	Provide materials, resources, and training for all teachers.	At least 10 teachers are involved in establishing clubs related to outdoor education.	Participants create well-defined lesson plans integrating the natural world within the curriculum.	Participants design lesson in the outdoor space that meet or state standards.	Participants experience new ways to integrate the natural world in the curriculum.
There is renewed interest in using the space; however, many teachers are not comfortable using the space, particularly in all subject areas.	Infrastructure for integrating outdoor instruction within the curriculum.	Deliver instruction on creating lesson plans within the outdoor classroom.	At least 80% of lesson plans meet a proficiency level based on a pre-established rubric.			

Assumptions	External Factors
With training on integrating the outdoor classroom within the curriculum, teachers will have increased self-efficacy and will be more likely to use the space with their students.	External factors include curriculum parameters, school logistics, and teacher interest in using the outdoor classroom. These factors could influence potential changes.

TABLE 9.7 ■ Questions for Outdoor Classroom Logic Model

Question	Response
How will the inputs in this situation support the outdoor classroom program?	The inputs will provide funding for personnel, professional development workshops, materials, infrastructure, and collaborations with local agencies and naturalists.
What activities support the program?	The activities include implementing professional development workshops on instructional practices to teach in the outdoors, providing teachers with materials and resources, and training on creating outdoor-based lesson plans.
What are the outputs of the program?	The outputs include a school-wide curriculum that integrates natural sciences in outdoor instruction; at least 40 teachers (from all subject areas) who are implementing the training for outdoor instruction; At least 10 teachers involved in establishing clubs based on the outdoor classroom; and at least 80% of lesson plans meet a proficiency level based on a preset criteria for outdoor instruction.
How are the program outcomes categorized?	The program outcomes are categorized based on (a) knowledge (e.g., ways to use the outdoor classroom), (b) action (e.g., actual use of the outdoor classroom), and (c) conditions (e.g., higher teacher self-efficacy for teaching outdoors).

Question	Response
How can it be helpful to consider program assumptions and external factors?	The assumptions are important in clarifying the goals of the evaluation sponsors and potentially revealing biases. External factors are taken into consideration that could influence change in the social setting. An assumption for the outdoor classroom program is that students will benefit from instruction in the outdoors. Some external factors could be time limitations due to the school day structure and access to the outdoor space.

Let's Do It! 9.3

Guided Practice: Logic Models in Program Evaluations

Goal: Creating a Logic Model

The purpose of this activity is to practice analyzing examples of logic models so as to subsequently create logic models. Figure 9.11 shows a WonderBox logic model (Sharp & Mason, 2021) created for the Mississippi Children's Museum. The evaluand for this model is WonderBox, a makerspace platform where students can collaborate to do STEM

FIGURE 9.11 ■ Logic model for WonderBox (Sharp & Mason, 2021) from the Mississippi Children's Museum

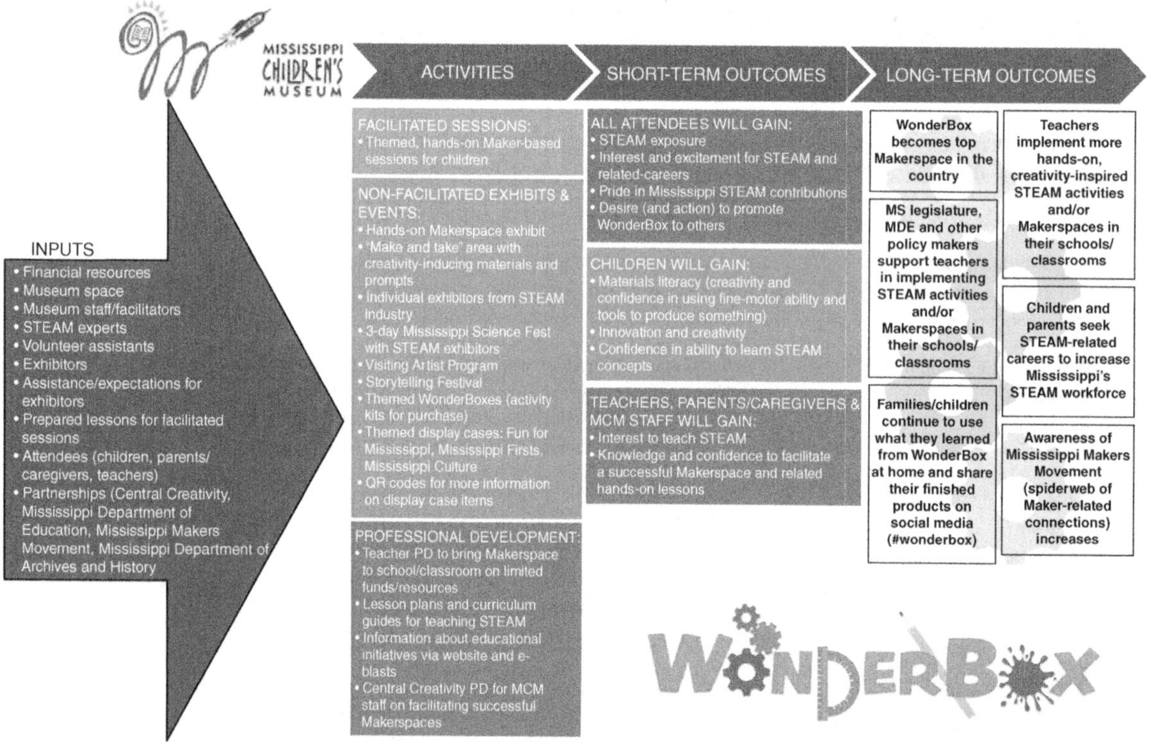

Sharp, S. R., & Mason, S. K. (2021). WonderBox logic model. Center for Research Evaluation, Oxford, MS. Created for Mississippi Children's Museum, Jackson, MS. https://cere.olemiss.edu/logic-models-vs-theories-of-change/

projects (Mississippi Children's Museum, 2023). To guide your thinking, we encourage you to use the Let's See It! Figure 9.12 and Table 9.7. Then review the logic model that follows and answer the corresponding questions in Table 9.8. We also provide an answer key in the appendix at the end of the chapter for you to check your work.

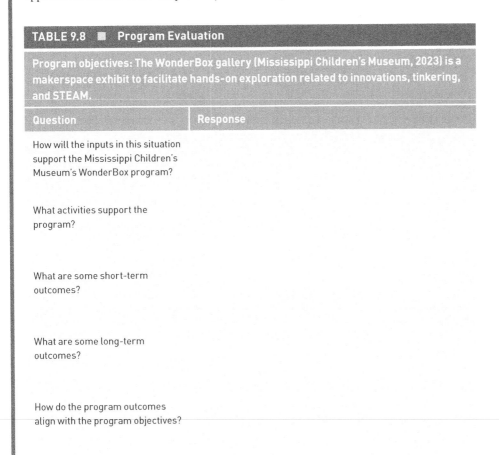

TABLE 9.8 ■ Program Evaluation	
Program objectives: The WonderBox gallery (Mississippi Children's Museum, 2023) is a makerspace exhibit to facilitate hands-on exploration related to innovations, tinkering, and STEAM.	
Question	**Response**
How will the inputs in this situation support the Mississippi Children's Museum's WonderBox program?	
What activities support the program?	
What are some short-term outcomes?	
What are some long-term outcomes?	
How do the program outcomes align with the program objectives?	

The logic model is an effective way to describe elements of the program evaluation. The model and corresponding description help to convey key processes to clients, sponsors, and stakeholders. Another important feature would be to have a clear plan and description of elements within the method section.

The Method Section

The method section of the program evaluation report is similar to research studies with features that include participants and settings, timelines, sources of data/measures, and proposed data analysis. These characteristics should be described in detail within the method section. For example, the evaluator will want to specify the criteria for participant selection to gather pertinent information for how the evaluand impacts the target population. If an organization wanted to survey members of the community who were involved in a local garden patch, an "X" could be placed on the ground. Individuals who crossed the marking would be a way to select participants for interviews and/or surveys.

Developing a program evaluation has many components to consider. A program evaluation decision tree can be a practical tool for creating a preliminary plan, which includes considerations for the program theory, logic model, and method section, as shown in Figure 9.12.

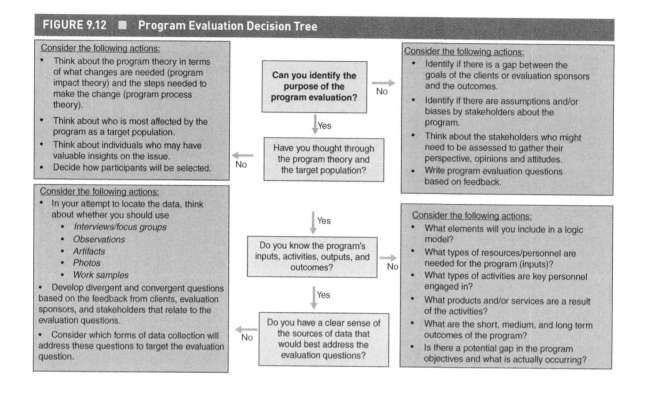

FIGURE 9.12 ■ Program Evaluation Decision Tree

In terms of data collection, program evaluations can include both quantitative and qualitative methods. To gauge the impact of an evaluand on the target population, an evaluator will often create original survey items and qualitative questions. A distinct feature in developing these surveys is to create selected response and constructed response items. This type of questioning stems from the evaluation questions. Selected response and constructed response items are written in part from the perspective of clients, evaluation sponsors, and stakeholders as part of discussions prior to and during the development of the program evaluation.

Selected response questions provide the participants in a study with a finite number of choices to select from in a survey (e.g., Likert-type scales). In contrast, constructed response questions allow for a variety of perspectives (e.g., open-ended questions on surveys and interviews). Consider that a district is examining a high school STEM career development program and one evaluation question is: "In what ways does the career development program support students in their career goals?" An example of a selected response item is "To what extent do different characteristics of the career development program support students' goals?" Figure 9.13 shows how survey items would reflect both the broad evaluation question and the corresponding selected response items.

The survey questions listed in Figure 9.13 would directly link to the broad evaluation question; however, participants would only be able to select from the provided responses. For the same evaluation question, "To what extent do different characteristics of the career development program support students' goals?" a corresponding constructed response items could be "Are there additional ways the STEM career development program could assist students?" Figure 9.14 shows how constructed response items steer an open-ended reply for the same topic.

FIGURE 9.13 ■ Survey Questions Based on Selected Response Items

1. General Questions: For starters, this section focuses on how the STEM career development program supports students. Please select from the following options: (1) strongly disagree, (2) disagree, (3) agree, (4) strongly agree.

Statement
I benefit from attending the STEM career development program.
I am able to learn techniques that can be used in my future career.
The STEM career development program provides me with the opportunity to learn about different careers.
The activities at the STEM career development program have helped me learn about a career I might be interested in for the future.

2. Level of Need for Service and Opportunities: This section will develop an understanding of what support students need to reach their goals. Rank the following needs by (1) low, (2) moderate need, (3) high need

Statement
Opportunities to work with mentors
Opportunities for internships
Presentations
Demonstrations
Hands-on activities
Bimonthly newsletter

FIGURE 9.14 ■ Open-Ended Questioning Based on Constructed Response Items

Please describe any service or opportunity needs that would assist you in the STEM career development program.

Selected response and constructed response items serve as a bridge between program evaluation questions and the items that appear on a survey or interview format. Table 9.9 provides a model for creating constructed response and selected response items in alignment with evaluation questions based on merit and worth and using the backdrop of the STEM career development program.

TABLE 9.9 ■ Selected Response and Constructed Response Items for Program Evaluations

Merit (Intrinsic value)	Worth (Extrinsic value)
Evaluation Question Is the STEM career development program a worthwhile initiative?	**Evaluation Question** Are students in the STEM career development program entering 4-year colleges?
Selected Response Item To what extent do students utilize the resources of the STEM career development program? (Often, somewhat, minimal, never)	*Selected Response Item* To what extent are students interested in entering a 4-year college for STEM careers? (Very interested, interested, little interest, not interested at all).
Constructed Response Item In what ways has the STEM career development program helped students?	*Constructed Response Item* How has the STEM career development program encouraged students to enter 4-year college STEM programs?

Analyzing and Interpreting Data

Once data collection has occurred, the evaluator will analyze and interpret data as part of the overall report. For selected response questions using quantitative information, a variety of graphs are suitable. This strategy is appropriate for presentations to convey information in a way that is easily understood by the audience. The use of visuals and tables helps the audience understand the findings and suggestions for the program. There are a range of data analysis techniques that would be relevant to use, depending on the program evaluation design (see Chapters 12, 13, and 14 for more information).

Let's See It! 9.4

Goal: Analyzing a Program Evaluation Report

The objective of this activity is to apply your knowledge of program evaluation by analyzing the Outdoor School for All program evaluation conducted by Braun (2019). This program evaluation focused on improving outdoor educational experiences for students across the state of Oregon. In addition to reviewing the content in Table 9.10, focus on the overall presentation to the audience as well. Then review Table 9.11 that follows to see how we identified key pieces of information from this program evaluation report.

TABLE 9.10 ■ Analyzing a Program Evaluation Report	
Study	Braun, S. M. (2019) Outdoor school for all: Diverse programming and outcomes in Oregon: 2018 pilot study evaluation. Portland, Oregon. The Gray Family Foundation. OSfA-Evaluation-highres-2.19.19.pdf (grayff.org)
Table of Contents	The table of contents provides background information about the need for the program evaluation, methods for the research design, findings, and recommendations.
Stakeholders	"Outdoor School for All (OSA)" is an Oregon state mandate to include outdoor education for all students. The stakeholders include members of OSA extension office, policymakers, educators, and administrators.
Goals	The goals center on determining the best practices to achieve equitable outcomes across all communities, identify strategies used by outdoor school educators that could be utilized across the state of Oregon, and identify how outdoor programs could be improved for students, particularly in terms of environmental literacy.
Findings	The findings showed that the outdoor school program had strong positive effects on students' environmental attitudes, problem-solving self-efficacy, and social/emotional well-being. The lowest gains were in interest for learning.
Recommendations	Recommendations included (a) increase the rigor of outdoor experience; (b) improve safety and support for students with nonbinary gender identities, particularly for overnight trips; and (c) improve initiatives that promote inclusivity of students of all racial groups, as some examples.
Figures and Graphs	A variety of colorful tables, figures, and photographs appear throughout the program evaluation report.

Let's Do It! 9.4

Guided Practice: Program Evaluation Reports

Goal: Analyzing a Program Evaluation Report

The objective of this activity is for you to independently practice reviewing a program evaluation on school lunch procedures (Atkins & Atkins, 2010) and identify the key characteristics emphasized in this chapter (Table 9.11). To guide your thinking, we encourage you to use the *Let's See It!* Table 9.10 and the guided questions. We also provide an answer key in the appendix at the end of the chapter for you to check your work.

TABLE 9.11 ■ Program Evaluation	
Study	Atkins, R. C., & Atkins, V. (2010). *An evaluation of the school lunch initiative.* University of California at Berkley. https://www.schoollunchinitiative.org/downloads/sli_eval_full_report_2010.pdf

Guiding Questions

1. Who are the stakeholders for this program evaluation?
2. What are the overall goals of the program evaluation?
3. What were key findings?
4. What were key recommendations?
5. How did the authors present information visually?

Table of Contents

Stakeholders

Goals

Findings

Recommendations

Figures and Graphs

THE TAKEAWAY

Program evaluators share findings to clients, sponsors, and/or stakeholders with reports. These reports should be created with the audience in mind.

ETHICAL CONSIDERATIONS

LEARNING OBJECTIVE	
9.6	Demonstrate knowledge of ethical issues when engaging in program evaluations.

Oversight in the field of program evaluation is reflective of high quality, ethical work. In the United States, a prominent organization providing guidelines for the process of program evaluation is the Joint Committee on Standards for Educational Evaluation (2022). The organization, composed of representatives from professional organizations and subject matter experts, created a series of standards for program evaluations, which are utilized in the United States and Canada. There are five standards, including utility (standards starting with "U"), feasibility (standards starting with "F"), propriety (standards starting with "P"), accuracy (standards starting with "A"), and evaluation accountability (standards starting with "E") as shown in Table 9.12.

TABLE 9.12 ■ Description of Standards by the Joint Committee on Standards for Educational Evaluation		
Standard	**Description**	**Standard Example**
Utility: Making use of services to the greatest extent to meet individual needs	Utility refers to providing evaluation services that can be utilized to the greatest extent to meet individual needs.	U2 Attention to Stakeholders. Evaluations should devote attention to the full range of individuals and groups invested in the program and affected by its evaluation.
Feasibility: Maximize program effectiveness and efficiency	The focus of the feasibility standard is to maximize program effectiveness and efficiency.	F2 Practical Procedures. Evaluation procedures should be practical and responsive to the way the program operates.
Accuracy: Relates to the dependability and trustworthiness of evaluation findings	Accuracy relates to the dependability and trustworthiness of evaluation findings.	A6 Sound Designs and Analysis. Evaluations should employ technically adequate designs and analyses that are appropriate for the evaluation purposes.
Evaluation accountability: Providing documentation that soundly supports evaluation processes, products, and outcomes	In terms of evaluation accountability, evaluators are able to provide documentation that soundly supports evaluation processes, products, and findings.	E1 Evaluation Documentation. Evaluations should fully document their negotiated purposes and implemented designs, procedures, data, and outcomes.
Propriety: Imparting services that provide fair, legal, right, and just evaluations	When considering propriety, the evaluator focuses on providing services that provide fair, legal, right, and just evaluations.	P3 Human Rights and Respect. Evaluations should be designed and conducted to protect human and legal rights and maintain the dignity of participants and other stakeholders.

Utility refers to making use of services to the greatest extent to meet individual needs. A sample standard that falls under the general utility standard includes the following: "Evaluations should devote attention to the full range of individuals and groups invested in the program and affected by its evaluation." This consideration refers to meeting the needs of all individuals in the target population of the evaluand. For this reason, the model, methods, and procedures utilized capture the factors and impacts for all individuals.

The focus of the feasibility standard is to maximize program effectiveness and efficiency. A sample standard that reflects this goal is "Evaluation procedures should be practical and responsive to the way the program operates." When evaluators develop a program model, considering how to gather the necessary data and information in an expedient way without overly impacting the daily operations in an evaluand would be indicative of feasibility. Further, the evaluator considers whether a program can be implemented with the context and structure of one's existing role.

Accuracy (in program evaluation) relates to the dependability and trustworthiness of evaluation findings. In this regard, "Evaluations should employ technically adequate designs and analyses that are appropriate for the evaluation purposes." Addressing elements represents the topics of program theory, logic models, methods, analysis and interpretations, and reporting findings as outlined in this chapter. With the ultimate goal of improving practices, accuracy is necessary in creating valid and trustworthy interpretations.

To maintain evaluation accountability, evaluators are able to provide documentation that soundly supports evaluation processes, products, and outcomes. In this way, findings are substantiated with detailed and extensive organization of data information and analysis and interpretations. A sample standard of evaluation accountability includes the following: "Evaluations should fully document their negotiated purposes and implemented designs, procedures, data, and outcomes."

When considering propriety, the evaluator focuses on imparting services that provide fair, legal, right, and just evaluations. This standard reflects considerations utilized for research design as well. An example evaluation standard for propriety is "Evaluations should be designed and conducted to protect human and legal rights and maintain the dignity of participants and other stakeholders." These standards are reflective of the Belmont Principles utilized in research as well as program evaluations.

Upholding the principles of the *Belmont Report* (U.S. Department of Health and Human Resources, 2022), respect for persons, beneficence, and justice are underlying considerations in program evaluations. These guidelines for ethical principles, commissioned in 1974 by the National Commission for the Protection of Human Subjects, create a framework for ethical research and evaluation.

Respect for persons describes the need to obtain permissions for individuals to participate in studies and to maintain privacy. This principle is particularly relevant for program evaluations, which center on issues within specific social organizations. For this reason, when reporting findings, the evaluator needs to be aware that the presentation of information requires that individuals in the organization cannot decipher personally identifiable information about other participants. This issue is not as large of a concern when reviewing information on an aggregate level (e.g., quantitative data on students receiving free and reduced level). However, when analyzing data at a smaller level (e.g., individual performance or qualitative data), changing descriptive information may be necessary (e.g., gender, role). For instance, there may be an instructor who has unique characteristics in contrast to the other individuals in the educational setting, such as the only male in the organization. In this case, the evaluator would want to be careful not to describe the information in a way that this individual's responses could be easily identified by others in the organization.

In addition, in some instances it may be best to remove information that could be harmful or jeopardize someone's position in the community (e.g., a controversial statement that could affect continued employment). This strategy would reflect beneficence where steps are taken to ensure there is no harm to participants. Finally, justice refers to ensuring that the members of a target population have equal opportunities to access services and would be relevant to identifying target populations.

It is generally required that organizations seek approval from the institutional review board (IRB) through a university or research department approval in a local school district. Nonprofit groups without affiliations may file for private IRB approval with organizations such as WCG IRG (wcgirb.com). It is possible that a program evaluation could be exempt from IRB oversight; however, checking approval guidelines is advisable.

While the program evaluation standards provided by the Joint Committee on Program Evaluations is widely known by program evaluators in North America, there are additional guidelines provided by specific organizations. For instance, the National Policy Board for Educational Administration outlines key considerations of program evaluation specifically for district and building leaders (2015).

THE TAKEAWAY

Based on the Joint Committee on Program Evaluations, ethical standards relate to utility, feasibility, accuracy, evaluation accountability, and propriety. These ethical standards are integral to the framework of a program evaluation.

AMERICAN PSYCHOLOGICAL ASSOCIATION STYLE

LEARNING OBJECTIVE

9.7   Utilize the *Publication Manual of the American Psychological Association* in reporting and presenting findings in program evaluation.

The guidelines for the use of APA style are similar in both program evaluation and research, with the notable exception of the use of color. For professional research studies, the use of color based on APA style is generally reserved for tables and figures, which are not discernible without color. However, the needs of a program evaluation require that color runs throughout the report. Color is useful in guiding the audience to read through a lengthy document, maintain focus and continuity as someone is reading, and provides clarity for tables and figures. For this reason, the use of color throughout the program evaluation report is appropriate.

When selecting color, consider the use of a color palette. Include a limited number of colors in the palette to create consistency. If the organization has a logo, utilize this design feature and corresponding palette in the evaluation. To account for individuals who have color blindness, avoid using greens and reds together in the image as individuals perceive shades of brown. See Table 9.13.

TABLE 9.13   ■   Checklist for Using Color in Program Evaluation Reports

1. Does the organization have a logo that could be utilized in the report?

2. Is there a color palette that corresponds with the organization's logo?

3. Has the color palette been used with consistency across the report?

4. Have a limited number of colors been selected from the palette?

5. Are there any figures that include red and green?

THE TAKEAWAY

Program evaluation reports contain visuals, graphs, and tables following a color palette. These elements help the audience to read the many components of the evaluation.

CHAPTER SUMMARY

Program evaluations are as diversified as the evaluands under study. Evaluators work closely with clients, evaluation sponsors, and stakeholders to develop evaluation designs that will inform decision making. The findings of the program evaluations center on making suggestions to improve programs, curriculum, and logistical processes. This chapter provided a broad spectrum of information on the differences between program evaluation and research studies; the types and purposes of program evaluation; and methods for planning, conducting, and reporting findings. Many variations of these guidelines are appropriate as the program evaluation design is custom-built for specific purposes.

In educational settings, the use of a program evaluation is an effective tool to monitor the worth and merit of educational initiatives, logistical procedures, and teacher professional development, as some examples. When designed and conducted effectively, the findings from a program evaluation can result in efficiency, better allocation of funds and resources, and improved services for students.

EXTENSION ACTIVITIES

You Do It! 9.1

Self-Directed Practice: Identifying Evaluation Questions Based on Merit and Worth

The purpose of this exercise is to identify evaluation questions based on merit and worth. Remember, merit refers to programs that add value to an organization (intrinsic value), whereas worth describes the utility of a program and its impact on a larger community (extrinsic value). After reviewing Table 9.2, consider an evaluand that you are familiar with that could be a topic for a program evaluation. Based on this topic, create evaluation questions based on merit and worth. Provide a rationale for why each question represents either merit or worth.

Evaluation Question	Merit (intrinsic value)	Worth (extrinsic value)

You Do It! 9.2

Self-Directed Practice: Identifying the Components of a Program Evaluation

In this chapter, we reviewed how to identify components of a program evaluation. Locate a program evaluation of a topic of interest. Use the following guide sheet to identify the components of a program evaluation. As a follow-up, share the components with a classmate.

Study
Type of Program Evaluation
Evaluand
Purpose
Data Collection Tools
Data Analysis
Findings
Recommendations

You Do It! 9.3

Self-Directed Practice: Creating a Logic Model

Using a topic that you would be interested in studying for a program evaluation, consider the elements of a logic model. First review the decision-tree diagram Figure 9.15. Then complete the corresponding decision-tree guide sheet. Then, create a draft logic model with the template (Figure 9.16).

FIGURE 9.15 ■ Decision Tree

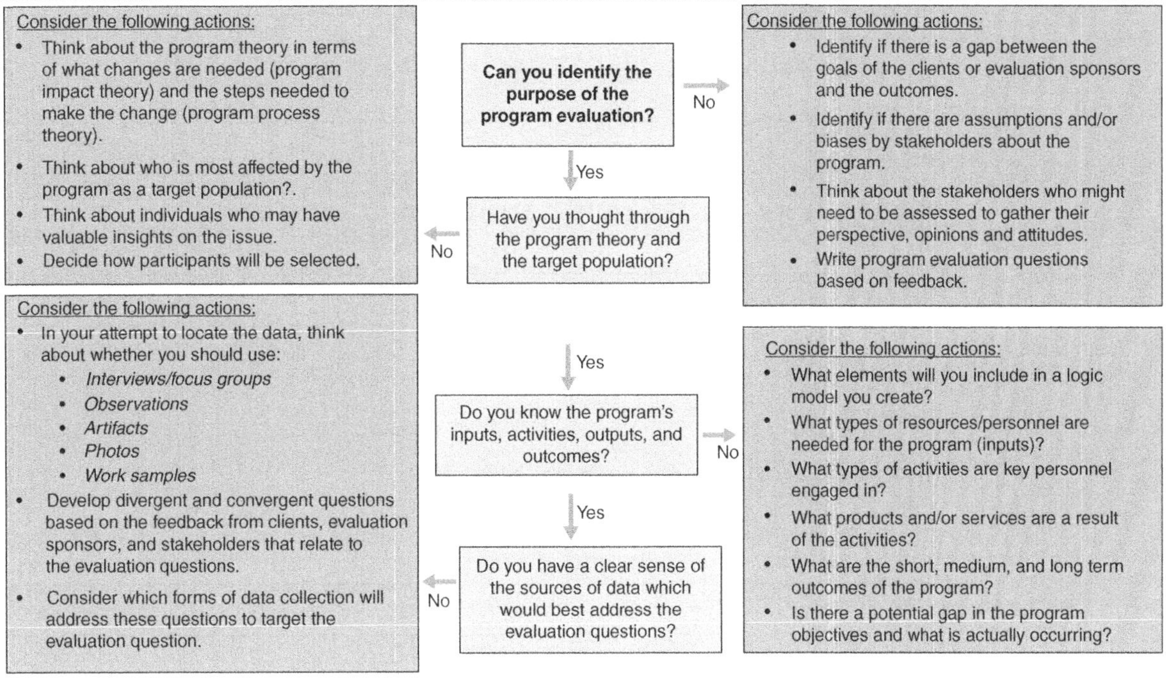

Consider the following actions:
- Think about the program theory in terms of what changes are needed (program impact theory) and the steps needed to make the change (program process theory).
- Think about who is most affected by the program as a target population?.
- Think about individuals who may have valuable insights on the issue.
- Decide how participants will be selected.

Can you identify the purpose of the program evaluation? No

Yes

Have you thought through the program theory and the target population? No

Consider the following actions:
- Identify if there is a gap between the goals of the clients or evaluation sponsors and the outcomes.
- Identify if there are assumptions and/or biases by stakeholders about the program.
- Think about the stakeholders who might need to be assessed to gather their perspective, opinions and attitudes.
- Write program evaluation questions based on feedback.

Consider the following actions:
- In your attempt to locate the data, think about whether you should use:
  - Interviews/focus groups
  - Observations
  - Artifacts
  - Photos
  - Work samples
- Develop divergent and convergent questions based on the feedback from clients, evaluation sponsors, and stakeholders that relate to the evaluation questions.
- Consider which forms of data collection will address these questions to target the evaluation question.

Yes

Do you know the program's inputs, activities, outputs, and outcomes? No

Yes

Do you have a clear sense of the sources of data which would best address the evaluation questions? No

Consider the following actions:
- What elements will you include in a logic model you create?
- What types of resources/personnel are needed for the program (inputs)?
- What types of activities are key personnel engaged in?
- What products and/or services are a result of the activities?
- What are the short, medium, and long term outcomes of the program?
- Is there a potential gap in the program objectives and what is actually occurring?

You Do It! 9.4

Self-Directed Practice: Creating a Logic Model Worksheet

Guiding Questions

Purpose and Evaluation Questions

What is the nature of the critical issue you want to examine?

How would your idea contribute to understanding the merit and worth of the evaluation program?

Can you create any specific evaluation questions that relate to the critical issue?

Background

Are there gaps between the goals of the clients or evaluation sponsors and the outcomes?

_____

_____

_____

Have the assumptions and potential biases of stakeholders been identified?

_____

_____

_____

Program Theory

What changes need to be made (program impact theory)?

_____

_____

_____

What steps will need to occur to make the change (program process theory)?

_____

_____

_____

Logic Model

What elements will you include in a logic model that you create?

_____

_____

_____

What are some underlying assumptions and external factors?

_____

_____

_____

What types of resources/personnel are needed for the program (inputs)?

_____

_____

_____

What type of activities are key personnel engaged with?

_____

_____

_____

What products and/or services are a result of the activities?

_____

_____

_____

What are the short-, medium-, and long-term outcomes of the program?

_____

_____

_____

Is there a potential gap in the program objectives, and what is actually occurring?

_____

_____

_____

Data Collection Tools

Who are the sources of data for the program evaluation?

_____

_____

_____

What are the types of data that will be used for the evaluation?

_____

_____

_____

What types of selected response (convergent questions) and constructed response (divergent questions) will help to address the overarching evaluation questions?

_____

_____

_____

Self-Directed Practice: Creating a Logic Model Template

FIGURE 9.16 ■ **Logic Model Template**

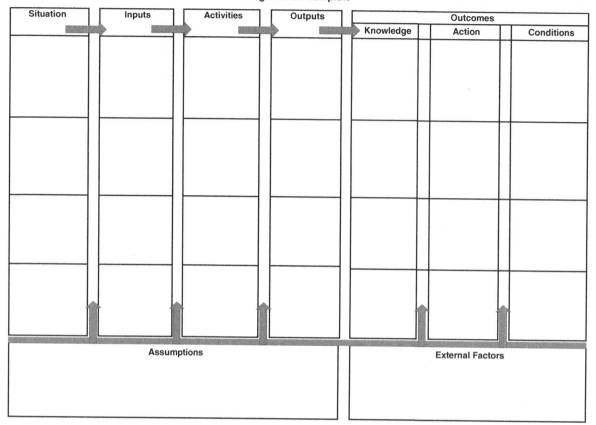

Logic Model Template

Guiding Questions for Data Analysis

1. What type of software can be used to analyze the data?

2. What type of graph will best display the data?

3. What features will be included in the graph to assist readers?

4. What will be the title of the graph?

5. What will be the axes (x and y) labels?

Data Analysis

Guiding Questions for Interpretation

1. What does the graph show about the limitations of using the outdoor classroom?

2. What are some important features of the graph to describe.

3. What do these findings mean in terms of addressing the evaluation question?

Interpretation

Self-Directed Practice: Analyzing a Program Evaluation Report

In this chapter, we addressed the major components of program evaluation reports and guidelines for formatting and reporting information. Locate a program evaluation on a topic of interest. Complete the following worksheet, and then share an overview with classmates.

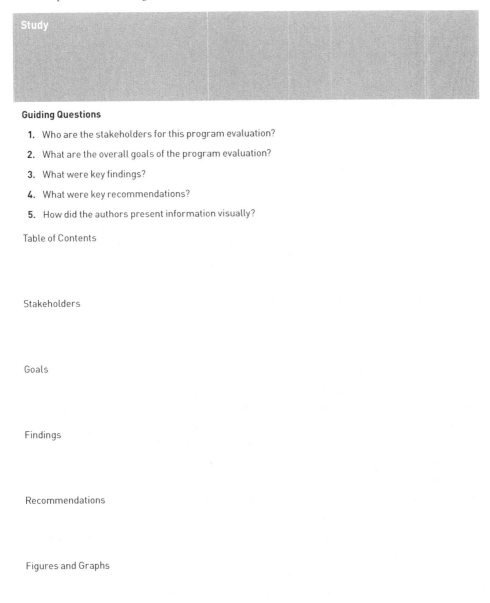

Study

Guiding Questions

1. Who are the stakeholders for this program evaluation?

2. What are the overall goals of the program evaluation?

3. What were key findings?

4. What were key recommendations?

5. How did the authors present information visually?

Table of Contents

Stakeholders

Goals

Findings

Recommendations

Figures and Graphs

KEY TERMS

Accuracy (in program evaluation)

Activities

Assessment (in program theory)

Audience

Client

Collaborative evaluation

Consumer-oriented evaluation

Constructed response questions

Cost-benefit analysis

Cost-effectiveness analysis

Context evaluation

Empowerment evaluation

Evaluand

Evaluation accountability

Evaluation sponsor

Expertise-oriented evaluation

Feasibility

Formative evaluation

Independent evaluation

Input evaluation

Inputs

Logic model

Management-oriented evaluation

Merit

Object

Objectives-oriented evaluation

Outputs

Outcomes

Participant-oriented evaluation

Post-assessment

Pre-assessment

Process evaluation

Product evaluation

Propriety

Program evaluation

Program impact theory

Program process theory

Program theory

Selected response questions

Social structure

Stakeholders

Summative evaluation

Utility

Worth

ANSWER KEY

Stop and Think Activities

STOP AND THINK 9.1

There are many possible options to answer Stop and Think #1. The purpose of the evaluation could be to conduct a needs assessment to see if there is a need for the product. Another option would be a consumer-oriented evaluation to determine the worth and merit of a program (e.g., such as a math-based program). Clients typically commission the evaluation, whereas stakeholders have a vested interest in the program. An audience member may not be directly impacted by the program; however, they are interested in the findings. A teacher learning about the benefits of a math-based program at a school staff member would be an example of a stakeholder.

STOP AND THINK 9.2

There are many issues to consider when reflecting on a program or initiative within a school program. Possible options would include the overall goals of the program, the target population, personnel and resources, processes to run the initiative, costs, and impacts as some examples.

STOP AND THINK 9.3

This topic varies based on the social structure of each educational institution. An example would be a school that adopts a Wednesday afternoon club initiative. The administrator's goal is to provide social time for students and capitalize on student interest in hobbies. In this club, each block on Wednesdays would be shortened to provide time for clubs. While this idea may seem to be beneficial, a needs assessment may be conducted to see if the students need/want to attend clubs as well as the impact on student achievement for shortened class periods. This type of needs assessment would be conducted prior to launching the initiative. Possible factors could include student interest for the program, the impact on teacher planning, lack of by-in from teachers, and parental support for the program. Possible stakeholders include students, teachers, administrators, teacher assistants, counselors, and parents.

Stop and Think 9.4

The response to this question varies based on the context. For example, a school that is considering a computer-assisted program in mathematics may want to conduct a consumer-oriented evaluation. An increase in school absenteeism across a district may require an expertise-oriented evaluation. Another example would be a district interested in creating a teacher to principal pipeline through leadership training. In this case, a participant-oriented evaluation may yield information about the best way to support individuals through this transition.

A possible evaluand in a school could be a peer-mentoring program. Students who are trained in conflict resolution serve as mentors when two students have a dispute. This type of program is often run by counselors who train students, attend sessions, and monitor student interactions and outcomes. In this case, a participant-oriented evaluation would be appropriate to evaluate the impact of the program from the perspective of students, teachers, counselors, and administrators.

Let's Do It! Activities
Let's Do It! 9.1
Guided Practice: Identifying Evaluation Questions Based on Merit and Worth

The purpose of this exercise it to identify evaluation questions based on merit and worth. Remember, merit refers to programs that add value to an organization (intrinsic value), whereas worth describes the utility of a program and its impact on a larger community (extrinsic value). After reviewing Table 9.2, consider a school district that wants to implement workshops on improving instruction in the outdoor classroom. Following are a series of evaluation questions. Identify whether the questions are examples of merit or worth and provide the rationale. To guide your thinking, we encourage you to use the *Let's See It!* Table 9.2.

Evaluation Question	Merit (intrinsic value)	Worth (extrinsic value)
How effectively are teachers able to utilize the strategies from the outdoor classroom workshops?	Merit: This question relates to merit as the goal and is to determine if training is translating to effective practices as a form of intrinsic worth to the school district.	
Will the outdoor classroom workshops be worth the financial costs associated with program implementation?		Worth: In this case, the emphasis is on the value of the program associated with the costs that are allocated.

(Continued)

Evaluation Question	Merit (intrinsic value)	Worth (extrinsic value)
Are the outdoor classroom workshops leading to increased student achievement?	Merit: Targeting student achievement reflects merit. In other words, "Is this program any good?"	
Has there been increased enrollment in the environmental science course with the implementation of outdoor classroom workshops?		Worth: Increased enrollment reflects the value of the program to support students in ways that would help the community at large.

LET'S DO IT! 9.2

Guided Practice: Identifying the Components of a Program Evaluation

The objective of this activity is to identify the types and purposes of program evaluation designs. Identify the components of the program evaluation using the guide sheet as a *Let's Do It!* activity. To guide your thinking, we encourage you to use the *Let's See It!* Table 9.5 and the program evaluation article by Berk (2018) on out-of-school academic support.

Study	Berk, S. (2018). Assessment of public schools' out-of-school time academic support programs with participant-oriented evaluation. *Journal of Education and Learning, 7*(3), 159–175. https://doi.org/10.5539/jel.v7n3p159
Type of Program Evaluation	Participant-oriented approach.
Evaluand	The evaluand was an out-of-school, academic support program known as the Out-of-School Time Academic (OSTAS) program, which took place in public schools in Turkey.
Purpose	The purpose of the evaluation program was to determine if the OSTAS programs were effective in meeting the needs of students as well as running efficiently.
Data Collection Tools	Surveys were administered to teachers, administrators, students in and not in OSTAS, and parents. Participants took one of five surveys, which included selected response (close-ended questions) and constructed response (open-ended questions) items. The measures included (a) the Administrator Questionnaire, (b) the Teacher Questionnaire, (c) Attending Student Questionnaire, (d) the Non-attending Student Questionnaire, and (e) the Parent Questionnaire.
Data Analysis	Analysis for constructed response item (close-ended) questions involved frequency and percentages. For selected response items (open-ended), participant responses underwent content analysis.
Findings	Findings revealed that there was adequate administrative support for the OSTAS program; however, administrators indicated that charging a normal fee would encourage students to take the program seriously. Teachers generally had less understanding of the concepts taught and the rationale for the program, while students were not invested in the program. Although participating students saw benefits to the program, findings revealed that student input was not part of the program design.

Recommendations

The recommendation is that at each institution, student perspectives should be taken into account when developing OSTAS. Students should be encouraged to take responsibility and ownership for learning, and higher quality resources would improve instructional delivery. Further, logistical issues related to transportation required attention. Each institution should create contingency plans to deal with absenteeism and low motivation on the part of students.

LET'S DO IT! 9.3

Guided Practice: Creating a Logic Model

The purpose of this activity is to practice analyzing examples of logic models so as to subsequently create logic models. Figure 9.11 shows a WonderBox logic model (Sharp & Mason, 2021) created for the Mississippi Children's Museum. The evaluand for this model is WonderBox, a makerspace platform where students can collaborate to do STEM projects ((Mississippi Children's Museum, 2023). To guide your thinking, we encourage you to use the *Let's See It!* Figure 9.12 and Table 9.7. Then review the logic model that follows and answer the corresponding questions in Table 9.8.

Questions on WonderBox Logic Model	
Program objectives: The WonderBox gallery (Mississippi Children's Museum, 2023) is a makerspace exhibit to facilitate hands-on exploration related to innovations, tinkering, and STEAM.	
Question	**Response**
How will the inputs in this situation support the Mississippi Children's Museum's WonderBox program?	The inputs focus on financial resources; museum resources and logistics (e.g., space, staff, volunteers, exhibits); needs of attendees; and collaborative partnerships. These inputs are central to providing services for student learning.
What activities support the program?	The activities fall into three categories: hands-on, facilitated sessions for children; self-directed, hands-on activities in the museum; and professional development for teachers.
What are some short-term outcomes?	To motivate interest for STEAM and an awareness of Mississippi STEAM innovations. For students, there will be stronger self-efficacy for STEAM and a platform to use creativity. Teachers will be more self-efficacious in facilitating makerspaces.
What are some long-term outcomes?	WonderBox becomes a leader of makerspaces with support from policy makers. Families and children utilize the WonderBox as a resource to upload creations on social media. Teachers will increase the use of makerspaces for instruction, and children will develop an interest for STEAM careers.
How do the program outcomes align with the program objectives?	The outcomes generally align with the objective of facilitating hands-on exploration related to innovations, tinkering, and STEAM.

LET'S DO IT! 9.4

Guided Practice: Analyzing and Interpreting Data Based on an Evaluation Question

The purpose of this activity is to practice analyzing and interpreting data from a program evaluation on the use of an outdoor classroom with quantitative data. To guide your thinking, we encourage you to use the *Let's See It!* Table 9.8.

Evaluation Question: Is the outdoor classroom being underutilized?

Selected Response Question on Survey: Outdoor classroom limitations: This section will help to identify limitations in using the outdoor classroom. Please rank the limitations of using the outdoor classroom from (1) not a limiting factor, (2) limiting factor, (3) extreme limiting factor

Limitation	1	2	3
Time			
Testing requirements			
Lack of materials			
Difficulty in reaching the outdoor classroom			
Lack of lesson plans			
Limited environmental training experiences			
Subject area does not lend itself to outdoor experiences			
Lack of technology available outside			

Quantitative Data

	Not a Limiting Factor	Limiting Factor	Extreme Limiting Factor	No Response
Time	17	50	33	0
Testing requirements	27	58	15	0
Lack of materials	23	56	21	0
Difficulty in reaching . . .	60	33	8	0
Lack of lesson plans	13	65	19	2
Limited training	17	65	15	2
Subject area does not . . .	46	33	21	0
Lack of technology . . .	44	35	19	2

Guiding Questions for Data Analysis

1. *What type of software can be used to analyze the data?* Excel

2. *What type of graph will best display the data?* This example uses a bar graph; however, other options include pie charts and/or box and whisker plots.

3. *What features will be included in the graph to assist readers?* Title, labeled axes legend, and data labels.

4. *What will be the title of the graph?* Limitations

5. *What will be the axes (x and y) labels?* Factors and Number (responses)

Data Analysis

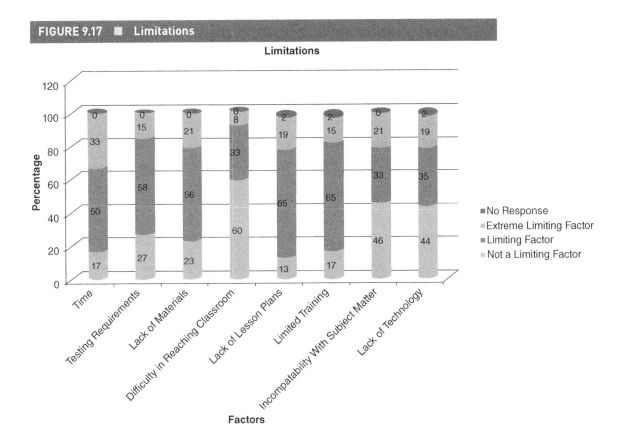

FIGURE 9.17 ■ Limitations

Guiding Questions for Interpretation

1. *What does the graph in Figure 9.17 show about the limitations of using the outdoor classroom?* Notice that the greatest limitations related to the light blue and light green columns. Compare the image with actual data.

2. *What are some important features of the graph to describe?* For this graph, it is helpful to include a key and labeled axes.

3. *What do these findings mean in terms of addressing the evaluation question?* Future resources should be allocated to train teachers and provide lessons for the outdoor classroom.

Interpretation

When it comes to limitations of using the outdoor classroom, the greatest barriers are lack of training (80% extreme and limiting factor) and lesson plans (84% extreme and limiting factor).

Some teachers felt that they could not allocate instructional time outside (83% extreme and limiting). These limitations prevent teachers from utilizing the outdoor classroom fully.

LET'S DO IT! 9.5

Guided Practice: Analyzing a Program Evaluation Report

The objective of this activity is for you to independently practice reviewing a program evaluation and identify the key features emphasized in this chapter. Complete the worksheet that follows, using Table 9.9 to guide your thinking on a school lunch initiative.

Analyzing a Program Evaluation Report

Guiding Questions (see answers in the table below.)

1. Who are the stakeholders for this program evaluation?
2. What are the overall goals of the program evaluation?
3. What were key findings?
4. What were key recommendations?
5. How did the authors present information visually?

Study	Atkins, R. C., & Atkins, V. (2010). *An evaluation of the school lunch initiative.* University of California at Berkley. https://www.schoollunchinitiative.org/downloads/sli_eval_full_report_2010.pdf
Table of Contents	The table of contents starts with a summary of findings, an introduction, and the evaluation design. Fine-grained details related to each evaluation question follows in the sequence of topics.
Stakeholders	Members of the Chez Panisse Foundation, the Center for Ecoliteracy, and the Berkeley Unified School District.
Goals	To examine in what ways the School Lunch Initiative would influence students' knowledge of food and nutrition, attitudes toward healthy eating and environmental stewardship, and decision making with food selection.
Findings	The School Lunch Initiative positively influenced students' knowledge and attitudes about food and nutrition, eating habits, and knowledge of environmental impacts related to food choices.
Recommendations	Integrate garden and cooking classes with hands-on learning environments, include parents and community members in programs, encourage changes in the quality of food brought from home, increase children's physical activity in the classes.
Figures and Graphs	Figures and graphs appeared throughout the text to support the discussion.

©iStockphoto.com/LumiNola

10 SAMPLING AND MEASUREMENT

LEARNING OBJECTIVES

Upon completion of this chapter, students should be able to

10.1 Define sampling-related terminology

10.2 Describe probability and non-probability sampling techniques

10.3 Compare sampling across quantitative, qualitative, mixed methods, and action research

10.4 Clarify the difference between measurement and measurement error in research

10.5 Differentiate between levels of measurement

10.6 Describe different types of validity in measurement

10.7 Describe different types of reliability in measurement

10.8 Demonstrate knowledge of ethical issues when collecting, managing, and communicating information on sampling and measurement

10.9 Utilize the *Publication Manual of the American Psychological Association* when reporting information on sampling and measurement

A DAY AT WORK

Measuring the Unique Abilities of Exceptional Learners!

©iStockphoto.com/Prostock-Studio

Mrs. Riegler is a second-grade general education teacher in a suburban city who has been teaching at an elementary school for almost 10 years. Her school district places a heavy emphasis on inclusion programs for students who are diagnosed with multiple disabilities. Prior to the start of the school year, Mrs. Riegler was introduced to Myron, a new student in her class. He had been diagnosed with oppositional defiant disorder (ODD) and attention deficit hyperactivity disorder (ADHD). Myron's Individualized Education Plan (IEP) shows he was barely meeting grade level reading; however, his testing scores have shown him to be gifted in oral comprehension and mathematics. To find the most developmentally appropriate instruction for Myron, Mrs. Riegler needs to assess and evaluate Myron's current reading level, which has proven to be a challenge due to his acting out. Many of Myron's previous teachers and counselors have been cautious around him because he has frequent anger and defiant outbursts, which include becoming irritated or lashing out. Myron's IEP team wants to develop a plan to help him manage his behavior and to build rapport; however, how should they approach data collection to adequately understand the behavior and needs of this individual student?

INTRODUCTION

Sampling is a critical component of research. Researchers must ensure that the sample of research participants selected is appropriate for the type of research study being conducted, the goals of the research, and the research questions being answered (see Figure 10.1). If the sample is not appropriately representative of the population the researchers wish to study, researchers may not be able to effectively understand and make generalizations about the population. Another important issue is that researchers must make sure the measurement instruments used to assess the sample are psychometrically strong and appropriate for that sample. Thus, it is important for educators as researchers to be able to make informed choices about who to include in the study and how to approach assessing that sample. In this chapter, we describe sampling techniques across quantitative, qualitative, mixed methods, and action research designs. We also discuss important measurement-related concepts such as levels of measurement, validity, and reliability. The final portion of this chapter focuses on ethical issues in sampling, measurement, ethics, and reporting in APA style.

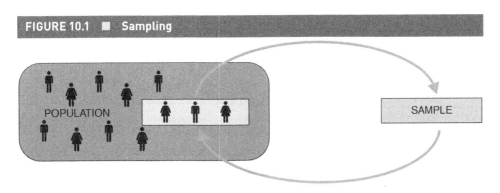

FIGURE 10.1 ■ Sampling

POPULATION

SAMPLE

SAMPLING-RELATED TERMINOLOGY

LEARNING OBJECTIVE

10.1   Define sampling-related terminology

Define Sampling in Research

The goal of many types of research is to understand a population by using a sample. The target population (or the sampling frame) is defined as the entire group of individuals that represent who the researcher wishes to understand and make generalizations (e.g., students who are twice exceptional). All members of the population are connected in some way, or share similar characteristics. For example, students who are twice exceptional are all gifted learners who have been clinically diagnosed with a learning disability. Therefore, when conducting research, the sample, or a subset of individuals taken from the population, is used to represent the population of interest. In most situations, the members of the sample are referred to as participants.

This process involving the selection of participants to represent the population in a particular study is called sampling. Decisions on who to include in the sample are based on about whom the researcher would like to be able to make generalizations. When effective sampling procedures are used, researchers can then generalize from samples to the population, even if not everyone from the population participated in the study. When sampling for a study, it is important to begin by fully understanding the population of interest and the total set of characteristics, or parameters, that are represented within that population. A population parameter is a numerical value that describes a characteristic of the population (e.g., age, biological sex, level of education, socioeconomic status). Any numerical value that is computed from a sample is then called a sample statistic (e.g., averages, medians, standard deviations). However, in many cases, the population parameter and sampling statistic may not be the exact same thing; therefore, a sampling error is calculated to indicate the difference between the sample statistic and the population parameter. Thus, **sampling error** is the difference between the sample mean and the population mean on one or more characteristics or variables. A good sampling technique serves to ensure that the sample is properly representative of the variation included within the population. When the sample mean is less than the population mean, the sampling error will be displayed as a negative number. When the sample mean is greater than the population mean, the sampling error will be positive (i.e., an overestimate). If the sampling error is calculated as zero, then this indicates the two means are equal. Researchers understand that regardless of the sampling approach, the sample will never be identical to the population across all characteristics. In essence, there will be sampling error.

Let's return to our opening scenario for an illustrative example. Perhaps the school psychologist at Myron's school would like to draw inferences about the twice exceptional population (learners who are considered gifted and talented but also are considered for special education services) at the school district. Let's say there are 20 students who have been identified as twice exceptional. Those 20 students represent the population the school psychologist is interested in learning more about. Because it is probably not feasible for her to survey or interview all 20 students, she randomly selects a sample of five of those students to be included as participants in her study. A population parameter that might be used for students that are twice exceptional is that, similar to Myron, they may be clinically diagnosed with a learning disability or portray behavioral challenges in the classroom, but they tend to be high scorers on specific subject tests (e.g., math, science) in comparison to their peers within the classroom. An example of a sample statistic then would be the average test scores of these students—specifically in our scenario, the school psychologist might measure behavior and math test scores in their sample and calculate a sample statistic that can be used to generalize and estimate that population parameter. However, it is important to keep in mind that although the population and sample have similar characteristics, they also carry unique characteristics that could impact the research such as socioeconomic status, behavioral disorders, type of learning disability, and age. Understanding these characteristics of a population will give researchers an important roadmap for selecting a sample that adequately represents that population. In other words, when the sample exhibits the same characteristics of the population, we can say the sample is effectively representative of that population. Researchers can only generalize (i.e., apply) the results from a sample to a population if that sample is truly representative of that population.

STOP AND THINK 10.1

Take a moment to think why obtaining a representative sample is important.

Sampling Terminology

Statistical terminology in sampling can be depicted in one of two ways—either with words or with a dedicated symbol. Statistical symbols are commonly used in research to help communicate findings to the research community in a way that is efficient and universally understood. Generally, italicized Greek and Roman letters are used to depict specific terms in American Psychological Association (APA) style. For terminology and statistics that refer to the population, researchers primarily use Greek lettering. For example, the symbol μ (mu) represents the population mean, and the symbol σ (sigma) represents the population standard deviation. For sample terminology and statistics, researchers emphasize Roman lettering. For example, *SD* represents the sample standard deviation, and *r* represents the sample correlation. In Table 10.1, we provide specific details about some of the more commonly used statistical notations for the population and sample.

TABLE 10.1 ■ Common Statistical Symbols

Population		Sample	
Statistical Symbol	**Meaning**	**Statistical Symbol**	**Meaning**
μ	Population Mean	$\bar{X}$ or M	Sample Mean
Σ	Standard Deviation of a population	s or SD	Standard deviation of a sample
σ^2	Variance of a population	s^2	Variance of a sample
μ	Mean of a population	SD	Standard Deviation of a sample
ρ	Correlation coefficient of a population	r	Correlation coefficient of a sample
N	The number of elements in a population	n	The number of elements in a sample

Sample Size

In research, sample size (*n*) is the number of individuals selected from a population for participation in a study. As we have already discussed, the sample generally consists of a subset or small handful of all individuals from a particular population. After deciding how the sample will be collected (e.g., probability or random sampling, or non-probability sampling [which we will talk about later in the chapter]), determining an appropriate sample size for the goals of the study can be a bit more challenging.

It is important for research to include a sufficiently sized sample. A large sample is ideal for several reasons: it allows researchers to draw credible generalizations about the population from which the sample is drawn (a larger sample provides a greater quantity of information and represents more individual differences within the population); it can help improve the representation of the population, increase the statistical power of a study, and provide greater opportunities for complex data analyses. The sample size required for a particular study is dependent on the design of the study and can be determined by conducting a power analysis prior to beginning the study. A power analysis is a systematic approach used to identify an appropriate sample size through the order of magnitude. Generally, a sample size of 30 participants per variable is recommended for correlational research: 12 participants in each group for experimental studies where an intervention is implemented and 350 for studies with an administration of surveys. Overall, your power analysis will vary based on the unique characteristics of your study. Having a study design with multiple groups or categories would require a larger sample size to ensure that each group/category is represented adequately. Generally speaking, the larger the sample the better able researchers are to draw accurate conclusions about the population.

STOP AND THINK 10.2

A seventh-grade mathematics teacher is interested in examining the relationship between homework completion and performance on tests among struggling students who have Individualized Education Programs (IEPs). The teacher begins by defining the school as the population, and from there, the teacher takes a random sample of students on IEPs from all seventh-grade mathematics classrooms. Is this sample a good, generalizable representation of the target population?

The following *Let's See It!* and *Let's Do It!* activities will help you think about important issues in sampling and why it is so important for researchers to be able to make informed sampling decisions before initiating data collection. Read through the following scenario and answers to key sampling questions.

Let's See It! 10.1

Goal: Identify Why Sampling Matters

Read the scenario that follows and then review Table 10.2 to help you think through the importance of proper sampling techniques in a study.

Imagine you are a school psychologist at a local elementary school that takes seriously the issue of inclusivity and integration of students who are twice exceptional into general education classrooms. One of your goals for this academic year is to assess how students who have been identified as gifted and also have an IEP (i.e., learning disability, developmental disability, intellectual disability, etc.) can be better supported. Suppose you had the research expertise to conduct a mixed methods study to address this critical issue. As one component of your study, you decide to survey two groups of students: (1) those with an IEP; and (2) those without an IEP but who are enrolled in a class with students who have one. The survey focuses on perceptions of the needs, feelings, and experiences of students in an integrated classroom environment. An average classroom has about 25 students with anywhere from 2 to 5 students having an IEP. You want both "groups" of students to be equally represented in your study. Suppose you decide to take a random sample from the population of ALL students who attend this elementary school. Does this type of sampling procedure make sense? See Table 10.2 for the answer to this question. How can you go about sampling for your study?

TABLE 10.2 ■ Key Sampling Questions to Consider

Sampling Question	Response
What is the population of interest?	Twice exceptional students at the elementary school—both those with an IEP and those without one.
Are characteristics/individuals equally represented in the population?	No. In a general education classroom of 25 students, anywhere from two to five students are twice exceptional.
Is it important that characteristics/individuals be equally represented in the study?	Yes. The study is designed to better support students with an IEP, but the input of students without an IEP is also important to consider.
Is the proposed sampling approach appropriate for this scenario?	Random sample taken from all students who attend the elementary school would not produce enough twice exceptional students with an IEP to make an adequate comparison because there are significantly fewer students with an IEP at the school compared to those without one.

Let's Do It! 10.1

Guided Practice: Think About Important Sampling Issues in Your Own Study

Think through a critical issue you might like to address in your own classroom or school from the perspective of a student, an educator, or an administrator. After you have a critical issue and population of interest in mind, think about how you might obtain a representative sample from this population to address your critical issue. Fill out Table 10.3 using Table 10.2 and *Let's See It!* 10.1 for guidance, specifically focusing on how each question informs the next. Focus on whether or not the characteristics represented in your population must be equally represented in your study, and your reasoning behind the answers to these questions.

TABLE 10.3 ■ Key Sampling Questions to Consider

Sampling Question	Response
What is the population of interest?	
Are characteristics/individuals equally represented in the population?	
Is it important that characteristics/individuals be equally represented in the study?	
Is the proposed sampling approach appropriate for this scenario?	

PROBABILITY AND NON-PROBABILITY SAMPLING TECHNIQUES

LEARNING OBJECTIVE
10.2   Describe probability and non-probability sampling techniques and sampling error

There are two major classes of sampling to consider when deciding which approach is best for determining your sample for a research project—probability and non-probability sampling. How you choose to sample will depend on your research interests. Will the participants be selected deliberately for their characteristics (e.g., age, sex or gender, disability status)? Are they selected at random from the larger population? Or are the participants selected out of convenience due to limited time and resources of the researcher? In this section, we delve into the differences between probability and non-probability sampling and provide guidance about identifying the most effective approach for your study.

Probability Sampling

Random, or probability sampling occurs when each individual in a population has an equal probability of being selected for inclusion in a sample. Random sampling is the best way to ensure the sample accurately represents the characteristics of the population. This type of sampling is used in quantitative research or in the quantitative portion of mixed methods research. There are two important yet distinct terms to make note of under the umbrella of random sampling: random selection and random assignment. Random selection involves choosing your participants for a study at random from the population, whereas random assignment is when you take your participants and you randomly assign them to the different groups in your study (i.e., experimental group or control group). Overall, probability sampling includes any method that gives an equal opportunity for all members of a population to be selected for a study. There are several types of probability sampling. The four main types include simple random sampling, systematic random sampling, stratified random sampling, and cluster sampling. Figure 10.2 and Table 10.4 briefly summarize these four types of probability sampling. Table 10.4 also provides some examples that will help you understand how these four types of probability sampling techniques differ.

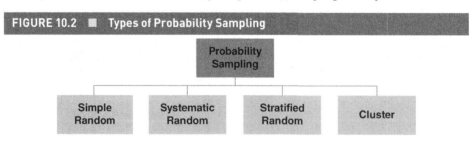

FIGURE 10.2   ■   Types of Probability Sampling

TABLE 10.4   ■   Types of Probability (Random) Sampling

Type	Definition	Example
Simple Random Sampling	A random sampling method where each member of the population has an equal chance of being selected.	Ms. Tabatha Smith, a school psychologist at Myron's school, wants to randomly select five students out of the 20 students who are twice exceptional who attend the school. She writes each student's name on a piece of paper and draws five from a hat.

Type	Definition	Example
Systematic Random Sampling	All members of a population are arranged into a list, and every *n*th person from that list is selected.	Ms. Tabatha Smith takes the list of every student who is twice exceptional at the school and selects every fourth student from the list to participate in a study.
Stratified Random Sampling	A population is divided into groups based on certain characteristics, and participants are randomly selected from within each of those groups.	Ms. Tabatha Smith wants to select five girls and boys (10 total students) out of the students who are twice exceptional at the school. She divides the students into two groups based on biological sex and randomly selects five students from each group.
Cluster Sampling	A researcher selects a random sample of naturally occurring groups (clusters) from a population to include in their study.	Ms. Tabatha Smith randomly selects two classrooms out of the 10 classrooms with students who are twice exceptional at the school and asks every student who is twice exceptional in each of those two classrooms to participate in the study.

STOP AND THINK 10.3

Why do we use the term "random" when describing these techniques? Does it make sense?

Simple Random Sampling

Simple random sampling involves an approach whereby each sampling unit (e.g., single piece of data in a sample—single student within the sample of students) has an equal chance of being chosen. Meaning, each member of the population has an equal chance of being selected for participation in the research, and the selection process is completely random (e.g., picking names or numbers from a hat or a lottery method). Suppose a researcher wants to examine teacher efficacy in mainstreaming students with behavior problems. If the researcher chose to proceed with simple random sampling, then every teacher within that school would have an equal chance to be selected to participate. The researcher could use one of various random procedures, such as randomly picking the names out of a hat, assigning each teacher a number and then randomly selecting those numbers, or utilizing a random number table or generator. The idea is that a simple random sample takes a small, random portion of the entire teacher population wherein each teacher has an equal probability of being selected simply by chance.

Advantages of simple random sampling are that it requires little knowledge of the population in advance and is free of possible classification errors such as correctly identifying the individuals who are being studied to have specific skills to qualify for the study. Further, unlike other probability sampling techniques, the researcher does not need any prior knowledge to implement this sampling strategy. Disadvantages of this method are that it might be challenging to gain access to a list of a larger population, and when a sample set of the larger population is widely diverse, representation of the full population might not be possible and the data collected may not match the sample requirements. Overall, this sampling method is advantageous because it limits human error and subjectivity, assuming that any bias in the targeted population would be equally distributed.

Simple random sampling gives every sampling unit an equal chance of being selected, such as reaching your hand in and pulling a single candy out of a jar.
©iStockphoto.com/fcafotodigital

Systematic Random Sampling

Systematic random sampling is another effective probability sampling technique that involves obtaining a list of every member in the population and selecting every *n*th individual for participation in the study. The sampling interval (i.e., distance between each *n*th term) is calculated by dividing the size of the population (*N*) by the size of the desired sample (*n*), and a random number between one and that value is selected to count off every *n*th individual through the list of all population members. For example, thinking back to the example mentioned for simple random sampling, if you have a population of 20 teachers, but your sample requires five participants, then your *n*th term would be between 1 and 5. From there you would arrange your population of teachers in a line, and select every *n*th teacher in the study. Let's say you chose the number 3, then from your alphabetized list of teachers numbered from 1 through 20, you would choose teachers numbered #3, #6, #9, #12, #15, and #18 from your list to participate in your study (Figure 10.3).

FIGURE 10.3 ■ Systematic Random Sampling

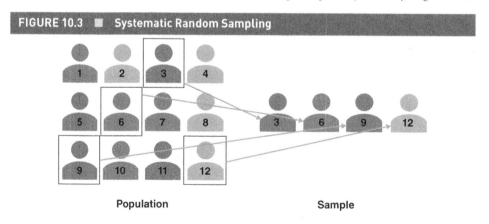

Population   Sample

Systematic Random Sampling (every third person)

An advantage to using systematic random sampling is that it makes the sample easy to select; however, a disadvantage is that any preexisting lists of population members may be organized in a way that makes the list nonrandom, such as if the population was grouped by ability or a list was alphabetized by last name where some ethnicities might not have an equal chance of being selected. Overall, this method of sampling is low cost and simple, but ultimately using systematic sampling with a list could result to over- or under-representation of particular groups in the data.

Stratified Random Sampling

Stratified random sampling is an approach where the researcher divides the population into several groups (i.e., strata) based on a certain characteristic of sampling units (e.g., geographical areas) and then takes a random sample from each stratum (singular). Note, the size of the random sample within the stratum or group is proportional to the size of the strata or groups. For example, if the study focuses on the prevalence of learning disabilities in the third grade within a specific county, the researcher may group the students who have been diagnosed with a learning disability (e.g., ADD/ADHD, dyslexia, intellectual disability, dysgraphia, aphasia, etc.). From there, the researcher would randomly select the number of individuals from each of the groups to create the sample. This approach can also be illustrated using the scenario targeting the self-efficacy of teachers across subject areas who work with students who have learning disabilities. In this example, the researcher could group teachers by subject area. This method is highly effective for ensuring proper representation of a population when different aspects of the population are important to consider; however, it may be difficult to avoid generalization and can be costly/time consuming.

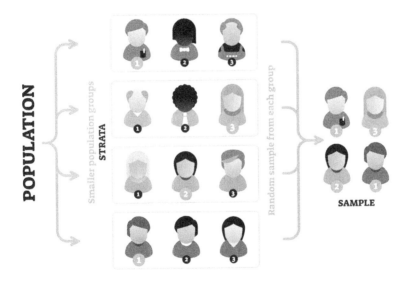

Stratified random sampling involves dividing the population into groups based on certain characteristics and taking a random sample from each group.

©iStockphoto.com/VectorMine

An advantage to using stratified sampling is that it ensures that the sample captures the key characteristics that the researcher is interested in including in the sample. As a result, there is homogeneity in each group or stratum, so each group can be represented by fewer cases, thus there is less need for a larger sample. Disadvantages of this sampling method are that it requires more planning and accurate information on a proportion of the population in each stratum. Keep in mind it may be costly to obtain and prepare lists of classification information, and there are typically risks of improper classification of individuals in strata because of clerical errors or poor measurement.

Cluster Sampling

Finally, cluster sampling occurs when the researcher randomly selects clusters or a sample of naturally occurring groups within a population for inclusion in the study (e.g., students in certain schools, in a school district, or households on different streets in a neighborhood). There are many types of cluster sampling. A single-stage cluster is a type of cluster sampling in that the naturally occurring clusters are directly sampled. In a two-stage sampling approach, clusters are created in the same way as in the one-stage cluster sampling (e.g., students who are twice exceptional learners in a school), but additionally there is random sampling within the selected clusters. For example, if our first cluster is a sample of classrooms, then stage-two clusters would be a random sample from those individual classroom clusters. Finally, multi-stage cluster sampling takes two-stage sampling further by adding multiple stages and steps. Going back to our scenario of a researcher using this type of sampling who randomly selects school districts in a country, and then obtains a list of the twice exceptional students in each of those school districts. The next step then is to randomly sample within each school district. Regardless of the number of stages, all individuals in the selected clusters are used in the sample.

Advantages of this method of sampling are that it is easy to perform, and it ensures adequate representation of a population. Cluster sampling may also reduce travel and that the sampling frames (characteristics of people within that population) need to be constructed only for units used in the sample. A disadvantage of this method would be that it may result in a larger error in comparison to other sampling methods.

Cluster sampling involves selecting a random sample of naturally occurring groups within a population, such as selecting only the red and blue candies from a bowl of mixed colored candies.

©iStcokphoto.com/in-finity

Other Sampling Methods

Other random sampling methods that are not often used include proportional and disproportional stratified sampling and adaptive cluster sampling. Table 10.5 provides a brief summary of these three types of less frequently used sampling methods. Proportional stratified sampling is when the proportions of the sample match that of the population (i.e., the population shows 50% males and 50% females, and so the sample will also consist of 50% males and 50% females), and disproportional stratified sampling is when the proportions of the sample are different than that of the population (e.g., the population is made of 40% males and 60% females, but the sample will consist of 50% males and 50% females). Adaptive cluster sampling is used when the population of interest is within a rare or unique sampling frame; that is, there is not enough people within the population from which to draw an appropriate sample. For example, if a researcher is working with a unique population of students, such as students with autism spectrum disorder (ASD) who also have savant syndrome, there will likely be very small numbers of such students from which to select an adequately sized sample. Thus, the only way to appropriately use adaptive clustering is if they include multiple schools in their school district or perhaps other school districts to expand their sample size. Table 10.6 provides a checklist to help you determine what type of random sampling to use in a study.

TABLE 10.5 ■ Other Types of Random Sampling		
Type	**Definition**	**Example**
Proportional Stratified Sampling	A random sampling method when the proportions of the sample match that of the population.	A third-grade classroom consists of 50% boys and 50% girls, so the sample selected from that classroom will also consist of 50% boys and 50% girls.
Disproportional Stratified Sampling	A random sampling method when the proportions of the sample are different than that of the population.	A fifth-grade classroom consists of 70% high-achieving students and 30% low-achieving students, but a researcher selects a sample that includes 50% high-achieving students and 50% low-achieving students.
Adaptive Cluster Sampling	A random sampling method used for populations with unique or rare sampling frames. What this method entails is that a researcher is able to identify surrounding clusters that they may use within their study.	A researcher wants to identify how accessibility is being offered to deaf-blind students at a certain district. Using adaptive cluster sampling, the researcher can expand their sample size by including neighboring districts with similar demographics.

STOP AND THINK 10.4

Think about the critical issue you want to tackle. Do you think probability sampling would be the best technique to obtain a representative sample of the population? If so, which sampling technique would best serve you? Is there more than one technique that could work? Why or why not? Take a look at Table 10.6 for some guiding prompts and questions!

Now that you have learned about probability sampling and the various types of probability sampling that can be used in research, the following *Let's See It!* and *Let's Do It!* activities provide you with an opportunity to practice. The key theme for these activities is to identify the nature of the probability sampling techniques used in two published research studies.

TABLE 10.6 ■ Checklist for Determining What Type of Random Sampling to Use
Stop and Think

1. Simple random sampling: Is it feasible to randomly select a sample of participants from the entire population? Do you have access to every member of the population?

2. Systematic random sampling: Can every member of the population be placed into a list? Is this list non-random in some way that could affect the selection of your sample?

3. Stratified random sampling: Are you interested in the characteristics of different groups within your population? Does your study seek to compare groups in some way?

4. Cluster sampling: Is your population already divided into naturally occurring groups? Is it important for the purposes of your study to compare these groups in some way?

Let's See It! 10.2

Goal: Identify the Use of Probability Sampling in Research

Locate and read the research article by Alexander et.al. (2020). As you read, focus on information that is provided about the sampling technique used to obtain student participants for the study and review Table 10.7 to see how we identified that information.

TABLE 10.7 ■ Probability Sampling in Research	
Study	Alexander, C., Wyatt-Smith, C., & Plessis, A. D. (2020). The role of motivations and perceptions on the retention of inservice teachers. *Teaching and Teacher Education, 96,* 1–12. https://doi.org/10.1016/j.tate.2020.103186
Probability Sampling Question	**Response**
Do researchers provide adequate information to help readers identify the sampling technique used to obtain participants in this study?	Yes. The researchers explicitly describe how they obtained their sample by indicating that from their target population 1 in 3 registered teachers were randomly selected to participate.
What type of sampling was used to identify the sample—that is, simple random, cluster, and so forth?	Systematic random sampling
How do you know what type of sampling was used to identify the student sample?	Researchers identified their target population through registered teachers ($n = 38,560$) in Queensland, Australia, and from this population 1 in 3 teachers were randomly selected to participate ($n = 12,854$). The researchers saw a 9% response rate, leaving their final sample size to be 1,165 inservice teachers.
Do you think this is an appropriate sampling method for the goals of this study? Why or why not?	Yes. The research questions align with the sampling approach. Probability sampling techniques improve the generalizability of the study's findings and are likely highly representative of the population of interest, and in this case, of inservice teachers' characteristics, perceptions, and motivations regarding teacher retention.

Can you identify any limitations to using this sampling method in this study?

The researchers do note that their sampling method does hold a limitation in that it can be difficult to control for the age of their participants when randomly selecting. Meaning, it is hard to ensure that there will be a variety of ages represented in the sample; however, one benefit to this study is that there is a large sample size ($n = 1,165$), so that improves the likelihood that there will be a distribution of demographic characteristics represented.

Let's Do It! 10.2

Guided Practice: Practice Identifying the Use of Probability Sampling in Research

Locate and read Carlson et al. (2004). As you read, focus on information that is provided about the sampling technique used to obtain participants for the study. Following the example in Table 10.7, answer the questions in Table 10.8 to help you identify the sampling technique.

TABLE 10.8 ■ Probability Sampling in Research	
Study	Carlson, E., Lee, H., & Schroll, K. (2004). Identifying attributes of high-quality special education teachers. *Teacher Education and Special Education, 27*(4), 350–359. https://doi.org/10.1177/088840640402700403
Probability Sampling Question	**Response**
Do researchers provide adequate information to help readers identify the sampling technique used to obtain participants in this study?	
What type of sampling was used to identify participants—that is, simple random, cluster, and so forth?	
How do you know what type of sampling was used to identify the sample?	
Do you think this is an appropriate sampling method for the goals of this study? Why or why not?	
Can you identify any limitations to using this sampling method in this study?	

Non-probability Sampling

When a sample is collected in a manner that is not random it is considered non-probability sampling. This means that every individual in a population does not have an equal chance of being selected for participation in a study. Some of the more common non-probability sampling techniques include convenience sampling, purposive sampling, quota sampling, and snowball sampling. Figure 10.4 and Table 10.9 summarize the four main types of non-probability sampling.

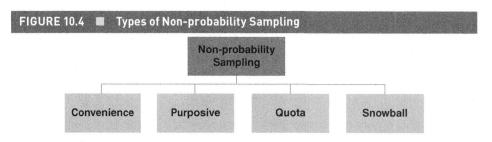

FIGURE 10.4 ■ Types of Non-probability Sampling

TABLE 10.9 ■ Types of Non-probability Sampling		
Type	**Definition**	**Example**
Convenience Sampling	The researcher selects participants for a study that are easily accessible and available.	Ms. Tabatha Smith a school psychologist, asks the first 10 students who are twice exceptional who enter the cafeteria one day to complete an open-ended response survey about their experiences in school.
Purposive Sampling	Participants are selected based on certain characteristics of interest in the study.	Ms. Tabatha Smith selects students who are twice exceptional of a low socioeconomic status in order to assess the factors that contribute to the unique needs of these students.
Quota Sampling	Researchers decide on a quota, or the number of individuals they would like to include in their study, and then they take a convenience sample from each stratum (group) of interest until they have met their quota.	Ms. Tabatha Smith wants to obtain 20 student participants from sixth, seventh, and eighth grade for a total of 60 participants. She selects the first 20 students from each grade who agree to participate for inclusion in her sample.
Snowball Sampling	Researchers begin with a convenience sample of volunteers who would like to participate in the study, and those volunteers are asked to recommend others who fit the study's criteria who would also be interested in participating.	Ms. Tabatha Smith asks a group of students who are twice exceptional to take a survey regarding their experiences in school and asks them to share the survey with any of their friends who are also twice exceptional who might be interested in participating in the study.

Convenience Sampling

In convenience sampling, the researcher selects subjects for participation in the study because they are easily accessible and available. A commonly used example of convenience sampling is when researchers at a university use self-selected students in a general psychology class as participants in their study. While this is certainly convenient for the researchers, convenience samples will often lack generalizability in that they are not appropriately representative of a well-defined population. Another example of convenience sampling would be if a researcher stood outside of a university's dining hall for two hours around lunchtime and asked each student who walked through the doors if they would be willing to fill out a survey or participate in a study in another capacity. Although many researchers use convenience sampling, it is imperative they discuss the characteristics of their participants in their study and the limitations or lack of generalizability their convenience sample may present. While convenience sampling is arguably the easiest method to obtain participants, this method can present a weakness or limitation in a study because convenience samples are not likely to be adequately representative of the population for many different reasons. For example, people who agree (self-select) to participate in research may be systematically different than those who do not agree to participate in research. Researchers must find a careful balance between ease of sample selection and adequate representation of the population.

STOP AND THINK 10.5

In what ways might students in a general psychology course not be representative of the population when researchers are attempting to draw conclusions about college students at large?

Purposive Sampling

In purposive sampling (also sometimes referred to as purposeful sampling), researchers will select individuals who meet the specifications of a particular study (i.e., "qualified" individuals). Purposive sampling is ideal when a study is looking to focus on a certain characteristic of the sample. For example, if a researcher wants to investigate the struggles faced by a family who has a child with ASD, the researchers would purposively choose families that fit this specific criterion. Or, if a researcher is investigating mathematics teachers and their pedagogical approaches in geometry with students diagnosed with ADHD, the researcher would specifically target teachers who teach geometry and who work with students diagnosed with ADHD.

Depending on the research questions, there are many types and/or variations of purposive sampling. We review a few here, including **criterion**, **maximum variation**, and critical case. Criterion (or homogeneous) sampling is used when a researcher is seeking to understand a group.

If a researcher wants to examine the challenges faced by families with a child with ASD, they would likely use purposive sampling to select only families that fit this criterion.

©iStockphoto.com/dragana991

It entails selecting participants from a well-defined subgroup, which ensures a sample with shared characteristics. Maximum variation (or heterogenous sampling) is used when a researcher aims to maximize the differences between participants to understand all perspectives. Critical case sampling is used to predict or explain other cases. A researcher needs to have the information necessary to select a critical case based on the presence or absence of specific knowledge or experience. Advantages of a purposive sample include that it is cost-effective, it can obtain data quickly using small samples, and it does not require having a complete population list as with random sampling. Disadvantages include that purposive sampling is subject to researcher biases. As the result, researchers should be cautious using their judgment in the selection process of participants (e.g., specific criteria), as it may be difficult to make generalizations from the sample to the population.

Quota Sampling

Quota sampling is a non-probability version of stratified random sampling where the researcher takes a convenience sample of each stratum, or group. In quota sampling, the researchers determine the number of individuals they would like to include in their sample within each group at the beginning of the study, which then becomes the fixed number of participants. For example, say a researcher is planning on asking special education teachers their preference of virtual or in-person classrooms. The researcher could say they will interview the first 50 male teachers who agree to participate in the study and the first 50 female teachers who agree to participate, setting the quota for 100. Another example could be that a researcher is interested in the students' perspectives and opinions of virtual versus in-person mathematics course modality. If the researcher wants a sample of 150 students, they will accept the first 150 students that provide assent. An advantage to this method of sampling is that it is easy to conduct and is more likely to accurately represent a population than other non-probability sampling methods. However, the sample may not be representative of the population and there are many factors (e.g., region, social factors, and geographic) that can play a role in the individuals selected for the study. As a result, researchers should try to eliminate the possibility of biases as they make the final decision on who is included in the sample.

Snowball Sampling

Snowball sampling (also sometimes referred to as network sampling) occurs when researchers begin by using a convenience sample, asking for volunteers, and then request that the participants go out and ask others to join the study. Snowball sampling also describes the process where the sample grows through word of mouth from participants to other potential participants. The sample may continue to grow as the study is continuously being conducted. For example, say the researcher puts a survey on their social media asking special education teachers to report their levels of burnout and what factors may contribute, and once completed, the researcher requests the current participants share it on their social media. From this point, say the 20 individuals who took the survey have now exposed the survey to their colleagues, expanding the sample from 20 to say 100. Some advantages of this form of sampling are that it is easy to implement and the sample size will be large; however, given the individual/participant who is making the referrals has a role in the direction the sampling takes, you have no control of knowing exactly what participants will be in your sample. Although snowball sampling is considered to be non-probability sampling, it is still possible for it to be probabilistic in part if the researcher chooses to randomly select from their pool of individuals identified through snowball sampling.

THE TAKEAWAY

Probability sampling occurs when the sample is selected at random. In non-probability sampling the sample is not selected at random but rather is selected either due to convenience/ease for the researcher or if the researcher wants to deliberately and intentionally focus on specific groups or individuals (Figure 10.5).

FIGURE 10.5 ■ Comparison of Probability and Non-probability Sampling

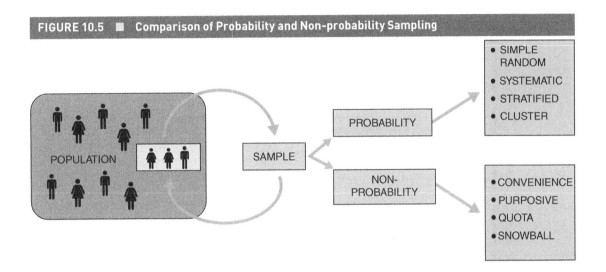

Now that you have learned about non-probability sampling and the various types of non-probability sampling that can be used in research, the following *Let's See It!* and *Let's Do It!* activities provide you with an opportunity to practice identifying the use of non-probability sampling in research with two published research studies.

Let's See It! 10.3

Goal: Identify the Use of Non-probability Sampling in Research

Locate and read the following research article by Matthews et al., (2021). As you read, focus on information that is provided about the sampling technique used to obtain participants for the study. Answer the questions in Table 10.10 to help you identify the sampling technique on how the teacher sample was identified in this study.

TABLE 10.10 ■ Non-probability Sampling in Research

Study	Matthews, H. M., Lillis, J. L., Bettini, E., Peyton, D. J., Pua, D., Oblath, R., Jones, N. D., Smith, S. W., & Sutton, R. (2021). Working conditions and special educators' reading instruction for students with emotional and behavioral disorders. *Exceptional Children, 87*(4), 476–496. https://doi.org/10.1177/0014402921999825

Non-probability Sampling Question	Response
Do researchers provide adequate information to help readers identify the sampling technique used to obtain participants in this study?	Yes. On page 479 the researchers describe using a purposive sampling technique to recruit their participants.
What type of sampling was used to identify the participants—that is, convenience, snowball, quota, and so forth?	Purposive sampling
How do you know what type of sampling was used to identify the sample?	The researchers explicitly stated that they selected their seven special education teachers across six public schools. The reasoning behind this was that the researchers aimed for similar characteristics amongst their participants and the students they worked with (homogeneity).
Do you think this is an appropriate sampling method for the goals of this study? Why or why not?	Yes. Non-probability sampling techniques are not usually used for studies that want to generalize findings to a specific population of interest. In the case for this study, the researchers very specifically wanted to explore working conditions of special education teachers within a specific context (reading instruction) as they work with specific students.
Can you identify any limitations to using this sampling method in this study?	A limitation that was also discussed by the researchers would be the fact that the findings of this study cannot be generalized across all special education teachers. Findings may vary across multiple factors, such as school status (e.g., Title I, public, private), subject areas, service delivery models, or other student populations. Further research would need to be conducted to explore these nuances.

Let's Do It! 10.3

Guided Practice: Practice Identifying the Use of Non-probability Sampling in Research

Locate and read the following research article by Mandouit and Hattie (2023). As you read, focus on information that is provided about the sampling technique used to obtain participants for the study. Following the example in Table 10.10, answer the questions in Table 10.11 to help you identify the sampling technique.

TABLE 10.11 ■ Non-probability Sampling in Research

Study	Mandouit, L., & Hattie, J. (2023). Revisiting "The Power of Feedback" from the perspective of the learner. *Learning and Instruction, 84*, 1–9. https://doi.org/10.1016/j.learninstruc.2022.101718
Non-probability Sampling Question	Response
Do researchers provide adequate information to help readers identify the sampling technique used to obtain the sample in this study?	

What type of sampling was used to
identify the sample—that is, convenience,
purposive, and so forth?

How do you know what type of sampling was
used to identify the sample?

Do you think this is an appropriate sampling
method for the goals of this study? Why or
why not?

Can you identify any limitations to using this
sampling method in this study?

SAMPLING ACROSS QUANTITATIVE, QUALITATIVE, MIXED METHODS, AND ACTION RESEARCH

LEARNING OBJECTIVE
10.3   Compare sampling across quantitative, qualitative, mixed methods, and action research

Although the concept of sampling is used across all research designs, the specific procedures or steps will often vary. Generally, the sampling technique will be determined by the research goals and purposes, research questions, and the design approach used in the study (e.g., quantitative, qualitative, mixed methods). In quantitative research, the sampling technique should be able to produce a sample of sufficient quality and size so it can be generalized to the population. For example, if a school principal Ms. Irene Burns wants to examine how students at her school feel about school climate and their happiness and well-being while in school, she might administer a survey to a random sample of 250 students out of the 1,000 students at the school. In comparison to selecting a few students she knows at the school to interview, this larger sample size will provide more data and include more perspectives and experiences. The larger (and randomly selected) sample is likely a strong representation of the population.

In qualitative research, the goal is often to select a more modest or small sample size. Even though the sample size is much smaller in qualitative research, the participants within the sample will often provide more in-depth and detailed information. Hence, it is important that the selected participants fit the criterion for inclusion in the study. For example, a teacher may want to interview a few students who participate in an advanced reading program to better understand what they are gaining from the program and if any changes should be made to the structure of the program. Mixed methods research and action research approaches will use a combination of quantitative and qualitative techniques to answer their research questions. In this section, we detail the various sampling techniques utilized by quantitative, qualitative, mixed methods, and action research designs. Table 10.12 provides a general overview of sampling techniques and their links to different research methodologies.

A teacher is interested in interviewing a few students who participate in an advanced reading program in their schools to learn about their experiences.

©iStockphoto.com/Wavebreakmedia

TABLE 10.12 ■ Research Designs and Commonly Associated Sampling Techniques		
Research Design	**Sampling Technique**	
Quantitative Research	Probability Sampling	• Simple random sampling
		• Systematic random sampling
		• Stratified random sampling
		• Cluster sampling
Qualitative Research and Action Research	Non-probability Sampling	• Convenience sampling
		• Snowball/Network sampling
		• Quota sampling
		• Purposive sampling
		• Criterion sampling
		• Maximum variation sampling
		• Critical case sampling
Mixed Methods Research		• Combination of qualitative and quantitative sampling

Participant Selection in Quantitative Research

Sampling in quantitative research may use a combination of both probability (e.g., simple random sampling, systematic random sampling, stratified random sampling, and cluster sampling), and non-probability sampling (e.g., convenience sampling, purposive sampling, snowball sampling, and quota sampling). In regard to sample size, there is no absolute guideline. However, a key rule of thumb to remember is to minimize sampling error by utilizing a larger sample. This may pose a challenge if using non-probability sampling. The biggest limitation in using non-probability sampling is that it is more difficult to use the sample to generalize about the population. If a researcher is selecting a sample out of convenience, then the sample characteristics would only pertain to those individuals within that context, not necessarily the population as a whole.

In general, when selecting participants for a quantitative study, the goal is for the participants to meet the characteristics of interest in the study. In other words, the sample should be representative of the population. By adhering to this, the sample can be said to be generalizable to the population. For example, if a researcher is investigating in a school district how student behavior is managed in inclusive classrooms where 20% of the students have learning disabilities, then a representative quantitative sample would include classrooms that meet that proportion. In summary, quantitative research studies with probabilistic and non-probabilistic samples are both valuable and informative provided that the purpose is for statistical inferences from the sample to the population or just drawing descriptive interpretations based on a sample respectively.

THE TAKEAWAY

When selecting participants for a quantitative study, the focus should be on selecting individuals who are representative of the characteristics of the population.

Participant Selection in Qualitative Research

Sampling and sample size in qualitative research is one of the most important components in qualitative studies. Qualitative researchers may use a variety of sampling techniques (e.g., purposive, convenience, snowball, etc.). The first step is to identify and describe the participants that a researcher needs to answer their research questions. Once the most pertinent sample characteristics have been listed then various sampling strategies can be used to gain an in-depth understanding of the study phenomenon. For example, purposive sampling is a very common approach used in qualitative research and includes selection of participants who are knowledgeable about the phenomenon being studied.

Ultimately, qualitative research differs a bit in what researchers expect from their participants. Qualitative research is based on experience, and it is important for the researcher to select participants whose experiences are in line with their purpose and goal of the study. As a result, there is no rule of thumb for determining the number of participants in qualitative research. Sample sizes are much smaller than those needed for quantitative studies as the goal is not to make generalizations to a larger population but rather focus on understanding, the how and why, of the phenomena of interest within a context.

THE TAKEAWAY

When selecting participants for a quantitative study, it is important to be mindful of how the participants' experiences are tied to your research study and that they are in line with your research purpose and questions.

Participant Selection in Mixed Methods Research

Mixed methods sampling typically consists of a combination of qualitative and quantitative sampling methods which makes the sampling and sample size process a bit more complex. The overall sampling plan depends on the type of research design used. As mentioned in chapter 7, in a concurrent triangulation design, data are collected simultaneously and the researcher integrates the findings of the two strands once the data are collected. In this case the sampling plan is clearly defined at the outset of the study. In sequential designs (i.e., explanatory and exploratory), the data collected from phase 1 informs decisions regarding data collected in phase 2. In this case, data analysis takes place before all the data are collected which might provide additional information for the sampling strategy in the second phase of the study. Thus, a researcher when sampling in mixed methods designs with two or more phases must determine whether the samples will be measured concurrently or sequentially and how the samples are linked together in a meaningful way.

That being said, the researcher engaging in mixed methods research needs to have a solid understanding of both quantitative and qualitative sampling techniques in order to establish a sample that is not only representative of the population but also provides experienced grounded information. As in all research studies, a clear rationale for the sampling strategy used in the various phases of the study should be described in detail. Finally, in regards to the size of the samples, the researcher should follow the guidelines that exist for qualitative and quantitative methods.

THE TAKEAWAY

Mixed methods require an understanding of both quantitative and qualitative sampling techniques.

Participant Selection in Action Research

Action research will generally use purposive sampling, which is a form of non-probability sampling. Purposive sampling is similar to stratified sampling in that the individuals selected will be part of a cohort of sorts. However, convenience sampling is also a common sampling procedure among educators (e.g., a teacher's classroom). What makes this sampling unique is that the researcher must have knowledge of the participant and their ability to play a role in the action research. Whatever sampling technique is utilized, a rationale should be provided explaining the basis of selecting the sample. In action research, most samples are selected from a population that the researcher aims to study. For example, a fourth-grade teacher may be interested in studying the effectiveness of a new classroom management intervention based on student perceptions. The teacher may choose to study all students in class or focus on a few students who exhibit behavioral issues. Although the teacher can collect data from all participants within the classroom, it is recommended for practical considerations to select a smaller sample using specific inclusion and exclusion criteria. In regards to sample size, typically action research involves small-scale studies and the sample consists of a small number of participants.

THE TAKEAWAY

During action research, the participants play a key role in the research, hence there is a greater emphasis on really knowing the participants and their ability to play their role in the research.

MEASUREMENT AND MEASUREMENT ERROR IN RESEARCH

LEARNING OBJECTIVE	
10.4	Clarify the difference between measurement and measurement error in research

The process of measurement requires assigning symbols or numbers to objects, events, people, characteristics, and so forth. Because measurement involves gathering data about people or situations, it is an essential component of data-based decision making in school contexts. Let's look at our scenario example of Mrs. Riegler and Myron. If Mrs. Riegler and her team wanted to create an intervention for Myron, there would need to be a sufficient amount of data collected that could help Mrs. Riegler and her team inform the decisions they make; however, how exactly should these data be collected (i.e., how do we measure Myron's behavior)? Some educators may recommend that Myron and his family/teachers take a survey to reveal information about his behaviors, while others may suggest conducting observations of Myron throughout the school day or perhaps interviewing Myron to gain his perspective on his behavior. All types of measurement can produce valid and reliable data, yet each route will paint a different picture. It is up to you, as the researcher, to determine what kind of picture you want to paint and which form of measurement can best accomplish the purpose of the study.

That being said, modes of measurement can range from scales and questionnaires to observations and even interviews. Modes of measurement, therefore, are related to how you, as a researcher, operationalize the variables targeted in the study. An operational definition specifies how you measure the variable in your study. You can find these types of definitions in the literature. There might be lots of ways to operationally define and measure a construct. As you think about the operational definition consider the variable being measured and its attributes (i.e., level of measurement that will be discussed later in this chapter) and then identify an actual measure for the variable of interest. Overall, it is essential to take note of how operational definitions directly impact the nature of the measures that are selected.

Measurement Error

When considering the best form of measurement to assess a specific variable, it is important to consider the types of error that can be associated with those measures. Measurement error is any factor that affects a person's true score on a measure. This error may either be random or systematic. Random error is defined as the chance difference between the true and the observed value. Random errors occur as a result of sudden, random changes while conducting the study. It is important to note that an increase in random error can cause high levels of variability. The researcher in this case might deal with this type of error by revamping the measure to make it more reliable and precise. This type of error is out of the control of the researcher. Systematic error can be the result of many things; however, this error affects the participants as a whole versus select individuals (e.g., poor test-taking conditions, unreliable measurement tool, etc.) and can be controlled or changed by the researcher. Systematic error is predictable and can be minimized by selecting better instruments or improving the experimental techniques or procedures. For example, it is highly recommended that the measures be pilot tested with the sample before conducting the study. Pilot testing can help to ensure that the participants are clear on the directions and that the items are working as intended. In summary, systematic errors are much more problematic to deal with in research because they can lead to inaccurate conclusions about the data, whereas random errors are typically not a problem when collecting data from large samples.

Now that we've talked about the importance of how we operationalize our variables and the impact they have on our design, from the purpose to the procedure, let's practice! In the following *Let's See It!* and *Let's Do It!* activity, you will be given the opportunity to identify how different variables are operationalized using our scenario with Mrs. Riegler.

Let's See It! 10.4

Goal: Identify How Different Variables Are Operationalized

Go back to the opening scenario. Think about what variables Mrs. Riegler might want to assess in her study to answer the critical issue of how to best assist Myron. Look at Table 10.13 to see how we identified how these variables might be operationalized or measured.

TABLE 10.13 ■ Mrs. Riegler's Research

What are the research questions?	What are Myron's specific and individualized needs? 1. What classroom behaviors does Myron need to work on? 2. What extra supports does Myron need to help him succeed (academic or social/emotional)?
What are the variables of interest?	1. Myron's behavior in the classroom. 2. Myron's experiences and well-being in school. 3. Myron's academic performance (reading, math, etc.).
How are these variables measured or operationalized?	1. Myron's behavior in the classroom is operationalized by the targeted challenging behaviors observed by Myron's current educator team. The variable will be measured through classroom observations by the school psychologist. 2. Myron's well-being experiences are operationalized by how Myron feels during school and what events lead to those feelings. An interview with Myron will be conducted. 3. Myron's academic performance is operationalized by the grades he receives during school (test scores, report card, etc.).

Let's Do It! 10.4

Guided Practice: Practice Identifying How Different Variables Are Operationalized in Research

Read the following article by Kitsantas et al. (2017) and answer the questions in Table 10.14 to help you understand how variables are operationalized and measured in research, following the example in Table 10.13.

TABLE 10.14 ■ Identification of Variables

Study	Kitsantas, A., Bland, L., & Chirinos, D. S. (2017). Gifted students' perceptions of gifted programs: An inquiry into their academic and social-emotional functioning. *Journal for the Education of the Gifted, 40*(3), 266–288. https://doi.org/10.1177/0162353217717033

What are the research questions?

What are the variables of interest?

How are these variables measured or operationalized?

LEVELS OF MEASUREMENT

LEARNING OBJECTIVE

10.5 Differentiate between levels of measurement

As indicated earlier in this chapter, measurement is the process of assigning numbers to empirical properties of variables according to rules. One aspect to measurement that helps to understand these numerical values involves levels of measurement. There are several different kinds of scales: nominal, ordinal, interval, and ratio (see Table 10.15). Knowing the distinction among these scales is important when we analyze data using statistical tools. Based on the scale of measurement for a variable one can make a decision to select an appropriate type of statistical analysis of the data. Thus, the process of measurement is a complex set of steps that generates numerical values for one or more variables for the research participants. Determining the scale of measurement to use for a variable can be a challenging task for students. Keep in mind that these four levels increase in complexity as there is an implied hierarchy (see Figure 10.6) where analysis of nominal and ordinal data tends to be the least complex, while interval and ratio scales lend themselves to more sophisticated statistical analysis. Table 10.15 provides a summary of the four levels of measurement.

Nominal

The nominal scale is the most basic level of measurement. The scores on a nominal scale simply reflect categories of some type. For example, you may want to survey a classroom of kindergarten students about their favorite ice cream flavors—with a choice of chocolate, vanilla, or strawberry. Each of the three flavors represent a category and would be assigned a numeral to represent that category (1 = chocolate, 2 = vanilla, 3 = strawberry). There is no order or intervals between the ice cream flavors and thus each number reflects a distinct or meaningful category. Thus, a score of 3 (strawberry) is not better or larger than a score of 1 (chocolate). They are simply distinct categories. Frequency counts are often used to aggregate nominal data. For example, the number of

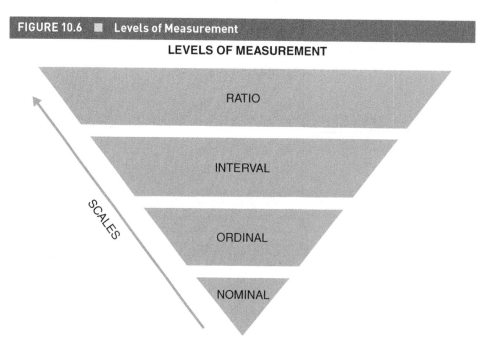

FIGURE 10.6 ■ Levels of Measurement

votes for each flavor would be added up to assess the frequency that each of the three flavors were selected as a favorite in the classroom. Another example of nominal data is if a researcher examined resource availability for families of children with disabilities and decided to group families by zip code to identify their location as part of the study. Nominal data can be represented with bar graphs, pie charts, or any other type of display that represents groups or frequencies.

Ordinal

Ordinal scales represent a more complex numerical system than nominal scales. Unlike nominal scales, ordinal scales are based on ordering, or rank, of the data points in relation to each other. For example, say you are measuring the heights of the students in your classroom from tallest to shortest. After placing the students in order according to height, you would then assign the tallest person rank one, next tallest would be two, then three, and so forth, until you get to the shortest person in the class who would be ranked last. Unlike differences in nominal scores or values,

TABLE 10.15 ■ Levels of Measurement

Scale Level	Scale of Measurement	Definition	Examples
1	Nominal	Simplest level of measurement Assigns categories to certain characteristics	Ethnicity
2	Ordinal	Based on rank order Distances between points may not be the same	Height ranking
3	Interval	Based on rank order that also represents equal distances between each point	Likert scales
4	Ratio	Similar to interval but includes an absolute zero, meaning the absence of the construct being measured	Age

ordinal data do reflect differences among individuals with different ranks. One important thing to note about ordinal scales is that the distance between each rank may not be equivalent (i.e., the height difference between the tallest student and the second tallest student may be three inches, but the distance between the second tallest student and the third tallest student may only be one inch). The rankings provide ordinal-level data on the heights of students but do not offer any information on the differences in height between each rank.

Lining up students from shortest to tallest and assigning each of them a rank would be an example of ordinal data.

©iStockphoto.com/zenstock

Interval

The interval scale is the third most complex level of measurement. Similar to ordinal scales, interval scales can be ranked and ordered; however, with an interval scale, the distance between each score or value is equal. A commonly used form of interval level data is the Likert scale. Likert scales are forms of questionnaires where the participant is asked a question and responds on a number scale representing the least amount of the construct on one end and the greatest amount of the construct on the other end (strongly agree to strongly disagree). Each level is ranked from least to greatest and represents an equal interval between each level. There is debate whether Likert scales should be treated as ordinal or interval data, which has implications for how to analyze data (i.e., whether to use a parametric or nonparametric test, see chapter 13).

Certain achievement tests are also considered interval data when looking at the number of items correct. Scores can be ranked from lowest to highest, and the distance between each possible score is equal in distance. If a student earned a zero on a test, it wouldn't mean there is a complete absence of knowledge on that topic, just that they did not get any questions correct or did not take the test at all. It is very important to note that for interval scales, there is no absolute zero, meaning a zero does not represent a true absence of the construct being measured. Interval scales are the most common levels of measurement used in educational settings mainly because they can be used to assess measures of central tendency (e.g., mean, median, mode, and range) that may provide educators with useful information.

Ratio

The ratio scale is the final and most complex level of measurement. The ratio scale is very similar to the interval scale but includes an absolute zero. A score of zero indicates an absence of the construct being measured. This allows for ratios to exist when comparing data (e.g., 1:2, 3:7, etc.). One example of this scale is speed while driving. It is clear that 50 mph is twice as fast as 25 mph (1:2 ratio). Similar to interval scales, ratio scales are also used to describe both the order and the value between each level/item choice. For example, if we examine the relationship between years of teaching experience and teacher efficacy beliefs in classroom management, a ratio scale could be used to assess the number of years of teaching experience. In this case, we know responses are ordered from the least teaching experience to the most teaching experience, as well as the interval between each level (i.e., the amount of experience between 5 and 10 years is the same as the amount of experience between 10 and 15 years). If a teacher indicates they have zero years of experience, then that would represent a true absence of experience such as if they had just graduated from their teaching program.

STOP AND THINK 10.6

What are some examples in your everyday life where you come across the four levels of measurement (nominal, ordinal, interval, and ratio)?

Now that we've gone over the four levels of measurement, it's time to practice! In the following *Let's See It!* and *Let's Do It!* activities, you will practice distinguishing between the different levels of measurement with examples that might be relevant to an educator.

Let's See It! 10.5

Goal: Identify Examples of Nominal, Ordinal, Interval, and Ratio Scales

Read the following measurement examples and the type of scale each measurement uses in Table 10.16 and think through why the scale corresponds with that measurement.

TABLE 10.16 ■ Levels of Measurement Examples

Measure	Scale	Explanation
Student gender: • Male • Female • Other • Do not wish to respond	Nominal	Gender is another categorical variable. One participant can't have "more" gender than another participant.
Grade level in high school	Ordinal	Freshman, sophomore, junior, and senior grade levels indicate a student's class rank

Measure	Scale	Explanation
Measuring teacher satisfaction with professional development: ● Not satisfied ● Slightly satisfied ● Somewhat satisfied ● Satisfied ● Completely satisfied	Interval	This can be considered a Likert scale.
Percentage/number of inclusive classrooms in each school district	Ratio	Each school district is likely to have different numbers of inclusive classrooms, and it is possible for some to have none.

Let's Do It! 10.5

Guided Practice: Practice Distinguishing Between the Different Levels of Measurement

Going back to our opening scenario with Myron and Mrs. Riegler, think through some potential forms of data collection that could be used to gather information on and assist Myron in his difficulties at school and identify what level of measurement corresponds to each measure. Several examples of measures are included in Table 10.17 for you to think through, but feel free to come up with additional examples of measures that could be useful in this scenario. Consider how data for each measure are collected and the level of measurement that they might fall under. Use the examples in Table 10.16 to help you in your thinking.

TABLE 10.17 ■ Assessing Levels of Measurement		
Measure	**Level of Measurement**	**Explanation**
Myron's race		
Myron's reading ability (e.g., beginner, intermediate, fluent)		
Assessment of Myron's anxiety		
Counselor observations on the number of times Myron gets out of his seat, has an outburst, and so forth during the day		
Myron's grades on science tests administered during class		

TYPES OF VALIDITY IN MEASUREMENT

LEARNING OBJECTIVE
10.6   Describe different types of validity in measurement

Validity (in measurement) refers to the degree to which researchers actually measure what they intend to measure. For example, to what extent does an emotional engagement scale actually measures a student's emotional engagement? There are several different types of validity in educational research but typically researchers use three forms: content, criterion-related, and construct validity. Each form of validity utilizes a different way to assess the extent to which a measure actually measures what is supposed to measure or the construct using both established theoretical and empirical approaches.

Content Validity

Content validity is the extent to which the items in an instrument are representative of the domain or construct of interest. Hence, the domain of interest needs to be clearly defined in order to assess the content validity of a particular measure. Usually, objectives or dimensions (lists of behaviors as descriptions of domain) are clearly stated in the test specifications and are all equally weighted. For example, if a researcher is constructing an instrument about student academic self-regulation and we only focus on goal setting, we would clearly lack content validity as we have omitted other processes of self-regulations such as self-monitoring or self-evaluation. A review of the literature will help the researcher identify all the dimensions of a construct.

During this process, each item is examined to see how well it aligns with the larger construct. Experts in that particular subject area (other than the writers of the items) are typically asked to evaluate the adequacy of the items on the measure. Decisions on whether or not each item in a scale aligns with the intended construct can be made dichotomously (yes or no), or by rating the degree of matching to the construct (e.g., 5-point scale). Finally, the results are summarized by looking at the percentage of items matched to objectives or dimensions. This form of validity is useful when useful when the possible items are identifiable.

Criterion-Related Validity

In criterion-related validity, measures how well the scores on an instrument predict outcome. The SAT test, for instance, is said to have criterion validity because high scores on this test are correlated with a students' freshman grade point averages. This can be determined through predictive validity (e.g., SAT scores predict GPA in college or some other outcome) or concurrent validity (i.e., the agreement between two assessments). In other words, if an achievement test was administered followed by a standardized version of the test, how well the two different scores were in agreement would be concurrent validity. The strength of the relationship between test scores and criterion performance is determined by the correlation coefficient. For example, does measurement of student academic self-regulation predict academic grade point average? This form of validity requires that the researcher clearly identifies appropriate outcomes.

Construct Validity

Construct validity refers to the degree to which an instrument represents the construct it claims to represent. A measure has construct validity when it conforms to the theoretical framework underlying the construct such as student motivation that cannot be observed directly. As part of the construct validation process, a researcher must provide both evidence of what the instrument is supposed to measure, but also what it does not measure. As a result, the researcher might use two additional types of validity such as convergent and discriminant to further demonstrate that a measure of emotional engagement yields an accurate assessment of this construct that cannot be directly observed. Convergent validity refers to when scores on one measure correlate with the scores on other similar measures that are designed to assess the same or similar constructs. For example, if you administer two different tests of reading ability to a group of third third-grade students, individual scores on each of the two measures should correlate with one another, indicating the two measures assess reading ability in similar ways. To support the evidence collected for convergent validity, many researchers will use discriminant validity to justify validity by demonstrating that the scores on one measure do not correlate with the scores on other measures that are designed to assess different constructs. Ultimately, when discriminant evidence is presented, this means your measure and other measures are measuring two completely different constructs.

Now that we have gone through the different types of validity used in educational research, let's take a moment to practice differentiating between them. In the following *Let's See It!* and *Let's Do It!* activities, you are going to see how to identify the different types of validity used in research studies.

Let's See It! 10.6

Goal: Identify Types of Measurement Validity

Read through the following article by Zimmerman and Kitsantas (2007) and think about the types of validity the authors used to validate the SELF, a scale that measures students' self-efficacy beliefs regarding their use of self-regulatory processes in various academic tasks. Then, let's review Table 10.18 to see how we identified the types of evidence of t validity the authors used to validate the SELF scale.

TABLE 10.18 ■ Types of Validity	
Study	Zimmerman, B., & Kitsantas, A. (2007). Reliability and validity of Self-Efficacy for Learning Form (SELF) scores of college students. *Zeitschrift für Psychologie/Journal of Psychology, 215*(3), 157–163. https://doi.org/10.1027/0044-3409.215.3.157
Type of Validity	Evidence
Criterion	Researchers established the predictive validity of the original and shortened versions of the SELF by examining the correlations between each of the two versions and the other variables of interest in the study, such as student grades.
Construct	Researchers used additional statistical procedures (e.g., factor analysis) to assess the factors in the SELF that accounted for the largest percentage of the variance and used these factors to create the shortened form of the SELF.

Let's Do It! 10.6

Guided Practice: Practice Identifying Types of Measurement Validity

Read through the following article by Varier et al. (2021) and fill out Table 10.19 using the example above in Table 10.18 for guidance. The SEESA-AW scale for argumentative writing measures college students' self-efficacy beliefs for self-assessment in the domain of argumentative writing. As you work on this task your focus should be to determine the type of validity the authors used to validate the SEESA-AW scale.

TABLE 10.19 ■ Types of Validity	
Study	Varier, D., Kitsantas, A., Zhang, X., & Saroughi, M. (2021). Self-efficacy for self-assessment: Development and validation of the SEESA-AW scale for argumentative writing. *International Journal of Educational Research, 110*, 1–11. https://doi.org/10.1016/j.ijer.2021.101885
Type of Validity (e.g., content, construct, convergence, etc.)	Evidence

TYPES OF RELIABILITY IN MEASUREMENT

LEARNING OBJECTIVE
10.7   Describe different types of reliability in measurement

Reliability is often referred to as consistency of the scores generated by a measure or assessment. For example, if you hear three different accounts of how an IEP meeting went but each account differs from what actually happened at the meeting, the accounts are inconsistent and therefore not reliable. Reliability is usually determined by a correlational coefficient, also called a reliability coefficient. A measure can be reliable (i.e., consistently produces the same results), but not valid (i.e., does not measure the actual construct). Likewise, a measure can be valid but not reliable if it is measuring the intended construct, but not in a consistent manner. A data collection instrument must be reliable and valid.

As with validity, there are different forms of reliability: test–retest reliability, equivalent forms reliability, internal consistency reliability, and interrater reliability. Test–retest reliability is used to test the reliability over time by repeated administration of the same test to the same participants. Equivalent form reliability is used when one group of participants are asked to take two different versions of the same test. The goal of equivalent forms reliability is to determine the pattern of scores participants earn on both Test A and Test B. The closer the two scores are in relevance, the higher the reliability coefficient. Internal consistency is used to determine how homogenous the items are of the test, meaning how well each item measures the intended construct; there are numerous empirical methods to measure internal consistency (i.e., Kuder-Richardson, Cronbach's alpha). Cronbach's alpha is the most commonly reported reliability coefficient, which refers to the extent to which items are intercorrelated. High reliability is usually indicated by a reliability score that is close to ±1.00 (strong, positive or negative correlation). Generally, the reliability coefficient must be above 0.7 to be considered acceptable. Finally, interrater reliability is used when you have two individuals take the same test and then you compare their scores. The closer the scores are to each other the stronger the reliability.

It is not typically possible for psychological measurements to be perfectly reliable, but we still want to know how reliable the scores from a test/instrument. This information helps to determine how consistently the test/instrument measures what we would like to measure. In summary, reliability demonstrates that the results obtained are consistent whereas validity shows the degree to which the measure actually measures what it is trying to measure. A good measure is both reliable and valid. Figure 10.7 compares reliability and validity.

FIGURE 10.7 ■ Validity Versus Reliability

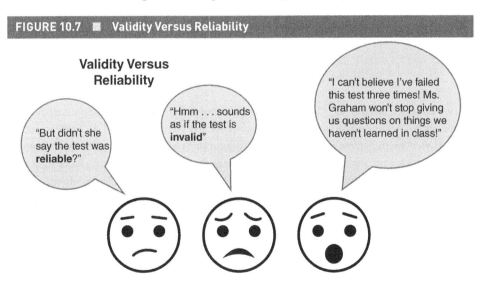

THE TAKEAWAY

When comparing validity to reliability, remember validity refers to whether the instrument is measuring what it is intended to measure, whereas reliability is how consistently the instrument produces a measure.

ETHICAL CONSIDERATIONS

When considering sampling and collecting data, there are strict guidelines to adhere to for ethical purposes. First, in regards to sample size, it is unethical to include an over-sized sample or an under-sized sample than what is effectively required to conduct a study. A researcher must ensure that participant burdens and the risks are minimized with the hope that new knowledge will be generated. The sample size should only be increased for potential expected attrition or nonresponses. Further, other guidelines in regards to sampling procedures include the restriction of measurements that can cause harm to the participants (i.e., appropriate for use and the least restrictive for the student), the importance of informed consent (i.e., many students with disabilities may be nonverbal or have low executive functioning, hence consent from parents and guardians is pertinent), avoiding an invasion of privacy (i.e., releasing parts of the students' medical records without consent; ignoring Health Insurance Portability and Accountability Act [HIPPA] laws), and deception.

STOP AND THINK 10.7

What are some ethical considerations Mrs. Riegler should keep in mind when conducting research with Myron as the case study?

In terms of collecting data in an educational setting—for example, special education—it is important to be mindful of maintaining a least-restrictive environment for the student participant. Under the Individuals with Disabilities Education Act (IDEA), all students are entitled to an education that is inclusive and not restrictive to their ability, and will be placed in a classroom environment that will adhere to their unique and individual needs. Hence, when sampling students in this population, it is important to keep in mind the students' characteristics and the mannerisms of how the sampling in data collection will proceed. Overall, in the context of sampling, the researcher should ensure the sample represents the intended population to avoid introducing any bias that might compromise the integrity of the research by producing inaccurate results.

THE TAKEAWAY

A researcher has an ethical obligation when designing a study to justify the sample size that will be collected.

AMERICAN PSYCHOLOGICAL ASSOCIATION STYLE

10.9 Utilize the *Publication Manual of the American Psychological Association* when reporting information on sampling and measurement

The methods section of an empirical study, the heart of the study, should be detailed and written in a manner that makes it replicable for others. When conducting a study, it is important to report the sample size, or the number of participants in a study as well as sampling procedures because it helps the reader evaluate the validity and applicability of a study's findings. In the participants section of the methods, the researcher reports the sample size ($N = 150$), which represents the number of participants in the study and any statistical power analyses performed to determine sample size. In addition, the researcher should explain how the sample was obtained (e.g., using simple random sampling, purposive sampling, etc.) and whether the final sample differed from the intended sample. All inclusion and exclusion criteria should also be described. The interpretations of the findings should be based only the final sample rather than the intended sample. Outline how the participants were selected. Finally, the researcher should describe any compensation (e.g., course credits) that was provided to participants and whether approvals from the institutional review board was obtained prior to recruitment of the participants.

Furthermore, it is also important to provide citations of any data collection instruments, describe the scoring and/or coding of the instrument, and present evidence of validity and reliability discussed in terms of the measurement. Researchers should list the measurement tools utilized in the study along with citations, describe the purpose of the instrument, the number items, scoring system, provide examples of a few items and evidence of reliability as predetermined from psychometric testing of that measure (e.g., Cronbach's alpha), and any biases that may be present. This process varies slightly when reporting validity and reliability based on a study that is meant to substantiate a data collection instrument. In general, this information gives the readers the ability not only to evaluate the validity of the measures but also to replicate the findings in follow-up studies.

THE TAKEAWAY

When reporting on sampling procedures, outline how the participants were selected to participate in the study, including any inclusion and exclusion criteria.

Recapping what we discussed in this chapter. when selecting a sample we begin by looking at the population (group of individuals) we want to focus on, the sampling frame (characteristics of individuals within that population), and then use some type of sampling technique to select the sample. These steps allow the researcher to generalize the results of the study to other individuals within that population. There are many methods to go about sampling that are either based in probability (e.g., simple random, systematic, stratified, cluster sampling) or non-probability (e.g., convenience, criterion, snowball, purposive) sampling. The specific sampling approach you choose will depend on the purpose and/or goal of the research study, the research questions, and the research design (qualitative, quantitative, action research, or mixed methods).

Participants come into studies with varying levels of ability, skills, and experiences. When sampling for a research study, it is important to keep all these characteristics in mind based on your research design. It is also relevant to determine an appropriate sample size that will lead to an adequate level of statistical power. Remember that sampling error will always be a threat in that there may be differences between your sample and the population on some of your constructs (i.e., no sample is exactly identical to the population). Once sampling is complete, the researcher can move on to measurement and collecting data from the sample. Levels of measurement (in order from least to most complex: nominal, ordinal, interval, and ratio) can be used to help guide measurement decisions and what instruments to use to collect your data. It is also very important to use measures that have strong evidence to support validity of inferences (whether the instrument is measuring what it's supposed to), and reliability (consistency, trustworthiness) of the scores generated by those data collection methods. Researchers typically report those psychometric properties (reliability, validity) for each measure used in a study that is published in a journal.

EXTENSION ACTIVITIES

You Do It! 10.1
Self-Directed Practice: Practice Thinking About Important Sampling Issues in Your Own Study

Think through a critical issue you might want to study. After you have a critical issue and population of interest in mind, think about how you might obtain a representative sample from this population to address your research questions. A key question to consider is: Are characteristics/individuals equally represented in the population and in the study?

You Do It! 10.2
Self-Directed Practice: Practice Developing and Thinking Through Validity and Reliability When Creating a Measurement

There are many things to consider when developing a measurement, including how to test for validity and reliability. In this *You Do It!* activity, you will be asked to create an educational measure that is related to your critical issue. When developing this measure, think about your population and sample and how they will engage with this measurement (e.g., survey, questionnaire, check-list), and if it is developmentally appropriate. After you have developed this measure, we encourage you to take a look back at the different types of measurement validity and reliability—how would you approach these processes?

You Do It! 10.3
Self-Directed Practice: Critiquing Empirical Articles for Their Use of Sampling and Validity and Reliability

A great way to improve our sampling and measurement skills is to read through published empirical articles. Empirical articles will almost always include sampling and measurement in their Method section. In this *You Do It!* activity, we are asking you to search for empirical articles related to your critical issue and to read through the method sections about sampling procedures and validity and reliability of measures. How did the researchers present this information? Did their method choices make sense based on what you have learned so far in this chapter? What are some recommendations regarding sampling strategies for future studies?

KEY TERMS

Cluster sampling

Construct validity

Content validity

Convenience sampling

Convergent Validity

Criterion-related validity

Critical case

Cronbach's alpha

Discriminant Validity

External validity

Internal consistency

Interrater reliability

Interval scale

Levels of measurement

Likert scale

Measurement

Measurement error

Network sampling

Nominal scale

Nonparallel sampling

Non-probability random sampling

Ordinal scales

Participants

Population

Population parameters

Power analysis

Probability/Random sampling

Purposive sampling/purposeful sampling

Quota sampling

Random error

Random selection

Ratio scale

Reliability

Sample

Sample relationship criterion

Sample size

Sample statistic

Sampling

Sampling error

Sampling frame

Simple random sampling

Snowball sampling

Stratified random sampling

Statistical symbols

Systematic error

Systematic random sampling

Test–retest reliability

Validity (in measurement)

ANSWER KEY

Stop and Think Activities

Stop and Think 10.1

A researcher uses a sample to draw inferences that are representative for the population from which the sample is taken. If the sample is not representative, the data collected will lead to findings that cannot be generalized with confidence to the target population.

Stop and Think 10.2

Yes. If the teacher wishes to understand only their students in the school (the target population), taking a sample of seventh-grade students enrolled in mathematics from their school who share similar characteristics (i.e., struggling students on Individualized Education Programs) would be a good representation of the population.

STOP AND THINK 10.3

The term *random* is used when describing these probability techniques because each individual in the population has an equal chance of being selected for inclusion in the sample. The term makes sense in that participants are not being selected in any kind of intentional way based off of certain characteristics or qualifications.

STOP AND THINK 10.4

A superintendent is interested in studying parental involvement with the schools in an affluent, middle-class school district. They are especially interested in examining parental involvement based on socioeconomic status broken into three levels (low, middle, and high). The best sampling strategy in this case would be to use a type of probability sampling. Because they have already divided the population based on SES and the population (affluent middle-class) reflects an imbalance on this characteristic, stratified sampling would enable them to sample randomly from each subgroup.

STOP AND THINK 10.5

Students in a general psychology course are typically first- or second-year students and are likely psychology majors (or interested in becoming a psychology major) and tend to be largely female. These students are unlikely to be representative of university students at large. A representative sample is one that reflects the general characteristics of the population (such as 50/50 male and female and a variety of undergraduate majors).

STOP AND THINK 10.6

Nominal-level data include variables like gender and ethnicity. Ordinal-level data may include the top three place winners at your school's spelling bee. Interval-level data include temperature in Fahrenheit or Celsius. Finally, ratio-level data may include things like yearly income or a grade on a mathematics test.

STOP AND THINK 10.7

There are a variety of ethical considerations that Mrs. Riegler should keep in mind when conducting research with Myron as the case study. For example, Myron is a minor; thus, Mrs. Riegler needs to obtain consent from Myron's parents as well as assent from Myron before collecting any data. Additionally, Mrs. Riegler should ensure that she maintains a least restrictive environment for Myron when conducting research. Finally, Mrs. Riegler should be careful to ensure that Myron's privacy is being respected and that she is not overburdening him with what she is asking of him.

Let's Do It! Activities

LET'S DO IT! 10.1

Think About Important Sampling Issues in Your Own Study

Answers may vary but here is hypothetical scenario.

Imagine that you are an elementary school principal. You received an invitation for your school to participate in an intervention that could help reduce mathematics anxiety among sixth-grade, female students. The research question considered was "What is the impact of peer-mentoring sessions on female student mathematics anxiety and achievement?" You were one of the two randomly selected schools in the school district to participate in the study. You are asked to select two mathematics teachers and their female students from your school. Does this type of sampling procedure make sense? See Table, 10.3.

Key Sampling Questions to Consider

Sampling Question	Response
What is the population of interest?	All sixth-grade female elementary school students in the school district
Are characteristics/individuals equally represented in the population?	Yes. Two mathematics teachers and their female students from two elementary schools are randomly selected to participate in the study
Is the proposed sampling approach appropriate for this scenario?	Yes. The sample is representative of the target population.

Let's Do It! 10.2
Probability Sampling in Research

Study	Carlson, E., Lee, H., & Schroll, K. (2004). Identifying attributes of high-quality special education teachers. *Teacher Education and Special Education, 27*(4), 350–359. https://doi.org/10.1177/088840640402700403

Probability Sampling Question	**Response**
Do researchers provide adequate information to help readers identify the sampling technique used to obtain participants in this study?	Yes. Researchers provide quite a bit of detail on their sampling technique, including discussion of a two-phase sample design that used simple random sampling and stratified random sampling.
What type of sampling was used to identify participants—that is, simple random, cluster, and so forth?	Stratified random sampling
How do you know what type of sampling was used to identify the sample?	Researchers discuss stratification based on geographic region, district size, and personnel type.
Do you think this is an appropriate sampling method for the goals of this study? Why or why not?	Yes. Researchers sought to develop a model of teacher quality in special education using a sample of teachers that was nationally representative.
Can you identify any limitations to using this sampling method in this study?	This is an effective sampling technique for the size and scope of the sample that the researchers sought.

Let's Do It! 10.3
Non-probability Sampling in Research

Study	Mandouit, L., & Hattie, J. (2023). Revisiting "The Power of Feedback" from the perspective of the learner. *Learning and Instruction, 84*, 1–9. https://doi.org/10.1016/j.learninstruc.2022.101718

Non-probability Sampling Question	**Response**
Do researchers provide adequate information to help readers identify the sampling technique used to obtain participants in this study?	Yes—On page 3, when the researchers are describing their participants they state that their sample ($n = 155$) was a convenience sample.
What type of sampling was used to identify the participants—that is, convenience, snowball, quota, and so forth?	Convenience sampling

(Continued)

(*Continued*)

How do you know what type of sampling was used to identify the sample?	The researchers stated that the participants of the study were from a school where one of the researchers worked as a teacher. These participants were convenient and easily accessible to the researchers due to this connection.
Do you think this is an appropriate sampling method for the goals of this study? Why or why not?	Yes, the sampling strategy is appropriate and is aligned with goals of the study.
Can you identify any limitations to using this sampling method in this study?	The researchers were not as transparent about potential limitations regarding their sample. Further research should be conducted across different schools with students from varying subject areas. Additionally, because the researcher was a teacher at the school there is a chance of bias in sample selection. Although this was addressed by the ethics board, participants may respond differently due to their familiarity with the researcher.

LET'S DO IT! 10.4

Identifying How Different Variables Are Operationalized in Research

Study	Kitsantas, A., Bland, L., & Chirinos, D. S. (2017). Gifted students' perceptions of gifted programs: An inquiry into their academic and social-emotional functioning. *Journal for the Education of the Gifted, 40*(3), 266–288. https://doi.org/10.1177/0162353217717033
What are the research questions?	In what manner do gifted students perceive that their all-day gifted program supports their academic and social-emotional functioning?
	How are gifted students' perceptions of their all-day gifted programs different for students in elementary and middle school?
What are the variables of interest?	Perceptions of academic functioning
	Perceptions of social-emotional functioning
How are these variables measured or operationalized?	These variables were measured through asking a set of questions during focus groups with students. Students had the opportunity to share their experiences in the all-day gifted program.

LET'S DO IT! 10.5

Practice Distinguishing Between the Different Levels of Measurement

Measure	Level of Measurement	Explanation
Myron's race	Nominal	Race has no numerical value.
Myron's reading ability (e.g., beginner, intermediate, fluent)	Ordinal	Categorize and rank reading ability data in an order.
Assessment of Myron's anxiety	Interval	Likert scale—can assume equal intervals among responses.

Measure	Level of Measurement	Explanation
Counselor observations on the number of times Myron gets out of his seat, has an outburst, and so forth, during the day	Ratio	There is a true zero point.
Myron's grades on science test administered during class	Ratio	There is a true zero point.

LET'S DO IT! 10.6

Practice Identifying Types of Measurement Validity

Study	Varier, D., Kitsantas, A., Zhang, X., & Saroughi, M. (2021). Self-efficacy for self-assessment: Development and validation of the SEESA-AW scale for argumentative writing. *International Journal of Educational Research, 110*, 1–11. https://doi.org/10.1016/j.ijer.2021.101885

Type of Validity	Evidence
Content	In developing the SEESA-AW Scale, researchers conducted a thorough review of the literature and utilized a rubric designed to assess argumentative writing in creating the items to ensure that all important aspects had been included. Additionally, researchers had three graduate students enrolled in an English academic writing class use the scale to assess their own writing and provide feedback on the measure.
Construct	Researchers used statistical procedures (e.g., exploratory and confirmatory factor analysis) to cluster items together and determine how much of the variance could be explained by each factor.
Convergent	Researchers compared the SEESA-AW Scale to the Writing Self-Efficacy Scale-Adapted (WSES-A) and the Self-Efficacy for Learning Form (SELF), two measures designed to assess similar constructs, to establish evidence for convergent validity.

11 DATA COLLECTION

LEARNING OBJECTIVES

Upon completion of this chapter, the reader should be able to

11.1   Describe the intersection between data collection instruments and the sources within educational settings

11.2   Identify the types, advantages, and disadvantages of data collection instruments used in quantitative research

11.3   Identify the types, advantages, and disadvantages of data collection instruments used in qualitative research

11.4   Outline ways to select data collection instruments

11.5   Demonstrate knowledge of ethical issues in collecting data for research studies

11.6   Utilize the *Publication Manual of the American Psychological Association* when reporting findings from data collection

A DAY AT WORK

What Training Do the Teachers Need?

Mr. Fernsby wants to collect data on how teachers are using technology tools within instruction in order to improve the upcoming professional development workshops.

©iStockphoto.com/monkeybusinessimages

Mr. Matt Fernsby, the district technology resource specialist, noticed that integrating technology within lessons is a common practice among the teachers in his school system. He also knew he was on to something in his professional development work with the school district when teachers in his last workshop said, "My kids will love this!" He also received positive feedback from surveys after his presentation.

One day, when he was visiting a local elementary school, he noticed that much of the student work with technology was created as substitutions for tasks that had been done in the past with paper and pencil. He wondered if the next series of professional development workshops should target more advanced ways of integrating technology and if teachers were interested in these topics. He also wanted to examine whether teachers' prior knowledge and self-efficacy for using technology related to their level of openness to using new technologies in the classroom. To address these issues, Mr. Fernsby needed to gather high quality information, so he asked himself, "Which instruments or approaches can I use to collect data?"

INTRODUCTION

Throughout this text, we have described many aspects of research design and the research process that educators and researchers can use to solve critical issues. Identifying appropriate data collection instruments (e.g., survey, interviews, observations) along with the most relevant sources of data (e.g., students, teachers, or parents) is fundamental to gathering data for a research study. Ultimately, it is this evidence from these instruments that will steer interpretations, findings, and recommendations. This chapter describes common data collection instruments across quantitative and qualitative research methodologies and highlights the advantages and disadvantages for each of these instruments. We then discuss multiple ways for collecting quantitative and qualitative data. The chapter concludes by detailing ethical issues surrounding methods of data collection and ways to assemble and organize data to adhere to the American Psychological Association (APA) style for subsequent writings and reports.

INTERSECTION OF DATA COLLECTION INSTRUMENTS AND SOURCES

11.1 Describe the intersection between data collection instruments and the sources within educational settings.

In the opening scenario, Mr. Fernsby realized that he did not have a clear understanding of the needs, attitudes, and skills of teachers in terms of technology integration within the classroom. He wanted to determine how to best serve the teachers and students in his local school district in upcoming workshops. To address this critical issue, Mr. Fernsby began to wonder about the type of information that was most important to assess, how he would assess it, and from whom he would collect the data. When researchers design a research study, one of the most critical things to figure out is the nature of data collection instruments to use and the most relevant people or sources for gathering these data.

At a general level, assessment (in school contexts) reflects a systematic approach for collecting data about people, learning contexts, or situations. Specifically, assessment can be used to gather information about people's attitudes, perspectives, or abilities; the nature of instructional practices; or the effects of intervention programs. Under this broad umbrella of assessment include the use of data collection instruments and the sources from which data are obtained. Data collection instruments are tools or approaches that gather different types of information for a research study. There are myriad assessment tools that researchers can use, such as observations, surveys or questionnaires, interviews, standardized or informal tests, interviews, or record review. In contrast, sources of data reflect the individuals or objects from which data and information are gathered. Common sources include students, teachers, administrators, and parents, as well as existing school records or artifacts. In a research study, researchers have great latitude in selecting assessment approaches. Further, they can administer multiple instruments to the same source, the same instrument to multiple sources, or multiple instruments to multiple sources.

To examine the issues about new types of technology to include as part of the school infrastructure, Mr. Fernsby decided to administer the same data collection instrument across different sources. For example, he conducted interviews with (a) teachers to uncover the ways they integrate technology in classroom instruction, (b) administrators to assess their perceptions regarding the role of technology in the schools, and (c) students to examine their favorite types of technology to use during learning. As we will describe throughout this chapter, Mr. Fernsby could have used many other data collection instruments, such as questionnaires (also called surveys), observations, artifacts created by teachers and students, lesson plans, or teacher-developed curriculum maps, to address aspect of the critical issue. Questionnaires represent a particularly popular form of assessment used to measure people's perceptions and attitudes about a given topic. Although not directly relevant to Mr. Fernsby and his critical issue, standardized tests and other forms for tests are quite popular in assessing students' abilities (e.g., intelligence), aptitudes (e.g., reasoning ability), or other types of academic skills (e.g., reading, writing). In short, researchers have access to a variety of assessment tools that can gather a wide array of quantitative data (i.e., number based) and qualitative data (i.e., language based).

Let's now examine some articles to see how researchers collect data to address their research questions. Identifying the data sources and data collection instruments is a key step that all researchers must take. In the Let's *See It!* activity, take look in the introduction section to identify the purpose of the study, then delve into the method section to identify sources of data and the data collection instruments.

Let's See It! 11.1

Goal: Identifying Sources of Data and Data Collection Instruments Within a Research Study

The primary objective of this activity is to identify the sources of data and data collection instruments from an article by Wang et al. (2014). Let's take a look at the Table 11.1, which includes a description of the purpose, sources, and the data collection instruments of the study.

TABLE 11.1 ■ Sources of Data and Data Collection Instruments	
Study	Wang, S.-K., Hsu, H.-Y., Campbell, T., & Longhurst, M. (2014). An investigation of middle school teachers and students use of technology inside and outside of classrooms: Considering whether digital natives are more technology savvy than their teachers. *Educational Technology Research Development, 62*(6), 637–622. https://doi.org/10.1007/s11423-014-9355-4
Purpose of study	The purpose of the study was to investigate the intersection of the "digital natives" and "digital immigrants" generations in regards to technology experiences and barriers in using these technologies with middle school students and their teachers.

| Identify sources of data | Twenty-four ($N = 24$) middle school science teachers and their students ($N = 1,060$) middle school students |
| Identify the data collection instruments | Quantitative survey measuring technology ownership, technology experience outside of school, and technology experience inside of school
Focus groups |

Let's Do It! 11.1

Guided Practice: Identifying Data Sources and Collection Instruments Within a Research Study

Goal: Identifying Sources of Data and Data Collection Instruments Within a Research Study

The primary objective of this *Let's Do It!* activity is for you to independently review a research article by Kule and Akcaoglu (2018) in Table 11.2 and identify the purpose of the study, sources of data, and the data collection instruments used in the study. To guide your thinking, we encourage you to use the *Let's See It!* information as well as the guiding headings. We also provide an answer key in the appendix at the end of the chapter for you to check your work.

TABLE 11.2 ■ Sources of Data and Data Collection Instruments	
Study	Kule, U., & Akcaoglu, M. (2018). The role of relevance in future teachers' utility value and interest toward technology. *Educational Technology Research & Development, 66*(2), 283–311. https://doi.org/10.1007/s11423-017-9547-9
Purpose of Study	
Identify sources of data	
Identify data collection instruments	

As you may recall from other chapters in this book, when a researcher identifies a critical issue and formulates research questions, the next step is for them to select a particular research methodology and design. As part of these methods, data collection instruments are identified and can represent either quantitative or qualitative approaches to gathering data. In Chapter 3, we outlined the differences between quantitative and qualitative methodologies. Quantitative research analyzes the relationships among variables, whereas qualitative research examines meanings, processes, and social interactions, often presented in narrative or language-based data. Thus, quantitative assessment methods yield numerical information used to assess how two or more variables are related or whether an intervention impacts another variable, while qualitative approaches generated language-based data to reveal the lived experiences of individuals or to highlight social dynamics within an educational setting. While referring to data collection instruments as quantitative or qualitative may be helpful, it is important to note that many data collection instruments can be used with either methodology. For example, while unstructured observations (i.e., writing a narrative about interactions among people) are prevalent in qualitative studies, structured observations (i.e., recording the number of times students get out of their seats during class) are quite common in quantitative studies. In general, the strategic selection of data collection instruments is often linked with the critical issue and the research question(s) (see Figure 11.1).

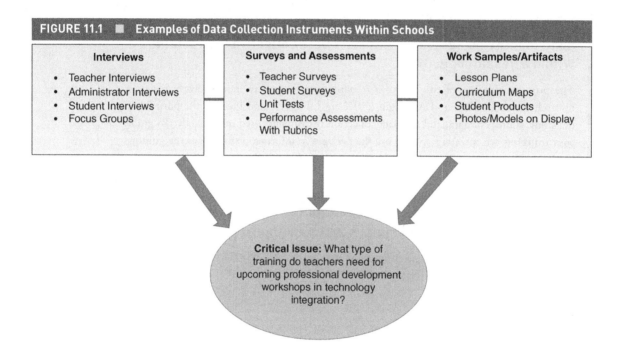

FIGURE 11.1 ■ Examples of Data Collection Instruments Within Schools

Interviews
- Teacher Interviews
- Administrator Interviews
- Student Interviews
- Focus Groups

Surveys and Assessments
- Teacher Surveys
- Student Surveys
- Unit Tests
- Performance Assessments With Rubrics

Work Samples/Artifacts
- Lesson Plans
- Curriculum Maps
- Student Products
- Photos/Models on Display

Critical Issue: What type of training do teachers need for upcoming professional development workshops in technology integration?

Suppose Ms. Jameson, a technology resource specialist assigned to several middle schools in a large school district, wanted to examine administrators' perceptions of technology integration and the structure of schools and resources allocated to accommodate new forms of technology. Specifically, she wanted to understand the values, attitudes, and behaviors of school personnel that shape the choices made to integrate technology within the school. In this situation, Ms. Jameson decided to conduct a series of interviews with the principals as well as multiple unstructured or narrative observations in the schools to examine block scheduling and utilization of the computer lab. These interviews and observations reflect data collection instruments designed to generate qualitative data.

In contrast, Mr. Carlson, who was a principal at one of the target middle schools regarding educational technology, was interested in examining whether teacher interest for innovations in educational technology increased over the course of several in-school workshops. Thus, he decided to provide teachers with a Likert-type questionnaire to assess their level of interest for technology integration. With this assessment, he gathered numerical information from questions such as, "On a scale of 1 to 5, with 5 being strong interest and 1 representing very low interest, please tell me how interested you are in learning about using the following types of technology-based activities in the classroom." Collecting this type of numerical information is useful to assess actual changes in teacher's level of interest, which is consistent with a more quantitative design (see Chapters 4 and 5)

Mr. Fernsby, who wanted to examine the impact of his professional development workshops on the level of technology integration, is interested in gathering both quantitative and qualitative data. In other words, he used mixed methods methodology (see Chapter 7). Mr. Fernsby used in-depth individual interviews with teachers to identify their perceptions and attitudes about technology integration. He also analyzed teacher lesson plans using a predetermined rubric to generate additional forms of qualitative data. On the other hand, he used questionnaires to assess teachers' level of interest in different types of technology as well as their self-efficacy for technology integration. These latter approaches reflect a quantitative set of data. Using data collection instruments that collectively generate both quantitative and qualitative types of data will often lead to deeper insights regarding some phenomenon.

STOP AND THINK 11.1

Here is a research question: What is the relationship between student self-efficacy for self-regulated learning and achievement in middle school mathematics? What are some potential data collection instruments you can use to answer this question? Please explain.

In sum, this section provided a general overview of the assessment process and a focus on how researchers can use different types of data collection instruments to gather quantitative and or qualitative information from different sources. The choices made about data collection and the subsequent data analysis process are intimately connected to the specific research methodology and design that one uses. In the next two sections of this chapter, we provide greater detail about specific quantitative and qualitative assessment approaches and a general overview of common advantages and disadvantages for these approaches.

THE TAKEAWAY

When conducting research, data collection instruments should gather the requisite information to adequately address the research questions.

QUANTITATIVE DATA COLLECTION INSTRUMENTS USED IN EDUCATIONAL SETTINGS

LEARNING OBJECTIVE

11.2 Identify the types, advantages, and disadvantages of data collection instruments used in quantitative research.

When examining most research methods textbooks, there are many ways in which authors have organized or categorized data collection instruments (please note that we use the term assessment tools interchangeably with data collection instruments). In this chapter, we classify the data collection instruments in terms of the two major research methodologies, quantitative and qualitative. Before we delve into the most common types of instruments, we wanted to offer a couple of qualifying statements. First, we recognize that our organizational structure is not perfect, nor is it the authoritative way to think about assessment. However, we use the qualitative–quantitative structure to help you more easily link data collection instruments with the type of data generated. Second, you will notice as you read further that several instruments are mentioned in both methodological categories. For example, observations are often used in both quantitative and qualitative research. As you will notice in the remainder of the chapter, the nature and characteristics of observations across the two methodologies are quite distinct and thus will lead to highly distinct forms of data.

In this section, we provide an overview of several common quantitative data collection instruments: (a) questionnaire or surveys; (b) structured observations; and (c) standardized tests (i.e., aptitude tests, standardized tests, norm-references tests, etc.). These three categories of assessment tools are not exhaustive of all potential instruments, but they are ones that are frequently used in school settings.

Questionnaires (Surveys)

Questionnaires reflect one of the most popular forms of quantitative assessment that entails asking the same questions using some type of response option or scale for all participants. There are two major ways to create questionnaire items—selected response (closed-ended) or constructed response (open-ended). *Selected response* items are used when an individual is given a series of predetermined responses to choose from, such as true/false, multiple choice, or Likert-type scales (e.g., agree, strongly agree, etc.). These types of items and measures are typically quantitative in nature because the responses naturally lead to numerical information that can be used to test relationships and trends with other variables, such as test scores, interest level, gender, or grade level. Questionnaires can also involve the use of *constructed responses* or open-ended questions. With this type of item, participants can respond with any answer they wish to express. These items can be scored with a rubric and then used as quantitative data or as qualitative data. For the remainder of this section, we illustrate in greater detail the key characteristics and distinctions between selected response and constructed response formats.

Selected Response Items

Selected response items are often used to gather information from a sample regarding demographic characteristics, attitudes, beliefs, and latent psychological constructs (e.g., anxiety, self-efficacy, happiness). Latent constructs are concepts that cannot be directly observed. As noted previously, the selected response options can be true/false, some type of multiple choice (select one option or all that apply), or Likert scale. To assess psychological constructs, researchers tend to emphasize Likert scales. The basic idea with a Likert scale format is that individuals will respond to a series of items that are collectively and theoretically supposed to be measuring the same construct. For example, suppose Mr. Fernsby wanted to assess students' perceptions regarding the frequency with which they engage in negative regulatory behaviors (e.g., procrastination, avoidance, and so on). He reviewed the literature and identified the Self-Regulated Strategy Inventory (SRSI; Cleary, 2006) as a viable questionnaire. The SRSI has three subscales, one of which includes eight items targeting maladaptive regulatory behavior ("I avoid going to extra help sessions"; "I wait to the last minute to begin studying"). Students are expected to read each item and then rate the frequency with which they engage in that behavior using a 7-point Likert scale ranging from 1 (never) to 7 (always). Thus, the use of the Likert scale with frequency anchors for each of the eight items allows researchers to draw conclusions about the frequency with which students display maladaptive regulation.

Questionnaires are typically self-report in format. That is, students or the other individuals complete the questionnaire to *self-report* their own perceptions, feelings, or beliefs. This differs from questionnaires that entail having sources other than the students, such as teachers and parents, provide ratings about student attitudes, beliefs, or psychological constructs. For example, the SRSI has a student self-report version as well as a teacher rating scale (SRSI-TRS) and a parent rating scale (SRSI-PRS). For these two rating scales, teachers and or parents are asked to provide ratings about *their* perceptions of students' regulatory behaviors. Another important feature of questionnaires involves how items are scored and interpreted.

In most cases, the scores for all items on a measure are aggregated and the mean score is used in the statistical analyses. After the researcher administered the eight-item maladaptive regulatory scale from the student version of the SRSI, the researcher would simply need to add the scores for each item and then calculate the mean or average score. This score would be interpreted as the frequency with which individuals display maladaptive regulation, on average.

©iStockphoto.com/ymgerman

Constructed Response Items

Constructed response items are frequently used in questionnaires and can be quite divergent in nature. With a more open-ended item, participants have more autonomy in what and how to provide a response. That is, they are not confined to the predetermined response options as with selected response formats. Constructed response items have several parts, including the item or prompt, a space for the respondent to provide a response, and the use of a rubric or coding scheme to transform the qualitative data into numerical format. The prompt is the part of the item that presents a question or situation to which a person responds. The response space is simply where the respondent provides their answer. Finally, the rubric is an assessment tool with preset criteria, descriptions of the criteria, and descriptions of levels of performance (e.g., outstanding, proficient, emerging).

Advantages and Disadvantages of Questionnaires

Questionnaires have many desirable features, which have resulted in their frequent use in schools and other contexts. They tend to be brief, easy to administer, and cost and time effective. Further, there are hundreds of questionnaires reported in the literature that show strong evidence for reliability and validity for assessing many important constructs (e.g., depression, anxiety, self-efficacy, school connectedness, self-concept, and so on). Thus, these measures can be quite useful when using inferential statistics in quantitative research to address questions pertaining to the relationships among variables. However, questionnaires are not without limitations. Because they rely on students' or other individual's self-reports, they simply reflect *perceptions of behavior* not actual behavior. Thus, if a student completes the SRSI maladaptive scale, the score does not reflect the students' actual behaviors; rather, it is simply their perceptions. Questionnaires are also often vulnerable to *socially desirable responses*. That is, people often wish to present themselves in a positive or favorable light. If a person responds to a questionnaire by providing socially desired responses, then the scores on the measure will be invalid (i.e., they do not represent the underlying construct the measure claims to measure).

Structured (Quantitative) Observations

Quantitative research emphasizes the use of structured and standardized ways to conduct observations. Structured observations reflect a set of quantitative data collection techniques for assessing and evaluating behaviors and events. When a researcher uses structured observations, they typically are interested in gathering information about behavior, such as whether it occurs, how often (frequency) or long (duration) it occurs, or the delay or time period before a behavior appears (latency). Typically, the first step when conducting quantitative observations is to identify and define the target behaviors of interest. Without a clear definition, an observer would not precisely know when or what to record. This issue is particularly important when multiple individuals are responsible for conducting the observations. For example, if the target behavior of interest was peer interactions, it is highly likely that different observers would have different interpretations of its meaning. Some may note that peer interactions reflect some type of sustained verbal conversation while others believe it includes both verbal conversations and non-verbal interaction. It is the responsibility of the researcher to define the target behavior and to provide examples and non-examples of that definition.

The next step when conducting these types of behavioral observations is to make decisions about the characteristics of behavior that one wishes to observe (e.g., frequency, duration) and the method for gathering the data. For instance, if a researcher wanted to assess the frequency with which teachers mention instructional strategies to support students during collaborative team meetings, they can simply record or tally every instance in which teachers mention a different type of strategy. If the researcher was interested in examining whether certain team members talk more frequently or longer than others, they could record the number of words spoken or the amount of time by each of the team members during the course of a meeting.

Another option for collecting data about behaviors would be to check off different points on a scale during each specific observation (e.g., to track student levels of engagement, social skills). Sometimes structured observational sheets will have a code with a legend on the sheet. When a researcher observes a targeted behavior, they enter the code within a designated space on the sheet. These codes can later be converted into numeric information. An example of a system of structured observations would be the Classroom Assessment Scoring System (CLASS; University of Virginia, 2023), designed to assess teacher behaviors in conjunction with student progress. The structured observation includes four, 15-minute observations with teacher behaviors and responses scored by trained observers and via manual guidelines. Ultimately, the goal is to improve student–teacher relationships to foster student growth.

Other methods would be to use a code to indicate observed behaviors based on intervals of time. This type of coding system would enable the researcher to track behavior with frequencies and graphs and compare student progress. Not only can structured observations support teachers and students in a specific context, but these tools can be useful in addressing hypotheses, particularly when used with other supporting data collection instruments. Regardless of the target behavior or the nature of the behavior that is recorded, these behavioral observations are quantitative because they generate numerical information that is used for interpretation.

Advantages and Disadvantages of Structured Observations

Structured observations are common in educational research, in part, because they are easy to implement and replicate. In fact, when the definitions of targeted behaviors are clear and multiple examples and non-examples are provided, it becomes much easier to train observers. A key benefit of structured observations is that they generate data reflecting behaviors as they occur within a specific situation or context. Thus, unlike questionnaires or surveys which rely on the respondents' perceptions and recall of behaviors, observations are highly objective in nature. Another advantage of behavioral observations is that they can easily be used to track behavior on a continuous basis or they can be used in certain research designs, such as single participant designs (see Figure 11.2 and Chapter 5).

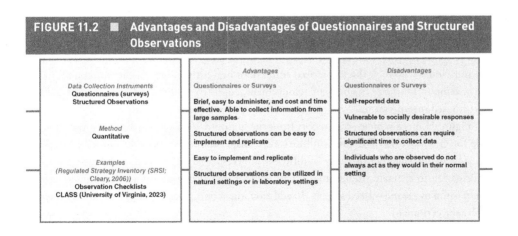

FIGURE 11.2 ■ Advantages and Disadvantages of Questionnaires and Structured Observations

	Advantages	Disadvantages
Data Collection Instruments **Questionnaires (surveys)** **Structured Observations**	Questionnaires or Surveys **Brief, easy to administer, and cost and time effective. Able to collect information from large samples**	Questionnaires or Surveys **Self-reported data**
Method **Quantitative**	**Structured observations can be easy to implement and replicate**	**Vulnerable to socially desirable responses** **Structured observations can require significant time to collect data**
Examples *(Regulated Strategy Inventory (SRSI; Cleary, 2006))* **Observation Checklists** **CLASS (University of Virginia, 2023)**	**Easy to implement and replicate** **Structured observations can be utilized in natural settings or in laboratory settings**	**Individuals who are observed do not always act as they would in their normal setting**

A limitation of structured observations is the increased time, number of personnel, and or cost. If a researcher wanted to conduct individual behavioral observations of 50 students in a school, they would either need a very large team of observers or multiple weeks to complete all of them. Another limitation is that the data reflect behavior as it occurs on a specific day and time and particular location. Thus, this type of data would not reveal what a student is typically like or how they tend to act in a general sense. Finally, if structured observations are conducted in a laboratory or more contrived setting, the data or information may not be representative of what individuals are like in a natural setting.

Measures of Abilities and Skills

Most educators are primarily concerned with students' cognitive abilities, potential to learn, and achievement skills. The preferred approach to address these areas is standardized tests. Standardized tests include assessments that are systematically administered, analyzed, and interpreted using set procedures and consistent guidelines. The rationale for using standardized procedures is to create a condition whereby all individuals who take the test experience the same questions in the same way and whose responses are scored in a uniform manner. Standardization allows one to make comparisons more easily and validly among groups of students while also identifying students' individual strengths and weaknesses. The use of standardized tests also allows school administrators and district leaders to evaluate students' mastery of learning and progress over time. To make determinations about student strengths and weaknesses, however, one needs to decide whether they will use norm-referenced or criterion-reference tests.

Norm-Referenced Tests

Norm-referenced tests are a type of assessment that uses the performance of a well-defined group (called the norm sample) as the basis for evaluating the performance of an individual. Thus, these scores generated from these tests are typically interpreted as, "How does this individual perform relative to a similar group of peers?" The raw score that an individual receives on a norm-referenced test is compared to the raw score for similar peers (in terms of age, grade level, ethnicity, and so on). The manuals of a standardized norm-referenced test will provide tables (or the use of computer software) that allows one to identify the person's standard score and percentile (metrics based on the use of the normal curve; see Chapter 12). The percentile is the easiest way to understand norm-based interpretation. Suppose a student takes a popular intelligence test, Weschler Intelligence Scale for Children (WISC). After completing this test, the examiner identifies that the students obtained an overall standard score of 115 and a percentile of 84. The latter score at the 84th percentile means that the individual who took the test scored equal to or better than 84% of the individuals in the norm sample. The large majority of achievement, cognitive ability, and aptitude tests rely on norm-based interpretation.

Figure 11.3 is a sample score report from the Stanford 10, a standardized test that is available for Grades K–12 (Pearson, 2009). In this image, the report provides information about the student and their performance in different subjects based on percentiles. Educators use this information to evaluate student mastery of content knowledge per subject and grade level in comparison to a standardized sample. In addition, the report gives a synopsis of skills covered in each subject domain.

FIGURE 11.3 ■ Sample Stanford 10 Report

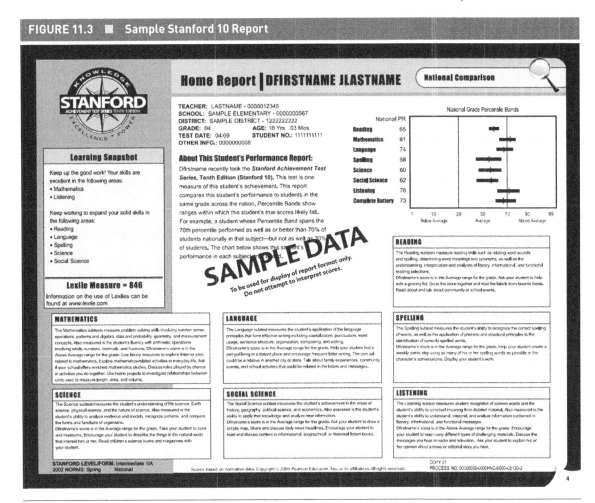

Criterion-Referenced Tests

A second type of standardized test is known as a criterion-referenced test (sometimes called domain-referenced). With this type of assessment, an individual's performance is judged relative to some professionally determined standard of performance. The scores derived from these tests are typically interpreted as, "How does this individual perform relative to some established criteria or standard?" Thus, norm-referenced and criterion-referenced tests are similar in that they both seek to generate data and making interpretations about student abilities and skills; the key difference is the nature of the comparative benchmark used to make interpretations. Norm-referenced tests use a clearly defined group as the benchmark while criterion-referenced tests use predetermined criteria. Some states adopt a criterion-referenced test as an end of the year assessment tool, which can have important consequences in terms of student promotion to a higher grade/course level or the overall accountability of schools, administrators, and educators. The metric used to interpret performance with criterion-referenced tests is typically some type of mastery benchmark, such as a percentage correct or expected level of questions answered. Based on the student's performance, they could be placed into different performance levels, such as developing, emerging, proficient, or advanced, or other similar terms that show a gradation of skill. Figure 11.4 includes an excerpt from a criterion-referenced test indicating levels of proficiency based on raw scores. Distinct from common norm-referenced test, criterion-referenced tests often provide specific information about student performance in sub strands. This information pinpoints student strengths and weaknesses.

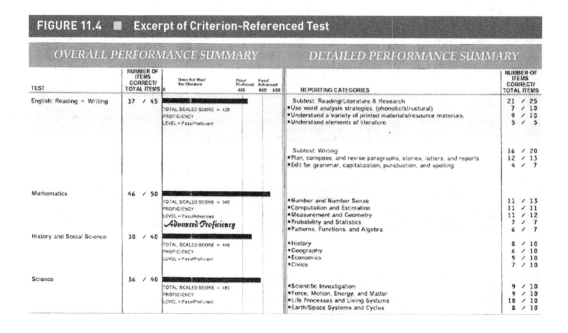

FIGURE 11.4 ■ Excerpt of Criterion-Referenced Test

STOP AND THINK 11.2

What experiences have you had with norm-referenced and criterion-referenced tests?

Types of Standardized Tests

There are many categories of standardized tests that are often used in education: (a) intelligence (cognitive ability), (b) achievement, (c) aptitude, and (d) diagnostic. These types of assessments are useful for both educators and researchers. The following section details the key characteristic of each type of standardized test and then provides a general overview of the key advantages and disadvantages of standardized tests.

Intelligence (Cognitive Ability) Tests

Intelligence tests have received an enormous amount of attention over the past century, particularly regarding their centra role in identifying students with learning difficulties or specific types of disabilities (e.g., learning disabilities, cognitive disabilities). These measures have become a staple of the assessment batteries used by psychologists in schools and clinical contexts. Although there is still debate regarding the ultimate importance, utility, and potential dangers of intelligence tests (i.e., role in discriminating against marginalized groups), they are important to evaluate and understand. Like any measure targeting a latent construct (not observable), intelligence tests were constructed to examine a broad range of cognitive abilities (i.e., spatial and verbal reasoning, visualization, processing speed) that collectively are labeled intelligence. Although there are many different theoretical models and definitions of intelligence, it is generally considered to reflect an ability to think abstractly, problem-solve, and adapt to experience. Some of the most common commercially available intelligence tests include the Wechsler scales (pre-school, children, and adult versions), Stanford-Binet Intelligence Scale, and Woodcock Johnson III Tests of Cognitive Abilities. There are several other tests that address different types of cognitive abilities, such as memory and executive functions. Regardless of the latent construct targeted by standardized tests, they all tend to rely on norm-based interpretations. Thus, if researchers wanted to assess intelligence of a sample used in a research study, they would rely on standard scores and percentiles as the basis for understanding their overall abilities.

Aptitude Tests

Aptitude tests are very similar to tests of intelligence or other cognitive ability but differ in their focus on student potential for success in school, work, or beyond. Aptitude tests are specifically designed to help understand student potential and their ability to succeed in specific situations or careers. For example, aptitude tests are often used to gauge student abilities as they transition to a new level of schooling (i.e., entering college) or employment (i.e., applying for a specific job). The Scholastic Aptitude Test (SAT) and Graduate Record Examination (GRE) are common examples of aptitude tests used by colleges and universities as a criterion in the admissions process. Although there is recent controversy regarding the appropriateness of these measures for marginally or underrepresented populations, the basic logic is that the norm-referenced scores generated from these tests are predictive of success in college. Aptitude tests are also used by high school counselors to advise students about career choice or by organizations to help identify individuals with high potential for success in a specific role or career, such as an airline pilot or police officer.

More recently, school districts have adopted computer adaptive tests with a scoring procedure based on a continuum of skills/content mastery that serves as a predictor of student success. A prominent difference between traditional aptitude tests and computer adaptive tests is the process of providing test items. Using computer adaptive testing (CAT), students receive a series of questions based on previous answers. As students answer questions correctly, the subsequent questions become more difficult. For instance, the Cognitive Ability (CAT4) test uses a series of quizzes/puzzles to assess student verbal, nonverbal, mathematical, and spatial reasoning. This aptitude test identifies the academic potential of students, assists in program/instructional placement, and predicts future academic success. Adaptive tests determine areas of student strengths and weaknesses to inform parents and teachers about next steps.

Achievement Tests

Achievement tests are designed to assess student mastery of content knowledge and/or skills acquired through specific experiences like school-based instruction. Thus, achievement tests are fundamentally distinct from aptitude or cognitive ability measures, the latter of which are affected by both informal learning experiences and those that occur in formal settings like schools. Achievement tests can vary in format, scope, and psychometric rigor. A major distinction is between standardized achievement tests and teacher-constructed tests (e.g., a test to assess knowledge of the respiratory system). Although both are designed to assess learning or skills in a specific area, standardized tests tend to have stronger evidence for reliability and validity. The lack of reliability and validity data is not a criticism of teacher-constructed tests; teachers simply do not have the time to evaluate each of their tests in this way. They teach a specific topic and then need to construct a test to immediately assess students' learning and overall knowledge for that topic.

Standardized tests also tend to be more fixed than teacher-constructed achievement tests. That is, to create "standardization," test developers need to include a particular set of content items and then develop specific procedures for administering and scoring the tests. Teachers can be nimbler and more adaptive in their development of classroom-based tests and are more free to use their personal experience to create tests that best meet the needs of their students. Further, standardized tests also rely on norm-referenced interpretations and thus will produce standard scores and percentiles as the basis for interpretation. Teacher-constructed tests tend to get evaluated using percentage accuracy or another criterion-based way to understand student performance. Informally, teachers can use some types of norm-based information to provide grades, such as when teachers only provide A's to students with grades within the top 25% of the class. This latter approach is often not viewed favorably by some scholars given that it promotes competition and shifts students' attention away from their individual learning to that of their peers. Common commercially available standardized tests of achievement include the Wecshler Individual Achievement Test (WIAT), Stanford Achievement Test (SAT 10), Woodcock-Johnson Tests of Achievement (WJ), Peabody Individual Achievement Test (PIAT), and the Kaufman Test of Educational Achievement (KTEA).

State-mandated achievement tests represent a special type of standardized test tied to state legislative initiatives, and they are often used for accountability purposes. Sometimes called "high stakes testing," the measure typically aligns with a state-developed instructional framework and can correspond with consequences, such as student promotion to a grade level/graduation, as well as school and teacher accountability. The Virginia Standards of Learning and Testing (Virginia Department of Education, 2022) is an example of a state-mandated test that utilizes a criterion-referenced system to assess student proficiency in core subjects across grade levels.

Diagnostic Tests

Diagnostic tests represent a special category of testing designed to identify specific areas of weakness or challenge for students, often in academic skills. Just like medical doctors use diagnostic tests to pinpoint the nature of a health condition, such as a CT scan, biopsy, or electrocardiogram, educators would use diagnostic tests to understand the nature of a students' reading, mathematics, or writing difficulties. There are a variety of standardized diagnostic tools used to pinpoint student needs and capabilities, such as the Stanford Diagnostic Reading Test (also has mathematics version), Woodcock Reading Mastery Test, and Group Mathematics Assessment and Diagnostic Evaluation. The primary goal for all types of diagnostic tests is to help educators or others identify and understand the nature of students' strengths and weaknesses and the nature of instructional or academic supports that are needed.

Advantages and Disadvantages of Standardized Tests

There are several advantages to using standardized tests, including strong psychometric properties as well as their ability to measure student progress in school, identify areas in need of improvement, reduce bias in scoring due to standardization, and enhance the overall accountability of schools. Most standardized tests that are commercially available tend to have robust psychometric properties, such as strong evidence to support the reliability of scores and the validity of inferences from these scores. This helps to reassure educators that the scores generated from these tests are in fact measuring the constructs that they claim to measure. Standardized tests are also used extensively within school contexts for clinical, educational, and practical purposes. For example, school psychologists often use standardized tests to assess students' cognitive abilities (e.g., intelligence, executive function skills) and academic achievement skills (e.g., reading, mathematics, and writing). These tests are foundational to identifying students who may need special education support programs and services. These tests can also be administered in the beginning and end of a school year to evaluate student progress and response to the curriculum. Standardized tests also offer multiple ways to interpret student performance, such as norm-referenced or criterion-referenced interpretations.

Like any data collection instrument, there are several drawbacks or limitations to standardized tests. Of greatest importance is that standardized tests can never really show a complete picture of students' achievement, skills, or abilities. Students may possess adequate knowledge, but for some, it does not manifest or reveal itself on standardized tests. Thus, standardized tests are not guaranteed to generate scores that accurately reflect students' capabilities. Furthermore, because most standardized tests use a standardized set of items and procedures, it is possible that these tests are "fairer" for some students than others. For example, students who have more experience in taking these tests and access to greater supports (i.e., those from more affluent background) are at a distinct advantage. This latter issue also reflects assessment bias; that is, when a measure unfairly and negatively impacts people based on certain personal characteristics like socioeconomic status, racial/ethnic backgrounds, gender identity, or other characteristics. When standardized tests are used as "high-stakes testing," there is often an increase in the level of stress and anxiety experienced by many stakeholder, such as administrators, teachers, students, and parents. When students take important standardized tests like different types of aptitude tests (e.g., SAT, GRE), they may underperform due to test anxiety.

Given that standardized testing focuses on one snapshot in time, there is also a potential risk that unpredictable factors influence the validity and accuracy of one's scores, such as poor sleep the night before the test, personal distractions (e.g., a student is distressed because they recently got cut from the baseball team), or family issues or crises (e.g., death of a family member). Finally, some districts have begun to use standardized tests to evaluate teacher effectiveness. This practice is questionable given that most of these tests have not been sufficiently vetted to serve this purpose. Figure 11.5 summarizes the advantages and disadvantages of standardized tests.

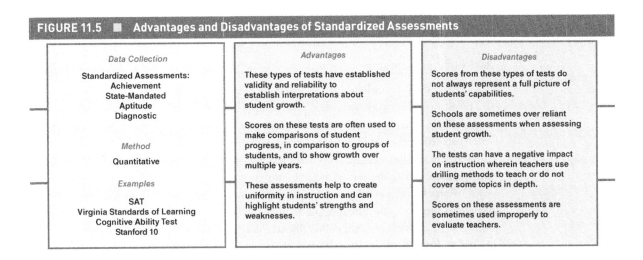

FIGURE 11.5 ■ Advantages and Disadvantages of Standardized Assessments

Data Collection	Advantages	Disadvantages
Standardized Assessments: Achievement State-Mandated Aptitude Diagnostic	These types of tests have established validity and reliability to establish interpretations about student growth.	Scores from these types of tests do not always represent a full picture of students' capabilities.
Method Quantitative	Scores on these tests are often used to make comparisons of student progress, in comparison to groups of students, and to show growth over multiple years.	Schools are sometimes over reliant on these assessments when assessing student growth. The tests can have a negative impact on instruction wherein teachers use drilling methods to teach or do not cover some topics in depth.
Examples SAT Virginia Standards of Learning Cognitive Ability Test Stanford 10	These assessments help to create uniformity in instruction and can highlight students' strengths and weaknesses.	Scores on these assessments are sometimes used improperly to evaluate teachers.

District/Teacher Developed Assessments

Not all assessments of student performance in schools reflect standardized tests. District or teacher developed assessments consist of benchmarks, unit tests, performance assessments, portfolio assessments, and course grades (Figure 11.5). This section provides a brief overview of these school-based assessment tools and their corresponding advantages and disadvantages. As a general rule of thumb, however, these types of assessments are not emphasized in research.

Benchmark Tests

Benchmark tests, commonly known as interim assessments, serve as standards or comparisons against which to monitor student progress throughout the year. Typically, these assessments are given in core subjects as a pretest, as a mid-year check, and then as a posttest. While the purpose of these tools is to prepare students for high stakes standardized tests and to track how well students are mastering and retaining information, from a research perspective, these assessments are viable as repeated measures. Examining student performance across the year in conjunction with the implementation of an intervention could help researchers examine the impacts.

Unit Tests

Another commonly available tool in classrooms is unit tests, a type of test to gauge student mastery of topics within a particular instructional unit (e.g., history—industrial revolution; science—plant and animal cells; mathematics—rationale numbers; language arts—figurative language). These tests can be used to determine student progress or differences among groups (e.g., special education students versus general education students).

Performance-Based Assessments

Performance-based assessments represent a form of assessment that requires students to demonstrate their knowledge and skills through authentic or open-ended activities. The key aspect of this type of assessment is students producing some type of artifact or product that can be evaluated. Examples of these types of assessments include writing a synthesis of a research literature, conduct a science investigation, or developing a portfolio of work that illustrates a specific skill set or knowledge base. Performance assessments are typically criterion-referenced and thus include a set of criteria of proficiency that correspond with a rubric. Unlike standardized tests that have highly objective and consistent scoring and evaluation procedures, the scoring of performance-based assessment can be highly subjective. Thus, the development of a clear, well-defined rubric and the provision of adequate training using such a rubric is often needed.

Portfolio Assessments

Portfolio assessments include a broad collection of student work products generated over time that involve a process whereby learners continuously collect and reflect on their work to improve their skills. In a sense, portfolios are reflective of self-regulatory processes given that students reflect on their work, refine strategies, and apply the revised strategies to create a product.

With a portfolio, students work with teachers to select items for the portfolio and gauge their progress, strengths, and areas for improved growth. Teachers sometimes provide skills-based rubrics for the students to self-critique their work. These portfolios are springboards for parent conferences or for students to articulate their growth across the year. In comparison to other assessment tools outlined in this chapter, a strong element of portfolio assessments centers around student interaction and reflection of materials.

Educators often assign performance assessments with corresponding rubrics to gauge student mastery of content. These assessments can be in the form of a project, report, model, or artifact, as some examples.

©iStockphoto.com/JGalione

Course Grades

Course grades reflect a type of performance indicator used in schools to reflect students' aggregated level of achievement in a particular class at defined points of a school year. This assessment tool capture trends across several grade levels; however, the use of grades as a research method has limitations based on differing grading scales across districts, teacher differences in scoring assessments, and varying modalities of instruction that can influence student performance, as some examples.

Advantages and Disadvantages of District/Teacher Developed Assessments

Teacher and district developed assessments can take a variety of forms, including benchmarks, unit tests, performance assessments, portfolio assessments, and course grades. For each type of assessment, there are specific advantages and disadvantages, not only for the student and educator but also in terms of a research study. Generally speaking, however, these types of assessments can assist teachers, district personnel, parents, and students in monitor student progress across the year. They can also generate information about students' context-specific or situational learning. Rather than waiting for an end of the year achievement score, the various forms of teacher-developed assessments provide more immediate and contextualized feedback. Collectively, these assessment tools provide useful supplements and alternatives to the more standardized and fixed assessment tools. As discussed previously, all students do not learn in the same way, nor do they demonstrate knowledge and skills in the same way. Thus, having an opportunity to demonstrate achievement and learning with a portfolio, performance-based assessment or some other local assessment tool can provide a more well-rounded approach to evaluating students.

A key limitation to this group of assessments is the lack of robust reliability and validity information. The scoring on these assessments tends to also be more subjective and variable than with more objective and standardized data collection instruments. Thus, with these contextualized forms of assessment, educators need to take special care to develop clearly defined guidelines and criteria that align with scoring procedures. In addition, these guidelines and criteria need to be explicitly described to students prior to the assignment. When these steps are not performed, students can become confused and anxious, thereby limiting their ability to perform and demonstrate their knowledge. Finally, for many of the reasons listed in this section, teacher-development assessments will often be de-emphasized in research contexts. When conducting a quantitative research study, researchers strive to emphasize the most reliable and valid measures so that there is strong confidence that the target constructs and variables are being assessed. Figure 11.6 summarizes the key points related to advantages and disadvantages of district/teacher developed assessments.

FIGURE 11.6 ■ Advantages and Disadvantages of District/Teacher Developed Assessments

Data Collection Instruments	Advantages	Disadvantages

Interim Assessment
Unit Test
Performance Assessment
Portfolio Assessment
Course Grade
 	
Method
 	
Quantitative
(with scores and rubrics)
 	
Examples
 	
District Benchmark
Unit Test on Photosynthesis
Project on Simple Machines
Student Selected Work in Science
Term Grade in Science
	District/Teacher developed tests can be predictive of student performance in subsequent assessments. A variety of district/school-based assessment tools can provide a multi-faceted view of what students know.
	    Some of these types of assessments account for students' reflection on their performance and can be used for parent conferences. Also, projects allow for divergent thought processes and encourage creativity and motivation. Grades provide an overall gauge of student performance.
		Poorly constructed assessment tools may provide teachers with incorrect perceptions of student progress.
		    Students may be able to guess correct answers from clues from other questions.
		    Some types of portfolio assessments may be difficult to manage, organize, and score with fidelity.
		    When scoring, some teachers may be influenced by the halo effect, which is when the educator has a positive preconceived perception of a student's capabilities prior to scoring work.
		    Grades can sometimes be inflated due to individual teacher standards and/or district policies.

THE TAKEAWAY

A researcher collects quantitative data to address research questions that focus on relationships among variables, trends, and predictions. The researcher should account for the advantages and disadvantages of the research tools prior to selection.

QUALITATIVE DATA COLLECTION INSTRUMENTS USED IN EDUCATIONAL SETTINGS

LEARNING OBJECTIVE

11.3   Identify the types, advantages, and disadvantages of data collection instruments used in qualitative research.

Researchers can utilize a variety of data collection instruments as part of qualitative research. Although it is possible for qualitative research to occasionally use numerical information as part of a study, the primary focus is on generating narrative or language-based information about people's experiences, perspective, and attitudes. In this section, we review the following four common qualitative data collection instruments: (a) interviews, (b) observations, (c) questionnaires, and (d) documents and artifacts. The following descriptions will also delineate the key advantages and disadvantages of each type of data collection instrument.

Qualitative Interviews

A common data collection instrument used within qualitative and mixed methods studies is the qualitative interview. Given that the experiences, perceptions, and attitudes of individuals in qualitative study are of paramount importance, it is often necessary to gather data directly from the participants through an interview format. The following section outlines three common ways to collect descriptions from individuals involved in research studies, participant interviews and focus group questions, and open-ended questionnaires.

Participant Interviews

Participant interviews represent a set of open-ended questions that are used to obtain the experiences and perspectives of individuals in great depth. These interviews can be informal and conversational in nature or they can adhere to a structured or semi-structured process. A semi-structured process is often desirable in qualitative research as it allows researchers to begin an interview session with a predetermined set of questions but be able to flexibly adapt or add questions during the interview process, as needed. This adaptation process is common in interviews, as the researchers strive to follow up or expand on participant responses that were lacking detail or were ambiguous.

When creating interview questions, researchers should consult the literature to highlight topics, concepts, or ideas that are relevant to a particular study. Although interview questions in a qualitative study should be distinct from other research, it is often helpful to review existing interview protocols used in prior research. Such an activity can provide ideas regarding formatting of sequencing of questions. It is also advisable to pilot test the interview with individuals like those used in the study and or experts in the field. Pilot testing is a fantastic way of refining and enhancing clarity of questions and to ensure that the interview protocol is effective in generating types of data that are expected. A researcher interested in studying teachers' experiences with technology in the classroom may gain insights from technology resource teachers, administrators, and computer specialists in the industry. A pilot study with experts can inform the framework of a subsequent study.

Finally, it is important to note that when individuals are speaking, the researcher should allow them to continue rather than redirecting them to address the questions the researcher wants to study. After all, the framing of the study centers on the voices of the participants. When the researcher seeks to learn more information, subsequent participants may provide additional accounts that enhance the direction of the study.

Focus Groups

An alternative to the individual interview format is to conduct a focus group. Focus groups center on interviewing several individuals at the same time about a particular issue. Usually, these individuals have common experiences and may even belong to the same organization. In the opening scenario, Mr. Fernsby wanted to improve the way teachers incorporated technology within their classrooms based on professional development. In this type of study, a focus group of five to six teachers who participated in the professional development program would be a way to gather deeper and potentially more information about the benefits of the program and subsequent needs of the teachers from a collective viewpoint. However, it is important to note that conducting focus groups typically exerts a higher level of demand and expectation on the interviewer. Unlike individual participant interviews, a focus group requires the interviewer to possess and effectively utilize group management skills while simultaneously asking and adapting questions relevant to the research questions of the study.

Advantages and Disadvantages of Qualitative Interviews

Participant interviews provide expansive information for researchers and often shed light on subtleties within educational contexts. This contribution is particularly true with well-defined selection criteria and well-constructed interview questions. Rich information provided by participants can be a major factor in analysis and interpretations of findings, theory development, and suggestions for effective educational practices. However, the participants may or may not provide information that addresses the overall goal or they might have minimal information to share. Conducting in-depth interviews can also be a time-consuming process. In Chapter 6, we discussed that sample size is often not a consideration for qualitative studies because the focus is on examining perceptions from the participants of the study rather than accepting or rejecting hypotheses. While meeting with individuals can yield critical information, even with a small number of participants, the process of interviewing, transcribing, and coding data and then conducting analysis and interpretations can be an overwhelming and time-intensive activity.

A common way to study a topic from participants' perspectives is through interviews. These interviews can provide rich information for findings, theory development, and effective educational practices with carefully defined participant sampling criteria.

©iStockphoto.com/SDI Productions

A major advantage of focus groups is the potential to generate data regarding the collective attitudes, values, and beliefs of the sample for a particular situation. For example, suppose a researcher wanted to examine the topic of computer science but wanted to assess males and females in separate groups due to historical differences between these groups with this topic. By conducting two separate focus groups to ascertain the attitudes and interest for entering computer science for each biological sex, the researchers would generate important information about the collective perspectives for each group. However, a major limitation of a focus group is the tendency for some participants to hijack or dominate the conversation. When one or two individuals dominate the conversation, a researcher may not truly capture the "collective voice" that they ultimately are attempting to gather. Figure 11.7 summarizes the advantages and disadvantages of interviews and focus groups.

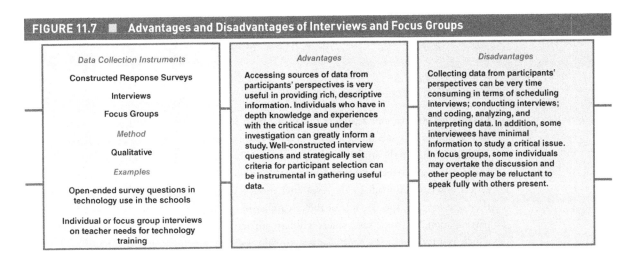

FIGURE 11.7 ■ Advantages and Disadvantages of Interviews and Focus Groups

Data Collection Instruments	Advantages	Disadvantages
Constructed Response Surveys Interviews Focus Groups *Method* Qualitative *Examples* Open-ended survey questions in technology use in the schools Individual or focus group interviews on teacher needs for technology training	Accessing sources of data from participants' perspectives is very useful in providing rich, descriptive information. Individuals who have in depth knowledge and experiences with the critical issue under investigation can greatly inform a study. Well-constructed interview questions and strategically set criteria for participant selection can be instrumental in gathering useful data.	Collecting data from participants' perspectives can be very time consuming in terms of scheduling interviews; conducting interviews; and coding, analyzing, and interpreting data. In addition, some interviewees have minimal information to study a critical issue. In focus groups, some individuals may overtake the discussion and other people may be reluctant to speak fully with others present.

Questionnaires (focus on open-ended items)

Earlier in this chapter, we discussed two primary types of questionnaire items; selected response and constructed response. While selected response items are emphasized in quantitative research, constructed response or open-ended items can be used in quantitative, qualitative, or mixed methods approaches. For example, researchers conducting quantitative studies can use constructed response or open-ended question to supplement the numerical, predetermined response categories found with selected response items. From a qualitative lens, however, the open-ended nature of questions is directly aligned with the nature of questions used during interviews. When respondents are provided with more general or open-ended questions, they are naturally prompted to provide deeper and more expansive perspectives on a particular topic. After the participants complete open-ended questions on a questionnaire, they would include these data as part of subsequent qualitative coding and analysis procedures.

Advantages and Disadvantages of Constructed Response Items

Incorporating constructed response items is an efficient and cost-effective way to gather additional qualitative information about participant perspectives and lived experiences. Surveying individuals minimizes or eliminates the time needed to locate participants, set up meeting times, interview individuals, and then conduct or locate a service to transcribe the interviews. Open-ended questionnaire items can also help a researcher gather information from a larger group of people than would be possible with an interview. This type of approach is suitable for research and program evaluations, the latter of which may entail a limited time frame from which to obtain data and then develop reports for stakeholders. In terms of limitations, open-ended questionnaire items can lead to more limited responses from participants than is the case with an interview. During an interview, a researcher can probe, ask follow-up questions, and delve into the weeds regarding comments from participants. Using an open-ended questionnaire format for items can limit the ability of researchers to extend participants experiences to theory development and/or implications.

STOP AND THINK 11.3

Consider a topic of interest. If you wanted to collect data on participants' perspectives, which data collection instrument would work best for your study?

Qualitative Observational Tools

Qualitative observations represent one of the most important data collection instruments used by researchers. In general, these types of observations seek to identify and record all interactions or ideas relevant to the study. Unlike quantitative observations which specify the target variables and precise ways to record information, qualitative observations are much less prescriptive. They reflect observations made by the researcher about research participants or the contexts in which they operate. The specific role of the researcher in qualitative research can vary in the level of participation. At times, researchers will have an active role within the participant community, which is a type of *participant observer*. In this case, the researcher has first-hand experiences within the group and participates in activities. In contrast, as a privileged observer, the researcher examines interactions in the community in a removed way. The following section outlines three common forms of observations: (a) observations and analytic memos; (c) audio/video recordings; and (d) observation checklists.

Field Notes and Analytic Memos

Observations are often a critical source of qualitative data. Researchers rely on observations, often in connection with other data sources, to interpret processes, social exchanges, or other phenomena. One way for researchers to collect observations is to write in a journal or on a laptop. These observations can be very useful in describing situations and social interactions by creating a rich narrative of the critical issue. In addition to collecting observations, a common practice is to write analytic memos of the observations. These memos can be written in the margins of a journal for instance. Analytic memos help the researcher with reflexivity, a process wherein the researcher reflects on their reactions to check potential personal biases (see Chapter 14 for more details). After writing observational field notes and analytic memos, the researcher will review their writings to consider the interpretations they have had for a given situation. Revisiting these notes helps the researcher to process information from a different lens, check for biases, and improve the rigor of the study.

Audio/Video Recording

Audio and video recordings represent technology-enhanced ways to gather observations about the behavior of individuals and the nature of their interactions within a social setting. Audio recordings and video recordings help a researcher to revisit the scene of an observation and to thoroughly examine or pinpoint important details that might not have been noticed during a live observation. Audio and video recordings are particularly helpful when observing the implementation of professional development activities or interventions in the classroom. If a researcher used audio recordings of teachers working in collaborative teams during a technology workshop, they will have a permanent record of the discussions. Again, a researcher would be able to revisit this professional development context to reveal important aspects of the conversations. For example, in listening to audio recording, the researcher may notice the high level of enthusiasm shown by teachers and thus could use a direct quote to support the importance of the program, "This Scratch Jr. card is great! My students would definitely understand the concept of looping from this task."

Observation Checklists

Another tool would be an observation checklist, a method for recording actions or processes that the researcher observes. Suppose a researcher wants to analyze the nature and range of events or behaviors in the classroom. Having an observation checklist prepared prior to implementing the study helps to prompt or remind the researcher about general things that one could examine. A researcher interested in how special needs students use technology in the classroom may want to create an observation checklist that centers on the types of assignments given, accommodations made for students, and access to assistive technologies. As a researcher moved between classrooms or observed rotating groups of students in a secondary school, a checklist would serve as a scaffold to steer observations. These observations can be in the form of tallies used for descriptions in qualitative research as well as accompanying narrative comments.

Advantages and Disadvantages of Qualitative Observations

Observational notes, analytic memos, audio and video recordings, and observational checklists are all instrumental in developing a rich understanding of some phenomenon. When several of these instruments are used, it allows researchers to triangulate data (i.e., assess convergence of data from multiple sources), particularly when comparing live field notes to a video recording. The use of these audio and video recordings is particularly important given that it may lead to new meanings beyond what was observed from the original situation. All these approaches are also important in that they create a permanent accounting of the observation scene or situation. In short, the use of multiple observation tools can enable researchers to have greater confidence in the accuracy and trustworthiness of the data.

A primary disadvantage of observation notes or memos is the high level of attention and memory required of an observer. It is virtually impossible to notice all nuances and details of a given situation, particularly situations that are complex. Although audio and video recording help to mitigate these issues, the use of technology can also be problematic. For example, if researchers were audio recording students using Scratch Jr. in the classroom following a professional development workshop for teachers, a hand-held audio device might inadvertently not record, or the data might be erased. For this reason, it is preferable to have several devices recording to offset this type of event. In addition, the quality of the recordings could be questionable. The filming of students outdoors could result in sound interference; there may be audio interference from wind, animals, air traffic, and so forth. The researcher would want to test the audio quality prior to conducting the investigation. In terms of observation checklists, a key disadvantage of this approach is that having predetermined topics to examine may cause the researcher to overlook an important interaction or element in the context of study. Figure 11.8 summarizes the advantages and disadvantages related to data based on researcher perspectives.

FIGURE 11.8 ■ Advantages and Disadvantages of Qualitative Observational Tools

Data Collection	Advantages	Disadvantages
Observations/Memos **Audio/Video Recordings** **Observation Checklists** *Method* **Qualitative** *Examples* **Observing/recording Teachers at an integrative technology workshop Using a checklist to examine the prevalence and types of assistive technology in classrooms**	**Data sources collected by researchers in the form of observations, memos, map making, recordings, and checklists can be used as a qualitative data source that can be coded and analyzed; descriptive information to describe an intervention, processes, or interactions; as a form of triangulation; and as a way for researchers to check potential personal biases.**	**When collecting these types of data sources, the researcher needs to be aware that their suppositions may be steering choices made (including types of data) and subsequent interpretations. The use and design of these elements may omit important topics. From a practical standpoint, the researcher needs to account for technical issues (recording devices failing) and interruptions (noise in the background). Potential problems should be tested prior to conducting research.**

Documents and Artifacts

Another important way to gather qualitative data is by collecting and analyzing artifacts, documents, or work products reflective of important ideas or themes. This data collection instrument is distinct from many other approaches because it does not require direct interaction between an observer and participant. A few general categories of artifacts that we review in this section include organizational documents and participant-created documents and products.

Organizational Documents

Within an educational framework, there are many organizational documents that can shed light on processes and interactions. Examples would be state-mandated learning standards, district curriculum guides, staff meeting agendas, faculty handbooks, student or faculty files, documentation of external communication, and so on. The importance of any organizational document or artifact is determined by its relevance and alignment with the objectives and purposes of a particular research study.

Participant-Created Documents and Products

Within a school setting, there is an abundance of work products and documents created by students, teachers, and staff members that can serve as artifacts for research studies. For example, student essays, writing journals, study notes, or emails to the teacher all represent a type of personal or participant product.

Advantages and Disadvantages of Documents and Artifacts

Qualitative research represents a multi-faceted, complex process that involves diverse types of data collection instruments. The following section outlines the advantages and disadvantages of incorporating these types of data within a study: organizational documents, participant-created products, and participant-created documents.

Artifacts can be useful for studying values, attitudes, and beliefs of participants; growth in a particular area or skill; and the impact of interventions. Because they represent extant data or records, the effort to obtain these records is much less intensive than conducting intensive live observations or interviews. Further, documents in educational settings represent a unique type of data that likely cannot be gathered using other qualitative data collection instruments.

However, the analysis of student work samples and other artifacts can be very time-consuming. Clearly articulating the methods for collecting data, including selection criteria, organization, and analysis techniques, maintains a level of transparency and checks assumptions and biases. A disadvantage would be if documents do not yield in-depth information that clearly addresses research questions. Figure 11.9 summarizes the advantages and disadvantages of school-based artifacts.

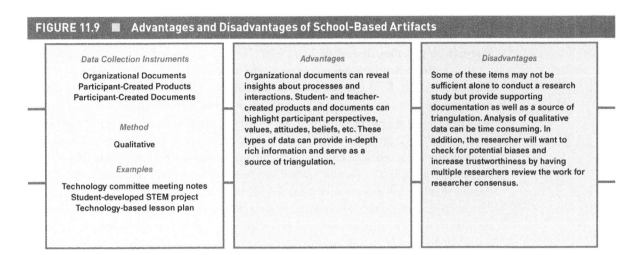

FIGURE 11.9 ■ Advantages and Disadvantages of School-Based Artifacts

Data Collection Instruments	Advantages	Disadvantages
Organizational Documents Participant-Created Products Participant-Created Documents *Method* Qualitative *Examples* Technology committee meeting notes Student-developed STEM project Technology-based lesson plan	Organizational documents can reveal insights about processes and interactions. Student- and teacher-created products and documents can highlight participant perspectives, values, attitudes, beliefs, etc. These types of data can provide in-depth rich information and serve as a source of triangulation.	Some of these items may not be sufficient alone to conduct a research study but provide supporting documentation as well as a source of triangulation. Analysis of qualitative data can be time consuming. In addition, the researcher will want to check for potential biases and increase trustworthiness by having multiple researchers review the work for researcher consensus.

THE TAKEAWAY

Qualitative researchers design studies that examine meaning, processes, and interactions. There are many options for qualitative data collection tools. The researcher will want to consider how specific tools correspond with the overall qualitative research design.

SELECTING DATA COLLECTION INSTRUMENTS

LEARNING OBJECTIVE

11.4 Outline ways to select data collection instruments

Researchers need to be strategic and intentional about the data collection instruments they choose given that those instruments provide the requisite information to address the key research questions of a study. Thus, when selecting one or more data collection instruments, researchers need to consider the type of research methodology and design, the nature of the research questions being asked, and the overall quality and appropriateness of the instrument.

As we have emphasized in this chapter, there are multiple data collection instruments that are used within quantitative or qualitative studies or in some instances, both methodologies. Central to quantitative studies include the use of questionnaires with a Likert scale format (i.e., response scale ranges from 1 to 5), structured or behavioral observations (i.e., frequency counts, duration of behavior), and standardized tests. A common characteristic of these instruments is the standardized approach to administration and the objective way in which scores are generated. For qualitative designs, researchers tend to emphasize interviews, informal or unstructured observations, open-ended items on questionnaires or surveys, and document or artifact review. These assessment tools are typically administered in a more dynamic and fluid way to align with specific situations and people involved in a study. However, the use of a questionnaire or an observation approach is not definitively aligned with one methodology over the other. The key guiding question to ask is, "What is the type of data that I need to best address my research question and what is the best approach for gathering those data?"

A key distinction between quantitative and qualitative assessment tools involves the importance of psychometric properties (i.e., reliability, validity) emphasized with quantitative measures. As discussed in Chapter 3, quantitative research seeks to assess variables (which represent a type of construct like anxiety or happiness) with specific assessment tools. Thus, it is essential that these measures have evidence to support claims that they consistently generate scores (i.e., reliability) that do in fact measure the target construct of interest (i.e., validity). If Mr. Fernsby wanted to assess students' sense of belonging in school, then he should select a measure that has already been developed and that shows evidence it does in fact measure sense of belonging. If researchers seek to develop their own quantitative measure, then they are responsible for providing this type of evidence before the measure is used in their study. In contrast, qualitative research does not specifically target variables or constructs as part of the assessment. They utilized more open-ended and exploratory data collection instruments to discover or generate conclusions about constructs. Thus, the requirement that empirical data supports reliability and validity about qualitative data collection instruments is not emphasized. That said, qualitative measures need to be administered and used in high quality ways and to be able to generate data that are credible and trustworthy. Thus, regardless of the research methodology, it is important for researchers to assess how credible or valid the information is generated by a data collection instrument. The way to determine how well a data collection instrument will yield usable results varies based on quantitative and qualitative methods (e.g., validity, reliability, trustworthiness; see Chapters 6 and 10).

On a more practical level, researchers need to consider the feasibility and usefulness of the data collection instruments for certain contexts or situations. For example, suppose a researcher sampled a group of 300 students and wanted to examine the relationship between student motivation and interest and success in school. Given that intelligence could impact student success, the researcher wanted to measure and include student intelligence as a control variable. However, because administering an intelligence test to 300 students can be quite expensive and time consuming for both students and the researchers, it may not be possible to administer a full measure of intelligence. Similarly, suppose a researcher working with Mr. Fernsby wanted to conduct a qualitative study examining student use and application of a new technology program for reading. As part of this study, the researcher wanted to conduct interviews with students and teachers while also observing students' use of the technology during authentic learning experiences. If the teacher or students find the observation approach overly intrusive or disruptive to the learning process, then it is likely that observations should not be used for that particular study. In Table 11.3 we provide a checklist of key criteria to consider when selecting data collection instruments. In the following two sections, we outline criteria for selecting quantitative and qualitative tools.

TABLE 11.3 ■ Checklist for Criteria for Selecting Data Collection Instruments
Checklist for Criteria for Selecting Data Collection Instruments

1. Does the instrument align with the purpose of the study?

2. Does the instrument align with the research questions?

3. Does the instrument reflect the overarching methodology of the study (quantitative, qualitative, mixed methods)?

4. Is it feasible to implement the instrument within an educational setting?

5. Is it cost effective to implement the instrument within a school setting?

6. Will the instrument provide enough information to yield findings?

7. Is the instrument feasible and user-friendly?

8. Does the use of the instrument adhere to ethical principles?

9. Will participants and the researcher be safe using the instrument?

10. Will the instrument provide credible findings based on validity/reliability (quantitative) or trustworthiness (qualitative)?

Criteria for Selecting Quantitative Instruments

We touched upon general guidelines for selecting data collection instruments in the introduction to this section. We now turn to some specific considerations for the several quantitative data collection instruments, including structured observational tools, surveys, standardized assessments, and performance-based assessments.

Structured Observations

Earlier in this chapter, we described the key characteristics and overall importance of structured or behavioral observations. As part of this process, one needs to define the target variables, identify the nature of the data to be collected (i.e., frequency count, duration), and then select the appropriate method for collecting the data (paper and pencil, behavioral counter, computer software). In determining these features, the researcher needs to also consider the relevance and appropriateness of the observational system in terms of the individual's developmental and behavioral characteristics. Further, the researcher should reflect on whether the specific observational system corresponds with the purpose and research questions of the study and the extent to which observers need to be trained in the use of the observation system. This step is necessary to establish calibration, a term that refers to the extent to which the scorers observe and interpret the behaviors in the same way.

Questionnaires

In addition to adequate evidence for reliability and validity, one of the most important considerations when selecting questionnaires is the quality and clarity of the items. A common mistake made with questionnaires is the use of double-barreled items; that is, items that reflect two or more characteristics or attributes. For example, the following question reflects a double-barreled item: "On a scale of 1 to 5, with 5 being high confidence and 1 being low confidence, how confident are you that you can teach about *coding* and *cloud storage?*" Including both coding and cloud storage is problematic and may lead to confusion for a respondent if they are quite confident in teaching about coding but possess very low confidence for teaching cloud storage. Thus, make sure the items on a questionnaire are clear and are likely to be interpreted in the same way by users.

Standardized Tests

Consistent with all quantitative measures, researchers need to carefully evaluate the psychometric quality of standardized tests in order to use them in a research study. Most commercially available standardized tests will typically exhibit excellent reliability and validity, but this may not always be the case. Given that there is great diversity in the type and corresponding purposes of standardized tests (e.g., cognitive ability tests, achievement tests, diagnostic tests), it is imperative that researchers not only ensure that the test measures the target construct of interest but that the scores generated by this measure reflects its objective. In other words, diagnostic reading tests may not be the best standardized test to administer if one wishes to assess changes in normative standing of students from pretest to posttest following a reading intervention. Finally, it is important to identify whether the standardized test has been normed on a sample that is similar in background and demographic information (e.g., age, biological sex, socio-economic status) to the sample used in the study. This same consideration should be made for questionnaires, which also tend to rely on norm-referenced interpretation.

District/Teacher Developed Assessments

Teacher developed assessments represent an alternative set of data collection instruments that could be used to supplement observations, questionnaires, and tests. However, in many instances, these forms of assessment (teacher developed tests, course grades, portfolios) do not generally possess the psychometric rigor and objective qualities that are desired in quantitative research.

This issue aside, we do offer some general recommendations for researchers if they believe teacher-developed tests could generate data of value to a research study. Regarding classroom tests, it is important that researchers employ some type of review and confirmation with content experts regarding the conceptual domain addressed by a given test. If you are designing a research study and want to incorporate a classroom test, one strategy would be to have another teacher or university professor with content expertise review the test for clarity of items. Similarly, make sure that the items directly link to the objectives of the study and that the test is clearly worded.

When using rubrics as part of a performance-based assessment or portfolios, it is critical to ensure that several individuals rate and evaluate a given work product to ensure high levels of interrater reliability. Attaining consensus and high levels of interrater reliability offsets a validity threat known as the halo effect, a type of bias that occurs when a teacher's positive preestablished perceptions of a student's capabilities influence their evaluations of that student.

If researchers want to use course grades as a type of data, they need to be wary about the many factors that could impact student grades but that are not reflective of content knowledge per se. For example, teachers may have a participation grade, extra point assignments, or other actions that can increase student grades. This creates a problem when interpreting the meaning of a course grade or when comparing course grades across teachers who may have varying expectations or grading methods. Thus, while including course grades can be useful in research, researchers should consider using alternative indicators of achievement or using course grades along with other achievement metrics. This latter strategy would enable researchers to engage in triangulation and to examine if the same conclusion is reached across achievement metric.

Criteria for Selecting Qualitative Instruments

In previous chapters, we have stressed that qualitative methods deal with participant perspectives and regularly utilize language-based data collection tools. In this section, we discuss some key consideration and criteria for selecting specific qualitative instruments.

Interviews and Focus Groups

When using an interview to collect qualitative data, researchers can use informal, semi-structured, or highly structured formats. In most situations, semi-structured formats reflect an approach that allows for some structure in preparing for an interview while also providing the interviewer with autonomy and freedom to adjust the interview as needed. To prepare, semi-structured questions should be written in advance of the session and used with all the participants for consistency. Over the course of the interview, it is appropriate to add other questions or adapt existing ones based on the participants' responses. Typically, researchers will create 8 to 10 questions (known as semi-structured interview questions) on the topic. They should also be mindful of the participants' time and stamina level and thus try to keep interviews within a 20- to 45-minute time frame. An additional strategy is to start with a question that creates some interest and puts the participant at ease. For example, if a researcher was interviewing a computer technology specialist in a school district, a starting question could be, "How did you first become interested in becoming a computer technology specialist?" Not only is this the type of question that a participant would likely be comfortable sharing, but this initial question sets a comfortable tone for the interview.

Another key strategy is to avoid using questions that have underlying assumptions that direct the interviewee. For example, asking a teacher about their perceptions of a technology workshop needs to be stated from an impartial stance. "How did the workshop help you with your students?" inherently assumes that the workshop was beneficial and that the teacher believes students profited from the strategies. In this case, the interviewee is initially directed to reply that the workshop had positive outcomes. Restating the question as "Can you describe your experiences with the workshop?" has a more neutral tone.

Another issue to be aware of is reactivity, which is when an interviewee receives verbal/visual cues from the interviewer, which influences the responses. Making comments after a response that have a value judgement can impact the interview. Imagine that after the initial question in the previous paragraph, a teacher responded that the technology workshop was extremely impactful for their students. A researcher who responded with a big smile, "I am really happy to hear that," will influence the remainder of the discussion. This statement implies that the researcher has an invested interest in positive benefits of the program.

Many of the principles described for writing semi-structured interview questions are relevant to working with focus groups. When creating questions for a group, select items that all participants can address. If the question was "How do you plan with other art teachers?" and most of the participants were not art teacher, this question would not be relevant. Questioning skills are paramount during focus groups to accommodate varying perspectives, personalities, and levels of engagement during the group session.

Questionnaires

The use of open-ended questions on a questionnaire will have value to a qualitative study, in part, because it is time and cost effective. When developing these questions, it is important to phrase the question that leads to a detailed response. For instance, a question for teachers on collaboration should be phrased in such a way that it encourages an informed and detailed response. A question like, "Do you enjoy collaborations?" is vague and may generate a limited response. However, if the question was phrased, "What are some effective strategies for collaborating with teachers in your department?" participants will likely have a clearer understanding of what is being asked and thus provide a more elaborate response.

Observational Tools

Selecting the specific type of observational tool (e.g., field notes, analytic memo, video recording) depends on the specific context and nature of the study. While audio/video recordings of IB teachers interacting during a professional development conference could aid in studying interactions and effective practices, adding an observational checklist would likely not be relevant. To determine what type of observational tool is needed, the researcher will consider the overall purpose of the study and other accompanying data collection instruments. For some studies, the researcher will focus on using field observations without integrating any other observational tools.

Documents and Artifacts

Educational settings provide access to a plethora of organizational documents as well as documents and artifacts generated by administrators, teachers, and students. Qualitative research can utilize one or more of these documents in data analysis (e.g., school schedules, trophy cases, student recognition displays, student work, etc.), depending on the purposes of the study. When selecting documents and artifacts, the researcher prioritizes tools that will provide rich information, whether that involves written and oral text or items that individuals create. What is most important is that the document/artifact will ultimately provide information to inform the topic of interest. Some key factors when selecting a document or artifact include (a) how the item reflects the topic of study, (b) who created the item, (c) the rationale for creating the item, and (d) the process for creating the item. Now, that we have discussed ways to select quantitative and qualitative instruments, let's take a look at peer review articles and describe the goals, research questions, and data collection instruments, and discuss their strengths and limitations! We also include a *You Do It!* activity for further practice.

Let's See It! 11.2

Goal: Identify Data and Evaluate Data Collection Instruments From a Peer-Reviewed Study

The primary objective of this activity is to identify and evaluate the data collection instrument(s) from the selected article, Stovner and Klette (2022), and list their strengths and limitations in Table 11.4.

Let's take a look at the following table, which includes a description of the purpose of the study, research question(s), the sample, data collection instruments, and the strengths and limitations of those instruments.

TABLE 11.4 ■ Identify and Evaluate Data Collection Instruments	
Study	Stovner, R. B., & Klette, K. (2022). Teacher feedback on procedural skills, conceptual understanding, and mathematical practice: A video study in lower secondary mathematics classrooms. *Teaching and Teacher Education, 110*, 1–12. https://doi.org/10.1016/j.tate.2021.103593
Purpose of Study	The purpose of this study was to explore teacher's oral feedback to their students in a lower-secondary school in Norway using a video study. The researchers wanted to specifically map out indicators of feedback (specific and non-specific), time spent giving feedback and during which activities, as well as what math competencies were discussed.
Research Question(s)	1. What is the quality of feedback as measured by the subject generic dimensions? 2. How much time do teachers spend providing oral feedback and in what activity formats? 3. To what extent and how do teachers in mathematics classrooms provide feedback focusing on procedural skills, conceptual understanding, and mathematical practices?
Sources of Data	The sample included 47 lower-secondary mathematics teachers from Norway (*n* = 47).
Data Collection Instruments	The researchers collected 172 video-recordings of lessons provided by the 47 teachers. The Protocol for Language Arts Teaching Observation (PLATO), a standardized observation tool, was used to analyse the video recordings and answer the research questions. PLATO subdivides the lessons into 15-minute segments, which are then rated on 12 quality indicators on a scale of 1 to 4 (4 being the highest). Observers must be trained and certified in order to use PLATO.
Strengths and Limitations	**Strengths** 1. Using a standardized observation tool is useful when analysing larger data sets, especially when there is a requirement that observers should be trained and certified—this supports the reliability of the data collected. 2. The PLATO is specifically designed to capture quality indicators of feedback, which aligns to the researcher's purpose. **Limitations** 1. When conducting an observation, it is important to be aware of how the presence of an observer or in this, case a video camera may have on the individuals being observed. This may be a limitation in that what is observed may not typically be the norm. 2. Finally, the researchers addressed the fact that PLATO is a language arts tool, yet they used it in mathematics. Sometimes researchers make minor adjustments to instruments to fit the needs of their study (e.g., changing a noun, not using all the items/questions), in this case, the researchers referenced other published peer-reviewed studies that used PLATO for mathematics to justify their decision. Although, this may still pose as a limitation given that the tool was not originally validated for mathematics observation.

Let's Do It! 11.2

Guided Practice: Identify Data and Evaluate Data Collection Instruments From a Peer-Reviewed Study

In this *Let's Do It!* activity we are going to identify and evaluate the data collection instrument(s) from the selected article, Kitsantas et al. (2020) and list their strengths and limitations in Table 11.5. Fill out this table to include a description of the purpose of the study, the sample, data collection instruments, and the strengths and limitations of those instruments.

TABLE 11.5 ■ Identify and Evaluate Data Collection Instruments	
Study	Kitsantas, A., Cleary, T. J., Whitehead, A., & Cheema J. (2020). Relations among classroom context, student motivation, and mathematics literacy: A social cognitive perspective. *Metacognition and Learning, 16*, 255–273. https://doi.org/10.1007/s11409-020-0924 9–1
Purpose of Study	
Research Question(s)	
Sources of Data	
Data Collection Instruments	
Strengths and Limitations	

THE TAKEAWAY

With secondary data, the researcher will want to consider if they have the right to access data, how to present attributes in an ethical manner, and if the data are complete and time relevant.

ETHICAL CONSIDERATIONS

While the prospect of selecting data collection instruments can be exciting, the researcher will need to consider how implementing the tool will impact the school day and student learning. The appropriate use of data collection instruments in applied context is essential to maintaining the integrity of research (e.g., detecting and documenting errors in the data collection process). Typically, administrators and educators are reticent to collaborate with researchers if the tool takes a great deal of time to administer and impacts learning. In all ways, the researcher should aim to be as unobtrusive and time efficient as possible. Preserving the natural educational environment and respecting the privacy and integrity of all individuals is reflective of high ethical standards.

It is also ethical practice to only select data collection instruments that have adequate reliability and validity (in the case of quantitative research) and that are appropriate relative to the target sample and situation. If a researcher knowingly uses assessment instruments that lack appropriate evidence for validity and then definitively discusses and interprets scores from these instruments, they can mislead the public about what the results actually mean. As we have frequently emphasized in this chapter and others in the book, when a data collection instrument does not have sufficient validity evidence, then researchers should not make interpretations about the latent constructs that the instrument is allegedly measuring. The reality is that without validity evidence, a researcher does not know whether the instrument does in fact target the intended construct. Further, selecting assessment tools and using them with samples that have not been supported by research can also create ambiguity and potential errors in interpretation.

When starting the process of data collection, researchers need to acknowledge that individuals possess the right to refrain from participating in research studies at any time without penalty or coercion (see Chapter 1 on the *Belmont Report*). When a researcher is meeting with participants, it is advisable to restate that there is no penalty from withdrawing from a study and that individuals have the option of withdrawing at any time. During data collection, if a participant expresses that they want to stop, the researcher should not question the decision or put pressure on the participant to continue. The rights of the participants in this regard are upheld above all other considerations.

As with all studies, the researcher will want to take great strides in protecting participant confidentiality. Re-use of an individuals' personal attributes or designations (e.g., free and reduced lunch, homelessness) should be approached in a sensitive manner. The researcher should note that participants may have given consent to participate in a specific study. The consent form may not extend to a new study, and/or the researcher may not have rights to the data.

THE TAKEAWAY

With all types of data collection instruments, researchers need to be unobtrusive within educational settings. The use of specific tools should not disrupt the educational environment or detract from student learning.

AMERICAN PSYCHOLOGICAL ASSOCIATION STYLE

LEARNING OBJECTIVE
11.6   Utilize the *Publication Manual of the American Psychological Association* when reporting findings from data collection.

Researchers describe the data collection instruments in the method section, which is the heart of a study. All instruments used should be described in detail. That is, for each instrument, the researcher should describe its purpose and provide a citation of the author that developed it. For example, if you used the Self-Regulated Strategy Inventory in your research, then you need to provide the appropriate citation (SRSI; Cleary, 2006). It is also helpful to include the number of items in the measure as well as format of the scoring system (e.g., a 5-point Likert-type scale ranging from 1 (strongly disagree) to 5 (strongly agree). Details about whether the instrument had subscales, how to interpret the instrument, and whether any items were reverse-scored, should be clearly outlined for the reader. Many readers also find it helpful if one or two example items or questions for each data collection instrument is provided. If a new instrument is created, the new instrument, should be included in an appendix.

In terms of qualitative data collection instruments, it is important to describe the purpose and structure of all interviews and provide example questions in the methods section. Authors are also encouraged to include the interview questions as an appendix. For other types of instruments like observational checklists, documents, and artifacts, the descriptive process is the same. For some techniques, it may be beneficial to include a figure within the method section with a description.

In addition to describing the characteristics of the data collection instruments used in a study, the actual procedures regarding when and how the instruments were used should be provided in the procedure section of the methods. There should be sufficient detail so that another researcher could easily replicate the study by simply reading the methods and procedure section. In sum, describing the data collection instruments with the use of APA style is a prominent portion of the method section. Including this information enables the reader to understand the link between the purpose of the study, the research questions, and the data collection instruments.

THE TAKEAWAY

Data collection instruments are described in the method section by including the title, author, year, purpose, scoring techniques and sample items. For quantitative tools, validity and reliability information is also provided.

CHAPTER SUMMARY

The focus of this chapter was to highlight an array of quantitative and qualitative data collection instruments that researchers can use to collect data as part of a research study. We also discussed the strengths and limitations of each data collection instrument. Given that selecting the instruments to use in a study is highly dependent on the purposes and research questions of a study, we also provided guidelines for selecting and evaluating data collection instruments. As with all elements of the research process, a most essential understanding is an awareness of how choices in data collection selection and procedures relate to ethical issues, particularly in terms of protecting participants as outlined by the *Belmont Report.*

EXTENSION ACTIVITIES

You Do It! 11.1
Identify Data Collection Instruments Within a Research Study

Self-Directed Practice: Identifying Data Collection Instruments Within a Research Study

Select three research articles based on a topic of interest. Make a listing of the data sources and the collection instruments data utilized in the study.

You Do It! 11.2
Self-Directed Practice: Identify Data and Evaluate Data Collection Instruments from a Peer-Reviewed Study

In *Let's See It! Let's Do It!* 11.2, we modeled how to identify and evaluate the strengths and limitations of data collection instruments within a research study. Select a research study related to your topic of interest. Identify the purpose of the study, the research questions, sources of data, and the corresponding data collection instruments. Consider other tools that could have been applied to this study.

KEY TERMS

Achievement tests
Analytic memos
Aptitude tests
Assessment (in school contexts)
Assessment bias
Benchmark tests
Calibration
Course grades
Criterion-referenced test
Data collection instruments
Diagnostic test
Double-barreled items
Focus group
Halo effect

Interim assessments
Latent constructs
Norm-referenced tests
Observation checklist
Performance-based assessment
Portfolio assessment
Questionnaires
Reactivity
Semantic differential
Sources of data
Standardized tests
State-mandated achievement tests
Structured observations
Unit tests

ANSWER KEY

Stop and Think Activities
STOP AND THINK 11.1
The research question is, "What is the relationship between student self-efficacy for self-regulated learning and achievement in middle school mathematics?" While they are many potential data collection instruments that one could use to measure self-efficacy for self-

regulated learning to answer this research question, one might be the Self-Efficacy for Learning Form (SELF) by Zimmerman and Kitsantas (2007). School mathematics achievement might be assessed using math grades, other related classroom assessments, and standardized scores.

STOP AND THINK 11.2

Educators have likely encountered both norm-referenced and criterion-referenced tests. An example of a norm-referenced test used in schools sometimes is the Stanford 10 and the SATs. In terms of a criterion-referenced test, an example is the Virginia Standards of Learning, which has a cut-off score of 400 to determine levels of proficiency.

STOP AND THINK 11.3

The response to this question varies based on the context. Using constructed response items on surveys, interviews, and focus groups are all ways to gather data from the perspective of participants. A researcher studying teacher collaborations could collect open-ended responses via surveys. For more detailed information, they may choose to interview individuals. As a third option, the researcher could conduct three focus groups (e.g., science teachers, language arts teachers, and art teachers).

Let's Do It! Activities
LET'S DO IT! 11.1

Study	Kule, U., & Akcaoglu, M. (2018). The role of relevance in future teachers' utility value and interest toward technology. *Educational Technology Research & Development, 66*(2), 283–311. https://doi.org/10.1007/s11423-017-9547-9
Purpose of Study	The purpose of the study was to examine preservice teacher's perceptions of the value and utility of integrating technology within lesson design based on reflective strategies.
Identify Data Sources	111 preservice teachers
Identify Data Collection Instruments	Survey with Likert-type scales Participant Prezi presentations (reflections of instruction) as textual information for thematic content analysis.

LET'S DO IT! 11.2
Guided Practice: Identify and Evaluate Data Collection Instruments From a Peer-Reviewed Study

In this *Let's Do It!* Activity we are going to identify and evaluate the data collection instrument(s) from the selected article, Kitsantas et al. (2020), and list their strengths and limitations. Fill out this table to include a description of the purpose of the study, the sample, data collection instruments, and the strengths and limitations of those instruments.

Study	Kitsantas, A., Cleary, T. J., Whitehead, A., & Cheema J. (2020). Relations among classroom context, student motivation, and mathematics literacy: A social cognitive perspective. *Metacognition and Learning, 16*, 255–273. https://doi.org/10.1007/s11409-020-09249-1
Purpose of Study	The purpose of this study was to investigate the relationship between teacher contextual variables (e.g., support and cognitive activations, student motivational beliefs, engagement, math literacy), as well as exploring whether the different forms of behavior and motivational engagement serve as mediators between student math literacy and classroom context.

Research Question(s)	This study utilized structural equation modelling (SEM), therefore there are no specific research questions. Instead, the researchers aim to find a best-fitting model showing the direct and indirect relationships between their variables.
Sources of Data	The sample consists on 4,978 (49%, girls) 15-year-old students across the United States. The data were collected from the U.S. segment of the Program for International Student Assessment (PISA) 2012.
Data Collection Instruments	This particular study utilizes a number of instruments in the form of surveys and questionnaires:

- Teacher Behavior: Teacher Support—five items on students' perception of teacher support in the classroom.

- Teacher Behavior: Cognitive Activation—nine items that capture and assess students' perceptions of their teachers' ability to activate cognition.

- Mathematics Self-Efficacy—eight items to capture student's perceptions of their capabilities to successfully answer math operations.

- Mathematics Intensions—five items used to determine student's intentions in math (i.e., "I am planning on pursuing a career that involves a lot of mathematics/science" or "I plan on <taking> as many mathematics/science classes as I can during my education"; Kitsantas et al., 2020, p. 264).

- Mathematics Work Ethic—nine items to capture student's perception of their work ethic.

- Perseverance—five items that capture a student's perception of their capability to persevere during academic tasks.

- Mathematics Literacy—this was provided by the PISA scores. The PISA is a standardized survey.

Strengths and Limitations	**Strengths**

1. One strength in using questionnaires and surveys is that they are time and cost effective.

2. By using portions of larger instruments in the study, the researchers were able to address all their variables.

Limitations

1. The researchers discussed that one of the limitations for the use of surveys and questionnaires is that the data are self-reported. Self-reported data can pose issues such as participants not honestly answering questions or even socially desirability bias (i.e., answering based on what they think other's want them to answer).

©iStockphoto.com/towfiqu ahamed

12 DESCRIPTIVE STATISTICS

A DAY AT WORK

How Can I Use School-Based Data More Effectively!

©iStockphoto.com/insta_photos

Ms. Emily Johnson, Ms. Jennifer Liptack, and Mr. Desmond James are middle school or high school teachers working in neighboring school districts in the Pacific Northwest. They are good colleagues who initially met as students enrolled in the same teacher education program. Ms. Johnson currently teaches high school English language arts, while Ms. Liptack teaches middle school science and mathematics. Mr. James is a middle school social studies and health teacher. Over the years, they have remained in touch and would try to attend the same professional development workshops or teacher education conferences, whenever possible. This past fall, they all attended a conference focused on the role of teacher expectations and student–teacher relationships on student learning and behavior in the classroom. Their interest in this conference stemmed from recent initiatives in their school districts to gather data about student–teacher interactions and to use these data to develop school programs to promote students' feelings of connection and sense of belonging in school. In each of their respective schools, Ms. Johnson, Mr. James, and Ms. Liptack volunteered to analyze these data and then present them to school administrators and the broader community. The question is, "how should they go about analyzing data and how can they be presented to others?"

INTRODUCTION

As you may recall, engaging in educational research can be a time consuming and rigorous multistep process. Researchers typically begin by conducting a literature review and then coming up with important research questions. They then select and utilize an appropriate research design (e.g., experimental, case study), which includes recruiting a sample and using different measures to collect data about relevant variables. For most researchers, however, the next step in the research process, *data analysis*, is the real "payoff." It is during data analysis that researchers get to answer their research questions and perhaps think about the broader conclusions and implications of their work. In quantitative studies, researchers rely on two types of statistical analysis: descriptive and inferential. Descriptive statistics reflect a set of procedures that describe or summarize one or more variables in a dataset, whereas inferential statistics use sample data to draw conclusions about the characteristics of a broader population (i.e., the larger group of people from whom the sample was collected).

In this chapter, we focus exclusively on descriptive statistics. After briefly reviewing the general format and structure of a quantitative dataset, we delve into various techniques for descriptively organizing and summarizing scores in a dataset. Through the use of authentic and hypothetical datasets, we illustrate the most essential and important characteristics of descriptive analyses. We also structure several practice opportunities to use different types of descriptive analyses via *Let's See It!* and *Let's Do It!* activities. As with the other chapters in the textbook, the current chapter ends with a discussion of ethical considerations and key APA formatting issues when engaged in data reporting.

KEY COMPONENTS AND NATURE OF DATASETS

LEARNING OBJECTIVE
12.1   Demonstrate knowledge of the key components of quantitative datasets.

A quantitative dataset can be thought of as a researcher's numerical workspace. It represents a highly structured, organized system that includes a set of data values representing the key variables in a study. Creating a high-quality dataset is one of the most important yet underemphasized aspects of the research process (see Figure 12.1). For this reason, we wanted to briefly review the key features of datasets and to underscore a few important principles to keep in mind when creating or using them.

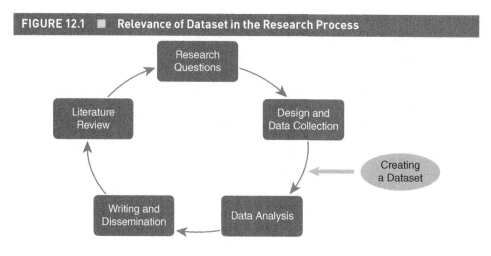

FIGURE 12.1 ■ Relevance of Dataset in the Research Process

In this chapter, we use an authentic dataset gathered from an ethnically and financially diverse group of middle school students (i.e., Connectedness Dataset) to illustrate the basic characteristics of a dataset and the different types of descriptive statistics that can be used. Most datasets reflect a matrix with rows and columns. Each column represents a variable that was measured in a study, while the rows signify the research participants. Table 12.1 illustrates each member of the participating sample (i.e., the rows) and their scores across six variables: biological sex, free and reduced lunch eligibility, teacher support, school connectedness, maladaptive behaviors, and mathematics grades (i.e., the columns). Please note that the values presented in Table 12.1 for several variables (i.e., teacher support, school connectedness, maladaptive behavior, and mathematics grades) represent average scores for each individual for those variables.

TABLE 12.1 ■ Screenshot of a Dataset for 20 Middle School Students

Research Participant	Biological Sex	FR Lunch	Teacher support	School Connectedness	Maladaptive Behavior	Mathematics Grades
1	0	0	4.00	3.40	2.25	90
2	0	0	3.67	3.60	2.38	94
3	1	0	4.83	3.20	1.88	88
4	0	0	3.50	2.00	2.75	85
5	1	0	3.50	3.80	1.50	90
6	1	1	4.33	3.20	1.50	90
7	0	0	3.67	4.20	2.00	74
8	1	0	3.83	4.20	2.75	90
9	0	0	1.33	4.60	3.88	78
10	0	0	3.17	3.40	1.75	90
11	1	1	2.83	3.00	1.00	99
12	1	1	3.33	3.40	3.13	90
13	0	0	3.67	3.40	2.25	86

Research Participant	Biological Sex	FR Lunch	Teacher support	School Connectedness	Maladaptive Behavior	Mathematics Grades
14	1	0	3.00	4.00	2.75	84
15	0	0	2.67	2.60	2.25	85
16	0	0	3.17	3.40	2.75	80
17	1	1	4.67	3.00	1.63	88
18	1	0	4.00	4.40	2.50	90
19	1	0	1.67	3.80	1.38	96
20	0	0	4.00	3.40	2.25	90

Note: The first column reflects a number linked with each research participant. All other columns reflect variables in the dataset. FR Lunch = free or reduced lunch. Biological Sex (0 = males and 1 = females) and Free and Reduced Lunch (0 = no, 1 = yes) were categorical variables.

When looking at a dataset, novice researchers may wonder, "What do the scores in the dataset mean?" and "Where do they come from?" The answers to these questions reveal important principles about quantitative data and the research process in general. The meaning of any quantitative score in a dataset depends on its level of measurement (i.e., rules for defining the meaning of data values or scores) and the measurement tool used to generate that score. As you may recall from Chapter 10, levels of measurement involve four basic categories: nominal, ordinal, interval, and ratio. Nominal scales include scores that reflect group membership (e.g., males and females), ordinal scales involve numerical ordering of scores (e.g., less than or greater than), interval scales involve scores that are equidistant from each other, and ratio scales include scores with an absolute zero point (i.e., absence of the essence or quality of a variable). These four levels can be further categorized into two superordinate categories: quantitative (i.e., ordinal, interval, ratio) or categorical (i.e., nominal). Scores for quantitative variables reflect variations in degree or quantity of a particular construct. Thus, the scores for the four quantitative variables in the Connectedness dataset (see Table 12.1; i.e., maladaptive, teacher support, connectedness, mathematics grades) reflect differences or variations in the *degree* to which participants exhibit those characteristics. For example, Participant 2 exhibited a numerically higher level of maladaptive behavior (i.e., 2.38) than research Participant 19, who received a score of 1.38.

Although categorical variables (i.e., nominal) are also reflected by numbers in a dataset, these values reflect membership in a category (e.g., giftedness status, biological sex) rather than degree or quantity. By convention, researchers use a (0, 1) coding scheme to represent two subgroups for a categorical variable. If there are more than two subgroups, then researchers add another number to represent that subgroup (i.e., 0, 1, 2, 3, 4, etc.). Researchers can also start the coding scheme with a 1 rather than 0 (i.e., 1, 2, 3, 4, etc.), although using 0 as the first value is the default or preferred method, particularly when using complex inferential statistical analyses (e.g., moderation analyses). To put it simply, the values or scores you see in a dataset for categorical variables do not possess any inherent meaning besides group membership. In the Connectedness dataset, there were two categorical variables, *biological sex* (0 = males, 1 = females) and *free/reduced lunch* (0 = no free or reduced lunch, 1 = yes free or reduced lunch). Each number represents a subgroup or category, not the degree or quantity of biological sex or lunch status. Given that researchers will often include many variables in a dataset, it is essential that they maintain a separate codebook (i.e., similar to an answer key) or use a labeling feature in a statistical program to track the specific meaning for these categorical values.

The scores that appear in a dataset are generated using one or more assessment methods (e.g., test, questionnaire, direct observations, review of educational record; see Chapter 11). In the Connections dataset (see Table 12.1), the scores for three of the variables were gathered from student ratings on different questionnaires (i.e., school connectedness, teacher support, and maladaptive behaviors). For each questionnaire, students read several items and then used a 5-point Likert scale (1 = not frequent at all to 5 = very frequently) to convey how often they engaged in a particular behavior. For example, the maladaptive self-report measure had eight items. These items reflected different aspects of students' maladaptive behaviors in the classroom, such as procrastination, avoidance of work, and forgetfulness (e.g., "I give up or quit when I do not understand something," and "I try to forget about topics that I have trouble learning)." If you look back to the maladaptive scores presented in Table 12.1, what do you think they mean, or what do they represent?

In this example, the scores for all 20 students in the dataset for the maladaptive, connectedness, and teacher support measures reflect the *average* or *mean score* for those variables. Although we discuss the meaning and procedures for calculating the mean score in Section 12.4, it generally reflects a score that best represents all individual scores included in a dataset for that variable. The mean score is of utmost importance to quantitative researchers because it is the most common way to identify the "typical" score in a group and because it is a required piece of information used in many types of inferential analyses (see Chapter 13).

We encourage you to keep in mind, however, that when creating or looking at a dataset, it is important to distinguish between scores for individual items on a questionnaire (or other measure) from scores reflecting the average or mean score representing all items on that measure. For example, in Table 12.2, we illustrate what a dataset might look like if a researcher included the specific scores for each of the eight items on the maladaptive measure. As you can see, the score from each item ranged from 1 to 5 (i.e., which is consistent with the 1–5 Likert scale) and are represented as separate variables in the dataset (i.e., remember that each column in a matrix reflects a separate variable). Although there may be times when researchers are interested in examining the individual item scores, in most instances, researchers focus primarily on interpreting and using the average or mean scores (see Table 12.1 and last column of Table 12.2).

TABLE 12.2 ■ The Use of Individual Item Scores and the Average Score in a Quantitative Dataset											
	Sex	FR Lunch	Mal1	Mal2	Mal3	Mal4	Mal5	Mal6	Mal7	Mal8	Maladaptive Average
1	0	0	2	1	3	3	3	3	1	2	2.25
2	0	0	2	1	2	4	2	3	2	3	2.38
3	1	0	2	1	2	3	2	1	2	2	1.88
4	0	0	3	2	3	3	3	3	2	3	2.75

As a final point about datasets, please note that not all scores that are included in a dataset are generated directly from assessment tools or measures administered to a sample (see Chapter 11). For demographic or background variables (e.g., biological sex, ethnicity, parent education level) and some performance outcomes (e.g., grades, GPA, scores), the data are often obtained from school records or from teacher and parental reports. Regardless of the source of the data, however, inputting scores into a dataset represents a key first step and foundation from which researchers use descriptive and inferential statistics.

THE TAKEAWAY

When creating a dataset, it is important to identify the meaning and level of measurement for each variable (i.e., categorical versus quantitative) and the nature of the scores that will be inputted (i.e., average score, individual item score).

PURPOSE AND IMPORTANCE OF DESCRIPTIVE STATISTICS

LEARNING OBJECTIVE

12.2 Explain the purpose and importance of descriptive statistics.

After data are entered into a dataset, researchers are ready to begin data analysis. In most instances, researchers rely on descriptive analyses to generate general conclusions about the sample. Thus, descriptive statistics reflect an array of tactics for summarizing, describing, or explaining the nature of scores in a dataset. Unlike inferential statistics, descriptive statistics do not answer questions about how well data in the sample reflect what one is likely to see in the broader population. To put it simply, you *describe a sample* with *descriptive statistics* but *make inferences from a sample to a population* with *inferential statistics* (see Figure 12.2).

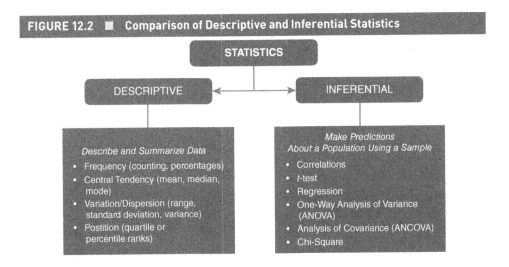

FIGURE 12.2 ■ Comparison of Descriptive and Inferential Statistics

The most common metrics used to convey descriptive information about variables include frequency counts (i.e., number of people who obtained a particular score; see Section 12.3), mean (i.e., average score in a distribution of scores; see Section 12.4), standard deviation (i.e., amount of variation of scores in a distribution; see section 12.5), and relative standing (i.e., comparison of individuals to a larger group). Each of these statistics can describe some aspect of the target sample as it naturally exists or occurs. Thus, Ms. Johnson can use descriptive statistics to determine the average essay grade (i.e., mean score) across all her English language arts classes, while Mr. James might be interested in collecting frequency data about student absences in his social studies classes. In sum, descriptive statistics are foundational to the data analysis process because they aggregate sample data into a more easily interpretable summary format that enables researchers to answer several basic, yet important, questions about the sample (see Figure 12.3).

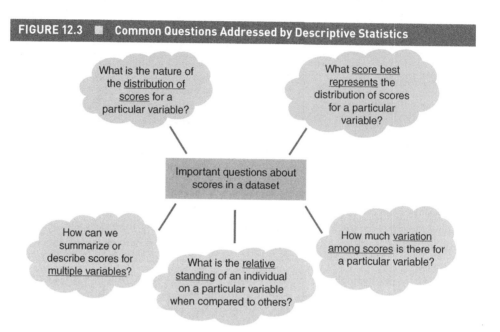

FIGURE 12.3 ■ Common Questions Addressed by Descriptive Statistics

What is the nature of the distribution of scores for a particular variable?

What score best represents the distribution of scores for a particular variable?

Important questions about scores in a dataset

How can we summarize or describe scores for multiple variables?

What is the relative standing of an individual on a particular variable when compared to others?

How much variation among scores is there for a particular variable?

Although we delve deeply into inferential statistics in Chapter 13, we wanted to make sure you clearly understand its distinction from descriptive statistics. Inferential statistics involve a set of procedures that helps researchers identify whether the scores or results from a study based on a particular sample represent a "true" or real effect in the broader population. Inferential statistics are much more complex than descriptive analyses because they require appropriate knowledge and use of high level, abstract concepts, such as hypothesis testing, probability analysis, and statistical significance. In some sense, descriptive statistics are quite advantageous to a novice researcher because of the ease with which one can use and interpret these statistics and because they are foundational to using inferential statistics.

Suppose a researcher wanted to examine whether two groups (e.g., high-school connectedness versus low-school connectedness) differed at a statistically significant level across anxiety and academic success. If examining "statistical significance" was of primary interest, the researcher would need some type of inferential test, such as an *independent* t-*test*. As you will learn in Chapter 13, the *t*-test is a great way to determine whether an observed difference between groups is a true or "real" effect in the broader population. However, just knowing whether the groups can be considered different does not tell the entire story. One must also know which group exhibited higher scores than the other. Descriptive statistics (e.g., the average score for anxiety and academic performance) serve this latter function. It is for this reason that almost all quantitative researchers will, regardless of the specific design (i.e., experimental comparative, correlational, etc.), include some type of descriptive analysis or descriptive summary for all the key variables in the study table (see Section 12.9). As you will learn in subsequent sections of this chapter, descriptive statistics help researchers understand the degree or quantity with which a group exhibits a certain construct.

Descriptive statistics are also helpful for identifying anomalies (i.e., rare or unusual characteristics) or potential problems in the data. Although we elaborate on this point in greater detail in Section 12.3, descriptive analysis techniques can help researchers identify scores in a dataset that are incorrect due to either human error (e.g., incorrectly inputting scores in a dataset) or a systematic problem with a scoring procedure. To learn more about how descriptive stats can be used in this way, please look at Table 12.3. This table represents a slight alteration of the data presented in Table 12.2. The changes are reflected in the bolded scores. Given that the average score for the maladaptive scale could range from 1 to 5 (which directly corresponds to the Likert rating scale that also ranged from 1 to 5), one can clearly see that an average or mean score of 6.88 is NOT possible. When reviewing each of the entered scores in the dataset, it is clear that the score of 22 for maladaptive items #3 and #7 is erroneous.

	Sex	FR Lunch	Mal1	Mal2	Mal3	Mal4	Mal5	Mal6	Mal7	Mal8	Maladaptive Average
TABLE 12.3 ■ Use of a Dataset and Descriptive Statistics to Reveal Inaccuracies in a Dataset											
1	0	0	2	1	3	3	3	3	1	2	2.25
2	0	0	2	1	2	4	2	3	2	3	2.38
3	1	0	2	1	**22**	3	2	1	**22**	2	**6.88**
4	0	0	3	2	3	3	3	3	2	3	2.75

Note: The maladaptive scores are based on a 5-point Likert scale ranging from 1–5.

THE TAKEAWAY

Although inferential statistics tends to be the primary focus of most quantitative research, descriptive analyses always play a central role in helping researchers understand the meaning of variables and accurately interpret the results.

EXAMINING DISTRIBUTION OF SCORES FOR A VARIABLE

LEARNING OBJECTIVE

12.3 Discuss the most effective ways for visually depicting a distribution of scores.

Most datasets include many variables. While some variables reflect demographic characteristics of the sample (e.g., biological sex, ethnicity), other variables represent psychological or educational variables (e.g., self-efficacy for learning, attitudes toward reading, anxiety), performance outcomes (e.g., test grades, report card grades), or types of experimental conditions (e.g., intervention versus no intervention). To begin the process of quantitative data analysis, researchers typically first focus on descriptive statistics, the latter of which can have a univariate (i.e., examine one variable at a time) or bivariate focus (i.e., examine two variables). Most of this chapter focuses on univariate techniques, although we do address the bivariate approach in the context of correlational analyses (see Section 12.7).

To begin the descriptive analysis process, most researchers are interested in answering the following question for all the variables in a dataset (Figure 12.4):

What is the nature of the distribution of scores for a particular variable?

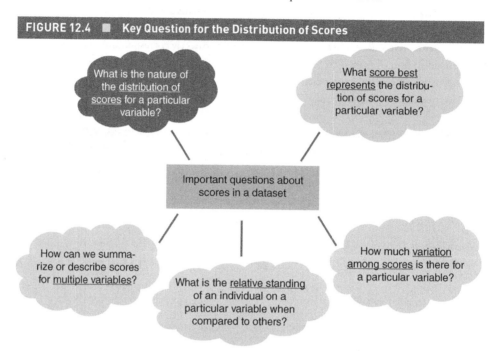

FIGURE 12.4 ■ Key Question for the Distribution of Scores

A distribution of scores reflects an organized listing of all scores obtained for a particular variable. Thus, when a researcher administers an assessment tool in a study, it will produce a set of scores of individuals that can be organized into a distribution. A specific type of distribution, a frequency distribution reflects a rank-ordered organization of scores (i.e., from low to high score) with reference to how often each score occurs. Frequency distributions, which are often reflected in terms of a frequency count (i.e., number of people obtaining a score) or percentage (i.e., proportion of a sample obtaining a particular score), are an important aspect of descriptive statistics because they help researchers quickly determine the most common scores in a set of scores.

Frequency distributions can be displayed in tabular or visual format and can be created for any variable in a dataset. When considering the original dataset presented in this chapter (Table 12.1), six different frequency distributions can be generated. Suppose Ms. Johnson was particularly interested in examining the distribution of essay grades for students in her English language arts classes. To create a frequency distribution, she could create a table with three columns. In the first column, she listed in ascending order all essay scores that were observed. These scores ranged from 1.7 to 4.0. In the next two columns, Ms. Johnson listed the frequency counts and percentages regarding how often each score occurred. In reviewing Table 12.4, an essay score of 2.7 was obtained by 10 students, whereas 19 students earned a score of 3.1. Ms. Johnson also elected to report percentages given that they are universally understood by most educators and because they can offer more nuanced insights regarding the overall performance of a group.

Essay grade	Frequency	Percentage (%)
TABLE 12.4 ■ Frequency Distribution for Essay Grades in Ms. Johnson's class		
1.7	2	1.5
2.1	4	3.0
2.2	1	0.8
2.4	5	3.8
2.7	10	7.6
2.8	4	3.0
2.9	10	7.6
3.0	13	9.8
3.1	19	14.4
3.2	12	9.1
3.3	10	7.6
3.4	12	9.1
3.5	7	5.3
3.6	6	4.5
3.7	6	4.5
3.8	4	3.0
3.9	5	3.8
4.0	2	1.5
	$n = 132$	100%

n = total number of students in the class.

STOP AND THINK 12.1

In looking at Table 12.4, can you identify how Ms. Johnson calculated the percentages included in the third column?

By creating this frequency distribution, Ms. Johnson was able to describe the essay grade data in terms of the number of students who performed well (i.e., high end of distribution = 3.8, 3.9, and 4.0) or struggled (i.e., low end of distribution = 1.7, 2.1, and 2.2), as well as the scores occurring most frequently (i.e., middle of distribution = 3.0, 3.1, and 3.2).

Please note that a frequency distribution is not simply restricted to quantitative variables (i.e., a variable that reflects variations in degree or quantity). For example, Ms. Johnson could produce a frequency distribution for biological sex (males and females) in her classes. However, given that only two scores are used for the biological sex variable (0 = males; 1 = females), the distribution is quite narrow and overly simplistic in nature (i.e., scores range from only 0 to 1; see Table 12.5). Nonetheless, this distribution still conveys a more organized summary of the scores than what would have been observed from simply looking at all the scores in the original dataset (see Table 12.1).

TABLE 12.5 ■ Frequency Distribution for Sex Variable		
Biological Sex	Frequency	Percentage (%)
0 (male)	73	55.3
1 (female)	59	44.7
	n = 132	100%

Graphical Representations of Frequency Distributions

Graphical or visual representations of distributions, which include bar graphs, histograms, line graphs, box-and-whisker plots, and stem-and-leaf graphs, are useful to show a distribution of scores. We provide a set of guidelines to consider when deciding which type of visualization would be most effective. A key first step is to identify the scale of measurement for each variable that you wish to describe. If the target variable is categorical or nominal in nature (e.g., biological sex, free and reduced lunch), a bar graph is most useful, but if the variable is quantitative, then a histogram or a line graph is more appropriate. Thus, to graph the biological sex variable, Ms. Johnson created a bar graph (see Figure 12.5). The number of bars equals the number of scores or subcategories for that variable. For the biological sex variable, because Ms. Johnson was concerned with only two groups, she only needed to create two bars. If religious affiliation was a variable in this dataset and there were five subgroups (i.e., Christianity, Islam, Judaism, Buddhism, and Hinduism), Ms. Johnson would create a bar graph with five bars (see Figure 12.6). The height of each bar reflects the frequency or percentage of individuals within a particular category.

For quantitative variables, researchers often use histograms, frequency polygons (i.e., line graph), stem-and-leaf displays, or box-and-whisker plots. A histogram is essentially a bar graph with a couple of important distinctions. First, the x-axis (i.e., horizontal axis that goes from left to right) includes many values given the quantitative nature of the variable. The values need to be rank ordered from lowest to highest. With bar graphs, the ordering of subcategories is not relevant given that each bar (i.e., subcategory of a nominal variable) is a conceptually distinct and stand-alone concept. A second and perhaps more subtle distinction between bar graphs and histograms involves the positioning of the bars. In a bar graph, the bars do not touch; however, they do touch in histogram (see Stop and Think to explore this latter distinction in greater detail).

STOP AND THINK 12.2

Why would the bars in a bar graph be separated by a space but the bars in a histogram directly touch each other?

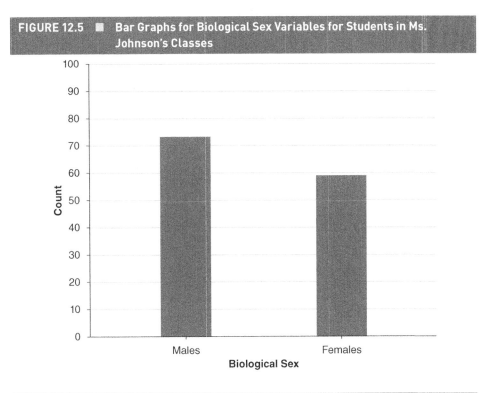

FIGURE 12.5 ■ Bar Graphs for Biological Sex Variables for Students in Ms. Johnson's Classes

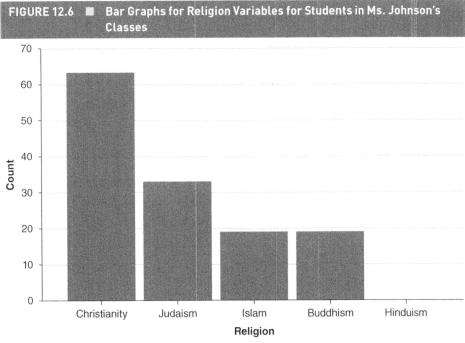

FIGURE 12.6 ■ Bar Graphs for Religion Variables for Students in Ms. Johnson's Classes

Conceptually, histograms are like frequency polygons in that they both can visually depict the shape of a distribution of scores (see Figure 12.7 and Figure 12.8). In contrast to histograms, which use bars to reflect frequencies of scores (i.e., or range of scores), frequency polygons use a continuous line. However, some researchers prefer frequency polygons to histograms because the straight line that connects the frequency scores can more easily illustrate a trend or pattern within the distribution scores.

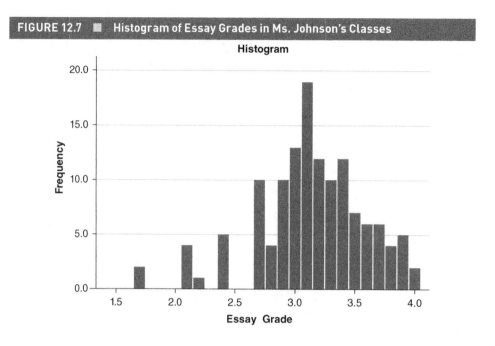

FIGURE 12.7 ■ Histogram of Essay Grades in Ms. Johnson's Classes

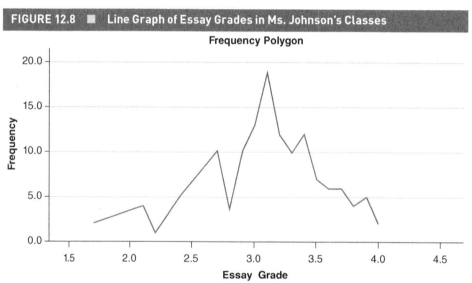

FIGURE 12.8 ■ Line Graph of Essay Grades in Ms. Johnson's Classes

Histograms and frequency distributions are very popular visual displays of distributions, but researchers may opt to use graphs that are less commonly used, such as a stem-and-leaf display or box-and-whisker plot. Stem-and-leaf plots are often used when there is a relatively small number of scores in a distribution or when researchers are interested in displaying each score in a distribution. The *stem* represents the first digit or set of digits of scores in a distribution. For example, consider the first stem-and-leaf figure presented in Figure 12.9. This figure represents essay grades in Emily's class ranging from 1.7 to 4.0. The *stem* value is placed in the second column of the figure while the *leaf* represents all remaining digits not included in the stem (last column). In this case, the stem is a single whole digit number, while all numbers under the leaf column represent decimal values. The frequency for each number category is presented in the first column. When looking at scores that range from 2.0 to 2.9 (i.e., second row), there are four people with a 2.1, one person has a score of 2.2, and five display scores of 2.4. If you are thinking that this first stem-and-leaf is too broad or coarse in nature to effectively visualize the distribution, you are correct! In fact, this first visual display is a bit silly when you think about it because there are 94 values within the 3s category.

A solution to this overly simplistic stem-and-leaf is to create more nuanced categories with a smaller range of scores. For example, in the second stem-and-leaf display in Figure 12.10, two distinct subcategories were created each for the broader 2s and 3s categories (e.g., [a] 2.0–2.4, [b] 2.5–2.9 and [a] 3.0–3.4, [b] 3.5–3.9). As you can see in this expanded stem-and-leaf display, the nature of the distribution is clearer and does a more effective job of representing the distribution shape that was conveyed in the histogram (see Figure 12.7). Hypothetically, one can create even more fine-grained categories to convey the distribution of scores (e.g., categories that only include two decimal values, such as 2.0–2.1 or 3.5–3.6). Although frequency polygons, histograms, and stem-and-leaf displays share the goal of visually depicting a distribution, many researchers prefer the stem-and-leaf option in certain circumstances because all values in a distribution are included.

FIGURE 12.9 ■ Stem and Leaf Graph for Essay Grades in Ms. Johnson's Class

Frequency	Stem	Leaf
2	1.	7
34	2.	1111244444777777777788889999999999
94	3.	00000000000001111111111111111111122222222222223333333333334444444444444555555556666667777778888899999
2	4.	00

FIGURE 12.10 ■ Expanded Stem and Leaf Graph for Essay Grades in Ms. Johnson's Class

Frequency	Stem	Leaf
2	1.	7
10	2.	1111244444
24	2.	7777777777888899999999999
66	3.	00000000000001111111111111111111122222222222223333333333334444444444444
28	3.	55555555666666777778888899999
2	4.	00

A final visual representation, infrequently used by many researchers but worthy of mention, is the box-and-whisker plot (see Figure 12.11). Compared to the other visual displays, a box-and-whisker plot is quite unique in its features. The box is represented by the rectangular shape in the figure, while the whiskers consist of single vertical and horizontal lines. Most notable is how this graph highlights specific scores in a distribution (i.e., lowest, median, and highest) and the clustering of scores into distinct *quartiles* (i.e., range of scores in the distribution that make up 25% of the scores at either the bottom, middle, or top; Figure 12.11). The top whisker represents the highest 25% of scores in the distribution, while the bottom whisker represents the lowest 25% of scores. The box contains the middle 50% of the scores. The dark blue line running horizontally through the box represents the median, which essentially divides this 50% of scores into two additional quartiles. Box-and-whisker plots can also include *extreme values*. These values are typically represented by circles and or numerals that signify the number of extreme scores. So what can Ms. Johnson determine by looking at Figure 12.11? She can easily identify that 50% of the scores in the distribution (the one that are not in the extreme ends) fall between a score of approximately 2.8 and 3.4. She also can identify that the non-extreme scores range from approximately 2.2 to 4.0 and that there are six extreme scores.

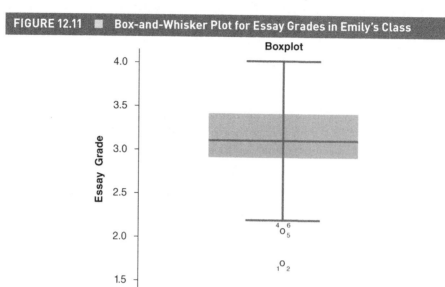

FIGURE 12.11 ■ Box-and-Whisker Plot for Essay Grades in Emily's Class

STOP AND THINK 12.3

What are your reactions or conclusions regarding the different graphical displays presented in this chapter for illustrating a distribution of scores?

THE TAKEAWAY

One of the first steps in descriptive data analysis is to examine the distributions of scores for each of the key variables in your dataset. Using visual displays can clearly illustrate the nature and characteristics of these distributions.

CENTRAL TENDENCY: IDENTIFYING THE MOST TYPICAL OR REPRESENTATIVE SCORE OF A DISTRIBUTION

LEARNING OBJECTIVE

12.4   Identify the most common measures of central tendency.

After creating a dataset and organizing the scores in terms of a distribution, most researchers shift their attention to a different descriptive statistic question (Figure 12.12):

What score best represents the distribution of scores for a particular variable?

FIGURE 12.12 ■ Key Question for the Most Typical Score in a Distribution

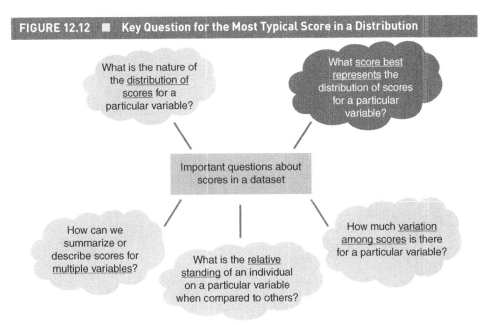

This notion of a "most typical" or "most representative" score lies at the heart of a core statistical concept called measures of central tendency. These metrics, which include the mean, median, and mode, reflect a single value that summarizes or describes a set of scores in a distribution. Each measure of central tendency is useful, but because the mean score is the most used and represents the key metric when conducting many types of inferential tests (see Chapter 13), readers are encouraged to focus most heavily on understanding this concept.

The Mean

The mean (M) represents the numerical average of a set of scores in a distribution. To calculate the mean, one simply needs to sum up all scores in a distribution, then divide that sum by the total number of scores.

$$\frac{\sum x}{n}$$

$\bar{x}$ = the sample mean

$\sum x$ = the sum of all scores for a given variable

n = the total number of scores obtained for that variable

Suppose Ms. Liptack wanted to calculate the average score for 11 students who took a recent science quiz in her class (2, 9, 1, 7, 8, 9, 10, 7, 6, 7, 10). The point total for this quiz ranged from 0 to 10. To calculate the mean, she would add all 11 student scores (2 + 9 + 1 + 7 + 8 + 9 + 10 + 7 + 6 + 7 + 10 = 76) and then divide that total by 11. Thus, the average quiz score for the students in Ms. Liptack's class would be 76/11 = 6.91. Although the mean is simple to calculate, it is widely considered to be the most robust measure of central tendency because it utilizes all scores in the distribution. It is also important because it is used when conducting other types of descriptive statistics, such as calculating standard deviations, effect sizes, or z-scores (see Sections 12.5 and 12.6), and several types of inferential statistics (e.g., t-test, ANOVA).

Measures of central tendency, like the mean, are a way for teachers/researchers to assess student performance.
©iStockphoto.com/Drazen Zigic

Researchers will use the mean as the measure of central tendency when the scores of a variable are based on an interval or ratio level of measurement. As you may recall from Chapter 10, an interval and ratio level of measurement includes the properties of rank-ordering _and_ equal distances between points on the scale (e.g., achievement test scores, GPA, anxiety scores on a rating scale). Thus, in situations when scores reflect a nominal (i.e., categories like ethnicity groups) or ordinal scale of measurement (i.e., ranks such as place in a science fair contest), the mean is not an appropriate measure of central tendency. For example, when considering the free and reduced lunch variable from our original dataset (see Table 12.1), two subgroups were coded as either a 0 (i.e., those who were not eligible to receive free or reduced lunch) or 1 (i.e., those who were eligible). If you followed the procedures for calculating a mean for this variable and thus added all 20 scores (i.e., total of 4) and then divided that number by the total number of scores (i.e., 20), you would get a value of .20. Unfortunately, this value does not represent the average score in the distribution or the more traditional understanding of the mean; rather, it reflects the proportion of cases who had a 1 score (i.e., .20 or 20%) on the free and reduced lunch variable.

The Median

As a measure of central tendency, the median reflects the midpoint of a distribution. As the center most score of a distribution, there will be 50% of the scores below and above the median value. To calculate the median, you can follow a simple three-step process: (1) rank order the scores (e.g., put in the order from lowest to highest), (2) identify whether the total number of scores is even or odd, and (3) find the midpoint. Using the same scenario with Ms. Liptack and the 11 student quiz scores, let's illustrate this process:

- _Rank order the scores_—order the quiz scores from lowest to highest. Ms. Liptack created a rank-ordered list as follows: 1, 2, 6, 7, 7, 7, 8, 9, 9, 10, 10.

- *Identify total number of scores*—note whether the total number of scores reflects an odd or even number. In this case, there is an odd number (i.e., 11).

- *Find the midpoint*—with an odd total number of scores, Ms. Liptack used the following rule to identify the midpoint: *divide the total number of scores by 2 and then round up.* Thus, Ms. Liptack divided 11 by 2 (11/2 = 5.5) and then rounded 5.5 up to 6; thus, a value of 6 communicates that the sixth score in the distribution (1, 2, 6, 7, 7, 7, 8, 9, 9, 10, 10) represents the midpoint or median (i.e., 7). Ms. Liptack knows that she correctly identified the median because there is an equal number or percentage of scores (i.e., 5 scores or 50%) below and above the third score of 7 (i.e., the 6th score in the ranked distribution).

STOP AND THINK 12.4

Using the three-step process for identifying the midpoint, can you identify the median in Ms. Liptack's distribution if one of the 7s was removed (i.e., there is now a total of 10 quiz scores—an even number)?

The Mode

Mode is another measure of central tendency that reflects the score that occurs most frequently in a distribution. In the preceding example, the mode score is a 7 (1, 2, 6, **7, 7, 7**, 8, 9, 9, 10, 10). Because the mode is directly linked to a frequency count, it tends to be most useful when scores are nominal or categorical in nature. While the mode may be used for quantitative variables in certain situations (e.g., when researchers are interested in identifying the frequency of specific scores or ranges of scores), it tends to be less useful than the mean or median in most circumstances in educational research.

Common Uses of Measures of Central Tendency

An important issue that novice researchers often grapple with involves which measure of central tendency to use for their data. As noted previously, our general recommendation is to use the mean score, given that it is the most precise measure of central tendency since it uses *every* score in a distribution. We also noted that the mean is central to calculating other types of descriptive statistics and when using many inferential statistics. However, there are situations when the mean is not the preferred metric, such as when there are extreme scores or outliers in a distribution. When a distribution contains one or more *outliers* (i.e., scores that are unusually different from most other scores), the mean becomes distorted and less meaningful. Consider the following scores on a recent exam for eight students in Mr. James's social studies class (100, 97, 94, 87, 86, 85, 80, 0). If Mr. James calculated the mean score for his class, he would obtain a mean of 78.6 (see the following Stop and Think activity for an elaborated discussion of this topic).

STOP AND THINK 12.5

In your opinion, does the mean of 78.6 serve as an adequate representation of the other seven scores in the distribution? What should you conclude?

The mean can also be problematic in situations when the distribution of scores is highly skewed. To understand this point, we first need to describe the meaning of two concepts: normal distribution and skewness. The normal distribution is an important concept that shares many of the characteristics of a frequency distribution or frequency polygon (line graph of a frequency distribution). The normal curve includes scores ranging from very low to high on the *x*-axis, with the peak of the distribution reflecting the score that occurs most frequently. However, the normal distribution has several special features that make it desirable when interpreting research results. It is perfectly *symmetrical* (i.e., an equal number of scores are below and above the mean), *unimodal* (i.e., only one most frequent score), and has an *equivalent* score for the mean, median, and mode (i.e., with all three values located in the middle position; see Figure 12.13). When constructing a frequency distribution with sample data, one cannot assume these normal distribution properties will be present. In fact, for most variables in educational contexts, the distributions of scores obtained from a sample will never reach perfect normality. The key point for you to remember here is that researchers are interested in making sure that the distributions of the key variables in their studies *approximate* this symmetrical and unimodal normal distribution.

THE TAKEAWAY

The mean score is central to most statistical approaches for describing or summarizing data and when making inferences about the results from a research study.

FIGURE 12.13 ■ Symmetrical, Unimodal, and Central Tendency Properties of the Normal Distribution

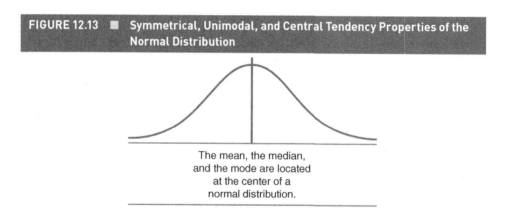

The mean, the median, and the mode are located at the center of a normal distribution.

Skewness refers to the extent to which the shape of a distribution deviates from the normal distribution. In skewed distributions, scores tend to cluster either to the right or left of the midpoint. Distributions are labeled as *positively skewed* if the scores cluster at the lower end for a given variable and *negatively skewed* when scores cluster at higher values of the variable (see Figure 12.14).

The simplest way to remember the difference between positive and negative skewness is to look at the direction of the tail of a distribution (i.e., where a minimal number or very few scores are found). If the tail stretches out and points in the direction of higher positive scores, then the distribution is positively skewed. If the tail stretches out and points toward zero or the negative side of the number line, then the distribution is negatively skewed. An interesting artifact of a skewed distribution is that, unlike the normal distribution, the values for the mean, median, and mode will be different. As a general rule of thumb, the mean will be closer to the tail side of a skewed distribution while the mode will be closer to the peak of the distribution. In more

FIGURE 12.14   ■   Types of Skewness Relative to the Normal Curve

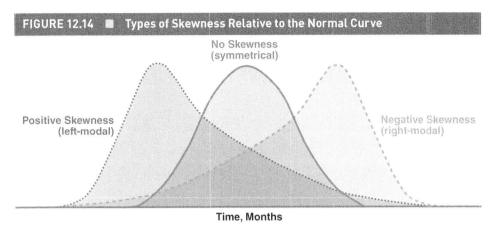

practical terms, if the mean score is lower than the median or mode, you will know that the distribution of scores cluster at high values (i.e., negatively skewed). If the mean score is higher than the median or mode, then the scores in a distribtuion cluster at the lower end (i.e., positively skewed). In these situations of high skewness, the median is the preferred measure of central tendency.

MEASURES OF VARIABILITY AMONG SCORES IN A DISTRIBUTION

LEARNING OBJECTIVE

12.5   Identify different metrics of variability of scores in a distribution.

Mr. James was speaking with one of his fellow social studies teachers. They both teach seventh-grade classes and recently had a conversation about student performance on a district-wide midterm exam.

Mr. James: "So how did your students do on the midterm exam?"

Ms. Brown: "They actually did very well. I was a bit worried given all the changes with online teaching and all the social distancing due to COVID."

Mr. James: "Yeah . . . I was very happy as well. They seemed to learn the material pretty well. Across my classes, the mean score was about 89."

Ms. Brown: "I guess we are doing something right as the class average for my sections is about an 88. It is amazing that our students performed in the same way."

Mr. James: "I know the district wants to use this test to gauge student progress during the year and to give remedial support to students in need. I guess our students are doing fine."

The exam data for the four sections of social studies classes (i.e., two for Mr. James and two for Ms. Brown) are presented in Table 12.6. Based on these data, were the comments made by Mr. James and Ms. Brown about student performance appropriate and valid? At first glance, it may seem so, given that, on average, the students performed reasonably well and consistent across all classes. However, communicating information that only reflects the central tendency (i.e., in this case the mean) is misleading because it only tells part of the descriptive analysis story. To give greater nuance and clarity when interpreting the exam scores, Mr. James and Ms. Brown should also have considered the variability or fluctuation of scores (Figure 12.15).

TABLE 12.6 ■ Raw and Mean Score Performance on Social Studies Exams			
Mr. James		**Ms. Brown**	
Section 1	Section 2	Section 1	Section 2
89	86	86	70
75	88	90	72
92	89	92	99
75	87	89	97
76	88	90	89
74	90	87	62
98	88	95	98
99	86	87	99
97	90	88	97
96	87	89	96
96	89	89	96
94	87	87	94
Mean = 88.4	**Mean = 87.9**	**Mean = 89.1**	**Mean = 89.1**

FIGURE 12.15 ■ Key Question for the Variability of Scores in a Distribution

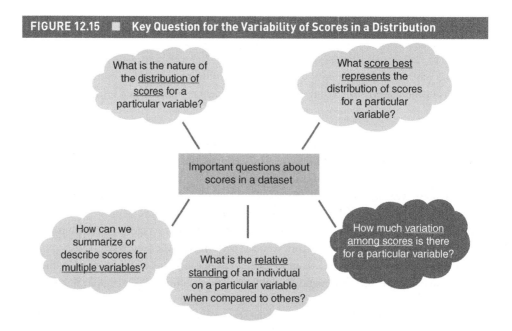

In looking at the data presented in Table 12.6, the test average in each of the four classes was remarkably similar (all around an average of 88 or 89). However, inspection of the individual exam scores reveals a noticeable pattern of variability (i.e., how different the scores are in a distribution) across the four sections of the class. To illustrate this point more clearly, let's first rank-order the scores. Like creating a frequency distribution or identifying the median score, rank ordering scores is helpful because it identifies the lowest and highest scores in a distribution as well as the frequency of scores. The rank-ordered scores for the four sections are presented in Table 12.7. When visually examining these rank-ordered scores, the pattern or variability among scores becomes quite clear. Students from Section 2 of Mr. James' class performed at a comparable level, but his students in Section 1 exhibited a much higher level of variability in performance. A similar pattern was observed between the two sections of Ms. Brown's class (i.e., greater variability for Section 2 than Section 1).

TABLE 12.7 ■ Raw Score, Mean, and Variability Indices of Social Studies Exam Performance			
Mr. James		**Ms. Brown**	
Section 1	**Section 2**	**Section 1**	**Section 2**
74	86	86	62
74	86	87	70
75	87	87	72
75	87	87	89
76	87	88	94
92	88	89	96
94	88	89	96
96	88	89	97
96	89	90	97
97	89	90	98
98	90	92	99
99	90	95	99
Mean = 88.4	**Mean = 87.9**	**Mean = 89.1**	**Mean = 89.1**
Range = 25	**Range = 4**	**Range = 9**	**Range = 37**
SD = 11.1	*SD* = 1.4	*SD* = 2.5	*SD* = 13.2

SD = standard deviation

While informal visual inspection of rank-ordered scores can uncover instances of variability, quantitative researchers typically want to calculate precise values, such as the range and standard deviation. The range is a fairly simple metric for variability that reflects the difference between the highest and lowest scores in a distribution. Thus, for students in Section 2 of Ms. Brown's class, the range was 37 (99–62) but only 9 (95–86) for students in Section 1. Although the range is useful for getting a general sense about variability relative to the extreme endpoints of a distribution, it has limited utility because it does not take into account the variation among all scores (i.e., a similar weakness noted for the mode and median as measures of central tendency).

STOP AND THINK 12.6

When examining Table 12.6 and 12.7, do you see the value of rank-ordering the scores in a distribution and how using both the mean and some indicator of variability can enhance understanding of student performance? Explain.

To generate a more robust metric of variability, researchers will often ask themselves two key questions: (1) what score best represents the distribution of scores for a particular variable (i.e., a central tendency question), and (2) how much variation among scores is there for a particular variable (i.e., a variability question)? In statistics, because researchers typically rely on the mean score as measure of central tendency, variability is conceptualized relative to the mean score. In other words, variability is conceptualized as an overall summary of the difference between each score in a distribution and the mean score. When most individual scores are close to the mean, variability will be low; when there is greater spread or difference among scores and the mean, the variability will increase. The standard deviation (*SD*), which is one of the most commonly used measures of variability, reflects the average difference between the individual and mean scores. The formula for a *SD* is reflected in the following equation:

$$SD = \sqrt{\frac{\sum (x - \bar{x})^2}{n}}$$

At first glance, this formula may seem daunting, but let's break it down. In short, to calculate the *SD* of scores, one needs to

- Subtract each score in the distribution from the mean score $(x - \bar{x})$

- Square each difference $(x - \bar{x})^2$

- Sum up these squared differences $(\sum [x - \bar{x}]^2)$

- Divide the sum of squared differences by the total sample size

- Take the square root of that number ($\sqrt{}$ = square root)

In some sense, a *SD* can be thought of as a special type of mean score. But rather than representing the average score in a distribution (i.e., the mean), an *SD* value represents the *average variability* of *scores around the mean*. It reflects the average variability because you are essentially dividing the sum of all individual variability scores $(x - \bar{x})$ by the sample size (i.e., similar in concept to how one would calculate the mean score).

THE TAKEAWAY

Measures of central tendency and variability each provide unique information about scores in a distribution. But they tend to have greater impact when used in complementary ways rather than in isolation.

Examining Central Tendency and Variability

Let's practice calculating different types of descriptive statistics using a dataset. As part of the *Let's See It!* activity, you will directly see how different measures of central tendency and variability are calculated. You can then demonstrate your mastery of these descriptive statistics principles as part of the *You Do It!* activity.

Let's See It! 12.1

Goal: To Learn About the Basic Procedures for Calculating Measures of Central Tendency and Variability

Directions: The primary objective of this activity is to illustrate the basic procedures for calculating three measures of central tendency (i.e., mean, median, mode) and two measures of variability (i.e., range, standard deviation).

TABLE 12.8 ■ Illustration of Procedures for Calculating Central Tendency and Variability

Measure of Central Tendency	Calculation Method	Example (rank-ordered distribution of scores: 15, 18, 24, 27)
Mean	Add up all the scores in a distribution and divide by the total number of scores.	Sum: 15, 18, 24, 27 = 84 Total number of scores = 4 Mean score = 84/4 = **21**
Median	Odd number of scores—divide the total number of scores by 2 and round up. Even number of scores—divide the total number of scores by 2, which gives you the positional value of a score. Calculate the average between that score and next highest value.	Even number of scores = 4 (rank ordered: 15, 18, 24, 27) Finding midpoint = 4/2 = 2. Using the score in the second position in the distribution (i.e., 18) and the next highest score (i.e., 24), find the average. 18 +24 = 42/2 = **21**
Mode	Conduct a frequency count for all scores and identify the most frequent score.	There is no mode. All scores occur one time in the distribution/

Measure of Variability	Calculation Method	Example (rank-ordered distribution of scores: 15, 18, 24, 27)
Range	Subtract the highest and lowest scores in a distribution.	27 – 15 = **12**
Standard Deviation	Divide the sum of squared deviations around the mean by the sample size. Then take the square root.	$SD = \sqrt{\frac{\sum(x-\bar{x})^2}{n}}$ Sum of squared deviations: 15-21 = 6^2 = **36**; 18-21 = 3^2 = **9** 24-21 = 3^2 = **9**; 25-21 = 4^2 = **16** 36 + 9 + 9 + 16 = 70/4 = **17.5** Square root of 17.5 = **4.18**

Let's Do It! 12.1

Goal: To Gain Experience in Calculating the Three Measures of Central Tendency (mean, median, mode) and Two Measures of Variability (range, standard deviation)

Directions: You will be given two datasets to practice. The first dataset reflects the number of pages of different books read by students in Ms. Johnson's English class during the third marking period. The other dataset represented scores that students received on a quiz in Mr. James' social studies class. Using the two datasets that follow, please complete the following questions in the second table.

TABLE 12.9 ■ Number of Pages Read and Quiz Score Depicted as Two Variables in a Dataset	
Number of Pages Read	**Social Studies Quiz Score**
367	17
519	19
218	27
486	11
24	15
385	22
225	15
307	3
367	22
n = 9	15
	n = 10

TABLE 12.10 ■ Calculating Central Tendency and Variability for Pages Read and Quiz Score		
	Number of Pages Read	**Social Studies Quiz Score**
Can you create a rank-ordered distribution?		
What is the mean of the distribution (round up to a whole number)?		
What is the midpoint or median of the distribution?		
What is the most frequently occurring score (i.e., mode)?		
Are any of the measures of central tendency misleading?		
What is the range of the distribution?		
What is the standard deviation of the distribution?		

METRICS TO CAPTURE THE RELATIVE STANDING OF INDIVIDUALS FROM A LARGER GROUP

Ms. Liptack recently administered a respiratory system exam to all of her biology classes. Billy, who struggled during the early part of the school year, received a grade of 80. This grade represented an improvement over his prior three exam grades of 60, 70, and 50. Billy was excited about this improvement given that he has been studying harder and giving more effort when completing homework. Using a self-standard to evaluate performance (e.g., comparing one's current grades to prior grades or a personal goals) is beneficial for students because it focuses their attention on their own behaviors and performance regardless of how their classmates or others perform. In many situations, however, administrators, teachers, and parents are interested in addressing a normative evaluative question (Figure 12.16):

"What is the relative standing of an individual on a particular variable when compared to others?"

FIGURE 12.16   ■   Key Question for Determining an Individual's Relative Standing

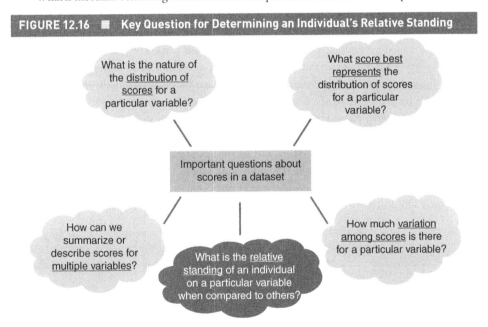

The concept of relative standing (i.e., how students compare to their peers or similar others) is of great importance to educators and administrators because it enables them to identify students who may be exceeding or falling behind their same age peers. In this section, we consider two of the most common metrics for determining how one student may compare to others on a particular variable (e.g., achievement scores, reading progress): percentiles and standard scores.

Percentiles

Percentiles represent a common and fairly simple way of expressing how individuals perform relative to others. A percentile signifies the percentage of individuals in a particular group that fall below a particular score. Thus, if Billy performed at the 34th percentile on a district-wide mathematics exam, this means that he scored equal to or better than 34% of the reference group (or

Marcus performed at the 98th percentile on a district-wide mathematics test, which means that he scored equal to or better than 98% of all school district students.

©iStockphoto.com/LumiNola

alternatively, 66% of the reference group scored higher than Billy). In general, a reference group (i.e., also called a standardization sample or norm group) reflects a group of people used to determine an individual's relative standing. A reference group can be conceptualized in many ways, such as a national sample of eighth graders, individuals from a particular school district, or individuals of a certain age or other demographic (i.e., socieconomic status). The specific characteristics of the reference group that educators or researchers wish to use will depend primarily on the nature of the interpretations they wish to make. In the preceding example with Billy, the reference group involved seventh-grade students in the school district.

Calculating a percentile score is also fairly straightforward. It can be computed by identifying the simple ratio between the ordinal rank of a particular score (i.e., the position of a score in a distribution) and the total number of scores in a dataset:

$$\text{Percentile} = (n/N) \times 100,$$

where n = ordinal rank of a given score and N = total number of scores in a dataset.

In the situation with Billy, suppose there were 200 individuals in the reference group (N = 200). Billy's exam score was found to be in the 68th rank-ordered position. Based on this information, one can conclude that Billy performed at the 34th percentile (68/200 x 100). Despite percentiles being a fairly universal and effective way to communicate relative standing, they are limited due to the *inequality of percentile scores* across a distribution, particularly when considering the extremes (i.e., end points) of a distribution. This notion of inequality can be illustrated with the following example. The differences in percentage of people receiving scores between the 4th to 10th percentile is not be the same as the percentage of people receiving scores at the 44th to 50th percentile (see Figure 12.17). The reason for this inequality is because larger percentages of people receive scores that hover around the midpoint or mean of the distribution (i.e., the height of a distribution reflects the greatest percentage of people receiving a particular score). Please refer to Stop and Think activity for an extended discussion of this concept (see also Table 12.11).

FIGURE 12.17 ■ Percentage of Scores in a Distribution at Various Standard Deviation Values

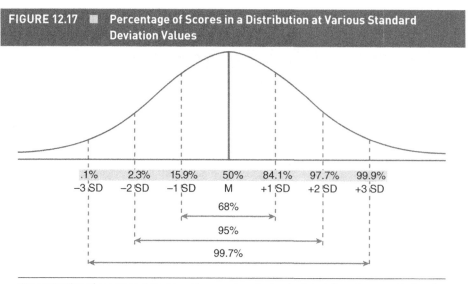

The proportion of scores under a normal curve at each standard deviation above and below the mean. The data are distributed as 20 ± 4 (*M* ± *SD*).

TABLE 12.11 ■ Advantages and Disadvantages of Relative Standing Metrics		
Relative Standing	**Definition**	**Advantages and Disadvantages**
Percentiles	Percentage of individuals in a group that fall below a certain score	Advantages: (a) easy to compute, (b) highly interpretable; (c) wide applicability Disadvantages: (a) unequal units between percentiles (percentage of people receiving scores between 40th and 50th percentile is much greater than the percentage between the 10th and 20th percentile).
Standard Scores	The difference between an individual's score from the mean expressed in standard deviation units	Advantages: (a) equal units between scores Disadvantages: (a) are not as interpretable and easy to understand as percentiles

STOP AND THINK 12.7

Using the normal curve in Figure 12.17, can you explain the concept of inequality of percentiles in a distribution?

Standard Scores

Standard scores represent a statistically more rigorous way of expressing relative standing or normative performance. In general, they convey how far an individual's raw score is from the group mean. Let's revisit a few concepts discussed earlier in the chapter (i.e., the mean, standard deviation, and normal distribution) to more fully grasp the meaning of standard scores. As you may recall, a mean score tells us about the most representative score of a distribution (i.e., measure of central tendency), while the standard deviation reveals information about the variability scores in a distribution around the mean. While Ms. Liptack was quite happy with Billy's score of 80 on the recent exam because it was an improvement over his prior grades earlier in the year (e.g., 68, 65), she wanted to be able to interpret this score (i.e., 80) in the context of the entire class. Her initial step in identifying Billy's relative standing was to first calculate the class exam average, which was observed to be an 87. If Ms. Liptack simply compared Billy's test score to the class averge, she could only conclude that Billy's score was numerically *lower* than the class average. She would not be able to precisely determine the meaning of this seven point difference (i.e., 80 [Billy score] - 87 [mean score]). In other words, simply knowing that Billy scored seven points below the mean does not give a lot of information about his relative standing to his peers. In some situations, a difference of seven points might be quite large, yet in others, it could reflect a small difference. The key factor in figuring out how meaningful the difference between a score and the mean is to identify the *SD* of scores within the distribution.

In technical terms, standard scores represent how far an individual's raw score is from the mean *in terms of SD units*. Thus, when researchers "standardize" a score (i.e., convert a raw score into a standard score), they are essentially doing two things:

- Determining how far an individual's score is from the overall group mean

- Dividing this difference by the *SD* of the reference group

As a general rule, dividing any value by a *SD* will convert or transform that value into *SD* units (i.e., the average variation of scores in a distribution). This transformed or derived value is called a z-score and is directly interpreted in terms of *SD* units. A z-score of zero reflects the average performance of the reference group, while positive z-scores reflect scores above the mean and negative z-scores indicate performance below the mean. Thus, if one of Ms. Johnson's students received an 85 on an essay and that score corresponded to a z-score of 0, she could conclude that the student performed at the same level as the average student within the larger group (i.e., 50th percentile). If a different student obtained a z-score of -.56, one can state that the latter student scored .56 standard deviations *below* the mean score for the reference group (see Basic Interpretation column of Table 12.12).

TABLE 12.12 ■ Examples of How to Interpret a z-score		
z-score	**Basic Interpretation**	**Normative-Based Interpretation**
+ .45	The individual performed .45 *SD* higher than the mean of the reference group.	The individual performed at approximately the 67th percentile.
0	The individual performed at the mean level of the reference group.	The individual performed at the 50th percentile.
− 1.0	The individual performed 1 *SD* lower than the mean of reference group.	The individual performed at approximately the 16th percentile.
+ 2.45	The individual performed 2.45 *SD* higher than the mean of the reference group.	The individual performed at approximtaely the 99th percentile.
− 1.56	The individual performed 1.56 *SD* lower than the mean of the reference group.	The individual performed at approximtaely the 6th percentile.

Note: The specific percentiles are fixed when dealing with a z-score distribution (which is a type of normal distribution).

When first learning about standard scores, many students often get confused and may even ask, "But what does it mean to say that a score is a certain *SD* below or above the average score?" This is a great question. To address this question, let's revisit the concept of a normal distribution. As you may recall, a normal distribution (also called the normal curve) is perfectly *symmetrical* (i.e., 50% of scores are above and 50% below the mean). This feature greatly facilitates interpretation of all types of standard scores. In looking back to Figure 12.17, you would observe that the percentage of individuals scoring between the mean score and 1 *SD* above the mean is identical (34.13%) to the percentage of individuals falling between the mean and 1 *SD* below the mean (34.13%). Thus, when using a normal curve, one can say that 68.26% of a reference group *is within* 1 *SD* of the mean of that group (i.e., above and below the mean).

More importantly, because a z-score is conveyed in *SD* units, it can be directly superimposed or embedded onto the normal curve. In fact, for any z-score value, one can determine the exact percentile (see Table 12.12 for examples). Do not worry, you will not need to perform this z-score to percentile conversions in most situations given the littany of z-score-to-percentile calculators or conversion tables that are easily accessible on the internet (https://measuringu.com/calculat ors/pcalcz/; retrieved March 13, 2013). Because z-scores are somewhat abstract and can be difficult for educators or others to easily understand in an applied sense, several alternative standard scores can be used (e.g., deviation IQ, *T*-score, subscale score). Although these alternative standard scores have the identical meaning or intepretation as a z-score, they are much more familiar to most people and easier to understand. Like a *z*-score, however, each of these alternative scores has a specific mean and *SD*:

- *z*-score: Mean = 0; *SD* = 1

- Deviation IQ score: Mean = 100; *SD* = 15

- T-score: Mean = 50; *SD* = 10

- Subscale score: Mean = 10; *SD* = 3

You can convert a *z*-score to any of these other standard scores by using the following formula: *New standard score = New mean score + New* SD *(z-score)*. Thus, to convert a *z*-score of .45 to a deviation IQ score, which has a mean = 100 and a *SD* =15, one would perform this simple calculation:

$$\text{IQ score} = 100 + 15\,(.45) = 106.75.$$

The IQ score of 106.75 has the identical interpretation of a *z*-score of .45 because they both convey that a person performed .45 *SD*s from their respective mean. For example, because a *z*-score directly corresponds to *SD* units, a *z*-score of .45 is the same as saying that the person scored .45 *SD*s above the mean. When using the IQ score with a mean = 100 and a *SD* =15, the score of 106.74 also means that the person scored .45 *SD* from the mean. You should note that the mean *z*-score (i.e., 0) corresponds to the mean score for every other standard score (i.e., mean *T*-score = 50; mean IQ score = 100, etc.). Similarly, the *SD* unit of a *z*-score (i.e., 1) corresponds precisely to a *SD* of 10 for the *T*-score and a *SD* of 15 for the IQ score on the normal curve. Thus, the interpretation of a *z*-score value of +1 is identical to *T*-score of 60 (i.e., 50 [mean] + 10 [1 *SD*]) and IQ score of 115 (i.e., 100 [mean] + 15 [1 *SD*]). Thus, the great thing about standard scores is that you can decide which one makes the most sense for you and how you want to share results with others.

STOP AND THINK 12.8

Using the normal curve, can you identify the percentile and the specific *z*-score, *T*-score, and IQ score associated with -1 *SD*? Will all these scores be interpreted in the same way?

Another derivation of the *z*-score concept is **Cohen's *d***, which is a type of effect size used when comparing the mean scores for two groups. In general, an effect size represents the meaningfulness or magnitude of the relationship observed between variables or the difference between groups. In simplistic terms, effect sizes help researchers draw conclusions about the size of an observed result (i.e., small, medium, large). In the case of Cohen's *d*, this value reflects the difference between two groups expressed in *SD* units (i.e., just like a *z*-score). If Mr. James was interested in identifying an effect size of the difference in test scores between a mathematics intervention group and a regular mathematics instructional group, he would use the following formula: (mean score for intervention group – mean score for traditional group)/standard deviation. If the intervention group earned a test score of 93 while the traditional group received an average score of 88 and the overall *SD* across groups was 15, the value of Cohen's *d* would be: (93 - 88)/15 = .33. By convention, a Cohen's *d* value of .20 = small effect, .50 = medium effect, and .80 = large effect. Thus, in the scenario with Mr. James, the Cohen's *d* value of .33 falls between a small and medium effect. This concept is different than statistical significance, which is discussed in greater detail in Chapter 13. Other common effect size metrics used by researchers include eta-squared (ANOVA) and different derivations of the correlation coefficient (e.g., Pearson correlation, semi-partial correlation).

THE TAKEAWAY

An effective way to understand student performance is to compare it to the performance of similar others (i.e., relative standing). The use of percentiles and standard scores are useful in addressing relative standing.

Working With Standard Scores and Percentiles

Because standard scores and percentiles are ubiquitous in educational circles, it is important for educators to become conversant and knowledgeable about interpreting these scores and being able to convert back and forth between them. To get more practice in relating z-scores to other types of standard scores and the normal curve, please consider completing the *Lets's See It!* and *Let's Do It!* activities. You can also extend your knowledge and skills by completing a companion *You Do It!* activity.

Let's See It! 12.2

Goal: To Understand the Link Between Raw Scores, z-scores, T-scores, and Percentiles

Directions: Consider Ms. Johnson and her calculating and interpreting z-scores and T-scores of essay grades for three students in one of her English language arts classes. In this activity, focus specifically on Whitney.

TABLE 12.13 ■ Illustration of Procedures for Calculating Standard Scores

Student	Essay Grade	z-score	T-score	Percentile
Whitney	1.7	−2.08	29.2	1.9
Jake	2.7			
Santiago	3.3			

Calculating z-scores

To calculate the z-score for all students, Ms. Johnson needs to first calculate the mean (3.07) and the SD (0.66) for her entire class of 18 students. She used Excel to get these values. These values were then used in the z-score formula, $z = $ (obtained score − mean score)$/SD$ to calculate the z-scores presented in the preceding worksheet.

The z-score calculation for Whitney $= (1.7 - 3.07)/.66 = -2.08$

Calculating *T*-scores

Given Emily's concern about interpreting *z*-scores, she decided to transform the *z*-score value to a *T*-score, which has a mean of 50 and a *SD* of 10. In the worksheet provided in this example, Whitney obtained a *T*-score values of 29.2, which can be interpreted in the same way as the *z*-score of -2.08. The *T*-score was calculated using the formula: *T*-score = 50 + 10 *(z*-score).
The *T*-score calculation for Whitney $= 50 + 10\,(-2.08) = 29.2$

Interpretation of the Results

Based on Whitney's essay grade of 1.7 and the corresponding *z*-score of -2.08, she performed more than two *SD*s below the class mean, which places her performance at approximately the 2nd percentile. Given that the *T*-score has a mean = 50 and a *SD* = 10, the observed *T*-score of 29.2 also shows that Whitney scored 2.08 *SD*s below the class mean and at the 2nd percentile.

Let's Do It! 12.2

Goal: To Gain Additional Practice in Calculating and Interpreting *z*-scores, *T*-scores, and Percentiles

Directions: Based on the information presented in the *Let's See It!* activity and other information in this chapter, please do the following:

- Identify the *z*-score and *T*-score for Jake and Santiago.
- Interpret the normative performance of Jake and Santiago (i.e., How did their performance stack up against the entire class?).

TABLE 12.14 ■ Calculating Standard Scores From a Raw Score, Mean Score, and Standard Deviation

Student	Essay Grade	z-score	T-score	Percentile
Whitney	1.7	-2.08	29.2	1.9
Jake	2.7			28.8
Santiago	3.3			63.7

EXAMINING THE CORRELATION AMONG VARIABLES IN A DATASET

LEARNING OBJECTIVE

12.7 Explain the purpose of correlational analysis as a descriptive assessment technique.

In this chapter, you have learned many key activities related to descriptive statistics, such as creating score distributions (e.g., frequency distribution, histogram, etc.), identifying the most "representative" score of the distribution (i.e., mean, median, mode), calculating the variability among scores (i.e., range or standard deviation), and describing an individual's performance relative to a reference group (i.e., percentiles, standard scores). All these descriptive statistics reflect univariate analysis approaches. That is, they focus specifically on scores collected from a sample for a *single variable*. Researchers typically use univariate descriptive approaches to describe the characteristics of the most relevant or important variables for a study. If five variables are measured in a study, researchers will likely perform descriptive statistics for each of them. In many instances, however, researchers want to answer a different type of question (Figure 12.18):

"How can we summarize or describe how scores from multiple variables fit or go together?"

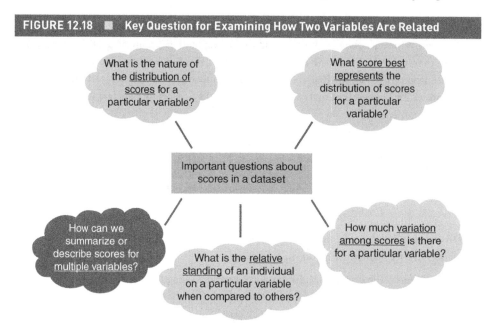

FIGURE 12.18   ■   Key Question for Examining How Two Variables Are Related

The most basic way for researchers to address this question is by examining how two or more variables relate to or covary with each other. Thus, Ms. Johnson might be interested in examining the relationship between students' attitudes about writing and their strategic approaches to writing, whereas Ms. Liptack wants to explore the statistical connection among teacher support, students' sense of connection to school, and student grades. When thinking about relationships among variables, one can focus on the *magnitude* or strength of that relationship (i.e., the numerical size of the correlation value) or the *direction* of the relationship (i.e., positive, negative, curvilinear). As with univariate approaches, visual displays and the calculation of specific statistical values are important.

Graphical Displays of Correlations

A scatterplot is a graphical representation of the statistical relationship between two variables. Using the original dataset presented in Table 12.1 (but with the full sample of 100 students), suppose Ms. Liptack wanted to examine the relationship between teacher support (i.e., student perceptions about the level of encouragement, feedback, and guidance from teachers) and students' perceived connection to school (i.e., positive feelings, valued in school). As a first step in understanding the nature of this statistical relationship, Ms. Liptack created a scatterplot. She placed the scores for one of those variables on the *x*-axis (horizontal line) and the scores for the other variable on the *y*-axis (vertical line). The dots in a scatterplot reflect the intersection between the scores on both variables for one person (see Figure 12.19). In other words, the location of the dots reveals how the scores for the two variables are linked or connected. To interpret this scatterplot, Ms. Liptack will try to identify one of three general patterns:

- As the scores for teacher support change in one direction (higher or lower), scores on connectedness change in the *same* direction (i.e., *positive relation*; high-high scores or low-low scores)

- As the scores for teacher support change in one direction (higher or lower), scores on connectedness change in the *opposite* direction (i.e., *negative relation*; high-low scores or low-high scores)

- No consistent pattern in the scores across the two variables can be identified (i.e., *no relation*)

FIGURE 12.19   ■   Scatterplots Illustrating a Positive and Negative Relationship Between Two Variables

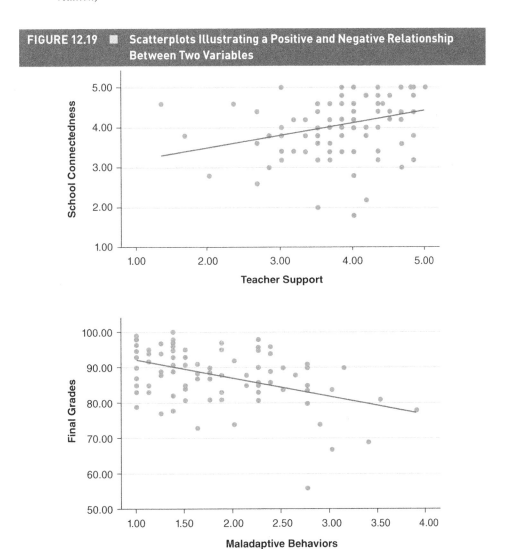

When looking at a scatterplot, researchers will often include a line of best fit, which is used to "summarize" the overall direction of the relation between the two variables. In looking at the first scatterplot in Figure 12.19, the line of best fit shows a positive relation between perceived teacher support and school connection; that is, on average, as students' perceptions of teacher support increase, so do their perceptions of school connection. We include a second scatterplot with different variables (i.e., grades, maladaptive behaviors [procrastination, avoidance] to reflect a different type of relationship. Can you explain the information presented in this second scatterplot (see Stop and Think activity)?

STOP AND THINK 12.9

How would you interpret the second scatterplot presented in Figure 12.19?

Measures of Correlation

Scatterplots can give researchers a sense or general feel about the nature of a correlation, but as we have mentioned repeatedly in this textbook, quantitative researchers prefer calculating specific numerical values to represent a concept. To understand the correlation among variables, researchers calculate a correlation coefficient. Correlation coefficients range in value from -1 to +1, with 0 indicating no relationship between the variables and the endpoints (1 or -1) representing perfect relationships. The positive and negative signs convey the direction of the relationship (i.e., do variables move together in the same direction or do they tend to move in opposite directions), while the size of numerical value reveals its strength. As correlation values approach either endpoint (e.g., .7, .8, -.8. -.9, etc.), the relationship is considered more robust or stronger. As the correlation values get closer to 0 (e.g., .3, -.3, .2, -.1), the nature of the relationship is weaker. It is important to note that a plus sign (+) is not needed to signify a positive relationship, but a minus sign (-) must be used to denote a negative relationship. The direction of the relation (- or +) is independent of the strength or magnitude of the relationship. Thus, a correlation coefficient of .78 is equivalent in magnitude to a coefficient of -.78.

The simplest type of correlation analysis involves two variables (i.e., bivariate or zero order correlation). On a conceptual level, a correlation is determined by examining the extent to which the scores from a group of individuals on a single variable show a *discernable pattern* with the scores on a different variable from the same group of people. To illustrate, let's think back to the scatterplot between maladaptive behavior and students' math grades (Figure 12.19). In order to obtain the scores for these variables, Ms. Liptack administered a measure of maladaptive regulation to students and then calculated their final math grades at the end of the marking period. Final math grades was a composite score reflecting exam performance, classwork, and homework. For these two variables (i.e., maladaptive behaviors, grades), a range of scores will be observed (e.g., maladaptive scores ranged from 1 to 5, while test scores varied from 50 to 100). Thus, a correlation coefficient will reveal the extent to which the pattern of scores for maladaptive behavior covaries or "is connected with" the pattern of scores in the other variable.

There are many different types of correlation coefficients that researchers can use to describe bivariate relationships. These coefficients largely differ in terms of the level of measurement for the variables (see Table 12.15). For example, while a Pearson product moment correlation reflects the relationship between two variables with an interval or ratio scale of measurement (i.e., equal distances between scores on the scale), a phi coefficient is used when only nominal or categorical variables are used, and the Spearman rho involves relations between variables with an ordinal scale of measure (i.e., rankings). While correlation coefficients are considered a type of descriptive statistic, if researchers are interested in discussing whether an observed correlation is likely to occur in the broader population, they would need to use inferential statistics and statistical significance (see Chapter 13).

TABLE 12.15 ■ Common Correlation Coefficients Used by Researchers			
Type of Relationship	**Variable 1**	**Variable 2**	**Example**
Pearson product moment (r)	Interval or ratio	Interval or ratio	School connectedness and teacher support
Spearman (p; rho)	Ordinal	Ordinal	Student ranking in physics class and student ranking in geometry
Biserial	Interval or ratio	Artificial dichotomy	Attitudes about school and achievement level (high or low)
Point-biserial	Interval or ratio	Natural dichotomy	Interest in math and biological sex (males, females)
Phi coefficient	Natural dichotomy	Natural dichotomy	Giftedness (gifted, non-gifted) and experimental condition (treatment, control)

THE TAKEAWAY

Correlational analyses are more complex than other types of descriptive statistics because they include multiple variables and consider the relations among them.

ETHICAL CONSIDERATIONS

As emphasized in all chapters throughout this textbook, ethical conduct is an essential and foundational component of the research process. When researchers collect data and engage in data analysis, several broad ethical principles are relevant, such as *integrity, respect for people's rights and dignity,* and *beneficence.* For the purposes of this chapter, we focus specifically on integrity; that is, the promotion of accuracy, honesty, and truthfulness when engaging in scientific or educational activities.

Reporting Descriptive Research Results

As previously emphasized in the various design chapters of this textbook, researchers and educators should never make interpretations that go beyond the data collected for a study. That is, it is never appropriate to discuss or present research results in a way that is misleading, inaccurate, or biased. This premise is quite relevant when using descriptive statistics, regardless of the research design that one may elect to use (i.e., experimental, descriptive survey, comparative). A common mistake made by emerging researchers is to confuse the term *numerical difference* with established statistical concepts, such as *effect size* and *statistical significance.*

Suppose Ms. Johnson conducted an experimental study to examine the effects of a writing strategy on students' essay grades. She randomly assigned one of her classes to receive the new writing strategy while the other class received the more typical or traditional writing instruction. She also administered pretest and posttest writing measures (i.e., pretest–posttest control group design; see Chapter 5). At posttest, Ms. Johnson found that students in the intervention condition exhibited an average essay grade of 87, while the traditional instruction group received an average score of 72. Technically speaking, Ms. Johnson would be correct in asserting that the two groups differed by fifteen points (i.e., a numerical difference). Further, at first glance, this difference might seem like a large and important effect. However, Ms. Johnson cannot make any claims about the *statistical significance* of this difference (i.e., the observed difference large enough to conclude that it is a real effect and did not occur by chance alone) or the overall importance or meaningfulness of this effect (i.e., effect size).

To address these latter two questions, Ms. Johnson conducted a statistical test (e.g., independent *t*-test) and found that the 15-point difference in the writing groups (i.e., intervention [87] and traditional [72]) was in fact statistically significant. Statistical significance simply means that the effect was a real effect or was too large to have occurred by chance alone. While this analysis helps Ms. Johnson with interpretation, it still does not allow her to make any claims about *how large of an effect* is represented by the 15-point difference. To make this claim, she must calculate an effect size, like Cohen's *d*. Using the same formula that was used in a previous scenario with Mr. James ([score 1 − score 2]/*SD*) and assuming a *SD* value of 15 was obtained, Ms. Johnson obtained a Cohen's *d* value of 1.0 ([87 − 72]/15). Any Cohen's *d* value above .80 reflects a meaningful and large effect. Thus, in this case, the writing intervention used with Emily's students had a *statistically significant* and *large effect* on their writing outcomes. In sum, it would be inappropriate and incorrect for Ms. Johnson to claim that the groups differed in a statistically significant or meaningful way if she only calculated the numerical difference. Researchers should only draw conclusions or make interpretive statements that directly align with the analyses that they perform; observing a numerical difference between two values is not enough to claim that they are statistically different or meaningful.

Researchers should avoid creating visual displays that mislead the readers or direct attention to a narrow component of the data.

©iStockphoto.com/lorenzoantonucci

It is also important for researchers to be cautious in how they present descriptive data in summary tables or figures. Specifically, researchers should avoid creating visual displays (e.g., histograms, bar graphs) that mislead readers or inappropriately direct their attention to a select aspect of the data. Consider the following two bar graphs in Figure 12.20. Suppose a researcher wanted to explore whether males were more likely to participate in an after-school sports program than females. Because the researcher hypothesized that more males would enroll in the program, he had a vested interest in showing that this was the case. Although the two bar graphs are based on the same raw data and accurately depict the same difference, the first bar graph shows a visually larger difference between males and females. This "visual difference" occurred because the second bar graph did not include frequency counts below 40 (i.e., a type of restriction of range). Researchers need to avoid this type of practice as it can mislead a reader and distort the nature of conclusions that should or can be made.

Another issue when using or reporting descriptive statistics is the omission of data that either contradict a researcher's hypotheses or create misleading or inaccurate results. For example, in Section 12.4 we presented a scenario with Mr. James and his desire to calculate the mean exam score for eight of his students. As you may recall, one of his students received a score of zero, which if used in the calculation of the mean score would greatly distort the results. However, it would be unethical for Mr. James to simply omit this score because he was concerned about reporting a

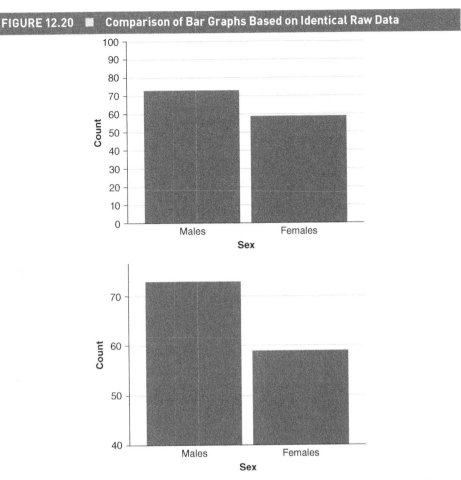

FIGURE 12.20 ■ Comparison of Bar Graphs Based on Identical Raw Data

distorted mean. A more ethical and appropriate choice would be to adapt his measure of central tendency and use the median score. This is not to say, however, that removing a score from data analysis is never appropriate. For example, if the student who obtained a score of zero did not take the exam due to an illness, then removing this score prior to calculating the mean would be appropriate because in that situation a score of zero reflects something conceptually different from a score of zero obtained by someone who took the exam. If researchers ever remove scores from a dataset, they are ethically bound to discuss this issue and the reasoning and logic behind one's decision.

A couple of other important ethical recommendations you should consider in the context of using descriptive statistics include the following:

- Only use data that were collected (i.e., do not fabricate or make up data)

- Only claim or report on your own data (i.e., do not plagiarize or pass off data from an external source as one's own)

AMERICAN PSYCHOLOGICAL ASSOCIATION STYLE

LEARNING OBJECTIVE

12.9   Utilize the *Publication Manual of the American Psychological Association* in reporting and presenting descriptive statistics.

There are several standard sections to a quantitative research article, including the introduction, method, results, and discussion. It is within a data analysis section of the methods or the results section of a paper that is most applicable to descriptive statistics. It is within these sections where researchers discuss the statistical approaches used to address the research questions and their methods for addressing potential problems with the data (e.g., missing data, assumption violations). In most cases, quantitative research articles include descriptive statistics for all variables and, as appropriate, information about inferential statistics (e.g., *t*-tests, ANOVA, etc.; see Chapter 13). For quantitative variables (e.g., scores on an exam, teacher ratings of satisfaction), researchers focus on measures of central tendency (e.g., mean) and variability (e.g., standard deviation). When variables are categorical in nature (e.g., ethnicity, grade level), frequency counts and percentages are more relevant. Given that descriptive statistics are designed to summarize or aggregate data in a meaningful way, we focus specifically on the creation and appropriate use of three descriptive summary tables: (a) demographics summary table, (b) descriptive statistics table for single variables, (c) correlational tables.

STOP AND THINK 12.10

Why do you think almost all quantitative research will include at least some descriptive statistics or summary tables in a journal article?

Most quantitative research involves recruiting a sample, collecting data from the sample, and then performing statistical analyses to answer the research questions. In studies that include a sample of people, it is customary to present and summarize the core characteristics of this group, such as biological sex, ethnicity, grade level, and/or family-related variables (e.g., free and reduced lunch status, parent education, etc.) in the form of a *demographic summary* table. Some demographic tables will convey information about an entire sample, whereas other tables will divide the sample into subgroups based on the purposes of the study. For example, Cleary et al. (2017) conducted an experimental study to examine the effects of a self-regulated learning intervention on several outcome variables in middle school students. There were two groups in this study: an intervention condition and a comparison condition (see Table 12.16). Because the key objective of the study was to examine the posttest differences between these two conditions, a summary table detailing the characteristics of each group was more relevant than presenting more general and aggregated information about the entire sample.

As another example, Cleary (2009) conducted a survey with a group of school psychologists across the United States. Because of the author's interest in showing that the participant sample was representative of the broader sample of school psychologists, demographic information for the entire sample and for the broader population of school psychologists based on membership in the National Association of School Psychologist (NASP) was included in the same table (see Table 12.17).

A second type of descriptive summary table focuses on the primary variables used in a study. With these tables, researchers typically report the means and standard deviations for all variables but may also include other descriptive statistics, such as the range or coefficient alpha values (i.e., a type of reliability index). These descriptive tables can also include both quantitative and categorical variables (see Cleary, 2009; Table 12.18)

TABLE 12.16 ■ Demographic Characteristics of SREP and WIN Conditions

Characteristics of Instruction	Intervention (n = 22) n (%)	Comparison (n = 20) n (%)
Ethnicity		
Black	10 (45.5%)	9 (45%)
Hispanic	7 (31.8%)	5 (25%)
White	3 (13.6%)	2 (10%)
Asian	2 (9.1%)	1 (5%)
Biracial	0 (0%)	3 (15%)
Biological Sex		
Male	13 (59.1%)	11 (55%)
Female	9 (40.9%)	9 (45%)
Free/Reduced Lunch	10 (45.5%)	9 (45%)
NJASK	200.3	201.5

Note: NJASK = New Jersey Assessment of Skills and Knowledge. SREP = Self-Regulation Empowerment Program; WIN = What I Need.

TABLE 12.17 ■ Demographic Characteristics of Respondent Sample and NASP Membership List

Demographic Characteristics	Current Sample Percent (%)	NASP Member List Percent (%)
Biological sex		
Female	68	74
Male	32	26
Ethnicity		
African American	2.8	1.9
Hispanic	3.7	3.0
Native American	0.9	0.8
White	90.7	92.6
Missing/Other	1.8	0.8
Mean age of respondents[a]	44	46.2
Type of degree		
EdS/Master's	75	68
Doctorate	25	32

Note: Under NASP member list, the percentages listed for gender, ethnicity, age, and type of degree refer to the 2004–2005 membership list.

[a] Reported in number of years

TABLE 12.18 ■ Frequency Ratings of Specific Referral Types Encountered by School Psychologists

	Frequency of Referrals[a]		Most Frequent Referral Problem		"Top Four" Referral Problem	
	Mean	SD	N	%	N	%
Academic skill deficits						
Reading skills	4.1	.72	66	61.1	85	78.7
Writing skills	3.7	.72	1	.9	37	34.3
Arithmetic skills	3.1	.65	0	0	19	17.6
Cognitive/Language deficits						
Intelligence skills	3.0	.70	1	.9	18	16.7
Language skills	2.9[b]	.80	1	.9	10	9.3
Academic enablers						
Task/Homework completion	3.6[b]	.79	8	7.4	38	35.2
Motivation	3.5[b]	.78	7	6.5	23	21.3
Study skills	3.4[b]	.94	3	2.8	30	27.8
Peer relationships	3.1	.70	1	.9	12	11.1
Internalizing disorder/symptoms					18	
Depression	2.9	.74	2	1.9	6	16.7
Anxiety	2.7	.70	2	1.9	2	5.6
Suicidal ideation	2.1	.90	0	0	6	1.9
Poor self-esteem	2.9	.79	0	0		5.6
Externalizing disorder/symptoms						
Inattention	3.8	.55	2	1.9	49	45.4
Hyperactivity	3.6[b]	.63	4	3.7	26	24.1
Oppositional	3.4[b]	.66	2	1.9	26	24.1
Conduct/Violent behaviors	3.3	.70	8	7.4	27	25.0

Note: Study skills and organization skills were combined into one category.

[a] Scores were based on Likert scale ranging from 1 "almost never" to 5 "almost always"

[b] $N = 107$

Correlation summary tables represent another table often included in quantitative research articles. Within these tables, researchers present bivariate or pair-wise correlations (i.e., a correlations coefficient for each pair of variables) and may include descriptive statistics (i.e., means, standard deviations) for each variable. To format this table, researchers will number the variables in the first column and then use those numbers to represent each of the variables across all columns. This numbering format allows researchers to insert information about the mean and *SD* and then list out the correlations for each pair of variables. Table 12.19 represents a correlation table for the Connection dataset discussed throughout the chapter.

TABLE 12.19 ■ Means, Standard Deviations, and Zero-Order Correlations Among All Measures						
Measures	M	SD	1	2	3	4
1. School connectedness	4.1	.73	–			
2. Teacher support	3.9	.74	-.31**	–		
3. Maladaptive behaviors	1.8	.66	-.28**	-.30**	–	
4. Grades	88.2	7.57	.14	.18	-.45**	–

Note: The first three variables are based on a 5-point Likert scale. Grades were based on scale ranging from 0 to 100. High scores for connectedness teacher support and grades are adaptive in nature, but high scores for the maladaptive scale reflect negative behaviors. *M* = mean score; *SD* = standard deviation.

* $p < .05$ ** $p < .01$

THE TAKEAWAY

Descriptive statistics tables are valuable for conveying information about the sample as well as the key variables used in a quantitative study.

CHAPTER SUMMARY

In this chapter, we reviewed several approaches for summarizing and describing scores included in a quantitative dataset. Descriptive statistics are valuable because they can help answer important questions, such as the following:

- What is the most typical or representative score for each variable?

- How much variability is there among scores for each variable?

- How does an individual perform relative to others?

- What is the size of an effect?

- How do variables relate to each other?

Although research studies can focus exclusively on descriptive statistics (see descriptive designs in Chapter 4), descriptive analyses tend to be used in a complementary way with inferential statistics. As you will learn in Chapter 13, inferential statistics are used to address the viability of hypotheses in a research study and to assist researchers in drawing conclusions about whether the results observed with a sample represent real or true effects within the broader population. Descriptive statistics, whether that includes means, standard deviations, or effect sizes, are essential to understanding inferential analyses because they give practical meaning to the variables included in the analyses.

KEY TERMS

Bar graph
Box and whisker plot

Correlation coefficient
Dataset

Descriptive statistics	Percentiles
Deviation IQ score	Range
Distribution of scores	Reference group
Effect size	Relative standing
Frequency count	Scatterplot
Frequency distribution	Skewness
Frequency polygon	Standard deviation
Histogram	Standard score
Mean (M)	Stem-and-leaf plot
Measures of central tendency	Subscale score
Median	T-score
Mode	z-score
Normal distribution	

EXTENSION ACTIVITIES

You Do It! 12.1

Using Descriptive Statistics in Practice

Self-Directed Practice: Understanding and Explaining the Descriptive Characteristics of Important Variables Linked to Teaching

Directions: Think about one of your classes that you teach and the various types of student information that you typically have access to or gather during instruction. Examples of important variables might entail student demographics (e.g., biological sex, ethnicity or race, disability status), behavioral indicators (e.g., out of seat behavior, discipline referrals, homework completion), and overall performance (e.g., grades for quizzes, tests, essays, other projects). You may also have access to information about students' cognitive abilities, academic achievement skills, anxiety, self-efficacy, or other psychological variables from testing conducted by other school staff. Using the worksheet that follows and Excel, SPSS, or other statistical software, perform the following actions:

a Select any three student variables about which you will conduct descriptive analyses.

b Using a sample of about 10 students from your classes (try to use students of varying ability or performance levels), create a dataset in Excel (or a statistical program like SPSS) that lists the student names in rows (use pseudonyms for this activity) and the three variables of interest as columns.

c Identify and calculate a measure of central tendency that is most appropriate for each variable.

d Calculate the standard deviation for each of the variables.

Target Variables	Central Tendency	Standard Deviation
Variable 1 _____		
Variable 2 _____		
Variable 3 _____		

You Do It! 12.2

Applying Descriptive Statistics and Relative Standing in Practice

Self-Directed Practice: Understanding and Explaining the Relative Standing of Students in Your Classroom

Directions: In the two sets of *Let's See It!* and *Let's Do It!* activities in this chapter, you practiced how to calculate measures of central tendency (mean, median, mode), variability (range, standard deviation), and relative standing (z-scores, T-scores). For those activities, we supplied the scenarios and datasets. Now we would like you to think about the students with whom you work in school to calculate these descriptive statistics. That is, in this activity you will calculate measures of central tendency and measures of variability and use those values to determine the relative standing of a few students from your classroom. Using the worksheet that follows and the formulas and information you learned in this chapter, complete the following actions:

a   Identify an exam, quiz, essay, or other academic activity that you recently assigned and graded using a numerical score (e.g., score of 93 on a quiz). Try to select an assignment that generated a wide range of student grades or scores.

b   List those student grades.

c   Using a sample of 10 to 12 students from your class, please calculate the mean and standard deviation for that group of students.

d   Select three students from your class who showed low scores, medium scores, and high scores. Using these individual scores
   1.   Calculate a z-score for each student.
   2.   Calculate a T-score for each student.
   3.   Using the link for the percentile calculator, calculate the percentiles for both variables for each student. https://measuringu.com/calculators/pcalcz/

e   Make some interpretive statements about these three students in terms of their relative standing as compared to their classmates.

Group Level Analysis	List of Scores on Assignment	Mean	Standard Deviation

Student Level Analysis	z-score and T-score	Percentile	Overall Interpretation
Student 1	z-score: _____ T-score: _____		
Student 2	z-score: _____ T-score: _____		
Student 3	z-score: _____ T-score: _____		

Note: z-score to percentile calculator: https://measuringu.com/calculators/pcalcz/

Stop and Think Activities

STOP AND THINK 12.1

To calculate the percentage, Ms. Johnson divided each frequency by the total number of observations. Thus, in this problem, 10 students received an essay grade of 3.3. Given that there was a total of 132 students who received an essay grade, the percentage of time that a grade of 3.3 occurred in her classes was 10/132 = 13.2%. Just note that when creating these types of tables, researchers also often include a column with cumulative percentages (see table that follows). The cumulative percentage reflects the number of observations for a given score plus all other scores lower than that value.

Essay Grade	Frequency	Percentage (%)	Cumulative Percentage (%)
1.7	2	1.5	1.5
2.1	4	3.0	4.5
2.2	1	0.8	5.3
2.4	5	3.8	9.1
2.7	10	7.6	16.7
2.8	4	3.0	19.7
2.9	10	7.6	27.3
3.0	13	9.8	37.1
3.1	19	14.4	51.5
3.2	12	9.1	60.6
3.3	10	7.6	68.2
3.4	12	9.1	77.3
3.5	7	5.3	82.6
3.6	6	4.5	87.1
3.7	6	4.5	91.6
3.8	4	3.0	94.6
3.9	5	3.8	98.4
4.0	2	1.5	100
	$n = 132$	100	

STOP AND THINK 12.2

A histogram and a bar graph serve the same basic function and are highly similar in terms of the visual representation; that is, to visually display the shape of a score distribution. The presence or absence of a space between the bars in these two visuals is due to the level of measurement for the variable (e.g., categorical, ordinal, interval). Bar graphs are used when a variable is nominal or categorical in nature. The space between the bars denotes that each of the subgroups or subcategories of a variable (e.g., males, females) represents mutually exclusive or distinct categories.

For histograms, the bars directly touch because the scores are quantitative or more continuous in nature; thus, there is an order and sequential aspect to the scoring system.

STOP AND THINK 12.3

A common observation about the various graphical displays is that despite differences in format or appearance, they all tend to have the same function; that is, to use a visual format to convey the frequency or scores and or characteristics of the distribution of scores. Another common observation is that each graphical display or visualization can be used for a specific purpose when dealing with a certain type of variable. For example, despite bar graphs and histograms having the same basic function and general appearance, bar graphs are specifically used when the variable is categorical in nature, while histograms are useful for quantitative variables. Finally, researchers tend to use the graphical displays that best serve their interests and conveys the type of information of greatest value to their analyses.

STOP AND THINK 12.4

In this situation, if one of the 7s in the distribution was removed, there would now be an even number of scores (i.e., 1, 2, 6, 7, 7, 8, 9, 9, 10, 10), which technically does not have an observed score at the midpoint. The midpoint in this situation will need to involve an average of the two middle-most scores in the distribution. To find the midpoint, Ms. Liptack needs to average the two middle scores (7 + 8 / 2 = 7.5). Identifying the two middle scores that you want to average is more challenging when the number of scores is very large (e.g., 350 scores). A simple procedure for finding the two middle scores in an even numbered set of scores is to divide the total number of scores by 2 (e.g., 10/2 = 5). The number you get denotes the number of scores below (i.e., 5 scores) and above the midpoint (i.e., 5 scores). The last score (7) in the set of lower scores (i.e., 1, 2, 6, 7, **7**) represents one of the middle scores while the first number (8) in the set of higher scores (i.e., 8, 9, 9, 10, 10) represents the other middle score. Dividing these two middle scores will give you the median score (i.e., 7.5).

STOP AND THINK 12.5

This question was designed to underscore a situation when it is not appropriate to use the mean score as the best representation of the set of scores. Specifically, when one or more scores in a distribution are extremely or unusually different from the other scores (i.e., outliers), it is likely that the mean does not adequately represent the nature of the entire distribution. The example presented in this scenario includes eight test grades for students in Mr. James's social studies class (i.e., 100, 97, 94, 87, 86, 85, 80, 0). Suppose the score of zero was omitted from the distribution. Based on the remaining seven scores, the mean average would be 89.9 rather than 78.6 when the score of 0 was included—quite a large difference! In looking back at the full distribution of scores, does the mean of 89.9 seems like an adequate representation of the distribution? It certainly does appear to capture or represent most of the scores. However, researchers cannot, without proper justification and acknowledgement, remove extreme scores from a dataset. Thus, in this specific situation, researchers should think about using an alternative measure of central tendency, such as the median. The median (i.e., [87 + 86]/2 = 86.5) would be a much better approximation of the central tendency than the original mean value of 78.6, given that a median score is unaffected by extreme scores.

STOP AND THINK 12.6

Rank-ordering scores in a distribution will help researchers more easily determine the range of scores in a distribution (difference between highest and lowest scores). It can also give them a clearer sense of how scores tend to cluster or group together. While identifying the measure of central tendency (i.e., median or mean) provides useful information, it is not until one identifies the variability among scores that one can truly understand group performance.

STOP AND THINK 12.7

The concept of inequality of percentiles in a distribution specifically refers to differences in the frequency or clustering of scores along different points of a score distribution. For example, approximately 34% of individuals in a normal distribution fall between the mean and 1 *SD* above the mean. When examining those individuals between 1 *SD* and 2 *SD* above the mean, however, approximately 13.5% of the individuals will fall within this range. Thus, as a score approaches the midpoint or mean of a normal distribution, the percentage of individuals receiving those scores will substantially increase. The further a score is from the mean, the more "rare" or unusual the score will be. Thus, there will be a lower percentage of individuals receiving this score. In sum, the percentage of scores between the mean and 1 *SD* will be "different" or "unequal" when compared to the percentage of scores that fall between 1 *SD* and 2 *SD*.

STOP AND THINK 12.8

In looking at the normal curve and scores that are 1 *SD* below the mean, the following scores are obtained:

- Percentile = approximately 16th

- *z*-score = -1

- *T*-score = 40

- Deviation IQ = 85

All these standard scores would be interpreted in the same way given that they all reflect performance that was 1 *SD* below the mean. For example, with a *z*-score, the mean is set at 0 and the *SD* =1. Thus, a *z*-score of -1 is synonymous with performance 1 *SD* below mean. For a *T*-score, the mean is set at 50 and one *SD* unit is 10. Thus, a score of 40 (50 [mean] − 10 [*SD*]) also reflects 1 *SD* below the mean. Finally, a deviation IQ score has a mean of 100 and an *SD* of 15. Thus, 1 *SD* (i.e., 15 points) below the mean (i.e., 100) would equal an 85. All three standard scores are 1 *SD* below the mean, which is represented by the 16th percentile.

STOP AND THINK 12.9

When attempting to analyze any scatterplot, a key first step is to identify the two variables of interest. In this case, maladaptive behavior (e.g., avoidance, forgetfulness) was placed on the horizontal or *x*-axis while the final grade variable was on the vertical or *y*-axis. The second step is to figure out what high and low scores for each of the variables mean. High scores on maladaptive measure signifies students who more frequently exhibit negative school behaviors, such as avoidance, forgetfulness, or procrastination. High scores on final grade indicate students who performed well on the various performance measures in a class. Finally, you want to identify the pattern that you see, specifically in terms of how changes in the scores for one variable predict or align with changes in the scores of the other variable. In this example, as scores for maladaptive behavior get higher (i.e., more negative behavior), the scores for final grades get smaller. Thus, there is an inverse or negative relationship between the two variables. As students behave in more maladaptive ways, they tend to perform more poorly, while those who exhibit very few maladaptive behaviors will, on average, tend perform at a higher level.

STOP AND THINK 12.10

Descriptive statistics help researchers and consumers of research understand, discuss, and interpret the scores collected as part of a research study. Before researchers can interpret inferential statistics or draw conclusions about the implications of the results, they need to have knowledge of the specific values about central tendency (e.g., mean) and variability (e.g., standard deviation). These values help researchers draw more meaningful interpretations based on relative standing and when using inferential statistics.

Let's Do It! Activities

LET'S DO IT! 12.1

Goal: To Gain Experience in Calculating the Three Measures of Central Tendency (mean, median, mode) and a Measure of Variability (range)

Directions: You will be given two datasets to practice. The first dataset reflects the number of pages of different books read by students in Ms. Johnson's English class during the third marking period. The other dataset represented scores that students received on a quiz in Mr. James' social studies class. Using the two datasets that follow, please complete the following questions in the second table.

Number of Pages Read and Quiz Score Depicted as Two Variables in a Dataset

Number of Pages Read	Social Studies Quiz Score
326	17
419	19
218	27
307	11
14	15
317	22
225	15
307	3
325	22
n = 9	15
	n = 10

Calculating Central Tendency and Variability for Pages Read and Quiz Score

	Number of Pages Read	Social Studies Quiz Score
Can you create a rank-ordered distribution?	24, 218, 225, 307, 307, 317, 325, 326, 419	3, 11, 15, 15, 15, 17, 19, 22, 22, 27
What is the mean of the distribution (round up to a whole number)?	273.1	16.6
What is the midpoint or median of the distribution?	307	16

	Number of Pages Read	Social Studies Quiz Score
What is the most frequently occurring score (i.e., mode)?	307	There are two modes: 15, 22
Are any of the measures of central tendency misleading?	The mean because of the extreme scores of 24	No
What is the range of the distribution?	405	24

LET'S DO IT! 12.2

Goal: To Gain Additional Practice in Converting z-scores to Other Types of Derived Scores

Directions: Based on the information presented in the *Let's See It!* activity and other information provided in this chapter, please do the following:

- Identify the z-score and *T*-score for Jake and Santiago

Calculating Standard Scores From a Raw Score, Mean Score, and Standard Deviation

Student	Essay Grade	z-score	T-score	Percentile
Whitney	1.7	-2.08	29.2	1.9
Jake	2.7	-.56	44.4	28.8
Santiago	3.3	.35	53.5	63.7

Calculating z-scores

Using the mean (3.07) and the *SD* (0.66) for the entire class of 18 students, Ms. Johnsoncan use the z-score formula, z = (obtained score – mean score)/*SD* to calculate the z-scores for Jake and Santiago.

$$\text{The } z\text{-score for Jake} = (2.7 - 3.07)/.66 = -.56$$
$$\text{The } z\text{-score for Santiago} = (3.3 - 3.07)/.66 = .35$$

Calculating *T*-scores

Ms. Johnsoncan use the general formula of a *T*-score = 50 + 10 (z-score) to calculate the *T*-score for Jake and Santiago.

$$\text{The } T\text{-score for Jake} = 50 + 10 (-.56) = 44.4$$
$$\text{The } T\text{-score for Santiago} = 50 + 10 (.35) = 53.5$$

- Interpret the normative performance of Jake and Santiago (i.e., how did their performance stack up against the entire class)

Based on Jake's essay grade of 2.7 and his z-score of -.56, he performed .56 *SD*s *below* the class mean, which places his performance at approximately the 29th percentile. The same logic is used to interpret his *T*-score of 44.4. Because the *T*-score has a mean = 50 and a *SD* = 10, the observed *T*-score of 44.4 is also .56 *SD*s below the mean of 50 on this scale.

Based on Santiago's essay grade of 3.3 and his z-score of .35, he performed .35 *SD*s above the class mean, which places his performance at approximately the 64th percentile. The same conclusion is reached when examining his *T*-score of 53.5. Because the *T*-score has a mean = 50 and a *SD* =10, the observed *T*-score of 53.5 is .35 *SD*s above the mean of 50 on this scale.

13 INFERENTIAL STATISTICS

LEARNING OBJECTIVES

Upon completion of this chapter, students should be able to

13.1   Describe the purpose of inferential statistics

13.2   Summarize data using measures of variability

13.3   Explain probability and statistical significance

13.4   Conduct hypothesis testing and interpret statistical significance

13.5   Compare and contrast various inferential tests (regression, *t*-tests, one-way ANOVA, ANCOVA, and chi-square).

13.6   Demonstrate knowledge of ethical issues in conducting, analyzing, and communicating findings of inferential statistics

13.7   Utilize the *Publication Manual of the American Psychological Association* in reporting findings of inferential statistics

A DAY AT WORK

How Can I Use School-Based Data More Effectively?

©iStockphoto.com/xavierarnau

Mr. Karr is an Algebra I math teacher at an urban high school and has been teaching for 10 years. He typically teaches afternoon classes, but this year, he is teaching two morning periods (first and second) and two afternoon periods (sixth and seventh). Although his teaching methods are consistent across class periods, he has noticed that students in his afternoon sections are far more engaged and attentive than students in his morning sections, the latter of whom seem tired and often fall asleep during class. He also noticed that students in his morning classes scored on average, nearly 10 points lower than those taking math in the afternoon.

Mr. Karr wondered if this trend was happening in other high schools. Hypothesizing that students in morning periods may be less attentive during class due to the early start time, Mr. Karr thought he might explore whether the difference between his morning and afternoon classes was statistically significant. That is, is the difference a real effect that would be observed in the broader population? He is thinking that perhaps mathematics classes should be offered in the afternoon to ensure students are more awake, but what evidence would he need before he presented this recommendation to the superintendent?

FIGURE 13.1 ■ Inferential Statistics

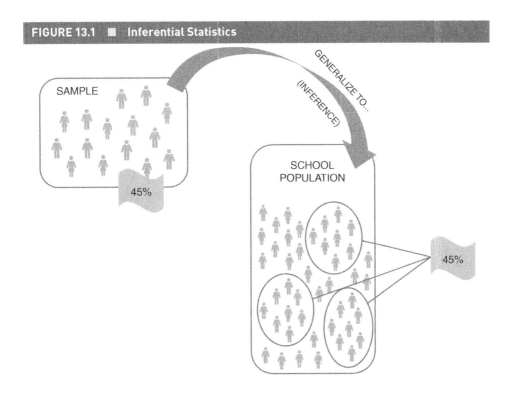

INTRODUCTION

From what we have learned so far in this textbook, there are two major categories of statistics used by researchers: descriptive statistics and inferential statistics. In Chapter 12, we talked about descriptive statistics as a set of procedures that summarize scores from a sample in terms of the most representative scores, level of variability among scores, and correlations among scores in a distribution. In this chapter, we shift focus and discuss inferential statistics. Inferential statistics are more complex and sophisticated than descriptive statistics because they go well beyond mere descriptions of sample characteristics; they enable researchers to draw conclusions about whether sample results are a real effect in the broader population from which the sample was drawn.

The primary focus of this chapter is on the broad range of inferential statistics that researchers can use to determine whether one can draw conclusions or inferences about a population based on results using a subgroup or sample of that population. We begin by discussing the overall purposes of inferential statistics and underlying concepts such as probability theory, hypothesis testing, and statistical significance. We then provide an overview of the most common types of inferential statistics including multiple regression, t-tests, one-way ANOVA, ANCOVA, and chi-square. Lastly, we describe ethical issues in using inferential statistics and the role of the APA's publication manual in helping educators such as Mr. Karr write about their findings.

THE PURPOSE OF INFERENTIAL STATISTICS

LEARNING OBJECTIVE
13.1   Describe the purpose of inferential statistics.

As a review (see Chapter 12), descriptive statistics are often used to describe and summarize sample data using graphs or charts (e.g., histograms, bar graphs, boxplots, scatter plots), measures of central tendency (e.g., mean, median, mode), variability (e.g., standard deviation), or relative standing (e.g., standard scores). These statistics are designed to provide information about a specific sample rather than draw conclusions about a population. For example, Mr. Karr may want to calculate the average test score for each of his three classes or create a histogram of scores across each class to visually see how the scores in his specific classes are distributed.

With inferential statistics, researchers use sample data to make predictions or inferences about the characteristics of the population (Figure 13.1). Because it is typically not possible or feasible for researchers to collect data on every member in a population, they collect data on samples. Ideally, the sample that is used in a study should be representative of the population about which one wishes to make estimations or predictions. Going back to our example with Mr. Karr, one of the issues he wanted to explore was whether there was a relationship between the number of hours of sleep high school students receive each night and their overall performance in mathematics. Thus, he collected data from a sample within the broader population of high school students and calculated a correlation coefficient ($r = .40$), observing a moderate relationship between these two variables. A correlation coefficient is a type of descriptive statistic, but it takes on a different meaning when inferential testing is used. With inferential statistics, Mr. Karr is interested in identifying whether the correlation of .40 is a true or real effect within the broader population. As we will explain in subsequent sections of this chapter, inferential testing assumes there is no effect or relationship among variables in the population. Thus, in this case, it is assumed that the correlation should be 0 in the population. Inferential testing conveys information to help Mr. Karr determine whether the correlation of .40 is a real effect (i.e., statistically different from 0) or not a real effect (i.e., not statistically different from 0). Again, because it would be virtually impossible to collect data from every single high school student in a school district, collecting data from a smaller number of representative students and using inferential statistics would allow Mr. Karr to make inferences about the whole population in that school district more broadly. Figure 13.2 shows different methods to describe a sample and several statistical techniques to draw inferences from a sample to a population.

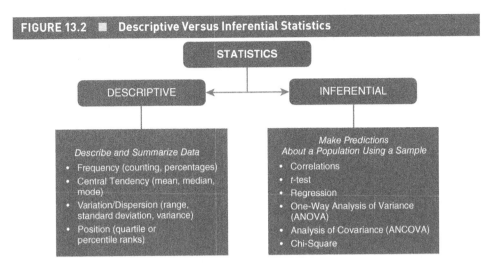

FIGURE 13.2 ■ Descriptive Versus Inferential Statistics

When determining which type of statistics to use, it is important to consider the goal of the specific research study. As discussed in Chapter 12, if the goal is simply to understand and describe a set of data, then descriptive statistics would be sufficient. If the goal of the research, however, is to draw conclusions or make generalizations about a defined population, then collecting data from a sample and using inferential statistics is the preferred choice. In other words, in inferential statistics, researchers use data and findings from a sample to make generalizations about the population. As we will discuss in subsequent sections, concepts such as probability and hypothesis testing allow researchers to draw conclusions from the sample to the population.

STOP AND THINK 13.1

What is a critical issue you are interested in exploring that might be answered through the use of inferential statistics?

As another example, say we have collected data from a single school about student scores on the PSAT/NMSQT (Preliminary SAT/National Merit Scholarship Qualifying Test), a standardized test administered by the College Board for 10th and 11th graders. As a researcher, we could analyze the data by looking at the percentage of students who score at a certain level based on race and grade level. We could also take a look at a distribution of scores within the sample. However, if we wanted to test the probability that the scores from our single school reflect the scores of other 10th and 11th graders within the district or even the state, then we would need to use inferential statistics.

Of course, it is important to note that researchers can only make generalizations or inferences about a population from a sample when the sample is truly representative of that population (see Chapter 10 on sampling and measurement). The larger the sample the more likely that it is representative of the population. For example, Mr. Karr should not attempt to use data from 10 high school students to draw conclusions about all high school students, nor should he use high school sample data to make generalizations about elementary school students.

THE TAKEAWAY

Descriptive statistics summarize data from a given sample, whereas inferential statistics make inferences that can be generalized to the population as a whole.

MEASURES OF VARIABILITY

LEARNING OBJECTIVE
13.2   Summarize data using measures of variability.

Classrooms are filled with diverse learners. Most educators are aware of the diversity of skills abilities, and performance of students—some students always perform at higher levels, whereas others may need additional support to achieve their very best.

Classrooms include diverse learners with a wide range, or variability, of abilities and performance levels across subject areas.

©iStockphoto.com/insta_photos

This range of student performance or abilities can be depicted in terms of variability. Just as it does in the classroom, the word *variability* refers to how spread apart the scores of the distribution are or how much the scores vary from each other. As discussed in Chapter 12, measures of variability include the range, variance, and standard deviation. The range represents the difference between the highest and lowest score in a distribution. For example, if Mr. Karr wanted to assess the range of test scores for each of his four classes, he would identify the highest and lowest scores in each class and subtract them. This would provide Mr. Karr with information about how spread out the scores are in his classes. The variance is the average of the squared differences

---

of each score from the mean. In order to calculate the variance, the difference between each score and the mean is squared and then added together. The sum is then divided by the total number of scores minus one, a concept called *degrees of freedom* (discussed later in the chapter). The standard deviation is then calculated by taking the square root of the variance. The standard deviation is typically reported in most quantitative research studies as it is the most useful and effective metric of variability and it is the metric most commonly used in inferential statistics. Both the variance and standard deviation are interpreted in terms of how far scores are from the mean. A standard deviation close to zero indicates that the scores tend to cluster close to the mean, whereas a high standard deviation reflects scores that fluctuate widely either above or below the mean (e.g., positive standard deviation reflect scores above the mean).

We remind readers about standard deviations, given that this concept is foundational to understanding many inferential tests of statistical significance. Table 13.1 presents an abbreviated set of data for a measure of student academic self-regulation, including calculations for measures of variability. In this case, the range (3.62), which is the difference between the lowest and highest value, is excessively altered by a few extreme values, whereas the variance (1.18) and the standard deviation (1.09) provide a better picture of the variability in student self-regulation because they take all data points into account.

TABLE 13.1 ■ Calculations for Measures of Variability			
Participant	Self-Regulation Scores	Subtract the Mean (3.19)	Square Each Number
1	2.69	- 3.19 = −0.50	$(-0.50)^2 = 0.25$
2	4.00	- 3.19 = 0.81	$(0.81)^2 = 0.66$
3	2.77	- 3.19 = −0.42	$(-0.42)^2 = 0.18$
4	3.31	- 3.19 = 0.12	$(0.12)^2 = 0.01$
5	1.92	- 3.19 = −1.27	$(-1.27)^2 = 1.61$
6	2.15	- 3.19 = −1.04	$(-1.04)^2 = 1.08$
7	4.62	- 3.19 = 1.43	$(1.43)^2 = 2.04$
8	4.38	- 3.19 = 1.19	$(1.19)^2 = 1.42$
9	4.54	- 3.19 = 1.35	$(1.35)^2 = 1.82$
10	2.54	- 3.19 = −0.65	$(-0.65)^2 = 0.42$
11	5.00	- 3.19 = 1.81	$(1.81)^2 = 3.28$
12	2.77	- 3.19 = −0.42	$(-0.42)^2 = 0.18$
13	3.15	- 3.19 = −0.04	$(-0.04)^2 = 0.002$
14	2.62	- 3.19 = −0.57	$(-0.57)^2 = 0.32$
15	1.38	- 3.19 = −1.81	$(-1.81)^2 = 3.28$

Total = 16.55
Variance = 16.55 / (15 — 1) = **1.18**
Standard Deviation = $\sqrt{1.18}$ = **1.09**

Range = Highest Score (5.00) — Lowest Score (1.38) = **3.62**

> ## THE TAKEAWAY
>
> Measures of variability—including range, variance, and standard deviation—help researchers understand how spread apart the scores are in a distribution.

PROBABILITY AND STATISTICAL SIGNIFICANCE

LEARNING OBJECTIVE
13.3   Explain probability and statistical significance.

Probability is central to understanding statistical significance and researchers' abilities to make inferences about a population when using inferential statistics. Simply put, probability is the likelihood that a certain outcome will occur based on some proportion of all possible outcomes. Probability (p) in inferential statistics helps researchers understand the relationship between a sample and the population by assessing whether the scores in the sample are typical or different from those in the population. The normal distribution illustrates the likelihood or probability of certain scores occurring relative to all other scores in the distribution.

Sampling Distribution and Statistical Significance

When using inferential statistics, researchers are essentially making judgments about how likely an observed result within a sample will be observed in the population (denoted as μ//II//). The first step in accomplishing this goal is for researchers to randomly select a sample from the population of interest. As noted previously, if the sample is not randomly selected from the population, it clouds the issue regarding whether one can accurately compare sample data to the assumed values in the population (i.e., the population values are estimated because there are no actual data for the full population).

The goal of many inferential statistics is to first identify a sample statistic (e.g., correlation value or mean difference between groups in a sample) and then use inferential testing (i.e., regression, t-tests, ANOVA, ANCOVA, and chi-square) to determine the probability with which the observed sample statistic would appear in the population. The meaning of the term *statistical significance* will be discussed in greater detail later in this chapter, but for now, just recognize that all inferential tests are grounded in the concept of a sampling distribution. A sampling distribution is a hypothetical distribution of all scores in a population that assumes a given statistic (e.g., correlation, mean difference) was collected over a very large or infinite number of studies. It is the sampling distribution that allows researchers to talk in terms of probabilities between sample data and population data. In fact, a sampling distribution is a type of normal distribution that allows researchers to identify the precise proportion of individuals who might receive any score in the distribution.

There are two forms of error associated with the sampling distribution. The first is sampling error, which indicates the difference in scores between the population parameter and the sample statistic. Thus, sampling error is associated with the quality of measurement of the population. This notion of error has important implications for drawing inferences about the population from a sample because it can lead to incorrect interpretations. Consequently, the goal of the researcher is to reduce the sampling error. On the other hand, the standard error estimates how far the sample statistic is likely to be from the true population statistic in the sampling distribution. Both standard deviation and standard error reflect a type of variability; thus, the higher the standard deviation or standard error, the more spread out the scores are in a distribution.

The standard deviation values depicted in Table 13.1 reflect the average amount with which scores vary around the sample mean. Thus, this value is directly calculated using sample data. In contrast, the standard error estimates how much discrepancy there likely is between the mean score of a sample with the hypothetical population mean in the sampling distribution. While the standard deviation is directly observed and calculated, the standard error is approximated and based on probability theory and sampling distribution. With inferential statistics, a goal is to create conditions that minimize standard error (i.e., we want the sample statistics to closely resemble the population parameter). In other words, researchers want to reduce any error in their study so they can be reasonably confident that any observed result (e.g., group difference, correlation between two variables) is a real effect and thus not due to chance or other extraneous factors. In short, inferential statistics make certain assumptions and use sampling distributions as the basis for drawing conclusions about how sample data are aligned with population data.

THE TAKEAWAY

Probability in inferential statistics allows researchers to make a judgement about how likely an observed result in a sample is to occur within the population.

HYPOTHESIS TESTING AND STATISTICAL SIGNIFICANCE

LEARNING OBJECTIVE

13.4   Conduct hypothesis testing and interpret statistical significance.

Researchers use hypothesis testing to make inferences about a population based on sample data. Hypothesis testing can be applied to many different situations, including testing whether groups differ on some variables or whether variables are correlated in some way.

In inferential statistics, two types of hypotheses exist, the null hypothesis and the alternative hypothesis. The null hypothesis, which is denoted as H_0, states there is no relationship or group difference that exists in the population. For example, if Mr. Karr was interested in examining differences in achievement scores between students taking math in the morning versus the afternoon, the null hypothesis indicates that there is no difference between these groups in the broader population. The null hypothesis always represents a null effect, such as no correlation or no group difference. In contrast, the alternative hypothesis, which is denoted as H_A, states there is a difference between groups on some dependent variable.

STOP AND THINK 13.2

Which hypothesis is associated with identifying that there is no significant effect in your results?

In hypothesis testing, researchers seek to either accept the null hypothesis (i.e., there is no effect) or reject the null hypothesis (i.e., there is a real effect). Thus, once the statistical test has been conducted with sample data, a researcher will decide whether to reject the null hypothesis or fail to reject the null hypothesis. When we reject the null hypothesis (which is typically what researchers hope to see), we are essentially concluding that a statistically significant difference exists between groups or that a significant relationship exists between variables. Conversely, if we fail to reject the null hypothesis, we are making a claim that there is *no difference* between groups or there is *no relationship* between variables. Accepting the null hypothesis (i.e., failing to reject) is akin to saying the sample results are not statistically significant (i.e., they are 0 as expected in the population), whereas rejecting the null hypothesis means there is evidence that the sample results are statistically significant (i.e., not 0 as we expected in the population).

THE TAKEAWAY

In hypothesis testing, it is important to remember that you are testing whether the sample data reflect the absence of a difference or relationship among variables.

To make this determination about accepting or rejecting the null hypothesis, researchers first need to identify the specific statistical inferential tests that best answer their research question(s). Various test statistics (e.g., *r, t*-value, *F*-value) are used by researchers to make decisions regarding rejecting or accepting the null hypothesis. In simplistic terms, the test statistic is generated from sample data that the researcher has collected. These values are then compared to a critical value, which is identified using the population sampling distribution. This critical value reflects a cutoff point used to denote how "rare" or unusual an observed sample score would be if the null hypothesis was actually true (i.e., no difference or no relationship). A general convention in inferential statistics is that to determine whether a sample result is statistically significant, one needs to show that the value is a rare occurrence (e.g., defined as occurring less than 5% of the time). Thus, statistical significance is merely a reflection of how rare a sample result is relative to the expected value of 0 in the population. When a sample statistic is found to be statistically significant, this means the assumption about "no relationship" in the population is wrong. That is, the observed sample statistic is so rare that the assumption made about no relationship or no group difference cannot realistically be true; thus, there is a "real effect."

Let's look at an example with Mr. Karr. Mr. Karr wants to assess whether there was a difference in mathematics performance between students in the morning and afternoon sections of his Algebra I class. Using the language of inferential testing, he wants to examine whether a difference observed in the sample is large or rare enough to be considered a real effect in the population (i.e., he defined the population as all of the algebra classes within the school district). Even if Mr. Karr does not have a specific hypothesis about whether there would be a *time-of-day* effect on mathematics scores, his use of an inferential test will allow him to make judgments about the statistical significance of the observed effect (see Figure 13.3). If statistical significance is observed, then Mr. Karr has essentially found that the observed difference between his morning and afternoon classes is too large or rare to have occurred by chance, and thus this difference cannot be 0 as predicted by the null hypothesis.

FIGURE 13.3 ■ Mr. Karr States a Null and an Alternative Hypothesis

H_0: $\mu_{\text{(Mr. Karr's class)}} = 0$
There is no difference between morning and afternoon algebra classes within the population.

H_A: $\mu_{\text{(Mr. Karr's class)}} \neq 0$
There is a difference between morning and afternoon algebra classes within the population.

We will delve into much further detail on conducing a hypothesis test as well as the various inferential tests later in the chapter using Mr. Karr's scenario as an example. For now, we want you to simply recognize that whenever you use any statistical test, you are ultimately testing the premise that there is no relationship or difference between groups. There are five general steps to conducting all hypothesis-based tests, which are outlined in Table 13.2 that follows. You may see some unfamiliar and or technical statistical terms in this table—do not worry, we will be introducing more definitions as we progress through the chapter.

TABLE 13.2 ■ Five Basic Steps to Conducting a Hypothesis Test

1. State the null and alternative hypotheses.

2. Determine desired significance level and whether to use a one-tailed or a two-tailed test.

3. Complete data collection and identify an appropriate statistical test.

4. Compute the sample statistic and look up the appropriate cutoff in a table.

5. Conclude whether to reject or fail to reject the null hypothesis.

STOP AND THINK 13.3

Think about the critical issue you want to tackle and the steps you would take to conduct a hypothesis test.

Determining Statistical Significance

So let's delve deeper into how to determine the probability, or *p*-value, of your results if you were to reject your null hypothesis (i.e., if you did find a real correlation or group difference). A measure of the level of significance of a particular statistic, the *p*-value indicates the probability that the difference between the groups is due to chance. There are two *p*-values that are used in inferential statistics. We will call the first *p*-value, which represents a fixed decision point about whether a result obtained with sample data is rare or unusual in the population of scores, alpha. The alpha level is the probability of being wrong in rejecting the null hypothesis and is the cutoff value for determining whether to reject or fail to reject the null hypothesis. An alpha value of .05 ($p < .05$) is generally accepted as the "cutoff score" for statistical significance in educational research. It is important though to note that there are three alpha levels that researchers commonly use (.05, .01, and .001), though .05 tends to be the most frequently used. Different fields tend to use different alpha levels depending on the ability to accept error or uncertainty in that field. For example, in the medical field, the alpha level is generally set at .001. Scientists studying the effectiveness of a new drug want to be as confident as possible that a drug will be effective in the population and will not be associated with serious side effects. In this context and situation, there is a very low tolerance for incorrectly concluding that a particular result is a real effect. On the other hand, let's say for example a school psychologist implements a reading program in a single classroom with the hopes of making the program available to all students at that school if it is shown to be effective. An alpha level of .05 will likely be acceptable for this situation. Even if there is a 5% chance that the reading program is not actually effective and that an observed difference in reading scores is due to chance or other factors, the implementation of the program will likely not have serious negative effects on students, unlike the situation with medical scientists and the commercial use of prescription drugs.

In contrast to alpha, there is a second *p*-value (i.e., observed *p*-value) that is computed using statistical analysis software (i.e., using the data you collected). In hypothesis testing, one is ultimately comparing the observed *p*-value to the fixed alpha level. A researcher can also obtain a critical value for most statistical tests (*t*-tests, ANOVA, chi-square) from critical value tables provided in most statistics books. If researchers elect to use a critical value, then one simply compares the observed sample statistic (e.g., *t*-value) to the critical *t*-value obtained from the critical value table. When the observed *p*-value is lower than the alpha, then you can conclude the observed result is statistically significant. In other words, if the observed *p*-value (one that is identified from sample data) is less than the critical or alpha value (e.g., observed *p*-value is .003 while alpha is set at .05), then a researcher will conclude that the observed result in the sample is too rare to have occurred by chance alone and thus is a real effect. Thus, if the observed *p*-value is less than .05 (which indicates how rare the observed result is), then your sample results are considered to be statistically significant and you would reject the null hypothesis (i.e., your sample is significantly different than the population).

In summary, when reading research reports, you will regularly encounter the null-hypothesis-testing approach, so you will need to understand at a basic level what it does and what conclusions can be reasonably drawn from it. When reading research, knowing how to use an observed *p*-value and critical or alpha value is the most important thing to keep in mind. That is, rejecting the null hypothesis (i.e., observed *p*-value is less than the alpha value) means that one is concluding that the results obtained in the sample are too rare to have occurred by chance alone. Thus, the alternative hypothesis is true. When the observed *p*-value is high (above the alpha level and communicating that the sample result is NOT rare), then you *cannot* reject the null hypothesis. You must conclude that there is no statistically significant difference between groups.

THE TAKEAWAY

A *p*-value (less than .05) will indicate significance in your results and a justification to reject the null hypothesis.

One-Tailed and Two-Tailed Hypothesis Tests

When a researcher is interested in a specific direction of an effect, then the researcher formulates a directional hypothesis (e.g., high school students will perform better in the morning than in the afternoon classes). As a result, in this case, the null hypothesis is also directional. Thus, if we were to describe this difference between classes, we would do so by labeling it as either one tailed (directional) or two tailed (non-directional). A one-tailed directional hypothesis indicates that the scores fall at a single end of the normal distribution. A two-tailed non-directional hypothesis, on the other hand, is split between both ends of the normal distribution. As in the example, the researcher might conduct a non-directional (two-tailed) test if they believe there is a difference between the groups but do not make any hypotheses about which group would perform better. This is considered two tailed in that the scores are split between both ends (tails) of the distribution. However, the researcher would choose to conduct a directional (one-tailed) test if they hypothesize that students in the morning classroom would outperform students in the afternoon sections. In this case, the researcher is expecting all of the scores to be located in one end of the distribution (see Figure 13.4).

FIGURE 13.4 ■ Critical Region and Significance

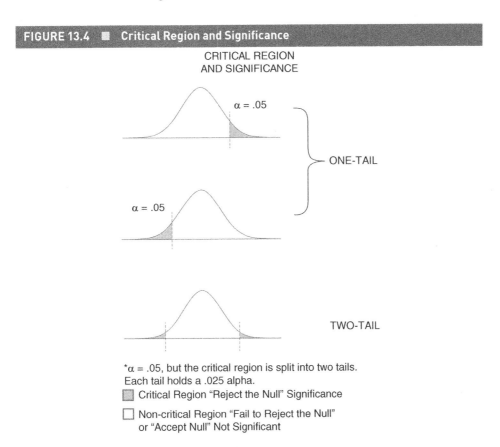

CRITICAL REGION
AND SIGNIFICANCE

$\alpha = .05$

ONE-TAIL

$\alpha = .05$

TWO-TAIL

*$\alpha = .05$, but the critical region is split into two tails.
Each tail holds a .025 alpha.
▨ Critical Region "Reject the Null" Significance
☐ Non-critical Region "Fail to Reject the Null"
  or "Accept Null" Not Significant

Visually, when a graph of the distribution is created, there are certain regions within that distribution that help determine whether or not a statistic is considered to be significant or not. This value, the p-value, is dependent on the distribution table that is specific to the inferential test being used (e.g., t-table, z-table, etc.), whether the researcher is using a one- or two-tailed approach, as well as the alpha value. Figure 13.4 visually displays what a distribution would look like with an alpha level set at .05, both in one tail as well as split between two tails (.025 in both ends). It is generally easier to reject a null hypothesis with a one-tailed test than with a two-tailed test; thus a researcher should use a one-tailed test when they make a clear directional hypothesis.

THE TAKEAWAY

Hypotheses can either be one tailed or two tailed. The main distinction between the two is that a one-tailed hypothesis is used when a researcher makes a prediction about the nature of an effect, whereas a two-tailed hypothesis makes no predictions about the nature of the observed effect or difference.

Degrees of Freedom

Degrees of freedom (df) estimate or make inferences about population parameters based on sample data. Researchers use degrees of freedom to identify the number of values that may have varied (or those that carry error) from the dataset. In other words, the degrees of freedom are set to represent the ability, or freedom, of a score to vary and can be presented differently for different tests; the greater the degrees of freedom, the more possibilities. For example, this value can be used to calculate the level of significance in a particular study or when trying to correct for variations in a calculation due to error. Degrees of freedom are important for finding critical cutoff values for inferential statistical tests such as t-tests because they relate to the size of the sample. A higher degree of freedom means more statistical power to reject a false null hypothesis. Most commonly, we will see df presented as N—1, with N being the total number of participants in a sample, but this may differ across statistical tests.

Types of Error in Hypothesis Testing

Due to the fact that hypothesis testing is based on comparing a sample statistic to a hypothetical population distribution, researchers need to be aware of different errors that can be made when determining statistical significance. A Type I error, also known as alpha, indicates that the researcher rejected the null hypothesis even though it is true (i.e., they concluded there is a real effect when there really is not). This is the same idea as the alpha level discussed previously. Thus, alpha sets the minimum threshold for making decisions about statistical significance. In the Mr. Karr scenario, he would make a Type I error if he rejected the null hypothesis (i.e., stated there is a real difference between morning and afternoon class sections) but should not have. In order to minimize Type 1 errors, researchers can set the significance level lower than .05, such as $p < .01$ or $p < .001$.

On the other hand, a Type II error, also known as beta, indicates that the researcher failed to reject the null hypothesis when it should have been rejected (i.e., the researcher did not detect a real effect). With a Type II error, the researcher would conclude there is no effect, or group difference, even though there is one in the population. For example, Mr. Karr would make a Type II error if he determined that there was no difference in exam scores between morning and afternoon class sections (potentially indicating that a lack of sleep does not affect his morning students), when in fact there was a significant difference in exam scores. In research, a Type II error most often occurs when the study is underpowered; that is, the sample size is not large enough to detect an effect. A basic principle in research is that larger samples lead to more powerful research designs because they help to minimize sampling error. As the sample gets larger, it becomes a more accurate representation of the population from which it was drawn. Figure 13.5 summarizes the two types of error and two correct decisions associated with hypothesis testing.

FIGURE 13.5 ■ Determining Chart for Type I and Type II Errors

Determining Error		DECISION: REJECT H_0	DECISION: FAIL TO REJECT H_0
TRUTH	TRUE H_0	TYPE I ERROR	CORRECT
TRUTH	FALSE H_0	CORRECT	TYPE II ERROR

SELF-CHECK 13.1

Can you explain in your own words the difference between a Type I and Type II error?

So far in this chapter, we have spent a lot of time talking about hypothesis testing, p-values, null and alternative hypotheses, and types of error. In the following *Let's See It!* and *Let's Do It!* activities, we are going to take the time and look at peer-reviewed articles and dissect how researchers engage in hypothesis testing!

Let's See It! 13.1

Goal: Identify Null and Alternative Hypotheses and Related Error in Research

Directions: Read the following article. As you read, think about the null and alternative hypotheses, whether the alternative hypothesis is one tailed or two tailed, and what the error associated with these hypotheses might be. Then, look at Table 13.3 to see how we answered some of these questions.

TABLE 13.3 ■ Identifying Hypotheses in Research

Study	Short, M. A., Gradisar, M., Lack, L. C., & Wright, H. R. (2013). The impact of sleep on adolescent depressed mood, alertness and academic performance. *Journal of Adolescence, 36*(6), 1025–1033. https://doi.org/10.1016/j.adolescence.2013.08.007
What is the null hypothesis?	There will be no difference in daytime alertness, depressed mood, and academic performance between adolescents who receive an adequate quantity and quality of sleep each night and those who do not.
What is the alternative hypothesis?	There will be a difference in daytime alertness, depressed mood, and academic performance between adolescents who receive an adequate quantity and quality of sleep each night and those who do not receive an adequate quantity and quality of sleep each night.

Is the alternative hypothesis one tailed or two tailed?	One-tailed—researchers hypothesized the direction of the relationship.
What are the potential Type I and Type II errors in this study?	*Type I:* Researchers concluded that there was a significant difference between adolescents who do and do not get an adequate quantity and quality of sleep each night in terms of the variables of interest when there was not a difference. *Type II:* Researchers concluded that there was no difference between adolescents who do and do not get an adequate quantity and quality of sleep each night in terms of the variables of interest when in fact there is a difference.
Where in the Determining Error chart do the actual conclusions of the study fall?	The bottom left quadrant—researchers rejected the null hypothesis when a difference actually existed (a correct decision).

Now that you have had the opportunity to read a research article using inferential statistics and see how we identified the null and alternative hypotheses and potential types of error present, read the article presented in the following *Let's Do It!* activity and practice identifying these components on your own! Recall that the null hypothesis indicates there is no difference between groups, while the alternative hypothesis indicates there is a difference between groups. Additionally, recall that a Type I error indicates the researcher rejected the null hypothesis even though it is true (i.e., false positives), while a Type II error indicates the researcher failed to reject the null hypothesis when it should have been rejected (i.e., the researcher missed a difference that existed). After completing the *Let's Do It!* activity and reviewing the answer key, try to work through the corresponding *You Do It!* activity at the end of the chapter relating to null and alternative hypotheses in your own research.

Let's Do It! 13.1

Goal: Complete the Chart Using the Article and the Let's See It! Activity

Guided Practice: Practice Identifying Null and Alternative Hypotheses and Related Error in Research

Directions: Read the following article in Table 13.4. Think about the null and alternative hypotheses, whether the alternative hypothesis is one tailed or two tailed, and what the error associated with these hypotheses might be. Answer the following questions, using the preceding example as a guide.

TABLE 13.4 ■ Identifying Null and Alternative Hypotheses	
Study	Lewin, D. S., Wang, G., Chen, Y. I., Skora, E., Hoehn, J., Baylor, A., & Wang, J. (2017). Variable school start times and middle school student's sleep health and academic performance. *Journal of Adolescent Health, 61*(2), 205211. https://doi.org/10.1016/j.jadohealth.2017.02.017

What is the null
hypothesis?

What is the
alternative
hypothesis?

Is the alternative
hypothesis one
tailed or two tailed?

What are the
potential Type I and
Type II errors in this
study?

Where in the
Determining Error
chart do the actual
conclusions of the
study fall?

Effect Size

Another concept that is often used in conjunction with inferential statistics is effect size. As mentioned in Chapter 12, effect sizes convey the magnitude (i.e., strength) of the observed result, whether that involves relationships among variables or differences between groups. An effect size typically is represented in terms of the amount of variation in a dependent variable that is explained by predictor variables or independent variables. Thus, an effect size represents a measure of practical significance. Whereas statistical significance simply communicates whether an observed result represents a real effect, an effect size reflects how important or meaningful that real effect might be. We should always take a look at effect size to determine how strong the relationship is between two variables—the larger the effect size, the greater the strength; the smaller the effect size, the weaker the strength. An intervention or treatment may create a statistically significant difference, but perhaps the more meaningful question is whether the size of the effect of the intervention or treatment is large enough to justify efforts in implementing the program throughout the school district. Thus, researchers and practitioners should consider the magnitude of effect associated with results when making decisions about implementation.

Effect size is generally measured using Cohen's d and can translate into power (Cohen, 1988). When you have a larger Cohen's d (.8 or above), then the study is considered to have high power, and a smaller Cohen's d (about .2) shows the study has a low power. Going back to Mr. Karr's scenario, his classroom students who were taking exams earlier in the day displayed exam scores which, on average, were lower in comparison to their peers across the school district. If Mr. Karr were to use inferential statistics, he would have to report whether these findings were statistically significant (i.e., is the difference between groups large enough to be considered rare or a real effect) *and* the magnitude or importance of the observed effect. Just because something is determined to be statistically significant does not tell us anything about the size, magnitude, or importance of that effect. Thus, in closing, effect size quantifies the degree of associations between variables or difference between groups after the correlations or observed difference have been determined to be significant.

Now that we have talked about all the moving parts when engaging in hypothesis testing using inferential statistics, it's time to do a *Let's See It!* and *Let's Do It!* activity to practice the steps of conducting a hypothesis test from beginning to end. As a reminder, the five basic steps to conducting a hypothesis test that will allow you to conclude whether to reject or fail to reject (accept) the null hypothesis are listed in the *Let's See It!* activity that follows. The focus at this point should be just on understanding how to use these five steps to conduct a hypothesis test, not the types of statistical tests used (e.g., analysis of variable), which will be discussed later in the chapter.

In this activity set and the ones that follow, you will see mention of SPSS (Statistical Package for the Social Sciences), which is one of several statistical software packages that is commonly used to analyze statistical data collected in educational research. This software and other similar ones make analyzing data a manageable process, even for those who do not enjoy statistics!

Let's See It! 13.2

Goal: Understand Steps for Conducting a Hypothesis Test

Model: How to Conduct a Hypothesis Test

Directions: Use the five basic steps from Table 13.2 to conduct hypothesis testing for Mr. Karr's critical issue.

Now that you have reviewed a step-by-step example of how to conduct a hypothesis test with an example, read the article included in the following *Let's Do It!* activity and see if you can outline the hypothesis testing steps the researchers followed while conducting their study. After completing the *Let's Do It!* activity and reviewing the answer key at the end of the chapter, work through the corresponding *You Do It!* activity to conduct a hypothesis test for your own research.

Let's Do It! 13.2

Goal: Use the Article to Set Up the Steps for Hypothesis Testing

Guided Practice: Practice Conducting a Hypothesis Test

Directions: Using the example in Table 13.5, outline the five steps for conducting a hypothesis test using the following scenario and the steps in Table 13.6.

TABLE 13.5 ■ Five Steps to Conducting a Hypothesis Test	
Step 1	State the null and alternative hypotheses.
	Mr. Karr's sample size: $N = 31$ students in the 8:00 a.m. class; $N = 30$ students in the 11:00 a.m. class; $N = 31$ students in the 2:00 p.m. class
	H_0: There are no differences in student mathematics scores among morning, midday, and afternoon algebra classes within the population.
	H_A: There are differences in student mathematics scores among morning, midday, and afternoon algebra classes within the population.
Step 2	Determine the desired significance level and whether to use a one-tailed or a two-tailed test.
	Level of Significance: $\alpha = .05$

Step 3   Complete data collection and identify an appropriate statistical test.

One-Way Analysis of Variance (ANOVA)

Step 4   Calculate the test statistic from the collected data.
Look up the appropriate cutoff in a *F* Table, then compare the test statistic to that critical value,
OR use statistical software such as SPSS by looking at the output table.

F-Value Statistic $F(2, 91) = 0.25$, $F_{Critical} = 1.32$

Step 5   Conclude whether to reject or fail to reject the null hypothesis.
Test Statistic > Critical Value: Reject the Null
Test Statistic < Critical Value: Fail to Reject the Null

Fail to Reject the Null

TABLE 13.6 ■ Five Steps to Conducting a Hypothesis Test

Step 1	State the null and alternative hypotheses.
Step 2	Determine the desired significance level and whether to use a one-tailed or a two-tailed test.
Step 3	Complete data collection and identify an appropriate statistical test.
Step 4	Calculate the test statistic from the collected data. Look up the appropriate cutoff in an *F* table, then compare the test statistic to that critical value, OR use statistical software such as SPSS by looking at the output table.
Step 5	Conclude whether to reject or fail to reject the null hypothesis. Test Statistic > Critical Value: Reject the Null Test Statistic < Critical Value: Fail to Reject the Null

Student writing performance throughout school continues to be a topic of educational concern because it has significant implications for academic and life success. A researcher is interested in testing the effectiveness of a writing intervention titled "Writing to Learn: Becoming a Self-Regulated Writer." They randomly assign classes of students to one of two conditions: the writing intervention group or the comparison group. Student class grades and standardized scores in writing were collected.

THE TAKEAWAY

Effect size can be considered a measure of practical significance or the meaningfulness of a certain result. Results can be statistically significant but have a small effect size.

VARIOUS INFERENTIAL TESTS

LEARNING OBJECTIVE

13.5 Compare and contrast various inferential tests (regression, t-tests, one-way ANOVA, ANCOVA, and chi-square).

In looking at the research questions in Figure 13.6, what do they all have in common? Each of these questions can be answered with a different type of inferential statistical test. Thus, inferential statistical tests can be of great value to educators and researchers seeking to answer a variety of practical questions.

FIGURE 13.6 ■ Inferential Statistics Research Questions

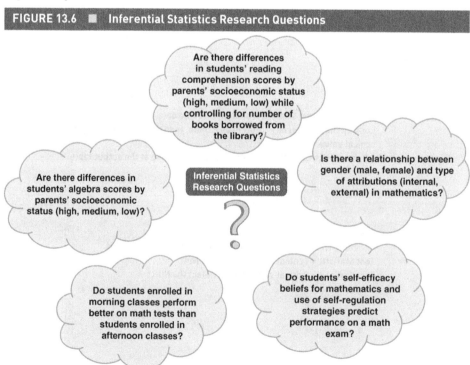

In this section, we discuss some common inferential statistical tests; multiple regression, *t*-tests, ANOVA, ANCOVA, and chi-square. These inferential tests can be used to address a variety of research questions as well as make generalizations about a population using a sample. See Table 13.7 for a description of some commonly used statistical tools that Mr. Karr might use to answer slightly different research questions. Although we will discuss these statistical tests and others in further detail, the selection of appropriate statistical tools depends largely on the research questions examined, level of measurement (i.e., data might be nominal, ordinal, interval, and ratio), and nature of the observations (i.e., same participants are measured at different time points, also known as paired data, or independent groups of participants are being assessed). Overall, it is important to note that the way a research question is written will help you determine the correct statistical tool to use.

TABLE 13.7 ■ Statistical Tests and Example Research Questions					
	Regression	**t-test**	**ANOVA**	**ANCOVA**	**Chi-Square**
Description of statistical test	Makes predictions about one variable based off of data from another	Compares differences between two groups' means to the *t* statistic	Compares the means of three or more groups to the *F* statistic	Similar to ANOVA but also controls for confounding or covariate variables	Tests whether two nominal or categorical variables are likely to be related or not
Example Research Question	"Does time of day and quality of sleep predict student test performance on math exams?"	"Do students enrolled in morning classes versus those enrolled in afternoon classes differ in math performance?"	"Do students enrolled in classes at three different times of day differ in their performance on math exams?"	"Do students enrolled in classes at three different times of day differ in their performance on math exams, controlling for prior performance on test scores?"	"Do male and female students differ in their preference of time of day to take an exam?"

Regression

The category of regression reflects a set of statistics that allow us to make predictions about one variable using data collected on one or more other variables. Let's start with the bivariate regression (also known as simple linear regression). In this case, we use the scores from a sample on one measure to make predictions about that the sample's scores on another variable. The variable used to make the prediction is called the *predictor variable* or the *independent variable*. The variable you make predictions about is called the *dependent variable*. A regression line depicts the relationship between values of the predicted values and the dependent variable.

On the other hand, multiple regression takes into consideration multiple predictor variables. It looks at the relationship between a dependent variable and two or more predictors or independent variables. The multiple correlation coefficient (known as R) describes the overall correlation between the set of predictors and the dependent variables. R ranges in value from 0 (no linear relationship between predictor and dependent variables) to 1 (perfect correlation between all predictors and the dependent variable). Another important coefficient in multiple regression is R^2. As its name suggest, it is calculated by simply squaring R. R^2 is an important metric in regression analysis because it conveys the percentage variance in the dependent variable that is accounted by all of the predictor variables in the model. R^2 ranges between 0% and 100% of the variance in the dependent variable. A research question presented in Figure 13.7, "Do students' self-efficacy beliefs for mathematics and use of self-regulation strategies predict performance on a math exam?" can be answered using a regression analysis.

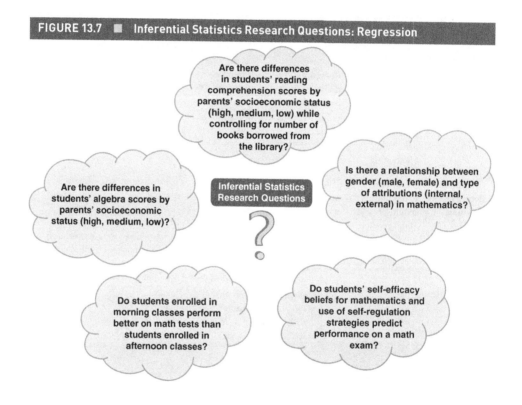

FIGURE 13.7 ■ Inferential Statistics Research Questions: Regression

Are there differences in students' reading comprehension scores by parents' socioeconomic status (high, medium, low) while controlling for number of books borrowed from the library?

Inferential Statistics Research Questions

Is there a relationship between gender (male, female) and type of attributions (internal, external) in mathematics?

Are there differences in students' algebra scores by parents' socioeconomic status (high, medium, low)?

Do students enrolled in morning classes perform better on math tests than students enrolled in afternoon classes?

Do students' self-efficacy beliefs for mathematics and use of self-regulation strategies predict performance on a math exam?

THE TAKEAWAY

A regression is used to make predictions about one variable using data collected on another.

In the next *Let's See It!* and *Let's Do It!* activity, we are going to practice how to conduct a regression analysis using the same dataset from the previous activities.

Let's See It! 13.3

Goal: Learn How to Conduct a Regression

Model: How to Use a Dataset When Engaging in a Regression Analysis

Directions: Look at the following data Table 13.8, which depicts data collected from a study conducted with middle school students. The dataset includes information on final math grades, a teacher rating scale of student self-regulation, a self-efficacy for self-regulated learning scale, a task interest scale, and student standardized math scores. The variable labels represent each measure used in this study. As this is a real dataset, you will notice that there is some missing data on student final math grades and standardized test scores. It is common to have missing data in educational research, and researchers have developed strategies to deal with missing data. Generally, it is fine when the percentage of missing data is low. Take a look at the research questions following the table to learn more about this statistical technique.

Variable Labels

Math Grades = Final Math Grades

SRST = Self-Regulation Strategy Inventory—Teacher Rating Scale

SELF = Self-Efficacy for Self-Regulated Learning

TI = Task Interest

SMS = Standardized Math Scores

All Likert scales for SRST, SEL, and TI ranged from 1–5.

TABLE 13.8 ■ Middle School Student Motivational Beliefs and Math Performance					
Participant	Final Grades	SRST	SELF	TI	SMS
1	84	2.69	3.57	3.00	690
2	84	4.00	4.00	4.67	849
3	75	2.77	3.29	2.50	710
4	86	3.31	4.43	3.17	.
5	71	1.92	3.14	1.67	664
6	94	4.62	4.57	5.00	802
7	94	4.38	4.71	4.33	946
8	88	4.54	4.29	5.00	823
9	87	2.54	4.00	3.33	828
10	84	3.15	4.14	3.50	719
11	87	2.62	2.71	1.83	837
12	59	1.38	4.14	3.83	611
13	92	4.69	4.71	4.83	843
14	80	2.54	4.14	5.00	792

Participant	Final Grades	SRST	SELF	TI	SMS
15	83	2.38	4.00	5.00	867
16	89	4.46	4.86	4.50	854
17	89	1.31	4.43	3.83	827
18	84	2.31	4.43	4.83	744
19	78	1.54	4.14	5.00	820
20	85	2.08	3.29	3.17	920
21	92	2.54	3.71	4.83	750
22	86	3.00	3.71	4.00	843
23	94	2.92	3.43	4.83	.
24	94	4.00	2.57	3.00	766
25	90	3.69	3.71	3.50	735
26	90	4.00	4.43	4.17	865
27	74	1.54	3.57	4.00	598
28	90	3.38	2.43	3.00	876
29	96	2.85	3.00	2.50	912
30	72	2.15	4.57	3.83	.
31	95	4.69	4.71	5.00	768
32	60	2.15	3.57	5.00	693
33	90	5.00	3.14	3.33	943
34	92	2.77	2.57	2.33	857
35	74	2.31	2.00	1.50	567
36	77	4.00	3.57	3.83	627
37	84	4.00	4.71	3.33	751
38	83	4.54	4.57	3.83	844
39	75	3.46	4.43	4.80	945
40	90	4.08	3.71	3.50	601
41	85	3.77	4.00	3.17	.
42	84	3.08	3.14	2.67	829
43	84	3.08	3.43	3.67	792
44	71	2.23	3.00	3.00	723
45	91	4.15	4.71	4.83	805
46	90	2.46	3.43	3.33	914

Participant	Final Grades	SRST	SELF	TI	SMS
47	73	1.69	3.57	4.17	756
48	99	4.23	4.86	4.50	812
49	91	4.69	4.86	4.67	769
50	86	4.38	3.57	2.33	966

Note. Typically, larger samples are needed for regression analyses.

Set of Questions

1. To what extent do student self-efficacy beliefs for self-regulated learning and prior standardized math scores predict their final math grades? What test would we use to answer this question?

   Multiple regression would be used to answer this question. Both student self-efficacy beliefs for self-regulated learning and prior standardized math scores (predictor or independent variables) were analyzed together in order to predict final math grades (dependent variable). This model is a significant predictor of students' final math grades.

2. Do the two predictor variables predict or explain a statistically significant portion of the variance in final grades? What do we look at to know this information?

Yes, the regression equation is significant, R^2 = .28, F (2,43) = 8.35, p = .001. Thus, because the observed p of .001 is less than the critical p-value (alpha of .05), we can conclude that the observed value was large enough to be considered rare. Thus, we reject the null hypothesis that the R^2 is 0.

Figure 13.8 provides a copy of the SPSS output that will help you understand how to answer these research questions.

FIGURE 13.8 ■ Regression SPSS Output

Regression

Descriptive Statistics

	Mean	Std. Deviation	N
Math Grades	84.5217	8.82103	46
SELF	3.8106	.73281	46
SMS	792.4565	99.06557	46

Model Summary

Model	R	R Square	Adjusted R Square	Std. Error of the Estimate
1	.529[a]	.280	.246	7.65824

a. Predictors: (Constant), SMS, SELF

ANOVA[a]

Model		Sum of Squares	df	Mean Square	F	Sig.
1	Regression	979.586	2	489.793	8.351	<.001[b]
	Residual	2521.893	43	58.649		
	Total	3501.478	45			

a. Dependent Variable: Math Grades
b. Predictors: (Constant), SMS, SELF

We also provide a description on how to conduct a multiple regression analysis step-by-step using SPSS.

SPSS Steps

1. Click "Analyze"
2. Click "Regression"
3. Click "Linear"
4. Move [Math Grades] into the Dependent box.
5. Move [SELF] and [SMS] into the Independent(s) box.
6. Click "OK"

Now that you have reviewed the use of regression analysis to answer a set of questions for the included dataset, use the same dataset to answer the questions in the following *Let's Do It!* activity.

Let's Do It! 13.3

Goal: Understand How to Set Up and Conduct a Regression Analysis

Guided Practice: Practice Conducting a Regression

Directions: Using the data provided in the preceding table, conduct a regression analysis to answer the following questions. Follow the preceding example for guidance.

Set of Questions

1. To what extent do teacher ratings of self-regulation strategies and students' task interest predict students' final math grades? What test would we use to answer this question?
2. Do these variables predict a significant portion of the variance in final math grades? What do we look at to obtain this information?

---

t-tests

The *t*-test was first created by William Sealy Gosset (Devore et al., 2021), who worked as a quality control specialist for Guinness Breweries in Ireland, in 1908. In general, the goal of a *t*-test is to assess hypotheses involving a single mean or differences between two means across one dependent variable. There are three types of *t*-tests that are related but exhibit differences: the one-sample *t*-test, the independent-samples *t*-test, and the dependent- samples *t*-test. A research question "Do students enrolled in morning classes perform better on math tests than students enrolled in afternoon classes?" could be answered using a *t*-test presented in Figure 13.9. We will go into more detail on each of these types of *t*-tests next.

THE TAKEAWAY

There are three common types of t-tests: one-sample, independent-samples, and dependent-samples.

FIGURE 13.9 ■ Inferential Statistics Research Question: *t*-test

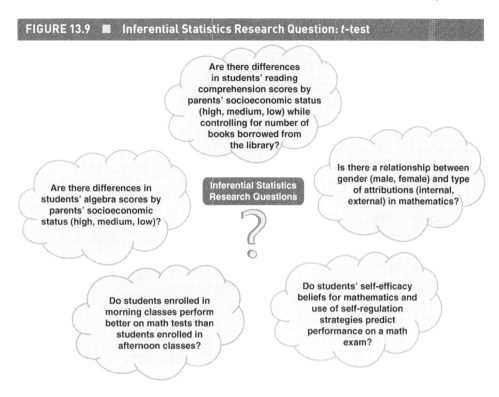

In the one-sample *t*-test, the researcher evaluates whether a mean for a population is the same to a hypothesized test value based on the study hypothesis. When we conduct a one-sample *t*-test, we need to make sure that the scores on the target dependent variable are normally distributed and independent from each other. Otherwise, the one-sample *t*-test will result in an inaccurate *p*-value.

The independent-samples *t*-test assesses the differences between the mean scores of the dependent variable across two independent groups. An independent *t*-test is appropriate when there are only two groups to be compared, such as difference sections of class. For example, Mr. Karr could use an independent-samples *t*-test to compare the mean test scores of his students in his morning class relative to the afternoon class. When conducting an independent-samples *t*-test, it is important that the participants selected represent a random sample from the population where the scores are normally distributed and the variances of the test variables for the populations are equal.

Finally, in the case of a repeated-measures statistical test, the same participants are tested at two different times, such as in a pretest/posttest design. Some key assumptions to keep in mind are that the data should be approximately normally distributed, that the participants represent a random sample from the population, and that the scores are independent of each other.

In the following *Let's See It!* and *Let's Do It!* activity, we will be using a dataset from a study to develop a research question and walk through a statistical analysis using one of the *t*-tests we reviewed.

Let's See It! 13.4

Goal: Learn How to Conduct a *t*-test

Model: How to Read a Dataset and Set Up a Statistical Analysis

Directions: Look at the following data Table 13.9, which includes data from a study conducted with middle school students. The data variables include grades, socioeconomic status, which is based on whether students were receiving free and reduced lunch, and their perceptions of school connectedness. Examine the variable labels to help you understand the observed data. Read the research question that follows and consider what type of inferential test could be used to answer it.

Variable Labels

Grade Level

0 = sixth grade

1 = seventh grade

SES (socioeconomic status, based on free and reduced lunch**)**

0 = No

1 = Yes

SCS = School Connectedness Scale

Likert scale ranging from 1 (strongly disagree) to 5 (strongly agree)

TABLE 13.9 ■ Middle School Student School Connectedness and SES			
Participant	Grade Level	SES	SCS
1	0	0	3.80
2	0	0	3.60
3	0	0	4.40
4	0	0	4.00
5	0	0	3.40
6	1	0	4.00
7	0	0	5.00
8	0	0	5.00
9	0	0	5.00
10	0	0	4.20
11	1	0	3.40
12	1	0	3.40
13	0	0	5.00
14	0	0	4.20
15	0	0	4.50
16	0	0	4.80
17	1	0	3.80

Participant	Grade Level	SES	SCS
18	0	0	5.00
19	0	0	4.60
20	0	0	5.00
21	1	0	4.80
22	1	0	3.20
23	1	0	3.60
24	0	0	4.20
25	0	0	4.40
26	0	1	4.40
27	0	1	3.80
28	0	1	4.80
29	0	1	3.60
30	0	1	3.80
31	1	1	4.00
32	1	1	3.40
33	0	1	3.60
34	1	1	2.00
35	0	1	3.80
36	0	1	3.20
37	1	1	3.40
38	0	1	4.20
39	1	1	3.80
40	1	1	3.00
41	1	1	3.80
42	1	1	3.40
43	1	1	4.40
44	1	1	3.00
45	0	1	3.40
46	0	1	3.00
47	0	1	3.80
48	0	1	4.80
49	1	1	4.80
50	1	1	3.40

Set of Questions

1. Do students who receive free and reduced lunch differ in their feelings of school connectedness from those who do not receive free and reduced lunch? What test do we use to compare these two groups?
   An independent t-test would be used to answer this question. We want to compare two separate groups (those who receive free and reduced lunch and those who do not).
2. Are these differences statistically significant? What do we look at to determine this information?

Yes, there is a significant difference. We look at the t-test value, which is t (48) = 3.08, p = .003, and the corresponding p-value to answer this question. We can conclude that students who do not receive free and reduced lunch (M = 4.25) report a significantly higher level of feelings of school connectedness than students who do receive free and reduced lunch (M = 3.70).

See Figure 13.10, which depicts the SPSS output to help you answer this research question for this dataset.

FIGURE 13.10　■　*t*-test SPSS Output

T-Test

Group Statistics

Free and Reduced Lunch Program/SES		N	Mean	Std. Deviation	Std. Error Mean
SCS	No	25	4.2520	.60767	.12153
	Yes	25	3.7040	.64838	.12968

Independent Samples Test

		Levene's Test for Equality of Variances		t-test for Equality of Means						95% Confidence interval of the Difference	
		F	Sig.	t	df	Significance One-Sided p	Significance Two-Sided p	Mean Difference	Std. Error Difference	Lower	Upper
SCS	Equal variances assumed	.110	.741	3.083	48	.002	.003	.54800	.17773	.19066	.90534
	Equal variances not assumed			3.083	47.800	.002	.003	.54800	.17773	.19062	.90538

We also provide a description on how to conduct an independent-samples *t*-test step-by-step using SPSS.

SPSS Steps

1. Click "Analyze"
2. Click "Compare Means and Proportions"
3. Click "Independent-Samples T Test"
4. Move [SCS] to the Test Variable(s) column.
5. Move [SES] to the Grouping Variable column.
6. Click "Define Groups"
7. Group 1: 0
8. Group 2: 1
9. Click "Continue"
10. Click "OK"

Now that you have reviewed how to use a *t*-test, use the same data as used in the *Let's See It!* activity to answer the questions in the *Let's Do It!* activity.

Let's Do It! 13.4

Guided Practice: Practice Conducting a *t*-test

Goal: Understand How to Set Up and Conduct a *t*-test

Directions: Using the data provided in the preceding table, use a *t*-test to answer the following questions. Follow the preceding example for guidance.

Questions to Consider

1. Do sixth- and seventh-grade students differ in their perceptions of school connectedness?
   a. What test do we use to compare these two groups?
   b. Are these differences statistically significant? What do we look at to know this information?

THE TAKEAWAY

The t-tests allow researchers to assess the difference between the means of two different groups.

One-Way ANOVA

There are several univariate (i.e., one dependent variable) and multivariate analysis of variance procedures (i.e., multiple dependent variables) that can examine differences between three or more groups. In this book we are only going to focus on a simplistic analysis called one-way analysis of variance (ANOVA). We consider two basic versions of ANOVA: (1) when there is a single independent and dependent variable and (2) when there are two independent variables and one dependent variable. See Figure 13.11, which depicts a research question "Are there differences in students' algebra scores by parents' socioeconomic status (high, medium, low) that could be answered with an ANOVA?"

FIGURE 13.11 ■ Inferential Statistics Research Question: ANOVA

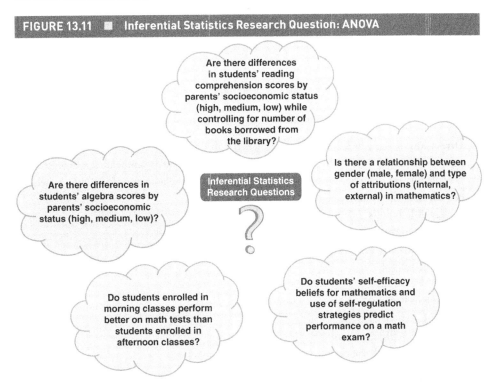

In a one-way ANOVA, one independent variable is analyzed with one dependent variable. Each participant or case must have scores on both variables. The independent variable must be categorical in nature, while the dependent variable is continuous. The ANOVA *F*-test assesses whether the group means on the dependent variable differ significantly from each other. As with *t*-tests, there are also some key assumptions to consider. The dependent variable must be normally distributed and the variances should be the same for all populations. In addition, the researcher must ensure that the participants or cases represent random samples from the populations and that the scores on the test variable are independent from each other. Although ANOVA is similar to the *t*-test, it is more flexible in that it can assess differences between two, three, four, or even more groups. For example, a research question that could be explored using an ANOVA is, "Do freshmen, sophomores, juniors, and seniors differ with regard to their drinking habits?" An ANOVA would be used to compare those four groups of students, while an independent *t*-test cannot examine all four groups simultaneously. If a researcher finds there is an overall difference among these four groups, then they can conduct *t*-tests to examine each paired difference or differences among selected pairs.

In a factorial ANOVA, two or more independent variables are included in the analysis. In Chapter 5, we discussed how this type of analysis will lead to two types of effects: (1) main effects for each independent variable, and (2) an interaction effect between the two independent variables. For the main effects, the researcher is interested in determining whether the level for each independent variable (e.g., biological sex [male, female]; achievement group [high achieving, low achieving]) differ across the dependent variable. In order to proceed with this *F*-test, the assumptions of normally distributed and equal variances of the dependent variables must be met. Also, participants or cases must be randomly selected samples from the populations, with the scores on the dependent variables independent from each other.

In the following *Let's See It!* and *Let's Do It!* activities, we will be using a dataset from a study to develop a research question and walk through a statistical analysis using a one-way analysis of variance only.

Let's See It! 13.5

Goal: Learn How to Conduct an ANOVA

Model: How to Read a Dataset and Set Up a Statistical Analysis

Directions: Take a look at the dataset depicted in Table 13.10, which includes data on a number of variables collected using high school students. The data include scores on student sleep quality, self-efficacy beliefs for learning, year in high school, and their GPA. Labels are provided for all variables.

Variable Labels

Sleep Quality Group (sleep quality as measured by a Fitbit)

1 = Poor

2 = Fair

3 = Good

4 = Excellent

SELF (self-efficacy for learning)

0–10 = Definitely Cannot Do It

20–30 = Probably Cannot

40–50 = Maybe

60–80 = Probably Can
90–100 = Definitely Can Do It
Grade Level = Year in High School
9 = Freshman, 10 = Sophomore, 11= Junior, and 12 = Senior
GPA = Grade Point Average

TABLE 13.10 ■ High School Student Sleep Quality, Self-Efficacy for Learning, and School Performance				
Participant	Sleep Quality Group	GPA	SELF	Grade Level
1	1	3.30	80.00	10.00
2	1	3.30	80.00	10.00
3	1	2.00	80.00	10.00
4	1	3.00	80.00	9.00
5	1	3.00	80.00	9.00
6	1	2.50	90.00	9.00
7	1	3.00	80.00	9.00
8	1	3.00	70.00	9.00
9	1	3.00	70.00	9.00
10	1	3.00	80.00	9.00
11	1	3.00	50.00	9.00
12	1	2.00	70.00	9.00
13	1	2.00	60.00	10.00
14	2	2.97	60.00	10.00
15	2	3.23	80.00	10.00
16	2	3.30	80.00	10.00
17	2	3.00	70.00	10.00
18	2	3.33	70.00	10.00
19	2	3.00	80.00	10.00
20	2	3.00	60.00	10.00
21	2	2.00	70.00	10.00
22	2	2.90	90.00	10.00
23	2	2.90	80.00	10.00
24	2	3.90	70.00	10.00

Participant	Sleep Quality Group	GPA	SELF	Grade Level
25	2	3.00	70.00	10.00
26	2	3.00	80.00	10.00
27	2	3.00	90.00	11.00
28	3	3.23	90.00	9.00
29	3	3.23	60.00	9.00
30	3	3.29	60.00	9.00
31	3	3.30	80.00	9.00
32	3	3.30	90.00	9.00
33	3	3.34	70.00	9.00
34	3	3.35	60.00	9.00
35	3	3.56	70.00	9.00
36	3	3.79	90.00	9.00
37	3	3.79	80.00	10.00
38	3	3.00	90.00	10.00
39	3	3.90	90.00	10.00
40	3	3.84	90.00	10.00
41	4	3.90	90.00	10.00
42	4	3.88	100.00	10.00
43	4	3.88	90.00	10.00
44	4	4.00	90.00	10.00
45	4	3.90	90.00	10.00
46	4	3.90	90.00	10.00
47	4	3.90	90.00	10.00
48	4	3.90	90.00	10.00
49	4	3.90	90.00	10.00
50	4	4.00	90.00	10.00
51	4	3.83	90.00	11.00
52	4	3.88	90.00	11.00
53	4	3.88	80.00	11.00
54	4	3.88	90.00	11.00
55	4	3.88	90.00	11.00
56	4	3.90	100.00	11.00

Participant	Sleep Quality Group	GPA	SELF	Grade Level
57	4	3.90	100.00	11.00
58	4	3.90	90.00	11.00
59	4	3.90	80.00	11.00

Research Question

Let's assume that an educator was interested in the following research question. Are there differences in student self-efficacy beliefs for learning among the four sleep quality groups (poor, fair, good, or excellent)?

A one-way ANOVA would be used to answer this question. We want to compare four artificial groups (those students with poor, fair, good, and excellent quality of sleep) to determine if their self-efficacy beliefs for learning differ. Let's first take a look at the means and standard deviations for each of the four groups. As you can see, Figure 13.12 shows the SPSS output that displays the means and standard deviations for this dataset. You will notice that the means are different among the four groups.

FIGURE 13.12 ■ Descriptive Statistics and ANOVA SPSS Output

Oneway

Descriptives

SELF

	N	Mean	Std. Deviation	Std. Error	95% Confidence interval for Mean Lower Bound	95% Confidence interval for Mean Upper Bound	Minimum	Maximum
Poor	13	74.62	10.500	2.912	68.27	80.96	50	90
Fair	14	75.00	9.405	2.514	69.57	80.43	60	90
Good	13	79.46	12.810	3.553	70.72	86.20	60	90
Excellent	19	90.53	5.243	1.203	88.00	93.05	80	100
Total	59	80.68	11.576	1.507	77.66	83.69	50	100

ANOVA

SELF

	Sum of Squares	df	Mean Square	F	Sig.
Between Groups	2835.837	3	945.279	10.531	<.001
Within Groups	4937.045	55	89.764		
Total	7772.881	58			

Take a look at the ANOVA output provided by SPSS. Are these differences statistically significant? What do we look at to determine this information?

Yes. The ANOVA was significant based on the SPSS output, see Figure 13.13. We look at the F value, $F(3, 55) = 10.53$, $p = .001$. Thus, we can conclude that the four sleep quality groups differ significantly in their self-efficacy for learning. Follow-up tests may be conducted to evaluate pairwise differences among the means to determine whether they are significantly different from one another.

We also provide a description on how to conduct an ANOVA step-by-step using SPSS.

SPSS Steps

1. Click "Analyze"
2. Click "Compare Means and Proportions"
3. Click "One-Way ANOVA"
4. Move [SELF] to the Dependent List box.
5. Move [Sleep Quality Group] to the Factor box.
6. Click "OK"

Now that you have reviewed how we conducted a one-way ANOVA to answer a set of questions for the included dataset, use the same dataset to answer an additional set of questions in the following *Let's Do It!* activity.

Let's Do It! 13.5

Goal: Understand How to Set Up and Conduct an ANOVA

Guided Practice: Practice Conducting a One-Way Analysis of Variance (ANOVA)

Directions: Using the data provided in the preceding table, conduct a test to answer the following research question:

1. Are there differences in student GPA across the four sleep quality groups (poor, fair, good, or excellent)?
   a. Are these differences statistically significant? What do we look at to find this information?

THE TAKEAWAY

An ANOVA is used to compare the difference in means between two or more groups by assessing the variance between them.

ANCOVA

What if Mr. Karr wants to run an ANOVA for these data analyzing sleep, time of day, and math performance but realized that some of the students in the general education class may have a learning disability (e.g., ADHD, dyslexia, dysgraphia, or dyscalculia)? This can be a problem if one thinks the confounding variable (i.e., type of disability) has a strong relation to dependent variable (self-efficacy). Researchers can use a variation of ANOVA called the analysis of covariance (ANCOVA). With this approach, a researcher tells the computer software program to consider learning disability status a control variable. The statistical approach adjusts or equates all four groups in terms of the covariate. The program then uses those adjusted scores to determine if there would be statistically significant group differences across sleep quality. In other words, it is designed to address confounding effects of variables other than the target variables on the dependent variable. That being said, the ANCOVA may also be used to reduce error or residual variance caused by the design. Adding another covariate in the design may potentially help with reducing error, thus making the relationship between the independent variables and the dependent variable clearer. In addition to the other assumptions related to ANOVA analyses, the researcher needs to keep in mind that the covariate is linearly related to the dependent measure within all levels of the independent variable. Further, the slopes relating the covariate to the dependent variable must be equal across all levels of the independent variable. Here is an example of a research question that could be answered with an ANCOVA, "Are there differences in students' reading comprehension scores by parents' socioeconomic status (high, medium, low) while controlling for number of books borrowed from the library?" see Figure 13.13.

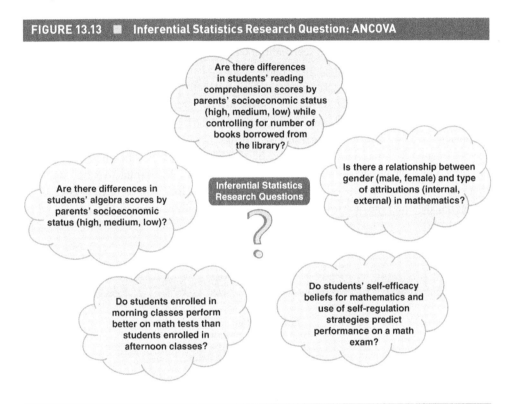

FIGURE 13.13 ■ Inferential Statistics Research Question: ANCOVA

Are there differences in students' reading comprehension scores by parents' socioeconomic status (high, medium, low) while controlling for number of books borrowed from the library?

Are there differences in students' algebra scores by parents' socioeconomic status (high, medium, low)?

Inferential Statistics Research Questions

Is there a relationship between gender (male, female) and type of attributions (internal, external) in mathematics?

Do students enrolled in morning classes perform better on math tests than students enrolled in afternoon classes?

Do students' self-efficacy beliefs for mathematics and use of self-regulation strategies predict performance on a math exam?

THE TAKEAWAY

An ANCOVA is similar to an ANOVA but is able to control for confounding or other covariate variables in the analysis; this approach helps to reduce error and enhances the likelihood of observing a real effect.

Parametric and Nonparametric Tests

Inferential statistics consists of both parametric statistics and nonparametric statistics. Parametric statistics require (a) interval or ratio data and (b) that certain assumptions are met (e.g., assumption of normality). All of the statistical tests discussed thus far in this chapter were considered a type of parametric test. What happens though if a researcher cannot fulfill the necessary assumptions required to conduct a parametric statistical test, such as a *t*-test or ANOVA? Typically, for every parametric test, there is a nonparametric equivalent that can be used. The nonparametric statistics, such as the chi-square test for independence, are used for data on a categorical scale. For data on an interval/ratio scale that do not satisfy the assumption of normality, researchers use the Wilcoxon test and the Mann–Whitney, which are equivalents to *t*-tests. In this chapter, we are just going to focus briefly on chi-square tests.

Chi-Square Test

The chi-square test of independence looks for a relationship between two categorical variables. For example, say a researcher wants to examine the relationship between biological sex (male versus female) and text anxiety (low versus high). In this case, the data can be displayed in a contingency table of two rows and columns. These columns and rows represent the different levels of the first (biological sex) and the second (test anxiety) variable respectively. As with any hypothesis testing, the null hypothesis states that there is no relationship between the two variables, while the alternative hypothesis states that there is a relationship between the two variables. Thus, when testing for independence, a researcher is essentially examining whether the relationship between two categorical variables (e.g., when comparing the frequencies of two groups) is statistically significant. One key assumption associated with the chi-square test is that the data must have been randomly selected. The chi-square statistic is always a positive number (similar to that of the ANOVA). An example research question that could be answered with a chi-square test, "Is there a relationship between biological sex (male, female) and type of attributions (internal, external) in mathematics?" is displayed in Figure 13.14.

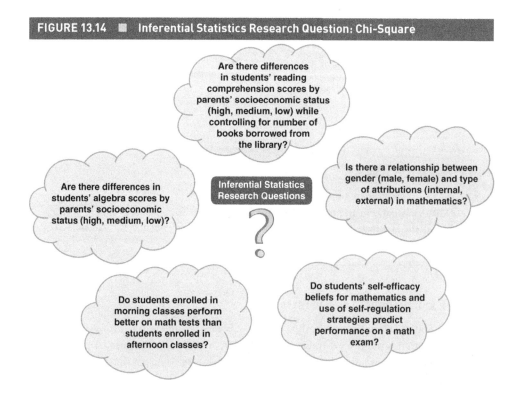

FIGURE 13.14 ■ Inferential Statistics Research Question: Chi-Square

Are there differences in students' reading comprehension scores by parents' socioeconomic status (high, medium, low) while controlling for number of books borrowed from the library?

Is there a relationship between gender (male, female) and type of attributions (internal, external) in mathematics?

Inferential Statistics Research Questions

Are there differences in students' algebra scores by parents' socioeconomic status (high, medium, low)?

Do students enrolled in morning classes perform better on math tests than students enrolled in afternoon classes?

Do students' self-efficacy beliefs for mathematics and use of self-regulation strategies predict performance on a math exam?

THE TAKEAWAY

The chi-square test for independence determines the significance of the relationship between two *categorical* variables.

Table 13.11 summarizes the types of statistical tests we have learned about in this chapter. This table might be helpful in identifying which statistical test is most appropriate to address the given research questions you are trying to answer and the type of dependent variables used in the study. For additional practice, use the *You do it!* 13.3 and 13.4 activities to distinguish between the different types of inferential tests and test your research questions that require some type of inferential statistics.

TABLE 13.11 ■ Inferential Statistical Tests

Type of Test	# of Variables	Type of Variable	Purpose
Pearson Correlation	2	Continuous	Relationship/Association
Regression (simple linear)	1 IV 1 DV	IV (any—must be coded if nominal or ordinal) DV (interval or ratio)	Prediction
Multiple Regression	2+ IVs 1 DV	IV (any—nominal must be "dummy" coded) DV (interval or ratio)	Prediction
Dependent *t*	1 IV (2 levels) 1 DV	IV (nominal) DV (interval or ratio)	Compare 2 conditions
Independent *t*	1 IV (2 groups) 1 DV	IV (nominal) DV (interval or ratio)	Compare 2 groups
One-Way ANOVA	1 IV (2+ groups) 1 DV	IV (nominal) DV (interval or ratio)	Compare 2+ groups
Factorial ANOVA	2+ IVs 1 DV	IVs (nominal) DV (interval or ratio)	More than 1 factor
Chi-Square Test for Independence	1 IV 1 DV	IV (nominal) DV (nominal)	Compare 2 groups (Categorical data)

Now that we have reviewed several of the most common inferential statistics, it's time to refer back to Mr. Karr and his dilemma regarding whether students in the morning sections are more engaged and perform better on exams than students enrolled in his afternoon sections. Following data collection using an engagement scale (interval data) and math exam scores (ratio data), Mr. Karr can use either an independent *t*-test or one way ANOVA to compare the two groups (morning and afternoon). If he found that his afternoon classes exhibited significantly lower engagement and math exam scores than his morning classes, then Mr. Karr could make a case to persuade the superintendent of his school district to have mathematics classes offered in the afternoon. Inferential statistics might help him make some decisions about when is the best time to offer his math classes!

ETHICAL CONSIDERATIONS

13.6   Demonstrate knowledge of ethical issues in conducting, analyzing, and communicating findings of inferential statistics.

There are a variety of ethical standards researchers must adhere to when conducting and analyzing results using inferential statistics. As a general rule, it is vital that researchers be aware of their own biases while conducting a study. Researchers should be aware of any personal biases they might hold and how those biases might affect their ability to objectively collect, analyze, and report their data findings.

Researchers must adhere to ethical standards when conducting and analyzing research to avoid misleading readers or bringing harm to participants.

©iStockphoto.com/Paul Bradbury

Furthermore, the sample used in a study should be representative of the population as well as of an adequate size to answer a research question. For example, it would be problematic for Mr. Karr to assume based on the poor test performance of a few students in his morning class who reported not getting enough sleep the night before that the academic performance of all high school students is negatively impacted by a lack of sleep. His sample size, a sample of convenience, might be too small and not appropriately representative of the population. Thus, it would be unethical if Mr. Karr reported his conclusions based on the performance of a few students and then petitioned the school board to have all schools in the school district have a later school start time. The data must support the conclusions.

In terms of the data themselves, it is important for researchers to appropriately handle missing data and to consider how outliers may affect the analysis and reporting of quantitative data. Because participants do not always answer every question on a survey or researchers may not always have access to each participant's grades, demographics, and so forth, it is common to have missing data, as we illustrated in our sleep quality study. However, when presenting their findings, researchers must be upfront about the existence of missing data and whether this missing data occurred in some systematic way. For example, was there a particular section of a survey that some participants declined to answer due to fears of upsetting an employer or colleague? If missing data occurs systematically, researchers may need to address the issue in their research. Additionally, outliers can skew the findings of a study in important ways. Thus, it is critical for the researcher to systematically clean the data to remove any outliers from the dataset that might lead to false inferences, for example, statistical significance. Overall, researchers must be truthful and thorough when presenting data so the findings of a study can be trusted and other researchers can continue work in that area of study.

Researchers must also be careful to select the appropriate statistical test for the research question and sample. A researcher might also be unfamiliar with all the different methods of analyses, which might result in the wrong types of statistical tests being used in their study, which may lead to a misinterpretation of findings. Going back to the example, if Mr. Karr was unsure about which statistical test was most appropriate or how the test should be conducted, he should seek advice from a colleague to ensure that his data analysis is done ethically and that he has a clear reason for selecting a specific statistical test. Moreover, following the data analyses, during the interpretation phase of the study, researchers must be careful not to state that a particular result is significant when it is not, even if the result is "approaching" significance (i.e., observed $p = .06$, which is greater than alpha = .05). When an observed p-value for any sample statistic (e.g., t-value, F-value, etc.) is larger than the your alpha critical (e.g., .05 or .01), then it is not significant. In addition to accurately reporting statistical significance, researchers should also report the effect size of their findings. As previously discussed, effect size assesses the magnitude of an effect and gets at the idea of practical significance. A finding may be statistically significant but have a very small effect size. There is nothing inherently wrong with that, and it may mean the sample needs to be larger or further research needs to be conducted. But it is important for researchers to report the effect size and not attempt to overstate the effect or make it seem larger than the data support.

Another consideration to keep in mind involves the generalizability of findings and implications for practice. That is, it is important for researchers to be careful not to overgeneralize when discussing the implications of their study's findings. If further research is required to understand how the variables of interest interact in a different sample, that should be stated. A single study can never be expected to address a research question relative to every potential context, situation, or population. Thus, researchers should always think about how well the sample is representative of the targeted populations and never overstate conclusions about the entire population. This balance is a challenge.

Although it is important to be able to conduct statistical tests in an ethical manner, it is also important to be an educated consumer of research and to recognize ethical concerns in the research articles you read. You must know how to evaluate research performed by others and be aware of the appropriate standards that certain types of statistics presented by others must meet. One key question is whether the researcher has selected the appropriate statistical techniques to answer their research questions. For example, if trying to compare the exam scores of students before and after implementing an intervention, you would NOT use a t-test for independent means, instead, a more appropriate test would be a dependent samples t-test. Table 13.12 provides a checklist of questions to consider when reading and conducting ethical research.

TABLE 13.12 ■ Checklist of Ethical Issues to Consider in Inferential Statistics

1. Is the sample representative of the population and of an adequate size?

2. Are there missing data present in the study?

3. Are there outliers in the data collected?

4. Is the appropriate statistical test used to answer the research question?

5. Is the statistical significance reported accurately?

6. Do the data support the inferences drawn?

THE TAKEAWAY

There are multiple ways to approach a study. Your approach, if followed ethically, will likely be acceptable as long as you are able to justify your reasoning for taking a certain approach over another.

AMERICAN PSYCHOLOGICAL ASSOCIATION STYLE

LEARNING OBJECTIVE

13.7 Utilize the Publication Manual of the American Psychological Association in reporting findings of inferential statistics.

When using APA style writing, there are a few things to keep in mind. First, it is important that data are presented in a way that is easily understood by your reader. Tables can be an especially useful way to present information that is easily understood by others, regardless of their familiarity with your study or content area. Researchers use tables to report means and standard deviations of different comparison groups and correlations when they use inferential tests. Means and standard deviation are mostly presented in parentheses ($M = 90.22$, $SD = 10.45$). Correlations among variables are also reported sometimes in text (e.g., there was a positive correlation between the two variables, $r(80) = .48$, $p = .001$) to make the information easier to understand. Figure 13.15 presents an example of an APA style table that includes means and standard deviations among variables across three experimental groups representing an intervention.

When reporting inferential statistics, the researcher reports the test statistic (F-ratio, t-value, etc.), degrees of freedom, and typically the exact or a rounded-off p-value that is provided in an inferential test from a software program (i.e., SPSS). For example, a t-statistic for a significant result would be reported as follows: $t(22) = 4.90$, $p = .001$. Non-significant results are also reported in a similar way $t(22) = 1.20$, $p = .350$.

Finally, a key part of writing about research involving inferences is related to the implications and limitations of the findings. Elaborating on implications for research and practice can assist others in the field to extend this research and use the findings to improve practice respectively. For example, if a researcher implements three different types of reading interventions with different groups of third-grade students in a school and uses an ANOVA test to determine which

FIGURE 13.15 ■ Example APA Style Table

Table 2

Dependent measure means and standard deviations for each group

| Dependent Measure | | Experimental Groups | | |
		No Modeling	Mastery	Coping
Interest	*M*	2.53	4.40	5.42
	SD	.59	.66	.35
Self-Efficacy	*M*	55.13	70.25	90.62
	SD	9.85	9.16	7.55
Self-Reaction	*M*	70.00	88.00	96.00
	SD	10.17	8.22	5.16

intervention was most effective at increasing the reading abilities of those students, educators reading about that research study are going to want to know in clear terms what the implications of that research are for their classroom or school district. Which intervention was most effective? Was the intervention more effective for a certain subset of the sample than others? What factors should teachers consider when implementing this reading intervention with their students? All of these questions fall under the topic of implications for practice and are important to elaborate on in the writing and presentation of a study's findings. The best way to improve your skills in writing while presenting research using inferential statistics is to practice by writing consistently and seeking feedback from those in your community.

THE TAKEAWAY

It is important to engage in APA style writing when reporting the results of inferential statistics in order to provide clarity and replicability for the reader.

CHAPTER SUMMARY

Inferential statistics go beyond descriptive statistics. They allow researchers to make inferences or predictions about a population based on a sample drawn from that population. In this chapter, we provided an overview of inferential statistics techniques that researchers frequently use and that can be used even by inexperienced researchers or educators. Major inferential statistics including the t-test, ANOVA, ANCOVA, regression, and chi-square analyses are all designed to help researchers make probability judgments about whether an observed difference between groups is due to chance or not in a research study. Inferential statistics are useful because they enable researchers to talk about populations even though we are never really able to assess the entire population. When a result is found to be statistically significant from one of the inferential tests, researchers can conclude that effect is a real effect; it was too large to have occurred by chance alone.

EXTENSION ACTIVITIES

You Do It! 13.1

Self-Directed Practice: Identify Null and Alternative Hypotheses and Related Error in Your Research

Directions: After reviewing *Let's See It! and Let's Do It!* 13.1, consider the null and alternative hypotheses involved in your own research and think about whether the alternative hypothesis is one tailed or two tailed and what the error associated with these hypotheses might be. Fill in the table that follows.

Study	
What is the null hypothesis?	
What is the alternative hypothesis?	
Is the alternative hypothesis one-tailed or two-tailed?	
What are the potential Type I and Type II errors in this study?	
Where in the Determining Error chart do the actual conclusions of the study fall?	

You Do It! 13.2

Self-Directed Practice: Conduct a Hypothesis Rest for Your Own Research

Directions: After reviewing *Let's See It! and Let's Do It!* 13.2, outline the five steps for conducting a hypothesis test for your own research using the table that follows.

Step 1	**State the null and alternative hypotheses.**

Step 2   Determine the desired significance level and whether to use a one-tailed or a two-tailed test.

Step 3   Complete data collection and identify an appropriate statistical test.

Step 4   Calculate the test statistic from the collected data.
                Look up the appropriate cutoff in a *F* table, then compare the test statistic to that critical value,
                OR use statistical software such as SPSS by looking at the output table.

Step 5   Conclude whether to reject or fail to reject the null hypothesis:
                Test Statistic > Critical Value: Reject the Null
                Test Statistic < Critical Value: Fail to Reject the Null

You Do It! 13.3

Self-Directed Practice: Practice Distinguishing Between the Types of Inferential Statistical Tests

Directions: Following is an activity to help you better understand when to conduct the various types of tests discussed in this chapter. Please read through each research scenario and decide the inferential test that should be used to best answer the research question of interest.

1. An elementary teacher wants to determine which type of teaching approach provides the greatest benefit for students struggling to learn to read: a focus on phonics, a focus on sight words, or reading aloud to students. Which inferential test should she use?
    a. One-way ANOVA
    b. Regression
    c. Factorial ANOVA
    d. Independent *t*-test
        Please provide a brief explanation: _____

2. A science and technology magnet school admissions committee is interested in determining what factor(s) are the most important in determining potential success in high school: middle school GPA, standardized scores, or extracurricular activities. Which inferential test would best answer this question?

    a. Simple regression
    b. Factorial ANOVA
    c. Multiple regression
    d. Pearson correlation

        Please provide a brief explanation:

_____

3. A high school health education teacher wants to determine whether the number of hours of sleep students get each night is associated with attentiveness in class. Which inferential test should she use?

    a. Pearson correlation
    b. Independent *t*-test
    c. Chi-square test of independence
    d. One-way ANOVA

        Please provide a brief explanation:

_____

4. A seventh-grade teacher wants to determine whether there is a difference in mathematics scores between the seventh-grade boys and girls at her school. Which inferential test should she use to answer this question?

    a. Pearson correlation
    b. Dependent *t*-test
    c. Chi-square test for independence
    d. Independent *t*-test

        Please provide a brief explanation:

_____

YOU DO IT! 13.4

Self-Directed Practice: Use Inferential Statistics in Your Own Research

Directions: Think about a research study you might like to conduct, perhaps related to your role as an educator or a student. Think about how you might use inferential statistics in your study to help you answer your research question. Answer the questions in the following table, using the corresponding *Let's See It!* and *Let's Do It!* activities presented earlier in the chapter as a guide.

What are your variables of interest?

What is your research question(s)?

What is the rationale behind the use of inferential statistics in this study? How would it help answer your question?

What assumptions would you test?

What inferential test would you use?

What might you expect the findings of this study to look like?

How would inferential statistics help you address your research question?

KEY TERMS

Alternative hypothesis (H_A)

ANOVA (analysis of variance)

ANCOVA (analysis of covariance)

Chi-square test

Cohen's d

Critical value

Degrees of freedom (*df*)

Directional (one-tailed) test

Fail to reject the null hypothesis

Hypothesis testing

Inferential statistics

Non-directional (two-tailed) test

Nonparametric statistics

Null hypothesis (H_0)

Parametric statistics

Probability

p-value

Regression

Reject the null hypothesis

Sampling distribution

Standard error

Test statistic

t-test

Type I error (alpha)

Type II error (beta)

Variance

ANSWER KEY

Stop and Think Activities

STOP AND THINK 13.1

There are numerous potential answers to this question. One critical issue that is pressing among mathematics educators is how to help middle school students develop attributional styles that enhance learning and achievement mathematics. Thus, a researcher may be interested in developing an intervention to teach students to attribute their failures to lack of strategy use and effort rather than ability. They randomly select four middle school mathematics teachers out of all teachers in a school district to participate in the study. Two are assigned in the intervention group and the other two in the comparison group. Inferential tests will enable the researcher to compare and contrast the two groups and make inferences about a population based on a sample of individuals taken from that population.

STOP AND THINK 13.2

The answer is the null hypothesis. The null hypothesis states that there is no significant difference between samples drawn from the same population, whereas the alternative hypothesis states that there is a significant difference.

S<small>TOP AND</small> T<small>HINK</small> 13.3

There are many critical issues you may face as an educator. For example, you may work in a low-income school where a significant number of students does not have access to resources at home (e.g., internet, a quiet place to study, books, etc.). You might want to investigate this issue further to determine the pervasiveness or impact of this issue. You would start out by stating the null and alternative hypotheses: Your null hypothesis might be that students' lack of resources at home has no effect on their academic achievement, for example. The alternative hypothesis then would be that students' lack of resources at home does have a significant impact on their academic achievement. You would also need to determine who the population is in your study. Is it all students at your school? In your school district? You would then use inferential statistics to help you better understand and draw conclusions about this critical issue.

Self-Check Activity
S<small>ELF-</small>C<small>HECK</small> 13.1

A Type I error indicates that the researcher concluded that there is a real effect or difference when in reality there is not in the population. A Type II error indicates that the researcher concluded that there is not a real effect or difference when in reality there is in the population.

Let's Do It! Activities
L<small>ET'S</small> D<small>O</small> I<small>T</small>! 13.1

Guided Practice: Practice Identifying Null and Alternative Hypotheses and Related Error in Research

Study	Lewin, D. S., Wang, G., Chen, Y. I., Skora, E., Hoehn, J., Baylor, A., & Wang, J. (2017). Variable school start times and middle school student's sleep health and academic performance. *Journal of Adolescent Health, 61*(2), 205–211. https://doi.org/10.1016/j.jadohealth.2017.02.017
What is the null hypothesis?	There will be no difference in sleep duration or academic performance between students with an earlier school start time (SST) and students with a later SST.
What is the alternative hypothesis?	Students with an earlier SST will report shorter sleep duration; additionally, longer sleep duration and later SST will be associated with improved academic performance.
Is the alternative hypothesis one tailed or two tailed?	One-tailed—researchers hypothesized which direction the relationship would work in.
What are the potential Type I and Type II errors in this study?	*Type I*: Researchers concluded that there was a significant difference between students with an earlier SST and students with a later SST in terms of the variables of interest when there was not. *Type II*: Researchers concluded that there was no difference between students with an earlier SST and students with a later SST in terms of the variables of interest when in fact there is.
Where in the Determining Error chart do the actual conclusions of the study fall?	The bottom left quadrant—researchers rejected the null hypothesis when a difference actually existed (a correct decision).

LET'S DO IT! 13.2

Guided Practice: Practice Conducting a Hypothesis Test

Step 1   **State the null and alternative hypotheses.**
H_0: There will be no difference in student class grades and standardized scores in writing between students in the writing intervention group and students in the comparison group.
H_A: There will be a difference in student class grades and standardized scores in writing between students in the writing intervention group and students in the comparison group.

Step 2   **Determine the desired significance level and whether to use a one-tailed or a two-tailed test.**

Level of Significance: $\alpha = .05$

Step 3   **Complete data collection and identify an appropriate statistical test.**

Two-tailed independent t-test

Step 4   **Calculate the test statistic from the collected data.**
Look up the appropriate cutoff in a F table, then compare the test statistic to that critical value,
OR use statistical software such as SPSS by looking at the output table:

Writing Grade: $t = 0.97$, $df = 48$, $p > .05$
Standardized Score in Writing: $t = 0.82$, $df = 48$, $p > .05$

Step 5   **Conclude whether to reject or fail to reject the null hypothesis:**
Test Statistic > Critical Value: Reject the Null
Test Statistic < Critical Value: Fail to Reject the Null

Fail to reject the null hypothesis

LET'S DO IT! 13.3

Guided Practice: Practice Conducting a Regression

1. Yes, teacher ratings of student self-regulation (SRST) and students' task interest can be used to make predictions about students' math grades. A multiple regression analysis would be used to answer this question. In the SPSS output in Figure 13.16, you can view the means and standard deviations of all variables (i.e., SRST, TI, final grades). Figure 13.16 provides a copy of the SPSS output that will help you understand the process of conducting a multiple regression.

2. SRST and TI would be used to predict final math grades. The key is to look for the $R^2 = .35$ and the corresponding p-value. This model is a significant predictor of students' final grades. We look at the p-value to make this decision. In this case for the overall model, $p < .001$. The regression equation is significant, $R^2 = .35$, $F(2,47) = 12.58$, $p = .001$. Thus, because the observed p of .001 is less than the critical p-value (alpha of .05), we can conclude that the observed value was large enough to be considered rare. Thus, we reject the null hypothesis that the R^2 is 0.

We also provide a description on how to conduct a multiple regression analysis step-by-step using SPSS.

SPSS Steps

1. Click "Analyze"

2. Click "Regression"

3. Click "Linear"

4. Move [Math Grades] into the Dependent box.

5. Move [SRST] and [TI] into the Independent(s) box.

6. Click "OK"

FIGURE 13.16 ■ Regression SPSS Output

Regression

Descriptive Statistics

	Mean	Std. Deviation	N
Math Grades	84.5000	8.74876	50
SRST	3.2015	1.03587	50
TI	3.7693	0.98032	50

Model Summary

Model	R	R Square	Adjusted R Square	Std. Error of the Estimate
1	.590[a]	.349	.321	7.20979

a. Predictors: (Constant), TI, SRST

ANOVA[a]

Model		Sum of Squares	df	Mean Square	F	Sig.
1	Regression	1307.392	2	653.696	12.576	<.001[b]
	Residual	2443.108	47	51.981		
	Total	3750.500	49			

a. Dependent Variable: Math Grades

b. Predictors: (Constant), TI, SRST

LET'S DO IT! 13.4

Guided Practice: Practice Conducting a t-test

Yes, they do differ in their perceptions of school connectedness.

An independent t-test would be used to answer this question. We want to compare two groups (sixth-grade students and seventh-grade students).

Yes, the differences are statistically significant. We look at the t-test value, which is $t(48) = 3.27$, $p = .002$, and the corresponding p-value to answer this question. In this case for a two-tailed test, $p = .002$ is significant. Sixth-grade students reported ($M = 4.20$) significantly higher levels of school connectedness than seventh-grade students ($M = 3.61$).

See Figure 13.17 that depicts the SPSS output that help you answer this research question for this dataset.

FIGURE 13.17 ■ *t*-test SPSS Output

T-Test

Group Statistics

	Grades Level	N	Mean	Std. Deviation	Std. Error the Mean
SCS	6th Grade	31	4.2032	.60359	.10841
	7th Grade	19	3.6105	.65140	.14944

Independent Samples Test

		Levene's Test for Equality of Variances		t-test for Equality of Means						95% Confidence interval of the Difference	
		F	Sig.	t	df	Significance One-Sided p	Significance Two-Sided p	Mean Difference	Std. Error Difference	Lower	Upper
SCS	Equal variances assumed	.088	.767	3.271	48	<.001	.002	.59270	.18121	.22835	.95705
	Equal variances not assumed			3.210	35.955	.001	.003	.59270	.18462	.21825	.96715

We also provide a description on how to conduct an independent-samples *t*-test step-by-step using SPSS.

SPSS Steps

1. Click "Analyze"

2. Click "Compare Means and Proportions"

3. Click "Independent-Samples T Test"

4. Move [SCS] to the Test Variable(s) column.

5. Move [Grade Level] to the Grouping Variable column.

6. Click "Define Groups"
   a. Group 1: 0
   b. Group 2: 1

7. Click "Continue"

8. Click "OK"

LET'S DO IT! 13.5

Guided Practice: Practice Conducting an ANOVA

Yes, students do differ in their GPA across the four groups. Here are the means and standard deviations of the student GPA for each sleep group.

See Figure 13.18 that depicts the SPSS output that helps you answer this research question for this dataset.

A one-way ANOVA would be used to answer this question. We want to compare four groups (those with poor, fair, good, and excellent quantity/quality of sleep) in terms of their GPA. Yes, the groups do differ significantly in their GPA. The ANOVA was significant based on the SPSS output, see Figure 13.18. We look at the *F* value, $F_{(3, 55)} = 36.08$, $p = .001$. The means and standard deviations for each of the four groups are also displayed in the SPSS output. Follow-up

FIGURE 13.18 ■ ANOVA SPSS Output

Oneway

Descriptives

GPA

	N	Mean	Std. Deviation	Std. Error	95% Confidence interval for Mean		Minimum	Maximum
					Lower Bound	Upper Bound		
Poor	13	2.7769	.48158	.13357	2.4859	3.0679	2.00	3.30
Fair	14	3.0379	.39833	.10646	2.8079	3.2678	2.00	3.90
Good	13	3.4554	.28716	.07964	3.2819	3.6289	3.00	3.90
Excellent	19	3.9005	.03894	.00893	3.8818	3.9193	3.83	4.00
Total	59	3.3502	.54771	.07131	3.2074	3.4929	2.00	4.00

ANOVA

GPA

	Sum of Squares	df	Mean Square	F	Sig.
Between Groups	11.536	3	3.845	36.077	<.001
Within Groups	5.863	55	.107		
Total	17.399	58			

tests may be conducted to evaluate pairwise differences among the means to determine whether they are significantly different from one another.

We also provide a description on how to conduct an one-way ANOVA analysis step-by-step using SPSS.

SPSS Steps

1. Click "Analyze"

2. Click "Compare Means and Proportions"

3. Click "One-Way ANOVA"

4. Move [GPA] to the Dependent List box.

5. Move [Sleep Quality Group] to the Factor box.

6. Click "OK"

14 QUALITATIVE ANALYSIS

A DAY AT WORK

Planning and Teaching With the International Baccalaureate Curriculum

©iStockphoto.com/fizkes

Working in the International Baccalaureate (IB) program in the local high school, Mrs. Gul and Mrs. Choi became close colleagues and friends. The teachers have a common understanding that the IB curriculum is an international initiative with a standardized program emphasizing inquiry, action, and reflection. They also share the same level of passion for working with high school students through the IB language arts curriculum. The "dynamic duo," as many teachers and students refer to them, regularly attends conferences and professional development workshops focused on IB issues.

Dr. Gustav Giordano, who is an expert in qualitative research, met Mrs. Choi and Mrs. Gul during a professional development workshop on teaching and creative writing that he sponsored through a local university and a grant. Based on his interactions with them, Dr. Giordano became intrigued by how the two teachers partnered, planned, and thought about classroom instruction. He felt that conducting a qualitative case study about their personal experiences with IB and implementation in schools would be illuminating. Given the strong interest and experience of the two teachers collaborating on an IB curriculum, they agreed to engage in the case study, which would involve in-depth interviews, observations, and a review of important documents and artifacts—like meeting notes and authentic lesson plans—. Intrigued by this study and the potential findings it might generate regarding the collaboration between the two teachers, Dr. Giordano thought to himself, "I wonder what I will discover?"

INTRODUCTION

Qualitative research focuses on the in-depth exploration of the lived experiences, perceptions, and attitudes of individuals or other phenomena that generates language-rich data, such as interviews, observations, and documents or artifacts. Ideally, qualitative research leads to the development of new insights and themes that could lead to further investigations and research. The goal of this chapter is to provide an overview of the key characteristics of qualitative analysis. Clearly, the details provided in this chapter are not exhaustive of qualitative analyses, given that such analyses reflect a multifaceted, complex process that may vary depending on the specific design that is selected (e.g., case study, ethnography). We begin by briefly discussing the key role of the researcher as a data collection instrument. We then provide specific strategies for analyzing qualitative data and describe common approaches to qualitative data analysis. Third, we outline variations in the structure of qualitative data analysis across different research designs and end with an overview of how to present qualitative research findings while adhering to ethical standards and APA style.

THE RESEARCHER AS THE INSTRUMENT IN QUALITATIVE RESEARCH

LEARNING OBJECTIVE

14.1 Outline the aspects of the researcher as the instrument in qualitative research.

Qualitative data analysis can be a stimulating, meaningful, and rewarding activity. Although statistical analyses as used in quantitative analyses is also incredibly meaningful and important, the process through which researchers analyze qualitative data analysis is much more fluid, dynamic, and perhaps even more complex and time-consuming. In this chapter, we structure our overview of the qualitative data analysis process in three parts: (1) the researcher as an "instrument" in the analysis; (2) a process and set of strategies for coding and building themes; and (3) exploring specific approaches for analyzing data across qualitative designs (see Figure 14.1). We begin with a discussion of the researcher as a data collection instrument.

FIGURE 14.1 ■ The Researcher, Strategies, and Approaches to Qualitative Data Analysis

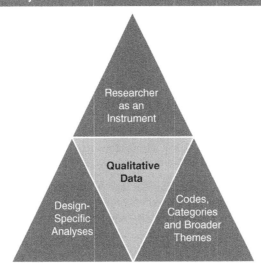

Researcher as an Instrument

Qualitative research is an important and useful approach for examining a critical issue, often focusing on the lived experiences and perspectives of participants. Qualitative data are gathered from a myriad of instruments such as interviews, memos, observations, and documents/artifacts. Researchers not only serve as key people in the data collection process, they also play a pivotal role in organizing and coding the data and then analyzing and interpreting the data to generate themes or more broad, integrative ideas. Both data collection and analysis in qualitative research operates as an ongoing and continuous process that may evolve and adapt based on new insights, discoveries, or information. In this way, the inductive reasoning that underlies much of qualitative analysis (i.e., identifying how details fit together to form a bigger idea) can be thought of as a spiraling endeavor. The integral role of the researcher in this spiraling sequence can be thought of as the "researcher as the instrument."

In qualitative studies, the researcher can be thought of as the instrument. Their role is to collect, organize, analyze, and interpret data in an iterative, spiraling sequence to provide a rich, detailed account of the critical issue.

©iStockphoto.com/piranka

Qualitative researchers need to clearly describe the ways in which they intend to collect, analyze, and interpret data when describing the methods of a study. When referring to qualitative research, it is important to differentiate the terms analysis and interpretation. *Analysis* refers to a strategic and systematic use of tools to create information to inform explanations. On the other hand, *interpretation* relates to the use of diverse methods to generate conclusions about a critical issue. In other words, qualitative analysis involves a review of mostly non-numerical data that is then subject to the process of interpretation and meaning-making based on the context being studied. Since qualitative research relies on the views and experiences of participants, the types of data tend to be heavily language based. While many examples included in this chapter relate to coding language-based data, we would like to note that it is possible for qualitative data to be numeric. Utilizing numbers in qualitative research is appropriate when describing the dynamics or processes of the critical issue. In this case, integrating descriptive information like frequencies, tallies, and percentages can be part of qualitative research for descriptive purposes.

As noted previously, Dr. Giordano's attempt to gain insight into the instructional approach of Mrs. Choi and Mrs. Gul reflects qualitative research. Through interviews, observations, field and the use of artifacts, he hopes to develop "thick" descriptions that accurately and meaningfully convey the experiences and voices of the teachers. This diverse set of data collection instruments will aid in developing a more complete picture of the way the two IB teachers plan, coordinate, and instruct in a naturalistic setting. Despite Dr. Giordano only serving as a *participant observer* (i.e., an observer who does not directly interact with participants) rather than a *privileged observer* (i.e., an observer who interact with participants), he will gain insights into teachers' co-constructed understandings of their instructional approaches in the IB context. In his role as a data collection instrument, it is essential for Dr. Giordano to continuously reflect on the rationale behind choices he makes about analysis and interpretation and to be transparent and forthcoming about his inherent biases that may influence or reshape his interpretations.

Qualitative analysis refers to a strategic and systematic use of tools to create information to inform explanations. In contrast, interpretation relates to activities in which often diverse methods generate conclusions for a critical issue.

©iStockphoto.com/FrankRamspott

Qualitative researchers strive to establish high quality rigor for all phases of the data collection, analysis, and interpretation. Because the researcher is an important piece of the puzzle in qualitative data analysis, we will now discuss important factors that should be taken into consideration as part of the interpretation process—such as trustworthiness, reflexivity, subjective lens, intercoder reliability, member checking, and triangulation. We focus on these topics at the outset of the chapter, given that they are foundational to assisting researchers in conducting qualitative analyses.

Trustworthiness

Trustworthiness is a foundational element of qualitative research design in that it aims to illustrate or substantiate the fidelity of findings. Four tenets of trustworthiness include credibility, transferability, confirmability, and dependability. Credibility specifically addresses the way the research design and methods promote accuracy of findings. *Transferability* describes the ways the implications of a current study can relate to other similar situations, whereas *confirmability* outlines steps taken to address potential issues of researcher bias. With the notion that other people may want to replicate a study, *dependability* entails providing detailed information about the processes in a study for others to reproduce the procedures in a subsequent study.

At times, qualitative researchers use naturalistic generalizations, wherein the findings from a qualitative study transfer to other case studies and/or contexts in broad terms. In this way, there is potential for other educators to use qualitative data and findings to inform or address critical issues within their own school settings. The integration of these four components of trustworthiness provides a rigorous and ethical framework to engage in data analysis (see Chapter 6 for more information on trustworthiness). A cornerstone of qualitative research is for researchers to continuously reflect on and minimize researcher bias to the greatest extent possible. Some useful strategies for reducing this type of bias include reflexivity, subjective lens, intercoder reliability, member checking, and triangulation.

Reflexivity

In qualitative studies, the researcher is often thought of as the primary instrument of data collection, so mitigating their biases is critical. The principle of reflexivity, which can be thought of as a researcher acknowledging their own role in the research process, is a fundamental underlying principle of qualitative analysis; that is, it involves an examination of the choices and interpretations made throughout a research study. Further, because qualitative researchers construct knowledge jointly with participants during a research study, an intrinsic awareness of the role of the researcher is necessary. Inherently, the researcher's values, beliefs, attitudes, identity, personal philosophies, and experiences can be lurking behind the scenes and unwittingly disrupt the data analysis process. Reflexivity aims to examine and curtail these potential influences on data analysis.

When conducting qualitative analysis, there are multiple ways to interact with data (e.g., reading and rereading transcripts). In this aspect of research, as with other procedures, reflexivity stems from a researcher's self-awareness in reflecting on choices made throughout the study. It requires continuous introspection regarding how the researcher's subjectivity may influence the study. The researcher may want to reflect on whether the participant interviews and semi-structured interview questions are effective in the overall research purpose. For instance, Dr. Giordano initially might want to ask the teachers, "How do you maintain positive interactions when working together?" Upon reflection, he realizes that this question could be leading given that the two teachers may not always have positive interactions. He also recognizes that some questions provide brief or monosyllabic responses from the participants and do not capture participant responses that align with the research questions. These are potential issues to which he needs to improve.

When engaged in the data collection process of interviewing, reflexivity takes on a particularly important function. As an interviewer, researchers need to maintain a neutral stance, both in terms of questioning skills and absence of reactions like, "That's a great response." This latter type of response is not neutral because it can easily lead to reactivity on the part of the participant. *Reactivity* refers to the extent that verbal and physical cues from the researcher influence participant responses. Participants can sometimes become self-conscious when being interviewed and/or observed, and when this occurs, they could become prone to providing socially desirable responses (i.e., answers to questions that please the researcher). From a slightly different perspective, researcher behaviors can also unintentionally influence the participant. If Dr. Giordano was typing observations at a rapid pace on his laptop, the teachers could become distracted during their meetings. These participant reactions are not desirable because they can alter the dynamics during the study and may not be reflective of more typical behaviors in a naturalistic setting (i.e., without the observer). Thus, striving to mitigate reactivity is advisable.

Reflexivity is applicable across all phases or steps of a qualitative study. Thus, qualitative researchers should continually reflect on and question the way in which the methods are executed and how the qualitative analyses unfold or evolve during a study. In other instances, a researcher should consider the completeness of the data collection process and whether there were lost opportunities to generate more details from observations or interviews. Also, if some information was excluded from analysis, the use of reflexivity as a guiding principle for researchers can prompt them to make sure that this choice did not stem from a personal bias.

Since a qualitative researcher is often the instrument, checking potential biases is imperative. Reflexivity is one way to check biases during data collection and analysis.

©iStockphoto.com/SDI Productions

Researchers should also use reflexivity when analyzing and presenting information from the participants' perspectives. A key goal is for researchers to frame their work from an emic stance rather than an etic perspective. *Emic* perspectives situate the study from the viewpoint of the participant rather than from the lens of an insider. The goal is to analyze, interpret, and share findings that reflect the experiences of the individuals who have encountered the phenomenon. Framing studies from an etic viewpoint places the participant as an outsider. The concern with using an *etic* framework is that it can lead researchers to present findings in a biased way, often "othering" the participants studied and marginalizing groups. The use of reflexivity can enhance the likelihood that an emic approach is utilized.

Typically, researchers create a system or set of actions to practice reflexivity. One way to incorporate this principle is daily journal writing. This activity can be an effective way to detect biases in terms of choice of sampling method, such as purposeful sampling (the criteria for selecting participants), the questions selected for interviews, and/or the way data are interpreted. To amplify the importance of reflexivity in the mind of researchers, they should remember the need to discuss how reflexivity was addressed when writing or seeking to publish a journal article about a qualitative study. An in-depth explanation of reflexivity in a journal article ensures that readers have a firm understanding of the researchers' potential biases across methodological approaches and their interpretive lens. In short, reflexivity is akin to a mental guide or compass that helps researchers remain neutral and balanced in their data collection, analysis, and interpretation approach during the research process. When this principle is followed, there is a much greater chance that threats of researcher bias are minimized.

Subjective Lens

Qualitative researchers also need to be mindful of their subjective lens. The subjective lens refers to the researcher's perceptions and their positionality regarding the study. By describing their personal perspectives, in addition to reflexivity, qualitative researchers provide a high level of transparency in the presentation of findings. Clarifying one's subjective lens as a researcher will help others understand their particular beliefs or research orientation, the way data were analyzed, and the approach to disseminating information. Dr. Giordano, who in the past has studied IB programs and STEM as part of his research agenda, frequently and openly conveys his strong belief that IB programs have great potential for enhancing students' conceptual skills in science as well as their motivation to pursue STEM careers. By integrating this type of statement in a journal article, he directly clarifies his stance on the topic. Similar to reflexivity, the qualitative researcher should take steps to minimize the threat of potential biases that may arise from their positionality and subjective lens. Other steps or actions to be taken that can mitigate the threat of personal biases include intercoder reliability, member checking, and triangulation.

Intercoder Reliability

Intercoder reliability is a common tool for checking researcher biases in qualitative studies' data analyses. In essence, intercoder reliability is used to examine consistency in data analysis. This approach may be familiar to educators who have collaborated to assess the quality of student writing prompts in subjects such as language arts or history. The underlying premise of intercoder reliability is to ensure that different observers or researchers engaged in data analysis interpret the data in similar ways. If researcher biases are in effect, they will likely be revealed through formal intercoder reliability checks.

Although we describe the process for coding qualitative data later in this chapter, one step researchers can take to achieve a high level of intercoder reliability is by using a detailed codebook for coding and analyzing data. As part of this process, training is typically provided to all coders regarding how to proceed with coding. Ideally, all coders will review all qualitative data in a study. However, this is not realistic when a large amount of data is gathered in a study. In these instances, one coder may review 100% of the data while a partner coder reviews 30% of the data. Coders will typically meet to discuss the level of agreement in their codes. If there are discrepancies, the two researchers discuss their interpretations to reach consensus or bring in a third individual when discrepancies are not resolved. The level of agreement among coders is often reported as a percentage. The use of intercoder reliability is a common way to counter biases to promote trustworthiness of the data analyses.

Member Checking

Interviewing participants, either individually or as part of a focus group, is a highly common and effective approach to gathering data about an individual's perspective. During these group discussions, the researcher will ask several questions developed prior to engaging with the participants. As the focus group interview evolves, the researcher will often adjust questions based on the participants' responses or ask follow-up questions to enhance clarity or elaboration. Following the interview, the dialogue will be transcribed by the researcher or through an online service. To ensure the accuracy of the participants' responses during an interview, researchers can use the technique called member checking. Member checking refers to procedures that involving checking with participants to verify the accuracy of the collected data and or the interpretations of those data. This step enables the participant to reflect on the discussion, clarify any points that were made, and validate that their statements in the transcript reflect what they intended to say. Member checking adds an additional check for researcher biases and provides both the participant and researcher with a further check on the collected data.

Triangulation

Triangulation is a method to reduce bias that is frequently used across many qualitative research designs. Triangulation involves the use of multiple methods, data collection instruments, or methodologies to ensure credibility of the data. This approach also serves as a type of researcher bias check. For qualitative research, using multiple data collection instruments and several types of data would be reflective of triangulation. Multiple instruments and forms of data are helpful for creating rich descriptions and understandings of some phenomenon. The process of triangulation is also useful for determining if the same conclusions are drawn across instruments and data sources and whether potential biases are steering data analysis and interpretation. While Dr. Giordano examines the collaborative efforts of Mrs. Gul and Mrs. Choi as two IB teachers, he uses interviews, meeting notes, organizational documents, and his personal observations. In triangulating the data across these data instruments and sources, he can determine whether the same conclusions are reached while also questioning whether and how certain data were more biased than others.

STOP AND THINK 14.1

If you were analyzing data for a qualitative study, what steps would you take in support of trustworthiness?

When researchers present findings without an explicit description of the analysis methods and procedures used in a study, there is a danger that individuals reading about the qualitative research may perceive the process as merely involving the deconstruction of participant statements to create summaries. By clearly articulating the rationale and processes used during analysis, the researcher adheres to the principles of trustworthiness (e.g., dependability, credibility, transferability, and confirmability) to provide sound findings that promote a deeper understanding of a research topic.

THE TAKEAWAY

Qualitative researchers strategically use different organizational systems to keep track of the rationale and processes in methods and analyses, actions that will often lead to rigorous, high-quality studies with strong levels of trustworthiness (dependability, confirmability, transferability, and credibility).

STRATEGIES FOR DEVELOPING CODES IN QUALITATIVE DATA

14.2   Describe strategies for coding qualitative data.

A notable characteristic of qualitative research designs is the iterative, dynamic, and creative aspects of data collection and analysis. Given this level of flexibility, it is not surprising that qualitative data analysis is quite varied and complex. In fact, the specific type of qualitative analysis that one elects to use in a given research study depends on its purpose, type of research design, and the type of data collected. While there is no formulaic approach to analyzing qualitative data, the following section provides general guidelines and a five-step approach for engaging in qualitative analysis (see Figure 14.2).

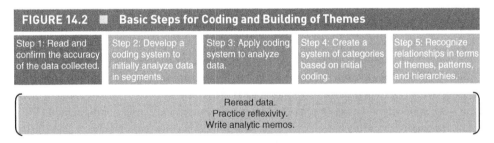

FIGURE 14.2 ■ Basic Steps for Coding and Building of Themes

| Step 1: Read and confirm the accuracy of the data collected. | Step 2: Develop a coding system to initially analyze data in segments. | Step 3: Apply coding system to analyze data. | Step 4: Create a system of categories based on initial coding. | Step 5: Recognize relationships in terms of themes, patterns, and hierarchies. |

Reread data.
Practice reflexivity.
Write analytic memos.

As you review the five-step process presented in Figure 14.2, please keep a few points in mind. First, the process of coding is foundational to analysis and interpretation. Thus, regardless of the qualitative design that is used, converting narrative or language-based text to some type of code is the basic building block for detecting patterns needed in inductive reasoning to identify broader themes. Thus, it is important that we be very clear about the nature of the coding process before detailing steps for engaging in thematic analysis or other high-level analyses.

Second, a researcher's positionality and subjective lens can seep into and adversely affect any aspect of the qualitative analysis process. To offset the potential for research bias, we encourage qualitative researchers to continually engage in reflexivity as a daily practice and to engage in other actions, such as repeatedly reviewing or reading the raw data and writing analytic memos.

Engaging in these behaviors should help to remind researchers that the qualitative data analysis process is recursive and iterative. Thus, while we present and discuss this process in a linear manner, it is expected that qualitative researchers spiral back to return to previously completed steps as new data are collected, analyzed, and interpreted.

Finally, the five-step process does not necessarily encompass the full range of analyses that researchers may elect to use in a qualitative research study. However, most qualitative analyses use inductive reasoning that, to a large degree, involves integrating smaller ideas (codes) into higher-level categories, themes, theories, or essences. Further, we believe that this five-step process organizes several critical concepts of qualitative analysis into an easy to digest format. In this section, we focus on the first three steps of this process and then shift to the higher-level analyses (Steps 4 and 5) in the subsequent section.

Step 1: Reading and Confirming the Accuracy of Data

After collecting qualitative data, researchers will want to carefully read and review the various types of data that were collected (often from multiple data collection instruments). In the context of interview data, this step is particularly relevant. Researchers will need to transcribe the interview, ideally with some type of web service or external source. Rereading the transcripts carefully in comparison to the audio is advisable. Many services provide an editing tool for this purpose. Secondly, the researcher will want to become very familiar with the transcriptions from interviews as well as the data gathered from other instruments before engaging in the data analysis process. Much like an initial screening that may occur during quantitative data analysis (e.g., looking for outliers or missing data in a dataset), reviewing and identifying inaccuracies, gaps, or problems with qualitative data are essential for the proper analysis of qualitative data. Finally, an identification code to each participant or interview should be added to keep track of the source of the information.

Step 2: Developing a Coding System

Coding data is central to qualitative data analysis. *Codes* reflect the symbols or phrases that are assigned to parts or segments of qualitative data, while *coding* involves the process through which researchers assign codes to the different parts of narratives and other types of text or forms of qualitative data. Further, a *codebook* refers to a type of master list in which all codes are listed, defined, and described. This codebook becomes the basis for assigning codes to all data, training new coders, and sustaining a high level of reliability during the coding process.

When first reviewing the data, researchers can begin formulating codes for the codebook. During the early part of reviewing qualitative data, researchers will often generate codes to represent small segments of data or to what they perceive as a meaningful unit of information. There are many options regarding how to code data, such as focusing on nouns, frequency of particular words, strongly emphasized words, or longer segments of text that represent meaningful units of information. Being detailed and clear about all codes within the codebook is essential for optimizing consistency in the analysis and for helping researchers accurately report in a publication how the qualitative data were segmented and then analyzed. Further, while most qualitative research involves the development of a coding scheme or codebook during the process of data analysis, there may be select occasions when researchers utilize an *a priori coding scheme;* that is, a coding scheme established prior to a study that was based on a particular theory or prior research. On other occasions, a researcher may wish to begin with initial codes that are closely linked to or relevant to the overall purposes of the study or the research questions. Regardless of how a codebook is created, it is important to recognize that its development and use represents a foundational feature of qualitative data analysis. In Table 14.1, we offer some suggestions for creating a coding system.

TABLE 14.1 ■ Quick Checklist: Creating a Coding System

1. Was each code clearly labeled and defined?

2. Does each code only correspond with one text segment/concept/idea/noun?

3. Do I need to add new codes at any point during the analysis process?

4. Have I documented the steps I have taken during each step of the coding process?

5. Are there any discrepancies in the coding system that need to be reviewed?

6. Is my codebook complete, organized, and clearly defined?

7. Have I utilized reflexivity when reviewing my notes?

Step 3: Applying a Coding System

Once the initial codebook has been created, the researcher is ready to begin initial coding. One way to proceed, especially for researchers new to coding, is with descriptive coding, a technique of open coding where small sections of phrases or words are labeled with a letter often denoting a noun or description. There are actually many distinct approaches to this initial coding. Examples include *values coding* (e.g., identifying individuals' beliefs, values, and attitudes during the coding process), *in vivo coding* (e.g., the researcher focuses on words with strong connotations), or *frequency coding* (e.g., the number of times that words appear; see Saldaña [2021] for other options).

Figure 14.3 shows a transcript from an IB focus group interview on effective practices of teachers who integrated self-regulated learning principles in the classroom. In this case, the IB teachers discussed how students utilize self-regulatory processes in their classroom. Each letter/symbol represents a code that corresponds with a noun label referenced in the transcript. The researcher will want to define the meaning of each code so the label is used with consistency. In this sample, only example segments are coded. However, when the full analysis is completed, all meaningful segments will have received codes.

FIGURE 14.3 ■ Descriptive Coding

```
103   09:07 Michael k could speak for us, I guess. And it's be t rollercoast s You ce t ly have
104   a group of kids. So, we have rough t n hour and a half a day of self-regulated time. Which
105   sometimes shifts to unregulated time and those are the skills k trying to teach along the
106   way. And we've been upd t as we go. We have. Some kids are just, they're on their own.
107   They can do it all day every day, and then you get the middle of the pack, and k e end of
108   the back, and kind of s g to what Bethany was talking about is once the kids latch onto
109   their project, that self-regulation turns into a real thing. It really does, and they get frustrated
110   when they're not making progress. But until that point, the struggle I think, s tting them to
111   latch onto something. And so, I think it's that purpose [that] leads to self-regulation rather
112   than self-regulation leads to purpose.
```

Sample Codebook Excerpt

t = time; description of time lapse or time constraints.

s = self-regulation; the process of setting a goal, detailing strategies to reach the goal, trying the strategies, and then reflecting on the strategies.

k = kids; K-12 students.

As noted previously, there are many possibilities for coding transcripts beyond descriptive coding (see Saldaña [2021] for other options). As with all parts of the research design process, the researcher will want to take notes on the rationale and processes used for all steps taken.

These steps will help the researcher to be explicit about the processes used in coding with specific examples when writing a report.

It is also relevant to point out that Steps 2 and 3 of the five-step process do overlap to a large degree. That is, researchers do not simply create a codebook at the outset of analysis and then rigidly apply and use it to engage in the coding process. In fact, it is often customary and appropriate for new codes to be added to the codebook during data analysis, particularly as new pieces of text or transcripts are encountered or when reviewing text from individuals with varying perspectives. If researchers do add new codes to the codebook during the analysis process, it is important that they make sure to apply these new codes to the previously reviewed transcripts as well as to all new transcripts or text. This continuous updating and refinement of the codebook underscores the iterative and recursive nature of qualitative analysis.

The following *Let's See It!* activity illustrates how to develop initial codes from a transcript of a teacher implementing self-regulatory strategies for students as part of instruction. The *Let's Do It!* is a guided follow-up practice activity on the same topic but with different data.

Let's See It! 14.1

Modeling: How to Code Qualitative Data

Goal: Analyzing Data With Descriptive Coding

Directions: The primary objective of this activity is to analyze data using descriptive coding. Table 14.2 includes an excerpt from an IB focus group on integrating self-regulation in class work followed by an example of how to create a codebook for descriptive coding. Note that only a few codes are included as examples to guide your thinking. As you complete the *Let's See It!* activity, we encourage you to use Figures 14.3 and Figure 14.4. You should first read the transcript from Mark and then review the coding system and codebook excerpt.

FIGURE 14.4 ■ Open Coding With Descriptive Coding

10:42/**Mark:** …and that makes me think about it from a different angle. We have some groups that are hilarious in terms of solid self-regulation. One group, particularly we asked them how far along in their project they are and they reported they were about 85% done. Which is hilarious because they're probably 5% done. So there, that's just coming from another angle, they see themselves in a much different place than they are, which is fine, and you work with them.

G 42/**Michael:** …and that makes me think S but it from a diffe G angle. We have some groups that are hilarious in te P of solid self-regulation. One group, particularly we asked them how far along in their project they are and they reported they were about 85% done. Which is A arious because they're probably 5% done. So there, that's just coming from another angle, they see themselves in a much different place than they are, which is fine, and you work with them. A

Sample Codebook Excerpt

A = angle; a way of approaching or considering an issue

G = group(s); a number of people that are considered together

P = project; an individual or group task

S = self-regulation; the process of planning, doing, and reflecting on a specific task

Let's Do It! 14.1

Guided Practice: How to Code Qualitative Data

Goal: Analyzing Data With Descriptive Coding

Directions: After reviewing Figure 14.4, use this second transcript excerpt to practice descriptive coding. Create a codebook with definitions and apply the system to the transcript from "Carmel." Answers will vary, so compare your process to that of a classmate's as well as the accompanying answer key. We provide an answer key in the appendix at the end of the chapter for you to check your work.

> Carmel: Yeah, definitely. We said a weekly goal, which could be a very long-term goal. So, they just look at it every week and then they also set daily goals. That way they have a plan of action for their day. Cause sometimes if you're just looking at a gigantic longterm goal, that's hard to like . . . okay, well, where do I get started? It's like hard to focus. So, it narrows it down. It gives them kind of like a stepping stone or little baby steps to get there.

Effectively engaging in the process of coding is an activity that takes much practice. We encourage you to practice developing an initial coding scheme via the *You Do It!* You can refer to Figure 14.2 to help guide your thinking when developing the coding scheme for the collected data.

STRATEGIES FOR BUILDING THEMES IN QUALITATIVE DATA

LEARNING OBJECTIVE

14.3   Integrate codes to inform higher-level themes, theories, and essences.

In the previous section, we highlighted the first three steps in our qualitative analysis process, which focused primarily on the initial coding process. In this section, we dig deeper and engage in more advanced forms of inductive reasoning to establish integrated categories and overarching themes, essences, or theories. We begin with Step 4, which focuses on building categories.

Step 4: Building Categories or Themes

The initial codes that were applied to the qualitative text convey important information to the analysis process. However, this initial process for establishing meaning for the qualitative data is not the end of the overall analysis. Researchers use and integrate these initial codes into more meaningful or conceptual ways to form *categories*, which can be thought of as broader conceptual groupings integrating related individual codes. In a simplistic sense, the researcher attempts to create an organizational system that moves coded segments from individual transcripts or texts into broader categories. An analogy would be having coded phrases on index cards from each participant and then placing those cards into different shoeboxes. Each shoebox would represent a distinct category.

Another option is to create individual Word documents representing each category. For instance, in a study of IB teachers' perceptions of integrating self-regulation within a course structure, one category in a Word document could be *self-regulation*, another could be the *role of the teacher*, while a third reflects *collaboration*. Then individual phrases can be copied and pasted from each participant into the corresponding category. If this technique is used, it is helpful to include pseudonyms for each participant, with that same pseudonym used by the researcher when providing quotes in written publications or reports.

More recently, qualitative researchers use software programs to code and analyze qualitative data. For those individuals who want to use technology, computer assisted qualitative analysis (CAQDS) is a broad term for platforms that can be utilized in qualitative data analysis. Online tools like NVivo, MAXQDA, Dedoose, and ATLAS.ti provide a highly structured environment within which researchers can organize codes and categories. We strongly recommend that researchers explore these different platforms to identify those that offer the most ideal organizational structure or features to support their research objectives and goals. From our experience, these tools typically reduce the cognitive load for a researcher during the coding process and optimize the overall coding process. Figure 14.5 shows how descriptive labels are grouped to reflect individual categories. In this case, four categories have been formed by combining excerpts from the open-coding phase (using descriptive coding). However, please note that these technological platforms are relevant and appropriate for all phases of the coding process outlined in the five-step process.

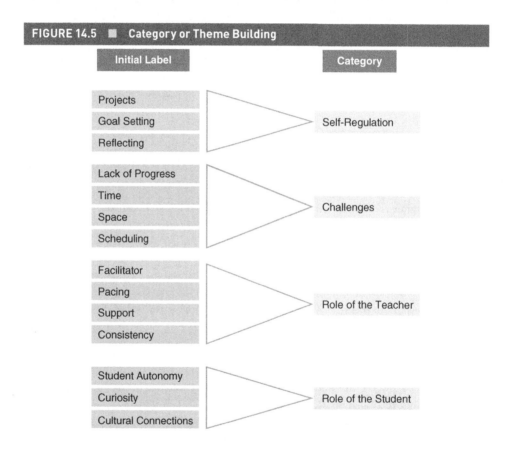

FIGURE 14.5 ■ Category or Theme Building

STOP AND THINK 14.2

How will taking notes about the rationale and choices made during the coding and data analysis process help the researcher when reporting findings?

Step 5: Approaches to Analyzing Qualitative Data

Steps 3 and 4 of the coding and analysis accomplish two key objectives: (1) generate codes to represent meaningful pieces of information from text, and (2) generate integrative categories that typically include two or more related codes. This process of going from specific details (codes) to broader concepts (categories) is at the heart of what researchers call inductive reasoning. However, in most instances, researchers go even further and use special types of inductive analyses to develop even broader categories called theories, essences, or themes. Themes can be thought of as overarching patterns of ideas that encapsulate many of the established codes and categories. To generate this superordinate or higher-level concept, researchers can use a variety of unique approaches, such as constant comparative analysis, thematic analysis, narrative analysis, and discourse analysis, to name a few. For the purposes of this chapter, we focus specifically on thematic analysis, given that it represents one of the most commonly used approaches and is often easiest for beginners to understand. That said, we provide a brief overview of other analysis approaches so that readers can appreciate the diverse nature and application of several analysis options for qualitative researchers. In many cases, the analysis approach closely corresponds with the particular qualitative design, such as constant comparative analysis in grounded theory designs and narrative analysis for narrative inquiry designs.

Thematic Analysis

As noted previously, we devote primary attention to thematic analysis in this section given its wide applicability and utility for novice researchers. However, as you read about this approach, you will likely notice many similarities with the three other analysis approaches (i.e., constant comparative analysis, narrative analysis, discourse analysis). Thematic analysis focuses on the search and generation of themes from a collection of data. It uses the established codes and categories to identify and apply themes. After completing the process of coding and category formation (as described in Steps 2–4), the researcher will begin to look for patterns, themes, and hierarchies in the data to establish interpretations. The patterns could be reflective of the way individuals interact, the actions they display, or their interpretation of events. For instance, qualitative researchers could identify themes based on the sources of conflict among individuals and the ways in which they cope and respond. Events and individual reactions could be detailed as a repeated sequence of events. However, it is noteworthy that it would not be appropriate to infer a cause-and-effect relationship from a qualitative method of this nature (see Chapter 5 for information on cause and effect).

As an alternative approach, themes can be constructed from tiers of coding and described in detail with specific pieces of data, such as participant quotes. From a layered approach of initial coding, category formation, and theme generation, a researcher can report findings clearly to the audience. However, it would not be uncommon for the researcher to loop together the data collection, analysis, and interpretation while creating these themes. Creating this type of cyclical process is reflective of the inductive, iterative framework of qualitative analysis.

Another way to proceed in recognizing relationships is to analyze a hierarchy of structures, roles, and interactions within the study. As with any type of analysis, the researcher needs to apply reflexivity to avoid generalizing based on preconceived notions or biases. An adept researcher will stay attuned to their own perspectives as well as the anomalies, inconsistencies, and points of conflict during analysis, making interpretations, and ultimately reporting findings.

Thematic analysis is particularly relevant for qualitative research designed to specify theoretical explanations of specific situations. Thematic analysis is an approach wherein a researcher reviews a set of data to detail patterns and/or themes. Utilizing thematic analysis is helpful to understand meanings and experiences of one or more participants. Theme development occurs through inductive and/or deductive data analysis, although inductive analysis (i.e., from specific details to broader categories) tends to predominate.

At times it can be challenging to know when and how to move from tiers of coding to create rich descriptions from conducting thematic analysis. The process entails more than creating codes in a cycle of phases and then writing a summary. In fact, when a researcher is developing themes and writing a description, it may be necessary to revisit open and/or axial coding (i.e., categories) to redefine the codes. While some methodologists consider coding and analysis to be mutually exclusive processes, other individuals believe they are more integrated.

There are several actions that researchers can use to transition from open coding to category formation and then on to developing themes. When using interviews as a data collection instrument, researchers can ask themselves the same questions presented to participants and then compare their own responses to the participants. Although the data provided by the researcher would obviously not be included in the analysis, this step could provide useful insights into the participants' perspectives and could give the researcher a more useful framework for understanding how participants experience the interview process. In addition, the researcher can continually reflect on the process by asking what they are learning throughout the study.

As part of this higher level process, each code is reviewed for associated meanings while noting potential patterns in the data, identifying inconsistencies or anomalies in the information, and determining the frequency with which certain key phrases or ideas appear in the data. Finally, keeping observational notes helps the researcher revisit their own perspective and insights to clarify understanding. These notes can be quite instrumental when writing a report or research article begins. Table 14.2 includes a checklist of considerations as a researcher conducts qualitative analysis.

TABLE 14.2 ■ Checklist for Thematic Analysis Approach
Has the Researcher . . .
1. reread the transcripts and codes multiple times?
2. asked themselves the same questions they asked the participants?
3. asked themselves while reviewing codes and categories what they are learning?
4. identified patterns in the data?
5. identified inconsistencies and/or anomalies in the data?
6. tabulated the frequency with which certain phrases are used?
7. compared codes to summarize main ideas?
8. kept analytic memos?

Researchers may find it helpful to create a table that links coding to the theme-generation process. One example of a table includes columns depicting open coding, categories from axial coding, descriptions of the categories, and analytic memos (notes taken by the researcher to process information). Table 14.3 illustrates such a table using the category, *Role of the Teacher* selected from the example provided in Figure 14.4. In this case, the labels of *facilitator, pacing*, and *support* have been combined to form the category of *Role of the Teacher*. The description defines the meaning of this category as developed by the researcher. The analytic memo is a reflection by the researcher of what the findings show during the process of analysis.

TABLE 14.3 ■ Transitioning From Coding to Form Rich Descriptions			
Open Coding (labels)	Axial Coding (categories)	Descriptions	Analytic Memo
Facilitator Pacing Support Consistency	Role of the Teacher	The Role of the Teacher category centers on how participants viewed their part in working with students to be self-regulated learners.	The teachers viewed themselves as facilitators and were interested in finding ways to support students to be independent through self-regulation. It seems that many teachers were concerned about having enough time and embedding self-regulatory techniques on a consistent basis. I wonder if the teachers all have the same level of buy-in for using self-regulation as part of instruction. Some individuals seemed very concerned about time.

Researchers can clarify distinct aspects of the analysis process using templates like Table 14.3. In essence, this technique serves as a bridge between coding, analysis, and emergent theme development. The descriptions and analytic memo sections are important precursors to writing thick descriptions of emergent themes. Thus, when completing this type of table, researchers are essentially laying the foundation for creating meaning and writing a published manuscript. Another way to illustrate and describe the thematic analysis process is with visualizations or figures. These images help to show how the researcher has examined patterns, meanings, and processes through the system of coding. Figure 14.6 depicts the structure of analysis with categories (e.g., from axial coding) and emergent themes in a study examining the impact of IB professional development on teachers. The data collection instruments in this example are interviews and observations of teachers from a professional learning community (PLC) tailor-made for IB instruction.

Based on the qualitative data generated, the researchers need to create codes and a codebook, engage in multiple iterations of coding and analysis, and conduct thematic analyses to identify emergent themes, such as the three themes: (1) *Collaborative Partnerships*, (2) *Sense of Belonging*, and (3) *Self-efficacy for Teaching the IB Curriculum*.

Narrative Analysis

Narrative analysis reflects a variety of analytic methods for interpreting the stories or lived experiences of others. It focuses on accurately depicting the stories of participants as conveyed through their voices. Interviews and written texts are common data collection instruments used to generate data. The individual is the unit of analysis, and the focus is on understanding how that individual makes meaning of their life story and experiences. From a research perspective, the central area of focus is the nature and scope of the transcription and the need to utilize multiple researchers to ensure the accuracy of the life story. In terms of transcription, researchers do not simply focus on the words as they appear in written form or the transcript from an interview. Researchers will also pay particular attention to the words, nonverbal gestures or communication, tone of voice, and pace or rate of speech (including pauses). Thus, researchers will look to include audio and video recordings of the interviews or will take copious notes about nonverbal behaviors, gestures, affect, or tone of the participant during the interview.

In a narrative analysis, researchers are interested in examining the content and structure of the narrative as well as the context within which the narrative occurs. Structural analysis is concerned with key components of the story, such as the plot, problem, and settings, while

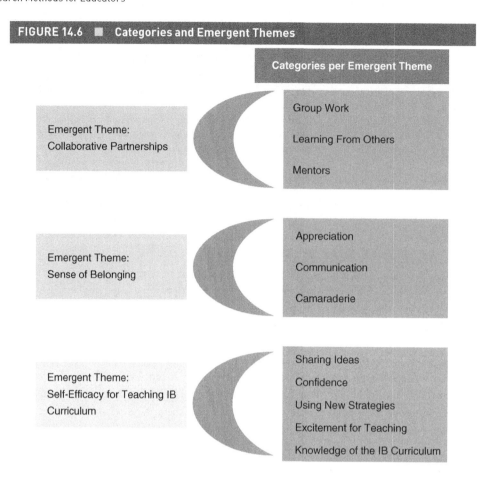

FIGURE 14.6 ■ Categories and Emergent Themes

Categories per Emergent Theme

Emergent Theme:
Collaborative Partnerships

Group Work

Learning From Others

Mentors

Emergent Theme:
Sense of Belonging

Appreciation

Communication

Camaraderie

Emergent Theme:
Self-Efficacy for Teaching IB
Curriculum

Sharing Ideas

Confidence

Using New Strategies

Excitement for Teaching

Knowledge of the IB Curriculum

content analysis pertains to the major themes, ideas, or patterns that emerge or are prominent in the story. If there are multiple stories included within a particular research study, qualitative researchers can even seek to identify themes across these stories. In short, by examining the content, structural, and contextual or social aspects of a story, researchers can develop a greater understanding about individuals' identities, relationships with others, and their experiences in the broader world. Because the goal of narrative analysis is to accurately share the life story of an individual through the voice of that individual, establishing trustworthiness and credibility of interpretations is key. Thus, the primary researcher will often have one or more other researchers read and reread their initial interpretations to ensure that the initial conclusions are viable. For example, suppose that Dr. Giordano was interested in documenting novice teachers' experiences with course delivery and satisfaction with the IB program. He might conduct a narrative study to document how teachers engage in instructional delivery of the content and feel within the IB community. After he analyzes and interprets the collected data, he would then ask other individuals to evaluate the viability and appropriateness of the interpretations.

Discourse Analysis

Discourse Analysis is a qualitative method of data analysis that focuses on developing a rich, in-depth understanding of written, spoken, non-verbal, and symbolic communication, both in terms of the meaning of discourse or communication as well as the social context within which it occurred. It is helpful to break the term discourse analysis into its two key parts: discourse and analysis. A *discourse* refers to a discussion about a topic. It is any form of communication that has meaning and purpose. Researchers using this type of analysis are primarily interested in understanding (analyzing) what is behind the meaning of the discussion or discourse. If educators conducting qualitative research would like to use discourse analysis, it is important that they understand the *language of communication*—this includes the meaning of the words used by individuals, inflection and tone in word usage, body language while communicating, the sentence structure, location and time, cultural influences, and so on. The social context in which communication is made is of critical importance to understanding the meaning of the language. For example, Mr. Giordano observed his colleagues, Mrs. Gul and Mrs. Choi, talking together in the teachers' lounge. He noticed they smiled and laughed with one another, engaged in lengthy discussions about their students, made frequent eye contact, and sat beside each other. Dr. Giordano's observations included the words the teachers expressed, their body language, and the context: the location and proximity to which they sat from one another. From his observations, he surmised the presence of a genuine respect and fondness between the two of them.

Images and symbols are forms of communication that are also examined in discourse analysis. Many images and symbols have universal applications. For example, while the word "stop" is different in languages throughout the world, all stop signs are red. In many countries, stop signs are an octagonal shape; in others, they are a circle shape; and in a few countries, they are triangular shaped. Regardless of the shape, the stop signs are red and easily understood to mean *go no further!* Yet there are other signs or symbols that mean different things based on the society, cultural context, or country. For example, animal alert signs are often yellow but with different pictures of animals on them, depending on the location of the sign. Kangeroo crossing signs are found in Australia, deer crossing signs are found in the United States, and elk crossing signs are found in Sweden. It would be strange to see a camel crossing sign, commonly found in South Africa, on a street corner of New York City! In other words, the context of the discourse is critical for understanding the meaning behind what is being communicated. When educators conduct a discourse analysis, it is important to understand that words, nonverbal behavior, and signs are symbolic and have distinct meaning, just as the stop sign reflects the message to go no further.

In short, the concepts presented in this section should remind those who conduct a discourse analysis about the need to understand the motivation and underlying messages behind the communication. In essence, the intended audience, climate, time of day, language, cultural background, and political viewpoints are all important because they help analysts interpret the communication. It is also important to note that discourse analysis extends beyond the conventional interpretation of language as only written text and speech. In other words, language is thought of as a multimodal way of communicating (e.g., written and oral language, body gestures, and verbal and nonverbal cues). Furthermore, the use of language in society often becomes the impetus for action and greatly shapes power dynamics, the availability of resources, and barriers and supports within societal communities. Thus, in educational settings, discourse analysis is useful in examining best practices for teaching and learning, school and district systems of interactions, and the benefits of professional development, as some examples.

Constant Comparative Analysis

The final type of qualitative analysis approach reviewed in this book involves the constant comparative analysis. Developed by Glaser and Strauss (1967), this approach is closely intertwined with ground theory design given its focus and goal of identifying new theories. Researchers use interviews or focus groups as the primary data collection instrument and seek to interview 20 or more individuals (the precise number will vary based on the nature of the research design and overall goals). Like its name suggests, the basic premise of constant comparative analysis is to continually compare new data with previously collected data. The comparisons that are made could entail data from different sources (interviews versus focus groups), the codes and themes that are generated, or even different researchers involved in the research study.

After the data are gathered for a grounded theory study, researchers go through a coding sequence from basic to more complex coding. With this approach, the researcher begins with *open coding* (similar to Step 3 of the five-step process) but then shifts to axial coding and then selective coding. Open codes essentially reflect new ideas that form the foundation for more advanced analysis. Axial coding involves attempts to establish relations or connections between the open codes to form categories (similar to Step 4). Axial coding is considered a more advanced level than open coding because it entails a higher level of inductive thinking and because researchers continually seek to modify or refine their emerging theoretical framework as new data are collected. *Selective coding* is the highest level of coding in this process and relates to the formation of a broad theme (similar to Step 5). However, for the constant comparative approach, researchers describe this highest inductive category as a theory or unified theory. In other words, this last phase of the coding process should either lead to a new theory or assist in refining an existing one. Selective coding works well when *saturation* has been achieved; saturation reflects the extent to which no new information can be obtained with additional rounds of data collection. If saturation is not reached, the researcher states that emergent themes have been developed rather than describing selective coding with themes. For example, a researcher might want to study how teacher leaders in IB schools describe their experiences in these roles. The researcher might interview a few teacher leaders, analyze the data for themes, and arrange these themes into a theory or visual model that depicts the barriers and supports that teacher leaders encounter while working in these roles. The development of the theory should only be considered appropriate if the researchers notices that no new information was detected after additional rounds of data were collected.

THE TAKEAWAY

There are many approaches to analyzing qualitative data that vary depending on the goals of the study and the data collected. In many cases, the analysis approach corresponds with the particular qualitative design, such as constant comparative analysis in grounded theory designs.

COMPARISON OF DATA ANALYSIS PRINCIPLES ACROSS RESEARCH DESIGN

LEARNING OBJECTIVE

14.4   Describe distinctions in qualitative data analysis across designs.

Now that you have developed some basic knowledge in qualitative analysis, we shift the focus to specific data analysis issues for common qualitative designs: grounded theory, narrative inquiry, ethnography, case study, and phenomenology. We summarize the key data collection instruments and data analysis principles (see Table 14.4). Please note that although we identify primary and secondary data collection methods across designs, the secondary methods may serve as primary approaches to data collection in some instances.

TABLE 14.4 ■ Characteristics of Data Collection and Analysis Principles Across Qualitative Research Designs		
Research Design	**Data Collection Methods**	**Data Analysis Principles**
Grounded Theory	Primary: interviews with enough individuals to reach saturation Secondary: observations and documents	Constant comparative analysis Various level of coding (open, axial, and selective) Unified theory (new theory or replacement of older theory)
Case Study	Primary: integrated use of multiple instruments (documents, interviews, constructed responses, observations)	Descriptions of case Within case analysis and themes Cross case analysis and themes Conclusions about meaning of case
Ethnography	Primary: collection of a wide array of data on site via interviews, focus groups, and observations, Secondary: documents and artifacts	Detailed description of group Group themes Broad principles about group dynamics and processes
Phenomenology	Primary: multiple interviews with people who experienced phenomenon Secondary: observations, documents and artifacts	Description of experience Significance of statements, events Essence of the target experience
Narrative Research	Primary: multiple and time-intensive interactions with emphasis on several methods (interviews, documents, artifacts) Secondary: observations	Narrative analysis Restorying, in participant voice Theme development Narrative about life story

Grounded Theory Design

As noted in the previous section, researchers using grounded theory designs will emphasize constant comparative analysis. Through an iterative and recursive process, researchers continually refine, adapt, or expand the nature of codes until a unified theory is attained. This theory may represent a new interpretive finding or replace an older theory. A primary data collection principle in this design is conducting interviews (often semi-structured in format) with enough people so that researchers can reach saturation. Unlike other qualitative research designs that may include a small number of participants (i.e., in some cases only one participant), grounded theory designs may target 20 individuals or more.

Although the constant comparative analysis approach is preferred with this design, it is possible for researcher to utilize another system—a blend of systems, or a self-created system. Again, the key analysis principle in grounded theory is to reach saturation during the selective coding process. Without reaching saturation, full grounded theory is difficult to achieve; therefore, emergent themes are more appropriate to report.

For grounded theory designs, it is often very helpful to use visuals and tables to articulate the coding procedures and overall analysis. For example, Figure 14.5 (see Section 14.3) shows an example of how to present the coding procedures during open coding, axial coding, and the development of emergent themes associated with constant comparative analysis. This visual can help readers more fully understand the relevant steps in analysis. As another example, in Table 14.5, we illustrate an approach to present themes in the beginning section of the results narrative. An effective way to represent each theme is to provide a sample quote. This structure enables readers to focus on key aspects of the theme that are ultimately developed more fully in the narrative.

TABLE 14.5 ■ Illustration of Link Between Themes and Quotes in Ground Theory Designs	
Themes	Sample Quote
Supports for the use of self-regulatory processes in instruction	"I think like one of our biggest successes last year was working [with] all four of us together and being a support for all of our students. So that way they had knowledge from all four teachers and they created awesome projects." Carmel
Barriers for the use of self-regulatory processes in instruction	"So, we have roughly an hour and a half a day of self-regulated time. Which sometimes shifts to unregulated time and those are the skills we're trying to teach along the way." Mark
Student autonomy and self-regulation	"So then, I went into . . . it was really hard to tie in the projects without telling them what to do, or we give them choices, but yet at the same time they would use that as a bounce, as a, um, sounding board to go in and develop this thing." Brianna

While figures and tables are useful for all forms of qualitative research, a hallmark of grounded theory is the systematic, layered approach to analyses to construct themes. Clearly articulating the grounded theory approach within a specific study through writing, visuals, and tables provides a clear and straightforward structure for readers to both understand the research study and the procedures for replication, if that is of interest.

Narrative Inquiry

Narrative inquiry designs focus on the experiences of an individual or individuals to accurately convey a life story or experience. To collect data in this design, researchers will often repeatedly engage with participants, typically in the form of interviews and observations. Audio and video recordings are particularly useful in creating these narratives, supporting theme development, and describing interventions. Of particular interest to researchers using this design is to collect information on the sequences of events and verbal and non-verbal cues amongst participants. Further, photographs (with appropriate permissions), participant-created artifacts, and objects of importance are other ways to encapsulate the experiences of the participant and can be integrated within the narrative writing as part of restorying.

After the data are collected, researchers will use narrative analysis to create a narrative about the participant's lived experiences. This process of creating a personal narrative is known as *restorying*, where the researcher recounts the story through the lens and voice of the participant.

Within school systems, teachers constantly develop new instructional and assessment tools, such as lesson plans, specific activities, and formative and summative assessments. Suppose Dr. Giordano wanted to convey the life story of a science teacher who was hired a few years ago after immigrating from China. This teacher has an excellent reputation as a strong teacher and recently received the Teacher of the Year award from a regional organization. Over the course of several interviews and observations, Dr. Giordano generates enough data to create a narrative about the teacher's life but with particular emphasis on his overcoming multiple personal and political challenges to become a master teacher. To ensure the trustworthiness of the life story, Dr. Giordano asked two researchers with expertise in qualitative analysis to review collected data and the life story.

Ethnography

An ethnography is a type of qualitative research wherein the goal is to examine the cultural behaviors, attitudes, and customs of a specific group. In this design, researchers often live amongst the cultural group for an extended time period, either as a privileged observer or participant observer. As you may recall, a participant observer assimilates within the community under study, while a passive or privileged observer observes the processes and dynamics of the culture from an outside lens. In either case, the researcher strives to collect data while "on site" using multiple data collection instruments including interview, observations, and documents or artifacts.

While many qualitative researchers seek to study patterns of behavior, a specific focus on identifying and describing cultural dynamics is a hallmark of ethnographies. Ethnographers aim to not only comprehend the individuals' daily experiences and practices but also the cultural norms shaped by collective and individual beliefs, values, and attitudes. It is for this reason why ethnographers strive to amass large quantities of data from an array of data collection instruments.

One approach that ethnographers use after collecting data is to discern patterns depicting larger concepts reflecting cultural domains. The cultural domain is a way to identify features or prominent elements within the study. A label would be used to distinguish the domain (e.g., district leaders). Next, each cultural domain is subdivided into subdomains or categories (e.g., teachers, mentorship, sense of community). Then, the ethnographer identifies relationships among categories.

For instance, when studying professional development on IB collaborative teaching, Dr. Giardono might identify that district leaders within the workshops exhibit a dominant role in steering the interactions. Categories within this framework could be teachers, mentorship, and sense of community. He might notice that the relationships among teachers and leaders through mentorship was shaping a sense of community in different ways, depending on the partnerships. As he continues to add data through school visits, workshops, and interactions with teachers and district leaders, he would strive to refine emerging themes about the cultural group.

Given the time commitment required of ethnographers and the massive amount of information that is typically obtained, they often write analytic memos to notate their thoughts relative to the observations. These analytic memos move beyond mere descriptions and seek to encapsulate higher order, inductive thinking skills. Figure 14.7 shows some potential topics for analytic memos.

Ethnographers also emphasize the use of visualizations to underscore group characteristics and dynamics. For example, map making reflects diagrams that highlights the processes and interpersonal interactions within a system, such as a school district. For instance, Dr. Giordano could expand his study to examine when, where, and how IB teachers collaborate. Using a map-making technique, he could keep a record of where teachers meet in the school library by department and at what time as shown in Figure 14.8. Visualizations such as these provide additional information to correspond with other forms of data.

Map making can be applicable in many ways to illuminate content and context. In a study of teachers attending a professional development workshop, the research design incorporated a map to show the relationship between teachers' school districts, gender, grade level, and PLC groups by creating a diagram (see Figure 14.9). Analysis of this map could illuminate interactions among the group members in tandem with other types of data. For instance, when reviewing this map, it is clear that School District 1 (SD) and its corresponding teachers played an integral role in the workings across all of the PLC groups by examining the preponderance of a left shift of the PLC loops. Whether individuals from SD1 had a strong influence needs further examination from different types of data. To extend the use of map making, qualitative researchers may use software tools like NVivo to create conceptual maps and tree diagrams.

FIGURE 14.7 ■ Potential Topics for Analytic Memos

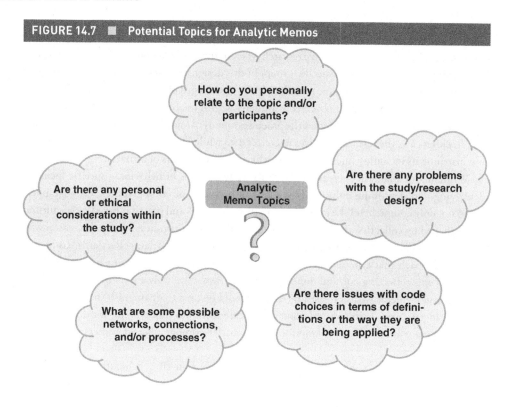

FIGURE 14.8 ■ Sample Map Making for IB Collaborative Meetings

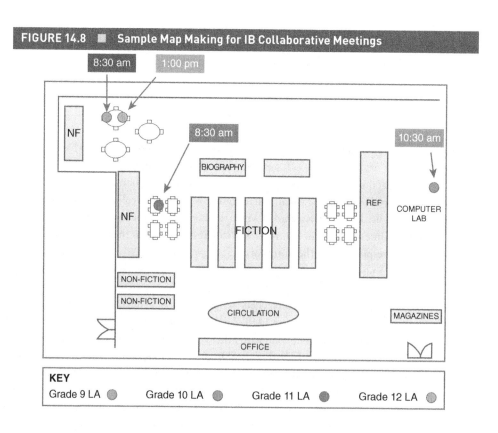

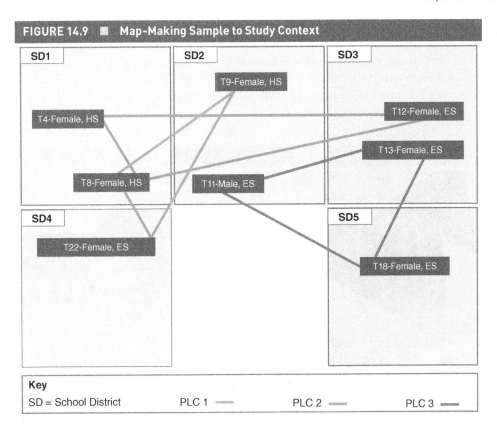

FIGURE 14.9 ■ Map-Making Sample to Study Context

SD1

T4-Female, HS

T8-Female, HS

SD2

T9-Female, HS

T11-Male, ES

SD3

T12-Female, ES

T13-Female, ES

SD4

T22-Female, ES

SD5

T18-Female, ES

Key

SD = School District   PLC 1 ——   PLC 2 ——   PLC 3 ——

Case Study Design

The primary goal of a case study design is to create an in-depth description and analysis of one or more individuals, although this design can also target an event, activity, or program (like the IB program in the case scenario). While a single individual is often the target, case studies often include multiple individuals who are either highly similar or distinct (i.e., extreme case). In most instances, pre-established criteria are used to identify and select the case. Given the in-depth focus of case studies, researchers need to administer and use several data collection instruments, such as interviews, observations, organizational documents, and artifacts. Researchers will use triangulation to identify areas of convergence and divergence and then seek to settle on the most consistent and important themes within the sample. Importantly, case studies can consist of both *within-case* and *cross-case* analyses theme development. That is, researchers often seek to describe each individual case and the themes linked to that case while also considering how multiple cases compare. It is with cross-case analyses that researchers can identify broader and more insightful themes.

Given the wide array of data collection instruments used in a case study, researchers need to be mindful of the distinctiveness of the data provided by each approach and how the interpretive process may also vary. Consider a less common but interesting type of artifact that could be used in a case study: a visual art work created by a secondary student (see Figure 14.10). We illustrate how this artifact can lead to insights into what individuals value as well as the potential meanings and processes within a given context. While a teacher may analyze this work for elements required in the curriculum, a qualitative researcher can use a different kind of lens, such as considering the use of color, imagery, and terms to convey meanings. The researcher will consider how shapes, objects, and terms have been laid out in the image to draw inferences from the work.

In addition, the researcher may analyze what has been omitted in the work (e.g., the student's self-image or other influential people in their lives) or interview the student about the processes involved in creating the work, challenges associated with making the art, and what the art represents/means to the individual. In summary, engaging in data analysis for a case study can be an exciting but complicated process, primarily because of the varied nature of the data generated from the multidimensional assessment focus.

FIGURE 14.10 ■ Sample of Visual Image

Permission to reprint artwork by Ava Kelley.

Phenomenology

A phenomenology design is distinct from the other qualitative designs in its focus on a shared experience of individuals regarding an intense, severe, or significant event (e.g., survivors of a mass school shooting; victims of the effects of significant weather storms, like tornados or hurricanes). The ultimate goal when using this design is to delineate the essence of the lived experience of this event. In most instances, researchers seek to administer interviews with a group of people with this shared experience, although other data collection instruments can be used—such as observations, documents, and artifacts. In collecting data, the researchers are primarily interested in identifying highly relevant and significant pieces of information that relate to the essence of the intensive experience. The researchers also strive to examine the collective experiences and insights of individuals to understand how they make sense and meaning out of the experience. Creating meaning through the human consciousness is known as Lifeworld (see Chapter 6 for more details) and a central concept of phenomenology.

Given that phenomenologists rely heavily on interviews and focus groups to explore group dynamics, the following section highlights the structure of this type of data and presents a composite account of a phenomenon. Individual interviews and focus groups are heavily emphasized in these designs, in part because they can illuminate the collective attitudes, beliefs, values, and/or goals of multiple people with a shared experience of an event. Focus groups can be particularly beneficial because they are cost effective and can provide a broad and diverse range of responses from a seemingly homogeneous group. The nature of the groupings based on participant availability, the roles of the individuals in the group, and the cohesiveness of innerworkings will play a role in the interactions during the focus group. Educators who form a cohesive network (e.g., Facebook group for IB teachers, central office for curriculum specialists) would offer very different information in a focus group compared to teachers who did not have a commonality.

Focus groups are one way to gather data from a phenomenological perspective to highlight group dynamics, points of agreement and conflict, and needs of the group. Using a checklist to reflect on the focus group transcripts is useful in data analyses.

©iStockphoto.com/Eva-Katalin

Analysis of focus group interviews often follow the same guidelines as individual participant interviews. However, when conducting a focus group, the researcher should take steps to not favor one participant over others. For instance, individuals can sometimes dominate the conversation while others are quieter. This lack of participation can be an individual's preference or style or may represent a certain type of reactivity, where the participant is self-conscious of others' reactions to their comments within the organization. Being mindful of the level of engagement of each individual during a focus group is paramount. Then, as needed, direct or guide the conversation so as not to overemphasize one perspective over others.

Many of the techniques suggested throughout this text for displaying tables and figures would be applicable to the study of phenomenology, particularly in sharing findings from the collection of interviews. An ethnographer could use a matrix to identify key elements to explore during observation in detail with subsequent types of data. Table 14.6 exemplifies how a researcher could integrate a matrix within a professional development program for IB teachers with a PLC component. The matrix displays the progress of each PLC group in terms of a given project, questions asked, interest of PLC members, or progress on a project. In addition, the researcher could compare the groups' interests, questions, needs, and meetings. Counting the number of meetings and types of questions could yield some information to further gauge how the professional development program that incorporates PLC groups supports individuals in their instructional effectiveness.

TABLE 14.6 ■ Sample Matrix for IB Teacher in a PLC Professional Development Program						
Topic	PLC Team 1	PLC Team 2	PLC Team 3	PLC Team 4	PLC Team 5	PLC Team 6
Meetings						
Questions						
Interests						
Requests for Workshops						
Progress on PLC Project						

A next step would be to review the data gathered from interviews and observation matrix to create diagrams and charts. Consider IB teachers who attended professional development workshops. Based on data provided by interviews and checklists, a diagram was created to highlight specific systems and their relationships, as shown in Figure 14.11. When used in conjunction with other data collection instruments, diagrams can assist researchers in drawing conclusions and conveying meanings. Thus, the diagram in Figure 14.11 can serve as a springboard to interpret participant interests and perceptions of the benefits of collaboration and mentorship. In addition, descriptive verbs are indicative of actions that participants emphasize.

Throughout this section, we focused on describing distinctions in qualitative data analysis across designs. In the *Let's See It!* in Table 14.7, we provide a study by Shaunessy-Dedrick et al. (2015) related to IB programs for you to gain some experience on how these types of qualitative designs are conducted. This example is followed by a *Let's Do It!* activity as guided practice with an article by Kwong and Churchill (2023).

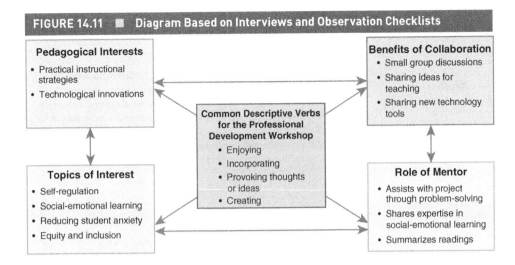

FIGURE 14.11 ■ Diagram Based on Interviews and Observation Checklists

Pedagogical Interests
- Practical instructional strategies
- Technological innovations

Benefits of Collaboration
- Small group discussions
- Sharing ideas for teaching
- Sharing new technology tools

Common Descriptive Verbs for the Professional Development Workshop
- Enjoying
- Incorporating
- Provoking thoughts or ideas
- Creating

Topics of Interest
- Self-regulation
- Social-emotional learning
- Reducing student anxiety
- Equity and inclusion

Role of Mentor
- Assists with project through problem-solving
- Shares expertise in social-emotional learning
- Summarizes readings

Let's See It! 14.2

Goal: Review and Describe the Qualitative Data Analysis Process in a Peer-Reviewed Study

Directions: The main objective of this activity is to describe the design and the process of analysis using the selected article, Shaunessy-Dedrick et al. (2015). Let's take a look at the table, which includes a description of the purpose of the study, research question(s), the sample, type of qualitative design and analysis, and the process of analysis leading to the generated themes.

TABLE 14.7 ■ Qualitative Data Analysis

Study	Shaunessy-Dedrick, E., Suldo, S. M., Roth, R. A., & Fefer, S. A. (2015). Students' perceptions of factors that contribute to risk and success in accelerated high school courses. *High School Journal, 98*(2), 109–137.
Purpose of Study	The researchers sought to explore the influence of student-perceived stressors, coping strategies, and environmental factors from 30 high school students on their success in college-level courses.
Research Question(s)	1. What are the primary types of stressors faced by AP and IBD students?
	2. What coping strategies are effective and ineffective in managing such stressors?
	3. What personal characteristics contribute to student success in AP and IBD programs?
	4. What social, familial, and educational supports and barriers influence students' success in AP and IBD?
	(Shaunessy-Dedrick et al., 2015, p. 115)
Sample	Participants were recruited using extreme case sampling and consisted of 30 (*n* = 30) high school students; 15 were identified as successful students and the other 15 were identified as struggling students. These students were either enrolled in the International Baccalaureate Diploma Program or in advanced placement (AP) courses.

(Continued)

TABLE 14.7 ■ Qualitative Data Analysis (*Continued*)	
Qualitative Design	This study utilized a case study design.
Codes, Categories, and Broader Themes	The researchers analyzed the data using an applied thematic analysis. They began by transcribing all of their interview data and compared these data to the field notes that were taken. After the initial readthrough, the researchers developed several code categories and themes of student academic concerns. A codebook was iteratively developed and included detailed descriptions of the coding system.

Let's Do It! 14.2

Guided Practice: To Practice Reviewing and Describing the Qualitative Data Analysis Process in a Peer-Reviewed Study

Directions: In this *Let's Do It!* activity, you will be asked to review and describe the qualitative design and analysis used in the article, Kwong and Churchill (2011). Fill out this table to include a description of the purpose of the study, the sample, the type of qualitative design and analysis, and a description of the process of analysis leading to the generated themes.

TABLE 14.8 ■ Qualitative Data Analysis Process	
Study	Kwong, C.-Y. C., & Churchill, D. (2023). Applying the Activity Theory framework to analyse the use of ePortfolios in an International Baccalaureate Middle Years Programme Sciences classroom: A longitudinal multiple-case study. *Computers & Education, 200*, 1–14. https://doi.org/10.1016/j.compedu.2023.104792
Purpose of Study	
Research Question(s)	
Sample	
Qualitative Design	
Codes, Categories, and Broader Themes	

Many qualitative research studies reference various analyses. Now that you have had the opportunity to review research articles that describe different designs, review the *You Do It!* 14.4 for further exposure to qualitative data analysis.

THE TAKEAWAY

Qualitative research approaches to data analysis differ in sources of data and context, but they all share similar characteristics in the data analysis process.

ETHICAL CONSIDERATIONS

Given the nature of qualitative studies, the interaction between researchers and participants can pose challenges as the researcher is also considered to be the research instrument of the study. First, with large amounts of data (some including video/audio recordings), the researcher has a responsibility to secure data, maintain anonymity and confidentiality, create a clear organizational record system, and keep an organized and secure account of data and analysis to substantiate claims as a form of audibility. The researcher should describe their subjective lens or their personal perspectives and positionality about the target topic and the steps that were proactively taken to curtail biases to strengthen trustworthiness and rigor of the study. In qualitative research in particular, it is important for the researcher to build a rapport with the participants due to the fact that qualitative research by nature asks more from participants, potentially requesting that they share sensitive information in a face-to-face setting where complete anonymity is not possible. Thus, it is imperative that participants be able to trust the researcher to maintain confidentiality so that they will feel comfortable sharing information with the researcher. It is also critical that the participants feel comfortable ending their participation in the research if desired. The researcher/participant relationship is an especially important one in qualitative research.

While establishing a trusting relationship is paramount, there are some added factors to consider. First, the two parties work together to co-construct meaning, particularly during the interview process. However, to maintain impartiality, the researcher needs to acknowledge that they are not engaging in the interview as a friend. Building a trusting relationship based on a mutual partnership while maintaining impartiality requires some adeptness.

Next, the researcher needs to present the results in a balanced account from all participants. The researcher should maintain a clear approach to presenting information, so as to share the experiences of the participants with one individual while not overshadowing others. One strategy is for the researcher to review quotes to check whether one participant's viewpoint is predominant. If Mrs. Choi is more talkative than Mrs. Gul, Dr. Giordano will want to be sure that the presentation of findings balances the perspective of both individuals. It is also important for researchers to ensure that every participant feels comfortable sharing their ideas in group research settings, such as focus groups. It is common in these settings for some participants to be more talkative and open than others; thus, the researcher should ensure that each participant has the time and space to share their ideas.

While there are many ways to uphold ethical standards for qualitative research, establishing a researcher–participant partnership as well as sharing findings in an ethical manner is a central issue. The overarching goal is to utilize a neutral and comprehensive stance and share findings in a way that conveys the individuals' viewpoint, all while protecting the confidentiality of participants.

THE TAKEAWAY

In qualitative research, it is imperative that participants are able to trust the researcher to maintain confidentiality so that they will feel comfortable sharing information. Building a trusting rapport with participants while maintaining impartiality is a hallmark of ethical research.

AMERICAN PSYCHOLOGICAL ASSOCIATION STYLE

LEARNING OBJECTIVE

14.6   Utilize the *Publication Manual of the American Psychological Association* for reporting findings in qualitative research.

Many of the APA guidelines shared in this text are relatable to presenting qualitative analyses and findings. In general, qualitative data analyses sections of a journal article are typically longer and have more built-in flexibility than in quantitative studies. These features allow one to engage in deeper presentation of the data and to vary the reporting of the analyses and findings based on the qualitative design. For example, depending on the design, findings and discussion sections of a paper may be combined. Nevertheless, transparency of the qualitative analysis process is highly recommended. A well-described results section includes a description of coding procedures, including the development of themes when applicable. Researchers should describe data coding approaches in detail. Themes or categories that emerged from the analyses or those developed a priori should also be specified. Moreover, researchers are encouraged to include information about the coders and the training received and as appropriate, the nature of the computer software used to assist the coding process.

In addition, it is important that the researcher includes a section in the manuscript about methodological integrity (i.e., additional checks to the qualitative analysis) to provide evidence that produced findings are valid. Support for findings is offered with documentation, such as participant quotes or other qualitative data. Figures and tables support the interpretations drawn by the researchers. These elements coupled with writing make it clear to the reader how conclusions were drawn. In fact, the processes should be so clear as to be replicable by other researchers. Another important element of the results section is that the writing centers on the participants' perspectives. After all, much of qualitative research focuses on the viewpoint of those individuals studied or affected by a given situation.

A key topic with qualitative analysis and APA style is the use of figures and tables. These visuals or images are useful to show theoretical models, timelines for procedures, coding schemes, analysis of data (e.g., map making), and theme development, as some examples. For example, figures are often effective in guiding the reader in understanding the research design procedures and meanings that unfold within the study. Similarly, tables are helpful in relaying coding schemes, the process of analysis, interrelationships among individuals, and theme development. Table 14.7, referred to earlier in this chapter, highlights sample quotes of emergent themes from a study of integrating self-regulatory processes within an IB curriculum.

The discussion or conclusion section of a qualitative research study focuses on summarizing the current findings in relationship to the existing literature and considers alternate interpretations to researchers' own interpretations. In addition, there should be a limitations section that describes issues that may have affected the researcher's ability to draw conclusions. Finally, the author(s) should provide information in terms of implications and suggestions for future research. Table 14.9 includes a checklist to remind the researcher of some key aspects of qualitative analyses that should be included in a manuscript.

TABLE 14.9 ■ Checklist for Inclusion of Key Aspects in Qualitative Data Analysis Sections of a Manuscript

1. Has the researcher(s) described their subjective lens?

2. Have coding procedures been described in detail?

3. Does the work establish rigor by using multiple methods of triangulation?

4. Does the work show methodological integrity (e.g., include ways to counter researcher bias through intercoder reliability)?

5. Does the work support findings with participant quotes?

6. Is the writing centered from the participants' perspectives?

7. Does the conclusion include limitations?

8. Does the conclusion relate findings to previous literature?

These types of components in the checklist assist the audience in following the flow of the research design and findings. Integrating APA style further supports consistency in the presentation of findings.

THE TAKEAWAY

Utilizing APA style in tables and figures supports consistency in the presentation of findings and clarifies processes in a qualitative research study.

CHAPTER SUMMARY

Qualitative analysis is a dynamic, inductive, and often innovative process. This chapter provides a broad overview of the diverse methods used to analyze qualitative data. We discussed the important role that the researcher plays in the data analysis process and provided specific strategies for analyzing qualitative data across different research designs. We also emphasized that although there are many variations of data analysis procedures, particularly in relationship to the type of qualitative research design, the researcher should adhere to the same principles of trustworthiness in data collection, analysis, interpretations, and dissemination of findings. As technological features of qualitative software continue to expand and improve, researchers will likely have access to even greater supports that facilitate the qualitative analysis process.

EXTENSION ACTIVITIES

You Do It! 14.1

Analyzing Qualitative Data in the Open-Coding Phase

Self-Directed Practice: Analyzing Qualitative Data Using Open Coding

Directions: Table 14.3 provided an example of how to code data in the open-coding phase. Using data collected on your topic of interest, create a coding system for the initial phase to analyze transcripts. As a form of researcher consensus, provide one of your classmates with 30% of the data to analyze with the system you created. Once they have finished analyzing the data, meet with them to see if you have a consensus. For areas where there is not consensus, discuss your viewpoints to reach an agreement.

You Do It! 14.2

Using Thematic Analysis to Analyze Data

Self-Directed Practice: Using Thematic Analysis to Analyze Data

Directions: Table 14.9 provided an example of a qualitative article that used thematic analysis. Using data that you have collected, complete the table that follows with the open-coding labels and axial-coding categories that your created. Write a description of these codes to help with future descriptions.

Open Coding (labels)	Axial Coding (categories)	Descriptions

KEY TERMS

Axial coding
Computer Assisted Qualitative Analysis (CAQDS)
Constant comparative analysis approach
Cultural domain
Descriptive coding
Discourse analysis
Emergent themes

Map making
Member checking
Narrative analysis
Naturalistic generalization
Open coding
Selective coding
Theme
Thematic analysis

ANSWER KEY

Stop and Think Activities

STOP AND THINK 14.1

Qualitative researchers utilize a complex, tiered system of coding, analysis, and interpretation. Based on this process, the researcher will write a narrative to present findings from the study. Explicitly stating the process of data collection, analysis, and interpretations provides a layer of transparency that supports rigor and the four elements of trustworthiness (credibility, confirmability, transferability, and dependability).

STOP AND THINK 14.2

The researcher will want to be explicit when describing the process of analysis, both in the method and results section of a report or at a conference presentation. Taking notes will aid in recalling and relaying this information. In addition, the researcher will use reflexivity to check for aspects of bias, which are reflective of integrating trustworthiness in a study.

Let's Do It! Activities
LET's DO IT! 14.1

Guided Practice: How to Analyze Qualitative Data

Goal: Analyzing Data in the Open-Coding Phase

Directions: After reviewing Table 14.2, use this second transcript excerpt to practice descriptive coding. Create a codebook with definitions and apply the system to the transcript from "Carmel." Answers will vary, so compare your process to that of a classmate's as well as the accompanying answer key. Figure 14.12 is an example of the types of codes that could be created.

FIGURE 14.12
Examples of Descriptive Codes

13:46/Carmel: Yeah, definitely. We said a weekly goal, which could be a very long-term goal. So, they just look at it every week and then they also set daily goals. That way they have a plan of action for their day. Cause sometimes if you're just looking at a gigantic long-term goal, that's hard to like… okay, well, where do I get started? It's like hard to focus. So, it narrows it down. It gives them kind of like a stepping stone or little baby steps to get there.

[G] 13:46/Carmel: Yeah, definitely. W[W] aid a weekly goal, which could [G] a very long-term goal. So, they just [P] at it every week and then they also set daily goals. That way they hav[G] plan of action for their day. Cause sometimes if you're just looking at a gigantic long-term goal, that's hard to like… okay, well, v[S] re do I get started? It's like hard to focus. So, it narrows it down. It gives them kind of like a stepping stone or little baby steps to get there.

Sample Codebook Excerpt

G = goal; a person's aim or desired outcome

P = plan of action; a strategic system to reach a goal

S = stepping stone; an action that helps someone progress to reach a goal

W = week/weekly; 7 days/within 7 days

LET's DO IT! 14.2

Guided Practice: Identify and Describe Qualitative Design and Analyses From a Peer-Reviewed Study

Directions: In this *Let's Do It!*, fill out this table to include a description of the purpose of the study, the sample, the type of qualitative design and analysis, and a description of the process of analysis leading to the generated themes.

Qualitative Data Analysis Process

Study	Kwong, C.-Y. C., & Churchill, D. (2023). Applying the Activity Theory framework to analyse the use of ePortfolios in an International Baccalaureate Middle Years Programme Sciences classroom: A longitudinal multiple-case study. *Computers & Education, 200*, 1–14. https://doi.org/10.1016/j.compedu.2023.104792
Purpose of Study	The researchers in this study evaluated the use of ePortfolios in an International Baccalaureate (IB) Middle Years Programme (MYP) science classroom in China using an Activity Theory framework.
Research Question(s)	"How can Activity Theory be applied as a framework to analyse longitudinally the effects of introducing ePortfolios into a secondary classroom?" (Kwong & Churchill, 2023, p. 3).
Sample	The sample consisted of eight ($n = 8$) students who were consecutively enrolled in the IB MYP for two years.
Qualitative Design	This study used a longitudinal multiple-case study design.
Codes, Categories, and Broader Themes	The researchers analyzed the data using an inductive content and constant comparison method of analyses. The researchers collected data using multiple data sources (e.g., interviews, images and videos of lab sessions, reflections and summative assessments, to name a few) throughout the longitudinal study. The researchers conducted content analysis to code the various sources of data with themes developed in relation to the Activity Theory Elements through constant comparison analysis.

COMMUNICATING RESEARCH

A DAY AT WORK

Where and When to Begin? How Do We Share Our Research With Others?

Being proactive and using classroom management strategies can help prevent disruptions in learning.
©iStockphoto.com/JBryson

First-grade teacher Mrs. Smith and seventh-grade teacher Mr. Krahl have several students in their classrooms diagnosed with attention deficit hyperactivity disorder (ADHD). The teachers noticed that these students tend to exhibit impulsive behaviors such as inappropriately shouting out answers to questions or jumping out of their seats during class lessons. Similarly, they observed that many of these students seem to become overstimulated during class and struggle to remain focused. Mrs. Smith and Mr. Krahl feel inadequate in their understanding of ADHD and have low self-efficacy beliefs in their classroom management skills. They suspect other teachers have similar concerns and decide to conduct a district-wide experiment by randomly assigning teachers to an intervention program or control group. The intervention consists of a series of workshops designed to educate teachers in their district about ADHD and effective classroom management strategies for all students. Mrs. Smith and Mr. Krahl conducted this experiment and found that the posttest scores of teachers regarding their understanding of ADHD and self-efficacy for using classroom management techniques were significantly stronger than the scores demonstrated by those in the control group. Given these impressive findings, a teacher who participated in the treatment group suggested to Mrs. Smith and Mr. Krahl that they try to publish this study in a journal so that other teachers can learn and benefit from it. Surprised by this idea, they asked each other, "How do we go about doing that?"

INTRODUCTION

In previous chapters, we presented various research designs and discussed the benefits and complexities of conducting research. In this chapter, we shift our focus away from how to conduct research to the process of communicating research. We begin with a description of the importance of communicating research and identifying approaches to written and oral communication as they relate to educational research. These sections are followed by a discussion of the key considerations in communicating research and a description of how the three phases of self-regulated learning (planning, doing, and reflecting) can help researchers effectively engage in the communication process. Lastly, as with most other chapters of this book, we describe ethical issues and the role of the *Publication of the American Psychological Association* (APA) in helping educators communicate information about their research studies.

THE IMPORTANCE OF COMMUNICATING RESEARCH

LEARNING OBJECTIVE
15.1   Describe the importance of communicating research.

It is very exciting to embark on a research project. However, if the results from research are not read by others and thus are only known to the researchers themselves, the research will be of little use. Educators often do not think of themselves as researchers, but as you likely realized from reading this book, we believe all educators possess the capability to conduct and report on research findings! The prospect of communicating about research can be daunting, which can lead educators to avoid it or feel ill-equipped to overcome natural barriers. Thinking back to the original purpose for conducting the research and examining why the research is important can help motivate and inspire educators who do research to learn more about how and what to communicate about a research study. Communicating research is analogous to telling a story. The story has a beginning, middle, and end and can leave the reader with insights that can be used for multiple purposes. While there are many reasons why educators may want to share their research, we discuss three common ones: the desire to influence teaching and practice, an interest in professional growth and recognition from others, and the possibility it is a requirement from a funding source or by supervisors. Each of these reasons, which are not mutually exclusive, will to some degree determine the type of story you choose to tell.

Communicating about research is similar to storytelling.

©iStockphoto.com/FatCamera

Desire to Influence Teaching or Instructional Practices

Conducting research in a silo may benefit one's own work but limits the potential and powerful impact the research may have on others locally or throughout the world. Research that is published or shared at professional conferences, for example, and viewed by teachers and administrators can lead to dramatic improvements in classrooms and schools. In this situation, the story (i.e., research study) can provide readers with information that empowers them to make changes to their teaching practices, educational policies, and challenging problems that are beyond the scope of where the researchers live and work. The famous poet, memoirist, and civil rights activist Maya Angelou once said: "The idea is to write it so that people hear it, and it slides through the brain and goes straight to the heart." (Brownwell, 2014). While researchers are not writing poetry, their research has the potential to change the lives of others.

In our opening scenario, Mrs. Smith and Mr. Krahl conducted a study to examine the effects of a professional development program on teachers' knowledge about ADHD and their self-efficacy for using effective classroom management strategies. Given the importance and potential relevance of this study, taking the steps to share the findings within the educational community can have a snowball effect for teachers and students. Teachers who read this research may gain a greater sense of control over their classroom while also learning innovative ways to create a more positive educational environment for students with ADHD and their peers without disabilities. Using research to help improve one's work is often referred to as evidence-based practice. More specifically, evidence-based practice is the use of programs or practices that have been shown to be effective based on rigorous research (Slavin, 2020). The concept that evidence-based practice is important because it conveys that not all teaching approaches, academic strategies, or instructional programs are effective; some might improve student performance while others do not. In a sense, evidence-based practice take the guesswork out of identifying an effective intervention or instructional method during the problem-solving process used in schools. By sharing your research you can contribute to the evidence-based practice literature and thus potentially have a positive impact on other educators and their students.

Inappropriate classroom behavior can interfere with learning. Research can help educators solve this problem by studying innovative classroom management strategies.

©iStockphoto.com/TerryJ

Interest in Professional Development, Growth, and Recognition From Others

Communicating research can provide educators with opportunities for growth in many ways. To share your research, you will need to make several decisions, including the format of the communication—such as a presentation versus writing a manuscript for publication, the latter of which prompts the need to develop certain skill sets. In almost all chapters, we emphasized the importance of using the APA's publication manual when preparing a research paper for publication. This manual can also serve as a very useful guide when preparing a poster session or verbal presentation at a conference. Although having to learn and rely on a technical manual can be challenging and tedious, it can also result in a stronger skillset for effectively communicating your research.

We encourage educators to present or publish their research with appropriate permissions. Publishing, in one format or another, may not only contribute to practice but also impact educational theory. Publishing refers to communicating about research in ways that make it available to the public. To be effective as communicators, researchers must be like storytellers who continually seek to improve their ability to share information through written products (journal articles), oral presentations (at conferences or professional development meetings), and visual displays (diagrams, tables, and figures).

STOP AND THINK 15.1

Why would communicating your research be particularly important to you? What value do you see in communicating your research to others?

After completing their experiment, Mrs. Smith and Mr. Khral decided to first present their results at a conference. Unfortunately, they have no idea to which conference they should submit their research. As a first step to educating themselves about this proposal submission process, they spoke with the director of disability services at their school, who recommended presenting at the annual Council for Exceptional Children (CEC) Convention & Expo. Upon searching through the CEC website, Mrs. Smith and Mr. Khral read that the CEC is the largest international educational organization focused on helping students with disabilities succeed. Members of the CEC include those from a variety of fields related to special education, such as teachers, counselors, school psychologists, school social workers, physical and speech therapists, and administrators.

The next step was for the teachers to search the CEC website to learn about the different formats for presenting their research (i.e., posters versus paper sessions) and for the instructions and deadlines for submitting a proposal to the review panel of the convention. In browsing the website, they discovered several requirements and guidelines for submitting proposals and that each proposal undergoes competitive peer-review process that may lead to the proposal not getting accepted. Even with these challenges and the prospect that their proposal could be rejected, Mrs. Smith and Mr. Krahl decide to go ahead with their plan to submit it.

Similar steps are followed when researchers decide to submit a research paper to a journal for publication. In Table 15.1, we provide suggestions on how to decide which journal to submit your research to for publication.

TABLE 15.1 ■ Deciding Which Journal to Submit Your Research to for Publication		
Step	**Main Idea**	**Strategies**
1	Identify relevant journals and make a list.	• Ask colleagues, mentors, and others who have published their research for recommendations of journals. • Examine familiar journals and journals in your field. • Search the internet for journals on your topic.
2	Determine the journal's scope and overall purpose.	• Review the journal's table of contents to see what types of research are published in the journal. • Skim some of the articles—are they very quantitative or qualitative focused? Would your research study fit with the others in the journal?
3	Find the impact factor, journal rank, article influence, or h-index.	• These numbers provide insight into the citation rates for the articles published and usually provide insight about into the rigor of the articles appearing in the journal. • Review various databases, such as *Cabell's Journal Metrics*, which organize and rank scholarly journals. • Try to find out the rejection rates; typically, the higher the rank and rejection rate the more prestigious the journal and the greater challenge to having your research paper accepted for publication.
4	Narrow down your list to two–three journals.	• Read through the submission guidelines, overall requirements, and deadlines. These are usually found in the instructions for authors section. • Think about whether these requirements seem doable.

Step	Main Idea	Strategies
5	Examine the editorial board and the peer-review process and timeframe.	● Do a quick search on members of the editorial team to determine how knowledgeable they are in the subject. ● Determine if the timeframe (submission deadlines, reviewers' feedback timeframe, time needed to make revisions and resubmit) works with your schedule.
6	Decide on a journal.	● Based on the preceding factors, make a decision about the journal to which you will submit your research study.

In addition to enhancing your own learning and professional growth, submitting conference proposals or journal articles for publication help others get to know your work. Name recognition occurs as one conducts professional presentations and publishes research in high quality journals. In communicating research results in these ways, educators can expand their professional network, which can lead to practice-based or research-focused collaborations that extend beyond one's local or immediate community. In addition, sharing research on critical issues can help other educators by sharing important new knowledge. In sum, communicating one's research can give researchers name recognition, influence theory and further research, and provide opportunities for professional development and growth.

Communication of Research May Be Required

There are situations in which communication of research may be required by your principal, superintendent, or other individual. In fact, at times educators will only receive approval from administrators to conduct research if they agree to provide periodic progress reports as well as an end-of-project summary to interested parties. Members of your school or community may be interested in learning about the important observations, experiences, and the outcomes of your research study to enhance their own understanding or thinking about a given issue and how they might improve as an educator. At a broader impact level, policymakers could also view your research reports and consider implementing changes based on your findings.

To implement a research study, educators or researchers may need to obtain financial support, such as through a grant funding agency. Grants are financial awards given to researchers by a nonprofit, profit, or governmental agency that support or fund a research study. They differ from loans, the latter of which must be paid back. To obtain a grant, one must submit an application that, depending on the agency and the amount of the award, can be extremely time-consuming. The amount of money from grants can range from a few hundred dollars to millions of dollars. Most educators would typically apply for grants to cover the costs of conducting a research study. Mrs. Smith and Mr. Krahl have decided to do a preliminary or pilot study before their experiment. They want to first conduct a qualitative study to obtain information that may help determine whether an intervention-type of experiment might be beneficial at a later time. In their qualitative study, they plan to interview teachers and students. They are hoping the pilot study will give them the credibility they need to apply for a grant so they can then purchase video equipment to record classroom observations during the intervention study.

Finding sources for grant funding can be challenging. If educators are affiliated with universities, they could contact a designated research or grants office at the university. These offices are specifically focused on helping researchers find out about available grants while also providing support for submitting proposals to the funder. In addition, educators can speak with district and school administrators and colleagues to find out whether research grants are available through local or state governmental entities or foundations. Many professional organizations, such as the Association for Child and Adolescent Counseling or the National Counsel of Teachers of English, among others, also provide funding to members. Researchers may also search the internet for funding sources that are available for educational research, and there are numerous books dedicated entirely to grant writing, which may be helpful for educators who are unfamiliar with the grant proposal application process.

To write a successful grant application, one must be able to clearly and effectively communicate the purpose and rationale of the study, a clear and realistic timeline for the study, the key personnel to execute the study, an estimated budget regarding the use of the funds, a description of how the results will be disseminated in scholarly and non-scholarly contexts, and any legal or compliance issues that might need to be addressed (Ludlow, 2014). For school-based research, the grant proposal should also include permission from the principal, superintendent, or other body that approves such requests. The process of writing a grant proposal parallels the process and skills used by researchers. Thus, the outline created for the grant application—statement of the problem or critical issue and literature review, methodology, intended analyses, potential impact from findings, and the names and credentials of collaborators—can ultimately serve as the outline for the manuscript you may write or for presentations you may make in the future.

Most grants are competitive and therefore, receiving any type of grant can be very exciting! When funded, it suggests that others see value in your research and are willing to provide the financial support needed to execute your research vision. With this financial support comes great responsibility. Funding organizations or agencies often require researchers to write periodic reports throughout the grant timeframe, including a final report. Sometimes they will also require that applicants submit their research to a journal for publication within a certain timeframe or that they present their research to the community, at conferences, or some other public forum.

Regardless of whether one receives a grant to conduct research, all researchers need to become skilled at communicating research plans, methods, results, and implications. In the next section, we describe the different modalities of formal research communication (written, oral) followed by critical issues to be considered across these modalities.

THE TAKEAWAY

Communicating your research should be an integral part of your research proposal and plans.

APPROACHES TO WRITTEN AND ORAL COMMUNICATION OF RESEARCH

LEARNING OBJECTIVE

15.2   Identify approaches to written and oral communication of research.

Communicating research can be daunting, not only because of the necessary effort and time but because of the various ways of doing so. The specific communication approach you select is likely to correspond with your original purpose for conducting research and the type of story you want to tell. The two most common approaches are written communication and oral presentations. As we review each of these approaches, you will see they are not mutually exclusive. In fact, according to Lopez (2004, p. 15), "We remember 10% of what we read, 20% of what we hear, 30% of what we see, and 50% of what we see and hear"!

Written communication can take many forms, such as manuscripts for publication; reports for key stakeholders, such as principals or grant funding organizations; articles in newspapers and magazines; advertising brochures; blogs; or training manuals. For example, university professors often publish their research in scientific journals to contribute new knowledge to the literature. As described earlier in this book, these manuscripts undergo a rigorous and independent peer-review process by other academic experts and scholars in the field to ensure the overall quality and credibility of the research.

Educators who engage in research may also opt to submit a manuscript to scientific journals with the intended audience being scientists or researchers. However, other educators may prefer to target an audience of fellow educators or others in the school system. In this situation, they would likely submit the manuscripts to journals focused on practice, applied issues, or to those targeting specific content areas or academic subjects. For example, *The Mathematics Teacher* and *Social Studies and the Young Learner* are practitioner-based journals targeting educators in the mathematics and social studies disciplines. Practice-based journals are also often peer-reviewed journals, but the peers typically consist of practitioners in schools rather than exclusively university professors. The decision about the type of journal to which one submits an article will depend, to some extent, on your original purpose for conducting the research. The teachers in our opening scenario may want to publish their study in a scientific journal because they want to share their research with a broad range of special education educators as well as others with an interest in special education.

Teachers can collaborate and provide each other with feedback.
©iStockphoto.com/FG Trade

Another option is to submit a written report to your school leaders or to publish your research in a non-peer-reviewed journal, local parent or trade magazine, blog, or newspaper. For these types of publications, along with obtaining the necessary approvals from all stakeholders (superintendent, principal, parents, and students), the educator would likely prepare a much shorter document than one prepared for publication in a scientific journal or journal of practice. While magazine articles typically do not undergo a peer-review process, they often must be approved by the editorial team, and researchers would need to adhere to the publication's submission guidelines.

In previous chapters in this book, we discussed the need for educators conducting research to obtain written approvals from research participants and the participating organization prior to conducting a study. As part of this approval process, educators need to submit a formal application to the institutional review board (IRB), along with consent letters conveying the purpose, goals, and activities of the study and the intentions to publish the research. This ethical governance process is important because it helps to protect the public and highlights the need for researchers to use forethought when planning to conduct research. In other words, one must also make decisions about the goals of the study and what one will do with the results in advance of even beginning the study! Let's say a principal wanted to collaborate with a professor from a local university on the influence of teacher attrition in their school on reading achievement and then wanted to publish the research in a journal upon completion. They would need to acknowledge and directly state their intention to publish the research as part of their original IRB application. Thus, there are many decisions to be made when preparing to conduct a research study, including whether you intend to submit your work for publication to a wider community.

Oral communication can also occur in different ways and typically includes a written component. Sometimes educators are not interested in submitting their research for publication but want to share it with their colleagues and others who have an interest in education. Oral presentations are a unique modality of communication that provides researchers with this alternative. Educators may choose to communicate their research with professionals in the school, district, or community. The purpose of these presentations is to help others learn from their experiences, encourage others to conduct research, and to share best practices.

Educators often attend professional conferences. When they are interested in presenting research or educational ideas at such a conference, they need to prepare and submit a written proposal. Conferences vary in scope and size, ranging from district wide to regional, national, or even international levels. The nature of the specific proposal will often vary based on the conference, but generally speaking, the proposal requires a concise explanation of rationale, purposes, results, and implications and potentially the format of the presentation. Earlier, we mentioned that Mrs. Smith and Mr. Krahl wanted to share their research at the CEC Convention, a major educational professional conference. They were also motivated to talk about their research at the conference because of their interest in getting feedback from reviewers as well as the researchers and educators attending the conference. Many researchers purposefully present their research at conferences with the intention of using the provided feedback to improve the quality of a written manuscript to be submitted to a peer-reviewed journal in the future. What a great idea!

Most professional conferences offer a wide variety of presentation formats. One format includes a *theme-based paper session*, whereby each presenter is allotted a set amount of time to discuss their research related to the theme or specific topic. Typically, presenters develop and use PowerPoint slides to guide their presentation. Following each oral presentation, another individual is often tasked with summarizing and providing insights about the talks, which is then followed by a question-and-answer session between all presenters and the audience. Another option is an *interactive symposium session* where there may be several presenters who briefly discuss their research (with or without PowerPoint slides), with much more time allocated for interaction with the audience than the paper sessions. Both oral presentation formats include a designated chair who organizes the order of the speakers, monitors the time, and assists with the audience participation.

Presenting your research as a poster at conferences is another common presentation option. Researchers strive to create posters that summarize the key elements of their study and its outcomes. A *poster session* will often include many posters in a large space that provides attendees the opportunity to circulate at their leisure among the posters. Researchers have the option of openly discussing their entire poster or responding to select questions posed by the attendees. Poster sessions often promote a more intimate and informal exchange between researchers and the attendees than more formal paper and symposium formats.

Posters are another venue for communicating about one's research.

©iStockphoto.com/SDI Productions

Another format for presenting research at conferences is a *round table session* where researchers sit at tables and share their work with one another. Like poster sessions, round tables tend to be somewhat informal. While one does not need to prepare a formal "talk" or a poster, researchers will often provide a one- or two-page handout about their research findings to share with others or a QR code on the presentation that attendees can scan for additional information. The purpose of a round table discussion is to provide multiple presenters with the opportunity to briefly share their research in a more intimate context than large audience presentations. Seating at round tables tends to be limited, and there is usually an assigned moderator who guides the discussion and keeps presenters on track and within appropriate timelines. Regardless of the oral communication format, researchers need to prepare and submit a proposal to undergo a peer-review process. Similar to the journal submission process, not all conference proposals are accepted, although there tends to be a much higher rate of acceptance of conference proposals. It is important to also recognize that researchers not only need to spend time preparing the proposal but also the actual oral presentation, such as identifying the topics to discuss, developing PowerPoint slides, and practicing the presentation ahead of time.

Researchers often get very excited about sharing and discussing their work! Attending conferences and discussing your research can be both rewarding and challenging. Educators have a great forum to talk about meaningful topics and issues when presenting to colleagues or other educators with similar interests. However, there are often time constraints in a conference presentation, such as limiting the number of minutes one has to summarize their work—*but how does one condense months' or a year's worth of research into a 10 to 15 minute presentation?* Presenting research as an oral presentations will help you develop some of the skills needed to be an effective presenter, including brevity!

STOP AND THINK 15.2

What approach to communicating about research do you most prefer and why?

While we encourage readers to consider presenting their research at conferences, there are times when educators may choose to share their research in nonscientific platforms. Consistent with the notion of publicly engaged scholarship, researchers should also think about discussing their work with a broader nonscientific community via blogs, podcasts, videos, or as a guest on a radio show. The *Journal of Teacher Education*, considered the flagship journal of the American Association of Colleges of Teacher Education, for example, provides podcasts on innovative and notable research studies that have been conducted.

With any form of communication (written or oral), it is critical to consider the many ethical issues involved, such as maintaining confidentiality and anonymity of participants, schools, teachers, and staff in your writing and when speaking publicly. In addition, though communicating your research can be considered analogous to storytelling (the story of your research: why it was conducted, how it was conducted, what the results are, and what they mean), it is important that it is done so with integrity and honesty and free from bias. While ethics is covered more extensively in a later section of this chapter, we mention it here to emphasize that ethics should be a thread in every decision you make from beginning to end in conducting and communicating research.

THE TAKEAWAY

When you are planning to conduct a research study, include in your plans the way(s) in which you will communicate your research to others.

KEY CONSIDERATIONS WHEN COMMUNICATING RESEARCH

LEARNING OBJECTIVE

15.3   Identify the key considerations when communicating research.

As you begin to think about communicating the findings of your research study, there are several things to keep in mind. We have organized these key considerations into two broad categories that will make it helpful to the researcher: audience awareness and presenting data. These two issues are important regardless of the communication modality you choose.

Audience Awareness

Audience awareness is an expression often used in writing and public speaking. It refers to being cognizant of the population who will be reading or listening to you present your research. Characteristics of audience awareness include tone, clarity, and conciseness. Before we delve further into these characteristics, take a look at the *Let's See It!* activity that follows to see two examples of different types of writing about research based on the intended audience.

Let's See It! 15.1

Goal: Identify the Intended Audience From an Abstract

Directions: As you read the following abstract in Table 15.2, pay careful attention how the abstract is written and see if you can identify clues as to who the intended audience might be.

- Using these cues, we identify whether this research is geared toward the intended audience of practitioners in the field and/or other researchers.
- Now look at our explanation in Table 15.2 of how we identified important components in determining the intended audience.

TABLE 15.2 ■ Intended Audience of Research	
Study	Martin, A. J., Burns, E. C., & Collie, R. J. (2017). ADHD, personal and interpersonal agency, and achievement: Exploring links from a social cognitive theory perspective. *Contemporary Educational Psychology, 50*, 13–22. https://doi.org/10.1016/j.cedpsych.2016.12.001
Abstract	Harnessing social cognitive theory (SCT), we investigated the roles of personal agency (self-efficacy and perceived control) and interpersonal agency (relational support) in the academic achievement (via literacy and numeracy testing) of students with attention-deficit/hyperactivity disorder (ADHD) and their non-ADHD peers. A sample of $N = 164$ students diagnosed with ADHD were investigated alongside $N = 4658$ non-ADHD peers in the same schools and year levels. Using structural equation modeling, findings showed that self-efficacy and relational support were consistently associated with better academic achievement for both groups, but with positive effects significantly stronger for students with ADHD than for students without ADHD. Although perceived control was significantly associated with achievement for students without ADHD and not significantly so for students with ADHD, there was not much difference in absolute size of perceived control effects for the two groups. Findings are relevant to theory, research, and practice identifying motivational factors and processes that may assist in closing well known achievement gaps for students with ADHD whilst also maintaining positive outcomes for students without ADHD. (Martin et al., 2017, p. 13)
Explanation of Audience	While the focus of this research study is on students with ADHD, there is a lot of scientific jargon used that is associated with social cognitive theory. In particular, the abstract of this article specifies that motivational factors may be used to close the achievement gap for students with ADHD. Although this study may have been conducted and written with teachers in mind, it seems to be primarily targeted toward other researchers or educators who are familiar with social cognitive theory. The clues are the references to SCT and the vocabulary associated with this theory. In addition, the authors describe a sophisticated data analysis and terminology related to the results that many educators may not be familiar with.

Now try the *Let's Do It!* activity to practice identifying the targeted audience when reading journal abstracts.

Let's Do It! 15.1

Guided Practice: Identify the Intended Audience From an Abstract

Directions: As you read the following abstract in Table 15.3, pay careful attention to how the abstract is written and see if you can identify clues as to who the intended audience might be.

- Identify whether this research is geared toward practitioners in the field and/or other researchers.
- Use the example in Table 15.2 to write a brief explanation of who you believe the intended audience of this research is as well as what components of the abstract led you to this conclusion.

TABLE 15.3 ■ Practice Identifying the Intended Audience From an Abstract

Study	Bolinger, S. J., Mucherah, D., Markelz, D., & Andrew, M. (2020). Teacher knowledge of attention-deficit/hyperactivity disorder and classroom management. *The Journal of Special Education Apprenticeship*, 9(1), 1–14. https://scholarworks.lib.csusb.edu/josea/v019/iss1/5
Abstract	There is limited research on teacher knowledge of attention deficit hyperactivity disorder (ADHD) and classroom management; however, research suggests that teacher knowledge of ADHD influences teaching behaviors. This study investigates general education teachers' and special education teachers' knowledge of ADHD and the interaction with classroom management. In this study, 17 teachers responded to surveys about knowledge of ADHD and classroom management. Teachers scored an average of 61% on the knowledge of ADHD questionnaire. Contrary to the hypothesis, teacher knowledge of ADHD was not significantly related to classroom management. The relationship between knowledge of ADHD and classroom management needs further examination to determine if the two constructs are significantly related. (Bolinger et al., 2020, p. 1–14)
Explanation of Audience	Use these questions to help guide your response: • Who is the intended audience? • What components (or clues) help you identify the intended audience?

The two abstracts provided in the above *Let's See It!* and *Let's Do It!* activities differ greatly in many ways. Perhaps one of the most obvious ways is that the abstracts seem to be targeting different types of readers. At the end of this chapter, we provide readers with the opportunity in the *You Do It!* activity to independently practice identifying the target audiences for different abstracts. Practicing this skill will help readers become more familiar with the ways in which articles are written with the audience in mind.

Being aware of the target audience can help writers and speakers frame their communication with intentionality, meaning they strategically plan and monitor their communication based on who their audience will be. In our opening vignette, the two teachers would likely use a different approach to describe their study to colleagues than they would to students and parents. Usage of tone and choice of vocabulary, along with being concise and clear are components of audience awareness the two teachers in our opening scenario need to consider in their communication planning just as the two abstracts have done in the previous *Let's See It!* and *Let's Do It!* activities. Next, we describe each of these characteristics in further detail.

Tone typically refers to the voice in written work or oral presentation. While there are many different tones that writers and public speakers can use (such as optimistic, moody, encouraging, or exaggerated), in the communication of research, the tone is usually more formal and objective; that is, the authors use language that is free from opinion, bias, emotion, and hyperbole. Essentially, when researchers communicate their research, they should do so by describing the research in a straightforward manner without adding adjectives or adverbs that place unnecessary emphasis on content. The authors should also use bias-free language and refrain from providing personal beliefs. In each of the abstract examples found in the preceding *Let's See It!* and *Let's Do It!* activities, the authors used a more formal voice; attitudes and opinions are not provided, and the content is "neutral" per se. Note also that the abstracts use past tense verbs. Research studies are typically presented in past tense, even when reporting on a study that is currently in progress.

Tone is influenced by the strategic use of vocabulary. In the first abstract by Martin et al. (2017), the authors use a more formal voice. The abstract contains vocabulary words familiar to researchers who know about social cognitive theory and complex statistical procedures. The article is likely written for professors or others with expertise in academic research. The second abstract also uses a formal voice; however, the vocabulary is simpler, easier to understand, and more likely targeted toward practitioners. There is also less reference to complex statistical analyses, although there may, in fact, be some found within the article.

Conciseness refers to the ability to get right to the point! Whether communicating in writing or verbally, educators must be able to articulate the most essential points about their research in fairly short sentences. The longer the sentences, the more readers and listeners need to process to comprehend, which then can affect the clarity in understanding the message. Most of us have read publications or have heard lectures where we were clueless as to the actual message being delivered!

Clarity refers to information that is easy to understand. Sentences that have clarity are written or spoken with less technical language and are less ambiguous, meaning the reader or listener will not have any misunderstandings from the communication.

Longer sentences are more likely to be used in scholarly journal articles and will likely contain more technical jargon than practitioner publications or presentations where the focus or purpose of the research is to make immediate, critical decisions. Most journals will have word and page limitations for submission, just as oral presentations will have time limits and specific requirements (such as usage of visual aids, equipment required, and adaptations for those who have visual or hearing impairments) based on the journal's intended audience. In the *Let's See it!* and *Let's Do It!* activities that follow, using both Abstracts 1 and 2 presented earlier we first provide an example and then ask readers to dissect the introductory sentences by looking at the tone, vocabulary, conciseness, and clarity using the table provided.

Let's See It! 15.2

Goal: Identify the Audience Awareness Characteristics in an Abstract

Directions: Read the following introductory sentence in Table 15.4 This sentence is from the abstract presented in the previous Let's See It! activity. Pay careful attention to the tone, vocabulary, conciseness, and clarity used in the introductory sentence. Then, look at these qualities of the characteristics that help us determine the targeted audience.

TABLE 15.4 ■ Characteristics of Audience Awareness	
Study	Martin, A. J., Burns, E. C., & Collie, R. J. (2017). ADHD, personal and interpersonal agency, and achievement: Exploring links from a social cognitive theory perspective. *Contemporary Educational Psychology, 50*, 13–22. https://doi.org/10.1016/j.cedpsych.2016.12.001
Introductory Sentence	Harnessing social cognitive theory (SCT), we investigated the roles of personal agency (self-efficacy and perceived control) and interpersonal agency (relational support) in the academic achievement (via literacy and numeracy testing) of students with attention-deficit/hyperactivity disorder (ADHD) and their non-ADHD peers.
Characteristics	Qualities of the characteristics that help us determine the targeted audience.
Tone	Formal but geared more toward theoretical experts (researchers)
Vocabulary	Several terms associated with SCT: personal agency, self-efficacy, perceived control, interpersonal agency, and relational support
Conciseness	Word count = 40
Clarity	Message is clear to those familiar with SCT that this study examines the relevant constructs using comparison groups

Let's Do It! 15.2

Guided Practice: Identify the Audience Awareness Characteristics in an Abstract

Directions: Read the following introductory sentence in Table 15.5. This sentence is from the abstract presented in the previous *Let's Do It!* activity. Pay careful attention to the tone, vocabulary, conciseness, and clarity used in the introductory sentence. Complete the table *by explaining the qualities of these characteristics that can help you determine the targeted audience.*

TABLE 15.5 ■ Practice Identifying Characteristics of Audience Awareness	
Study	Bolinger, S. J., Mucherah, D., Markelz, D., & Andrew, M. (2020). Teacher knowledge of attention-deficit/hyperactivity disorder and classroom management. *The Journal of Special Education Apprenticeship, 9*(1), 1–14. https://scholarworks.lib.csusb.edu/josea/v019/iss1/5
Introductory Sentence	There is limited research on teacher knowledge of attention deficit hyperactivity disorder (ADHD) and classroom management; however, research suggests that teacher knowledge of ADHD influences teaching behaviors.

Characteristics	Qualities of the characteristics that help us determine the targeted audience.
Tone	
Vocabulary	
Conciseness	
Clarity	

In these examples, one can easily distinguish the different audiences the publications are targeting. Keeping in mind the original purpose(s) for conducting the research can help researchers determine who the audience will be when submitting a manuscript for publication. We encourage you to practice independently to identify the characteristics of audience awareness in the *You Do It!* exercise at the end of this chapter.

STOP AND THINK 15.3

In our opening scenario, we describe how two teachers collaborated on a research study. What considerations of audience awareness would they need to take into account when preparing a manuscript for publication in a practitioner's journal?

Presenting Data

Presenting data is one of the most important activities of the research process and, perhaps, one of the most challenging. We began this text by making the analogy of researchers as investigators, trying to find answers or solutions to critical problems. The term data has been used quite often throughout this textbook. As a reminder, it refers to both quantitative information (numerical values) and qualitative information (information that typically describes characteristics or abilities that is language based or narrative). The data we obtain from conducting research reflects evidence that can often provide us with clues in support of a new body of knowledge. Once we have gone through the process of analyzing and making sense of the data, we need to decide how best to display data in our communication. This can have a critical impact on how the research is understood, viewed by others, and used and can inform educators on what decisions are to be made.

Data are at the heart of research and provide guidance on which direction one might take depending on the original purpose for conducting research. The term *data* is plural; therefore, when discussing data, one must use the appropriate verbs such as *the data show* versus *the data shows*. We will focus on two areas to consider when reporting data: content and design.

Presenting data is part of telling a story. Data may be collected at various times during a research study, and figuring out how to present the data content in a concise, simple but clear way can be challenging. We recommend that as a first consideration, the data should be directly linked to each of the researchers' research questions and/or hypotheses. This may result in more than one representation of the data (such as a few different tables or multiple excerpts from interviews, for example), or perhaps multiple research questions and/or hypotheses may be addressed within one grouping of data. A second recommendation is that the data are presented in a simple and clear way. One of the key features of communicating data is the ability to objectively tease out what is most relevant, significant, and necessary and to present the data in a format that is understandable for the reader or listener, even if an abundance of data has been collected.

Data can be presented and shared in several different ways.

©iStockphoto.com/Anchiy

A third recommendation is for researchers to keep the complexity of data in mind when presenting data. It is easy to assume readers or listeners will understand the verbiage, terms, and concepts used by researchers, but the reality is that most people in the audience will be largely unfamiliar with the concepts or study you present. From our opening scenario, Mrs. Smith and Mr. Krahl spent a great deal of time discussing the critical issue at hand, the research they wanted to conduct, and the methodology of the study. Regardless of whether they used a quantitative, qualitative, or mixed methods research design, they were the ones collecting, analyzing, and interpreting the data. Whether they decide to present the data in tables, diagrams, graphs, or in some combination, researchers need to identify which approach will enable the targeted audience to most easily understand the results.

A fourth consideration involves the ways in which researchers write or speak about the data. It is important to think about the types of data to present and how you will discuss the data so others will understand their meaning. When discussing data, one should avoid discussing every number presented in a table or graph or every statement from an interview or every detail of the data analysis. Making this decision about amount of data to include can be tricky because the data may be comprehensive, and researchers may have several variables they examined. While you do not want to provide every detail in your explanation or description of the data or analyses, you want to be sure to provide sufficient information about the types of tests you used and how the data were analyzed. Researchers will need to think carefully and make decisions about what is most necessary to communicate about in the visual representations. One approach can be to ask yourself, "How can I best share the findings from my data analysis without overburdening the reader or listener?" or "What information is critical for them to know in order to understand the results and conclusions of my research?"

In discussing data, researchers should also be careful not to make sweeping statements, unfounded assumptions, unsound inferences, or express the presence of relationships among variables when there are no supporting data. In adhering to the metaphor of storytelling relative to research communication, one must consider the necessary information to provide readers and listeners so they can follow along and understand the results and how these data relate to the research questions and/or hypotheses. The tone should remain neutral, and like an investigator, one should "stick to the facts." Lastly, as emphasized earlier, in communicating about data, one should always keep the audience in mind! Table 15.6 presents a checklist to help you remember the four key issues to consider when organizing and preparing data content for a written or oral communication.

TABLE 15.6 ■ Checklist on Key Issues to Consider When Preparing to Communicate Data
Am I aware of the complexity of my data? Who is my audience, and have I prepared my communication appropriately?
Are the data directly linked to each of the research questions and/or hypotheses ?
Are the data presented in a simple and clear way?
Am I adequately explaining the data to help readers and listeners understand the results and conclusions?

Mrs. Smith and Mr. Krahl have completed their study and have decided to begin organizing their findings. They want to create some visual representations that highlight their data, but what are their options? There are many books written exclusively about the presentation and communication of data because this is such a critical part of both written and oral communication (See books by Edward R. Tufte, for example). Using tables, bar or pie charts, lists, figures, or other graphical representations are options to highlight relevant data that correspond to the research questions and/or hypotheses. These visual representations may appear within written manuscripts as well as in the visual resources one uses when making a presentation (i.e., PowerPoint slides, posters, flipcharts, whiteboards). The data presented should always be tied to the research questions and/or hypotheses.

Visual representations in a publication or other communication are often presented from simple to complex. For example, presenting a frequency table or a table with means and standard deviations may be followed by a correlational table, followed by a diagram of a sophisticated data analysis (i.e., structural equation modeling). While we may want to share all the data we collected, we need to be selective due to space limitations in addition to being sensitive to the possibility of mentally overloading the reader and listener. Researchers will often discuss descriptive data in a paper or discuss them verbally in a presentation and use tables or figures for more complex data.

One suggestion is to read through previous articles and identify ones you believe are well written and use them as models. Attending conferences or professional development workshops and observing the presentations' styles and formats can also be quite helpful as these examples can give one insight into how best to communicate your results. Always keep in mind that features such as color, size of font, quantity of numbers, and complexity can impact how well the data are understood by the reader or viewer. In addition, journals may have specific requirements for formatting that should be checked beforehand. For example, many journals require authors to use the APA manual's guidelines, which indicate color should only be used when necessary. As with writing, the simpler the better when communicating data results.

Using the *Let's See It!* activity that follows, review the ways in which the previously mentioned article presents data and connects them to the research questions and/or hypotheses. In the *Let's Do It! activity*, try to identify the ways in which data are presented and how the data are connected to the research questions and/or hypotheses. At the end of the chapter, you will find a *You Do It!* exercise that relates to these other activities. We encourage you to practice independently to help you become more comfortable with connecting data with research questions and/or hypotheses.

Let's See It! 15.3

Goal: Connecting Data to the Research Questions and/or Hypotheses

Directions: Read pages 15 through 20 of the Martin et al., 2017, article listed in Table 15.7. As you read the article, try to identify the ways in which data are presented, the research questions and/or hypotheses and how the data are connected to the research questions and/or hypotheses. Take a look at Table 15.7 to see how we answered some of these questions using information from the article.

TABLE 15.7 ■ Practice Connecting Data to the Research Questions and/or Hypotheses	
Study	Martin, A. J., Burns, E. C., & Collie, R. J. (2017). ADHD, personal and interpersonal agency, and achievement: Exploring links from a social cognitive theory perspective. *Contemporary Educational Psychology, 50,* 13–22. https://doi.org/10.1016/j.cedpsych.2016.12.001

How are the data presented?	• Data are described in detail in the results section
	• There are three tables.
	   ○ Table 1 presents descriptive data (means and standard deviations, as well a factor loadings and reliability scores)
	   ○ Table 2 presents correlational information
	   ○ Table 3 presents findings from SEM (structural equation modeling)
	• There is also a two-part figure that describes the parameters for both groups of students (those with and those without ADHD diagnosis)

What are the research questions, if any?	The research questions are not clearly delineated in this study, however, on page 15, the authors describe the "aims of the present study." One can infer they are asking whether there are differences on the impact of personal agency (self-efficacy and perceived control) and interpersonal agency (relational support) on achievement among students with ADHD versus those without ADHD.
What are the hypotheses, if any?	The hypothesis is also not clearly delineated in this study. However, it appears to be that they are hypothesizing that there will be differences between the students with ADHD and those without ADHD on the impact of personal agency and interpersonal agency on achievement.
Explain Tables 1–3 and Figures 1a and 1b and how they relate to the hypotheses and/or research questions.	As discussed earlier, the complexity of the information increases as we work through the tables and figure. Table 1 begins with simple descriptive information, whereas the last table, Table 3, provides results from a sophisticated type of data analysis called *structural equation modeling*. In looking at the data presented in the tables and described in the Results section, the findings suggest: Table 1 shows that there appears to be differences across all variables between the two groups of students and that the measurement scales used were reliable. Table 2 is interesting because it shows the correlations for both groups, but each group's correlations are separated by a diagonal line (see dashes). The non-ADHD group's correlations are on the bottom left diagonal, and the ADHD group's correlations are on the upper right diagonal. Look for the correlations with asterisks; those correlations marked with asterisks indicate there are significant relationships between the two variables. The table shows that for the ADHD group, self-efficacy and relational support are significantly related to achievement. However, perceived control was not significantly related to achievement, whereas all three were significantly correlated for the non-ADHD group. Table 3 and Figures 1a and 1b indicate that self-efficacy and relational support show medium to large effects for the ADHD group but small effects for the non-ADHD group.
What can one infer about the hypothesis (if any) from the data found in the tables and figures?	Taken together, these findings suggest self-efficacy and relational support were associated with academic achievement for the ADHD group, more so than for the non-ADHD group. Perceived control was found to play a minor role in predicting achievement for students without ADHD and a non-significant role for students with ADHD. Therefore, the hypothesis was only partially accepted in that achievement seems to be related to self-efficacy and personal agency for students with ADHD.

Let's Do It! 15.3

Guided Practice: Identify How Data Connect to Research Questions and/or Hypotheses

Directions: Read pages 4 through 8 (method, results, and discussion) of the Bolinger et al., 2020 article listed in the following table.

As you read through these pages, try to identify the ways in which data are presented and how the data are connected to the research questions and/or hypotheses and complete Table 15.8 using the information illustrated in Table 15.7 as a guide.

TABLE 15.8 ■ Practice Connecting Data to the Research Questions and/or Hypotheses	
Study	Bolinger, S. J., Mucherah, D., Markelz, D., & Andrew, M. (2020). Teacher knowledge of attention-deficit/hyperactivity disorder and classroom management. *The Journal of Special Education Apprenticeship, 9*(1), 1–14. https://scholarworks.lib.csusb.edu/josea/vol9/iss1/5
How are the data presented?	
What are the research questions, if any?	
What are the hypotheses, if any?	
Explain how Table 1 corresponds to the hypothesis or research questions.	
Explain how Table 2 corresponds to the hypothesis or research questions.	
What can one infer about the hypothesis (if any) from the data found in Tables 1 and 2?	

Each of the articles does a nice job connecting the data to the research questions and/or hypotheses. This is an important consideration to keep in mind when communicating about your research study.

THE TAKEAWAY

When communicating about data, researchers need to be sure they link the data to the original research questions and/or hypotheses and that the results are conveyed in ways that are simple, easy to understand, and at the appropriate level of complexity given the targeted audience.

THE ROLE OF SELF-REGULATED LEARNING IN THE COMMUNICATION OF RESEARCH

LEARNING OBJECTIVE
15.4   Apply self-regulated learning to the process of communicating about research.

We have introduced and highlighted the three phases of self-regulated learning: *planning* (setting goals, plans or strategies to reach the goals, and self-efficacy or confidence beliefs), *doing* (self-observing as we record and keep track of our progress and engage in metacognitive monitoring), and *reflecting* (evaluating and reacting to one's performance) in different chapters of this book. Educators may not be aware of when they are regulating their behavior, but it is something they naturally engage in at work as they plan for the day (*planning*), make observations about themselves and others in relation to their work (*doing*), then reflect on areas for improvement (*reflecting*). In the following section, we describe how self-regulated learning can help educators prepare to communicate about their research.

STOP AND THINK 15.4

Are there times when you have used the self-regulated learning cycle of planning, doing, and reflecting without even realizing you were doing so? How was it beneficial to you in reaching your goals?

For the purpose of brevity, we will discuss recommendations relative to written forms of communication; however, these recommendations can also apply to oral communication. In Chapter 2, we outlined the sections of a research manuscript that follow the first page which lists the title, authors' names, and their affiliations: the abstract, introduction, method, results, discussion, and references. In that chapter, we also presented *Let's See It!* activities that incorporated guidance on how to conduct a literature review using the three phases of self-regulated learning: planning, doing, and reflecting. Using the three phases can help researchers accomplish the task of writing about their research, thus maximizing the probability of publishing a paper in a peer-reviewed journal. The three phases of self-regulated learning can be used to organize oneself to write the entire paper, as well as for each individual section of the paper.

Mrs. Smith and Mr. Krahl have agreed to write a paper on their research. In thinking about completing the entire paper, they realize they need to set a plan, such as when and how each section of the paper will be written, implement the plan (doing), then reflect on the paper in its entirety.

Planning, Doing, and Reflecting in Communicating About Research

Researchers have plans for how to conduct the study but often do not plan or think about writing up the result of their research until after it has been completed. We would like to recommend a different approach. We believe that the process of writing a paper for publication coincides with the process of conducting the research study.

Researchers should include their intentions for communicating research when planning to conduct research; in fact, consent letters often need to describe if and how the research will be communicated to others. Researchers, however, often make the mistake of completing the research study *and then* beginning the writing process. Self-regulated learning suggests a more effective approach is to begin writing as one is conducting the research. We may not be surprised if some of you are thinking, "What? What does that mean? Am I supposed to write about my research while conducting the research?"

Where to begin when writing can be overwhelming and anxiety provoking. There are no rules on which section to begin with, but we believe it can be beneficial to follow a particular order when writing about your research. While the completed product will have a beginning, middle, and end, it is not necessarily the best idea to proceed in that way when writing about research. We recommend planning to write about your research using the order outlined in Table 15.9.

TABLE 15.9 ■ Planning to Write a Research Paper for Publication		
Writing Order	**Section**	**When and Why?**
1	Method	This section is best written *while engaging in the research* because researchers are actively engaged with the participants, the protocol and procedure, and any instruments being used. If completed at the end of the study, one might forget about subtle but important nuances that occurred several months before the time in which the study was taking place.
2	Results (including tables, charts, and diagrams)	This section is typically *completed after the study is completed and shortly upon completion of the data analysis.* It is helpful to complete this section at this time, due to recency—it is easier to recall the analyses if they were just completed. As a reminder, the results should correspond directly to the research questions and/or hypotheses and should flow from the method section.
3	Discussion	The discussion is typically *completed after the results* section and should describe, in a narrative style the significance of the findings. Researchers will often include educational implications in this section, along with limitations of the current study and recommendations for further research.
4	Introduction	*Once the method, results, and discussion are completed, the introduction section should be easy to write.* Remember, we discussed describing research as analogous to telling a story. In this section, authors want to "hook" the readers into understanding why their research is important. The introduction also lays the groundwork for how your research contributes to the body of knowledge and how it differs from other published research. While identifying, reviewing, and understanding the literature is essential when designing a study, this section can be fully written after you have written the previous three sections. It is imperative to clearly delineate the problem you are investigating and how your research makes a valuable contribution as these are things reviewers will look for when making decisions about whether to accept your manuscript for publication. Theoretical foundations and synthesis of research studies addressing similar issues would be described here following the presentation of the problem and your rationale for conducting the study. Toward the end of the introduction section, authors present their research questions and/or hypotheses.

Writing Order	Section	When and Why?
5	References	While you can compile your list of references when you are writing, *it is typically organized after the main sections of the paper have been written.* This section can be tedious as one needs to be careful to follow APA style. Be sure to carefully check that all citations are referenced. Most of the articles are typically cited in the introduction and discussion sections, although there can also be a few citations in the method and results sections.
6	Abstract	The Abstract is a concise paragraph describing the reason for the research, the methodology, and the outcomes and is *often written once the paper is completed* because it presents a short summary of the other sections. The Abstract can be written before the References section, but it is best to write your references while they are fresh in your mind.
7	Title Page	This page is typically written last, and its content may vary slightly depending on the journal to which you are submitting your publication. Titles can be challenging to develop, and usually once the study is written, the appropriate title will become more evident. This page often includes the names of the authors and their affiliations.

Now that Mrs. Smith and Mr. Krahl have decided to start with the method section, they are wondering if using the planning, doing, and reflecting cycle could help them with writing that section as well. In other words, they decided to set a plan for writing the method section, engage in writing this section, and reflect on their writing. Using the same format used in earlier chapters, the two teachers implement the three phases of self-regulated learning as seen in the following *Let's See It!*

Let's See It! 15.4

Goal: Use the Planning, Doing, and Reflecting Cycle of SRL for Writing the Method Section for Submission to a Publication

Mrs. Smith and Mr. Krahl plan to conduct a research study on teachers' knowledge about ADHD and their self-efficacy for effective classroom management techniques. They have received all required approvals and have a well-defined plan of how to conduct their study and analyze the data. Their study involves randomly assigning teachers to experimental (professional development) and comparison groups and then gathering information on teachers' knowledge of ADHD and self-efficacy for using effective classroom management strategies before and after the intervention.

Directions: Look at the example that follows to see how Mrs. Smith and Mr. Krahl might engage in planning, doing, and reflecting on writing and completing a manuscript about their study for publication.

From this example, using planning, doing, and reflecting can not only help researchers get organized but also minimize feeling overwhelmed about writing for submission to a professional publication.

TABLE 15.10 ■ A Model of Planning, Doing, and Reflecting in Writing About Research		
Planning	1. Setting goals 2. Feeling self-efficacious 3. Planning strategies	1. Mrs. Smith and Mr. Krahl set a goal to write about their research in a manuscript format using APA guidelines. They plan to submit the manuscript to a peer-reviewed journal within six months of completion of the study. 2. Mrs. Smith and Mr. Krahl do not feel 100% capable of conducting the research and of writing it up and getting it published, but they are willing to work together to give it a try. 3. The two teachers decide they will use the three phases of self-regulated learning for *each* of the sections of the manuscript along with a timeline for completing the writing and to begin with the method section. They also plan to begin writing *while the study is taking place* rather than waiting until the end.
Doing	1. Recording and keeping track of progress 2. Engaging in metacognitive monitoring	1. Each teacher focuses on a subsection of the method section (participants, instruments, protocol) and allots time on weekends to write. They take notes on their progress and decide to report weekly to one another as a way of keeping track. 2. Mrs. Smith and Mr. Krahl have started writing the method section of their study while the study is taking place. They notice that writing is coming easier than they anticipated because everything is fresh in their minds. While getting the content written is easy to do, the teachers realize as they read each other's drafts that it is challenging to take into account the considerations described earlier in this chapter when writing. They also notice that each of them has a different "tone" when writing.
Reflecting	1. Thinking about what worked well and 2. What needs to be changed to make things better?	1. Mrs. Smith and Mr. Krahl really like the idea of writing the method section while implementing the study. They also think that breaking down the individual subsections helped with the workload. They also are beginning to feel more self-efficacious in their capability to continue with the research study and the writing. 2. Mrs. Smith and Mr. Krahl decide to spend a Saturday afternoon together to review each other's feedback and to collaborate on getting one tone. They also decide that as they continue working on the manuscript, they will meet more often to review each other's feedback rather than wait until the entire section is completed. 3. The teachers plan to follow a similar cycle when writing the remaining portions of the manuscript. They agree that they will focus next on the results section, which they plan to start as soon as they have completed the data analysis.

Using the *Let's Do It!* activity that follows, practice how to apply the three phases of self-regulated learning—*planning, doing,* and *reflecting*—for writing the method section of a research study you might consider conducting.

Let's Do It! 15.4

Guided Practice: Practice Using the Planning, Doing, and Reflecting Cycle of SRL for Writing the Method Section for Submission to a Publication

TABLE 15.11 ■ Practice Using Planning, Doing, and Reflecting in Writing About Research
Directions
Planning—Select a research topic and describe your plans (your goals, feelings of confidence or self-efficacy, and your strategies) for writing the method section of your research study in the "doing cell." What might the study look like? What type of design will you use? What procedures might you follow? Do you plan to share your research with colleagues?
Doing—How do you envision yourself keeping track of your progress? Indicate in the "doing" cell how you might record and keep track your progress. How might the feedback you receive from recording and keeping track of your performance affect your thoughts (metacognitive monitoring) about your progress?
Reflecting—When the method section is completed, in the "self-reflecting cell," describe what type of self-evaluative feedback will you look for to evaluate the effectiveness of your communication? What changes might you consider making in your plans for communicating about your research next time or in the next section you plan to write?

Planning
1. Setting goals
2. Feeling self-efficacious
3. Planning strategies

Doing
1. Recording and keeping track of progress
2. Engaging in metacognitive monitoring

Reflecting
1. Thinking about what worked well and
2. What needs to be changed to make things better

At the end of the chapter, we provide you with an opportunity to work practice independently on using the three phases of self-regulated learning to create a poster for a professional development workshop in the You Do It! activity. As with all of the activities, we strongly encourage you to take the time to complete these exercises to strengthen your understanding, skills, and self-efficacy beliefs in learning about research.

Putting It All Together

Once each section of the research paper is written, it is necessary to review the entire paper from beginning to end. This phase of the writing process represents an opportunity for the authors to make corrections and edits, as well as any necessary revisions. Making changes to a paper are likely to occur after the completion of each section and again following the combination of all sections into one paper. Recall we have suggested the publication should be like a story. Once all the components are complete, the manuscript should be read through thoroughly to ensure there is a beginning, middle, and end and that it flows.

Authors must be extremely careful not to plagiarize. This is particularly important when writing the introduction and discussion sections, as those are typically the parts of the paper where authors will summarize others' work and use many citations. Authors must also cite themselves if they have previously published articles or research in which they are referencing. The results section can often be the most challenging section to write because authors are attempting to succinctly describe the analyses conducted in a manner that makes it easy for readers to comprehend. It is also the section where visual representations of data are usually presented, and creating diagrams, charts, and tables can be extremely time consuming. Chapter 2 provides additional details on the content of each of these sections of a published manuscript. Next, we emphasize the importance of ethical issues in communicating your research followed by the importance of following APA guidelines in written and oral communication.

THE TAKEAWAY

The cycle of planning, doing, and reflecting should be used with each section of the research paper.

ETHICAL CONSIDERATIONS

LEARNING OBJECTIVE

15.5   Demonstrate knowledge of ethical issues in communicating research.

Ethical issues are critical to consider when conducting research and when communicating research results. Earlier we discussed intentionality in the context of deciding who is the audience. There is also a more subtle association of the word intentionality, such as to intentionally communicate research in an ethical manner. In fact, the United States Public Health Service Commissioned Corps (USPHS), a governing agency, provides codes of ethical behavior for conducting and communicating research. According to the USPHS, research misconduct is considered the "fabrication, falsification, or plagiarism in proposing, performing, or reviewing research, or in reporting research results" (United States Department of Health and Human Services, 2005). In Table 15.12, we define several terms related to ethics in communicating research. In the far-right column, we provide examples of how Mrs. Smith and Mr. Krahl were careful not to breach ethical issues associated with these terms in their communication of their study.

Ethically communicating one's research study can be easy to do when keeping these key ethical issues in mind. They are necessary, not just for legal reasons but to ensure the integrity and honesty of the research. Following, we provide some advice on using the *Publication Manual of the American Psychological Association's* guidelines for communicating your research.

TABLE 15.12 ■ Ethical Issues in Communicating Research		
Ethical Issues	**Definitions**	**Applications**
Fabrication	Making up information such as data and results.	Mrs. Smith and Mr. Krahl did not obtain all of the results they were hoping for but decided to present their results as they were. They had heard stories in the past about how researchers might "embellish" their findings so that the hypotheses were met, but they knew that was wrong.
Falsification	Manipulating, misrepresenting data, omitting, or changing results so that the results do not accurately reflect the research findings.	Mrs. Smith and Mr. Krahl found that teachers' self-efficacy did not change after the intervention. Though disappointing, they realized they needed to report these results and try to explain why there may have been no change.
Plagiarism	Presenting someone else's work as your own without acknowledging them or without their consent.	Mrs. Smith and Mr. Krahl were careful to use their own words in the introduction and discussion sections of the paper and to use citations and quotation marks where needed.
Copyright Violations	Copyrighting laws protect the intellectual property rights of others. Directly copying tables or diagrams from others and using them in your paper without seeking permission can be a violation of copyright laws.	Mrs. Smith and Mr. Krahl saw a diagram in a published paper they thought would be helpful to use as part of their introduction. They contacted the author and requested permission to use the diagram and agreed to provide an acknowledgment of who the true author was in the paper.
Confidentiality	Collecting information about participants that only you, as researchers, can link to the individual participants and not sharing that information with others.	Mrs. Smith and Mr. Krahl collected surveys from teachers in their schools and aggregated all of the responses for their analysis. They did not write about any individual responses or provide any information linking a teacher's response to their name even though they were able to identify who completed which survey.
Anonymity	Collecting information about participants that does not include personal identifiers (such as names, social security numbers, emails) or not being able to link participant responses to their identity.	Mrs. Smith and Mr. Krahl provided randomly assigned numeric identifiers to each of the participants. They did not know which responses belonged to which teacher and were only able to refer to each survey based on the numeric identifier.

(Continued)

TABLE 15.12 ■ Ethical Issues in Communicating Research (*Continued*)		
Ethical Issues	**Definitions**	**Applications**
Purpose	The reason for conducting and communicating about research (i.e., for the purpose of advancing a body of knowledge).	Mrs. Smith and Mr. Krahl have a genuine concern about improving behavior management strategies in the classroom. They conducted a thorough literature review and did not find any studies similar to their own. Their goal is to not only improve their own practice but to provide insight to other educators struggling with similar issues.
Accuracy (in reporting research data)	Using caution and avoiding carelessness in analyzing and reporting data; it also involves not making sweeping statements or inappropriate generalizations.	Mrs. Smith and Mr. Krahl kept careful records of the protocol and measures. They checked each other's work and conducted their analyses a few times to ensure accuracy.
Openness	As contributors to knowledge, researchers should be prepared to share their instruments or additional information when inquiries are made; researchers should also be willing to receive constructive feedback.	Mrs. Smith and Mr. Krahl included an appendix in their paper, which contained the surveys used and information about the professional development training workshops. They also recognized the importance of feedback to ensure the information provided is accurate and complete.

THE TAKEAWAY

Ethical issues should be considered throughout a research study, including communicating about the research.

AMERICAN PSYCHOLOGICAL ASSOCIATION STYLE

LEARNING OBJECTIVE

15.6   Utilize the *Publication Manual of the American Psychological Association* in reporting and presenting research.

We have emphasized using the latest *Publication Manual of the American Psychological Association's* (APA) throughout this book. APA tends to publish an updated version of its guidelines every decade, and it is strongly recommended you review the latest version prior to preparing your manuscript. While these guidelines should be followed, they are in addition to the manuscript preparation guidelines specific to the journal to which you may plan to submit your paper. APA's general guidelines include double spacing all sections, using size 12 Times New Roman font, with one-inch margins on the sides, top, and bottom. In Table 15.13, we provide a general overview of several key features of each section, following the order we previously recommended (See Table 15.9) of which section to complete first.

TABLE 15.13 ■ APA Style Guidelines for Writing About Research			
Writing Order	Actual Order in Manuscript	Section	APA Style Guidelines
1	4	Method	The word "Method" is centered and bolded	• Subheadings: "Participants," "Materials," "Variables," "Measurement Tools," and "Procedure" are typically used • Subheadings are flushed left and bolded
2	5	Results	The word "Results" is centered and bolded	• Include tables, charts, and diagrams here • Describe the data analysis conducted • Include descriptive statistics • Relate analyses and conclusions to the research questions and/or hypotheses. Check APA manual's for guidelines on: • Formatting titles (i.e., tables versus graphs) • Reporting correlations, p-values, and other results within the written text
3	6	Discussion	The word "Discussion" is centered and bolded	• Discuss the analysis and relate it to the literature review discussed in the introduction section • Often includes the subsections: limitations, educational implications, and recommendations for future research. These subsections would be bolded and flushed left Check APA's manual for guidelines on in-text citations. Note: the procedure for citations applies to any section of the manuscript when citations are made
4	3	Introduction	There is typically no heading or title for this section, rather authors begin with the nature of the problem and the rationale for the current study	• After introducing the topic and rationale for your study, authors summarize theoretical foundations and synthesize research to date • Research questions and/or hypotheses should flow from the previous descriptions and should be close to the end of this section

(Continued)

TABLE 15.13 ■ APA Style Guidelines for Writing About Research (*Continued*)

Writing Order	Actual Order in Manuscript	Section	APA Style Guidelines	
5	7	References	The word "References" is centered and bolded	• References are listed in alphabetical order with the last name flushed left and the second line indented • These are also double-spaced • Authors with multiple references should be listed in chronological order Check APA's manual for titles of articles, books, chapters, government reports, conference presentations, and internet resources
6	2	Abstract	The word "Abstract" is typically centered and bolded	• The abstract is typically limited to typically about 120 words, but this varies based on journal stipulations • Include the critical issue studied, an overview of the method, results, and discussion • The abstract is written as a paragraph and in block formatting and it follows the title page
7	1	Title Page, Running Head, & Numbering		• **Running head:** This is an abbreviation of the title and should appear on the left side in the header; it is in all capital letters and should appear on every page of the manuscript. • **Page numbering:** Using the automatic page numbering in Microsoft Word, the title page is page number 1. Numbers should appear on the right side in the header on the same line as the running head. • **Title:** The title should be placed three to four lines from the top. It should be centered and bolded with the major words capitalized. Titles should be succinct and convey the research as clearly as possible. • **Authors names:** Authors need to decide who will be listed first. Usually, the ranking is based on contributions to the study. Names should be centered and on their own line. Professional affiliations (school names, for example) should be listed under each author's name.

Clearly, there are many little details involved in preparing a manuscript for publication. Similarly, while poster presentations can be a fun and creative way to share your research with others, there are specific recommendations one should consider implementing to ensure the poster is easy to read and follow. Unlike preparing a manuscript for publication, however, there is no specific "order" for completing the poster, but there are strongly suggested recommendations based on formatting.

Posters can be easily created using PowerPoint or other software programs such as Adobe Illustrator, Photoshop, and Indesign. Research posters summarize the research and are typically presented in a similar, organized way as a written paper and can consist of tables, graphs, pictures, and anonymous quotes from case studies or participants in addition to text. The APA publication manual's recommendations on the various sections to include on the poster and how to use citations and references should be followed as much as possible when creating posters, although, unlike manuscripts written with the intention for submission to a journal, colorful images and tables and graphs can be used to grab the interest of viewers. Table 15.14 presents recommended guidelines for developing research posters that can be helpful.

TABLE 15.14 ■ Guidelines for Creating Research Posters

White space is a good thing!	Posters should not be cluttered with too much text or data making them difficult to read.
Use a large font	As a rule, viewers should be able to read your poster from about 10 feet away.
Minimize details and be selective on color choice	Always keep the audience in mind when developing posters. Too many details and a variety of colors can overload readers. Keep details focused on the main points and use only two to three colors.
Word count should be 300–800 words	The content should be succinct and used as a "conversation starter." Carefully wording your research can help you grab the reader's attention and give you an opportunity to conversationally describe you study in more detail.
Include tables, charts, graphs, pictures, and anonymous quotes from case studies or participants	Including these items can help make your poster standout while succinctly providing readers with key information. Follow APA's manual for guidelines on formatting, although using colors in moderation can be helpful in grabbing viewers' interest.
Create a title that can grab readers' interest	Create a title that is short but can catch a readers' attention. You want viewers to stop and read your poster. Oftentimes, the first thing viewers will look at it is your title. They will then make a quick decision about whether to stop and read some more or to move on to the next poster.
Include your name, title, and professional affiliation	Viewers may ask you for additional information, and this is an opportunity for you to provide them with your contact information so that they can reach you at a later time for a more in-depth discussion of your research.
Summarize the purpose, participants, methodology, and results	This is the tricky part because you need to be concise due to limited space. Researchers will often use textboxes that are placed on the poster in a way that has a logical flow. It is recommended that textboxes have about 10 sentences within them—enough of a description to highlight the main points and to spark a viewer's interest.
Include headings	Including headings such as "Introduction," "Methodology," "Participants," "Instruments," "Results," and "Discussion" creates a flow and makes it easier for readers to follow along.
Bullet points are helpful	Using bullet points can help readers easily identify the key elements of your research.
Include definitions	Define terminology that readers may not be familiar with to help them better understand your research.
Use formatting tricks	Formatting tricks such as single-spacing text, using bold and larger fonts for headings, using italics rather than underlining, and placing items symmetrically on the poster can help with the clarity of the poster and the "eye appeal" as viewers walk by your poster and become curious enough to want to learn more about your research."

In sum, it is highly recommended that researchers obtain a copy of the latest *Publication Manual of the American Psychological Association* and become familiar with the guidelines prior to beginning to write a manuscript for publication or preparing a poster for a presentation at a conference or other professional forum. Doing so will help researchers not only be organized and prepared for the communication of their research but will also save time!

THE TAKEAWAY

The Publication Manual of the American Psychological Association should be consulted for all methods of communication of research.

CHAPTER SUMMARY

The purpose of this chapter was to provide researchers with information on how to effectively communicate research in written or oral form. We presented information on the importance of communicating research and how communicating about your research should be an integral part of the research proposal and plans. We discussed the necessity to link the data to the research questions and/or hypotheses when communicating about research, the importance of audience awareness, and how the self-regulated learning cycle of planning, doing, and reflecting can be used to help researchers effectively work through and complete the communication process. Lastly, as in the preceding chapters, we described critical ethical issues that can arise in communicating about research and the role of the APA publication manual in helping educators write and report research.

EXTENSION ACTIVITIES

You Do It! 15.1
Self-Directed Practice: Identify the Intended Audience From Two Abstracts

Directions: Find an educational research article that targets practitioners and one that targets researchers. Pay careful attention to how each abstract is written and see if you can identify clues as to how the abstracts seem to be targeting a particular audience. After reading the abstracts, write a brief explanation of each of them and describe the clues that helped you identify the target audience.

You Do It! 15.2
Self-Directed Practice: Identify the Audience Awareness Characteristics in an Abstract

Directions: Using the two abstracts found for the *You Do It!* 15.1, read the introductory sentence from each abstract and pay careful attention to the tone, vocabulary, conciseness, and clarity used in the introductory sentence. Complete the table that follows, identifying the qualities of the characteristics that help determine the targeted audience.

Study #1 Practitioner

Introductory Sentence

Characteristics	Evidence
Tone	
Vocabulary	
Conciseness	
Clarity	

Study #2 Researcher/Scientist

Introductory Sentence

Characteristics	Evidence
Tone	
Vocabulary	
Conciseness	
Clarity	

You Do It! 15.3

Self-Directed Practice: Identify How to Connect Data to the Research Questions and/or Hypotheses

Directions: Find a peer-reviewed article on a topic of your choice in education and identify the ways the data are connected to the research questions and/or hypotheses. Describe this information in the table that follows.

Study	
How are the data presented?	
What are the research questions, if any?	
What is the hypotheses, if any?	

(Continued)

(*Continued*)

Table 1?

Table 2?

Figure 1?

Figure 2?

What can one infer
about the research
questions and/or
hypotheses from
the data?

If your article has more than two tables or figures, add more rows as needed.

You Do It! 15.4

Self-Directed Practice: Use the Planning, Doing, and Reflecting Cycle of SRL to Communicate Research

Directions: You have been asked by the principal to speak for 15 minutes at a professional development workshop for teachers. The principal wants you to design a poster presentation on the research study conducted in the following article and to include all components of a research article (title, introduction, method, results, discussion, references) in your slides.

Review the article and complete the table that follows on preparing the poster for your presentation.

Planning—What are your goals for working on the poster? Do you feel self-efficacious to create a professional poster? What strategies will you employ to prepare and complete the poster?

Doing—How do you envision yourself keeping track of your progress? Indicate in the "doing" cell how you might record and keep track your progress. How might the feedback you receive from observing and monitoring yourself affect your thoughts about your progress (metacognition)?

Reflecting—When the communication is completed, in the "self-reflecting cell," what type of self-evaluative feedback will you look for from the principal, your colleagues, and yourself to evaluate the effectiveness of your communication? What changes might you consider making in your plans for communicating about your research next time or in the next section you plan to write?

Study	DiBenedetto, M. K., & Zimmerman, B. J. (2010). Differences in self-regulatory processes among students studying science: A microanalytic investigation. *The International Journal of Educational and Psychological Assessment, 5*(1), 2–24.
Planning	1. Setting goals 2. Feeling self-efficacious 3. Planning strategies
Doing	1. Recording and keeping track of progress 2. Engaging in metacognitive monitoring
Reflecting	1. Thinking about what worked well 2. Thinking about what needs to be changed to make things better

KEY TERMS

Accuracy (in reporting research data)
Anonymity
Audience awareness
Clarity
Conciseness
Confidentiality
Copyright violations
Data
Fabrication
Falsification

Grants
Intentionality
Openness
Oral communication
Plagiarism
Publishing
Purpose
Research misconduct
Tone
Written communication

ANSWER KEY

Stop and Think Activities

STOP AND THINK 15.1

Responses may vary; however, we would like to emphasize the importance of sharing your research with others. Even when research studies do not have the outcomes that we expected or hoped for, the information obtained from research can be useful to others in conducting future research or in problem-solving solutions to critical issues of practice.

STOP AND THINK 15.2

While responses will likely vary, educators should consider the initial purpose for conducting research as that might help them decide whether they want to submit a paper for publication in a journal or present their research at a conference or a combination of both.

STOP AND THINK 15.3

Researchers should take into account the characteristics of audience awareness, such as tone, vocabulary, conciseness, and clarity, as well as any specific guidelines provided by the journal.

STOP AND THINK 15.4

Responses will vary but may include a variety of daily activities. For example, teachers plan when they prepare lesson plans, counselors plan when they prepare for their sessions, and principals plan when they prepare agendas for meetings. Educators are constantly monitoring their performance (doing) and reflecting on outcomes. When encountering critical issues, it is particularly important to use the three phases of self-regulated learning as it can help educators define and refine their goals and plans, monitor their performance, and reflect on the outcomes and potential solutions to problem-solving.

Let's Do It! Activities
LET'S DO IT! 15.1
Practice Identifying the Intended Audience From an Abstract

Study	Bolinger, S. J., Mucherah, D., Markelz, D., & Andrew, M. (2020). Teacher knowledge of attention-deficit/hyperactivity disorder and classroom management. *The Journal of Special Education Apprenticeship, 9*(1), 1–14. https://scholarworks.lib.csusb.edu/josea/v019/iss1/5

Explanation of Audience

Use these questions to help guide your response:

- *Who is the intended audience?*
    The intended audience are general education teachers and special education teachers as well as anyone interested in understanding the relationship between ADHD and classroom management.

- *What components (or clues) help you identify the intended audience?*

The abstract begins by indicating there is limited research on teacher knowledge of ADHD and classroom management and by suggesting there may be a relationship between the two. The abstract indicates that the study showed a little more than half the teachers in the sample were knowledgeable about ADHD and that they found no relationship between knowledge and classroom management. The topic of classroom management is an important topic for educators and one that many teachers struggle with; therefore, one can presume the target audience was teachers of students diagnosed with ADHD.

LET'S DO IT! 15.2
Practice Identifying the Audience Awareness Characteristics in an Abstract
Practice Identifying Characteristics of Audience Awareness

Study	Bolinger, S. J., Mucherah, D., Markelz, D., & Andrew, M. (2020). Teacher knowledge of attention-deficit/hyperactivity disorder and classroom management. *The Journal of Special Education Apprenticeship, 9*(1), 1–14. https://scholarworks.lib.csusb.edu/josea/v019/iss1/5

Introductory Sentence

There is limited research on teacher knowledge of attention deficit hyperactivity disorder (ADHD) and classroom management; however, research suggests that teacher knowledge of ADHD influences teaching behaviors.

Characteristics	Qualities of the characteristics that help us determine the targeted audience
Voice	Formal but geared more toward practitioners
Vocabulary	Several terms associated with classroom practice: *classroom management, teacher knowledge,* and *influences* (of) *teaching behaviors*

Conciseness	Word count = 27
Clarity	Message is clear to educators that the article examines teacher knowledge of ADHD and teacher classroom management behaviors

Let's Do It! 15.3

Practice Connecting Data to the Research Questions and/or Hypotheses

Study	Bolinger, S. J., Mucherah, D., Markelz, D., & Andrew, M. (2020). Teacher knowledge of attention-deficit/hyperactivity disorder and classroom management. *The Journal of Special Education Apprenticeship, 9*(1), 1–14. https://scholarworks.lib.csusb.edu/josea/v019/iss1/5
How are the data presented?	The data are presented primarily in two tables. Table 1 shows means and standard deviations, while Table 2 shows correlations. Data are also described within the text in the results section.
What are the research questions?	1. To what extent are teachers knowledgeable about ADHD? 2. Does knowledge of ADHD impact self-reported management skills?
What is the hypothesis, if any?	Teachers with a higher level of knowledge of ADHD will be more likely to implement classroom management strategies that support students with ADHD and more frequently use procedures for appropriate social and academic behavior.
Explain how Table 1 corresponds to the research questions and/or hypotheses.	Table 1 presents means and standard deviations based on the participants' responses to the survey. The results correspond with the first research question on how knowledgeable the teachers are about ADHD.
Explain how Table 2 corresponds to the research questions/ and or hypotheses.	Table 2 is an interesting table. Notice the authors present the variables (knowledge of ADHD and classroom management) across the top and again in the first column. Each of these variables has different categories: ADHD has the same three categories presented in Table 1. In addition to those, Table 2 has the two categories of Classroom Management: Proactive or Negative Classroom Management and shows correlations. Each of these variables and categories is presented across the top and on the left column, but you will see that *only half the table has numbers.* That is because if you put a diagonal line from one corner of the table down to the other corner, the numbers would be identical; therefore, the protocol is to place dashes in those cells. What does Table 2 tell readers about the second research question? Here the authors are presenting correlations. You may recall that correlations show relationships among variables, and the asterisks indicate whether there is a "significant" relationship or whether the relationship may just be by chance. Notice some of the correlations are positive with asterisks, others are negative with asterisks, and others have no asterisk. The row in the table that is most relevant to the second research question is the row that indicates Proactive Classroom Management. If you look across that row, you will see that none of the correlations have asterisks, which implies there is no relationship between knowledge of ADHD and proactive classroom management techniques.
What can one infer about the hypothesis from the data found in Tables 1 and 2?	This study does NOT support the hypotheses, and we can tell this by looking at the data in the tables. On average, teacher participants scored correctly on a little over 61% of the items on the survey (See Table 1), suggesting that these participants were somewhat knowledgeable about ADHD—however, this knowledge does not seem to relate to classroom management techniques (See Table 2). Therefore, the study does NOT support the hypothesis.

Practice Using the Planning, Doing, and Reflecting Cycle of SRL to Communicate Research

Responses vary for this activity; however, educators can model their responses using the example provided in the *Let's See It!* activity. The three phases of self-regulated learning can serve as a template for planning, doing, and reflecting on their communication of research. This cyclical model of planning, doing, and reflecting can be implemented across many tasks to assist educators in successfully accomplishing their goals.

16 USING RESEARCH TO GUIDE PRACTICE

A DAY AT WORK

Immigrants in a New School: A Place of Learning for All Students

©iStockphoto.com/Ridofranz

Second-grade teacher Mrs. Toddle recently spoke to Principal Anne Chandler about Ali, who recently immigrated to the United States and was just placed in her class. Ali's family did not know his grade level because he did not attend school in Iran, his home country. He does not speak, read, or write in English. As a result, he seems lost and unable to keep up with the day's schedule. Mrs. Toddle felt unsure of how to help Ali succeed in her class and asked Principal Chandler for guidance.

In the same school, fourth-grade teacher Mr. Eklund seemed flustered when he met with Assistant Principal Mark Harris. He explained that Nazanin, an immigrant from Afghanistan, spontaneously runs out of the classroom screaming the word "HOME!" in Dari, her native language. Mr. Eklund is worried about Nazanin's safety and well-being as well as the disruptions she is causing in class.

These two scenarios, coupled with concerns expressed by other faculty and staff, have left the principal and assistant principal feeling confused and unsure about how to deal with the unexpected enrollment of children whose families immigrated from the Middle East. To engage in effective problem-solving, Principal Chandler and Assistant Principal Harris decided to call a "special meeting" with all school personnel, but what will they focus on so that the meeting is productive?

INTRODUCTION

Principal Chandler and Assistant Principal Harris have their hands full. Their school is in a small rural community where most families are white with limited education. Many of the children new to the school are part of the American Refugee Resettlement Program, and schools across the United States are grappling with ways to help recent immigrant children learn successfully. In this chapter, we focus on the power of research to guide and improve practice—practice that can be within the classroom as well as beyond. We begin by describing the interdependent relationship between research and practice, followed by guidelines on how to evaluate research to ensure its quality and potential applicability. We then describe the uses of research for educators, administrators, the community, and policymakers. Next, we discuss the influence of research on higher education programs and professional and personal growth. In the next section, we provide an example of how to apply self-regulated learning based on a prior research study. Lastly, as with previous chapters in this book, we discuss the critical role of ethics and the importance of using the *Publication Manual of the American Psychological Association* (APA) in applications of practice.

CONNECTING RESEARCH WITH PRACTICE

LEARNING OBJECTIVE
16.1   Connect research with practice.

The link between research and practice may seem obvious yet many educators experience a disconnect between research and its application, even though information from many research studies are readily accessible or available globally. Most journals have several volumes (i.e., number of years the journal has been in circulation), and issues (i.e., the number of times that journal is published in a given year). Each issue typically includes several articles that are often focused on a theme. For example, the journal *Research in the Teaching of English* (*RTE*) of the National Council of Teachers of English, is published four times a year, and each issue typically presents research articles focused on a particular topic.

As an alternative to conducting your own research, conducting a review of the research literature can help you better understand an education-related problem and help you identify potential solutions that could be applied in your school. Universities provide educators and researchers access to research databases that include scholarly publications in hundreds of journals from around the world. Educators, who are not affiliated with universities, may search through open-access journals and their school libraries as well as through Google Scholar, which provides many articles for free. The idea of implementing research to guide one's own work is often called evidence-based practice. Evidence-based practice refers to identifying and evaluating scientific evidence, such as from an experimental study, to determine its application to a current problem. Using evidence-based practice can assist educators in improving the quality of instruction, decision making, and other professional-based practices.

After conducting an initial literature review (see Chapter 2), you may find some articles that appear relevant to your topic of interest. You can take it a step further by searching the journal's table of contents on a computer database to see if there are additional articles that might be more directly applicable to the critical issue or problem in schools that you wish to address. Following, we provide an example of how the table of contents in a journal may provide additional studies and articles to review in the *Let's See It!* activity. Upon reviewing this activity, take a moment to practice using the *Let's Do It!* exercise.

Let's See It! 16.1

Goal: Understand How to Use Peer-Reviewed Research Articles and Journals to Find Additional Relevant Studies That Can Guide Practice

TABLE 16.1 ■ Demonstration of Searching a Journal's Table of Contents for Relevant Articles	
Directions: Step 1	Dr. Chandler from our opening scenario has decided to conduct research on teaching English to students from families who have migrated to the United States and came across the article that follows. Notice how she listed the journal name, year of publication, volume number, and issue.
Study	Alefesha, H. M. N., & Al-Jam, D. A. H. (2019). Syrian refugees' challenges and problems learning and teaching English as a foreign language (EFL): Jordan as an example. *Journal of Ethnic and Cultural Studies*, 6(1), 117–129.
Journal Name:	*Journal of Ethnic and Cultural Studies*
Year	2019
Volume	6
Issue	1
Directions: Step 2	Dr. Chandler then wanted to examine the entire volume to see if there are other articles that might be helpful, so she searched through a database and pulled up the entire journal. She then reviewed the table of contents to determine if there were any relevant articles. Following is a screenshot of a few articles listed in the table of contents from the preceding journal that she thought might be beneficial.

Let's Do It! 16.1

Guided Practice: Understand How to Use Peer-Reviewed Research Articles and Journals to Find Additional Relevant Studies That Can Guide Practice

TABLE 16.2 ■ Practice Searching a Journal's Table of Contents for Relevant Articles	
Directions: Step 1	Identify a critical issue in education that you would like to address. Search for a research study that examined this topic and complete the table that follows:
Critical Issue	
Study	
Journal Name	
Year	
Volume	
Issue	
Directions: Step 2	Search the journal's table of contents and screenshot some relevant articles and paste in the box that follows:

At the end of this chapter, we provide a *You Do It!* activity to help you see how searching through the references list of a research article can be a helpful strategy for identifying research studies that can be applied to practice. In the next section, we discuss using previously published research to help improve practice.

Using the Research of Others to Guide Your Research and Ultimately Improve Practice

Implementing recommendations from research studies can be beneficial to educators in many ways. In addition to providing implications and suggestions for practice, research studies can also provide educators insight into how the researchers went about investigating and generating a solution to a critical problem. But what if the research is somewhat relevant to a critical problem or issue but does not entirely match the same issues one is grappling with? For example, in an action research study that was conducted in Quebec, four teachers implemented the planning, doing, and reflecting model of action research (see Chapter 8) to teach students for whom English was a second language (Lau et al., 2020). In this study, they offered French and ESL classes designed to support immigrant students' bilingual learning and found that explicitly teaching strategies for reading and writing were beneficial in that they were transferable across languages. While this study may be helpful to educators who have students who are being taught two languages simultaneously, it may not necessarily be beneficial for English language learners who are in schools where they are not being taught two languages at the same time. Educators who plan to conduct research may choose then to modify elements of this study to conduct research that meets their specific interests and school's needs.

Research studies can provide educators with useful information for planning and conducting their own research study to address issues specific to a work situation. If Principal Chandler and Assistant Principal Harris wanted to discuss with colleagues the idea of conducting research on the implementation of a program they read about in published studies, they could adopt the program procedures used in prior studies or they can make modifications that are more appropriate for their students, faculty, staff, and school mission. Regardless of whether they use the precise procedures reported in a research study or slightly modified the program, they are replicating previous research. Replication of research refers to attempting to duplicate the original study.

There are two types of replication studies: exact replication or conceptual replication. Exact replication refers to duplicating a previously published study using the same number and types of participants, methodology, instruments, and analyses. Researchers may conduct an exact replication to check for validity of the results from the study (i.e., confirm that the interpretations for the original and subsequent studies are the same) before applying the study's recommendations at work. For instance, high school counselors may want to replicate a qualitative research study on the uses of therapeutic pets in school to reduce anxiety among students who experienced personal trauma. Having found a study that uses participants from a similar school, they repeat the study following the methodology as outlined in the published study. The counselors may want to conduct a pilot study replicating this research before conducting the study and implementing a long-term program in their school to ensure the validity of the conclusions that the program is effective.

STOP AND THINK 16.1

Have you ever done something exactly the same way as someone else because you wanted to see if you would get the same outcomes? For example, if a speech therapist tested children's use and understanding of directions, would you expect to get the same outcomes if you replicated this study and if so, why?

Conceptual replication refers to repeating the original study but making minor changes to procedures, such as using student participants who are a different age from those in the original study. Researchers may replicate a study while also making some modifications to the methodology or statistical analysis. Conceptual replications of previous research studies are common if changes are made to the study that advance a body of knowledge on the topic. Most published journal articles will include subsections in the discussion section labeled "limitations of the study" and "suggestions for future research." These subsections often provide recommendations for future researchers. For instance, if a study has shown that allowing second-grade students to have an additional 20 minutes of recess during the day leads to higher achievement on spelling test scores, the authors may want to point out that future research should explore whether the same approach works equally well for sixth graders. If this replication leads to similar results, then the findings from the original study will have greater validity and generalizability to older students.

Whether researchers choose to conduct an exact or conceptual replication, it is common for them to encounter challenges. In some situations, researchers may conduct an exact replication of a study and find they do not obtain the same results as those found in the original study. This is referred to as the replication crisis and can result from something being amiss in the original study, such as falsified or skewed data, poor or inappropriate data analyses, or biases in reporting and interpreting findings. However, a difference in results across studies may also provide nuance to the original findings, such that a given research finding depends on or varies across different samples, settings, or cultures. Another challenge in replication research is not being able to obtain specific information from the original study, such as gaining access to the full protocol, data collection instruments, and methodology. This can be especially difficult when the research was conducted several years ago or if the original authors do not wish to share their materials.

Even with these challenges, replication studies are important because they help to build directly on prior research and can serve as an exemplar or model for other researchers to follow. This can not only save time but also offer opportunities for educators to think about how conducting their own research study can lead to results that can offer guidance in making important decisions regarding current issues at work.

Benefits of Using Research for Yourself and Your Community to Improve Practice

There are many benefits of using research as a foundation for improving education and practice. As a researcher, you can expand your professional network to include other research-minded educators, whether at the local, national, and global levels. This sharing of problems and ideas can spark new ways of viewing a situation, lead to productive changes, and increase professional growth among educators. In preparation for the meeting with school staff about the recent surge in immigration in her school, Principal Chandler called a colleague who lives and works as a principal in a school in central Nebraska. Through email exchanges, Principal Chandler learned that her colleague's school has also received a recent influx of students who are refugees and that there is existing research examining the effects of specific instructional activities for students and parents transitioning to the United States. The principal from Nebraska shared the results from a study they conducted with colleagues in their school that focused on strategies to assist the American students to be more supportive, accepting, and inclusive of their new classmates, an approach Principal Chandler had not considered. While the two principals were not working together on a research study per se, their interactions and exchange of ideas inspired them to consider a potential research collaboration and possibilities for intervention approaches.

This sharing of ideas, discussing existing research, and brainstorming about solutions to critical issues can assist educators in making informed research-based decisions. In addition, when educators who have conducted research communicate with others about research, they are spreading knowledge, learning about what others may be doing, and engaging in networking.

Communities can also benefit from research related to student learning. For instance, many public schools in low-socioeconomic communities struggle with poor student attendance and retention. In these communities, students who frequently miss school may be working or caring for siblings and loved ones. Other times, their absences could reflect engaging in negative behaviors, such as delinquency, alcohol and drug abuse, and crime. A landmark study in Michigan conducted on the cost of educating public school students revealed that schools in the Detroit school system were grossly underfunded (Augenblick et al., 2018). For example, student-to-teacher ratios were higher; teacher salaries, availability of technology, special education services, and transportation funding was lower; the availability of preschool and afterschool programs was limited; and across many other variables, the disparity between funding for high-achieving schools across the United States and Michigan was great. The research shined a light on the challenges and financial burden public schools in low-income communities experience in educating students and keeping them in their schools.

Research conducted beyond the scope of one's school and district can impact students' learning and well-being.
©iStockphoto.com/: Prostock-Studio

Research that is not specific to schools can also have a powerful and influential effect on schools and communities. In studies examining environmental justice in North Carolina, for instance, researchers have found that the location of CAFOs (Concentrated Animal Feeding Operations) tend to be in poor black communities (Berger, 2018). North Carolina is among the top producers of pork in the United States, and thus the waste from the large number of hogs in the CAFOs has become an environmental problem; the hogs' waste odors infiltrate homes and the chemicals from the hogs' wastes contaminate the drinking water. Residents in many of these communities have come down with illnesses such as cancer; heart and lung disease; emphysema; irritation of the eyes, nose, and throat; and nausea. Research has also shown that school children in these communities have higher levels of asthma and wheezing, likely leading to increased absences in school compared to children attending schools further away. While the Michigan and the North Carolina research studies were conducted using a much wider lens than conducting a research study in one's classroom or principals collaborating to conduct a district-wide study, one can see that research findings may reveal information related to the education, well-being, and lives of the students in our schools and communities.

STOP AND THINK 16.2

Is there a research topic that you are interested in that can have an impact on practice in multiple schools and communities?

Collaborating on Research to Improve Professional Practice

Researchers will often collaborate, or work together, on a research study. Research collaborations can have many benefits for educators and administrators. We briefly discuss four benefits that impact practice for these professionals: expanding personal and professional expertise, learning from others, strengthening communication skills, and enhancing buy-in from others. Research that involves a diverse and collaborative team often brings together individuals with different and unique areas of expertise. Principal Chandler has administrative expertise and knowledge about her student body, staff, and the local community. She may want to conduct a research study with someone from a university with expertise in qualitative research. In this situation, Principal Chandler could collaborate on a research study that involves observing and interviewing students in her school and local community and therefore, wants to also invite someone with expertise on Middle Eastern cultures. With the use of the internet and availability of resources throughout the world, the opportunities are endless and therefore depend to some degree on several factors, such as the intent, cost, and time constraints for conducting the research.

Collaborating with others provides educators and researchers alike with the added opportunity of learning from others with different perspectives. As we previously mentioned, Principal Chandler's phone call to a colleague provided a different perspective to consider in problem-solving about the emergent and critical issue in her school. She learned that her colleague focused on promoting inclusiveness and acceptance by working with the American students in addition to trying different instructional approaches. Listening to the perspectives of others can provide educators with unexpected ideas and solutions to problems they would not have thought about otherwise. It also enhances one's communication skills.

When we involve multiple collaborators in our research, we need to keep in mind how to properly and effectively communicate ideas to others with less-developed or different expertise (see Chapter 15). A statistician who is discussing the statistical analyses to be used in your collaborative research study should do so in a way that helps you understand how the data will be analyzed without using unfamiliar statistical jargon. In addition, when you discuss a problem of practice with someone unfamiliar with your school, you need to do so in a way that will help your collaborators understand the issue.

STOP AND THINK 16.3

If you were to create a research study, who might you invite to collaborate with? How might this collaboration help you to successfully conduct a research study and improve issues of practice?

Lastly, obtaining buy-in from your research collaborators, partners, or other personnel is necessary for you to be able to execute a planned research study. Buy-in is a term used to describe the acceptance and support of something. In large-scale research studies, there are often multiple researchers on a project. There may be university faculty, school administrators and teachers, companies or governmental organizations that are providing financial support, and local politicians who are interested in the research and its potential outcomes. Collaboratively, they contribute ideas and perspectives on the research as they work together on developing the research study, applying for funding, implementing the study, analyzing the results, communicating the research, and ultimately, implementing the findings. Obtaining buy-in can be extremely important for the implementation and success of research. If Principal Chandler decides to conduct a research study using an intervention program on her faculty and staff to promote cultural awareness and acceptance, she will likely need her superintendent's approval and the buy-in and overall openness of her colleagues to learn and change.

Creating Opportunities to Create Change and Transformations in Oneself and Others

In Chapter 8, we discussed the idea of transforming our learners when we conduct research. However, when we work with others, we can also experience a transformation that is similar to the experience of students when they work with teachers during learning. This collaborative transformation experience can greatly impact our practice. Researchers learn as they go through the process of conducting research, and often what they learn can be implemented in schools to impact change.

Research can be a powerful impetus for change.
©iStockphoto.com/Willowpix

Educational research is conducted for many reasons, but it often involves gaining a greater understanding of a critical issue, explaining a phenomenon, helping with decision making and developing solutions, or making improvements to practice. As researchers, we transform our ways of thinking and doing things through research, therefore the breadth of our work can extend beyond the participants in the research study. We learn from our research, and we can use the findings where appropriate to promote student learning or to transform students into a state that was different from where they began. However, before we can use existing research or even our own research experiences to guide practice, we need to be able to effectively evaluate the quality of the research; that is, are there research studies or research results that we should trust more than others, and how do we determine that?

THE TAKEAWAY

Collaborating with others on research can help educators improve professional practice, and when we conduct research, we can create transformations in ourselves and others.

EVALUATING THE QUALITY OF RESEARCH

LEARNING OBJECTIVE
16.2   Evaluate the quality of research.

Educators need to be good consumers of research before they implement changes or replicate a study based on prior research. In this section, we address three important questions associated with evaluating the quality of research

- What does good research look like?

- Is the research applicable to my current professional role and situation?

- What are the benefits to implementing the research findings relative to my professional role and situation?

What Constitutes "Good" Research?

During the 17th century, there were two famous astronomers, Galileo Galilei and Francesco Sizi, who disagreed on the number of planets in our solar system (Baxter & Reddy, 2006). Galileo, who had built a telescope, said he discovered new planets and moons. Francesco Sizi ridiculed Galileo's findings saying that there could only be seven planets. Sizi based his findings on the understanding that there were (a) seven windows in the head—two nostrils, two ears, two eyes, and a mouth—(b) seven known metals, and (c) seven days of the week. Sizi also declared that because Galileo's sightings were invisible to the naked eye, they had no influence on Earth and did not exist.

In this short story in astronomy history, there were two different astronomers making claims about the number of planets in our universe (a controversial subject even today!) based on their experiences, research, and conclusions. As educators, how do we distinguish good research from poor research, including our own? As researchers and consumers of research we need to evaluate research using specific *criteria*—preestablished scientific guidelines that are widely accepted in the scientific community. Using agreed-upon standard criteria is important because the conclusions made from research evidence can influence the decisions educators make, the strategies and programs they decide to implement, and their understanding of psychological development and learning.

In evaluating quantitative research, educators should look for a sound theoretical foundation, whereas in evaluating qualitative research, the role of the theoretical framework depends on whether the study involved deductive or inductive reasoning (see Chapter 14). In both quantitative and qualitative research, educators should look for the presence of systematic and objective procedures to collect data and the use of rigorous data analyses linked to the research question(s) and/or hypotheses. Educators should also examine the appropriateness of the quantitative and qualitative data analyses used, and for quantitative studies, issues related to the sample size, generalizability, effect size, and significance (also for qualitative) should also be reviewed. In quantitative research, educators should search for evidence of reliability and validity, and in qualitative research, they should search for evidence of trustworthiness and credibility. In both research methodologies, educators should look for any potential ethical issues related to the research and whether the publication has undergone a peer-review process (Margolin & Buchler, 2004). We provide more information on each of these criteria in the sections that follow.

The Role of a Theoretical Framework

In quantitative research, the theoretical framework is like the organizational structure of a story; it gives the reader critical information needed to understand a phenomenon, how different aspects of the phenomenon relate to each other, and the reasoning behind conducting the research. A theoretical or conceptual framework may be relevant in qualitative research, particularly when the researcher is using deductive reasoning; however, in qualitative research that is inductive, findings may be used to help develop a theory.

Theories do not necessarily reflect established facts. Most theories used in practice have undergone numerous and rigorous testing to ensure that they are accepted or viewed as credible within the scientific community. For instance, Principal Chandler would like to conduct a research study examining the beliefs of her faculty to effectively teach students who have migrated from the Middle East. When reviewing the literature, she finds that Bandura's (1986, 1997) social cognitive theory provides a strong foundation for understanding the importance of self-efficacy beliefs (i.e., the belief in one's capability to accomplish a task or goal) in school contexts and how these beliefs develop. Within this broader theory, Principal Chandler read about the role of modeling in observational learning. Modeling refers to a process whereby individuals learn by watching a more capable person demonstrate some behavior or way of thinking. Principal Chandler begins to wonder if the use of observational learning could somehow be incorporated into a research study. There are many other concepts discussed in Bandura's social cognitive theory that Principal Chandler thinks can be relevant to her study and that can assist her in identifying variables to frame the hypotheses. In quantitative research without a theoretical framework, research would have no foundation or initial understanding to work from.

Using a sound theoretical framework in quantitative research is useful because it can help researchers make predictions about what they expect to occur, and it can guide thinking about the specific research design to use. If a given theory suggests that English language learners who feel self-efficacious about their capability to correctly conjugate English verbs will engage in those types of tasks in a more positive way, then one would predict that students with high self-efficacy beliefs will be able to perform well on an English verb conjugation test. Using this example, when conducting a research study that is quantitative in nature, we may want to include an intervention program that builds students' competency beliefs. In sum, the theoretical framework used in research can provide insights and explanations about learning and behavior in addition to helping educators and researchers make predictions about important outcomes or how to implement changes to practice to enhance these outcomes.

In qualitative research, relating theories to the study depends on whether the study is deductive or inductive. In deductive qualitative research, researchers conduct their study using a theoretical lens or framework, whereas in inductive qualitative research, researchers may use their findings to contribute to theory development. Therefore, regardless of the research methodology, one should look for some connection to theory when evaluating the study.

STOP AND THINK 16.4

Is there a theoretical framework that you learned about in your education program that you feel has been particularly insightful and useful for practice? Please explain.

Systematic Procedures to Collect Data

When evaluating research, one must also consider the methods and instruments the researchers systematically use. Systematic refers to carrying out all procedures and methods of the study (e.g., collecting of data, interacting with the sample) in an organized, logical, and careful manner. For example, experimental designs (discussed in Chapter 5) include randomization and the use of control and experimental groups. Before collecting data, highly detailed descriptions that include how randomization will take place and the steps involved in conducting the experiment (that are adhered to across control and experimental groups) must be provided, regardless of who or how many researchers are conducting the experiment. In addition, when evaluating evidence, one must be sure the measures selected were appropriate for the sample.

All types of quantitative and qualitative studies must convey a systematic approach whereby data collection is described in detail. This level of detail is needed so that readers of a published study can accurately and fully discern what was done in the research and how it was accomplished. Often, researchers may leave out some key information when writing the method section, which would make it difficult for readers to evaluate the quality and strength of the study.

For instance, the school social worker and school psychologist in Principal Chandler's school read about an intervention program that assisted students who are refugees transition more successfully to a new school. However, because the study did not provide specific details about the individuals who directly implemented the intervention, the ways in which it was implemented, or even the different components of the intervention, they disregarded the potential relevance of the study and continued the literature search.

Rigor of Data Analysis and Link to Research Questions and/or Hypotheses

The quality and overall rigor of data analysis procedures in quantitative research refers to the appropriate and accurate use of statistical procedures that are relevant and directly linked to the research questions and/or hypotheses. Often these statistical procedures involve technical skills and knowledge in conducting the analyses and interpreting the findings that can be difficult for readers unfamiliar with the statistical procedures to understand. In qualitative research, the data analyses and findings may lead to generating hypotheses. As with quantitative data, the procedures used to analyze and interpret the data in qualitative studies should be rigorous, systematic, and transparent.

There are several things to consider when reviewing statistical analyses in a research article, such as the appropriateness of the analyses used, sample size and generalizability, effect size and significance. While these terms have been discussed in other chapters in this book, we briefly describe why they are important when evaluating research for the potential application to your practice.

Appropriateness of the Quantitative and Qualitative Analyses Used

Several chapters in this book have introduced you to the different types of research methods, but we have only provided introductory or foundational information about data analyses. Data analyses, whether focused on quantitative or qualitative data, is often complex and requires a certain level of expertise in statistical techniques and data analyses. However, as consumers of research, it is important that we possess a general understanding of when and how quantitative statistical approaches or qualitative data analyses (e.g., coding, thematic analyses) are appropriate or not. Using the wrong statistical procedures will call into question the meaningfulness and overall accuracy of the findings. Thus, researchers who publish a study should describe the reasoning behind their use of a particular analysis and why this approach makes sense in relation to the research questions and/or hypotheses. Failure to do so can lead to others casting doubts about the validity of the claims made from the results.

Sample Size and Generalizability

The size of the sample or number of participants in the study is an important factor when evaluating research. The general rule of thumb in quantitative research is the sample size is 10% of the general population but typically not more than 1000 participants. This guideline, however, can change depending on the number of variables in the study or the complexity of the research questions and analyses. Generally speaking, studies with a greater number of variables (i.e., self-efficacy, parental educational level, achievement scores, retention) should have a larger sample size. The sample should also be representative of the population from which it was selected. In other words, the sample should exhibit similar characteristics, skills, and so forth expected in a population in order for the results in the study to generalize to that population. For example, it would be of little benefit to Principal Chandler to review a study on a new instructional program for students in marginalized populations who were born and raised in the United States when she is interested in understanding how to improve the educational transition of Middle Eastern students who have immigrated to the United States.

In qualitative research, the focus is less on generalizability and more on obtaining an understanding of human experiences within a contextualized setting; thus, within this methodology, the samples are often carefully selected based on certain criteria. A counselor in a school may be interested in understanding the effects of experiencing homelessness on a student's study and play habits and may observe and interview a student without a home over a period of time, in addition to asking the student to write in a daily diary. The data obtained are specific to this student and thus will likely not generalize to all students experiencing homelessness.

Effect Size and Significance

Effect sizes and statistical significance levels are emphasized in quantitative studies utilizing statistical analyses. Although these topics were directly addressed in Chapters 12 and 13, we want to emphasize the importance of educators considering these concepts when reading and evaluating research. As a reminder, statistical significance refers to the probability the observed results from a sample in a study occurred by chance. It reflects whether one can conclude that a correlation or observed difference is a real effect in the population In contrast, effect sizes measure the magnitude or size of associations between variables or the differences between group means. It tells us about the practical or clinical significance of the statistically significant results that were observed in quantitative research. In this way, effect size and statistical significance concepts contribute to our understanding of the rigor of the research and should be reported in the research studies you are reviewing. Effect sizes and statistical significance are important considerations when evaluating a research study and when making decisions about replicating a study or examining the effects of an intervention in your own classroom or school.

Reliability, Validity, Trustworthiness, and Credibility

Reliability and validity are critical factors to consider in your evaluation of quantitative research. Specifically, researchers are interested in demonstrating that the measures can consistently generate scores (i.e., reliability) and that the conclusions made from these scores are meaningful and accurate (i.e., validity). These studies are also concerned with making valid claims about the causal effects of intervention (i.e., internal validity) or that the observed results generalize beyond the sample used in a study (i.e., external validity). In qualitative research, researchers focus more on concepts like trustworthiness and credibility of the data that are collected. As discussed in Chapter 3, these latter concepts overlap with the terms *reliability* and *validity*. Regardless of methodology, consumers of research should look for evidence that the data and reported results are reliable, valid, trustworthy, or credible. Without this information, educators who engage in research or who are making decisions or implementing programs are doing so without all of the evidence needed.

Ethical Issues Are Addressed and Implemented

Ethical issues should be described in every research study to make readers aware of any potential negative outcomes. Educators are constantly making decisions based on what they believe to be in the best interest of their students, school, and community, and therefore, ethical issues are an essential component of an educator's decision making. When evaluating research and reflecting on whether it is something you would like to replicate or implement, you need to be aware of any potential negative consequences. Many publications will describe ethical issues within the context of the method or discussion sections of the study. As knowledgeable consumers of research, it is important for you to search through the article and to reflect and weigh-in on the ethics of the study.

Peer-Reviewed Publications

The requirement of peer review to publish scholarly work is not something to be taken lightly. When studies have undergone the peer-review process, readers can be assured the study has been evaluated by members of the scientific community with expertise on the topic and research methodology. Articles submitted to journals that require peer review undergo a thorough examination of the study and claims made by the researchers. As indicated in previous chapters, not all publications undergo peer review, but when evaluating research for the purposes of replication, decision making, or implementing change, it is highly recommended you seek publications that are published in peer-reviewed journals.

We suggest using the checklist in Table 16.3 when evaluating a research study of your choice to determine if these important factors are addressed. On the left side of the table is the list of items you should check for when evaluating a research publication; the right side is left blank for you to take notes. Following the checklist, we describe the various ways educators can use their own research or the research of others to guide practice.

Did I check this?	Question?	My Notes
	Is there a discussion about a theoretical framework or conceptual framework in relation to the research?	
	Did the researcher(s) use systematic and objective procedures to collect data?	
	Did the data appear to have been analyzed with rigor and are the analyses linked to the research questions and/or hypotheses?	
	Are the data analyses appropriate in relation to the research questions and/or hypotheses?	
	Did the researchers discuss sampling and issues of generalizability where appropriate?	
	Did the researchers discuss effect sizes and significance of the findings?	
	Is there evidence of reliability, validity, trustworthiness, and credibility of the data collected?	
	Are ethical issues addressed and implemented?	
	Did the manuscript undergo the peer-review process?	

TABLE 16.3 ■ Checklist of Criteria for Evaluating the Quality of Research

THE TAKEAWAY

Evaluating the quality of research is an essential component of conducting research and should include specific criteria depending on the methodological approach, such as the role of theoretical framework; data collection procedures; data analyses in relation to research questions/and or hypotheses; appropriateness of the analyses used; sample size, generalizability, effect size; and significance, reliability, validity, trustworthiness, and credibility; ethical issues; and peer-review.

USES OF RESEARCH FOR TEACHERS

Many teachers rely on their own observations and experiences in the classroom to make decisions related to instruction and classroom management. Informal observations can be useful and informative, especially when done over time. However, information generated from systematic and rigorous research can also assist educators in becoming more effective decision makers in schools. When educators have access to information vetted by the scientific community about child development, diversity and equity issues, instructional strategies, educational programs, healthy classroom environments, approaches to behavior management, and other education-related topics, they have greater chances of making more effective decisions. Research can provide educators with information that can be used to establish a strong rationale and justification for their decisions and the opportunity to gain insights into novel approaches that have been tested. While there are many issues teachers encounter on a regular basis, we chose to focus on three of the most common topics in which research can guide professional practice: pedagogy, problem-solving, and classroom management.

Using Research to Guide Pedagogy

Research can be a powerful tool for educators, regardless of whether they are students in a teacher education program or more experienced teachers with several years into their career. Pedagogy is defined by Merriam-Webster's online dictionary as "the art, science, or profession of teaching" (https://www.merriam-webster.com/dictionary/pedagogy). The term *art* is used in this context to describe a skill or talent. For instance, a teacher who recognizes that students in her college preparatory class feel less efficacious than students in her honors classes will likely differentiate instruction by providing assignments and activities that build self-efficacy for performing well.

Research studies conducted by you or others can inform educators about new instructional methods that have been shown to be effective relative to the developmental level of students. Research can be used to help educators understand the cognitive, psychological, social, and emotional developmental levels of the students they are teaching and to assist with lesson planning and goal setting. Research can also be used to guide curriculum and instruction that is developmentally appropriate. It is unlikely a mathematics teacher would teach first graders how to solve an algebraic problem. In algebra, students must understand that the variable x represents an unknown number, and most young students do not have the capability to understand this level of abstract reasoning.

Research can help educators by providing them with a justification for their decisions. Rather than go through a trial-and-error process or a sink-or-swim approach to teaching, teachers can rely on their own research findings or that of others on different instructional approaches that can be implemented in the classroom. Evidence-based research can provide educators with information on what has been shown to work well and why. Research can also provide teachers with insights into new and current trends in education and strategies for grappling with instructional approaches for students who have disabilities, are English language learners, recent immigrants, gifted, or struggling in one way or another.

STOP AND THINK 16.5

You are not sure why, but your students seem to be struggling to understand the current unit you are teaching. How could you locate and use existing research to help you with this dilemma?

Research can show which instructional programs promote retention and recall and are fun and enjoyable for students and themselves. Reviewing existing research studies or conducting a research study of your own gives you opportunities to use the most effective instructional approaches that can lead to better performance on classroom assignments or standardized tests. Many teachers experience anxiety around high-stakes testing (DiBenedetto & Schunk, 2022). Learning about different instructional approaches that have been shown to improve performance and enjoyment in the classroom can alleviate the pressure and stress teachers and students experience. If reading and conducting research can help teachers assist their students, then why not do it?

Using Research to Assist With Problem-Solving

As teachers, we can encounter problems daily and some are easier to solve than others. While there are numerous resources available in schools such as mentors, colleagues, and administrators, the research literature offers additional insight into problem-solving specific to one's own work-related issues. When we conduct our own research investigation, we pose research questions addressing critical issues or problems we want to solve. When we conduct research by reviewing research studies that have been published, we are seeking information from the world outside of our classroom to see how others may have addressed similar problems. For example, one of the teachers in Principal Chandler's school decided to conduct research on their own on how other schools have assisted students who are recent immigrants transition to American schools. They thought that perhaps there were some studies that might be beneficial to them when they did their lesson planning and parent-teacher conferences.

Conducting a thorough literature review or your own research study can be a powerful way to guide your problem-solving. Teachers who conduct research can use this opportunity to find solutions to problems in their classroom, school, district, or community. Researchers have the luxury of picking the specific "problem" or critical issue they want to investigate. This can help teachers gain clarity and enhance their understanding, skills, and knowledge needed to make informed decisions. For instance, the mathematics department faculty at a local high school is grappling with finding ways to assist students who are taking calculus succeed on the college Advanced Placement (AP) exam (students who perform well on these exams are awarded college credit.). The faculty has already tried different strategies, but none of these have worked. Together they decide to "test" the effects of a new instructional program that they read about in a research study that had successful results. These teachers are clearly using research to problem-solve!

Using Research to Learn About Classroom Management Practices

A 2019 report on the United States teacher shortage indicated that only about four out of ten classroom teachers reported their teacher education programs adequately focused on strategies for classroom management (Garcia & Weiss, 2019). Most teachers would agree that classroom management is one of the most challenging and demanding skills needed by teachers, regardless of the students ages, skill level, or academic discipline. Even university faculty members struggle with issues of classroom management in their classrooms—including students who show disrespectful or hostile behavior, excessive and inappropriate cellphone use, or absenteeism. Poor classroom management will likely increase frustration among teachers and students, inhibit learning, and affect teacher retention. Conducting or reviewing research can provide educators with information about effective and appropriate classroom management strategies for fostering learning and excitement in the classroom.

Classroom management is critical for creating a welcoming, orderly, and supportive learning environment. It involves educators being proactive in preventing and treating disruptive behavior and in establishing an effective climate where students feel comfortable and eager to learn. Not all behavior management strategies are equal, and it is beneficial for teachers to have a toolbox of different strategies they can use depending on the situation in their classroom. By conducting research, we can learn about new strategies and approaches.

STOP AND THINK 16.6

How can research be used to provide information and strategies not previously learned to help educators develop as professionals?

In our opening scenario, fourth-grade teacher Mr. Eklund was concerned about with how to manage a new student who is a refugee in his class. His student's frequent outbursts and running out of the classroom present safety issues and disrupt learning for many students in the class. Research evidence supports the idea that effective classroom management strategies can promote a safe environment where students understand teacher expectations and are less concerned about unexpected disruptions to the flow of the lesson. Although there are many different behavior management strategies and situations in which they may be applied, we present a few of the most common behavior management strategies research has supported in Figure 16.1. Notice how the strategies we provided in Figure 16.1 are primarily positive in focus.

Now that you have read through some of the strategies for behavior management techniques, read the *Let's See It!* on finding and using a research article that targets one of these classroom behavioral management strategies. Upon reviewing the example provided, it is your turn to search for an article on one of the strategies from Figure 16.1 and to provide an example in the *Let's Do It!*.

FIGURE 16.1 ■ Sample Classroom Behavioral Management Strategies

Behavioral Management Strategies

– Develop classroom rules with students
– Send positive emails or phone calls to parents or guardians
– Demonstrate ideal behavior by modeling
– Provide praise that is genuine and deserved
– Encourage initiative and provide students with academic choices
– Use nonverbal communication such as eye contact
– Teach mindfulness to enhance emotional regulation
– Address inappropriate behavior immediately and privately, if possible
– Have lessons that are fun and engaging
– Be aware of cultural differences

Let's See It! 16.2

Goal: Implementing Research on Classroom Management Practices

TABLE 16.4 ■ Demonstration of Finding a Peer-Reviewed Journal Article on Classroom Behavior Management

Directions: Step 1	Example of a peer-reviewed journal article on one of the classroom behavior management strategies listed in Figure 16.1 and a description of two situations when teachers might apply this strategy in their classrooms.
Study	Trussell, R. P. (2008). Classroom universals to prevent problem behaviors. *Intervention in School and Clinic, 43*(3), 179–185. https://doi.org/10.1177/1053451207311678
Directions: Step 2	Describe two situations when a teacher might apply this behavior management strategy.

This study describes the importance of positive behavior support and discusses various ways to prevent behavior management problems from arising in the classroom. One of the ways described in the study is to have classroom rules posted and visible to all students.

This is an important behavior management strategy to use in all grade levels. If an elementary school teacher takes the time to develop classroom rules with her students and then displays them publicly in the classroom, students are aware of the expectations for the classroom. The rule should be framed in a positive way, such as "We always raise our hands when we have a question or an answer to a question," versus a negative way. such as "We do not call out loud when we have a question or an answer to a question.

A second way to promote positive behavior suggested by the authors is to have a daily schedule. A daily schedule helps teachers reduce the likelihood of downtime and also provides students with a plan for how class will proceed.

This is another important behavior management strategy because it provides structure and organization to the class schedule. When there is downtime, students are more likely to engage in disorderly or disruptive behavior. A simple of way of using this strategy is to announce the plan before each class period as well as what will be covered in the subsequent period or day.

Let's Do It! 16.2

Guided Practice: Finding a Peer-reviewed Journal Article on One of the Classroom Behavior Management Strategies Listed in Figure 16.1

TABLE 16.5 ■ Practicing Finding a Peer-Reviewed Journal Article on Classroom Behavior Management	
Directions: Step 1	Using your knowledge of how to conduct a review of the literature, find a peer-reviewed journal article that presents research in support of one of the classroom behavior management strategies listed in Figure 16.1.
Study	
Directions: Step 2	Describe two situations when a teacher might apply this behavior management strategy.

Conducting research on multiple behavior management strategies and then trying them out in your classroom can assist you in building a repertoire to support a smooth, happy classroom. At the end of the chapter, we provide a *You Do It!* activity whereby you can practice independently the skills you have learned in the previous *Let's See It!* and *Let's Do It!* activities. We will now describe how administrators can use research to guide practice.

THE TAKEAWAY

Research can be used to help teachers learn new methods and techniques related to pedagogy, problem-solving, and classroom management.

USES OF RESEARCH FOR ADMINISTRATORS

LEARNING OBJECTIVE
16.4 Demonstrate knowledge about the uses of research for administrators.

School administrators may include educators with different titles. Principals, assistant principals, deans, heads of school, directors, department chairs, head teachers, and curriculum directors are examples of the many different types of administrators in schools. Although there are other examples of school administrators, these individuals are often in leadership positions that not only involve overseeing the learning and curriculum but also the safety, growth, and well-being of everyone on campus. With the ever-changing needs of our students, parents, and communities, administrators face new challenges and opportunities on a regular basis. Research can support and guide decision making and problem-solving skills and assist school administrators in addressing unanticipated and unpredictable events. School administrators can also significantly impact research, not only by conducting their own research but by supporting research activities in their schools. This can be done in several ways—such as allowing university faculty to conduct research in their schools, encouraging teacher-university faculty collaborations, providing funds and granting permission to colleagues to conduct research.

When administrators conduct research, they can use the results to obtain buy-in from others. This buy-in may be a necessary step in implementing a significant change in the school or in requests for financial support. In the following section, we focus on two important ways, research can guide practice for school administrators: using research to guide practice regarding school-wide issues, and using research to demonstrate a need for the school.

Using Research to Guide School-Wide Practice

Recall our emphasis on the power of research to contribute new knowledge. School administrators are often in positions of leadership and are typically held accountable when situations arise. Most principals would not want to be in a situation where violence has become a frequent occurrence in their schools. School administrators can serve as role models for other professionals in schools based on their willingness to conduct, participate, and review research. Research can be used to facilitate school and programmatic improvements, to empower administrators to take control of issues that have arisen, or to become pioneers for change. In our opening scenario, Principal Chandler needs to address a difficult situation, not just for the benefit of the students but also for the teachers, counselors, coaches, and other school staff. Examining a curriculum that embraces diversity can lead to beneficial outcomes for all, and by conducting research on programs that embrace diversity, Principal Chandler may find one that would work well in her school.

In addition to using research to facilitate change, school administrators can use research in making school-wide policy decisions that impact both learners and employees. Requiring all teachers and students to use laptops, instituting a daily rotating class schedule, eliminating all fried foods in the cafeteria or on school premises, standardizing school dress codes for students and employees, establishing an academic honor roll system across all grades, setting a minimum passing average of 75 for students, and purchasing a camera security system and mandating that all building access doors be locked are all examples of policies administrators could put in place if there is research to support these decisions.

STOP AND THINK 16.7

If you were a principal in a middle school with a high absenteeism rate, how might research help to remedy this problem? In conducting a research study, what initial steps would you take?

Using Research to Demonstrate a Need for Your School

Conducting research can help school administrators gain understanding about the root of a problem they are experiencing. For example, a principal is concerned about the consistently low test scores of students on standardized tests. The principal decides to conduct a literature review on studies involving schools with similar demographics to find out what new programs have been implemented and their effects on student achievement. Upon completing this review, the principal identifies a program with promise and decides to implement the program in the school.

Conducting research can also provide administrators with a rationale they may need to gain the support of parents, school boards, superintendents, and members of the local community. A high school principal believes the students and teachers in their school consistently have low morale because they live in a region where high school sports are widely publicized and they do not have a football field. The principal thinks that building a football field would have many benefits—such as connecting members of the school community with one another, supporting competition and commandry, providing students with opportunities to receive college athletic scholarships, and uplifting overall school morale and spirit. The principal decides to conduct a study comparing the opinions of students, staff, and parents in their high school and that of neighboring high schools with football fields. The principal is hoping the information gathered could support a request for funding of this endeavor. As you can see from each of these examples, research can have a real and potentially powerful impact on the lives of those in schools. Next, we address how using research can have a wider breadth in affecting practice on larger communities and policymakers.

THE TAKEAWAY

Research can be used to help administrators find solutions to problems or to demonstrate a need.

USES OF RESEARCH FOR THE COMMUNITY AND POLICYMAKERS

LEARNING OBJECTIVE

16.5   Demonstrate knowledge about the uses of research for the larger community and policymakers.

Research is often used to guide educational decisions that impact schools within communities, states, and nationally. Decisions that result in significant changes must be substantiated by research to be accepted by educators who will seek evidence for the effectiveness of the proposed changes. We will briefly discuss two uses of educational research that can be wider in breadth to beyond a school or classroom. These are to implement district-wide and national changes and to obtain funding.

Using Research to Implement District-Wide and National Changes

Educators are often expected to accept new standards, curriculum, and instructional methods. The National Reading Panel, a group of scientists with expertise in reading and education was appointed by Congress in 1997 to assess the effectiveness of different approaches to teaching reading. The panel completed their work three years later and found that teaching phonemic awareness, phonics, oral reading fluency, vocabulary, and comprehension were critical components of teaching children to read. What do you think was the impact of this research on instructional reading programs throughout the country?

Large-scale research studies such as the National Reading Panel provide evidence for making changes in policies such as that on reading instruction, and these changes when initiated by government agencies are then often mandated for federally-funded schools. The important point is that it can be helpful for educators to understand that the origins of mandated programs are often the result of large-scale scientific research.

Using Research to Obtain Funding

In Chapter 15, we described the benefits associated with receiving grants and provided a general overview of the grant writing process. Researchers may seek funding or grants for many reasons. We will now briefly discuss two common reasons researchers may seek funding.

Seeking Funding to Support Research

There are several governmental agencies and foundations that provide funding support for research in schools. For example, the Institute of Education Sciences and the National Science Foundation are government organizations that provide funding based on different topics of research, including those related to education. Public funding agencies such as these often have rigorous and competitive application processes with grant requests in the hundreds of thousands or millions of dollars. Research projects on this large of a scale are often wide in breadth, such as the Michigan study described earlier, and will include a diverse group of experts, educators from many schools, and other stakeholders with an interest in the research. The findings generated from a large-scale grant project can potentially lead to policy changes that affect many schools.

In addition to public sources for funding, there are several private organizations that will fund research. These are equally competitive and tend to focus on specific topics or causes. For example, the Annie E. Casey Foundation supports funding opportunities for research on underserved children and their families. The amount of the award from private source funds is typically not as large as those by federal funding agencies but may still be in the low-mid thousands or as high as one million dollars. In sum, each of these types of funding sources requires a considerable amount of preparation and typically, extensive knowledge and expertise to conduct the research along with a thorough understanding of the potential impact of the outcomes.

Seeking Funding as a Result of Research

Research findings can be used to support requests for funding. Principal Chandler is trying to figure out a way to assist new students' transitions to her school and create positive classroom learning experiences for all. She has begun a literature review and has engaged in outreach with peers who are grappling with similar issues. She discovers an intensive program that was conducted in another school with positive results and decides to ask one of her teachers to participate in a pilot study using this program with her students. Principal Chandler has a small budget for professional development activities and allocates part of these funds to train the teacher on the new program. Contingent on positive outcomes, she plans to contact her superintendent for additional financial support to implement a larger study involving selecting classrooms throughout the district. The principal is hoping the research outcomes will be equally positive and the school board would then support a request for federal funding to implement the program throughout all schools in the district. In this example, money is needed to implement the pilot study, the research study, and eventually the new program across several schools.

While research can affect the availability of funding and inform curriculum, it can also affect higher education programs and have an impact on one's professional and personal growth. We now highlight these connections.

THE TAKEAWAY

Research can be used to make large-scale improvements that extend beyond the scope of one's classroom or school, and funding sources can help researchers accomplish this goal.

USING RESEARCH TO IMPACT HIGHER EDUCATION PROGRAMS AND PROFESSIONAL AND PERSONAL GROWTH

LEARNING OBJECTIVE

16.6   Use research to impact higher education programs and professional and personal growth.

University faculty who teach courses in education-related programs are also affected by educational research. Research impacts the curriculum, instructional methodology, the theories taught, licensure requirements, degree requirements and length, and expectations for ongoing professional development. For example, findings from the research by the National Reading Panel described earlier resulted in dramatic changes in instructional reading strategies taught in higher education reading methods classes throughout the country. Faculty teaching future school leaders need to be abreast of recent research focusing on issues of diversity, equity, and inclusion and belonging (DEI). How would you feel if you graduated from a leadership program and were hired as a principal for a high school that has been experiencing a large dropout rate among students from marginalized communities? Would you be equipped to problem-solve without having learned about DEI in research in education in your graduate program?

As proponents of research, it is our hope that you will view research (both as a consumer and producer of research) as an opportunity for professional and personal growth. When educators conduct research, they acquire many new skills and abilities. They learn and experience what it is like to carry out a research study and to collaborate with others on research. Researchers also acquire new communication, critical thinking, problem-solving, and abstract reasoning skills. Research studies can help educators solve problems of practice that impact their students, school, and community.

STOP AND THINK 16.8

Describe some ways in which you would grow professionally by conducting research.

As educators, we often get excited when our students experience that "Ah ha!" moment. As researchers, you can experience that when conducting research! Principal Chandler in our opening scenario was surprised to hear that her colleague tested a program on how to make the American students more accepting and inclusive of students who are new to the country. It is clear from her surprise that her initial focus was on developing strategies that targeted assisting the children who had immigrated adjust rather than developing strategies for her *American students to adjust!* This insight opened her up to considering other possibilities for her school. Thus, the use of research is not only critical to guide practice but essential for promoting professional and personal growth in educators. In the next section, we briefly describe how the three phases of self-regulated learning can help educators apply research to practice in a systematic, a.k.a., regulated, way!

THE TAKEAWAY

Research can be used to impact higher education programs and professional and personal growth.

APPLYING RESEARCH FINDINGS TO PRACTICE USING THE CYCLE OF SELF-REGULATED LEARNING

LEARNING OBJECTIVE
16.7   Apply research findings to practice using the cycle of self-regulated learning.

Self-regulated learning has been a unique feature of this research methods textbook. There is much scientific evidence to support the use of self-regulation to promote learning, for us as educators and our students. Self-regulated learning can be a tool that educators use to not only conduct research but to implement findings from research into practice. It can organize our thinking and provide a framework of where to begin. A beneficial feature of self-regulated learning is that it is cyclical in nature, therefore assisting educators in continually becoming agents of change. Thus, we begin this section with an example of how a teacher may use a published research study to help guide high school science instruction. This is followed by an example of how a teacher may use the findings from the study to self-regulate instruction (i.e., setting personal goals for lesson planning) and to teach students to self-regulate (i.e., setting personal goals for homework completion).

Using Findings From Previous Research to Make Decisions About Implementing Changes to Practice

DiBenedetto and Zimmerman (2010) conducted a study on 51 high school students' self-regulated learning of studying science. They included three groups of 11th-grade students that were grouped by the schools into high achieving, average achieving, and low achieving in science. They tested students to see if there were differences in their use of the three phases of self-regulated learning (planning, doing, and reflecting). Students were individually told they would be given a three-page textbook passage to read about tornado development, time to study, and then a short test. The test involved two parts, the Tornado Knowledge Test and the Conceptual Model Test. The test looked as if it was just one exam, but it was measuring two different things: students' ability to perform well on basic scientific facts and students' ability to engage in abstract reasoning that was measured by a more challenging question embedded in the test. The investigators were looking to see if there were differences in the way students *planned, acted (doing), and reflected.* Students were asked questions throughout the protocol session to capture their thoughts during each of the three phases. Following are a few of the results from the study.

TABLE 16.6 ■ Excerpt of Means and Standard Deviation Scores From DiBenedetto and Zimmerman (2010)						
Self-Regulated Phases and Processes	**High Achievers**		**Average Achievers**		**Low Achievers**	
	M	*SD*	*M*	*SD*	*M*	*SD*
Tornado Knowledge Test (out of 100)	75.74	9.97	61.01	12.70	29.27	14.77
Conceptual Model Test (out of 6)	5.18	.95	3.29	1.83	1.94	1.60
Planning						
Strategy plans—students described the study strategies they were going to use	2.44	.22	2.31	.21	1.27	.21
Doing						
Strategy use—students described the strategies they were using—reading (and rereading)	2.71	.27	1.83	.26	1.61	.26
Strategy use—students described the study strategies they were using, such as note-taking, rehearsing, and testing themselves	3.48	.34	2.46	.32	1.96	.32
Reflecting: Based on seeing their grade on the Conceptual Model Test						
Self-evaluative standards—students indicated whether they thought they did as well as they should have	88.38	4.70	72.89	4.48	55.61	4.48
Self-satisfaction—students indicated whether they were satisfied with their grade	5.97	.35	4.57	.34	3.27	.34

Suppose you are a ninth-grade science teacher and are interested in the findings from this study. You have students who are struggling with course assignments and exams, and you would like to use research to learn about ways to help them perform better in class. What information can you gather from the preceding findings? In looking at the means and standard deviations, what observations can you make?

Findings from previous research studies, including your own, can be used as part of evidence-based practice. The preceding study presents a table of descriptive data (means and standard deviations) and not the results of an experimental design. The means, or averages, of test scores of the students in the high-achieving group appear to be higher than those in the average and low-achieving groups. The variance among the test scores appears to get larger when we look across the row from left to right. This suggests that low-achieving students' test scores may have varied more from one another than average students' tests scores and high-achieving students' test scores. This can suggest that most high-achieving students earned about the same grades as one another, whereas the low-achieving students' grades differed greatly from one another. Overall, on both tests, high-achieving students performed better than average-achieving students, and average-achieving students performed better than low-achieving students. While a teacher would likely think this is consistent with how they expected students from each category to perform, they would need to know whether the differences are significant before they make inferences about the students' use of self-regulated learning processes.

Next, we turn our attention to the self-regulated learning processes. The means were higher for each process by achievement group. A teacher may expect students who are high achieving to do a better job planning to study, using more study strategies, and feeling satisfied as they reflect on their performance as compared to lower-achieving students. But what can a teacher infer from these data? The teacher knows that they can use descriptive data as a guide but not to make claims about statistical differences; in order to do that they would need to use inferential statistics. The teacher also wonders if the means are significantly different from one another across groups, because if so, the teacher would feel more comfortable with connecting the self-regulated learning processes with the students' test scores. The teacher thinks: "I would consider teaching my students how to use self-regulated learning based on these research findings if I at least knew there were significant differences between the students' use of these processes."

DiBenedetto and Zimmerman (2010) further analyzed the data using two-way ANOVA to determine if there were significant differences in the means of the three groups of students. Table 16.3 shows their findings:

What could teachers infer from the findings in Table 16.7? Overall, it seems that high-achieving students used self-regulated learning more than low-achieving students (and in some cases, average-achieving students) when reading a passage and taking an exam, and average science students used more of the self-regulated learning processes more than low-achieving students. Although one cannot make causal conclusions that self-regulated learning directly impacted student achievement given that a non-experimental design was used, it appears that self-regulated learning is closely connected to how well students perform. Looking closely at this research study may help a teacher decide whether teaching the low-performing students how to self-regulate their learning could help bring their grades up. Again, the teacher understands this study did not involve an intervention and so one cannot claim with certainty that the use of self-regulated learning processes led to the high-test scores, but the teacher is willing to give it a try. Next, we describe how Mrs. Wilson, ninth-grade teacher, will engage in self-regulated learning to teach her students a science unit on Mendel's gene theory based on the preceding research study.

TABLE 16.7 ■ Excerpt of Two-Way ANOVA Findings (DiBenedetto & Zimmerman, 2010)			
Self-regulated Phases and Processes	High Achievers	Average Achievers	Low Achievers
Planning			
Strategy plans—students described the study strategies they were going to use	Significantly differed from low achievers	Significantly differed from low achievers	Significantly differed from high and average achievers
Doing			
Strategy use—students described the strategies they were using—reading (and rereading)	Significantly differed from low achievers	No significant differences	Significantly differed from high achievers
Strategy use—students described the study strategies they were using, such as note-taking, rehearsing, and testing themselves	Significantly differed from low achievers	No significant differences	Significantly differed from high achievers
Reflecting: Based on seeing their grade on the Conceptual Model Test			
Self-evaluative standards—students indicated whether they thought they did as well as they should have	Significantly differed from average achievers and low achievers	Significantly differed from high achievers and low achievers	Significantly differed from high achievers and average achievers
Self-satisfaction—students indicated whether they were satisfied with their grade	Significantly differed from average achievers and low achievers	Significantly differed from high achievers and low achievers	Significantly differed from high achievers and average achievers

Using the Three Phases of Self-regulated Learning to Teach a Lesson Based on Previous Research Findings

As indicated earlier, Mrs. Wilson is a ninth-grade science teacher. She is eager to help her students learn and enjoy science as much as she does. She has been having difficulty motivating the students in her science class, and their lack of motivation is reflected in their grades. She read the DiBenedetto and Zimmerman (2010) study described earlier as well as several other research articles on self-regulated learning and has decided to try to use the three processes of planning, doing, and reflecting in her own lesson planning and instruction, in addition to teaching her students how to self-regulate. Her focus is the next science unit where she will be teaching students about Mendel's gene theory. She knows this unit is particularly challenging for students because the lesson involves using matrices (Mendel's Punnett square) to determine inherited gene patterns. She prepares three diagrams of the processes described in the DiBenedetto and Zimmerman (2010) study along with self-efficacy and goal setting because she has read additional research studies that indicates self-efficacy and goal setting are good predictors of achievement. Mrs. Wilson prefers visuals for herself, and she decides to create these diagrams of how she and her students will engage in self-regulated learning.

Planning

During planning, Mrs. Wilson analyzes the tasks to be done and plans the strategies she will use to teach and motivate her students. She sets attainable goals for herself as well as content learning goals and objectives. She also plans strategies for gaining professional support to keep herself motivated. During planning, Mrs. Wilson will teach students how to be self-regulated by helping them set learning goals and study strategies. She hopes to build students' self-efficacy for learning about Mendel's theory and to teach them how to use self-talk to learn and sustain motivation. In addition, Mrs. Wilson will use Universal Design for Learning (UDL), an approach to instruction that gives all students the opportunity to succeed by using a variety of instructional methods and assessments. Mrs. Wilson plans to use these strategies while teaching the Mendel science unit so that students will be learning the content while also learning how to self-regulate.

Faculty can implement research findings such as the importance of strategic planning to help students succeed.
©iStockphoto.com/AndreyPopov

Mrs. Wilson's science students learn how to *plan for learning*. She has them articulate short goals related to content and assignments. She discusses with the students which new learning and study strategies would work given the science content and has students practice using self-talk in anticipation of working through the matrix problems and activities. See Figure 16.2 for examples of how Mrs. Wilson and her students will engage in the planning phase of self-regulated learning.

Doing

During the this phase, Mrs. Wilson uses her plans to teach. She teaches chunks of content at a time and models "thinking" by talking aloud to herself as she teaches. Based on the research Mrs. Wilson has read, she knows to reinforce students' self-efficacy by encouraging her students when working on difficult tasks and highlighting their successes. She teaches using hands-on activities, videos, songs, and memes for instruction. Mrs. Wilson is flexible in her approach, a

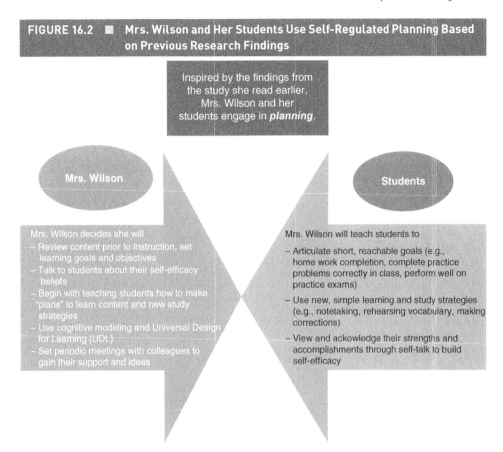

FIGURE 16.2 ■ Mrs. Wilson and Her Students Use Self-Regulated Planning Based on Previous Research Findings

Inspired by the findings from the study she read earlier, Mrs. Wilson and her students engage in *planning*.

Mrs. Wilson

Students

Mrs. Wilson decides she will

– Review content prior to instruction, set learning goals and objectives
– Talk to students about their self-efficacy beliefs
– Begin with teaching students how to make "plans" to learn content and new study strategies
– Use cognitive modeling and Universal Design for Learning (UDL)
– Set periodic meetings with colleagues to gain their support and ideas

Mrs. Wilson will teach students to

– Articulate short, reachable goals (e.g., home work completion, complete practice problems correctly in class, perform well on practice exams)
– Use new, simple learning and study strategies (e.g., notetaking, rehearsing vocabulary, making corrections)
– View and ackowledge their strengths and accomplishments through self-talk to build self-efficacy

critical characteristic of UDL, and gives students "choices" to demonstrate proficiency. Mrs. Wilson also asked her science colleagues to meet biweekly to discuss the challenges and accomplishments she is experiencing in using self-regulated learning.

Mrs. Wilson's students implement the strategies learned during the *doing* phase. They have written down their goals, and before each class meeting, Mrs. Wilson has them review them and make changes if necessary. The students are actively learning as they engage in more hands-on activities and make decisions about how they will be evaluated. Mrs. Wilson read research about the importance of practice and has her students practice completing the Punnett square—a matrix that is the visual representation Mendel's pattern of inheritance. She also has the students keep track of their schoolwork and performance. The students feel embarrassed talking out loud at first but then accept this as part of their class environment. Mrs. Wilson notices a change in the students' morale and the classroom learning environment, which seems more upbeat and livelier than it has been. Figure 16.3 describes some of the ways Mrs. Wilson and her students engage in the "doing" activities.

Reflecting

Upon completion of the science unit, Mrs. Wilson uses the time to reflect and has her students do the same. She is astounded at the change in her students. They seem much happier and more confident. The classroom has been a noisy room, with students using self-talk, practicing the strategies they observed her model, and laughter as students had fun learning and demonstrating their learning through a variety of self-chosen assessments. Mrs. Wilson evaluated her

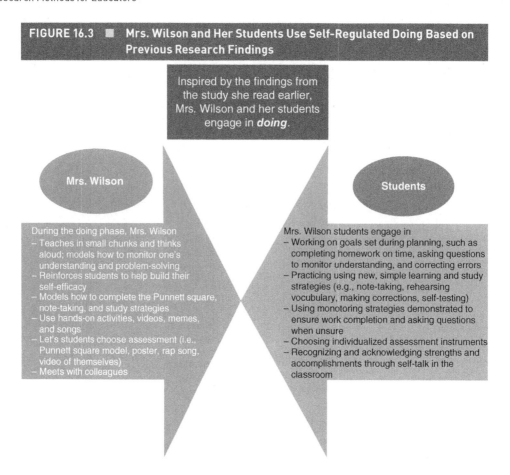

FIGURE 16.3 ■ Mrs. Wilson and Her Students Use Self-Regulated Doing Based on Previous Research Findings

Inspired by the findings from the study she read earlier, Mrs. Wilson and her students engage in *doing*.

Mrs. Wilson

During the doing phase, Mrs. Wilson
– Teaches in small chunks and thinks aloud; models how to monitor one's understanding and problem-solving
– Reinforces students to help build their self-efficacy
– Models how to complete the Punnett square, note-taking, and study strategies
– Use hands-on activities, videos, memes, and songs
– Let's students choose assessment (i.e., Punnett square model, poster, rap song, video of themselves)
– Meets with colleagues

Students

Mrs. Wilson students engage in
– Working on goals set during planning, such as completing homework on time, asking questions to monitor understanding, and correcting errors
– Practicing using new, simple learning and study strategies (e.g., note-taking, rehearsing vocubulary, making corrections, self-testing)
– Using monitoring strategies demonstrated to ensure work completion and asking questions when unsure
– Choosing individualized assessment instruments
– Recognizing and acknowledging strengths and accomplishments through self-talk in the classroom

instructional approach and is satisfied overall. She makes notes about a few things she would like to modify for the next unit and evaluates her own performance to some degree based on her students' increased achievement scores. She is also quite pleased with students' self-reflections.

Students stated they felt more self-efficacious about learning in her classroom. They indicated they learned new strategies that can be applied to other classes and while satisfied with their grades, several students indicated they wanted their grades to continue to improve. Students evaluated themselves as much stronger in science than they had previously thought and indicated they were excited to attend class. Figure 16.4 shows some of the ways that Mrs. Wilson and her students used self-reflection processes.

In the preceding example, Mrs. Wilson applies the research she has read about on self-regulated learning and UDL. Now in the final two sections of this chapter, we highlight the importance of ethical issues in using research to guide practice and the American Psychological Association's perspective on the application of research to practice.

THE TAKEAWAY

Using research studies that have been published in peer-reviewed journals can be beneficial to practice. Self-regulated learning provides educators with a framework to apply findings from research to their professional work.

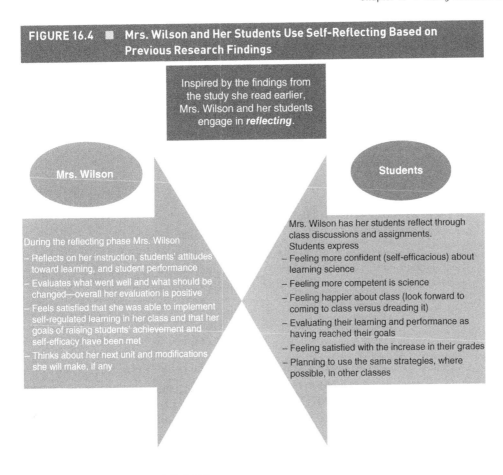

FIGURE 16.4 ■ Mrs. Wilson and Her Students Use Self-Reflecting Based on Previous Research Findings

Inspired by the findings from the study she read earlier, Mrs. Wilson and her students engage in *reflecting*.

Mrs. Wilson

During the reflecting phase Mrs. Wilson

– Reflects on her instruction, students' attitudes toward learning, and student performance
– Evaluates what went well and what should be changed—overall her evaluation is positive
– Feels satisfied that she was able to implement self-regulated learning in her class and that her goals of raising students' achievement and self-efficacy have been met
– Thinks about her next unit and modifications she will make, if any

Students

Mrs. Wilson has her students reflect through class discussions and assignments. Students express

– Feeling more confident (self-efficacious) about learning science
– Feeling more competent is science
– Feeling happier about class (look forward to coming to class versus dreading it)
– Evaluating their learning and performance as having reached their goals
– Feeling satisfied with the increase in their grades
– Planning to use the same strategies, where possible, in other classes

ETHICAL CONSIDERATIONS

LEARNING OBJECTIVE

16.8   Demonstrate knowledge of ethical considerations in using research to guide practice.

We will now discuss common ethical issues to consider when applying research to practice. When educators read or conduct research, it is often with the hope of gaining knowledge that can be useful to them in solving critical problems. Unfortunately, there are often situations where the consumers of research do not fully understand the implications or limitations of the research prior to implementing it into practice. As noted in the preceding scenario with Mrs. Wilson and her students, correlational studies do not provide evidence of cause and effect. Therefore, when implementing an instructional program that was examined using correlational research, one must understand that such a study cannot support claims that the program will or should, on average, have a causal impact on student outcomes. This is important because of various factors that one must consider in implementing a new program—such as cost, time, training, and potential outcomes. If Principal Chandler came across a study showing that teachers who administered a survey to new refugees assessing their needs tended to have happier students, she cannot assume that completing surveys is what is causing students to be happier. There may be many different factors that are impacting students' moods unrelated to completing surveys.

Another ethical concern is harm to human subjects or biases in the research. We discussed in detail in Chapter 1 Stanley Milgram's Obedience to Authority Study and the Tuskegee Syphilis Study. Both studies used methods that were harmful (and even deadly) to the participants. When reviewing research studies that have been previously published, you may also come across research that appears to go against your own values. You may also encounter research that draws conclusions based on a biases or ones that did not consider cultural or socioeconomic factors. Therefore, when reviewing research, educators must decide whether it is justified or not to apply the research to current issues of practice.

STOP AND THINK 16.9

What would you do if your principal told you she read a research study on student punishment and indicated teachers must now inflict some type of punishment (such as not allowing students to attend educational field trips) if they failed two or more exams? Is that ethical and would you do it? Please explain.

A final ethical consideration involves the importance of critically evaluating each research study to determine whether it was in fact, a research study or simply a statistical report. Often, people who are unfamiliar with research will use something they have read or cite statistics as if it were based on research. In 1980, one of the most respected scientific journals in medicine, *The New England Journal of Medicine*, published a five-sentence letter to the editor indicating that in 11,882 hospital medical patients who were administered narcotics, there were four cases of addiction and only one of these four cases had severe addition (Hawkins, 2017). None of these patients had previous addictions. The authors concluded that even though narcotics were widely used in hospitals, it is rare for someone without a history of addiction to become addicted. This letter is considered to have been the springboard to what became the "opioid crisis" in the United States. Pharmaceutical companies who may or may not have understood what constitutes good research used this letter for the promotion and marketing of oxycontin. They cited the prestigious journal's name in their marketing campaigns and indicated research showed that less than 2% of people who used oxycontin became addicted to the drug, thus emphasizing the rarity of addiction and justifying the use of the opioid for pain management. As a result, oxycontin was overly prescribed for pain management beginning in the 1990s and lasting until recently, resulting in thousands of deaths, many of whom were school-age children who gained access to the drug or were prescribed it. Using the checklist presented earlier (see Table 16.3) in this chapter can help educators evaluate whether reported information that appears to be research is in fact research—the implication being that misrepresenting or reporting data can have significant ethical consequences on others.

While the description on the misrepresentation of research is on drug prescriptions, educators may find themselves in meetings where colleagues present statistics that are not grounded in research. If Principal Chandler read an article in a local newspaper that indicated that 80% of recent refugees fail all courses in their first year of school and she presented this information to her teachers, the teachers may be influenced unfairly in their expectations and grading of students who are refugees. The ethical consequences of reciting statistics could be significant, which is why it is not only important to evaluate the research based on merit but also on the potential ethical outcomes of misrepresenting the data.

THE TAKEAWAY

Three key ethical considerations when reviewing prior research for applications to practice include the following:

1. Limitations due to the nature of the study
2. Harm to human subjects or biases in the research
3. Evaluating the quality of research reported before using the data

AMERICAN PSYCHOLOGICAL ASSOCIATION STYLE

LEARNING OBJECTIVE

16.9   Utilize the *Publication Manual of the American Psychological Association* in applications to practice.

While the *Publication Manual of the American Psychological Association* is primarily focused on preparing manuscripts for publication, it emphasizes the importance of using data and results appropriately. When data are analyzed, reported, and used, the data should not be falsified in any way or used to manipulate the behavior of others. Educators can also strengthen their instructional approaches when evaluating claims made from researchers by asking themselves whether there are alternative explanations for the outcomes. One suggestion is to speak with colleagues about the research. In working with others, educators can discuss the research and examine whether an instructional program would work effectively with their students. Educators need to ascertain whether the research provides information that can assist them in refining their teaching and administrative skills. The American Psychological Association has many books and articles available on preparing, conducting, and applying research to practice in appropriate, ethical ways. We encourage educators to take advantage of these books and to enjoy the adventure that comes with conducting research!

THE TAKEAWAY

Using the latest edition of the Publication Manual of the American Psychological Association is critical for all aspects of conducting, communicating, and applying research to practice.

CHAPTER SUMMARY

This chapter discussed the ways in which research can be used to guide practice. We discussed using one's own research as well as the research of others to help problem-solve. We described the importance of replication studies and how through reading research studies, educators may gain ideas of potential research studies they may wish to conduct. This was followed by a description of the ways in which research can be specifically used by teachers, administrators, the community, and policymakers. Research can also have an impact on educational programs in universities as well as provide educators with opportunities for professional and personal growth. We provided guidance on how self-regulated learning can be used to implement research-based changes and discussed the importance of ethical considerations in using research to guide practice. Our last section provided a general overview on how the American Psychological Association can be a useful resource in applying research to practice.

EXTENSION ACTIVITIES

You Do It! 16.1

Self-Directed Practice: Searching How to Use Peer-Reviewed Research Articles and Journals to Find Additional Relevant Studies That Can Guide Practice

Directions: Step 1	Identify a critical issue in education that you would like to address. Search for a research study that examined this topic and complete the table that follows:
Critical Issue	
Study	
Journal Name	
Year	
Volume	
Issue	
Step	
Directions: Step 2	Search the journal's table of contents and screenshot some relevant articles and paste in the following box:
Directions: Step 3	Select a couple of articles from the table of contents that appear relevant and read their abstracts. If they seem helpful, look at the references to identify other possible studies you might want to read for additional information. Make a list of five articles found in the references that could be beneficial to your issue in the following boxes:

You Do It! 16.2

Self-Directed Practice: Implementing Research to Practice

Directions: **Step 1**	Using your knowledge of how to conduct a review of the research, find a peer-reviewed journal article that presents research on a critical issue YOU are concerned about and list that article below.

Study

Directions: **Step 2**	Describe two situations when you might apply this behavior management strategy.

KEY TERMS

Buy-in
Conceptual replication
Evidence-based practice
Exact replication

Pedagogy
Replication
Replication crisis
Systematic

ANSWER KEY

Stop and Think Activities

STOP AND THINK **16.1**

While responses will vary, replicating research can make it easier for educators because it provides the opportunity to build on prior work and a template for researchers to work from. If one were to replicate the study involving the speech therapist teaching, one might expect to obtain the similar results if the study were replicated in exactly the way as the original study.

STOP AND THINK **16.2**

Responses will vary, however, research topics that affect multiple schools and communities could include the impact of school funding on student achievement, the over disciplining students of color, the effects of textbook censorship on students' understanding of American history and/or current events, and the impact of COVID 19 on student outcomes.

Stop and Think 16.3

Responses will vary depending on the critical issue; however, a good recommendation is for educators is to include colleagues with similar interests and/or expertise in areas that add to the richness of the design, development, and analysis.

Stop and Think 16.4

Responses will vary; however, educators may select a theory they studied in school and use this as a framework for conducting research. In the example in this chapter, we discuss Bandura's (1986, 1997) social cognitive theory.

Stop and Think 16.5

Responses will vary; however, teachers can conduct a literature review on the specific content area and grade level to see if there are studies that have already been done. Many journals that are specific to teaching methods in a content area will have research studies that may assist teachers in employing new instructional strategies to improve achievement.

Stop and Think 16.6

Conducting a literature review and conducting research on one's critical issue can assist educators in problem-solving and finding solutions. Research studies may offer recommendations for instruction and assessment as well as offer novel approaches not previously considered. Research can also empower educators by providing them with a rationale or justification for making changes to supervisors, parents, and students.

Stop and Think 16.7

A principal might, as a first step, conduct a careful literature review to determine if there are research studies that have been conducted on schools struggling with attendance and absenteeism that have similar demographics (i.e., grade level, student population, family SES) to their school. The principal could also discuss the situation with other principals and the superintendent to see if they have any recommendations. If neither of these approaches offer a remedy, the principal should consider conducting a research study.

Stop and Think 16.8

Conducting research will help educators grow in many ways. Educators will develop their professional, analytical, and communication skills. They will learn to become consumers and users of research as well as how to adhere to scientific guidelines and criteria in conducting research. Educators who conduct research can obtain recognition from peers and contribute to the existing body of knowledge. Research can help educators understand more about how students learn and new methods and techniques for their professional work, and it can help educators become more competent and successful at work.

Stop and Think 16.9

This is clearly an ethical issue and a situation that is not supported by research. Research, including studies conducted using operant conditioning, show that punishment weakens behavior. If teachers want students to improve performance on exams, they need to examine their instructional and assessment strategies, provide multiple practice and feedback opportunities, reinforce students when they succeed, and help improve students' self-efficacy for performing well. Conducting a literature review and using research to show that punishment is an ineffective and unethical way to improve achievement can help the principal understand there are more effective and ethical ways to foster student success.

Let's Do It! Activities

Let's Do It! 16.1

Guided Practice: Understand how to use Peer-reviewed Research Articles and Journals to Find Additional Relevant Studies that can Guide Practice

Practice Searching a Journal's Table of Contents for Relevant Articles

Directions: Step 1	Identify a critical issue in education that you would like to address. Search for a research study that examined this topic and complete the table that follows:
Critical Issue	
Study	
Journal Name	
Year	
Volume	
Issue	
Directions: Step 2	Search the journal's table of contents and screenshot some relevant articles and paste below:

Responses vary for this activity; however, educators can model their responses after reviewing the example provided in the *Let's See It!* 16.1.

Let's Do It! 16.2

Guided Practice: Finding a Peer-reviewed Journal Article on One of the Classroom Behavior Management Strategies Listed in Figure 16.1

Practicing Finding a Peer-Reviewed Journal Article on Classroom Behavior Management

Responses vary for this activity; however, educators can model their responses after reviewing the example provided in the *Let's See It!* 16.2.

TABLE 16.11 ■	
Directions: Step 1	Using your knowledge of how to conduct a review of the literature, find a peer-reviewed journal article that presents research in support of one of the classroom behavior management strategies listed in Figure 16.1.
Study	

(Continued)

TABLE 16.11 ■ *(Continued)*

Directions: Step 2	Describe two situations when a teacher might apply this behavior management strategy.

GLOSSARY

Accuracy (in program evaluation): the dependability and trustworthiness of evaluation findings

Accuracy (in reporting research data): the extent to which researchers use caution and avoid carelessness and inappropriate generalization when analyzing and reporting data

Achievement tests: used to assess student mastery of content knowledge and/or skills acquired through instruction

Acting: a component of the action research cycle where we implement the plans to address the critical issue or goal, making observations along the way

Action research: a research method in which the practitioner has a real-life problem or issue in their schools that needs to be resolved

Activities: actions or resources used to reach the needs of the target audience (e.g., students at the school)

Alternative explanation: explanation of an observed effect or result that is different from the presumed or expected explanation

Alternative hypothesis (H$_A$): a statement that reflects what a researcher believes is true regarding the relationship among variables

Analytic memo: a brief summary in which the researcher assesses what they have learned over the course of the study

Analytic memos: a process wherein the researcher reflects on their reactions to check potential personal biases

ANCOVA (analysis of covariance): an inferential test similar to ANOVA but that also controls for other variables that may influence the dependent variable

Anonymity: an aspect of research in which there is no way to connect participant responses to their identity

ANOVA (analysis of variance): an inferential test used to compare the means of two or more groups by assessing the variance between them

Applied research: a type of research that is focused on solving a specific problem or testing a theory to determine its usefulness to problems of practice

A priori hypothesis: type of prediction based on past research or theory that is made prior to a study taking place

Aptitude tests: a type of assessment that measures student potential and acts as a predictor of future academic success

Assessment (in program theory): a phase of the needs assessment that informs the evaluators and stakeholders about the program details in terms of meeting program objectives

Assessment (in school contexts): a systematic approach to collect, analyze, and make inferences about instruction practices and student development and learning

Assessment bias: refers to assessments that unfairly and negatively impact people based on certain personal characteristics like socioeconomic status, racial/ethnic backgrounds, gender identity, or other characteristics

Audience: group who may have an interest in the outcomes of a program evaluation but who are not directly involved in the implementation of the program

Audience awareness: being cognizant of the population to whom one is writing or speaking

Axial coding: a phase of the coding process associated with the constant comparative analysis approach in which labels from open coding are grouped into categories

Bar graph: a visual representation that uses vertical bars to represent the frequency of categorical scores in a distribution

Baseline phase: a phase of data collection in a time series design that occurs prior to implementing an intervention

Basic research: a type of research that is focused on understanding a phenomenon or developing or expanding a theory

Benchmark tests: also commonly known as interim assessments; serve as standards or comparisons against which to monitor student progress throughout the year

Beneficence: an ethical principle requiring researchers to cause no harm to research participants and to ensure their well-being and possible benefits from participation in a study

Bias-free language: writing or communication that is not offensive, demeaning, perpetuating of negative assumptions about groups of people

Bivariate correlation: a correlation coefficient between two variables

Bounded system: associated with case studies, encompasses the case within the context and parameters of the study, setting boundaries that can be an individual, a community of practice, an organization, or event

Box and whisker plot: a graphical display that summarizes the key aspects of a distribution including the middle 50% of scores, the median score, and the range of scores and potential outliers

Buy-in: a term used to describe the acceptance and support of something

Calibration: refers to the extent to which the scorers observe and interpret the behaviors in the same way

Case study design: a qualitative design involving an in-depth description of a bounded or individual, group, activity, or process

Causal comparative design (ex post facto): a particular type of comparative design in which researchers systematically attempt to rule out alternative explanations of observed group differences

Chi-square test: an inferential test designed to analyze the difference between the observed and expected values for categorical variables

Clarity: a characteristic of audience awareness that involves presenting information in written and spoken form that is clear and easy to understand

Classical grounded theory: emphasizes systematic analysis of data to generate the formation of a theory based on the perspectives of individuals. The researcher studies a problem with minimal background knowledge and in a detached way

Client: individual who is responsible for seeking an outside evaluation

Cluster sampling: a method of sampling where one randomly selects a sample from pre-established groups (clusters) within a population where the individual characteristics in the cluster vary

Cohen's d: a common measure of effect size reflecting the difference between two groups

Collaborative evaluation: reflects the dual roles of evaluators and stakeholders in shaping all aspects of the program evaluation process (also known as participatory evaluation)

Collective case study: a type of case that involves multiple cases that are conducted simultaneously or sequentially

Comparative design: a quantitative design that examines differences among naturally occurring groups

Comparison group: a group used in an experiment that receives some intervention but not the target intervention in the study

Computer Assisted Qualitative Analysis (CAQDS): a broad term for technological

platforms that are utilized to enhance qualitative data analysis

Conceptual definition: provides the meaning of a construct and often relates to a theoretical basis

Conceptual replication: repeating what was done in the original study with slight changes

Conciseness: a characteristic of audience awareness that involves articulating essential information in a brief and comprehensive way

Concurrent designs: a data collection process where all data are collected at the same time

Concurrent triangulation: a type of triangulation method for merging quantitative and qualitative results

Confidentiality: an ethical principle that safeguards the privacy of research participants including not sharing personal information with others

Confirmability: a characteristic of trustworthiness that reflects the strategies a researcher uses to remove personal bias from findings

Constant comparative analysis approach: a process of coding, analyzing, and interpreting data in an iterative process

Construct: an abstract idea or principle that is not directly observable but can be inferred from observed data

Constructed response questions: questions that allow for a variety of perspectives, often in the form of open-ended questions on surveys or interviews

Constructivist grounded theory: a type of grounded theory where the researcher and participants are actively engaged in constructing a theory without a predetermined theory in place prior to the study

Construct validity: a form of psychometric analyses that determines whether a test/instrument measures the construct or domain of interest that it claims to measure

Consumer-oriented evaluation: a type of program evaluation focused on assessing the effectiveness and worth of resources available for purchase

Content validity: evidence of validity generated from experts of a given domain that reveals whether a given test/instrument adequately represents the conceptual domain of the target construct

Context evaluation: examines how an organization can address gaps in a current societal structure by determining the needs of a target population and assessing if program goals align with these needs

Control group: a group in an experiment that does not receive the target intervention

Convenience sampling: refers to the selection of your participants based on who is easily accessible and available to the researcher

Convergent Validity: evidence of validity showing the extent to which scores on a test/instrument relate to other measures of the same or similar constructs

Copyright violations: a situation in which copyrighted materials are accessed or used without receiving the proper permissions

Correlational design: a quantitative design that focuses primarily on the statistical relationships between two or more variables

Correlation coefficient: a value between -1 and 1 that reflects the magnitude and direction of a relationship between two variables

Correlation matrix: a summary table of the correlations among pairs of variables

Cost-benefit analysis: a process that measures the costs and benefits of a program in monetary terms

Cost-effectiveness analysis: analyzes costs of a program in comparison to the final outcomes

Course grades: a type of performance indicator used in schools to reflect students' aggregated level of achievement in a particular class at defined points of a school year

Credibility: a characteristic of trustworthiness, credibility refers to how confident a researcher is that their findings reflect a correct and accurate interpretation of the data

Criterion-referenced test: a type of test in which an individual's performance is judged relative to some professionally determined standard of performance

Criterion-related validity: evidence of validity reflecting how well scores on a test/instrument relate to levels of performance or other outcomes in a domain of interest

Critical case: a type of a purposive sampling technique of a single case (or small number of cases) that can be pivotal in explaining the phenomenon of interest

Critical ethnography: a type of ethnography in which the goal is to empower a marginalized group of individuals

Critical friend: A person who can give constructive feedback while being supportive

Critical issue: an important topic, issue, or experience that often necessitates systematical exploration, review, and or analysis

Critical value: a value used to determine whether a researcher can reject the null hypothesis or conclude that a sample mean is statistically different from the population

Cronbach's alpha: a type of internal reliability that examines the consistency of the relationship among all items on a test/instrument

Cross case comparison: a qualitative approach to comparing multiple case studies

Cross-Sectional design: a research approach that involves collecting data at a single point in time

Cultural domain: a way to identify features or prominent elements within an ethnographic study

Data: quantitative information (numerical values) and qualitative information (information that typically describes characteristics or abilities) collected during research

Data collection instruments: tools that gather information for a research study

Dataset: a structured and organized collection of data values

Deductive reasoning: a type of top-down logical process that progresses from general ideas or hypotheses to specific conclusions

Degrees of freedom (df): the number of values that may vary or carry error within a dataset

Dependability: a characteristic of trustworthiness that reflects the ability of researchers to replicate a study with similar findings

Dependent variable: type of variable that is measured and predicted or caused by other variables

Descriptive coding: when noun labels are used to represent individual words

Descriptive design: a quantitative design that entails describing the characteristics of a sample, measurement tool, context, or some other phenomenon

Descriptive phenomenology: a type of phenomenology that includes the processes of exploring, analyzing, and describing shared and unique experiences

Descriptive statistics: a branch of statistics that involves describing, summarizing, and explaining scores of one or more variables

Deviation IQ score: a standard score with a mean of 100 and a SD of 15

Diagnostic test: a type of test used to identify specific areas of challenge or weakness and that likely needs instructional support

Directional (one-tailed) test: a type of analysis in which the researcher hypothesizes the direction of an expected result

Discourse analysis: a broad approach to qualitative analysis that focuses on the way individuals make meaning and draw on past knowledge and experiences with human interactions through oral and written communication

Discriminant Validity: evidence of validity showing a lack of relationship between a test/instrument and conceptually distinct constructs

Distribution of scores: the full range of scores that are recorded for a particular variable

Doing: the second phase of the self-regulated learning cycle where we carry out plans and engage in self-observing and monitoring our behavior and use metacognitive monitoring as we work toward accomplishing our goal

Double-barreled items: an item on a questionnaire that includes multiple characteristics or attributes

Educational research: a process that involves the organized or systematic collection of information to study teaching and student learning

Effect size: a metric used to denote the meaningfulness or practicality of a result, often in terms of the magnitude of the relationship between variables or difference between groups

Emergent themes: a type of theme or integrated idea that emerges from analyzing codes across the categories developed during the axial-coding phase

Emic: an approach related to studying a phenomenon from the participant's perspective

Empirical research: observations and measurements of a particular event based on actual experiences

Empowerment evaluation: a type of program evaluation that centers on transferring the knowledge from evaluator to stakeholders so the stakeholders can take ownership of the evaluation process

Emulation level: the second level in the development of self-regulatory competency that involves the act of replicating what was observed

Epoché: refraining from drawing conclusions during a study until rich sources of data have been accumulated

Ethnographic design: a qualitative design involving an analysis of the shared norms and behaviors of a particular cultural group

Etic: an approach related to studying a phenomenon from a researcher's perspective

Evaluand: the topic under investigation for a program evaluation, such as an initiative, strategy, or process

Evaluation accountability: documentation to support evaluation processes, products, and findings

Evaluation sponsor: an individual who is responsible for seeking an outside evaluation

Evidence-based practice: a process through which scientific evidence and applied knowledge are used to inform decision making and applications to real-world contexts

Exact replication: duplicating a previously published study using the same number and types of participants, methodology, instruments, and analysis

Experimental design: a quantitative design that is tightly controlled and involves intentionally manipulating variables to examine cause and effect

Expertise-oriented evaluation: a type of program evaluation conducted by subject matter experts to make judgments about the merit and worth of programs

Explanatory case study: focuses on addressing a specific question through analysis

Explanatory sequential design: a type of sequential design where Phase 1 incorporates quantitative data, which are then explained through the qualitative data in Phase 2

Exploratory case study: allows for a researcher to investigate a context for which they have minimal background knowledge or experience

Exploratory sequential design: a type of sequential design where the qualitative data is gathered first and followed by the quantitative phase of data collection

External validity: evidence of validity regarding the extent to which research results can be generalized to other subjects and settings

Fabrication: the act of making up information, such as data and results

Factorial design: a type of experimental design that examines the main and interaction effects of two or more independent variables on the dependent variable

Fail to reject the null hypothesis: in hypothesis testing, a situation in which the observed data in a sample does not allow researchers to conclude that there is not real effect in the population

Falsification: the act of manipulating, misrepresenting, omitting, or changing results so that the findings do not accurately reflect the research findings

Feasibility: A concept linked to maximizing program effectiveness and efficiency

Field notes: observational records used in qualitative research

Focus group: an approach that involves interviewing several individuals about a particular issue at the same time

Formative evaluation: a process of ongoing assessment to gauge the continuous improvements of a program throughout the process

Frequency count: the number of people, characteristics, or other phenomenon that occur

Frequency distribution: a type of distribution that illustrates the frequency with which each score occurs within the set of scores

Frequency polygon: a type of line graph that indicates the frequency scores in a distribution

Gatekeeper: a person in an organization who is not typically part of the research team, who provides access to a research location and/or participants

Grants: financial awards given to researchers by nonprofits, profits, or governmental agencies that support or fund a research study

Grounded theory design: a qualitative design that uses systematically collected data from multiple individuals to develop a theory

Grouping variable: type of variable used in comparative designs that distinguishes naturally occurring groups using specific criteria or group characteristics

Halo effect: a type of bias that occurs when a teacher's positive preestablished perceptions of a student's capabilities influence their evaluations of that student

Histogram: A visual representation that uses vertical bars to represent the frequency of quantitative scores in a distribution

History: a threat to internal validity involving the events, experiences, or situations that occur during the same time period when an intervention is administered

Hypothesis: a stated belief about the relationship between two or more variables or a proposed explanation stemming from your observations and literature review

Hypothesis testing: a process used to test a theory about the relationship between a sample and the population

Independent evaluation: a process in which evaluators create the design of the program with input from stakeholders and are hired on a commissioned basis

Independent variable: type of variable used in experimental research that is systematically manipulated by a researcher to examine cause and effect

Inductive approach: an analysis approach whereby the researcher enters the study with broad questions to uncover the nature of a given context without any preconceived notions

Inductive reasoning: a type of bottom-up process that progresses from specific observations and ideas to form general conclusions

Inferential statistics: a statistical method where the researcher(s) use data generated from a sample drawn from a defined population to make predictions or inferences about the characteristics of the population

Informed consent: a process through which research participants are informed about the purposes, scope, procedures, risks, and benefits of participating in a research study and are given the chance to accept or decline participation

Input evaluation: a process that focuses on how a project should be run through the perspective of clients, evaluation sponsors, and stakeholders

Inputs: the available resources provide structure or supports to the program, such as space, personnel, or materials

Institutional review board: an administrative body established to review, monitor, and approve human research with the broader goal of protecting the rights and welfare of research participants

Instrumental case study: used to learn about another topic that is tangential to the original topic of study

Instrumentation: a threat to internal validity involving changes in the nature or accuracy of a measurement approach over time

Intentionality: an important component of audience awareness where researchers plan who their audience will be and monitor their communication style to the audience

Intentionality of consciousness: notion that the nature of a phenomenon is intrinsically paired with the perceptions of individuals who experienced the phenomenon

Interaction effect: a type of effect whereby the relationship between an independent variable and a dependent variable depends on or varies based on a third variable

Interim assessments: commonly known as benchmark tests, are used in school districts to monitor student progress throughout the year

Internal consistency: a broad approach to reliability analysis that involves correlating different items on the same test

Interpretive grounded theory: a type of grounded theory with a systematic coding scheme in support of emergent themes and theories wherein the researcher is actively engaged with data analysis throughout the process

Interpretivist: a philosophic paradigm in which reality is dependent on individual experiences and the social world in which they operate

Interpretivist phenomenology: a type of phenomenology that emphasizes gaining deeper understandings through interpretations, particularly when there are further implications for the topic of study

Interrater reliability: a type of reliability evidence targeting the consistency with which different raters score the same behavior or skill

Interrupted time series design: a type of quasi-experimental design in which intervention effectiveness is determined by examining the pattern of multiple pretest data points to multiple posttest data points

Interval scale: a level of quantitative measurement that involves rank and order to the data as well as equal distance between each rank

Intervention group: one or more groups in an experiment that receive an intervention or program as stipulated by the researchers

Intervention phase: in a time-series design, a phase in which the intervention is implemented and data is collected over multiple time points

Intrinsic case study: a type of case study whereby the researcher selects the focus or topic of study

Justice: an ethical principle that requires researchers to ensure all individuals in research have access to and can benefit from programs, procedures, or other services

Latent constructs: construct that cannot be directly observed

Levels of measurement: a measurement structure that specifies how variables can be measured and recorded, typically in terms of four levels (nominal, ordinal, interval, and ratio)

Lifeworld: a principle in phenomenology whereby an individual's internal perceptions of life experiences linked to the consciousness

Likert scale: a type of questionnaire that allows respondents to rate different items on an ordinal scale from least to greatest

Literature reviews: original, interpretive overviews of research on a topic of interest

Logic model: visual representation of the inputs, resources, activities, and outputs of a given program; the elements in an evaluand that contribute to the issues of study and ways to bring about change

Longitudinal design: a research approach in which data is collected on repeated occasions over time

Main effect: the individual effect of an independent variable on the dependent variable

Management-oriented evaluation: emphasizes the use of information to assist individuals in the decision-making process

Map making: the process through which diagrams or other visualization are made to highlight the processes and interactions within a school organization

Matching: a process to establish initial group equivalence on one or more variables that relate to the dependent variable

Maturation: a threat to internal validity reflecting natural developmental or maturational changes that occur within individuals

Mean (M): the numerical or arithmetic average of a set of scores

Measurement: a process through which symbols or numbers are assigned to objects, events, people, characteristics, and so forth

Measurement error: factors that affect a person's true score on a measurement you are utilizing for your study

Measures of central tendency: a single score or numerical value that best represents or is most typical of the scores in a distribution

Median: the midpoint or most central score in a rank-ordered distribution of scores

Mediation: a type of statistical analysis in which the relationship between two variables is explained or clarified by including a third variable (mediator)

Member checking: checking with participants to confirm the accuracy of the collected data and or the interpretations of that data

Merit: refers to the value a program adds to an organization

Mixed methodology: broad category of research that combines features of both qualitative and quantitative methodologies

Mixed methods research: a mix of qualitative and quantitative approaches with different types of data and different research paradigms

Mode: the score that occurs most frequently in a distribution

Moderation: a type of statistical analysis in which the relationship between two variables depends or varies based on a third variable (moderator)

Multiple baseline design: a type of single-participant design in which intervention effectiveness is evaluated by comparing performance across multiple baselines (individuals, settings, behaviors)

Narrative analysis: reflects a variety of analytic methods for interpreting the stories or lived experiences of others

Narrative inquiry design: a qualitative design that records and retells the stories and lived experiences of an individual or group of similar individuals

Naturalistic generalization: the extent to which findings from a qualitative study transfer to other case studies and/or contexts in broad terms

Network sampling: a sampling strategy where initial participants identify other individuals to participate in the study.

Nominal scale: a level of measurement in which numbers reflect discrete categories or group assignment

Non-directional (two-tailed) test: a type of analysis in which the researcher does not specify the direction of an expected result

Nonequivalent control group design: a type of quasi-experimental design in which

multiple groups are pretested and posttested but the participants are not randomly assigned to condition

Non-experimental design: broad category of quantitative research that does not involve the manipulation of variables

Nonparallel sampling: a sampling approach whereby quantitative and qualitative samples are derived from different populations

Nonparametric statistics: a type of inferential statistics that are used for data on an ordinal scale or for data on an interval/ratio scale that do not satisfy the assumption of normality

Non-probability random sampling: a sampling approach in which samples are selected in a subjective non-random fashion

Normal distribution: a unimodal and symmetrical distribution that is the foundation for many statistical applications

Norm-referenced tests: type of assessment that uses the performance of a well-defined group as the basis for evaluating the performance of an individual

Null hypothesis (H_0): in hypothesis testing, a statement indicating no statistical significance or relationship exists between variables

Object: the topic under investigation for a program evaluation

Objectives-oriented evaluation: a type of program evaluation that centers on alignment between program objectives and outcomes

Observation checklist: a method for recording actions or processes that an individual observes

Observation level: the first level in the development of self-regulatory competency that involves learning by watching a model demonstrate an activity or by reading or seeing examples in written form

Observing: a component of the action research cycle where we make a concerted effort to pay careful attention, to be watchful, and to gather information by taking note of the observations

Open coding: a phase of the coding process associated with the constant comparative analysis approach in which labels or codes are assigned to discreet phrases or words

Openness: the extent to which researchers share their instruments or additional information when inquiries are made

Operational definition: clear and detailed statement about a variable to be measured

Oral communication: one of two broad approaches to communicating research that may involve presentations at a conference, webinars, podcasts, or other opportunities to verbally share research experiences with others

Ordinal scales: a level of measurement in which the numbers reflect order or rank

Othering: When a researcher presents a person or group of individuals as different or foreign to themselves, often with a negative connotation.

Outcomes: the indicators of effective changes to the program based on merit and worth

Outputs: the types of activities and participants involved in a program

Parametric statistics: a type of inferential statistics that require interval or ratio data and that certain assumptions be met

Participant observer: when a researcher has first-hand experiences in a community by participating in activities

Participant-oriented evaluation: concerned with the opinions of participants who are impacted by the evaluand

Participants: are individuals who are sampled from a target population of interest and who participate in the methods of a study

Participatory action research: research on social issues that aim to improve the quality of schools, districts, families, and communities and to develop an action plan that is then implemented

Pedagogy: the art, science, or profession of teaching

Peer-reviewed: articles that are anonymously evaluated by experts in a given field prior to publication

Percentiles: a metric that reflects the percentage of scores in a distribution that fall below a specific score

Performance-based assessment: represent a form of assessment that requires students to demonstrate their knowledge and skills through authentic or open-ended activities

Phenomenology: a qualitative design that explains the essence of an intense or important experience shared by multiple individuals

Pilot testing: a small-scale preliminary study designed to generate information about the adequacy of the procedures, measures, or other aspects of the research process

Plagiarism: presenting someone else's work as your own without acknowledging them or without their consent

Planning (in action research): a component of the action research cycle where we delineate the steps needed to take action and to reach one's goals

Planning (in self-regulated learning): the first phase of the self-regulated learning cycle where we set goals, develop strategies for reaching our goals, and feel a sense of self-efficacy for accomplishing our goals

Population: the group of individuals, objects, or events to whom researchers wish to draw conclusions

Population parameters: a number that describes a particular characteristic of a population

Portfolio assessment: an assessment that includes a broad collection of student work products across time

Positionality: an individual's worldview and the position they adopt about their research, including their beliefs about the nature of knowledge and agency

Positivism: a philosophical paradigm that emphasizes empirical scientific evidence to understand absolute truths and objective reality

Post-assessment: an assessment that focuses on proposed solutions to mitigate the problem under study

Posttest: an observation or measure of individuals' attributes, skills, or characteristics after an intervention has been completed

Posttest-only control group design: a type of experimental design without administering a pretest

Power analysis: a systematic approach used to identify appropriate sample size assuming a certain alpha, effect size, and power

Practical action research: research that involves an educator or team of educators working together to solve a pressing issue of practice of their choice that is localized and to develop an action plan that is then implemented

Pre-assessment: an assessment that gathers data about a problem from both an educational and social perspective

Predictor variable: a variable used in correlational designs to explain or predict other variables

Pre-experimental design: a simplistic version of an experimental design in which there is minimal control over extraneous variables

Pre-synthesis phase: a phase of the literature review process that involves activities that help to organize an approach to summarizing articles

Pretest: an observation or measure of individuals' attributes, skills, or characteristics prior to them receiving an intervention

Pretest–posttest control group design: a type of true experiment in which participants are randomly assigned to one of two conditions with both groups receiving pretest and posttest assessments

Primary sources: a source of information considered to be firsthand information or raw material related to the topic of interest

Privileged observer: as a privileged observer, the researcher is permitted to observe the interactions and behaviors but does not participate in activities

Probability: the likelihood that a certain outcome will occur relative to the total number of possible outcomes

Probability/Random sampling: a type of sampling that gives an equal opportunity for all members of a population to be selected for the study

Process evaluation: an evaluation approach that focuses on whether a program was implemented as intended

Product evaluation: an evaluation approach that determines how well the program met the needs of the target population via the objectives

Program evaluation: a systematic process of collecting information about the effectiveness of a program

Program impact theory: centers on what factors must be addressed to bring about change

Program process theory: a component of program theory that focuses on the processes that will be used to bring about change

Program theory: describes a proposed framework to tackle a specific problem in an educational setting and entails both the program impact theory and the program process theory

Propriety: a type of standard for ensuring that evaluations and services are provided in a fair, ethical, legal, and just way

Publication Manual of the American Psychological Association: provides a foundation for the scholarly communication of scientific information

Publishing: communicating research in ways that make it available to the public

Purpose: the reason for conducting and communicating about research

Purposive sampling/purposeful sampling: a form of non-probability sampling where individuals are selected based on possessing certain characteristics needed for the sample and study *p*-value: the probability that an outcome is a real effect or occurred by chance

Qualitative methodology: a broad category of research that entails collecting and analyzing non-numerical data to describe concepts or the lived experiences and perspectives of people

Quantitative methodology: a broad category of research that emphasizes collecting and analyzing numerical data to understand the nature of relationships or effects among variables and confirm hypotheses

Quasi-experimental design: an experimental design used to establish cause-and-effect relationships but does not involve random assignment

Questionnaires: assessments that contain a set of questions to which participants respond in writing

Quota sampling: a type of sampling in which a convenient sample is selected from each stratum

Random assignment: a procedure for assigning participants to conditions of an experiment whereby each person has an equal chance of being placed in any of the conditions or groups

Random error: a type of measurement error caused by factors outside of the researcher's control

Random selection: a type of sampling in which individuals from a population are selected in a random fashion

Range: a measure of variability that reflects the difference between the lowest and highest scores in a distribution of scores

Ratio scale: the most advanced level of measurement that includes a true zero value and equal intervals between points on the scale

Reactivity: a phenomenon in which individuals' responses on an assessment are influenced by the context

Reference group: a group of people used to determine an individual's relative standing

Reflecting (in action research): a component of the action research cycle where we not only make observations about

ourselves and others but also what we think about these observations and what they might mean

Reflexivity: the process of reflecting on one's own beliefs, values, and attitudes during the research process and how these aspects may shape findings

Regression: an inferential test used to examine the relationship between one or more predictor variables and a dependent variable

Reject the null hypothesis: a situation in which the observed data in a sample allows researchers to conclude that there is a real effect in the population

Relative standing: a set of procedures that reflect how one score in a distribution compares to other scores in the same distribution

Reliability: the consistency or stability of scores generated from a measure

Replication: the duplication of an original study

Replication crisis: conducting an exact replication of a study that does not end up with the same results as the original study

Research design: represents the overall blueprint, methods, and techniques for executing a study and answering research questions

Research methodology: the philosophical and theoretical perspective about research that is linked by its shared assumptions, practices, and concepts

Research methods: specific procedures for collecting and analyzing data to provide information or uncover a new finding

Research misconduct: fabricating, falsifying, or plagiarizing any aspect of the research process

Research questions: a question about some aspect of your problem that you want to explore or understand

Respect for persons: an ethical principle that requires that individuals should be treated as autonomous and vulnerable individuals that cannot act autonomously entitled to protection

Restorying: a technique qualitative researchers use to collect, analyze, and summarize the lived experiences of individuals

Sample: a group of participants selected from a population for the purposes of your research

Sample relationship criterion: refers to the extent to which samples are related to each other, such as identical, parallel, nonparallel, or multilevel

Sample size: refers to the number of individuals or observations taken in a given study

Sample statistic: a numerical value or characteristic representing the sample

Sampling: the process through which a researcher selects participants to represent the population in a particular study

Sampling distribution: the distribution of all possible sample statistics obtained from repeated sampling of a given population

Sampling error: a type of measurement error involving the difference between the population parameter sample statistic

Sampling frame: a list of elements forming a population from which a sample is taken

Scatterplot: a graphical representation of the relationship between two variables

Scientific method: a dynamic process that helps researchers conduct a study by following six distinct steps: (1) identifying a research problem, (2) reviewing the literature, (3) developing hypotheses, (4) collecting data, (5) analyzing and interpreting the data, and (6) drawing conclusions and communicating the research

Secondary sources: a source of information created by someone who did not experience firsthand or participate in the topic of interest

Selected response questions: type of questions that provide the participants in a study with a finite number of choices to select from a survey (e.g., Likert-type scales)

Selection: a threat to internal validity involving unexpected differences in the characteristics, attitudes, and beliefs of participants

Selective coding: a type of coding associated with the constant comparative analysis approach, selective coding involves theory development based on open and axial coding phases

Self-control level: the third level in the development of self-regulatory competency that involves the process of replicating what was observed under the watchful eye of someone who could scaffold as needed

Self-efficacy: beliefs in our capability to reach our goals

Self-reflecting: the third phase of the self-regulated learning cycle where we evaluate and react to outcomes and determine what worked well and what needs improvement in future iterations of the cycle

Self-regulated learning: the setting of personal goals and our motivation and strategies for reaching these goals

Self-regulation level: the fourth level in the development of self-regulatory competency that involves reaching competency as a self-regulated learner to successfully carry out tasks independently

Semantic differential: a type of survey or questionnaire that directs individuals to select their views about two statements across a continuum

Seminal work or author: scholarship or an individual that had a major influence in a given field of study

Sequential designs: a type of design that includes elements of longitudinal and cross-sectional designs

Simple random sampling: a random sampling method where each member of the population has an equal chance of being selected

Single group pretest–posttest design: a type of pre-experimental design involving the use of a single group with pretest and posttest data collection

Single participant research design: a type of experimental design that utilizes frequent and continuous assessment across baseline and intervention phases to evaluate the effects of an intervention on a single individual or very small group.

Skewness: the extent to which the shape of a distribution deviates from the normal distribution.

Snowball sampling: a form of convenience sampling where the sample grows through word of mouth from participant to participant

Sociality: associated with narrative inquiry, this term refers to cultural and social exchanges

Social structure: the patterned infrastructure in an organization and the way that individuals function in this arrangement

Sources of data: the variety of individuals or objects that provide data and information

Spatiality: associated with narrative inquiry, this term refers to environmental factors/place

Stakeholders: individuals who have an interest in the findings of the program evaluation and the implementation of a program

Standard deviation: a measure of variability reflecting the average amount of variation of scores around the mean

Standard error: the standard deviation of the sampling distribution.

Standardized tests: assessments that are systematically administered, analyzed, and interpreted using set procedures and consistent guidelines

Standard score: a type of derived score in which there is a fixed mean and standard deviation

State-mandated achievement tests: a type of standardized test tied to state legislative initiatives that are often used for accountability purposes

Statistical symbols: typically, Greek or Roman letters used to denote specific statistical concepts

Stem-and-leaf plot: a tabular display of scores in a distribution organized into a stem (initial digit[s] in a number) and leaf (the final digit[s] in a number)

Stratified random sampling: a sampling approach that divides the population into several groups (strata) based on shared characteristics of sampling units and then take a random sample from each stratum

Structured observations: a quantitative data collection technique for evaluating behaviors and events

Subjective lens: the perspective of an individual in terms of their feelings and/or beliefs

Subscale score: a standard score with a mean of 10 and a SD of 3

Summative evaluation: a type of evaluation focused on comparing the learning or skills of program recipients relative to some standard

Survey design: a quantitative study that involves assessing and discussing the attitudes, perceptions, and or practices of a group of individuals

Synthesis phase: a phase of the literature review process involving the integration of research ideas and trends typically through written communication

Systematic: carefully carrying out research procedures and data collection in an organized, careful manner

Systematic error: a type of measurement error in which deviations from a true score are predictable and consistent

Systematic random sampling: a probability sampling technique where all members of a population are arranged into a list and every nth person from that list is selected

Temporality: associated with narrative inquiry, temporality refers to people, events, and ideas as markers throughout time

Testing: a threat to internal validity in which the experience of taking a measure at one point in time influences subsequent responses or performance on that measure

Test–retest reliability: a type of reliability determined by administering the same test multiple times to the same group of individuals

Test statistic: the number that is calculated by using a particular statistical test, such as a t-score, F-value, correlation value

Thematic analysis: a broad approach to qualitative analysis wherein a researcher reviews a set of data to detail patterns and/or themes

Theme: encapsulated similar codes that represent an idea

Theoretical framework: the theoretical underpinnings and structure of a study that provides direction and guidance for developing and addressing research questions

Thick description: accounts of participant perspectives that move beyond summaries, to integrate both a description and the researchers' interpretations within an account

Threats to internal validity: one or more factors that can undermine the extent to which researchers can conclude that the manipulated variable caused the observed effect

Time series component: repeated administration of an assessment before (i.e., pretest) and after (i.e., posttest) an intervention

Tone: a characteristic of audience awareness that involves using a voice that is formal and objective in written and oral communication

Transferability: a characteristic of trustworthiness, transferability refers to ways that findings are applicable to other contexts

Transformative education: practices that result in changes in learners' thinking and understanding

Triangulation: an aspect of a mixed methods design study that refers to integrating quantitative and qualitative methods to determine if results show converging patterns

True experimental design: a type of experimental design using key methodological features and the use of control or comparison groups to help researchers have high levels of confidence that a particular intervention or instructional program was the primary cause of an observed change in outcomes.

Trustworthiness: a term used in qualitative research to convey the level of credibility, transferability, and confirmability of the data collection and analyses procedures

T-score: a standard score with a mean of 50 and a SD of 10

t-test: an inferential test used to compare the difference in means between two groups

Type I error (alpha): the probability of being wrong in rejecting the null hypothesis (false positive)

Type II error (beta): the probability of incorrectly concluding that a real effect does not exist in the population

Unit of analysis: an individual or group of individuals who are participants in the study

Unit tests: a type of test to gauge student mastery of topics within a particular instructional unit

Utility: the extent to which evaluation services can be utilized to the greatest extent to meet individual needs

Validity (in measurement): the extent to which a test/instrument measures what it intends to measure

Validity (in quantitative research): a term used in quantitative research to reflect the meaningfulness, accuracy, and appropriateness of inferences made about scores or research results

Variable: a characteristic, condition, or other phenomenon that is measured or quantified

Variance: the average of the squared differences of each score from the mean

Waitlist control group: a group of individuals, typically assigned to a control or comparison condition, who receive the same intervention as those in the experimental group but at a later time

Worth: the utility of an evaluand to the community at large

Written communication: one of two broad approaches to communicating research that may involve manuscripts, reports, posters, blogs, newsletters, or other written formats

z-score: a type of standard score with a mean of 0 and a SD of 1

REFERENCES

CHAPTER 1

Milgram, S. (1963). Behavioral study of obedience. *Journal of Abnormal and Social Psychology, 67*, 371–378.

Pickering, J. D., Bickerdike, S. R. (2017). Medical student use of Facebook to support preparation for anatomy assessments. *Anatomical Science Education, 10*(3), 205–214. https://doi.org/10.1002/ase.1663

Schunk, D. H., & DiBenedetto, M. K. (2020). Motivation and social cognitive theory. *Contemporary Educational Psychology, 60*, 1–10. https://doi.org/10.1016/j.cedpsych.2019.101832

Schunk, D. H., & Zimmerman, B. J. (1997). Social origins of self-regulatory competence. *Educational psychologist, 32*, 195–208. https://doi.org/10.1207/s15326985ep3204_1

U. S. Department of Health and Human Services (2022). *The Belmont report.* https://www.hhs.gov/ohrp/regulations-and-policy/belmont-report/index.html

Zimmerman, B. J. (2002). Achieving self-regulation: The trial and triumph of adolescence. In F. Pajares & T. Urdan (Eds.), *Academic motivation of adolescents* (Vol. 2, pp. 1–27). Information Age.

CHAPTER 2

American Psychological Association. (2019). *Publication manual of the American Psychological Association* (7th ed.). American Psychological Association.

Bell, C. V., & Pape, S. J. (2012). Scaffolding students' opportunities to learn mathematics through social interactions. *Mathematics Education Research Journal, 24*(4), 423–445.

Chen, P. P. (2003). Exploring the accuracy and predictability of the self-efficacy beliefs of seventh-grade mathematics students. *Learning and Individual Differences, 14*(1), 77–90. https://doi.org/10.1016/j.lindif.2003.08.003

Cleary, T. J., & Kitsantas, A. (2017). Motivation and self-regulated learning influences on middle school mathematics achievement. *School Psychology Review, 46*(1), 88–107. https://doi.org/10.17105/SPR46-1.88-107

Hiller, S. E., & Kitsantas, A. (2016). The validation of the citizen science self-efficacy scale (CSSES). *The International Journal of Environmental and Science Education, 11*(5), 543–555. https://doi.org/10.12973/ijese.2016.405a

Kitsantas, A., Cheema, J., & Ware, H. W. (2011). Mathematics achievement: The role of homework and self-efficacy beliefs. *Journal of Advanced Academics, 22*(2), 310–339. https://doi.org/10.1177/1932202X1102200206

Pajares, F., & Graham, L. (1999). Self-efficacy, motivation constructs, and mathematics performance of entering middle school students. *Contemporary Educational Psychology, 24*(2), 124–139. https://doi.org/10.1006/ceps.1998.0991

Schunk, D. H., & DiBenedetto, M. K. (2020). Motivation and social cognitive theory. *Contemporary Educational Psychology, 60.* https://doi.org/10.1016/j.cedpsych.2019.101832\

Usher, E. L. (2009). Sources of middle school students' self-efficacy in mathematics: A qualitative investigation of student, teacher, and parent perspectives. *American Educational Research Journal, 46*(1), 275–314. https://doi.org/10.3102/0002831208324517

CHAPTER 3

Hrastinski, I., & Wilbur, R. B., (2016). Academic achievement of deaf and hard-of-hearing students in an ASL/English bilingual program. *Journal of Deaf Studies and Deaf Education, 21*(2), 156–170. https://doi.org/10.1093/deafed/env072

Martin, A. J., & Lazendic, G. (2018). Computer-adaptive testing: Implications for students' achievement, motivation, engagement, and subjective test experience. Journal of Educational Psychology, 110(1), 27–45. http://dx.doi.org/10.1037/edu0000205

Maxwell, J. A. (2012). The importance of qualitative research for causal explanation in education. *Qualitative Inquiry, 18*(8). 7 pages. Doi: 10.1177/1077800412452856

National Research Act, 45 U.S.C. § 289 (1974). https://www.govinfo.gov/content/pkg/STATUTE-88/pdf/STATUTE-88-Pg342.pdf

CHAPTER 4

Cleary, T. J., & Zimmerman, B. J. (2001). Self-regulation differences during athletic practice by experts, non-experts, and novices. *Journal of Applied Sport Psychology, 13*(2), 185–206. http://doi:10.1080/104132001753149883

Cleary, T. J., & Kitsantas, A. (2017). Motivation and self-regulated learning influences on middle school mathematics achievement. *School Psychology Review, 46*(1), 88–107. https://doi.org/10.1080/02796015.2017.12087607

Cleary, T. J., Gubi, A., & Prescott, M. V. (2010). Motivation and self-regulation assessments: Professional practices and needs of school psychologists. *Psychology in the Schools, 47*(10), 985–1002. http://doi: 10.1002/pits.20519

Copur-Gencturk, Y., & Rodrigues, J. (2021).Content-specific noticing: A large-scale survey of mathematics teachers' noticing. *Teaching and Teacher Education, 101.* https://doi.org/10.1016/j.tate.2021.103320

Hartley, M. T., Bauman, S., Nixon, C. L., & Davis, S. (2015). Comparative study of bullying victimization among students in general and special education. *Exceptional Children*, *81*(2), 176–193. https://doi.org/ 10.1177/0014402914551741

Hendricks, D. (2011). Special education teachers serving students with autism: A descriptive study of the characteristics and self-reported knowledge and practices employed. *Journal of Vocational Rehabilitation*, *35*(1), 37–50. https://doi:10.3233/JVR-2011-0552

Hoogeveen, L., van Hell, J. G., & Verhoeven, L. (2012). Social-emotional characteristics of gifted accelerated and non-accelerated students in the Netherlands. *British Journal of Educational Psychology*, *82*, 585–605. https://doi:10.1111/j.2044-8279.2011.02047.x

Huk, O., Terjesen, M. D., & Cherkasova, L. (2019). Predicting teacher burnout as a function of school characteristics and irrational beliefs. *Psychology in the Schools*, *56*(5), 792–808. https://doi.org/10.1002/pits.22233

Kremer, K. P., & Kremer, T. R. (2019). Bullying victimization and disability status are associated with television watching in adolescence. *Journal of Child and Family Studies*, *28*(12), 3479–3486. https://doi.org/10.1007/s10826-019-01530-5

Mills, G. E., & Gay, L. R. (2019). *Educational research: Competencies for analysis and applications* (12th ed.). Pearson.

CHAPTER 5

Ansley, B. M., Houchins, D. E., Varjas, K., Roach, A., Patterson, D., & Hendrick, R. (2021).The impact of an online stress intervention on burnout and teacher efficacy. *Teaching and Teacher Education*, *98*, Article 103251. https://doi.org/10.1016/j.tate.2020.103251

Bui, Y., & Fagan, Y. (2013). The effects of an integrated reading comprehension strategy: A culturally responsive teaching approach for fifth-grade students' reading comprehension. *Preventing School Failure*, *57*(2), 59–69. https://doi.org/10.1080/1045988X.2012.664581

Cleary, T. J., Velardi, B., & Schnaidman, B. (2017). Effects of the Self-Regulation Empowerment Program (SREP) on middle school students' strategic skills, self-efficacy, and mathematics achievement. *Journal of School Psychology*, *64*, 28–42. http://dx.doi.org/10.1016/j.jsp.2017.04.004

Fuchs et al.(2021). A quasi-experimental evaluation of two versions of first-grade PAKS: One with and one without repeated reading. *Exceptional Children*, *87*(2), 141–162. https://doi.org/10.1177/0014402920921828

McDaniel, S. C., Houchins, D. E., & Robinson, C. (2016). The effects of Check, Connect, and Expect on behavioral and academic growth. *Journal of Emotional & Behavioral Disorders*, *24*(1), 42–53. https://doi.org/10.1177/1063426615573262

Zimmerman, B. J., & Kitsantas, A. (1999). Acquiring writing revision skill: Shifting from process to outcome self-regulatory goals. *Journal of Educational Psychology*, *91*(2), 241. https://doi.org/10.1037/0022-0663.91.2.241

CHAPTER 6

Arrazola, B. V., & Bozalongo, J. S. (2014). Teaching practices and teachers' perceptions of group creative practices in inclusive rural schools. *Ethnography and Education*, *9*(3), 253–269. http://dx.doi.org/10.1080/17457823.2014.881721

Bauml, M., & Patton, M. M. (2020). A qualitative study of teachers' perceptions of increased recess time on teaching, learning, and behavior. *Journal of Research in Childhood Education*, *34*(4), 506–520. https://doi.org/10.1080/02568543.2020.1718808

Benedict, A. E., Brownell, M., Bettini, E., & Sohn, H. (2021). Learning together: Teachers' evolving understanding of coordinated word study instruction within an RTI framework. *Teacher Education and Special Education*, *44*(2), 134–159. https://doi-org.mutex.gmu.edu/10.1177/0888406420930686

Brown, R. E. (2022). Using written teaching replays to learn what early career secondary mathematics

teachers notice. *International Journal of Science and Mathematics Education*, *20*, 1635–1657. https://doi.org/10.1007/s10763-021-10220-y

Bustamante, C. (2020). TPACK-based professional development on web 2.0 for Spanish teachers: A case study. *Computer Assisted Language Learning*, *33*(4), 327–352. https://doi.org/10.1080/09588221.2018.1564333

Charmaz. (2006). *Constructing grounded theory*. SAGE.

Corbin, J., & Strauss, A. (1990). Grounded theory research: Procedures, canons, and evaluative criteria. *Qualitative Sociology*, *13*(1), 3–21. https://doi.org/10.1007/bf00988593

Creely, E. (2018). "Understanding things from within." A Husserlian phenomenological approach to doing educational research and inquiring about learning. *International Journal of Research & Method in Education*, *41*(1), 104–122. https//doi.org/10.1080/1743727X.2016.1182482

Geertz, C. (1973). *Interpretation of cultures*. Basic Books.

Glaser, B. (1992). *Basics of grounded theory analysis: Emergence vs. forcing.* Sociology Press.

Glaser, B., & Strauss, A. (1967). *The discovery of grounded theory: Strategies for qualitative research.* Aldine de Gruyter.

Hite, R. L., & Milbourne, J. D. (2022). Divining the professional development experiences of K–12 STEM master teacher leaders in the United States. *Professional Development in Education*, *48*(3), 476–492. https://doi.org/10.1080/19415257.2021.1955733

Husserl, E. (2012). *Ideas: General introduction to pure phenomenology*. Routledge (First published in 1913).

Kaomea, J., Alvaret, M. B., & Pittman, M. (2019). Reclaiming, sustaining and revitalizing Hawaiian education through video-cued makawalu ethnography. *Anthropology & Education Quarterly*, *50*(3), 270–290. https://doi.org/10.1111/aeq.12301

Kayi-Aydar, H. (2019). A language teacher's agency in the development of her professional identities: A narrative case study. *Journal of Latinos and Education*, *18*(1), 4–18. https://doi.org/10.10 80/15348431.2017.1406360

Kuebel, C. R., Koops, L. H., & Bond, V. L. (2018). Cultivating teachers of general music methods: The graduate years. *Journal of Music Teacher Education*, *28*(1), 10–23. https://doi-org.mutex.gm u.edu/10.1177/1057083718761812

LeRoy, A. S., & Boomgaard, S. L. (2021). Empathy in isolation: Lived experiences of teachers of refugee children. *Integrative Psychological & Behavioral Science*, *55*(2), 430–443. https://doi.org/10.1007/ s12124-019-09508-0

MacDonald, M. (2007). The use of pedagogical documentation in early elementary classrooms. *Early Childhood Quarterly*, *22*, 232–242. https://doi. org/10.1016/j.ecresq.2006.12.001

Roybal-Lewis, A. (2021). Moving towards proficiency: A grounded theory study of early childhood teacher candidates and professional development schools. *Early Childhood Education Journal*, *50*, 913–924. https://doi.org/10.1007 /s10643-021-01229-7

Saldaña, J. (2021). *The coding manual for qualitative researchers* (4th ed.). SAGE.

Sciuchetti, M. B., Robertson, P. M., McFarland, L. A., & Garcia, S. B. (2018). Preservice special education teachers' reflections on their developing professional awareness via in-context learning. *The Teacher Educator*, *53*(2), 150–166. https://doi.org/10.1080/08878 730.2017.1419393

U. S. Department of Health and Human Services. (2022). *The Belmont Report. h ttps://www.hhs.gov/ohrp/regulations-an d-policy/belmont-report/index.html*

CHAPTER 7

Bandura, A. (1986). *Social foundations of thought and action: A social cognitive theory*. Prentice-Hall.

Cleary, T. J., Kitsantas, A., Peters-Burton, E., Lui, A., McLeod, K., Slemp, J., & Zhang, X. (2022). Professional development in self-regulated learning: Shifts and variations in teacher outcomes and approaches to implementation.

Teaching and Teacher Education, *111*. Advance online publication. https://doi. org/10.1016/j.tate.2021.103619

Hartwell, M., & Kaplan, A. (2018). Students' personal connection with science: Investigating the multidimensional phenomenological structure of self-relevance. *Journal of Experimental Education*, *86*(1), 86–104. https://doi.org /10.1080/00220973.2017.1381581

Mishna, F., Birze, A., & Greenblatt, A. (2022). Understanding bullying and cyberbullying through an ecological systems framework: The value of qualitative interviewing in a mixed methods approach. *International Journal of Bullying Prevention*, *4*, 220–229. https://doi.or g/10.1007/s42380-022-00126-w

CHAPTER 8

Haines, J., & Westmeyer, R. (2023). Show what you know: How girls' academic confidence increases with multiple and differentiated ways of sharing what the learned. *Journal of Teacher Action Research*, *10*(1). https://www.tea cheractionresearch.com/index.php/JT AR/article/view/67.\

Lewin, K. (1946). Action research and minority problems. *Journal of Social Issues*, *2*(4), 34–46.

CHAPTER 9

Atkins, R. C., & Atkins, V. (2010). *An evaluation of the school lunch initiative*. University of California at Berkley. http s://www.schoollunchinitiative.org/dow nloads/sli_eval_full_report_2010.pdf

Bandura, A. (1997). *Self-efficacy: The exercise of control*. Freeman.

Bell, L. (2019, October 4). *Legal fight over K–3 reading tool just beginning. Education NC*. https://www.ednc.org/lega l-fight-over-k-3-reading-tool-just-be ginning/

Berk, S. (2018). Assessment of public schools' out-of-school time academic support programs with participant-oriented evaluation. *Journal of Education*

and Learning, *7*(3), 159–175. https://doi. org/10.5539/jel.v7n3p159

Braun, S.M. (2019). *Outdoor school for all: Diverse programming and outcomes in Oregon: 2018 pilot study evaluation*. Portland, Oregon. The Gray Family Foundation. file:///C:/Users/S%20Hill er/Desktop/Books/SAGE%20Researc h/Chapter%208%20Program%20Eval uation/Articles/oregon2019_outdoor_ sschool_for_all-evaluation-lowres-2 1919.pdf

Byrne, J., Kardefelt-Winther, D., Livingstone, S., & Stoilova, M. (2016). *Global kids online research synthesis, 2015–2016*. UNICEF Office of Research Innocenti and London School of Economics and Political Science. http://globalkids online.net/synthesis-report/

Center for Research Evaluation. (2023, March 15). Logic models versus theory of change. *From the Blog*. https://cere. olemiss.edu/logic-models-vs-theorie s-of-change/

Jeynes, W. H. (2005). A meta-analysis of the relation of parental involvement to urban elementary school student academic achievement. *Urban Education*, *40*(3), 237–269. https://doi.org/10.1177/ 0042085905274540

Joint Committee on Standards for Educational Evaluation. (2022). *Program evaluation standards*. https://evaluation standards.org/program/

Mississippi Children's Museum. (2023). *WonderBox*. https://mschildrensmuseu m.org/exhibits/express-yourself-wond erbox/#:~:text=The%20WonderBox%2 0gallery%20is%20MCM's,explore%20v arious%20types%200f%20making. htt ps://mschildrensmuseum.org/exhibits /express-yourself-wonderbox/#:~:text =The%20WonderBox%20gallery%20is %20MCM's,explore%20various%20typ es%200f%20making

McTighe, J., & Silver, H. F. (2020). *Teaching for deeper learning: Tools to engage students in meaning making*. ASCD.

National Policy Board for Educational Administration. (2015). Professional standards for educational leaders. Pro fessionalStandardsforEducationalLea ders2015forNPBEAFINAL.pdf (ccsso. org)

Roberts, K. R., Sauer, K., Sneed, J., Kwon, J., Olds, D., Cole, K., & Shanklin, C. (2014). Analysis of school food safety programs based on HACCP principles. *Journal of Child Nutrition and Management*, *38*(1). https://schoolnutrition.org/5—News-and-Publications/4—The-Journal-of-Child-Nutrition-and-Management/Spring-2014/Volume-38,-Issue-1,-Spring-2014—Roberts,-Sauer,-Sneed,-Kwon,-Olds,-Cole,-Shanklin/

Scriven, M. (1967). The methodology of evaluation. In R. W. Tyler, R. M. Gagne, & M. Scriven (Eds.), *Perspectives of curriculum evaluation* (pp. 39–83). Rand McNally.

Sharp, S. R., & Mason, S. K. (2021). *WonderBox logic model*. Center for Research Evaluation, Oxford, MS. Created for Mississippi Children's Museum, Jackson, MS. https://mschildrensmuseum.org/exhibits/express-yourself-https://cere.olemiss.edu/logic-models-vs-theories-of-change/

Stufflebeam, D. L. (1971). The use of experimental design in educational evaluation. *Journal of Educational Measurement*, *8*(4), 267–274. https://doi.org/10.1111/j.1745-3984.1971.tb00936.x

U. S. Department of Health and Human Services . (2022). *The Belmont Report*. https://www.hhs.gov/ohrp/regulations-and-policy/belmont-report/index.html

CHAPTER 10

Alexander, C., Wyatt-Smith, C., & Plessis, A. D. (2020). The role of motivations and perceptions on the retention of inservice teachers. *Teaching and Teacher Education*, *96*, 1–12. https://doi.org/10.1016/j.tate.2020.103186

Carlson, E., Lee, H., & Schroll, K. (2004). Identifying attributes of high-quality special education teachers. *Teacher Education and Special Education*, *27*(4), 350–359. https://doi.org/10.1177/088840640402700403

Kitsantas, A., Bland, L., & Chirinos, D. S. (2017). Gifted students' perceptions of gifted programs: An inquiry into their academic and social-emotional functioning. *Journal for the Education of the*

Gifted, *40*(3), 266–288. https://doi.org/10.1177/0162353217717033

Mandouit, L., & Hattie, J. (2023). Revisiting "The Power of Feedback" from the perspective of the learner. *Learning and Instruction*, *84*, 1–9. https://doi.org/10.1016/j.learninstruc.2022.101718

Matthews, H. M., Lillis, J. L., Bettini, E., Peyton, D. J., Pua, D., Oblath, R., Jones, N. D., Smith, S. W., & Sutton, R. (2021). Working conditions and special educators' reading instruction for students with emotional and behavioral disorders. *Exceptional Children*, *87*(4), 476–496. https://doi.org/10.1177/0014402921999825

Varier, D., Kitsantas, A., Zhang, X., & Saroughi, M. (2021). Self-efficacy for self-assessment: Development and validation of the SEESA-AW scale for argumentative writing. *International Journal of Educational Research*, *110*, 1–11. https://doi.org/10.1016/j.ijer.2021.101885

Zimmerman, B., & Kitsantas, A. (2007). Reliability and validity of Self-Efficacy for Learning Form (SELF) scores of college students. *Zeitschrift für Psychologie/Journal of Psychology*, *215*(3), 157–163. https://doi.org/10.1027/0044-34010.215.3.157

CHAPTER 11

Cleary, T. J., & Zimmerman, B. J. (2006). Teachers' perceived usefulness of strategy microanalytic assessment information. *Psychology in the Schools*, *43*(2), 149–155. http://doi:10.1002/pits.20141

Fien, J., Yencken, D., & Sykes, H. (2002). Young people and the environment: An international study on environmental knowledge and attitudes questionnaire. In J. Fien, D. Yencken, & H. Sykes (Eds.), *Young people and the environment. An Asia Pacific perspective* (pp. 1–10). Kluwer Academic Publishers.

Kitsantas, A., Cleary, T. J., Whitehead, A., & Cheema, J. (2020). Relations among classroom context, student motivation, and mathematics literacy: A social cognitive perspective.

Metacognition and Learning, *16*, 255–273. https://doi.org/10.1007/s11409-020-09249-1

Kule, U., & Akcaoglu, M. (2018). The role of relevance in future teachers' utility value and interest toward technology. *Educational Technology Research & Development*, *66*(2), 283–311. https://doi.org/10.1007/s11423-017-9547-9

Maryland State Department of Education. (2018). *Maryland's K–12 computer standards*. Maryland Computer Science Standards by Grade Band (marylandpublicschools.org).

Pearson. (2009). *Stanford achievement series*. 10th ed http://images.pearsonassessments.com/images/assets/sat10/SAT10ScoreReportSampler.pdf

Stovner, R. B., & Klette, K. (2022). Teacher feedback on procedural skills, conceptual understanding, and mathematical practice: A video study in lower secondary mathematics classrooms. *Teaching and Teacher Education*, *110*, 1–12. https://doi.org/10.1016/j.tate.2021.103593

University of Virginia. (2023). *Classroom assessment scoring system*. https://education.virginia.edu/research-initiatives/research-centers-labs/center-advanced-study-teaching-and-learning/cast l-measures/classroom-assessment-scoring-system

Virginia Department of Education. (2022). *Standards of learning & testing*. https://doe.virginia.gov/testing/index.shtml#

Wang, S.-K., Hsu, H.-Y., Campbell, T., & Longhurst, M. (2014). An investigation of middle school teachers and students use of technology inside and outside of classrooms: Considering whether digital natives are more technology savvy than their teachers. *Educational Technology Research Development*, *62*(6), 637–622. https://doi.org/10.1007/s11423-014-9355-4

Zimmerman, B., & Kitsantas, A. (2007). Reliability and validity of Self-Efficacy for Learning Form (SELF) scores of college students. *Zeitschrift für Psychologie/Journal of Psychology*, *215*(3), 157–163. https://doi.org/10.1027/0044-3409.215.3.157

CHAPTER 12

Cleary, T. J. (2009). School-based motivation and self-regulation assessments: An examination of school psychologist beliefs and practices. *Journal of Applied School Psychology, 25*(1), 71–94. http://doi:10.1080/1537790080 2484190

Cleary, T. J., Velardi, B., & Schnaidman, B. (2017). Effects of the Self-Regulation.

Empowerment Program on middle school students' strategic skills, self-efficacy, and mathematics achievement. *Journal of School Psychology, 64*, 28–42. http://doi:10.1016/j.jsp.2017.0 4.004

CHAPTER 13

Cohen, J. (1988). *Statistical power analysis for the behavioral sciences*. Routledge Academic.

Devore, J. L., Berk, K. N., & Carlton, M. A. (2021). *Modern mathematical statistics with applications* (3rd ed.). Springer International Publishing. https://doi.or g/10.1007/978-3-030-55156-8

Lewin, D. S., Wang, G., Chen, Y. I., Skora, E., Hoehn, J., Baylor, A., & Wang, J. (2017). Variable school start times and middle school student's sleep health and academic performance. *Journal of Adolescent Health, 61*(2), 205–211. https://doi.org/10.1016/j.jado health.2017.02.017

Short, M. A., Gradisar, M., Lack, L. C., & Wright, H. R. (2013). The impact of sleep on adolescent depressed mood, alertness and academic performance. *Journal of Adolescence, 36*(6), 1025–1033. ht tps://doi.org/10.1016/j.adolescence.20 13.08.007

CHAPTER 14

Glaser, B. G., & Strauss, A. L. (1967). *The discovery of Grounded Theory: Strategies for qualitative research*. Aldine De Gruyter.

International Baccalaureate. (2021). *International baccalaureate diploma programme subject brief. Language A: language and literature*. https://www.i bo.org/contentassets/5895a05412144 fe890312bad52b17044/curriculum.br ief-languagea.language.and.literatur e-eng.pdf

Saldaña, J. (2021). *The coding manual for qualitative researchers* (4th ed.). Sage.

Shaunessy-Dedrick, E., Suldo, S. M., Roth, R. A., & Fefer, S. A. (2015). Students' perceptions of factors that contribute to risk and success in accelerated high school courses. *High School Journal, 98*(2), 109–137. https://doi.org/ 10.1353/hsj.2015.0002

Kwong, C.-Y. C., & Churchill, D. (2023). Applying the Activity Theory framework to analyse the use of ePortfolios in an International Baccalaureate Middle Years Programme sciences classroom: A longitudinal multiple-case study. *Computers & Education, 200*, 1–14. http s://doi.org/10.1016/j.compedu.2023.1 04792

CHAPTER 15

Bolinger, S. J., Mucherah, D., Markelz, D., & Andrew, M. (2020). Teacher knowledge of attention-deficit/ hyperactivity disorder and classroom management. *The Journal of Special Education Apprenticeship, 9*(1), 1–14. htt ps://scholarworks.lib.csusb.edu/josea /v019/iss1/5

Brownwell, R. (2014, May 29). Communications wisdom from Maya Angelou. *PRNEWS*. https://www.prnewsonline.c om/communications-wisdom-from-m aya-angelou/#:~:text=Here's%20a%20 brief%20sample%200 f,goes%20straig ht%20to%20the%20heart

DiBenedetto, M. K., & Zimmerman, B. J. (2010). Differences in self-regulatory processes among students studying science: A microanalytic investigation. *The International Journal of Educational and Psychological Assessment, 5*(1), 2–24.

Lopez, E. J. (2004). The art of using visual aids. *Nurse Practitioner*, 15–16. ht tps://login.libproxy.uncg.edu/login? ur

l=https://www.proquest.com/scholarl y-journals/art-using-visual-aids/docvi ew/222338708/se-2

Ludlow, B. L. (2014). Secrets of successful grant writing to support rural special education programs. *Rural Special Education Quarterly, 33*(2), 29–37. htt ps://doi.org/10.1177/875687051403300

Martin, A. J., Burns, E. C., & Collie, R. J. (2017). ADHD, personal and interpersonal agency, and achievement: Exploring links from a social cognitive theory perspective. *Contemporary Educational Psychology, 50*, 13–22. https://d oi.org/10.1016/j.cedpsych.2016.12.001

Slavin, R. E. (2020). How evidence-based reform will transform research and practice in education. *Educational Psychologist, 55*(1), 21–31. https://doi.or g/10.1080/00461520.2019.1611432

U.S. Department of Health and Human Services. (2005). Public Health Services Policies on Research Misconduct;. *Final Rule*. ori.hhs.gov/sites/def ault/files/42_cfr_parts_50_and_93_ 2005.pdf

CHAPTER 16

Alefesha, H. M. N., & Al-Jamal, D. A. H. (2019). Syrian refugees' challenges and problems of learning and teaching English as a foreign language (EFL): Jordan as an example. *Journal of Ethnic and Cultural Studies, 6*(1), 117–129.

Augenblick, Palaich and Associates, & Picus, Odden and Associates, . (2018, January). *Costing out the resources needed to Meet Michigan's standards and requirements*. http://www.fundmischo ols.org/wp-content/uploads/2018/01/ SchoolFinance-Research-Collaborativ e-Report.pdf, Retrieved from

Bandura, A. (1986). *Social foundations of thought & action: A social cognitive theory*. Prentice-Hall.

Bandura, A. (1997). *Self-efficacy: The exercise of control*. W H Freeman/Times Books/ Henry Holt & Co.

Baxter, S., & Reddy, L. (2006). *What is scientifically based research? A guide for teachers*. The National Institute for Literacy; The Partnership for Reading.

RMC Corporation, Retrieved from http://www.ncrel.org/sdrs/areas/issues/envrnmnt/go/g0900/#:~:text=This%20Critical%20Issue%20focuses%20on,research%20to%20improve%20student%20learning,

Berger, J. (2018). *How Black North Carolinians help pay the price for the world's cheap bacon.* Retrieved from https://www.vox.com/future-perfect/23003487/north-carolina-hog-pork-bacon-farms-environmental-racism-black-residents-pollution-meat-industry

Chu Lau, S. M., Brosseau, M.-C., Maegerlein, E., LeRisbé, M., & Blandford, M. (2020). Supporting immigrant students' academic and social integration: ESL and French college teachers' collaboration in promoting cross-linguistic teaching of language and strategies. *The Canadian Modern Language Review,* 76(4), 293–312. https://doi.org/10.3138/cmlr-2020–0001

DiBenedetto, M. K., & Schunk, D. H. (2022). Assessing academic self-efficacy. In T. Nielsen & M. S. Khine (Eds.), *Academic self-efficacy: Theory, measurement, and research* (pp. 11–37). Springer.

DiBenedetto, M. K., & Zimmerman, B. J. (2010). Differences in self-regulatory processes among students studying science: A microanalytic investigation. *The International Journal of Educational and Psychological Assessment,* 5(1), 2–24.

Garcia, E., & Weiss, E. (2018). The role of early career supports, continuous professional development, and learning communities in the teacher shortage (Report no. 5). *The Perfect Storm in the Teacher Labor Market Series: Economic Policy Institute*

Hawkins, D. (2017, June 2). How a short letter in a prestigious journal contributed to the opioid crisis. *The Washington Post.* Retrieved from https://www.washingtonpost.com/news/morning-mix/wp/2017/06/02/how-the-opioid-crisis-traces-back-to-a-five-sentence-scholarly-letter-from-1980/

Kurbegovic, D., & Cook, C. R. (2016). *A survey study examining teachers' perceptions in teaching refugee and immigrant students* (dissertation). University of Washington Libraries.

Margolin, J., & Buchler, B. (2004). *Critical issue: Using scientifically based research to guide educational decisions.* North Central Regional Educational Laboratory, Learning Point Associates.

Merriam, Webster. (n.d.). Pedagogy. In Merriam-Webster's online dictionary. Retrieved from https://www.merriam-webster.com/dictionary/pedagogy

Trussell, R. P. (2008). Classroom universals to prevent problem behaviors. *Intervention in School and Clinic,* 43(3), 179–185. https://doi.org/10.1177/1053451207311678

INDEX

Made in United States
North Haven, CT
13 January 2025